STATUTORY INSTRUMENTS 1968

PART III
(in two Sections)

SECTION 2

Published by Authority

LONDON
HER MAJESTY'S STATIONERY OFFICE
1969

2a

NOL

NOL

© *Crown copyright* 1969

PRINTED AND PUBLISHED BY HER MAJESTY'S STATIONERY OFFICE

To be purchased from

49 High Holborn, LONDON, W.C.1

13a Castle Street, EDINBURGH, 2   109 St. Mary Street, CARDIFF, CF1 1JW
Brazennose Street, MANCHESTER, M60 8AS   50 Fairfax Street, BRISTOL, BS1 3DE
258 Broad Street, BIRMINGHAM, 1   7 Linenhall Street, BELFAST, BT2 8AY

or through any Bookseller

1969

Price: £7 7s. 0d. the two Sections: the Volume, complete, £22 1s. 0d.

PRINTED IN ENGLAND

SBN 11 840020 7

Contents of the Volume

PART I, Section 1

PART I, Section 2

PART II, Section 1

PART II, Section 2

PART III, Section 1

PART III, Section 2

STATUTORY INSTRUMENTS

1968 No. 1875

INDUSTRIAL INVESTMENT

The Aluminium Industry (Invergordon Project) Scheme 1968

Laid before Parliament in draft

Made - - - -	*21st November* 1968
Coming into Operation	*26th November* 1968

WHEREAS in the opinion of the Board of Trade (hereinafter referred to as " the Board ") the project to which the following industrial investment scheme relates is likely to benefit the economy of the United Kingdom as being calculated to create new primary production capacity in the aluminium industry:

AND whereas in the Board's opinion the project would not be undertaken without such financial support as the scheme authorises the Board to provide:

AND whereas, for the purpose of providing such support, the Board, subject to the scheme's being approved by the House of Commons, propose to enter with the British Aluminium Company Limited into an agreement in the terms of the draft agreement set out in the Schedule hereto (hereinafter referred to as " the draft B.A. Co. Loan Agreement "):

AND whereas a draft of the scheme has been laid before Parliament and approved by the House of Commons:

NOW, therefore, in pursuance of sections 1 and 2 of the Industrial Expansion Act 1968(a), the Board, with the approval of the Treasury, hereby make the following industrial investment scheme:—

1. This scheme relates to the project of the British Aluminium Company Limited (hereinafter referred to as " the Invergordon project ") for the construction and operation at Invergordon in Ross and Cromarty of an aluminium reduction plant having an annual rated capacity of approximately 100,000 long tons of primary aluminium.

2. The Board may, for the purposes of the Invergordon project and in accordance with an agreement to be made between the Board and the British Aluminium Company Limited in the terms of the draft B.A. Co. Loan Agreement, make loans not exceeding in the aggregate £30,000,000 to the British Aluminium Company Limited.

3. The aggregate amount of expenditure which may be incurred by the Board under the scheme is £30,000,000.

4.—(1) This scheme may be cited as the Aluminium Industry (Invergordon Project) Scheme 1968, and shall come into operation on 26th November 1968.

(a) 1968 c. 32.

(2) The Interpretation Act 1889(a) shall apply for the interpretation of this scheme as it applies for the interpretation of an Act of Parliament.

21st November 1968.

Edmund Dell,
Minister of State,
Board of Trade.

Approved by the Treasury

21st November 1968.

Walter Harrison,
E. Alan Fitch,
Two of the Lords Commissioners
of Her Majesty's Treasury.

SCHEDULE

DRAFT B.A. CO. LOAN AGREEMENT

THIS AGREEMENT is made the   day of   1968 Between THE BOARD OF TRADE (hereinafter called " the Board ") of the one part and THE BRITISH ALUMINIUM COMPANY LIMITED whose registered office is at Norfolk House, St. James's Square, London, S.W.1 (hereinafter called " B.A.") of the other part.

WHEREAS : —

(1) B.A. proposes to undertake a project (hereinafter referred to as " the project ") providing for the construction and operation of an aluminium reduction plant at Invergordon in Scotland for which the North of Scotland Hydro-Electric Board (hereinafter called " NOSHEB ") would supply the electrical power required (hereinafter referred to as " the power supply element of the project ").

(2) In a contract of even date herewith (hereinafter referred to as " the power contract ") between B.A. and NOSHEB providing for the power supply element of the project there is included inter alia : —

    (a) a provision being clause 8 thereof whereby B.A. will pay to NOSHEB from time to time capital sums related to a proportion of the total cost (inter alia) of construction of the Hunterston " B " power station (the sums payable by B.A. pursuant to such provision being hereinafter called " the capital cost incurred by B.A. in relation to the power supply element of the project ") ; and

    (b) a provision being clause 19 thereof (hereinafter referred to as " the residual value clause ") whereby in the event of the power contract being determined in the circumstances therein specified NOSHEB are to pay to B.A. a sum to be calculated as therein provided after making such deductions as are therein specified.

(a) 1889 c. 63.

NOW IT IS HEREBY AGREED as follows:—

GENERAL INTERPRETATION

1.—(1) In this Agreement:—

(a) any reference to a principal sum outstanding at any time shall be a reference to a sum equal to the aggregate of—

(i) the sum of all advances theretofore made by the Board to B.A. in accordance with this Agreement, and

(ii) all sums (if any) deemed to be theretofore added to the sums so advanced, pursuant to the provisions of clause 6(2) and (3) and clause 12(5) hereof less any amounts attributable to such interest in earlier instalments,

less any amounts attributable to principal in earlier instalments ;

(b) " instalment date " means the 30th September ;

(c) " the appropriate actuarial principles " means the normal actuarial principles as exemplified in the " Tables for Repayment of Loans by way of Annuity " in Archer's Loan Repayment and Compound Interest Tables (10th Edition) or such other tables as the parties may agree ;

(d) " the contracted quantity " of electricity for any period for the purposes of clause 12 hereof shall be the number of kilowatt hours of the supplies of electricity contracted to be afforded to B.A. over such period under the provisions of clause 2 and Schedule 1 of the power contract ;

(e) " loan year " means any period of twelve months ending on (and including) 30th September.

(2) For the purposes of this Agreement the present value at any relevant 1st October of any sums advanced or expected to be advanced thereafter shall be the value thereof at that date calculated in accordance with the appropriate actuarial principles with interest at the specified rate discounted on each intervening instalment date between the subsequent date on which the advance was made or was then expected to be made, as the case may may be, and such 1st October.

WARRANTIES

2. B.A. hereby represents and warrants to the Board that it has obtained all necessary authorities and consents and has taken all corporate action necessary to enter into this Agreement and into the Assignment hereinafter mentioned.

ADVANCES BY THE BOARD TO B.A.

3.—(1) If at any time and from time to time B.A. by not less than two weeks' previous notice in writing shall notify the Board of its desire to borrow any sum for application in payment of the capital cost incurred by B.A. in relation to the power supply element of the project the Board will advance such sum to B.A. by way of loan, but so that:—

(a) the Board shall not be obliged so to advance any sum unless B.A. shall previously have furnished to the Board—

(i) such information as shall reasonably be necessary to satisfy the Board that B.A. will apply as hereinbefore mentioned the whole sum specified in the notice within two weeks of its receipt by B.A. ; and

(ii) (except for the purposes of the first such advance) a certificate or certificates by the Auditors of B.A. that the amount of the last preceding advance by the Board to B.A. has been so applied as hereinbefore mentioned within such period of two weeks as aforesaid ;

(b) the Board shall not be obliged so to advance sums aggregating more than £30,000,000 ;

(c) the Board shall not be obliged so to advance any sum after the 31st March 1977 or at any time if B.A. is in default in the performance or observance of any of its obligations to the Board under this Agreement unless such default has been made good or the written consent or waiver of the Board has been obtained by B.A. to its non-performance.

(2) Each advance shall for the purposes of this Agreement be regarded as being made and received when it is paid to the credit of B.A. at such bank in London as B.A. shall by notice to the Board specify for the purpose and as being applied as aforesaid when instructions shall have been given by B.A. to such bank to effect on B.A.'s behalf payment thereof to NOSHEB.

APPLICATION BY B.A. OF ADVANCES BY THE BOARD

4. Every such sum advanced by the Board shall be applied in payment of the capital cost incurred by B.A. in relation to the power supply element of the project and B.A. shall furnish to the Board:—

(a) not later than every 31st December (commencing on the 31st December next following the date of the advance of the first sum by the Board) until all such sums advanced shall have been applied such information as to the state of progress of the construction of the aluminium reduction plant and to the power supply element of the project as the Board may reasonably require ; and

(b) not later than three months after the date of payment of the final sum advanced by the Board a certificate by the Auditors of B.A. that the aggregate amount of all sums advanced has been so applied.

SECURITY FOR AND RANKING OF THE BOARD'S ADVANCES

5.—(1) B.A. shall on the date hereof enter into and deliver to the Board by way of security for all sums to be advanced by the Board under this Agreement and for all interest payable thereon as hereinafter provided an Assignment in the form set out in the Annexe hereto (hereinafter called " the Assignment ") of the benefits of the residual value clause and the right to any sum becoming payable to B.A. pursuant thereto.

(2) Immediately upon repayment by B.A. to the Board of all sums advanced by the Board pursuant to this Agreement together with all interest thereon as herein provided the Board will re-assign to B.A. the said benefit and right or otherwise discharge the said security.

(3) In the event of a winding up of B.A. the rights of the Board to the repayment of all sums advanced under this Agreement and of all interest thereon as hereinafter provided shall be postponed and subordinated to the rights of all other creditors of B.A. (whether secured or unsecured) to payment in full of amounts owing to them by B.A. except:—

(a) in so far as payment under the residual value clause is made to the Board by virtue of the Assignment which payment shall be applied by the Board first to the discharge of interest accrued and thereafter to or towards repayment of principal ; and

(b) that the Board shall rank pari passu with the unsecured creditors of B.A. for the whole or such part of any balance due to the Board (after applying payments under the residual value clause as hereinbefore provided) as shall be equal to any amounts which NOSHEB shall be entitled under the residual value clause to deduct in respect of accrued but unpaid annual charges for the supply of electricity arising under clauses 9 and 10 of the power contract and shall have deducted from the sum otherwise payable under the residual value clause ;

and the Board agree that they will not prove in any such winding up in competition with or to the detriment of the other creditors of B.A. except to the extent provided in paragraph (b) hereof and will authorise the liquidator to make such distributions and payments to the other creditors of B.A. in such manner as shall be necessary to give effect to the foregoing provisions of this sub-clause.

INTEREST

6.—(1) Every sum advanced by the Board under this Agreement shall carry interest at the rate of 7 per cent. per annum (hereinafter called " the specified rate ") from and including the day following the date of advance.

(2) Interest on every sum advanced on or before 30th September 1971 shall be compounded at annual rests on 30th September in each year up to and including 30th September 1971. Such interest shall for the purpose of calculating the instalments thereafter payable as hereinafter provided be deemed to be added to the principal sum outstanding on 1st October 1971 and the interest so added shall carry interest at the specified rate as from and including that date.

(3) Interest on sums advanced during each loan year from and including the loan year ending on 30th September 1972 and accruing to 30th September in such loan year shall for the purpose aforesaid be deemed to be added to the principal sum outstanding on 1st October next following such 30th September, to the extent of the amount (if any) by which the aggregate of that interest and of the interest accruing to such 30th September on the principal sum outstanding on the preceding 1st October exceeds the amount of the instalment payable on such 30th September, and any interest so added shall carry interest at the specified rate as from (and including) 1st October next following such 30th September.

(4) Any instalments payable to the Board under the following provisions of this Agreement or any partial repayment made to the Board under clause 13 hereof shall be applied first in or towards payment of interest already accrued due for payment and subject thereto in or towards payment of interest deemed to have been added to principal under the provisions of sub-clauses (2) and (3) of this clause and by virtue of clause 12(5) and subject thereto in or towards payment of principal.

(5) All interest payable under this Agreement is to be paid without deduction of income tax unless at any time B.A. shall be obliged by statute to deduct income tax before payment to the Board.

REPAYMENT OF ADVANCES WITH INTEREST BY YEARLY INSTALMENTS

7.—(1) B.A. will repay to the Board the sums advanced by the Board to B.A. under this Agreement together with interest thereon as aforesaid by yearly instalments comprising elements of capital and interest on 30th September (hereafter in this Agreement called " the instalment date ") in each year in accordance with the following provisions of this Agreement the first of such instalments to be paid on the instalment date in the year 1972.

(2) The amount of the instalment falling to be paid on any instalment date pursuant to sub-clause (1) of this clause shall be the appropriate amount for that instalment prescribed by the Board pursuant to clause 8 or 9 hereof, or, as the case may be, calculated in accordance with the provisions of clause 10.

8.—(1) Not earlier than 1st August nor later than 1st September in 1972 the Board shall by notice in writing to B.A. (hereafter in this clause called " the said notice ") given after consultation with B.A. prescribe the amount of the instalment payable by B.A. pursuant to clause 7 hereof in the year 1972, being the amount calculated for that purpose in accordance with the appropriate actuarial principles on the basis of a loan of the total sum referred to in sub-clause (2) of this clause carrying interest at the specified rate and repayable by equal yearly instalments over the period commencing on 1st October 1971 and ending on the instalment date in the year 1999 (including both such dates).

(2) The total sum for the purposes of sub-clause (1) of this clause shall be a sum equal to the aggregate of : —

    (a) the principal sum outstanding on 1st October 1971 ; and

    (b) the aggregate of the present values on 1st October 1971 of (i) each of the sums advanced to B.A. on or after 1st October 1971 but prior to the date of the said notice, and (ii) each of the sums then expected (according to the latest estimate then available) to be subsequently advanced to B.A. pursuant to this Agreement.

9.—(1) Not earlier than 1st August nor later than 1st September in the loan year ending on 30th September 1973 and in each subsequent loan year up to (and including) the loan year in which the final advance required to be made by the Board under this Agreement has been paid to B.A. the Board shall by notice in writing to B.A. (hereafter in this clause called "the said notice") given after consultation with B.A. prescribe the amount of the instalment payable by B.A. pursuant to clause 7 hereof on the instalment date next following the date of the said notice, being the amount calculated for that purpose in accordance with the appropriate actuarial principles on the basis of a loan of the total sum referred to in sub-clause (2) of this clause carrying interest at the specified rate and repayable by equal yearly instalments over the period commencing on the 1st October last preceding the date of the said notice and ending (subject to the operation of clauses 12 and 13 hereof) on the instalment date in the year 1999 (including both such dates).

(2) The total sum for the purposes of sub-clause (1) of this clause shall be a sum equal to the aggregate of—

(a) the principal sum outstanding on the 1st October last preceding the date of the said notice ; and

(b) the aggregate of the present values on such 1st October as aforesaid of (i) each of the sums advanced to B.A. on or after such 1st October but prior to the date of the said notice and (ii) each of the sums (if any) then expected (according to the latest estimate then available) to be subsequently advanced to B.A. pursuant to this Agreement.

10.—(1) The amount of the instalment payable by B.A. pursuant to clause 7 hereof on the instalment date in the loan year next following that in which the final advance is paid to B.A. and in every subsequent loan year shall be the amount calculated (in consultation between the Board and B.A.) for that purpose in accordance with the appropriate actuarial principles on the basis of a loan of the sum referred to in sub-clause (2) of this clause carrying interest at the specified rate and repayable by equal yearly instalments over the period commencing on the 1st October next following the payment of the final advance and ending (subject to the operation of clauses 12 and 13 hereof) on the instalment date in the year 1999 (including both such dates).

(2) The sum for the purposes of sub-clause (1) of this clause shall be a sum equal to the principal sum outstanding on 1st October next following the payment of the final advance.

INTEREST ON OVERDUE PAYMENTS

11. B.A. hereby covenants with the Board to pay to the Board interest (without deduction of tax) at the rate of 5 per cent. per annum or at a rate equal to 1 per cent. per annum above the official discount rate of the Bank of England for the time being (whichever rate shall for the time being be the higher) on any instalment as from the date on which that instalment becomes payable in accordance with this Agreement until the date on which it is paid.

REDUCED INSTALMENTS

12.—(1) Notwithstanding the provisions of clauses 8 to 10 of this Agreement, if (within the period commencing on 1st April 1972 and ending on the instalment date in the year 1998, both such dates included), over any period of six consecutive calendar months, or over each of two such periods neither of which includes any calendar month included in the other, the quantity of electricity actually supplied to B.A. pursuant to the power contract for the purposes of the project is less (by at least 100 million kilowatt hours) than the contracted quantity of electricity for such period or periods then B.A. may give to the Board (not later than 9th September next following the expiration of such period or both such periods) notice in writing to that effect (hereafter in this clause called a "notice of reduction") specifying therein the quantity of electricity (expressed in terms of kilowatt hours) actually so supplied to B.A. over such period or periods together with the contracted quantity for such period or periods.

(2) Upon a notice of reduction being duly given in any year, then, for the appropriate amount (hereafter in this clause called " the full amount ") of the instalment which would have been payable by B.A. on the instalment date next following the date of the notice there shall be substituted the reduced amount ascertained in accordance with the provisions of sub-clause (3) or sub-clause (4), as the case may be, of this clause: so, however, that no such instalment as aforesaid shall be so reduced if—

(a) (B.A. having elected under sub-clause (6) of this clause), the period of repayment would have to be extended in accordance with sub-cause (7) of this clause by reason of the amount of such reduction and all previous reductions (if any) beyond the instalment date in the year 2004; or

(b) (B.A. not having elected as aforesaid), the period of repayment (had B.A. so elected) would have had to be extended in accordance with sub-clause (7) of this clause by reason of the amount of such reduction and all previous reductions (if any) beyond the instalment date in the year 2004.

(3) For the purposes of sub-clause (2) of this clause, the reduced amount (in the case in which the notice of reduction relates to a single period of six months) shall be the aggregate of: —

(a) an amount equal to one half of the full amount ; and

(b) whichever is the greater of the following: —

(i) an amount which bears to one-half of the full amount the same proportion as the number of kilowatt hours of electricity actually supplied to B.A. over such period bears to the contracted quantity for that period ;

(ii) £500,000:

so, however, that the reduced amount shall not be less than the minimum amount which would permit of a reduction being made consistently with the provisions of sub-clause (2) of this clause.

(4) For the purposes of sub-clause (2) of this clause, the reduced amount (in the case in which the notice of reduction relates to two periods of six months) shall be the aggregate of: —

(a) whichever is the greater of the following: —

(i) an amount which bears to one half of the full amount the same proportion as the number of kilowatt hours of electricity actually supplied to B.A. over the first of such periods bears to the contracted quantity for that period ;

(ii) £500,000 ; and

(b) whichever is the greater of the following: —

(i) an amount which bears to one half of the full amount the same proportion as the number of kilowatt hours of electricity actually supplied to B.A. over the second of such periods bears to the contracted quantity for that period ;

(ii) £500,000:

so, however, that the reduced amount shall not be less than the minimum amount which would permit of a reduction being made consistently with the provisions of sub-clause (2) of this clause.

(5) To the extent that the reduced amount is insufficient to discharge the full amount of the interest accrued due for payment on the instalment date of the reduced instalment, the balance of that interest shall for the purpose of calculating the instalments thereafter payable (hereafter in this clause called " subsequent instalments ") be deemed to be added to the principal sum outstanding on the day next following the date on which the reduced instalment is payable, and accordingly shall carry interest on and from that date at the specified rate.

(6) Upon giving to the Board the first (and only the first) notice of reduction B.A. may (provided that the Board have first been satisfied as to the security

available or offered in respect of the extended period hereinafter referred to)
elect therein to have the amount of the instalment payable in each loan year
after that in which the first and any subsequent notice of reduction is given
calculated by reference to an extended period of repayment.

(7) In the event of B.A. having elected as aforesaid, then in order to give effect
to such election the amount of each subsequent instalment payable by B.A.
shall be calculated or recalculated, as the case may be, by reference to the
period then applicable under clause 9 or 10 hereof, as the case may be, extended
so as to end on the instalment date in that year which will result, upon the
application of the appropriate actuarial principles, in the amount of each of the
subsequent instalments approximating most nearly to but not being less than
the amount which would have been payable if the reduced instalment had not
been reduced ; and accordingly the provisions of clause 9 or 10 hereof, as the
case may be, shall apply for the calculation or recalculation of the amount of
each such subsequent instalment as if : —

> (a) in clause 9, for the reference in sub-clause (1) to the instalment date in
> the year 1999 (or other year then applicable by virtue of this clause or
> clause 13 hereof) there were substituted a reference to the instalment date
> in the year on which such extended period as aforesaid ends ;
>
> (b) in clause 10—
>
> > (i) for the period referred to in sub-clause (1) there were substituted the
> > period commencing on 1st October next following the instalment date
> > of the reduced instalment and ending on the instalment date on which
> > such extended period as aforesaid ends ; and
> >
> > (ii) the sum referred to in sub-clause (2) were the principal sum outstand-
> > ing on 1st October next following the instalment date of the reduced
> > instalment.

(8) In the event of B.A. not electing as aforesaid the amount of each subsequent
instalment shall be calculated or recalculated by reference to the principal sum
outstanding on the 1st October next following the instalment date of the reduced
instalment and the period then commencing and ending on the instalment date
in the year 1999 or other date then applicable under the provisions of clause 13
but, subject thereto, in accordance with the other provisions then applicable of
clause 9 or clause 10 hereof.

Early Repayment

13.—(1) Notwithstanding the foregoing provisions of this Agreement, B.A.
may not later than 31st August in any year give to the Board notice in writing
(hereafter in this clause called a " notice of repayment ") indicating its intention
to discharge on the 30th September next following the date of such notice the
principal sum outstanding on such 30th September (hereafter in this clause
called the " redemption date ") or such part of that principal sum as is specified
in the notice of repayment.

(2) In the case of a notice of repayment indicating its intention to discharge
the principal sum outstanding as aforesaid B.A. shall pay to the Board on the
redemption date a sum equal to the aggregate of the following amounts : —

> (a) the amount of the instalment payable by B.A. on that date ; and
>
> (b) the amount of all arrears (if any) then outstanding in respect of earlier
> instalments and of all interest thereon pursuant to clause 11 hereof ; and
>
> (c) the amount of the redemption value (as hereafter defined) of the principal
> sum outstanding as aforesaid ;

and upon payment of such sum by B.A. on the redemption date (but not otherwise) the indebtedness of B.A. under this Agreement shall thereupon be fully
discharged.

(3) In the case of a notice of repayment indicating its intention to discharge
a specified part of the principal sum outstanding as aforesaid (hereafter in this
clause called the " specified part of the principal sum outstanding ") B.A. shall

pay to the Board on the redemption date a sum equal to the aggregate of the following amounts : —

(a) the amount of the instalment payable by B.A. on that date ; and

(b) the amount of all arrears (if any) then outstanding in respect of earlier instalments and of all interest pursuant to clause 11 hereof ; and

(c) the amount of the redemption value (as hereafter defined) of the specified part of the principal sum outstanding as aforesaid ;

and upon payment by B.A. on the redemption date (but not otherwise) of such sum as aforesaid the indebtedness of B.A. in respect of the specified part of the principal sum outstanding shall thereupon be discharged and no further interest in respect of that specified part as such shall be payable by B.A.

(4) The payment made by B.A. on the redemption date pursuant to sub-clause (3) of this clause shall have effect to reduce the principal sum which would otherwise have been outstanding on 1st October next following the redemption date by an amount equivalent to the specified part of the principal sum included in such payment, and the instalments thereafter payable by B.A. shall be calculated or recalculated in accordance with clause 9 or 10 hereof, as the case may be, by reference to such reduced principal sum outstanding ; but so that the period to be taken into account for the purpose of such calculation or recalculation shall be the period commencing on such 1st October as aforesaid and ending on (and including) the instalment date in the year which would result from the application (upon the appropriate actuarial principles) of the specified part of the principal sum outstanding—

(a) first in eliminating the number of additional instalments (if any) which, by virtue of the operation of clause 12(6) and (7) hereof, are for the time being to be taken into account in calculating the appropriate amount of the instalments subsequently payable by B.A. or, if the specified part of the principal sum outstanding shall be insufficient to eliminate all the additional instalments, then in eliminating as many complete additional instalments as possible, and then, and subject thereto ;

(b) to the extent of any balance remaining, in reducing the amount of each of the instalments thereafter payable or, at the option of B.A. (to be expressly exercised in the notice of repayment), in reducing the number of instalments thereafter payable by B.A., so that the amount of each such instalment shall as nearly as practicable be the same as the amount which would have been payable if no such repayment had been made by B.A. on the redemption date.

(5) The expression " redemption value " in relation to the principal sum outstanding or the specified part of the principal sum outstanding, as the case may be, means that sum which shall be the equivalent of the present value, on the redemption date : —

(a) in the case of repayment of the principal sum outstanding, of the remaining instalments thereafter payable, or

(b) in the case of repayment of a specified part of the principal sum outstanding, of such of the instalments or amounts thereof which are discharged by such repayment ;

being the equivalent of the present value calculated in accordance with appropriate actuarial principles at the rate of interest applicable under section 5 of the National Loans Act 1968 seven days prior to the redemption date to British Government loans bearing a life equivalent to that which shall remain to the principal sum outstanding on the redemption date: Provided always that the minimum sum to be repaid in respect of each £100 principal sum outstanding shall be £100.

INFORMATION AND BORROWING LIMITS

14. B.A. further covenants and agrees with the Board that for so long as the sums owing to the Board or any part thereof remain outstanding : —

(1) B.A. shall keep books of account appropriate to the project and make them available for the inspection of the Board on the Board showing

reasonable cause in relation to the position of the Board under this Agreement; and

(2) B.A. shall furnish to the Board two copies of every Annual Balance Sheet, Profit and Loss Account and Director's Report presented or issued to its shareholders and also furnish to the Board such information relating to the project as the Board may reasonably require in relation to the position of the Board under this Agreement; and

(3) without the prior consent of the Board the aggregate amount outstanding of all monies borrowed by B.A. and its United Kingdom subsidiaries (excluding inter-Company borrowings) shall not exceed the greater of £35,000,000 or twice the aggregate of the paid up share capital of B.A. and the consolidated reserves of B.A. and its subsidiaries (adjusted as hereinafter provided).

Monies borrowed—

(a) shall include any premium on final repayment, acceptance credits, net borrowings from overseas subsidiaries of B.A. and guarantees of amounts borrowed by and share capital of others than B.A. and its United Kingdom subsidiaries; but

(b) shall not include borrowings for the purpose of repaying monies borrowed.

The consolidated reserves of B.A. and its subsidiaries shall be deemed to include any share premium account capital redemption reserve fund profit and loss account and other retained profits and shall be adjusted to exclude:—

(a) the amounts of reserves of overseas subsidiaries of B.A.;

(b) the amounts (if any) included in such consolidated reserves in respect of amounts set aside for tax equalisation or in relation to investment grants or building grants received or receivable under the Industrial Development Act 1966 or Local Employment Acts 1960 to 1966 respectively;

(c) amounts represented by goodwill and other intangible assets (provided that any asset representing interest arising under the provisions of this Agreement which is accrued but deferred or the capital cost incurred by B.A. in relation to the power supply element of the project shall be deemed not to be an intangible asset); and

(4) the amount of any net accretion thereto resulting from any revaluation of the land and buildings of B.A. and its United Kingdom subsidiaries made prior to the expiration of a period of 5 years from the date of this Agreement or from the date of any previous revaluation which is not excluded by virtue of this provision.

CIRCUMSTANCES IN WHICH ADVANCES BECOME REPAYABLE

15. The whole of the principal outstanding together with interest accrued thereon in respect of the advances made by the Board under this Agreement shall become repayable immediately on the happening of any of the following events:—

(a) if B.A. makes default in the repayment of any part of any sum advanced to B.A. under this Agreement or of any interest thereon for a period of 21 days from the date of delivery of a notice from the Board to B.A. specifying such default;

(b) if B.A. makes default in the performance or observance of any of the other conditions and obligations binding on it under this Agreement which default remains unremedied for more than 28 days from the date of delivery of a notice from the Board to B.A. of such default;

(c) if an order be made or an effective resolution be passed for the winding up of B.A. except for the purpose of reconstruction or amalgamation in respect of which the Board are satisfied that their position as creditor of B.A. under this Agreement will not be prejudiced thereby ; or

(*d*) if B.A. without the consent of the Board does not start to carry out the construction of the aluminium reduction plant by 31st December 1970 or does not start to operate the said plant by the 31st December 1972 or ceases permanently to operate the said plant unless the failure to start to construct such plant or the failure to start to operate it by the relevant date is due in whole or in part to force majeure, that is to say, Act of God, strikes, lockouts, government regulations or any other cause of whatsoever description beyond the control of B.A. or in the event of such failure being due in whole or in part to force majeure B.A. should fail to use reasonable endeavours to start to carry out such construction or to operate the said plant, as the case may be, as soon as is practicable in all the circumstances.

ASSIGNMENT

16. B.A. may with the consent of the Board assign its rights and obligations under this Agreement and/or under the Assignment to any company incorporated and registered in Great Britain which is controlled by B.A. or results from an amalgamation or reconstruction of B.A. provided that: —

(*a*) the Board are satisfied that their position as creditor will not be prejudiced as a result of such assignment ;

(*b*) B.A. execute or cause to be executed such supplemental agreement and other instruments and documents (if any) as the Board reasonably consider necessary to preserve their rights under this Agreement or under the Assignment ; and

(*c*) no order is made or effective resolution is passed for the winding up of B.A. prior to the completion of the assignment of its rights and obligations under this Agreement and to the execution of any agreement instrument and document mentioned in (*b*) above.

COSTS

17. B.A. shall be responsible at its expense for stamping this Agreement and the Assignment with the proper and appropriate stamp duty and will bear all legal costs and other expenses in connection with this Agreement the Assignment and any supplemental agreement and other instruments and documents required by virtue of clause 16(*b*) hereof.

NOTICES

18.—(1) Any notice certificate or other document given or furnished by B.A. to the Board shall be deemed to be effectively given or furnished under this Agreement or under the Assignment if but only if it is left at or is sent by registered post or recorded delivery addressed to the Board at 1 Victoria Street, London, S.W.1 or if another address has been notified in writing by the Board to B.A. as the address of the Board for that purpose that other address.

(2) Any notice certificate or other document given or furnished by the Board to B.A. shall be deemed to be effectively given or furnished under this Agreement or under the Assignment if but only if it is left at or is sent by registered post or recorded delivery addressed to B.A. at its registered office for the time being.

(3) Such notice certificate or other document if posted by prepaid post shall be deemed to be delivered to any address in Great Britain on the day following the day upon which such notice certificate or other document is posted.

(4) In proving delivery of any notice certificate or other document it shall be sufficient to prove that such notice certificate or other document was properly addressed, stamped and posted.

19. This Agreement shall be governed by English law.

IN WITNESS whereof the Official Seal of the Board of Trade has been hereunto affixed and B.A. has caused its Common Seal to be hereunto affixed the day and year first before written.

THE OFFICIAL SEAL of the BOARD OF TRADE
was hereunto affixed in the presence of:—   SEAL

THE COMMON SEAL of THE BRITISH
ALUMINIUM COMPANY LIMITED was hereunto   SEAL
affixed in the presence of:—

Director.

Director.

Secretary.

ANNEXE

FORM OF ASSIGNMENT

THIS ASSIGNMENT is made the   day of
1968 Between THE BRITISH ALUMINIUM COMPANY LIMITED whose
registered office is situate at Norfolk House, St. James's Square, London, S.W.1
(hereinafter called " B.A.") of the one part and THE BOARD OF TRADE
(hereinafter called " the Board ") of the other part:

WHEREAS in accordance with the provisions of an Agreement dated
       1968 made between the Board and B.A. (hereinafter referred
to as " the Loan Agreement ") the Board may advance to B.A. sums not exceeding
in the aggregate £30,000,000 to be applied (in relation to B.A.'s project for
the construction and operation of an aluminium reduction plant at Invergordon
in Scotland) in payment to the North of Scotland Hydro-Electric Board (herein-
inafter called "NOSHEB") as part of the consideration for the supply by
NOSHEB to B.A. of the electrical power required for the purposes of B.A.'s
project pursuant to a contract (hereinafter referred to as " the power contract ")
dated   1968 and made between NOSHEB and B.A.

AND whereas the power contract contains a provision being clause 19 thereof
(hereinafter referred to as " the residual value clause ") whereby in the event of
the power contract being determined in the circumstances therein specified
NOSHEB are to pay to B.A. a sum to be calculated as therein provided after
making such deductions as are therein specified:

AND whereas B.A. has agreed to secure the sums advanced by the Board pursuant
to the Loan Agreement by granting to the Board an assignment of the benefit
of the residual value clause and of any sum becoming payable to B.A. pursuant
thereto:

NOW THIS DEED WITNESSETH as follows:

1. In pursuance of the Loan Agreement and as security for repayment of
the sums to be advanced by the Board pursuant thereto (hereinafter referred to
as " the Board's loan ") together with interest thereon B.A. hereby assigns to the
Board the full benefit of the residual value clause and the rights of B.A. thereunder and all that sum becoming due or payable to B.A. in pursuance of that
clause less an amount equivalent to the amount of any liability of B.A. for tax
in respect of that sum TO HOLD the same unto the Board subject only to the
proviso for redemption hereinafter contained.

2. B.A. hereby covenants with the Board as follows:—

    (a) that B.A. will not without the previous consent of the Board do permit
        or suffer to be done any act or thing whereby the rights of B.A. under
        the residual value clause shall be lost or prejudiced ;

    (b) that B.A. will not without such consent receive compound or release
        the said sum or do any act or thing whereby the recovery of the said
        sum may be impeded delayed or prevented ;

    (c) that B.A. will from time to time execute and do all such assurances and
        things as the Board may reasonably require for perfecting the security
        hereby constituted and after the security hereby constituted has become
        enforceable for facilitating the realisation of the property hereby assigned.
        And B.A. hereby irrevocably appoints the Board to be the attorney of
        B.A. in the name and on behalf of B.A. to execute and do any assur-
        ances and things which B.A. ought to execute and do hereunder.

3. Provided always and it is hereby declared as follows: —

    (a) if B.A. shall repay the Board's loan together with all interest thereon in accordance with the terms of the Loan Agreement the Board will at the request and cost of B.A. re-assign to B.A. the property hereby assigned or otherwise discharge this security ;

    (b) it shall not be incumbent on B.A. to take any steps or institute any proceedings for the recovery of any sum becoming payable under and by virtue of the residual value clause nor shall B.A. be answerable for any loss arising from its having neglected to take such steps or institute such proceedings nor for any deductions from or reduction in the amount otherwise payable under the residual value clause resulting from the operation of the provisions of such clause ;

    (c) the Board shall not by virtue of this Assignment have or be entitled to any interest in or rights arising under the power contract apart from the residual value clause and nothing in this Assignment shall affect or inhibit in any way the right of B.A. to exercise and enjoy and implement for its own account and benefit the provisions of the power contract other than the residual value clause.

4. In this deed when the context so admits the expression " B.A." includes the persons deriving title under it.

5. This Assignment shall be governed by English law.

IN WITNESS etc.

EXPLANATORY NOTE

(This note is not part of the Scheme.)

This scheme, made under the Industrial Expansion Act 1968, authorises the Board of Trade to provide financial support by way of loans up to an aggregate of £30,000,000 to the British Aluminium Company Limited for the purpose of a project for the construction and operation of an aluminium reduction plant at Invergordon in Ross and Cromarty.

STATUTORY INSTRUMENTS

1968 No. 1880

CUSTOMS AND EXCISE

The Import Duties (General) (No. 12) Order 1968

Made - - - -	*25th November* 1968
Laid before the	
House of Commons	*29th November* 1968
Coming into Operation	*5th December* 1968

The Lords Commissioners of Her Majesty's Treasury, by virtue of the powers conferred on them by sections 1, 2 and 13 of the Import Duties Act 1958(a) and of all other powers enabling them in that behalf, on the recommendation of the Board of Trade hereby make the following Order:—

1. In Schedule 1 to the Import Duties (General) (No. 4) Order 1968(b) (which Schedule by reference to the Customs Tariff 1959 sets out the import duties chargeable under the Import Duties Act 1958), in heading 70.21 (articles of glass other than those specified in headings 70.01 to 70.20) the following shall be inserted after subheading (A), and the existing subheading (B) shall accordingly become (C):—

" (B) Face plates, cones or necks, being parts of glass   20%   — "
     envelopes for cathode ray tubes.

2.—(1) This Order may be cited as the Import Duties (General) (No. 12) Order 1968.

(2) The Interpretation Act 1889(c) shall apply for the interpretation of this Order as it applies for the interpretation of an Act of Parliament.

(3) This Order shall come into operation on 5th December 1968.

> *E. Alan Fitch,*
> *Walter Harrison,*
> Two of the Lords Commissioners
> of Her Majesty's Treasury.

25th November 1968.

(a) 1958 c. 6.   (b) S.I. 1968/679 (1968 I, p. 1519).   (c) 1889 c. 63.

EXPLANATORY NOTE

(This Note is not part of the Order.)

Following a Classification Opinion of the Customs Cooperation Council, certain parts of glass envelopes for cathode ray tubes, hitherto classified in subheading 85.21(B) of the customs tariff, now become classifiable under heading 70.21. This Order introduces a new subheading in that heading for the parts concerned, and prescribes the same rate of import duty (20% ad valorem, full rate) as that chargeable on the parts when classified in subheading 85.21(B).

STATUTORY INSTRUMENTS

1968 No. 1881

CUSTOMS AND EXCISE

The Import Duty Drawbacks (No. 10) Order 1968

Made - - - -	*25th November* 1968
Laid before the House of Commons - -	*29th November* 1968
Coming into Operation	*5th December* 1968

The Lords Commissioners of Her Majesty's Treasury, by virtue of the powers conferred on them by sections 9 and 13 of, and Schedule 5 to, the Import Duties Act 1958(a), and section 2(5) of the Finance Act 1965(b), and of all other powers enabling them in that behalf, on the recommendation of the Board of Trade hereby make the following Order:—

1.—(1) As respects import duty paid on any imported articles which on importation fell to be classified under any of the headings of the Customs Tariff 1959 listed in Schedule 1 to this Order, drawback shall be allowed in accordance with paragraph 2 of Schedule 5 to the principal Act on the exportation of the imported articles or goods incorporating the imported articles, but so that drawback under any entry in the said Schedule 1 shall be subject to the restrictions (if any) provided for in column 2 in that entry.

(2) Where in any entry in the said Schedule 1 the drawback is expressed in column 2 to be, or not to be, allowable for goods of a specified description, this is to be taken (unless the context otherwise requires) as restricting accordingly the description of imported articles in respect of which drawback may be allowed.

(3) Any reference in column 2 of the said Schedule 1 to a rate of duty shall, in a case where the imported articles were chargeable with duty at a preferential rate as being goods qualifying for Commonwealth preference or eligible for a Convention rate of duty within the meaning of the European Free Trade Association Act 1960(c), be construed as a reference to the full rate.

(4) No drawback of any duty shall be allowed by virtue of this Article if drawback in respect of that duty is allowable by virtue of Article 2 of this Order.

2.—(1) On the exportation of goods of a description mentioned in column 1 in any entry in Schedule 2 to this Order, being goods produced or manufactured from imported articles of any description mentioned in relation to those goods in column 2 in that entry, drawback as respects import duty paid on the imported articles shall be allowed in accordance with paragraph 3 of Schedule 5 to the principal Act and with the following provisions of this Article.

(2) Drawback under any entry in Schedule 2 to this Order shall, if a rate is shown in column 3 in that entry, be at that rate; and the quantity by reference to which any rate of drawback is stated is (according to the context)

(a) 1958 c. 6. (b) 1965 c. 25. (c) 1960 c. 19.

the quantity of the exported goods or the quantity actually contained in the exported goods of goods of the specified description, being either the imported articles or goods produced or manufactured from the imported articles.

(3) Where in the case of any entry in Schedule 2 to this Order no rate of drawback is specified in column 3, drawback under that entry shall be of an amount equal to the duty appearing to the Commissioners of Customs and Excise to have been paid in respect of the quantity of the imported articles which in their opinion has been used in the production or manufacture of the exported goods.

(4) Paragraph 3(2)(*a*) of Schedule 5 to the principal Act (under which, except in so far as an order provides to the contrary, rates of drawback in respect of duty on imported articles charged at a preferential rate are to be proportionately reduced) shall not apply to drawback on the exportation of goods of any description specified in Schedule 3 to this Order.

(5) The provisions of Schedule 4 to this Order shall have effect in relation to drawback under such of the entries in Schedule 2 to this Order as are specified in the said Schedule 4 (being entries relating to textiles and textile articles).

3.—(1) In this Order, " the principal Act " means the Import Duties Act 1958(**a**).

(2) The Interpretation Act 1889(**b**) applies for the interpretation of this Order as it applies for the interpretation of an Act of Parliament.

4.—(1) This Order may be cited as the Import Duty Drawbacks (No. 10) Order 1968.

(2) The Import Duty Drawbacks Orders specified in Schedule 5 to this Order are hereby revoked.

(3) This Order shall come into operation on 5th December 1968.

E. Alan Fitch,
Walter Harrison,
Two of the Lords Commissioners
of Her Majesty's Treasury.

25th November 1968.

(a) 1958 c. 6.   (b) 1889 c. 63.

SCHEDULE 1

DRAWBACKS ON EXPORTATION OF IMPORTED ARTICLES OR OF GOODS INCORPORATING IMPORTED ARTICLES

Tariff headings comprising imported articles for which drawback is allowable	*Restrictions on drawback*

Animal products

02.01 and 02.06 (meat and edible meat offals).	Allowable for beef and veal and edible offals of beef and veal; but, for boned or boneless beef or veal or edible offals of beef or veal, imported as such, allowable only on the exportation of the imported articles in the packages in which they were imported.
03.02 (fish, salted, in brine, dried or smoked).	Allowable for dried salted split fish.
04.06 (natural honey).	Allowable for honey which has been blended before exportation.

Vegetable products

07.05 (dried leguminous vegetables).	Allowable for seeds of a kind used for sowing.
08.02 (citrus fruit).	Allowable for fresh grapefruit and fresh oranges; but, for fresh oranges, allowable only on their exportation in the packages in which they were imported.
09.02 (tea).	Allowable for tea which has been blended before exportation.
10.02 to 10.05 and 10.07 (cereals).	Allowable for seeds of a kind used for sowing.
12.01 (oil seeds and oleaginous fruit).	Allowable for groundnuts, whether decorticated or not.
12.03 (seeds, fruit and spores, of a kind used for sowing).	—
12.06 (hop cones and lupulin).	Allowable for hops, but only on their exportation in the packages in which they were imported.
14.01 (vegetable materials of a kind used primarily for plaiting).	Allowable for bamboos and rattans, whether or not washed, cut to length, sorted, split or bleached, but not further prepared.
20.07 (fruit juices).	Allowable for lemon juice not containing added sweetening matter.

Products of the chemical and allied industries

28.06 (hydrochloric acid and chlorosulphonic acid).	Allowable for hydrochloric acid of analytical reagent quality.
28.08 (sulphuric acid; oleum).	Allowable for sulphuric acid of analytical reagent quality.
28.09 (nitric acid; sulphonitric acids).	Allowable for nitric acid of analytical reagent quality.
28.10 and 28.11 (phosphorus pentoxide and phosphoric acids; arsenic trioxide and pentoxide, and acids of arsenic).	Allowable for goods for which the rate of duty under the relevant heading was an ad valorem rate of $12\frac{1}{2}$ per cent. or over.
28.12 (boric oxide and boric acid).	Allowable for boric oxide.

Tariff headings comprising imported articles for which drawback is allowable	*Restrictions on drawback*
28.13 (other inorganic acids, and oxygen compounds of non-metals).	Allowable for goods for which the rate of duty was an ad valorem rate of 12½ per cent. or over, and for hydrofluoric acid of analytical reagent quality.
28.14 and 28.15 (halogen compounds of non-metals; sulphides of non-metals, and phosphorus trisulphide).	Allowable for goods for which the rate of duty under the relevant heading was an ad valorem rate of 12½ per cent. or over.
28.17 (sodium hydroxide, potassium hydroxide, etc.).	Allowable for potassium hydroxide of pharmaceutical quality, for solid potassium hydroxide of a purity of not less than 88 per cent. and not more than 92 per cent., and for sodium peroxide.
28.18 (oxides, etc., of strontium, barium or magnesium).	Allowable for goods for which the rate of duty was an ad valorem rate of 12½ per cent. or over, and for magnesium oxide of pharmaceutical quality.
28.19 (zinc oxide and peroxide).	Allowable for zinc peroxide.
28.20 (aluminium oxide and hydroxide; artificial corundum).	Allowable for aluminium oxide of analytical reagent quality.
28.21 (chromium oxides and hydroxides).	Not allowable for chromic oxide.
28.24 (cobalt oxides and hydroxides).	Allowable for cobalt hydroxides.
28.27 (lead oxides; red lead and orange lead).	Allowable for lead dioxide, and for lead monoxide of pharmaceutical quality.
28.28 (hydrazine and hydroxylamine, etc.).	Allowable for goods for which the rate of duty was an ad valorem rate of 12½ per cent. or over, for germanium dioxide, and for cupric oxide of analytical reagent quality.
28.29 (fluorides, etc.).	Allowable for goods for which the rate of duty was an ad valorem rate of 12½ per cent. or over.
28.30 (chlorides and oxide chlorides).	Allowable— (a) for goods for which the rate of duty was an ad valorem rate of 12½ per cent. or over, but not including ammonium chloride not of pharmaceutical quality or calcium chloride not of pharmaceutical quality; (b) for the following chlorides if of analytical reagent quality—barium, ferric or ferrous, magnesium, manganous, and stannic or stannous.
28.32 (chlorates and perchlorates).	Not allowable— (a) for the following chlorates—ammonium, barium, potassium or sodium; (b) for the following perchlorates—ferrous, lead, lithium, magnesium, potassium or sodium.
28.33 and 28.34 (bromides, etc.; iodides, etc.).	Allowable for goods for which the rate of duty under the relevant heading was an ad valorem rate of 12½ per cent. or over.

Tariff headings comprising imported articles for which drawback is allowable	*Restrictions on drawback*
28.35 (sulphides; polysulphides).	Allowable— (*a*) for goods for which the rate of duty was an ad valorem rate of 12½ per cent. or over, but not including antimony pentasulphide, antimony trisulphide, cadmium sulphide, mercuric sulphide (red), or zinc sulphide; (*b*) for sodium sulphide of analytical reagent quality.
28.36 (dithionites; sulphoxylates).	Allowable for goods for which the rate of duty was an ad valorem rate of 12½ per cent. or over.
28.37 (sulphites and thiosulphates).	Allowable for goods for which the rate of duty was an ad valorem rate of 12½ per cent. or over, and for sodium sulphite of analytical reagent quality.
28.38 (sulphates and persulphates).	Allowable— (*a*) for goods for which the rate of duty was an ad valorem rate of 12½ per cent. or over, but not including barium sulphate not of pharmaceutical quality, calcium sulphate or basic lead sulphate; (*b*) for the following sulphates if of pharmaceutical quality—aluminium ammonium, aluminium potassium, ferric or ferrous, magnesium, sodium and zinc; (*c*) for the following sulphates if of analytical reagent quality—aluminium, cupric or cuprous, manganic or manganous, potassium and sodium hydrogen.
28.39 (nitrites and nitrates).	Allowable— (*a*) for goods for which the rate of duty was an ad valorem rate of 12½ per cent. or over, but not including synthetic sodium nitrate; (*b*) for lead nitrate if of analytical reagent quality; (*c*) for sodium nitrite if of analytical reagent quality.
28.40 (phosphites, hypophosphites and phosphates).	Allowable for goods for which the rate of duty was an ad valorem rate of 12½ per cent. or over, for *di*ammonium hydrogen orthophosphate of analytical reagent quality, and for *di*sodium hydrogen orthophosphate of pharmaceutical quality.
28.41 (arsenites and arsenates).	Allowable for goods for which the rate of duty was an ad valorem rate of 12½ per cent. or over, and for sodium arsenate of analytical reagent quality.

Tariff headings comprising imported articles for which drawback is allowable	*Restrictions on drawback*
28.42 (carbonates and percarbonates).	Allowable— (a) for goods for which the rate of duty was an ad valorem rate of 12½ per cent. or over, but not including barium carbonate not of analytical reagent quality, basic copper carbonates or basic lead carbonate; (b) for the following carbonates if of analytical reagent quality—barium, calcium, potassium and sodium; (c) for sodium hydrogen carbonate of pharmaceutical quality.
28.43 (cyanides and complex cyanides).	Allowable— (a) for goods for which the rate of duty was an ad valorem rate of 12½ per cent. or over, but not including ferric ferrocyanide or ferrous ferricyanide; (b) for the following if of analytical reagent quality—potassium cyanide and potassium ferrocyanide.
28.44 (fulminates, cyanates and thiocyanates).	Allowable for goods for which the rate of duty was an ad valorem rate of 12½ per cent. or over.
28.45 (silicates).	Allowable for the following silicates—barium, cadmium, chromic or chromous, cobalt, cupric or cuprous, lead, magnesium, manganic or manganous, nickel, strontium and zinc.
28.46 (borates and perborates).	Allowable for goods for which the rate of duty was an ad valorem rate of 12½ per cent. or over, but not including hydrated *di*sodium tetraborate such that, if reduced to the dry anhydrous form, it would be of a purity not less than 99 per cent.
28.47 (salts of metallic acids).	Allowable— (a) for goods for which the rate of duty was an ad valorem rate of 12½ per cent. or over, but not including cobalt aluminate, cobalt zincate, lead chromate, basic lead chromate, lead titanate, zinc chromate or zinc tetroxychromate; (b) for potassium dichromate of analytical reagent quality.
28.48 (other salts, etc., of inorganic acids).	Allowable for goods for which the rate of duty was an ad valorem rate of 12½ per cent. or over, but not including ammonium cobalt phosphate.
28.49 to 28.52 (colloidal precious metals, etc.; fissile chemical elements and isotopes, etc.; compounds of thorium, uranium, etc.).	Allowable for goods for which the rate of duty under the relevant heading was an ad valorem rate of 12½ per cent. or over.
28.55 to 28.57 (phosphides; carbides; hydrides, etc.).	Allowable for goods for which the rate of duty under the relevant heading was an ad valorem rate of 12½ per cent. or over.

Tariff headings comprising imported articles for which drawback is allowable	Restrictions on drawback
28.58 (other inorganic compounds).	Allowable for goods for which the rate of duty was an ad valorem rate of 12½ per cent. or over, but not including lead cyanamide.
All headings of Chapter 29 (organic chemicals).	Allowable— (a) for goods for which the rate of duty under the relevant heading was an ad valorem rate of 12½ per cent. or over, or the greater of such an ad valorem rate and a specific rate, but not including 1,6-hexanolactam, emetine and its salts, nicotine or nicotine sulphate; (b) for amidopyrin, buta-1,2-diene and buta-1,3-diene; (c) for caffein and its salts; (d) for theobromine and its salts; (e) for the following if of analytical reagent quality—benzene, cupric or cuprous acetate and sodium acetate.
30.03 (medicaments).	Allowable for unmixed products which, if not put up in measured doses or in forms or in packings of a kind sold by retail for therapeutic or prophylactic purposes, would be classified in Chapter 28 or Chapter 29, and would be eligible for drawback.
30.04 (wadding, gauze, bandages and similar medical or surgical dressings, etc.).	Allowable for wadding containing more than 33⅓ per cent. by weight of man-made fibres.
37.02 (unexposed photographic film).	Allowable for film of a length of 12 feet or more.
37.07 (exposed and developed cinematograph film not consisting only of sound track).	—
38.03 (activated carbon and certain activated mineral products).	Allowable for activated carbon, not being of animal origin.
38.11 (disinfectants, insecticides, etc.).	Allowable for unmixed products which, if not put up as mentioned in heading 38.11, would be classified in Chapter 28 or in Chapter 29, and would be eligible for drawback.

Articles of plastic and other artificial materials, or of rubber

39.01 (condensation, poly-condensation and poly-addition products).	Allowable for polyoxymethylenes in the form of granules, being poly-addition products of not less than 90 per cent. by weight of formaldehyde and not being plasticised or otherwise compounded.
39.02 (polymerisation and co-polymerisation products).	Allowable for poly(vinyl chloride) tape not exceeding ¾ inch in width, 15/1,000 inch in thickness or 36 feet in length, whether or not backed with adhesive.

Tariff headings comprising imported articles for which drawback is allowable	*Restrictions on drawback*
39.07 (articles of artificial resins or plastic materials, or of cellulose esters or ethers).	Allowable— (*a*) for articles of apparel (finished, unfinished, complete or incomplete) and for material cut to shape for making into apparel; (*b*) for objects of personal adornment; (*c*) for book-ends; (*d*) for cigar and cigarette cases and boxes; (*e*) for clock and watch glasses; (*f*) for fancy blotters; (*g*) for inkstands; (*h*) for photograph frames; (*i*) for plastic combined bottle-stoppers and screw adaptors, but only on the exportation of lamp adaptors, of a kind suitable for the conversion of bottles into table lamps, incorporating such articles; (*j*) for powder bowls and boxes; (*k*) for receptacles imported as part of a brush, comb and mirror set; (*l*) for rosaries the beads of which are of plastic; (*m*) for smokers' ash receptacles; (*n*) for components for hand-operated appliances embodying a blade and working edge of base metal, and used for making labels or name-plates from plastic or metal strip, otherwise than by stamping the whole legend simultaneously; but not allowable, in the case of the articles referred to at (*d*) and (*j*) above, on the exportation of goods incorporating those articles as, or as part of, the packing, container or get-up of the goods.
40.06 (unvulcanised rubber in certain forms, and articles thereof).	Allowable for impregnated thread containing more than 10 per cent. by weight of silk, of man-made fibres, or of both together.
40.10 (transmission, conveyor or elevator belts or belting, of vulcanised rubber).	Allowable for goods containing man-made fibres.
40.11 (rubber tyres, tyre cases, inner tubes and tyre flaps).	—
40.13 (articles of apparel, etc., of unhardened vulcanised rubber).	—
40.14 (certain articles of unhardened vulcanised rubber).	Allowable— (*a*) for polychlorobutadiene impellers and shaft seals for self-priming flexible vane impeller pumps; (*b*) for components for hand-operated appliances embodying a blade and working edge of base metal, and used for making

Tariff headings comprising imported articles for which drawback is allowable	*Restrictions on drawback*

labels or nameplates from plastic or metal strip, otherwise than by stamping the whole legend simultaneously;

(*c*) for shock, sound and vibration damping devices consisting of bellows of synthetic rubber based on nylon fabric anchored at each end to a steel bead wire, being devices which on exportation are incorporated in machinery.

Leather and furskin, and articles of descriptions commonly made thereof

41.02 to 41.08 (leather). —

42.02 (travel goods and other cases or containers of leather or certain other materials).

Allowable—

(*a*) for cases, made wholly or partly of leather or material resembling leather, for musical instruments;

(*b*) for cigar and cigarette cases and boxes;

(*c*) for pocket wallets and for purses;

(*d*) for receptacles imported as part of a brush, comb and mirror set;

(*e*) for tobacco pouches;

(*f*) for transparent plastic pass-holders which, on exportation, are incorporated in wallets or billfolds;

(*g*) for women's handbags;

but not allowable, in the case of the articles referred to at (*b*), (*c*) and (*e*) above, on the exportation of goods incorporating those articles as, or as part of, the packing, container or get-up of the goods.

42.03 (articles of apparel, etc., of leather or of composition leather). —

42.04 (articles of leather of a kind used in machinery, etc.).

Allowable—

(*a*) for leather drafting bands of a kind used for textile machinery;

(*b*) for leather picking bands and tuggers.

42.05 (miscellaneous articles of leather or of composition leather).

Allowable for fancy blotters.

43.02 (furskins, tanned or dressed, and pieces thereof).

Allowable for furskins, tanned or dressed, not assembled.

43.03 (articles of furskin).

Allowable—

(*a*) for articles of apparel (finished or unfinished, complete or incomplete);

(*b*) for material cut to shape for making into apparel;

(*c*) for picking bands and tuggers.

43.04 (artificial fur and articles thereof).

Allowable for articles of apparel (finished or unfinished, complete or incomplete) and for material cut to shape for making into apparel.

Tariff headings comprising imported articles for which drawback is allowable	*Restrictions on drawback*

Wood and cork and articles thereof

44.03 to 44.08, 44.10, 44.13 and 44.14 (wood in various forms, not more than partly manufactured, wood paving blocks, railway and tramway sleepers of wood, veneer sheets and sheets for plywood).	Not allowable, in the case of heading 44.08, except for riven staves not further prepared. Not allowable, in the case of heading 44.14, except for veneer sheets and sheets for plywood, of a thickness not exceeding 5 mm.
44.15 (plywood and other laminated or inlaid wood products and the like).	Allowable for plywood, blockboard, laminboard and battenboard, containing no material other than wood and bonding material.
44.20 (wooden picture and photograph frames and the like).	Allowable for photograph frames.
44.21 (complete wooden packing cases, boxes, etc.).	Allowable for boxes of softwood boxboards not dovetailed, mortised or tenoned at the ends and not exceeding 22 inches in length, 11 inches in breadth, and 5¾ inches in depth, imported complete but unassembled; but allowable only on the exportation in the boxes of fresh or cured whole or filleted fish, other than shell-fish.
44.24 (household utensils of wood).	—
44.25 (wooden tools, tool bodies, tool handles and certain other articles of wood).	Allowable— (a) for tools; (b) for axe handles of the bent fawn foot type, not less than 24 inches in length; (c) for matchet handles; (d) for sticks of rectangular cross-section throughout, not more than 1 inch in width nor more than ¼ inch in thickness, and not more than 9 inches or less than 3 inches in length.
44.27 (certain articles of wood of a domestic, personal or ornamental kind).	Allowable— (a) for articles of personal adornment; (b) for book-ends; (c) for cigar and cigarette cases and boxes; (d) for inkstands; (e) for rosaries the beads of which are of wood; but not allowable, in the case of the articles referred to at (c) above, on the exportation of goods incorporating those articles as, or as part of, the packing, container or get-up of the goods.
44.28 (miscellaneous articles of wood).	Allowable— (a) for tops of bottle stoppers, but only on the exportation as such of bottle stoppers consisting wholly or partly of the imported top joined to a cork; (b) for curved handles pierced transversely at each end for attachment purposes, of a size and shape adapted for use in suitcases or attaché cases;

Tariff headings comprising imported articles for which drawback is allowable	Restrictions on drawback

    (c) for parts of matchet handles;

    (d) for spoons, flat, not more than 6 inches in length and not more than $\frac{1}{4}$ inch in thickness;

    (e) for sticks of circular cross-section throughout, not more than $\frac{1}{4}$ inch in diameter, and not more than 6 inches or less than 2 inches in length;

    (f) for sticks of rectangular cross-section throughout, not more than 1 inch in width nor more than $\frac{1}{4}$ inch in thickness, and not more than 9 inches or less than 3 inches in length;

but not allowable, in the case of the articles referred to at (b) above, on the exportation of goods incorporating those articles as part of the packing, container or get-up of the goods.

45.03 and 45.04 (articles of cork and agglomerated cork).

Allowable for corks, being parts of bottle stoppers, but only on the exportation as such of bottle stoppers consisting wholly or partly of the imported cork joined to a top.

Articles of paper and paperboard

48.16 (boxes, bags and other packing containers, of paper or paperboard).

Allowable for waxed paper cartons, with inner lid and closure cap, of a capacity of not less than 12 and not more than 13 fluid oz., or not less than 25 and not more than 26 fluid oz., but only on the exportation of syrup in the cartons.

48.18 (registers, exercise books, note books, blotting-pads, etc., of paper or paperboard).

Allowable for fancy blotters.

48.21 (miscellaneous articles of paper pulp, paper, paperboard or cellulose wadding).

Allowable for rolled paper sticks of circular cross-section throughout, not more than $\frac{1}{4}$ inch in diameter, and not more than 6 inches and not less than 2 inches in length.

Textiles and textile articles

50.03 (silk waste).

Allowable for goods containing more than $33\frac{1}{3}$ per cent. by weight of man-made fibres.

50.04 to 50.10 (silk yarn, silk-worm gut and imitation catgut of silk, and woven silk fabrics).

—

51.01 to 51.04 (yarn and the like, and woven fabrics, of man-made fibres, continuous).

—

52.01 (metalised yarn).

Allowable for goods containing more than $33\frac{1}{3}$ per cent. by weight of silk, of man-made fibres, or of both together.

Tariff headings comprising imported articles for which drawback is allowable	*Restrictions on drawback*
52.02 (Woven fabrics of metal thread or of metalised yarn, of a kind used in articles of apparel, as furnishing fabrics or the like).	—
53.03 (waste of sheep's or lambs' wool or of other animal hair, not pulled or garnetted).	—
53.04 (waste of sheep's or lambs' wool or of other animal hair, pulled or garnetted).	Allowable for goods containing more than 33⅓ per cent. by weight of man-made fibres.
53.06 to 53.10 (yarn of sheep's or lambs' wool or of other animal hair).	Allowable for goods containing silk or man-made fibres.
53.11 to 53.13 (woven fabrics of sheep's or lambs' wool or of other animal hair).	—
54.01 (flax, flax tow and flax waste).	Allowable for flax, flax tow or flax waste not hackled, carded or combed.
54.02 (ramie, ramie noils and ramie waste).	Allowable for ramie, ramie noils or ramie waste not carded or combed.
54.03 and 54.04 (flax or ramie yarn).	Allowable for yarn containing silk or man-made fibres.
54.05 (woven fabrics of flax or ramie).	—
55.03 (cotton waste, not carded or combed).	—
55.05 and 55.06 (cotton yarn).	Allowable for yarn containing silk or man-made fibres.
55.07 to 55.09 (woven fabrics of cotton).	—
All headings of Chapter 56 (man-made fibres, discontinuous, and yarn and fabrics thereof).	—
57.01 and 57.03 (true hemp, jute, and tow and waste thereof).	Allowable for hemp or jute, or tow or waste thereof, not carded or combed.
57.04 (miscellaneous vegetable textile fibres and waste thereof).	Allowable for goods, not carded or combed, containing more than 33⅓ per cent. by weight of man-made fibres.
57.05 to 57.07 (yarn of true hemp, jute and miscellaneous vegetable textile fibres).	Allowable for yarn containing man-made fibres.
57.09 to 57.11 (woven fabrics of true hemp, jute and miscellaneous vegetable textile fibres).	—

Tariff headings comprising imported articles for which drawback is allowable	Restrictions on drawback

Tariff headings comprising imported articles for which drawback is allowable

Restrictions on drawback

57.12 (woven fabrics of paper yarn).

Allowable for woven fabric of a weight not exceeding 12 oz. to the square yard, made either entirely from paper yarn, whether treated with cellulose solution or not, or from such material with the addition of one or more strands of other material in the selvedge.

All headings of Chapter 58 (carpets, etc., and tapestries; pile and chenille fabrics; narrow fabrics; tulle and other net fabrics; lace; embroidery).

Not allowable for chenille or gimped yarns of heading 58.07 not containing silk or man-made fibres.

All headings of Chapter 59 (wadding and felt; twine, cordage, etc.; special fabrics; impregnated and coated fabrics; textile articles of industrial use).

Not allowable for goods of heading 59.01 (wadding, flock, etc.) not containing more than 10 per cent. by weight of man-made fibres.

Not allowable for the following goods of heading 59.03—

(a) bonded fibre fabrics, impregnated or coated with rubber or in which rubber forms the bonding substance, which contain 50 per cent. or more by weight of non-textile material and 10 per cent. or less by weight of man-made fibres;

(b) articles of bonded fibre fabrics impregnated or coated with rubber or in which rubber forms the bonding substance which contain 50 per cent. or more by weight of non-textile material:

(c) rubber adhesive goods with backings of bonded fibre fabrics, being goods which contain 50 per cent. or more by weight of non-textile material.

Not allowable for goods of heading 59.04 (twine, cordage, etc.) not containing silk or man-made fibres.

Not allowable, in the case of articles of any of headings 59.01 to 59.05 (wadding, etc., felt, bonded fibre fabrics, twine, cordage, etc., and nets and netting), on the exportation of goods incorporating them as, or as part of, the packing, container or get-up of the goods.

Not allowable for the following goods of heading 59.11, namely, woven textile fabrics, impregnated, coated, covered or laminated with rubber, which contain 50 per cent. or more by weight of rubber.

Not allowable for the following goods of heading 59.17, namely, articles of woven textile fabrics, impregnated, coated, covered or laminated with rubber, which contain 50 per cent. or more by weight of rubber.

Tariff headings comprising imported articles for which drawback is allowable	*Restrictions on drawback*
All headings of Chapter 60 (knitted and crocheted goods).	—
All headings of Chapter 61 (articles of apparel, etc., of textile fabrics, other than knitted and crocheted goods).	—
62.01 and 62.02 (travelling rugs and blankets; household linen and textile furnishings).	—
62.03 and 62.04 (sacks and bags of a kind used for the packing of goods; tarpaulins, sails, awnings, sunblinds, tents and camping goods).	Allowable for articles containing more than 5 per cent. by weight of silk, of man-made fibres, or of both together; but not allowable on the exportation of goods incorporating the articles as, or as part of, the packing, container or get-up of the goods.
62.05 (miscellaneous made-up textile articles).	Allowable— (a) for articles containing more than 5 per cent. by weight of silk, of man-made fibres, or of both together; (b) for boot, shoe, corset and similar laces.
Both headings of Chapter 63 (old clothing, etc., and rags).	—

Footwear, headgear and miscellaneous articles of kinds suitable for personal use

64.01 to 64.04 (footwear).	—
64.05 (parts of footwear).	Allowable for shoe uppers incorporating woven strips of leather, whether or not containing furskin, on the exportation of shoes incorporating such shoe uppers.
All headings of Chapter 65 (headgear and parts thereof).	—
66.01 (umbrellas and sunshades).	Allowable for goods with covers or cases containing silk or man-made fibres.
67.02 (artificial flowers, foliage or fruit).	Allowable for artificial flowers, foliage or fruit, and for articles made of artificial flowers, foliage or fruit.
67.04 (wigs and other false hair, and other articles of human hair).	Allowable for hair nets.

Articles of stone, plaster, cement, asbestos, mica and similar materials; ceramic products; glass and glassware

68.04 and 68.05 (millstones, grindstones, etc. and hand polishing stones, whetstones, oil stones, etc.).	—
68.13 (fabricated asbestos and articles thereof, etc.).	Allowable for wheels of corrugated asbestos paper.
68.14 (friction material of a kind suitable for brakes, clutches or the like, with a basis of asbestos, other mineral substances or cellulose).	—

Tariff headings comprising imported articles for which drawback is allowable	*Restrictions on drawback*
69.03 (miscellaneous refractory goods).	Allowable for laboratory wares, but not on the exportation of goods incorporating those wares as, or as part of, the packing, container or get-up of the goods.
69.09 (laboratory, chemical or industrial wares of ceramics, and certain other articles).	Allowable for laboratory wares, but not on the exportation of goods incorporating those wares as, or as part of, the packing container or get-up of the goods.
69.11, 69.12 and 69.13 (tableware and other articles of a kind commonly used for domestic or toilet purposes, of porcelain, china or other pottery; certain ornaments and furniture of ceramic).	Not allowable on the exportation of goods incorporating the imported articles as, or as part of, the packing, container or get-up of the goods, and not allowable in respect of any exportation on or after 1st July 1970.
70.03 (glass in balls, rods and tubes, unworked, not being optical glass).	Allowable for tubing of a kind suitable for use for scientific purposes.
70.06 (cast, rolled, drawn or blown glass in rectangles, surface ground or polished, but not further worked).	Allowable for heat-absorbing glass, surface ground and polished on both faces, and having the properties of either of the categories specified in paragraph 23 of British Standard 952:1964, being glass imported in rectangles of 10 feet or more in length and $7\frac{1}{2}$ feet or more in width.
70.08 (safety glass consisting of toughened or laminated glass).	Allowable for safety glass in sizes and shapes ready for incorporation in motor vehicles.
70.09 (glass mirrors).	Allowable for hand mirrors, and for rear-view mirrors suitable for cycles or motor vehicles.
70.10 (certain containers of glass).	Allowable for syphon vases, but not on the exportation of goods incorporating the syphon vase as, or as part of, the packing, container or get-up of the goods.
70.11 (glass envelopes for electric lamps, etc.).	Allowable for glass envelopes other than those for filament lamps or for mercury arc rectifiers of the mercury pool cathode type.
70.12 (glass inners for vacuum flasks, etc.).	—
70.13 (glassware of a kind commonly used for table, kitchen, toilet or office purposes, for indoor decoration or similar uses).	Not allowable on the exportation of goods incorporating the imported articles as, or as part of, the packing, container or get-up of the goods, and not allowable in respect of any exportation on or after 1st July 1970.
70.14 (illuminating glassware, signalling glassware and optical elements of glass).	Allowable for illuminating glassware of a kind commonly used for table, kitchen, toilet or office purposes, for indoor decoration, or for similar uses, but not allowable on the exportation of goods incorporating any such articles as, or as part of, the packing, container or get-up of the goods, and not allowable in respect of any exportation on or after 1st July 1970.

Tariff headings comprising imported articles for which drawback is allowable	Restrictions on drawback
70.15 (clock and watch glasses and similar glasses).	Allowable for clock and watch glasses.
70.17 (laboratory, hygenic and pharmaceutical glassware, and glass ampoules).	Allowable for laboratory glassware and for glass ampoules; but not allowable on the exportation of goods incorporating the imported article as, or as part of, the packing, container or get-up of the goods.
70.18 (optical glass and elements of optical glass, other than optically worked elements; blanks for corrective spectacle lenses).	Allowable for optical glass and elements of optical glass.
70.19 (glass beads, imitation pearls, etc., and other decorative glass smallwares and articles thereof).	Allowable for articles wholly or partly of glass beads, and for objects of personal adornment.
70.21 (other articles of glass).	Allowable for face plates, cones or necks, being parts of glass envelopes for cathode ray tubes.

Jewellery, etc.

71.02 and 71.03 (unmounted precious and semi-precious stones, natural, synthetic or reconstructed).	—
71.12 (articles of jewellery and parts thereof of precious metal or rolled precious metal).	Allowable for buttons, but not on the exportation of goods (other than goods consisting only of buttons and any packing, container and get-up thereof) incorporating buttons.
71.15 (articles consisting of or incorporating pearls or precious or semi-precious stones).	Allowable— (a) for buttons, but not on the exportation of goods (other than goods consisting only of buttons and any packing, container and get-up thereof) incorporating buttons; (b) for cultured blister pearls (Mabe pearls), sorted and graded, but not on the exportation of the imported articles after they have been subjected to any process other than sorting and grading or of goods (other than goods consisting only of the imported articles and any packing, container and get-up thereof) incorporating the imported articles.
71.16 (imitation jewellery).	—

Base metals and articles of base metal

73.02 (ferro-alloys).	Allowable for ferro-molybdenum, for ferro-titanium containing not more than 2 per cent. by weight of carbon, for ferro-tungsten and for ferro-vanadium.
73.15 (alloy steel, etc.).	Allowable for stainless steel tape not exceeding $\frac{1}{2}$ inch in width, 6/1,000 inch in thickness or 21 feet in length, whether or not backed with adhesive.

Tariff headings comprising imported articles for which drawback is allowable	*Restrictions on drawback*
73.20 (tube and pipe fittings of iron or steel).	Allowable for specialised parts of aircraft, motor vehicles or machinery.
73.29 (chain and parts thereof of iron or steel).	Allowable for specialised parts of aircraft, motor vehicles or machinery.
73.32 (bolts, nuts, screws, rivets, etc. of iron or steel).	Allowable for specialised parts of aircraft, motor vehicles, clocks and watches, or machinery and for bolts, nuts and screws which are incorporated on exportation in complete hand-operated appliances embodying a blade and working edge of base metal, and used for making labels or nameplates from plastic or metal tape otherwise than stamping the whole legend simultaneously.
73.35 (springs and leaves for springs of iron or steel).	Allowable for specialised parts of aircraft, motor vehicles or machinery and for springs which are incorporated on exportation in complete hand-operated appliances embodying a blade and working edge of base metal, and used for making labels or nameplates from plastic or metal tape otherwise than by stamping the whole legend simultaneously.
73.37 (boilers, radiators and other appliances for room heating, not electrically heated).	Not allowable except for air heaters and hot air distributors (including those which can also distribute cool or conditioned air) not designed for connection to a central heating system.
73.40 (miscellaneous articles of iron or steel).	Allowable—

Allowable—

(a) for electrical insulator parts, being insulator caps of galvanised steel, but only on the exportation as such of electrical insulators of glass and metal incorporating the caps;

(b) for ladies' handbag frames, but only on the exportation as such of ladies' handbags incorporating the frames;

(c) for empty ribbon spools adapted for use in typewriters (including electric typewriters), accounting, adding, listing, book-keeping and billing machines, cash registers, weighing machines or time recorders and for parts of such spools;

(d) for cigarette boxes and tobacco boxes of iron or steel or both;

(e) for cigarette cases of iron or steel or both, on which the duty paid was not more than 4s. 0d. per dozen;

(f) for steel key-plates, brassed and lacquered and with a sliding bar, but without hooks or loops, being key-plates which on exportation are incorporated in key containers;

Tariff headings comprising imported articles for which drawback is allowable	*Restrictions on drawback*
	(g) for spherical-headed hooks and loops which on exportation are incorporated in key containers;
	(h) for articles which are incorporated on exportation in complete hand-operated appliances embodying a blade and working edge of base metal, and used for making labels or nameplates from plastic or metal tape otherwise than by stamping the whole legend simultaneously;
	but not allowable, in the case of the articles referred to at (d) and (e) above, on the exportation of goods incorporating those articles as, or as part of, the packing, container or get-up of the goods.
74.04 (wrought plates, sheets and strip, of copper).	Allowable for copper tape not exceeding ½ inch in width, 8/1,000 inch in thickness or 21 feet in length, whether or not backed with adhesive.
74.08 (tube and pipe fittings of copper or copper alloys).	Allowable for specialised parts of aircraft, motor vehicles or machinery.
74.11 (certain articles of copper wire or of wire of copper alloys).	Allowable for fourdrinier paper-machine wires.
74.13 (chain and parts thereof of copper or copper alloys).	Allowable for specialised parts of aircraft, motor vehicles or machinery.
74.15 (bolts, nuts, screws, rivets, etc., of copper or copper alloys).	Allowable for specialised parts of aircraft, motor vehicles, clocks and watches, or machinery.
74.16 (springs of copper or copper alloys).	Allowable for specialised parts of aircraft, motor vehicles or machinery.
74.19 (miscellaneous articles of copper or copper alloys).	Allowable— (a) for ladies' handbag frames, but only on the exportation of ladies' handbags incorporating the frames; (b) for plated drinking cups, finished bright both inside and out, of a capacity not exceeding 8 fluid oz.
75.04 and 75.06 (tube and pipe fittings and miscellaneous articles of nickel or nickel alloys).	Allowable for specialised parts of aircraft, motor vehicles or machinery.
76.04 (aluminium foil).	Allowable for aluminium tape not exceeding ½ inch in width, 6/1,000 inch in thickness or 16 feet in length, whether or not painted or backed with adhesive.
76.07 (tube and pipe fittings of aluminium or aluminium alloys).	Allowable for specialised parts of aircraft, motor vehicles or machinery.
76.15 (articles of a kind used for domestic purposes and certain other articles of aluminium or aluminium alloys).	Allowable for smokers' ash receptacles.

Tariff headings comprising imported articles for which drawback is allowable	Restrictions on drawback

76.16 (miscellaneous articles of aluminium or aluminium alloys).

Allowable—

(a) for cigar and cigarette cases and boxes, but not on the exportation of goods incorporating those articles as, or as part of, the packing, container or get-up of the goods;

(b) for rosaries the beads of which are of aluminium;

(c) for specialised parts of aircraft, motor vehicles or machinery;

(d) for terminal clamps for silicon carbide high temperature heating elements, but not on the exportation of goods (other than goods consisting only of the imported articles and any packing, container and get-up thereof) incorporating the imported articles;

(e) for articles which are incorporated on exportation in complete hand-operated appliances embodying a blade and working edge of base metal, and used for making labels or name-plates from plastic or metal tape otherwise than by stamping the whole legend simultaneously.

77.03 (miscellaneous articles of magnesium or magnesium alloys).

Allowable for specialised parts of aircraft, motor vehicles or machinery.

78.05 and 78.06 (tube and pipe fittings and miscellaneous articles of lead or lead alloys).

Allowable for specialised parts of aircraft, motor vehicles or machinery.

79.03 (wrought plates, sheets and strip, of zinc; zinc foil; etc.).

Allowable for zinc alloy tape not exceeding $\frac{1}{2}$ inch in width, 10/1,000 inch in thickness or 15 feet in length, whether or not backed with adhesive.

79.04 and 79.06 (tube and pipe fittings and miscellaneous articles of zinc or zinc alloys).

Allowable for specialised parts of aircraft, motor vehicles or machinery and for articles of zinc which are incorporated on exportation in complete hand-operated appliances embodying a blade and working edge of base metal and used for making labels or nameplates from plastic or metal tape otherwise than by stamping the whole legend simultaneously.

80.05 and 80.06 (tube and pipe fittings and miscellaneous articles of tin or tin alloys).

Allowable for specialised parts of aircraft, motor vehicles or machinery.

81.01 (tungsten and tungsten alloys, and articles thereof).

—

81.02 (molybdenum and molybdenum alloys, and articles thereof).

—

Tariff headings comprising imported articles for which drawback is allowable	Restrictions on drawback
81.04 (miscellaneous base metals and alloys, and articles thereof).	Allowable— (a) for chromium and vanadium and articles thereof; (b) for manganese metal (other than alloys of manganese) containing not more than 1 per cent. by weight of carbon; (c) for uranium depleted in U235.
82.01 (agricultural, horticultural and forestry hand tools).	Allowable for picks, for axes, bill hooks and similar hewing tools, for grass shears, and for timber wedges.
82.02 to 82.08 (tools and implements of various types, of base metal).	—
82.09 (knives).	Allowable for pocket knives.
82.11 (razors and razor blades).	Allowable— (a) for razors other than safety razors; (b) for blades and heads, and base metal parts of blades and heads, for electric shavers.
82.12 (scissors and blades therefor).	Allowable for scissors, including tailors' shears.
82.13 (miscellaneous articles of cutlery; manicure and chiropody sets and appliances).	Allowable for manicure sets, for manicure clippers and nippers, being articles not less than 4 inches in length, and for nail files.
83.01 (locks and padlocks, frames for handbags, etc., incorporating locks, and keys therefor, of base metal).	Allowable— (a) for spring-catch locks with spring hinged hasps, of a size and shape adapted for use in suitcases or attaché cases, but not on the exportation of goods incorporating the locks as part of the packing, container or get-up of the goods; (b) for ladies' handbag frames, but only on the exportation as such of ladies' handbags incorporating the frames.
83.06 (indoor ornaments of base metal).	Allowable for metal ornaments in the form of models of living creatures, flowers, foliage, fruit, or inanimate objects, being ornaments of a size and kind suitable for incorporation as decoration in clock cases, inkstands, ash trays, caskets and similar articles used for domestic or office purposes; but not allowable on the exportation of goods incorporating the ornament as part of the packing, container or get-up of the goods.
83.07 (lamps, etc., of base metal but not including electrical apparatus).	Allowable for cycle lamps.

Tariff headings comprising imported articles for which drawback is allowable	*Restrictions on drawback*
83.09 (clasps, frames with clasps for handbags, etc., buckles, buckle-clasps and certain other articles, of base metal, of kinds commonly used for clothing, travel goods, etc.).	Allowable— (a) for ladies' handbag frames, but only on the exportation as such of ladies' handbags incorporating the frames; (b) for fancy buckles and clasps; (c) for steel key-plates, brassed and lacquered and with a sliding bar, complete with spherical-headed hooks or loops, being key-plates which on exportation are incorporated in key containers.
83.11 (bells and gongs, non-electric, of base metal).	Allowable for cycle bells.
83.12 (photograph, picture and similar frames and mirrors, of base metal).	Allowable for photograph frames and for mirrors.

Machinery and electrical equipment

All headings of Chapter 84 (boilers, machinery and mechanical appliances).	Not allowable for water closet cistern mechanisms or parts thereof, being goods of heading 84.59 or 84.61.
85.01 (electrical goods of the following descriptions: generators, motors, converters, transformers, rectifiers and rectifying apparatus, inductors).	Allowable for generators and motors (other than synchros) and rotary converters, for laboratory induction coils, for calibrated inductors, and for parts of any of those articles.
85.02 (electro-magnets; permanent magnets and articles of special materials for permanent magnets, being blanks of such magnets; electro-magnetic and permanent magnet chucks, clamps, vices and similar work holders; and certain other electro-magnetic articles).	—
85.03 (primary cells and primary batteries).	Allowable for standard cells and for parts thereof.
85.04 (electric accumulators).	Allowable for positive plates and negative plates, made of nickel plated steel, not less than $5\frac{1}{10}$ inches nor more than $5\frac{1}{4}$ inches in length, and not less than $1\frac{1}{8}$ inches nor more than $1\frac{3}{8}$ inches in width.
85.05 to 85.09 (hand tools, domestic appliances, shavers and hair clippers, with self-contained electric motors; electrical starting and ignition equipment for internal combustion engines; certain electrical equipment for cycles and motor vehicles).	—
85.11 (industrial and laboratory electric furnaces, etc.; electric welding, brazing and soldering machines and apparatus and similar electric machines and apparatus for cutting).	Allowable for laboratory electric furnaces, for welding, brazing and soldering machines and apparatus and similar machines and apparatus for cutting, and for parts of any of those articles.

Tariff headings comprising imported articles for which drawback is allowable	*Restrictions on drawback*

85.12 (electric space and water heaters, electric hair dressing appliances and certain other electric appliances of a similar nature).

Allowable—

(*a*) for hair driers and parts thereof and for hand and face driers and parts thereof;

(*b*) for silicon carbide high temperature heating elements with a heating temperature range that exceeds 1100° centigrade, but not on the exportation of goods (other than goods consisting only of the imported articles and any packing, container and get-up thereof) incorporating the imported articles.

85.13 (electrical line telephonic and telegraphic apparatus).

Allowable for teleprinters, for morse transmitters and receivers, for morse re-perforators, and for parts of any of those articles.

85.14 (microphones, loudspeakers and amplifiers).

Allowable—

(*a*) for the following, if on exportation they are incorporated in complete deaf aids, namely—

(i) microphones of approximately cylindrical shape not exceeding 18 mm. in diameter and 8 mm. in thickness, exclusive of leads, or of approximately rectangular shape, with a maximum dimension not exceeding 20 mm., exclusive of leads;

(ii) transistor amplifier units containing not less than two and not more than five transistors and weighing less than $1\frac{1}{2}$ oz.;

(*b*) for the following, if on exportation they are incorporated in loudspeakers, namely—

(i) loudspeaker cones of paper pulp;

(ii) loudspeaker spiders comprising a disc, centre punched, with circular corrugation, manufactured from a plasticised fabric.

85.15 (radio etc. apparatus).

Allowable—

(*a*) for electrically operated extending and retracting aerials which on exportation are incorporated in motor-cars;

(*b*) for radio (including radar and television) transmitting sets, receiving sets and combined transmitting and receiving sets, complete, designed or adapted for fitting to aircraft or motor vehicles;

(*c*) for radio-broadcast reception apparatus (television or sound, or both) incorporating gramophones.

Tariff headings comprising imported articles for which drawback is allowable	*Restrictions on drawback*
85.18 (electrical capacitors).	Allowable—
	(*a*) for laboratory and standard capacitors and parts thereof;
	(*b*) for tantalum capacitors, approximately cylindrical in shape, with a maximum diameter not exceeding 3 mm. and a maximum length not exceeding 7 mm., exclusive of leads, and incorporated on exportation in complete deaf aids.
85.19 (apparatus for making and breaking, protecting, connecting, regulating or controlling electrical circuits).	Allowable—
	(*a*) for solenoid or motor operated switches;
	(*b*) for switches, switchboards and control panels, being specialised parts of machinery, aircraft or motor vehicles;
	(*c*) for precision, standard and laboratory resistors, and parts thereof;
	(*d*) for carbon track volume controls incorporated on exportation in complete deaf aids, being controls of drum type with a cylindrical drum not exceeding 12 mm. in diameter and 4 mm. in thickness, or of sliding type with a length of carbon track not exceeding 7 mm.;
	(*e*) for torpedo switches;
	(*f*) for lampholders fitted with a plastic combined bottle-stopper and screw adaptor and suitable for use with lamps having bayonet caps $\frac{7}{8}$ inch in diameter;
	(*g*) for lampholders suitable for use with lamps having Edison screw caps 1 inch in diameter;
	(*h*) for two-pin plugs with flat pins;
	(*i*) for two-pole 10 amp. 250 volt plugs having an earth socket and dual wiping earth contacts, and being suitable for use with socket outlets having a pin-type earthing contact or side earthing contacts, if—
	(i) the diameter of the plug base is not less than 1·418 inches or more than 1·456 inches, and
	(ii) the exterior length of the pins is not less than 0·688 inches or more than 0·728 inches, and
	(iii) the distance between the centres of the pins is not less than 0·740 inches or more than 0·756 inches, and
	(iv) the earth socket is capable of accepting pins of a diameter not less than 0·169 inches or more than 0·208 inches,
	and the plugs are on exportation fitted to portable electric tools;

Tariff headings comprising imported articles for which drawback is allowable	*Restrictions on drawback*
	(*j*) for terminal straps for silicon carbide high temperature heating elements, but not on the exportation of goods (other than goods consisting only of the imported articles and any packing container and get-up thereof) incorporating the imported articles;
	but not allowable, in the case of the articles referred to at (*e*), (*f*), (*g*) and (*h*) above, except on the exportation of lamp adaptors, of a kind suitable for the conversion of bottles into table lamps, incorporating such articles.
85.20 (electric filament lamps and electric discharge lamps; arc-lamps; electrically ignited photographic flash bulbs).	Allowable for discharge lamps and for arc-lamps for cinematograph projectors, and for parts of such lamps.
85.21 (thermionic, cold cathode and photo-cathode valves and tubes; photocells; mounted transistors, etc.).	Allowable—
	(*a*) for thermionic, cold cathode and photo-cathode valves and tubes, for photocells, for mounted piezo-electric quartz crystals, and for parts of any of those articles;
	(*b*) for junction transistors, approximately cylindrical in shape, not exceeding 4 mm. in diameter and 8 mm. in length, exclusive of leads, and incorporated on exportation in complete deaf aids.
85.22 (miscellaneous electrical goods and apparatus).	Allowable for standard signal generators, radio type, for oscillators, laboratory and standard, and for parts of any of those articles.
85.24 (carbon brushes, arc-lamp carbons and other carbon articles of a kind used for electrical purposes).	Allowable for arc-lamp carbons and parts thereof, and for amorphous carbon electrodes, other than primary battery carbons.
85.26 (certain insulating fittings for electrical apparatus, being fittings wholly of insulating material apart from certain components incorporated for purposes of assembly).	—

Vehicles, aircraft and vessels

86.01 to 86.04 (rail locomotives and mechanically propelled railway and tramway rolling-stock).	—
86.06 (railway and tramway rolling-stock, the following: workshops, cranes and other service vehicles).	Allowable for cranes.
86.09 (parts of railway and tramway locomotives and rolling-stock).	Allowable for parts of rail locomotives.

Tariff headings comprising imported articles for which drawback is allowable	*Restrictions on drawback*
All headings of Chapter 87 (vehicles other than railway or tramway rolling-stock), except headings 87.10 (cycles, not motorised) and 87.13 (baby carriages and invalid carriages, not mechanically propelled).	Allowable, in the case of goods of heading 87.14 (miscellaneous vehicles, not mechanically propelled), only for trailer units of flexible or articulated motor vehicles, and for parts of such units.
88.02 (flying machines, gliders and kites; rotochutes).	Allowable for flying machines.
88.03 (parts of goods falling in heading 88.01 (balloons and airships) and 88.02).	Allowable— (i) for parts of flying machines; (ii) for wing sections, fuselage sections and under-carriage parts for gliders, but only when exported as parts of complete gliders fully assembled or in kit form.
88.04 (parachutes).	Allowable for goods of silk or man-made fibres.
88.05 (catapults and similar aircraft launching gear; ground flying trainers).	—

Optical, photographic, measuring, etc., and medical and surgical apparatus; clocks and watches; musical instruments, and sound recorders and reproducers

90.01 and 90.02 (lenses, prisms, mirrors and other optical elements, etc.).	—
90.03 (frames and mountings for spectacles, etc.).	Allowable for frames of tortoise-shell.
90.05 and 90.06 (refracting telescopes and astronomical instruments).	—
90.07 (photographic cameras; photographic flashlight apparatus, photocopying apparatus (not contact type)).	Allowable for all goods except tripods and other stands, pistol grips and photographic flashlight apparatus.
90.08 (cinematographic cameras, projectors, sound recorders and sound reproducers).	Not allowable for tripods and other stands for articles of heading 90.08, or for pistol grips for cameras of that heading.
90.09 (image projectors; photographic enlargers and reducers).	Not allowable for tripods and other stands for image projectors.
90.10 (miscellaneous photographic and cinematographic equipment and apparatus).	Allowable— (a) for cinematographic editing machines incorporating means of projection; (b) for cinematographic enlargers and reducers (optical printers); (c) for re-recorders; (d) for other optical projection apparatus; (e) for film viewing magnifiers; (f) for photo-copying machines (being non-optical) of direct contact or transfer type (other than dyeline type) with semi-dry developing system.

Tariff headings comprising imported articles for which drawback is allowable	*Restrictions on drawback*
90.11 and 90.12 (microscopes and diffraction apparatus, electron and proton, and compound optical microscopes).	—
90.13 (miscellaneous optical appliances and instruments).	Not allowable for spotlights (non-focusing) or searchlights.
90.14 (surveying, navigational, meteorological and similar instruments).	Allowable— (*a*) for instruments incorporating optical elements, but not including instruments in which the optical element is for viewing a scale or for some other subsidiary function; (*b*) for the following surveying (including photogrammetrical surveying) and hydrographic instruments—clinometers, hypsometers, co-ordinatographs, cross staff heads, and plane tables; (*c*) for the following navigational instruments—accelerometers, altimeters, and horizons (artificial), gyroscopic type; (*d*) for the following geophysical instruments—magnetometers, seismographs and variometers; (*e*) for compasses.
90.15 (balances of a sensitivity of 5 centigrams or better).	—
90.16 (drawing, marking-out and mathematical calculating instruments; measuring or checking instruments, appliances and machines; profile projectors).	Allowable— (*a*) for instruments, appliances and machines incorporating optical elements, but not including instruments, appliances or machines in which the optical element is for viewing a scale or for some other subsidiary function; (*b*) for the following other instruments, appliances and machines— (i) calculating cylinders, dials and rules, isographs, half sets, compasses (including beam compasses), dividers (including proportional dividers), bows, spring bows, ruling pens, pantographs and eidographs, and slide rules; (ii) chronographs (barrel), clinometers, coordinatographs, dividing machines and engines (linear and circular), engine indicators, harmonic analysers (planimeter type), integraphs, integrators (planimeter type), opisometers, planimeters, and spherometers; (iii) curves, drafting machines, parallel rules, protractors, precision squares, set squares, and T squares, scribing blocks of precision or surface gauges, straight edges and surface plates;

Tariff headings comprising imported articles for which drawback is allowable	*Restrictions on drawback*

(iv) gauges and measuring instruments of precision of the types used in engineering machine shops and viewing rooms;

(v) tape measures in ornamental containers with a spring-operated rewind device.

90.17 (medical, etc., instruments and appliances).

Allowable—

(*a*) for instruments and appliances incorporating optical elements, but not including mouth mirrors not optically worked, or instruments or appliances in which the optical element is for viewing a scale or some other subsidiary function;

(*b*) for cardiographs;

(*c*) for optometers;

(*d*) for myographs;

(*e*) for glass barrelled hypodermic syringes.

90.19 (orthopaedic appliances, etc.; artificial parts of the body; deaf aids, etc.).

Allowable—

(*a*) for artificial human eyes of glass;

(*b*) for the following articles incorporated on their exportation in complete deaf aids, that is to say—

(i) chassis with a cylindrical drum volume control not exceeding 12 mm. in diameter and 4 mm. in thickness mounted thereon,

(ii) earphones of approximately cylindrical shape, not exceeding 18 mm. in diameter and 8 mm. in thickness, or of approximately rectangular shape with a maximum dimension not exceeding 16 mm., the measurement being made (in any case) exclusive of earmould nipples and of leads.

90.20 and 90.22 to 90.27 (X-ray apparatus, etc.; miscellaneous measuring and checking instruments and apparatus, etc.).

—

90.28 (electrical measuring, checking, analysing or automatically controlling instruments and apparatus).

Not allowable for—

(*a*) ammeters, voltmeters, wattmeters, thermostats and thermo-regulators (other than precision types);

(*b*) automatic regulators of electrical quantities (other than motor driven and vibrating contact automatic voltage regulators);

(*c*) automatic control instruments and apparatus for controlling non-electrical quantities (other than those for automatic control of flow, depth, pressure or other variables of liquids or gases, or of temperature);

(*d*) telemetering instruments and apparatus.

Tariff headings comprising imported articles for which drawback is allowable	*Restrictions on drawback*
90.29 (parts or accessories of measuring and checking instruments and apparatus, etc.).	Not allowable for parts or accessories of the following— (*a*) ammeters, voltmeters, wattmeters, thermostats and thermo-regulators (except parts and accessories of precision types, and parts and accessories incorporated in refrigeration controls, being parts and accessories suitable for use solely with, or of a kind mainly used with, such controls); (*b*) automatic regulators of electrical quantities (other than motor driven and vibrating contact automatic voltage regulators); (*c*) automatic control instruments and apparatus for controlling non-electrical quantities (other than those for automatic control of flow, depth, pressure or other variables of liquids or gases, or of temperature).
All headings of Chapter 91 (clocks and watches).	—
All headings of Chapter 92 (musical instruments and sound or television image recorders and reproducers).	Not allowable for television image and sound recorders and reproducers, magnetic (classified in heading 92.11) or parts and accessories thereof (classified in heading 92.13).

Miscellaneous manufactured articles

94.03 (miscellaneous furniture).	Allowable for wooden frames for camp beds, imported without metal fittings, but only on the exportation as such of complete assembled camp beds each incorporating a wooden frame and a canvas top.
94.04 (mattress supports and articles of bedding or similar furnishing).	Not allowable for articles of expanded, foam or sponge artificial plastic material, whether or not covered.
95.01 (worked tortoise-shell and articles of tortoise-shell).	Allowable for articles of tortoise-shell.
95.02 (worked mother of pearl and articles of mother of pearl).	Allowable for articles of mother of pearl.
95.05 (worked horn, coral or other animal carving material, and articles thereof).	Allowable— (*a*) for articles of coral or shells; (*b*) for matchet handles and parts thereof of horn.
95.06 (worked vegetable carving material, and articles thereof).	Allowable for rosaries the beads of which are of coco bean.
96.02 (miscellaneous brooms and brushes, paint rollers, etc.).	Allowable— (*a*) for hair, tooth, nail, clothes, hat and shaving brushes;

Tariff headings comprising imported articles for which drawback is allowable	*Restrictions on drawback*
	(b) for brooms and brushes with filling of man-made fibres (including monofil of heading 51.01 or 51.02).
96.05 (powder-puffs and pads for applying cosmetics or toilet preparations).	Not allowable on the exportation of goods incorporating the imported article as, or as part of, the packing, container or get-up of the goods.
97.01 to 97.03 (toys).	Not allowable for parts.
97.04 (equipment for parlour, table and funfair games).	Not allowable for playing cards, or for billiard tables.
97.06 (equipment for gymnastics, athletics, sports and outdoor games).	Allowable— (a) for blade blanks for electric foils or electric épées, but only on the exportation of such foils or épées or of blades therefor; (b) for dome-shaped cork pieces, but only on the exportation of shuttlecocks incorporating them.
98.01 (buttons and button moulds, studs, cuff-links and press-fasteners).	Allowable— (a) for buttons and button moulds, and parts and blanks thereof, but not on the exportation of goods (other than goods consisting only of the imported articles and any packing, container and get-up thereof) incorporating the imported articles: (b) for cuff-links.
98.03 (fountain pens, etc., pen-holders, pencil-holders and the like, propelling pencils and sliding pencils).	—
98.05 (pencils, with certain exceptions, crayons, chalks and the like).	Allowable for pencils.
98.07 (hand-operated date, etc., stamps and composing sticks, and certain hand printing sets).	Allowable for hand-operated appliances embodying a blade and working edge of base metal, and used for making labels or name plates from plastic or metal tape otherwise than by stamping the whole legend simultaneously.
98.10 (mechanical lighters and similar lighters, and parts thereof).	Allowable for flint wheels for mechanical lighters and for metal gas tanks incorporated in mechanical lighters.
98.11 (smoking pipes; cigar and cigarette holders).	—
98.12 (combs, hair-slides and the like).	—
98.14 (scent and similar sprays of a kind used for toilet purposes).	—
98.15 (vacuum flasks, etc.).	Allowable for vacuum flasks and other vacuum vessels, complete with cases.

SCHEDULE 2

DRAWBACKS ON EXPORTATION OF GOODS PRODUCED OR MANUFACTURED FROM IMPORTED ARTICLES

Exported Goods	*Imported Goods*	*Rate of Drawback (if any)*
Abrasive discs.	Vulcanised fibre imported in rolls.	—
Acetylcarbromal.	2-Ethylbutyric acid.	—
Adhesive tape, of a width not exceeding 6¼ ins. consisting of paper coated on one side with adhesive.	Creped paper, manufactured entirely of semi-bleached sulphate cellulose fibre, whether wet-strengthened or not but not otherwise treated or impregnated, being paper which is imported in rolls of a width not less than 23 ins. and which is of a weight when fully extended equivalent to more than 24·5 grammes, but not more than 98 grammes, per square metre on which the duty paid amounted to more than 2s. 6d. per cwt.	—
Animal black (other than ivory black and spent animal black).	Bones, de-fatted, crushed or uncrushed.	£2 13s. 0d. per ton of animal black.
Animal foodstuffs, canned.	Whale meat of heading 02.04 of the Customs Tariff 1959.	—
Apricot kernel products.	Apricot kernels, shelled but not further prepared.	18s. 2d. per cwt. of apricot kernels.
Beans: 1. Canned in tomato sauce, with or without sausages, pork, kidney or bacon. 2. Canned in curry sauce.	Dried white beans, other than butter beans.	—
Biscuits (other than chocolate biscuits), cake mixes, puddings and pudding mixes.	Sugar of either of the following descriptions: (a) sugar not qualifying for Commonwealth preference, of a polarisation exceeding 98°;	(i) 6s. 10·8d. per cwt. of sugar; (ii) 6s. 6·9d. per cwt. of anhydrous invert sugar.
	(b) sugar qualifying for Commonwealth preference, of a polarisation exceeding 99°.	(i) 1s. 0·8d. per cwt. of sugar; (ii) 1s. 0·19d. per cwt. of anhydrous invert sugar.

Exported Goods	Imported Goods	Rate of Drawback (if any)
Booklets, not exceeding 3½ ins. in length and 2½ ins. in width, and containing not less than 60 leaves consisting of paper coated on one side with powder.	Paper, coated on one side with powder, in sheets not less than 30 ins. in length and 18 ins. in width and of a weight when fully extended equivalent to not less than 35, and not more than 45, grammes per square metre.	—
Boots, bootees, shoes, slippers and sandals containing in the uppers (and not as linings, internal stiffening pieces, stitchings, fastenings or ornaments) leather of the following description, namely, dressed leather other than patent leather, and other than glace kid being chrome tanned goatskin of smooth polished finish.	Leather of the description referred to in column 1, not imported in the form of shaped pieces for making into footwear.	—
Bromvaletone.	isoValeric acid.	—
Carbromal.	2-Ethylbutyric acid.	—
Casings for sausages and prepared meats:		
1. Casings manufactured in the form of bags of which the sealed ends are curved.	Tubing of poly(vinyl chloride) imported in reels, whether or not plasticised or pigmented, on which the duty paid amounted to more than 6½d. per lb.	—
2. Other casings.	Tubing of any of the following materials imported in reels, whether or not plasticised or pigmented— (a) regenerated cellulose, (b) poly (vinyl chloride), (c) coated or impregnated paper of vegetable fibre, on which the duty paid amounted to more than 6½d. per lb.	—
Castor oil and goods made therefrom:		
1. Castor oil (including dehydrated oil); fatty acids derived from castor oil (including dehydrated fatty acids).	Castor seed.	—

Exported Goods	*Imported Goods*	*(Rate of Drawback if any)*
2. Dehydrated castor oil; fatty acids derived from castor oil (including dehydrated fatty acids).	Castor oil (other than hydrogenated castor oil).	—
3. Sebacic acid.	Castor oil.	—
Chewing gum and chewing confectionery.	Chewing gum base.	—
Chocolate:		
1. Block couverture, bakers' covering compounds, granulettes and other chocolate for further manufacturing purposes.	(A) Raw cocoa beans, whole or broken, and cocoa paste.	—
	(B) Cocoa butter (fat or oil).	
	(C) Sugar of either of the following descriptions:—	
	(*a*) sugar not qualifying for Commonwealth preference, of a polarisation exceeding 98°;	(i) 6s. 10·8d. per cwt. of sugar;
		(ii) 6s. 6·9d. per cwt. of anhydrous invert sugar.
	(*b*) sugar qualifying for Commonwealth preference, of a polarisation exceeding 99°.	(i) 1s. 0·8d. per cwt. of sugar;
		(ii) 1s. 0·19d. per cwt. of anhydrous invert sugar.
	(D) Lecithin and other phosphoaminolipins.	—
2. Chocolate confectionery, sugar confectionery containing cocoa, and chocolate biscuits.	(A) Raw cocoa beans, whole or broken, and cocoa paste.	—
	(B) Cocoa butter (fat or oil).	—
	(C) Sugar of either of the following descriptions:—	
	(*a*) sugar not qualifying for Commonwealth preference, of a polarisation exceeding 98°;	(i) 6s. 10·8d. per cwt. of sugar;
		(ii) 6s. 6·9d. per cwt. of anhydrous invert sugar.
	(b) sugar qualifying for Commonwealth preference, of a polarisation exceeding 99°.	(i) 1s. 0·8d. per cwt. of sugar;
		(ii) 1s. 0·19d. per cwt. of anhydrous invert sugar.
	(D) Liquid glucose.	
	(E) Milk powder; dried egg albumin; coconut, desiccated; pineapple, fresh; edible nuts other than coconuts, brazil, cashew, hazel, almonds and chestnuts; peel of melons and citrus fruit, fresh, frozen, dried or provisionally preserved; ginger; menthol, not synthetic; tartaric acid; essential oils, terpeneless —orange, lemon, lime, mandarin, tangerine, peppermint, spearmint, aniseed and eucalyptus; lecithin and other phosphoaminolipins; natural gums.	—

Exported Goods	Imported Goods	Rate of Drawback (if any)
Cigarette papers in the form of booklets.	Cigarette paper imported in bobbins or reels.	—
Cinematograph film (including sound tracks), exposed, whether positive or negative, and whether developed or not.	Unexposed film of a length of 12 ft. or more.	—
Cloth oil or wool oil but neither containing less than 70 per cent. by weight of oleine fatty acids.	Animal tallow or bone grease.	—

Cocoa:

1. Cocoa butter (fat or oil).	Raw cocoa beans, whole or broken, and cocoa paste.	—
2. Cocoa butter, blended or refined.	Cocoa butter (fat or oil).	—
3. Cocoa cake and cocoa paste.	Raw cocoa beans, whole or broken.	—
4. Cocoa powder, sweetened or unsweetened, and drinking chocolate.	Raw cocoa beans, whole or broken, and cocoa paste.	—
5. Cocoa powder, sweetened, and drinking chocolate.	Sugar of either of the following descriptions:— (a) sugar not qualifying for Commonwealth preference, of a polarisation exceeding 98°; (b) sugar qualifying for Commonwealth preference, of a polarisation exceeding 99°.	(i) 6s. 10·8d. per cwt. of sugar; (ii) 6s. 6·9d. per cwt. of anhydrous invert sugar. (i) 1s. 0·8d. per cwt. of sugar; (ii) 1s. 0·19d. per cwt. of anhydrous invert sugar.
Cod, dried and salted.	Fresh cod, with heads and tails, from which the entrails, livers and roes have been removed.	£4 2s. 0d. per ton of dried salted cod.

Coffee:

1. Roasted coffee beans.	Coffee beans, not being kiln dried or roasted or ground.	—
2. Roasted coffee in ground form, whether pure or mixed with other substances.		
3. Soluble coffee powder, whether of pure coffee or a mixture of pure coffee and other substances.		
Combing oil, being a mixture of refined sperm oil, castor oil and fatty acids.	Unrefined sperm oil and castor oil.	—

Exported Goods	Imported Goods	Rate of Drawback (if any)
Cuprammonium products, that is to say, manufactures wholly or partly of cuprammonium filament or fibres, the following:—		
1. Woven ribbons, woven labels and similar woven goods, whether in the piece or not; woven fabric.	Cuprammonium continuous filament yarn.	—
2. Warp knitted fabric, whether on a base or not.	Spun yarn of cuprammonium fibres or of cuprammonium fibres and wool.	—
3. Brushed warp knitted fabric.	Cuprammonium continuous filament yarn.	—
4. Warp knitted fabric other than brushed warp knitted fabric.	Cuprammonium continuous filament yarn.	—
Dextrins, soluble, and other modified starches, and starch adhesives (plain or compounded).	Starch, being maize starch or milo starch.	—
Doors, flush, faced with fibre hardboard.	Fibre hardboard, of a weight exceeding 50 lb. per cubic foot, imported in sheets of a length exceeding 5 ft. $11\frac{7}{8}$ ins. but not exceeding 7 ft. $0\frac{1}{8}$ in., of a width exceeding 1 ft. $5\frac{3}{8}$ in. but not exceeding 3 ft. $0\frac{1}{8}$ in., and of a thickness exceeding $0 \cdot 105$ in. but not exceeding $0 \cdot 145$ in.	—
Doors, flush, faced with plywood.	Plywood containing no material other than wood and bonding material, imported in sheets, sanded or scraped on one or both sides, of a length exceeding 5 ft. $11\frac{7}{8}$ ins., but not exceeding 7 ft. $1\frac{1}{4}$ ins., of a width exceeding 1 ft. $5\frac{3}{8}$ ins. but not exceeding 3 ft. $1\frac{1}{4}$ ins., and of a thickness exceeding $2 \cdot 85$ mm. but not exceeding $4 \cdot 4$ mm.	—
Drafting bands of a kind used for textile machinery.	Leather of either of the following descriptions:— (a) chrome tanned calf leather imported in skins or pieces weighing less than 4 lb. each; (b) dressed vegetable tanned calf leather.	—

Exported Goods	Imported Goods	Rate of Drawback (if any)
Dyeline natural tracing paper, sensitised but unexposed.	Natural tracing paper, coated with cellulose acetate, and— (a) weighing more than 120 but not more than 135 grammes per square metre; (b) on which the duty paid amounted to not less than 3d. per square metre.	—
Electrosensitive recording paper rolls of a width exceeding 8 ins.	Wet-strengthened uncalendered cellulose paper of a weight when fully extended equivalent to not less than 40 grammes and not more than 50 grammes per square metre, and containing not more than the following parts per million of the following metals:— Aluminium ... 20 Calcium ... ... 250 Iron ... ... 5 Magnesium ... 50 All other metals together (except sodium and potassium) 20	A rate for each complete 100 ft. of the exported paper calculated as follows:— where the width of the paper— does not exceed 9 ins., 4·7d. exceeds 9 ins. but does not exceed 11 ins., 6·4d. exceeds 11 ins. but does not exceed 18 ins., 6·5d. exceeds 18 ins., 10·8d.
Foodstuffs, canned or bottled, the following:— 1. Foodstuffs, canned in tomato sauce. 2. Foodstuffs, other than fish, bottled in tomato sauce. 3. Ketchups, sauces, chutneys and soups, canned or bottled.	Tomato purée or paste, containing not less than 25 per cent. by weight of tomato solids.	—
Fruit, fruit peel and fruit juice preserved with sugar, bottled or canned, or drained, glacé or crystallised; jams, lemon curd, fruit jelly preparations, marmalades, mincemeat, fruit purée and fruit pastes, containing added sugar.	Sugar of either of the following descriptions:— (a) sugar not qualifying for Commonwealth preference, of a polarisation exceeding 98°; (b) sugar qualifying for Commonwealth preference, of a polarisation exceeding 99°.	(i) 6s. 10·8d. per cwt. of sugar; (ii) 6s. 6·9d. per cwt. of anhydrous invert sugar. (i) 1s. 0·8d. per cwt. of sugar; (ii) 1s. 0·19d. per cwt. of anhydrous invert sugar.
Fruit cakes and other goods made with dried fruit:— 1. Fruit cakes, fruit puddings, biscuits and sweetmeat confectionery.	Raisins, sultanas, currants and other dried grapes and dried figs.	—
2. Mincemeat, pickles, sauces and chutneys.	Raisins, sultanas, currants and other dried grapes.	—
3. Fig jam.	Dried figs.	—

Exported Goods	Imported Goods	Rate of Drawback (if any)
Furniture.	(A) Woven textile fabrics.	—
	(B) Plywood of birch and beech, blockboard, laminboard and battenboard, excluding veneered panels and sheets.	—.
	(C) Wood in the rough, roughly squared or half squared or sawn lengthwise, sliced or peeled, of the following species, namely species of Acer, Betula, Fagus, Fraxinus, Juglans, Populus, Quercus and Ulmus; Castanea sativa; Eucalyptus diversicolor; Eucalyptus marginata.	—
Garments, the following:—		
1. Men's jackets, trousers, waistcoats and shorts, and women's trousers, shorts and skirts.	Silk fabric, being fabric— (a) woven wholly from spun yarns of mulberry silk; (b) of plain weave, showing a slub effect in both warp and weft directions; (c) free from metallic weighting; (d) weighing not less than $5\frac{1}{2}$ oz. and not more than 7 oz. per square yard; and (e) on which the duty paid amounted to not less than 2s. 6d. per lb.	.—
2. Women's and girls': (A) Dresses (whether lined or not). (B) Jackets, unlined. (C) Skirts, unlined and not falling within paragraph 1 of this entry. (D) Two-piece ensembles consisting of a dress and jacket (whether lined or not).	Fabric, containing silk or man-made fibres or both, on which the duty paid amounted to more than 4d. per lb.	—.
Garments, rain-proof, the following:— Raincoats; Jackets; Trousers; Over-trousers; Skirts; Headgear.	Woven fabric, whether or not proofed, being fabric of cotton or of cotton and man-made fibre and falling to be classified, on importation, under heading 55.09 of the Customs Tariff 1959, on which the duty paid amounted to not less than 6d. per lb.	—

Exported Goods	Imported Goods	Rate of Drawback (if any)
Glass, laminated, in sheets, consisting of two layers of glass with a middle layer of poly(vinyl butyral).	Poly (vinyl butyral) in sheet form.	—
Glue, gelatin and other bone products, the following:—	Bones, crushed or uncrushed.	—
1. Glue and gelatin produced by a process of degelatinisation, containing not more than 16 per cent. moisture.		
2. Ossein.		
3. Gelatin produced by a process of acidulation, containing not more than 16 per cent. moisture.		
4. Calcium phosphates; mineral supplements for animal feeding containing calcium phosphates; crushed or ground degelatinised bones.		
5. Calcined bones.		
Golf clubs.	Golf club head blocks of wood or of laminated wood, being either roughly shaped by sawing or shaped by sawing and by further manufacture but not fully machined and sandpapered.	—
Hats, bonnets, hat shapes, capelines, hoods and manchons.	Hatters' fur, unblown.	A rate per lb. of felt equal to 1·2 times the amount per lb. of the duty paid on the fur or, where the amount per lb. of the duty so paid was less than 1s. 6d., equal to 1·5 times the amount per lb. of the duty so paid.
Hazelnut products, the following:—	Hazelnuts, shelled but not further prepared.	—
1. Paste produced partly from hazelnuts.		
2. Chocolate, chocolate confectionery and sugar confectionery, containing hazelnuts, either whole, cut, broken or ground, or containing paste produced partly from hazelnuts.		

Exported Goods	Imported Goods	Rate of Drawback (if any)
Heat-absorbing glass, surface ground and polished on both faces, and having the properties of either of the categories specified in paragraph 23 of British Standard 952:1964.	Glass of the description specified in column 1, imported in rectangles of 10 ft. or more in length and $7\frac{1}{2}$ ft. or more in width.	—
Inked ribbons for typewriters or for other office machinery.	Woven fabric, wholly of silk, not inked, exceeding 30 cm. in width.	—
Insulated copper strip and winding wire, being, in both cases, of a high conductivity.	Polyvinyl acetal resins, polyester resins, polyurethane resins and linseed oil.	—
Leather, dressed, in complete skins.	Goat and kid skins, fresh, salted, dried, pickled or limed, but not further treated.	—
Leather goods, the following:— 1. Saddlery and harness (including horse boots). 2. Trunks, bags, wallets, pouches and other receptacles (whether fitted or not) other than handbags.	Dressed leather, other than patent leather, and other than glacé kid being chrome tanned goatskin of smooth polished finish.	
Linseed oil, and goods made with linseed oil (other than printers' inks): 1. Linseed oil, and mixtures consisting of linseed oil and driers.	Linseed.	£13 10s. 0d. per ton of linseed oil
2. Linseed oil, refined or heat-treated or both; mixtures consisting of linseed oil and driers; mixtures of linseed oil and other oils, with or without the addition of driers or of rosin or of both; mixtures of linseed oil and vegetable substances, with or without the addition of water; adducts of linseed oil; putty.	Linseed oil.	—
3. Mixtures consisting of cobalt linoleate, linseed oil and linseed oil fatty acids, and having a metallic content of not more than 6 per cent. by weight.	Linseed oil.	11s. 5d. per 100 kg. of the mixture.

Exported Goods	*Imported Goods*	*Rate of Drawback (if any)*
4. Linseed oil fatty acids (being the acids obtained by the hydrolysis of linseed oil).	Linseed oil.	£13 13s. 10d. per ton of linseed oil fatty acids.
5. Printed linoleum and floorcloth.	Linseed oil.	£1 18s. 5d. per ton of linoleum or floorcloth.
6. Linoleum, not printed manufactured on a base of jute canvas, cotton or spun rayon cloth.	Linseed oil.	£3 2s. 10d. per ton of linoleum.
7. Linoleum, not printed, manufactured on a base of bitumenised felt.	Linseed oil.	£2 2s. 2d. per ton of linoleum.
8. Linoleum, not printed, manufactured on a base of resin coated paper felt.	Linseed oil.	£2 16s. 3d. per ton of linoleum
9. Cork carpets; unpigmented linoleum composition manufactured on a base of flannelette.	Linseed oil.	£3 3s. 8d. per ton of cork carpet or linoleum composition.
10. Felt base.	Linseed oil.	7s. 11d. per ton of felt base.
11. Oil baize and leathercloth.	Linseed oil.	£2 4s. 0d. per ton of oil baize or leathercloth.
12. Blocks, tiles, and similar articles, of a kind used for floors, walls or staircases, consisting mainly (by weight) of cement, lime and plaster, and impregnated with linseed oil, of dimensions not greater than 10 ins. in length or width.	Linseed oil.	£1 8s. 11d. per ton of blocks, tiles or other articles.
13. Paint, enamel and varnish.	Linseed oil.	—
14. Synthetic resins.	Linseed oil.	—
Lubricating oil viscosity modifiers consisting of polymerised aliphatic methacrylates dissolved in lubricating oil.	Acetone cyanohydrin, containing not more than 0·10 per cent. by weight of free hydrogen cyanide.	—
Men's shirts.	Woven fabric of spun silk.	—
Methacrylates, falling within heading 29.14 of the Customs Tariff 1959, the following—butyl methacrylate, hexyl methacrylate, lauryl methacrylate and stearyl methacrylate.	Acetone cyanohydrin, containing not more than 0·10 per cent. by weight of free hydrogen cyanide.	—

Exported Goods	Imported Goods	Rate of Drawback (if any)
Moulding compounds in the form of granules, coloured, of polyoxymethylene, not compounded with any other substance.	Polyoxymethylenes in the form of granular powder, being polyaddition products of not less than 90 per cent. by weight of formaldehyde, and not being plasticised or otherwise compounded.	—
Neckties, bow-ties and cravats.	Woven fabric of heading 50.09, 50.10 or 51.04 of the Customs Tariff 1959.	—
Oat products.	Oats in husk.	4s. 7d. per cwt. of ground, rolled or flaked oats, or oatmeal, or oat flour.
Ophthalmic lenses, single vision, other than contact lenses.	Drawn ophthalmic raw sheet glass falling within heading 70.05 of the Customs Tariff 1959.	—
Orange marmalade,	Fresh bitter oranges.	—
Oranges, bitter, prepared for use in the manufacture of marmalade.	Fresh bitter oranges.	—
Packing cases of fibreboard, corrugated or solid.	Kraft paper or kraft board, bleached or unbleached, on which the duty paid amounted to more than £1 per ton.	A rate per ton of paper or board equal to £1 5s. 6d. for the first £1 5s. 0d. of the amount per ton of the duty paid on it, plus 5s. 8d. for each additional 5s. 0d. or part of 5s. 0d. of that amount.
Packing cases of plywood, reinforced with steel.	Plywood which contains no material other than wood and bonding material and is of a thickness not less than 3 mm. and not more than 9 mm.	A rate per 100 square feet of plywood equal to 9½d. for each complete millimetre of the thickness thereof.
Panama hats.	Natural straw hoods on which the duty paid was more than 3s. 0d. per dozen hoods.	—
Paper bags, open-topped without flaps, or closed except for a single opening of the valve type.	Paper of any of the following descriptions, being paper of a weight when fully extended equivalent to not more than 220 grammes per square metre:— (a) paper manufactured wholly of bleached or unbleached sulphate cellulose fibre; (b) sulphite wrapping paper, machine glazed; (c) greaseproof paper, bleached;	—

Exported Goods	*Imported Goods*	*Rate of Drawback (if any)*
	(d) greaseproof paper, unbleached; (e) glazed transparent paper— on which the duty paid amounted to more than £1 7s. 6d. per ton	
Photographic film, sensitised but unexposed; photographic film base prepared for colour photography, but not sensitised.	Photographic film base (other than nitro-cellulose) imported in rolls.	—
Pigment produced or manufactured from combined cadmium.	Cadmium metal.	1s. 11d. per lb. of combined cadmium.
Plastic-bonded asbestos panels, that is to say, board manufactured from asbestos, lime, silica, water, and no other materials, with a single piece of laminated plastic sheeting bonded to one side or to each side, in panels— (a) of a length not less than 7 ft. 11 ins. but not exceeding 10 ft. 1 in.; (b) of a width not less than 1 ft. 11 ins. nor more than 2 ft. 1 in., or not less than 2 ft. 11 ins. nor more than 4 ft. 1 in.; (c) of a thickness not less than 0·28 in. but not exceeding 1·35 ins.	Laminated plastic sheets, consisting of resin-impregnated papers, bonded together, or of such papers bonded together and coated on one side with melamine resin, and— (a) of a length not less than 8 ft. but not exceeding 10 ft. 2 ins., (b) of a width not less than 3 ft. but not exceeding 4 ft. 2 ins., and (c) of a thickness not less than 0·024 in. but not exceeding 0·081 in.— on which the duty paid amounted to not less than 6d.	—
Poly(vinyl chloride) tape, whether or not colour-coated, and whether or not backed with adhesive, for use in hand operated appliances for making labels or name plates otherwise than by stamping the whole legend simultaneously.	Tape of the descriptions referred to in column 1 exceeding 500 ft. in length.	—
Printers' inks and printing ink base.	(A) Carbon black. (B) Linseed oil.	— £13 10s. 0d. per ton of linseed oil.

Exported Goods	*Imported Goods*	*Rate of Drawback (if any)*
Products of "improved" wood within the meaning of Chapter 44 of the Customs Tariff 1959, the following:—	Wooden veneer sheets.	—

1. Picking sticks, being weaving loom parts.

2. Railway fishplates.

3. Steel-rule die-blocks.

4. Rectangular panels, boards, sheets, billets, strips or blocks.

Exported Goods	*Imported Goods*	*Rate of Drawback (if any)*
Quebracho extract and blends thereof:		
1. Ground insoluble quebracho extract.	Solid insoluble quebracho extract.	—
2. Soluble quebracho extract, powder or liquid.	Solid insoluble quebracho extract.	—
3. Blends in powder form of quebracho extract with the following materials—	Solid insoluble quebracho extract.	—

(A) lignite, in which the content by weight of soluble quebracho extract is 60 per cent.;

(B) mangrove extract, in which the said content is 75 per cent.;

(C) mimosa extract, in which the said content is 47 per cent.;

(D) myrobalan extract, in which the said content is $64\frac{1}{2}$ per cent.;

(E) mimosa extract and myrobalan extract, in which the said content is $33\frac{1}{3}$ per cent.;

(F) sulphite cellulose, in which the said content is 50, 60, 75 or 86 per cent.;

(G) sulphite cellulose, in which the content by weight of insoluble quebracho extract is 50 per cent.

Exported Goods	*Imported Goods*	*Rate of Drawback (if any)*
4. Ground soluble quebracho extract.	Solid soluble quebracho extract.	

Exported Goods	Imported Goods	Rate of Drawback (if any)
Seasoning, liquid, produced from tabasco red pepper mash and vinegar.	Tabasco red peppers (being the fruit of capsicum frutescens, var. tabasco), mashed and provisionally preserved in brine.	—
Shuttlecocks and shuttle-cock skirts	Poly(ll-aminoundecanoic acid) in the form of granules, containing fillers or plasticisers or both.	A rate of 0·021d. per gramme of the imported articles.
Soap (including medicated soap), and surface-active preparations and washing preparations containing soap.	Animal tallow.	—
Soft drinks, unconcentrated or concentrated; powders for such drinks; sweetened flavouring syrups and concentrates.	Sugar of either of the following descriptions:— (a) sugar not qualifying for Commonwealth preference, of a polarisation exceeding 98°; (b) sugar qualifying for Commonwealth preference, of a polarisation exceeding 99°.	(i) 6s. 10·8d. per cwt. of sugar; (ii) 6s. 6·9d. per cwt. of anhydrous invert sugar (i) 1s. 0·8d. per cwt. of sugar; (ii) 1s. 0·19d. per cwt. of anhydrous invert sugar.
Soya bean oil and other goods made from soya beans:		
1. Soya bean oil (whether hydrogenated or not), unmixed.	Soya beans.	£4 16s. 0d. per ton of soya bean oil.
2. Paint, enamel and varnish.	Soya beans.	—
3. Synthetic resins.	Soya beans.	—
Sperm oil, refined, and fatty alcohol derived from sperm oil.	Unrefined sperm oil.	—
Stearine fatty acids and oleine fatty acids.	Animal tallow or bone grease.	—
Sugar, refined in the United Kingdom: (a) of a polarisation exceeding 98°.	Beet sugar and cane sugar, solid, not qualifying for Commonwealth preference.	(i) where the duty paid was at the highest rate, 6s. 10·8d. per cwt. of refined sugar; (ii) where the duty paid was at less than the highest rate, 4s. 3½d. per cwt. of refined sugar.
(b) of a polarisation not exceeding 98°.		A rate per cwt. of refined sugar equal to the full rate of duty per cwt. chargeable on the importation into the United Kingdom of sugar of the like polarisation.

Exported Goods	Imported Goods	Rate of Drawback (if any)
(c) in the form of fine white powder, not flavoured, containing not less than 8 per cent., and not more than 10 per cent., invert sugar.		—
Sugar confectionery, not containing cocoa.	(A) Liquid glucose.	—
	(B) Sugar of either of the following descriptions:—	
	(a) sugar not qualifying for Commonwealth preference, of a polarisation exceeding 98°;	(i) 6s. 10·8d. per cwt. of sugar; (ii) 6s. 6·9d. per cwt. of anhydrous invert sugar.
	(b) sugar qualifying for Commonwealth preference, of a polarisation exceeding 99°.	(i) 1s. 0·8d. per cwt. of sugar; (ii) 1s. 0·19d. per cwt. of anhydrous invert sugar.
	(C) Milk powder; dried egg albumin; coconut, desiccated; pineapple, fresh; edible nuts other than coconut, brazil, cashew, hazel, almonds and chestnuts; peel of melons and citrus fruit, fresh, frozen, dried, or provisionally preserved; ginger; menthol, not synthetic; tartaric acid; essential oils, terpeneless —orange, lemon, lime, mandarin, tangerine, peppermint, spearmint, aniseed and eucalyptus; lecithin and other phosphoaminolipins; natural gums.	—
Suitcases, attaché cases and hat boxes; train cases, beauty cases and similar receptacles.	Board (other than vulcanised fibre board, leatherboard, imitation leatherboard and strawboard) made from paper or pulp, being board weighing more than 850 grammes per square metre of which one side only has been coloured and varnished and on which the duty paid amounted to not less than £3 per ton.	—
Syrups and treacles.	Beet sugar and cane sugar, solid, not qualifying for Commonwealth preference.	–

Exported Goods	Imported Goods	Rate of Drawback (if any)
Tinsel cord fabric.	Tinsel cord, consisting of yarn wholly of silk and man-made fibres, or either of them, wound with metal.	—
Toilet paper in rolls or packets.	Paper of any of the following descriptions:— (a) tissue paper or machine glazed paper of a weight when fully extended equivalent to not less than 19·5 grammes and not more than 24·5 grammes per square metre; (b) crepe paper of a weight when fully extended equivalent to not less than 24·5 grammes and not more than 39 grammes per square metre— on which the duty paid amounted to not less than £2 per ton.	—
Vegetables with added sugar, bottled or canned.	Sugar of either of the following descriptions:— (a) sugar not qualifying for commonwealth preference, of a polarisation exceeding 98°. (b) sugar qualifying for Commonwealth preference, of a polarisation exceeding 99°.	(i) 6s. 10·8d. per cwt. of sugar; (ii) 6s. 6·9d. per cwt. of anhydrous invert sugar. (i) 1s. 0·8d. per cwt. of sugar; (ii) 1s. 0·19d. per cwt. of anhydrous invert sugar.
Veneer sheets, being sheets cut cross-section from a laminate of wooden veneer sheets.	(A) Wooden veneer sheets. (B) Timber logs of the following species, namely, species of Acer, Betula, Fagus, Fraxinus, Juglans Populus, Quercus, and Ulmus; Castanea sativa; Eucalyptus diversicolor; Eucalyptus marginata.	— —
Vinyl chloride and vinylidene chloride products, the following: 1. Tubing, lay-flat. 2. Bags. 3. Film in rolls.	Copolymers of vinyl chloride and vinylidene chloride in the form of powder.	—

Exported Goods	Imported Goods	Rate of Drawback (if any)
Waste, textile, and yarn: 1. Textile waste which has been subjected to one or more of the following processes:— (a) pulling, (b) garnetting, (c) carding, (d) combing, (e) cutting to staple fibre lengths. 2. Yarn.	Textile fibre, in the form of waste, rags or scrap material, of man-made fibres or of man-made fibres and wool, not pulled, garnetted or further processed.	—
Weed-killer, compound, containing not less than 20 per cent. and not more than 75 per cent. by weight of sodium chlorate.	Sodium chlorate imported in the form of powder, not less than 99 per cent. pure.	—
Whey powder preparations, containing lactose but no substance other than whey powder, lactose or other sugar.	Whey powder.	—
Wood tar, refined by the removal by distillation of water and volatile oils, and either unmixed or mixed only with resinous material or hydrocarbon oil or both.	Unrefined wood tar.	—
Wood-faced plastic laminates, resulting from the lamination of a single melamine-impregnated wooden veneer sheet with a backing of phenolic resin core papers.	Wooden veneer sheets.	—
Yarn, metallic, that is to say, strip, of a width not exceeding ⅛ in., consisting of aluminium foil between two layers of plasticised cellulose acetate butyrate, whether or not doubled or twisted with yarn or thread.	Laminated aluminium foil, consisting of foil of a thickness not exceeding 0·15 mm., between two layers of plasticised cellulose acetate butyrate, imported in sheets of a width not less than 18 ins.	2s. 10d. per lb. of laminated aluminium foil.
Yeast products for human consumption.	Yeast and autolysed yeast, dried or liquid.	—

SCHEDULE 3

Goods Excluded from Operation of Import Duties Act 1958

Schedule 5, Para. 3 (2) (a)

1. The descriptions of goods referred to in Article 2 (4) of this Order are all descriptions of goods mentioned in column 1 of the entries specified below, except that words limiting any such entry to specified paragraphs thereof shall be taken as limiting the descriptions of goods to those mentioned in column 1 of the specified paragraphs.

2. The said entries are those in Schedule 2 to this Order beginning with or consisting of the following words:—

Animal black,
Electrosensitive recording paper,
Hats,
Linseed oil (paragraphs 3 to 12 only),
Packing-cases of fibreboard,
Packing-cases of plywood,
Printers' inks,
Yarn, metallic,

SCHEDULE 4

SPECIAL PROVISIONS AS TO TEXTILES AND TEXTILE ARTICLES

1.—(1) In the entries to which this paragraph applies, any loading or dressing taken into account in determining the weight of any man-made fibres or silk for the purposes of charging duty shall be treated for the purposes of drawback under the said duty as part of those fibres or, as the case may be, that silk.

(2) This paragraph applies to the entries in Schedule 2 to this Order beginning with or consisting of the following words:—

Cuprammonium products,
Garments, the following,
Garments, rain-proof,
Inked ribbons,
Men's shirts,
Neckties.

2.—(1) In the entries to which this paragraph applies references to silk do not include noil yarn or noil yarn doubled or twisted with other yarn.

(2) This paragraph applies to the entries in Schedule 2 to this Order beginning with or consisting of the following words:—

Garments, the following,
Inked ribbons,
Men's shirts.

SCHEDULE 5

IMPORT DUTY DRAWBACKS ORDERS REVOKED

Number and Year of Order				*Reference*
No. 6 of 1966	...	...	...	S.I. 1966/921 (1966 II, p. 2207).
No. 7 of 1966	...	...	...	S.I. 1966/1081 (1966 II, p. 2662).
No. 8 of 1966	...	...	...	S.I. 1966/1220 (1966 III, p. 3278).
No. 9 of 1966	...	...	...	S.I. 1966/1335 (1966 III, p. 3663).
No. 10 of 1966	...	...	...	S.I. 1966/1462 (1966 III, p. 3962).
No. 11 of 1966	...	...	...	S.I. 1966/1563 (1966 III, p. 4766).
No. 1 of 1967	...	...	...	S.I. 1967/78 (1967 I, p. 157).
No. 2 of 1967	...	...	...	S.I. 1967/204 (1967 I, p. 344).
No. 3 of 1967	...	...	...	S.I. 1967/470 (1967 I, p. 1415).
No. 4 of 1967	...	...	...	S.I. 1967/651 (1967 I, p. 2045).
No. 5 of 1967	...	...	...	S.I. 1967/780 (1967 II, p. 2307).
No. 6 of 1967	...	...	...	S.I. 1967/952 (1967 II, p. 2916).
No. 7 of 1967	...	...	...	S.I. 1967/1113 (1967 II, p. 3268).
No. 8 of 1967	...	...	...	S.I. 1967/1255 (1967 II, p. 3666).
No. 9 of 1967	...	...	...	S.I. 1967/1435 (1967 III, p. 4132).
No. 10 of 1967	...	...	...	S.I. 1967/1564 (1967 III, p. 4339).
No. 11 of 1967	...	...	...	S.I. 1967/1719 (1967 III, p. 4647).
No. 12 of 1967	...	...	...	S.I. 1967/1835 (1967 III, p. 4901).

Number and Year of Order				Reference
No. 1 of 1968	...	...	...	S.I. 1968/78 (1968 I, p. 260).
No. 2 of 1968	...	...	...	S.I. 1968/251 (1968 I, p. 763).
No. 3 of 1968	...	...	...	S.I. 1968/481 (1968 I, p. 1192).
No. 4 of 1968	...	...	...	S.I. 1968/644 (1968 I, p. 1480).
No. 5 of 1968	...	...	...	S.I. 1968/930 (1968 II, p. 2432).
No. 6 of 1968	...	...	...	S.I. 1968/1157 (1968 II, p. 3142).
No. 7 of 1968	...	...	...	S.I. 1968/1385 (1968 II, p. 3943).
No. 8 of 1968	...	...	...	S.I. 1968/1508 (1968 III, p. 4268).
No. 9 of 1968	...	...	...	S.I. 1968/1722 (1968 III, p. 4645).

EXPLANATORY NOTE

(This Note is not part of the Order.)

This Order:—

(1) consolidates all existing provisions for the allowance of drawback of import duty under the Import Duties Act 1958 and, in addition,—

(2) provides that there shall continue to be drawback of import duty in respect of certain glass parts of cathode ray tubes, notwithstanding their reclassification in a tariff heading (70.21) which would otherwise render them ineligible for drawback;

(3) amends the provisions for the allowance of drawback of import duty on rolls of electrosensitive recording paper so that the drawback is related to the total quantity of paper exported and not to the paper content of each roll;

(4) revokes the provisions for the allowance of drawback of import duty on handbags manufactured from imported leather; and

(5) revokes the existing fixed rates of drawback of import duty in respect of photographic film and prepared film base and provides for drawback to be related to the duty paid on the imported film base actually used in the manufacture of the exported goods.

STATUTORY INSTRUMENTS

1968 No. 1882

INDUSTRIAL TRAINING

The Industrial Training (Carpet Board) Order 1968

Made - - -	*25th November* 1968
Laid before Parliament	*4th December* 1968
Coming into Operation	*18th December* 1968

The Secretary of State after consultation with the Carpet Industry Training Board and with organisations and associations of organisations appearing to be representative respectively of substantial numbers of employers engaging in the activities hereinafter mentioned and of substantial numbers of persons employed in those activities and in exercise of her powers under section 9 of the Industrial Training Act 1964(**a**) and of all other powers enabling her in that behalf hereby makes the following Order :—

Citation, commencement and interpretation

1.—(1) This Order may be cited as the Industrial Training (Carpet Board) Order 1968 and shall come into operation on 18th December 1968.

(2) In this Order—

(*a*) "the Act" means the Industrial Training Act 1964 ;

(*b*) "the Board" means the Carpet Industry Training Board ;

(*c*) "levy Order" means the Industrial Training Levy (Carpet) Order 1967(**b**) or the Industrial Training Levy (Carpet) Order 1968(**c**) ;

(*d*) "the principal Order" means the Industrial Training (Carpet Board) Order 1966(**d**).

(3) The Interpretation Act 1889(**e**) shall apply to the interpretation of this Order as it applies to the interpretation of an Act of Parliament and as if this Order and the principal Order were Acts of Parliament.

Activities of the Board

2. The activities in relation to which the Board exercises the functions conferred by the Act upon industrial training boards shall, in lieu of the activities specified in Schedule 1 to the principal Order, be the activities specified in the Schedule to this Order, and accordingly in the principal Order the latter Schedule shall be substituted for the former Schedule.

Transitional provisions

3.—(1) The chairman and other members of the Board on the day upon which this Order comes into operation shall continue to be members of the Board and to hold and vacate their offices in accordance with the terms of the instruments appointing them to be members.

(**a**) 1964 c. 16.
(**c**) S.I. 1968/30 (1968 I, p. 88).
(**e**) 1889 c. 63.
(**b**) S.I. 1967/331 (1967 I, p. 1147).
(**d**) S.I. 1966/245 (1966 I, p. 499).

(2) The provisions of this Order shall not—

(a) extend the operation of either levy Order ;

(b) affect the operation of either levy Order in relation to the assessment of an employer within the meaning of that Order in respect of an establishment engaged in the first levy period or the second levy period, as the case may be, wholly or mainly in activities included in the Schedule to this Order ;

(c) affect the operation of any assessment notice served by the Board under the provisions of either levy Order before the date upon which this Order comes into operation or any appeal or other proceedings arising out of any such notice.

25th November 1968.

Barbara Castle,
First Secretary of State and Secretary of State for Employment and Productivity.

SCHEDULE

Article 2

THE CARPET INDUSTRY

1. Subject to the provisions of this Schedule, the activities of the carpet industry are the following activities in so far as they are carried out in Great Britain:—

(a) the manufacture (otherwise than wholly or mainly from jute) of carpets, carpeting, mats, matting, rugs or any similar floor coverings ;

(b) the manufacture of pressed or needle felt when carried out by an employer (or an associated company of the employer, being a company) engaged mainly in the manufacture of all or any of the products to which the foregoing sub-paragraph applies ;

(c) the manufacture, from paper, of yarn or woven fabric ;

(d) any of the following processes when carried out by an employer (or an associated company of the employer, being a company) engaged in the manufacture of any products to which sub-paragraph (a) of this paragraph applies for the purposes thereof—

(i) sorting, treating, dyeing, using or consuming textile fibres or tops, or packing, re-packing or warehousing such fibres, tops or yarn ;

(ii) carding, combing or re-combing textile fibres ;

(iii) making rovings from textile fibres or tops, or spinning yarn ;

(iv) twisting, doubling, folding, winding, warping, warp dressing, beaming, reeling, curling, sizing or dyeing yarn or any other process in the preparation of yarn for further processing ;

(e) any activities, being—

(i) related activities incidental or ancillary to principal activities of the carpet industry ; or

(ii) activities undertaken in the administration, control or direction of one or more establishments, being establishments engaged wholly or mainly in principal activities of that industry, in related activities incidental or ancillary thereto, or in the administration, control or direction of one or more other establishments engaged in such principal or related activities ;

and carried out, in either case, by the employer engaged in those principal activities or, where that employer is a company, by the company or by an associated company of the company ;

(*f*) any activities of industry or commerce (other than carpet activities) carried out at or from an establishment mainly engaged—

    (i) in carpet activities ; or

    (ii) in carpet activities and in activities described in the Appendix to this Schedule, but to a greater extent in carpet activities than in activities described in that Appendix in relation to any one industry.

2. Notwithstanding anything contained in this Schedule, there shall not be included in the activities of the carpet industry : —

    (*a*) the activities of any establishment engaged—

        (i) mainly in activities not being carpet activities or activities described in the Appendix to this Schedule ; or

        (ii) to a less extent in carpet activities than in activities described in that Appendix in relation to any one industry ;

    (*b*) the activities of any establishment engaged wholly or mainly in related activities, being activities—

        (i) incidental or ancillary to the activities of one or more establishments (in this sub-paragraph hereafter referred to as "the principal establishment") engaged wholly or mainly in any activities not being principal activities of the carpet industry ; and

        (ii) carried out by the employer carrying on the principal establishment or, where that employer is a company, by the company or by an associated company of the company ;

    (*c*) the activities of any establishment engaged wholly or mainly in the activities following or any of them, that is to say—

        (i) the manufacture of pressed or needle felt, not being manufacture specified in paragraph 1(*b*) of this Schedule ;

        (ii) the manufacture of any products wholly or mainly from cork ;

        (iii) the manufacture, wholly or mainly from candlewick or terry towelling, of mats, rugs or toilet sets ;

        (iv) the processing of rubber or of plastics material ;

        (v) the coating or impregnation of textile fabric with rubber or plastics material ;

        (vi) the manufacture of linoleum or any similar floor covering or of felt base floor covering ; or

        (vii) the manufacture, mainly from skins with the hair or wool on or from fur skins, of rugs or similar floor coverings ;

    (*d*) the activities of any company, association or body that is required by its constitution to apply its profits, if any, or other income in promoting its objects and is prohibited thereby from paying any dividend to its members, and that has for its sole or principal object or among its principal objects the provision of facilities for any of the purposes mentioned in section 15(1) of the Disabled Persons (Employment) Act 1944(**a**) (which relates to the provision for registered persons who are seriously disabled of work or training) ;

    (*e*) any work, occupation or training that is provided in accordance with arrangements made by a local authority under the Disabled Persons (Employment) Act 1958(**b**) or any other enactment that authorises or requires the provision of arrangements for persons suffering from illness, severe physical defect or disability or from mental disorder, or for persons who have been suffering from illness or whose care is undertaken with a view to preventing them from becoming ill, or for old people ;

    (*f*) the supply of food or drink for immediate consumption.

(**a**) 1944 c. 10.   (**b**) 1958 c. 33.

3. In this Schedule unless the context otherwise requires—

(a) "carpet activities" means any one or more of the principal activities of the carpet industry and the activities included in that industry by virtue of paragraph 1(e) of this Schedule ;

(b) "company" includes any body corporate, and "subsidiary" has the same meaning as by virtue of section 154 of the Companies Act 1948(a) it has for the purposes of that Act ;

(c) "felt base floor covering" means any floor covering made from bitumen saturated grey felt paper that is paint-coated and finished with an enamel paint or plastics surface ;

(d) "manufacture" includes any process or operation incidental or appertaining to manufacture ;

(e) "office premises" has the same meaning as in section 1(2) of the Offices, Shops and Railway Premises Act 1963(b) ;

(f) "principal activities of the carpet industry" means activities which, subject to the provisions of paragraph 2 of this Schedule, are specified in paragraph 1, other than sub-paragraphs (e) and (f) thereof, as activities of the carpet industry ;

(g) "processing" in relation to rubber or plastics material means any of the operations of masticating, compounding, mixing, calendering, moulding, pressing, casting, dipping, coating, heat sealing, laminating, machining (other than stitching), cutting, vulcanising or foaming ;

(h) "related activities" means any of the following activities, that is to say—

(i) research, development, design or drawing ;

(ii) buying, selling, testing, advertising, packing, distribution, transport or any similar operations ;

(iii) operations of a kind performed at office premises or laboratories, or at stores, warehouses or similar places ;

(iv) cleaning, washing or garaging vehicles, or carrying out running repairs or minor adjustments thereto ; or

(v) training of employees or apprentices ;

(i) "rubber" means the following products, whether or not vulcanised or hardened, that is to say, natural rubber, balata, gutta percha, and similar natural gums, synthetic rubber and factice derived from oils, and such substances reclaimed ;

(j) "textile fibres" means any fibres consisting, or including more than 15 per cent. by weight, of—

(i) animal fibres of any kind or mixture ;

(ii) the waste of any such fibres ; or

(iii) any mixture of such fibres or waste ;

and includes any other fibres or continuous filaments when used or intended for use in a textile factory for the production of yarn or fabric by a system of manufacture similar to one commonly employed in the production of woollen or worsted yarn or fabric ;

(k) "yarn" (except in paragraph 1(c) of this Schedule) means yarn consisting of textile fibres.

4. For the purposes of this Schedule two companies shall be taken to be associated companies if one is a subsidiary of the other, or both are subsidiaries of a third company, and "associated company" shall be construed accordingly.

(a) 1948 c. 38.   (b) 1963 c. 41.

APPENDIX

The activities that would be included in an industry specified in Column 1 hereof by virtue of the industrial training order specified in the corresponding entry in Column 2, if the provisions specified in Column 3 were omitted from that order.

Column 1	Column 2	Column 3
The wool, jute and flax industry	The Industrial Training (Wool Industry Board) Order 1964 as amended by the Industrial Training (Wool, Jute and Flax Board) Order 1968(a)	Schedule 1 Paragraph 1(s)
The iron and steel industry	The Industrial Training (Iron and Steel Board) Order 1964(b)	Schedule 1 Paragraph 1(j)
The construction industry	The Industrial Training (Construction Board) Order 1964 as amended by the Industrial Training (Construction Board) Order 1967(c)	Schedule 1 Paragraph 1(l)
The engineering industry	The Industrial Training (Engineering Board) Order 1964 as amended by the Industrial Training (Engineering Board) Order 1968(d)	Schedule 1 Paragraph 1(m)
The shipbuilding industry	The Industrial Training (Shipbuilding Board) Order 1964 as amended by the Industrial Training (Shipbuilding Board) Order 1968(e)	Schedule 1 Paragraph 1(g)
The ceramics, glass and mineral products industry	The Industrial Training (Ceramics, Glass and Mineral Products Board) Order 1965(f)	Schedule 1 Paragraph 1(n)
The furniture and timber industry	The Industrial Training (Furniture and Timber Industry Board) Order 1965(g)	Schedule 1 Paragraph 1(r)
The man-made fibres producing industry	The Industrial Training (Man-made Fibres Producing Industry Board) Order 1966(h)	Schedule 1 Paragraph 1(d)
The knitting, lace and net industry	The Industrial Training (Knitting, Lace and Net Industry Board) Order 1966(i)	Schedule 1 Paragraph 1(j)
The cotton and allied textiles industry	The Industrial Training (Cotton and Allied Textiles Board) Order 1966 (j)	Schedule 1 Paragraph 1(p)

(a) S.I. 1964/907, 1968/898 (1964 II, p.1928; 1968 II, p.2376).

(b) S.I. 1964/949 (1964 II, p.2127).

(c) S.I. 1964/1079, 1967/924 (1964 II, p.2384; 1967 II, p.2757).

(d) S.I. 1964/1086, 1968/1333 (1964 II, p.2402; 1968 II, p. 3694).

(e) S.I. 1964/1782, 1968/1614 (1964 III, p.3928; 1968 III, p.4432).

(f) S.I. 1965/1391 (1965 II, p.4062).

(g) S.I. 1965/2028 (1965 III, p.5998).

(h) S.I.1966/143 (1966 I, p.257).

(i) S.I. 1966/246 (1966 I, p.506).

(j) S.I. 1966/823 (1966 II, p.1907).

APPENDIX—*contd.*

Column 1	Column 2	Column 3
The agricultural, horticultural and forestry industry	The Industrial Training (Agricultural, Horticultural and Forestry Board) Order 1966**(a)**	Schedule 1 Paragraph 1(*m*)
The road transport industry	The Industrial Training (Road Transport Board) Order 1966**(b)**	Schedule 1 Paragraph 1(*o*)
The hotel and catering industry	The Industrial Training (Hotel and Catering Board) Order 1966**(c)**	Schedule 1 Paragraph 1(*e*)
The civil air transport industry	The Industrial Training (Civil Air Transport Board) Order 1967**(d)**	Schedule 1 Paragraph 1(*h*)
The petroleum industry	The Industrial Training (Petroleum Board) Order 1967**(e)**	Schedule 1 Paragraph 1(*h*)
The rubber and plastics processing industry	The Industrial Training (Rubber and Plastics Processing Board) Order 1967**(f)**	Schedule 1 Paragraph 1(*k*)
The chemical and allied products industry	Thc Industrial Training (Chemical and Allied Products Board) Order 1967**(g)**	Schedule 1 Paragraph 1(*s*)
The paper and paper products industry	The Industrial Training (Paper and Paper Products Board) Order 1968**(h)**	Schedule 1 Paragraph 1(*j*)
The printing and publishing industry	The Industrial Training (Printing and Publishing Board) Order 1968**(i)**	Schedule 1 Paragraph 1(*n*)
The distributive industry	The Industrial Training (Distributive Board) Order 1968**(j)**	Schedule 1 Paragraph 1(*h*)
The food, drink and tobacco industry	The Industrial Training (Food, Drink and Tobacco Board) Order 1968 **(k)**	Schedule 1 Paragraph 1(*q*)
The footwear, leather and fur skin industry	The Industrial Training (Footwear, Leather and Fur Skin Board) Order 1968**(l)**	Schedule 1 Paragraph 1(*v*)

(a) S.I. 1966/969 (1966 II, p.2333).   **(b)** S.I. 1966/1112 (1966 III, p.2712).
(c) S.I. 1966/1347 (1966 III, p.3669).   **(d)** S.I. 1967/263 (1967 I, p.968).
(e) S.I. 1967/648 (1967 I, p.2032).   **(f)** S.I. 1967/1062 (1967 II, p.3151).
(g) S.I. 1967/1386 (1967 III, p.4049).   **(h)** S.I. 1968/787 (1968 II, p.2194).
(i) S.I. 1968/786 (1968 II, p.2185).   **(j)** S.I. 1968/1032 (1968 II, p.2709).
(k) S.I. 1968/1033 (1968 II, p.2721).   **(l)** S.I. 1968/1763 (1968 III, p. 4785).

EXPLANATORY NOTE

(This Note is not part of the Order.)

This Order re-defines the activities in relation to which the Carpet Industry Training Board exercises its functions. The Board was established on 18th March 1966 by the Industrial Training (Carpet Board) Order 1966.

Amongst the activities henceforth to be included in the carpet industry is the manufacture from paper of yarn or woven fabric. The manufacture of pressed or needle felt will henceforth be included in the industry only if the employer is engaged mainly in the manufacture of carpets or similar floor coverings.

STATUTORY INSTRUMENTS

1968 No. 1883

SUGAR

The Sugar (Rates of Surcharge and Surcharge Repayments) (No. 7) Order 1968

Made - - - -	*26th November* 1968
Laid before Parliament	*27th November* 1968
Coming into Operation	*28th November* 1968

The Minister of Agriculture, Fisheries and Food, in exercise of the powers conferred on him by sections 7(4), 8(6) and 33(4) of the Sugar Act 1956(a) having effect subject to the provisions of section 3 of, and Part II of Schedule 5 to, the Finance Act 1962(b), and section 58 of the Finance Act 1968 (c) and of all other powers enabling him in that behalf, with the concurrence of the Treasury, on the advice of the Sugar Board, hereby makes the following order:—

1.—(1) This order may be cited as the Sugar (Rates of Surcharge and Surcharge Repayments) (No. 7) Order 1968; and shall come into operation on 28th November 1968.

(2) The Interpretation Act 1889(d) shall apply for the interpretation of this order as it applies for the interpretation of an Act of Parliament.

2. Notwithstanding the provisions of Article 2 of the Sugar (Rates of Surcharge and Surcharge Repayments) (No. 6) Order 1968(e), the rates of surcharge payable under and in accordance with the provisions of section 7 of the Sugar Act 1956, having effect as aforesaid, in respect of sugar and invert sugar imported or home produced or used in the manufacture of imported composite sugar products shall on and after 28th November 1968 be those rates specified in Schedule 1 to this order.

3. For the purpose of section 8(3)(b) of the Sugar Act 1956, having effect as aforesaid, the rates of surcharge repayments in respect of invert sugar produced in the United Kingdom from materials on which on or after 28th November 1968 sugar duty has been paid or, by virtue of paragraph 1 of Part II of Schedule 5 to the Finance Act 1962, is treated as having been paid shall, notwithstanding the provisions of Article 3 of the Sugar (Rates of Surcharge and Surcharge Repayments) (No. 6) Order 1968 be those specified in Schedule 2 to this order.

(a) 1956 c. 48.   (b) 1962 c. 44.
(c) 1968 c. 44   (d) 1889 c. 63.
(e) S.I. 1968/1717 (1968 III, p. 4635).

In Witness whereof the Official Seal of the Minister of Agriculture Fisheries and Food is hereunto affixed on 25th November 1968.

(L.S.)

R. P. Fraser,

Authorised by the Minister.

We concur.

26th November 1968.

E. Alan Fitch,
B. K. O'Malley,

Two of the Lords Commissioners of
Her Majesty's Treasury.

SCHEDULE 1

PART I

SURCHARGE RATES FOR SUGAR

Polarisation	Rate of Surcharge per cwt.	
	s.	d.
Exceeding—		
99°	28	0·0
98° but not exceeding 99°	26	4·8
97° ,, ,, ,, 98°	25	9·1
96° ,, ,, ,, 97°	25	1·0
95° ,, ,, ,, 96°	24	4·9
94° ,, ,, ,, 95°	23	8·9
93° ,, ,, ,, 94°	23	0·8
92° ,, ,, ,, 93°	22	4·8
91° ,, ,, ,, 92°	21	8·7
90° ,, ,, ,, 91°	21	0·6
89° ,, ,, ,, 90°	20	4·6
88° ,, ,, ,, 89°	19	8·5
87° ,, ,, ,, 88°	19	1·8
86° ,, ,, ,, 87°	18	7·1
85° ,, ,, ,, 86°	18	1·0
84° ,, ,, ,, 85°	17	7·0
83° ,, ,, ,, 84°	17	0·9
82° ,, ,, ,, 83°	16	6·9
81° ,, ,, ,, 82°	16	1·5
80° ,, ,, ,, 81°	15	8·1
79° ,, ,, ,, 80°	15	2·7
78° ,, ,, ,, 79°	14	9·4
77° ,, ,, ,, 78°	14	4·0
76° ,, ,, ,, 77°	13	10·6
Not exceeding 76°	13	6·0

PART II
SURCHARGE RATES FOR INVERT SUGAR

Sweetening matter content by weight	Rate of Surcharge per cwt.
	s. d.
70 per cent. or more	17 9
Less than 70 per cent. and more than 50 per cent.	12 9
Not more than 50 per cent.	6 3

SCHEDULE 2
SURCHARGE REPAYMENT RATES FOR INVERT SUGAR

Sweetening matter content by weight	Rate of Surcharge Repayment per cwt.
	s. d.
More than 80 per cent.	21 0
More than 70 per cent. but not more than 80 per cent.	17 9
More than 60 per cent. but not more than 70 per cent.	12 9
More than 50 per cent. but not more than 60 per cent.	10 1
Not more than 50 per cent. and the invert sugar not being less in weight than 14 lb. per gallon	6 3

EXPLANATORY NOTE
(*This Note is not part of the Order.*)

This order prescribes—

    (*a*) reductions equivalent to 4s. 8d. per cwt. of refined sugar in the rates of surcharge payable on sugar and invert sugar which become chargeable with surcharge on or after 28th November 1968;

    (*b*) correspondingly reduced rates of surcharge repayment in respect of invert sugar produced in the United Kingdom from materials on which surcharge has been paid.

STATUTORY   INSTRUMENTS

1968 No. 1884

SUGAR

The Composite Sugar Products (Surcharge and Surcharge Repayments—Average Rates) (No. 7) Order 1968

Made - - - -	*26th November* 1968
Laid before Parliament	*27th November* 1968
Coming into Operation	*28th November* 1968

Whereas the Minister of Agriculture, Fisheries and Food (hereinafter called " the Minister ") has on the recommendation of the Commissioners of Customs and Excise (hereinafter called " the Commissioners ") made an order(a) pursuant to the powers conferred upon him by sections 9(1) and 9(4) of the Sugar Act 1956(b), having effect subject to the provisions of section 3 of, and Part II of Schedule 5 to, the Finance Act 1962(c), to the provisions of section 52(2) of the Finance Act 1966(d), and to the provisions of Section 58 of the Finance Act 1968(e), providing that in the case of certain descriptions of composite sugar products surcharge shall be calculated on the basis of an average quantity of sugar or invert sugar taken to have been used in the manufacture of the products, and that certain other descriptions of composite sugar products shall be treated as not containing any sugar or invert sugar, and that in the case of certain descriptions of goods in the manufacture of which sugar or invert sugar is used, surcharge repayments shall be calculated on the basis of an average quantity of sugar or invert sugar taken to have been so used:

Now, therefore, the Minister, on the recommendation of the Commissioners and in exercise of the powers conferred upon him by sections 9(1), 9(4) and 33(4) of the Sugar Act 1956, having effect as aforesaid, and of all other powers enabling him in that behalf, hereby makes the following order:—

1.—(1) This order may be cited as the Composite Sugar Products (Surcharge and Surcharge Repayments—Average Rates) (No. 7) Order 1968; and shall come into operation on 28th November 1968.

(2) The Interpretation Act 1889(f) shall apply for the interpretation of this order as it applies for the interpretation of an Act of Parliament.

2. Surcharge payable on or after 28th November 1968 under and in accordance with the Sugar Act 1956, having effect as aforesaid, in respect of sugar and invert sugar used in the manufacture of the descriptions of imported composite sugar products specified in column 2 of Schedule 1 to this order shall, notwithstanding the provisions of the Sugar (Rates of Surcharge and Surcharge Repayments) (No. 7) Order 1968(g) and the Composite Sugar Products (Surcharge and Surcharge Repayments—Average Rates) (No. 6) Order 1968(a), be calculated by reference to the weight or value, as the case may be, of the products at the rates specified in relation thereto in column 3 of the said Schedule.

(a) S.I. 1968/1718 (1968 III, p. 4638).   (b) 1956 c. 48.   (c) 1962 c. 44.
(d) 1966 c. 18.   (e) 1968 c. 44.   (f) 1889 c. 63.
(g) S.I. 1968/1883(1968 III, p. 5024).

3. Imported composite sugar products other than those of a description specified in Schedules 1 and 2 to this order shall be treated as not containing any sugar or invert sugar for the purposes of surcharge payable on or after 28th November 1968.

4. Surcharge repayments payable on and after 28th November 1968 under and in accordance with the provisions of section 8 of the Sugar Act 1956, having effect as aforesaid, in respect of sugar and invert sugar used in the manufacture of the descriptions of goods specified in column 1 of Schedule 3 to this order shall, notwithstanding the provisions of the Sugar (Rates of Surcharge and Surcharge Repayments) (No. 7) Order 1968(**a**) and the Composite Sugar Products (Surcharge and Surcharge Repayments—Average Rates) (No. 6) Order 1968(**b**), be calculated by reference to the quantity of the goods at the rates specified in relation thereto in column 2 of the said Schedule.

In Witness whereof the Official Seal of the Minister of Agriculture, Fisheries and Food is hereunto affixed on 26th November 1968.

(L.S.)
R. P. Fraser,
Authorised by the Minister.

SCHEDULE 1

In this Schedule:—

" Tariff heading " means a heading or, where the context so requires, a subheading of the Customs Tariff 1959 (see paragraph (1) of Article 1 of the Import Duties (General) (No. 4) Order 1968(**c**)).

" Per cent." means, where it occurs in relation to any rate of surcharge, per cent. of the value for customs duty purposes of the product to which it relates.

Tariff heading	Description of Imported Composite Sugar Products	Rate of Surcharge
		per cwt. s. d.
04.02	Milk and cream, preserved, concentrated or sweetened, containing more than 10 per cent. by weight of added sweetening matter	12 5
17.02 (B) (2) and 17.05 (B)	Syrups containing sucrose sugar, whether or not flavoured or coloured, but not including fruit juices containing added sugar in any proportion:—	
	containing 70 per cent. or more by weight of sweetening matter	17 9
	containing less than 70 per cent., and more than 50 per cent., by weight of sweetening matter...	12 9
	containing not more than 50 per cent. by weight of sweetening matter	6 3

(**a**) S.I. 1968/1883(1968 III, p. 5024)   (**b**) S.I. 1968/1718 (1968 III, p. 4638).
(**c**) S.I. 1968/679 (1968 I, p. 1519).

Tariff heading	Description of Imported Composite Sugar Products	Rate of Surcharge
		per cwt. s. d.
17.02 (F) ...	Caramel:—	
	Solid	28 0
	Liquid	19 7
17.04	Sugar confectionery, not containing cocoa	22 9
18.06	Chocolate and other food preparations containing cocoa:—	
	Chocolate couverture not prepared for retail sale; chocolate milk crumb, liquid	12 5
	Chocolate milk crumb, solid	15 4
	Solid chocolate bars or blocks, milk or plain, with or without fruit or nuts; other chocolate confectionery consisting wholly of chocolate or of chocolate and other ingredients not containing added sugar, but not including such goods when packed together in retail packages with goods liable to surcharge at a higher rate	12 7
	Other	16 3
		per cent.
19.08	Pastry, biscuits, cakes and other fine bakers' wares containing added sweetening matter:—	
	Biscuits	6
	Other	3¾
20.01	Vegetables and fruit, prepared or preserved by vinegar or acetic acid, containing added sweetening matter	8⅘
20.03	Fruit preserved by freezing, containing added sugar	3
		per cwt. s. d.
20.04	Fruit, fruit-peel and parts of plants, preserved by sugar (drained, glacé or crystallised)	18 5
20.05	Jams, fruit jellies, marmalades, fruit purée and fruit pastes, being cooked preparations, containing added sweetening matter	17 7
		per cent.
20.06	Fruit otherwise prepared or preserved, containing added sweetening matter:—	
	Ginger	12
	Other	3

SCHEDULE 2

Tariff heading	Description of Imported Composite Sugar Products
17.05 (A) and (B)	Sugar and invert sugar, flavoured or coloured.

SCHEDULE 3

Description of goods	Rate of surcharge repayment per bulk barrel of 36 gallons
Lager	1s. 2d.
All beer other than lager	1s. 0·5d.

EXPLANATORY NOTE

(This Note is not part of the Order.)

This order provides for reductions on and after 28th November 1968 in the average rates of surcharge payable on imported composite sugar products of the descriptions specified in Schedule 1 and in the average rates of surcharge repayment in respect of exported goods of the descriptions specified in Schedule 3. These correspond to the reductions in surcharge rates effected by the Sugar (Rates of Surcharge and Surcharge Repayments) (No. 7) Order 1968 (S.I. 1968/1883). Provision is also made for certain imported composite sugar products to be treated as not containing any sugar or invert sugar.

STATUTORY INSTRUMENTS

1968 No. 1885

CUSTOMS AND EXCISE

The Anti-Dumping (Provisional Charge to Duty) Order 1968

Made - - - - -	*26th November* 1968
Laid before the House of Commons	*29th November* 1968
Coming into Operation - -	*30th November* 1968

The Board of Trade, in pursuance of the powers conferred upon them by sections 1 and 2 of the Customs Duties (Dumping and Subsidies) Act 1957(**a**), as extended by section 1(2) of the Customs Duties (Dumping and Subsidies) Amendment Act 1968(**b**), hereby make the following Order:—

1. Goods of the description set out in the Schedule hereto (being goods classified in accordance with the Customs Tariff 1959(**c**) under the heading mentioned in that Schedule) shall be subject to a provisional charge to duty in respect of a duty of customs at the rate set out in that Schedule.

2. This Order may be cited as the Anti-Dumping (Provisional Charge to Duty) Order 1968 and shall come into operation on 30th November 1968.

Edmund Dell,
Minister of State,
Board of Trade.

26th November 1968.

(**a**) 1957 c. 18.　　　　(**b**) 1968 c. 33.
(**c**) *See* S.I. 1968/679 (1968 I, p. 1519).

SCHEDULE

Relevant Tariff Heading	Description of Goods	Relevant Rate
12.01 (A)	Rape seed originating in Poland or the Soviet Zone of Germany	£4 per ton

EXPLANATORY NOTE

(This Note is not part of the Order.)

This Order makes imports of rape seed originating in Poland or the Soviet Zone of Germany subject to a provisional charge in respect of anti-dumping duty.

The making of the Order enables the Commissioners of Customs and Excise to require security for the payment of any anti-dumping duty which may be imposed retrospectively on such imports in accordance with section 1(1) of the Customs Duties (Dumping and Subsidies) Amendment Act 1968.

If any duty is imposed retrospectively, it may only be so imposed on goods imported while this Order is in force, and its rate may not exceed the rate mentioned in the Schedule to this Order.

This Order expires automatically after three months unless previously revoked or extended (for not more than three months) by a further Order.

STATUTORY INSTRUMENTS

1968 No. 1889 (S. 166)

LOCAL GOVERNMENT, SCOTLAND

The Rate Support Grant (Scotland) (Amendment) Regulations 1968

Made - - - -	22nd November 1968
Laid before Parliament	9th December 1968
Coming into Operation	10th December 1968

In exercise of the powers conferred on me by paragraph 5 of Part I of Schedule 1 to and section 45(2) of the Local Government (Scotland) Act 1966(**a**) and of all other powers enabling me in that behalf, and after consultation with such associations of local authorities as appear to me to be concerned, I hereby make the following regulations:—

1. These regulations may be cited as the Rate Support Grant (Scotland) (Amendment) Regulations 1968 and shall come into operation on 10th December 1968.

2. The Interpretation Act 1889(**b**) shall apply for the interpretation of these regulations as it applies for the interpretation of an Act of Parliament.

3. In the Rate Support Grant (Scotland) Regulations 1967(**c**):—

(1) In regulation 2(2)—

(*a*) there shall be omitted the words "certificated teacher" and the definition of "in-service course"; and

(*b*) there shall be added before the words "relevant expenditure" the words " "registered teacher" means a teacher registered under the Teaching Council (Scotland) Act 1965"(**d**).

(2) In paragraphs (2) and (3) of regulation 4 there shall be substituted for the word "certificated" the word "registered".

William Ross,
One of Her Majesty's Principal
Secretaries of State.

St. Andrew's House,
Edinburgh, 1.
22nd November 1968.

(**a**) 1966 c. 51.   (**b**) 1889 c. 63.
(**c**) S.I. 1967/715 (1967 II, p. 2162).   (**d**) 1965 c. 19.

EXPLANATORY NOTE
(This Note is not part of the Regulations.)

These Regulations amend the existing Regulations dealing with the pooling of expenditure incurred by certain local authorities among all local authorities, by means of adjustments to rate support grants; expenditure on the training of teachers attending in-service courses (which will in future not be subject to the limitations imposed by a precise definition) and on the training of teachers as educational psychologists will now be pooled only if the teachers are registered with the General Teaching Council.

STATUTORY INSTRUMENTS

1968 No. 1890

WAGES COUNCILS

The Wages Regulation (Retail Furnishing and Allied Trades) (Amendment) Order 1968

Made - - -	*26th November* 1968
Coming into Operation	*13th January* 1969

Whereas the Secretary of State has received from the Retail Furnishing and Allied Trades Wages Council (Great Britain) the wages regulation proposals set out in the Schedule hereto;

Now, therefore, the Secretary of State in exercise of her powers under section 11 of the Wages Councils Act 1959(a), and of all other powers enabling her in that behalf, hereby makes the following Order:—

1. This Order may be cited as the Wages Regulation (Retail Furnishing and Allied Trades) (Amendment) Order 1968.

2.—(1) In this Order the expression "the specified date" means the 13th January 1969, provided that where, as respects any worker who is paid wages at intervals not exceeding seven days, that date does not correspond with the beginning of the period for which the wages are paid, the expression "the specified date" means, as respects that worker, the beginning of the next such period following that date.

(2) The Interpretation Act 1889(b) shall apply to the interpretation of this Order as it applies to the interpretation of an Act of Parliament.

3. The wages regulation proposals set out in the Schedule hereto shall have effect as from the specified date.

Signed by order of the Secretary of State.
26th November 1968.

A. A. Jarratt,
Deputy Under Secretary of State,
Department of Employment and Productivity.

(a) 1959 c. 69.   (b) 1889 c. 63.

Article 3

SCHEDULE

STATUTORY MINIMUM REMUNERATION

The Wages Regulation (Retail Furnishing and Allied Trades) Order 1967(a) (Order R.F.A. (48)) shall have effect as if in the Schedule thereto:—

1. for paragraph 2 there were substituted the following paragraph:—

"SHOP MANAGERS AND SHOP MANAGERESSES

2. Subject to the provisions of this paragraph, the minimum remuneration payable to Shop Managers and Shop Manageresses employed in the areas specified in Column 2 of the next following table shall be the amount appearing in the said Column 2 against the amount of weekly trade shown in Column 1.

Column 1	Column 2					
	LONDON AREA per week		PROVINCIAL A AREA per week		PROVINCIAL B AREA per week	
	Male	Female	Male	Female	Male	Female
	s. d.	s. d.	s. d.	s. d.	s. d.	s. d.
WEEKLY TRADE						
Under £175	279 0	243 0	271 6	235 6	259 0	225 6
£175 and under £200	284 0	248 0	276 6	240 6	264 0	230 6
£200 ,, ,, £225	286 6	250 6	279 0	243 0	266 6	233 0
£225 ,, ,, £250	289 0	253 0	281 6	245 6	269 0	235 6
£250 ,, ,, £275	291 6	255 6	284 0	248 0	271 6	238 0
£275 ,, ,, £300	294 0	258 0	286 6	250 6	274 0	240 6
£300 ,, ,, £325	296 6	260 6	289 0	253 0	276 6	243 0
£325 ,, ,, £350	299 0	263 0	291 6	255 6	279 0	245 6
£350 ,, ,, £375	301 6	265 6	294 0	258 0	281 6	248 0
£375 ,, ,, £400	304 0	268 0	296 6	260 6	284 0	250 6
£400 ,, ,, £425	306 6	270 6	299 0	263 0	286 6	253 0
£425 ,, :, £450	309 0	273 0	301 6	265 6	289 0	255 6
£450 ,, ,, £475	311 6	275 6	304 0	268 0	291 6	258 0
£475 ,, ,, £500	314 0	278 0	306 6	270 6	294 0	260 6
£500 ,, ,, £525	316 6	280 6	309 0	273 0	296 6	263 0
£525 ,, ,, £550	319 0	283 0	311 6	275 6	299 0	265 6
£550 ,, ,, £575	321 6	285 6	314 0	278 0	301 6	268 0
£575 ,, ,, £600	324 0	288 0	316 6	280 6	304 0	270 6
£600 ,, ,, £625	326 6	290 6	319 0	283 0	306 6	273 0
£625 ,, ,, £650	329 0	293 0	321 6	285 6	309 0	275 6
£650 ,, ,, £675	331 6	295 6	324 0	288 0	311 6	278 0
£675 ,, ,, £700	334 0	298 0	326 6	290 6	314 0	280 6
£700 ,, ,, £725	336 6	300 6	329 0	293 0	316 6	283 0
£725 ,, ,, £750	339 0	303 0	331 6	295 6	319 0	285 6
£750 ,, ,, £775	341 6	305 6	334 0	298 0	321 6	288 0
£775 ,, ,, £800	344 0	308 0	336 6	300 6	324 0	290 6
£800 and under £825	346 6	310 6	339 0	303 0	326 6	293 0
£825 ,, ,, £850	349 0	313 0	341 6	305 6	329 0	295 6
£850 ,, ,, £875	351 6	315 6	344 0	308 0	331 6	298 0
£875 ,, ,, £900	354 0	318 0	346 6	310 6	334 0	300 6
£900 and over	356 6	320 6	349 0	313 0	336 6	303 0

For the purposes of this paragraph 'weekly trade' shall be calculated half-yearly and based on the period of 12 months immediately preceding the commencement of each half-year in the following manner:—

For the period of 26 weeks beginning (1) with the fifth week or (2) with the 31st week following the accounting date in any year, the weekly trade of a shop shall be one fifty-second of the amount of the total receipts for goods sold at that shop during the 52 weeks immediately preceding the accounting date (in the case of (1) hereof) or the 26th week following the accounting date (in the case of (2) hereof).

(a) S.I. 1967/907 (1967 II, p. 2707).

Except as provided as aforesaid, the weekly trade in respect of any week shall be the amount of the total receipts for goods sold at the shop in the preceding week.

In this paragraph—

(a) 'accounting date' means that date in each year on which the books of accounts of a shop are closed for the purpose of preparing the annual accounts in respect of that shop, or, in the absence of any such date, the 5th April in any year;

(b) the expression 'receipts for goods sold' includes receipts in respect of hire purchase transactions;

(c) 'shop' includes any part of the shop not engaged in the retail furnishing and allied trades."

2. for paragraphs 4 and 5 there were substituted the following paragraphs:—

"WORKERS OTHER THAN SHOP MANAGERS, SHOP MANAGERESSES, TEMPORARY SHOP MANAGERS, TEMPORARY SHOP MANAGERESSES OR TRANSPORT WORKERS

4. Subject to the provisions of paragraph 1, the minimum remuneration payable to male or female workers of the classes specified in Column 1 of the next following table employed in the London Area, Provincial A Area or Provincial B Area, as the case may be, shall be the appropriate amount set out in Column 2.

	Column 2					
Column 1	LONDON AREA per week		PROVINCIAL A AREA per week		PROVINCIAL B AREA per week	
	Male s. d.	Female s. d.	Male s. d.	Female s. d.	Male s. d.	Female s. d.
(1) CLERK GRADE I, AGED 23 YEARS OR OVER	250 6	187 0	240 6	182 0	228 0	172 0
(2) CLERK GRADE I, AGED UNDER 23 YEARS, CLERK GRADE II, SHOP ASSISTANT, CASHIER, CENTRAL WAREHOUSE WORKER, STOCKHAND OR VAN SALESMAN:—						
Aged 22 years or over	243 0	182 0	233 0	177 0	220 6	167 0
,, 21 and under 22 years ...	223 0	167 0	213 0	162 0	200 6	152 0
,, 20 ,, ,, 21 ,, ...	189 0	145 6	184 0	140 6	171 6	133 0
,, 19 ,, ,, 20 ,, ...	174 0	135 6	169 0	130 6	156 6	123 0
,, 18 ,, ,, 19 ,, ...	159 0	128 0	154 0	123 0	141 6	115 6
,, 17 ,, ,, 18 ,, ...	135 6	107 0	130 6	102 0	118 0	94 6
,, 16 ,, ,, 17 ,, ...	125 6	102 0	120 6	97 0	108 0	89 6
,, under 16 years	115 6	97 0	110 6	92 0	98 0	84 6
(3) ALL OTHER WORKERS (OTHER THAN TRANSPORT WORKERS):—						
Aged 22 years or over	233 0	177 0	223 0	172 0	210 6	162 0
,, 21 and under 22 years ...	218 0	164 6	208 0	159 6	195 6	149 6
,, 20 ,, ,, 21 ,, ...	179 0	140 6	174 0	135 6	161 6	128 0
,, 19 ,, ,, 20 ,, ...	164 0	133 0	159 0	128 0	146 6	120 6
,, 18 ,, ,, 19 ,, ...	154 0	125 6	149 0	120 6	136 6	113 0
,, 17 ,, ,, 18 ,, ...	133 0	104 6	128 0	99 6	115 6	92 0
,, 16 ,, ,, 17 ,, ...	123 0	99 6	118 0	94 6	105 6	87 0
,, under 16 years	113 0	94 6	108 0	89 6	95 6	82 0

TRANSPORT WORKERS

5. Subject to the provisions of paragraph 1, the minimum remuneration payable to Transport Workers employed in the London Area, Provincial A Area or Provincial B Area, as the case may be, shall be the appropriate amount set out in Column 3 of the next following table:—

Column 1	Column 2	Column 3		
Age of transport worker	Mechanically propelled vehicle with carrying capacity of	LONDON AREA per week	PROVINCIAL A AREA per week	PROVINCIAL B AREA per week
		s. d.	s. d.	s. d.
21 years or over ...	⎫	240 6	233 0	220 6
20 and under 21 years	⎪	199 0	194 0	181 6
19 ,, ,, 20 ,,	⎬ 1 ton or less	184 0	179 0	167 6
18 ,, ,, 19 ,,	⎪	169 0	165 0	157 6
under 18 years ...	⎭	145 6	140 6	130 0
All ages	Over 1 ton and up to 2 tons	245 6	238 0	225 6
	Over 2 tons and up to 5 tons	250 6	243 0	230 6
	Over 5 tons	255 6	248 0	235 6 "

3. **for the definition of "Transport Worker" in paragraph 20 there were substituted the following definition:—**

" *'Transport Worker' means a male worker (other than a van salesman) engaged wholly or mainly in driving a mechanically propelled road vehicle for the transport of goods and on work in connection with the vehicle and its load (if any) while on the road."*

EXPLANATORY NOTE

(This Note is not part of the Order.)

This Order, which has effect from 13th January 1969, amends the Wages Regulation (Retail Furnishing and Allied Trades) Order 1967 (Order R.F.A. (48)) by increasing the statutory minimum remuneration fixed by that Order.

New provisions are printed in italics.

STATUTORY INSTRUMENTS

1968 No. 1896

SOCIAL SECURITY

The National Insurance (Industrial Injuries) (Colliery Workers Supplementary Scheme) Amendment (No. 2). Order 1968

Laid before Parliament in draft

Made - - -	28*th November* 1968
Coming into operation	3*rd December* 1968

Whereas the National Committee for the time being constituted in accordance with the Supplementary Scheme set out in Schedule 1 to the National Insurance (Industrial Injuries) (Colliery Workers Supplementary Scheme) Amendment and Consolidation Order 1963(a) as subsequently varied and amended (b) is the body charged with the administration of that Scheme and has requested the Secretary of State to vary and amend the provisions of the said Supplementary Scheme in manner set out in the following Order :—

Now, therefore, the Secretary of State, in exercise of his powers under section 47(1)(*a*)(ii) of the National Insurance Act 1965(c) as applied by section 82(2) of the National Insurance (Industrial Injuries) Act 1965(d) and of all other powers enabling him in that behalf, hereby makes the following Order, a draft of which has been laid before Parliament and has been approved by resolution of each House of Parliament:—

Citation, commencement and interpretation

1.—(1) This Order, which may be cited as the National Insurance (Industrial Injuries) (Colliery Workers Supplementary Scheme) Amendment (No. 2) Order 1968, shall come into operation on 3rd December 1968.

(2) In this Order "the Scheme" means the Supplementary Scheme set out in Schedule 1 to the National Insurance (Industrial Injuries) (Colliery Workers Supplementary Scheme) Amendment and Consolidation Order 1963 as varied and amended.

Amendment of Article 12 of the Scheme

2. In paragraph (4)(*a*) of Article 12 of the Scheme for the date "3rd December 1968" there shall be substituted the date "3rd June 1969".

R. H. S. Crossman,
Secretary of State for
Social Services.

28th November 1968.

(a) S.I. 1963/934 (1963 II, p. 1559).
(b) The relevant amending instruments are S.I. 1967/1550, 1968/83 (1967 III, p. 4313; 1968 I, p. 266).   (c) 1965 c. 51.   (d) 1965 c. 52.

EXPLANATORY NOTE

(This Note is not part of the Order.)

This Order amends the provisions of the National Insurance (Industrial Injuries) Colliery Workers Supplementary Scheme by extending until 3rd June 1969 the period during which the rates of certain supplementary benefits that are related on a fractional basis of calculation to benefits payable under the National Insurance (Industrial Injuries) Act 1965 are not affected by any increases in such benefits payable under the said Act under or by virtue of the National Insurance Act 1967 and the National Insurance (Industrial Injuries) (Increase of Benefit and Miscellaneous Provisions) Regulations 1967.

STATUTORY INSTRUMENTS

1968 No. 1898

DEFENCE

The Rules of Procedure (Army) (Second Amendment) Rules 1968

Made - - -	*29th November* 1968
Laid before Parliament	*6th December* 1968
Coming into Operation	*1st January* 1969

The Secretary of State in exercise of the powers conferred upon him by sections 103, 104, 105 and 106 of the Army Act 1955(**a**) and of all other powers enabling him in that behalf hereby makes the following rules :—

Citation and Commencement

1. These Rules may be cited as the Rules of Procedure (Army) (Second Amendment) Rules 1968 and shall come into operation on 1st January 1969.

Interpretation

2. The Interpretation Act 1889(**b**) shall apply to the interpretation of these Rules as it applies to an Act of Parliament.

Amendment to the Rules of Procedure (Army) 1956(c)

3.—(1) The Rules of Procedure (Army) 1956, as amended (**d**), shall be further amended in accordance with the following provisions of this Rule.

(2) In part (2) of the Second Schedule (Statements of Offences—Army Act 1955) :—

(*a*) for the detail under Section 44(1)(*b*) there shall be substituted : —

"Handling stolen goods contrary to section 44(1)(*b*) of the Army Act 1955"

(*b*) for the detail under Section 45(*b*) there shall be substituted : —

"Handling stolen goods contrary to section 45(*b*) of the Army Act 1955"

(3) In Part (3) of the Second Schedule (Illustrations of Charge-Sheets) for the first illustration there shall be substituted the following : —

"CHARGE SHEET

The accused No. 87654321 Private John Black, 1st Battalion The Loamshire Regiment, a soldier of the regular forces is charged with :—

(a) 1955 c. 18.   (b) 1889 c. 63.   (c) S.I. 1956/162 (1956 I, p. 213).

(d) The relevant amending instruments are S.I. 1961/2223, 1967/46, 1967/1469 (1961 III, p. 3903; 1967 I, p. 113; 1967 III, p. 4157).

1st Charge —STEALING PUBLIC PROPERTY CONTRARY TO SEC-
TION 44(1)(*a*) OF THE ARMY ACT 1955
in that he
at Catterick on 1st January 1969 stole a pair of binoculars,
public property.

2nd Charge—HANDLING STOLEN GOODS CONTRARY TO SEC-
(Alternative TION 44(1)(*b*) OF THE ARMY ACT 1955
to the in that he
1st Charge) at Catterick on 1st January 1969 dishonestly received a pair of
binoculars, stolen public property, knowing or believing the
same to be stolen.

> *B. C. Green, Lieut. Colonel,*
> Commanding, 1st Battalion
> The Loamshire Regiment
> Commanding Officer of the accused.

Catterick
16th January 1969.

To be tried by   District Court-Martial.

> *A. D. White, Brigadier,*
> Commanding 1st Infantry Brigade.

Catterick
17th January 1969".

> *Denis Healey,*
> One of Her Majesty's Principal
Dated 29th November 1968.   Secretaries of State.

EXPLANATORY NOTE

(*This Note is not part of the Rules.*)

These Rules amend the Rules of Procedure (Army) 1956 to take account of
the amendments to section 44(1)(*b*) and 45(*b*) of the Army Act 1955 effected by
the Theft Act 1968 in substituting in those sections references to handling stolen
goods for the references to receiving stolen property.

STATUTORY INSTRUMENTS

1968 No. 1908 (C.25)

TOWN AND COUNTRY PLANNING, ENGLAND AND WALES

The Town and Country Planning Act 1968 (Commencement No. 1) Order 1968

Made	-	-	-	*29th November* 1968

The Minister of Housing and Local Government and the Secretary of State in exercise of the power conferred on each of them by section 105 of the Town and Country Planning Act 1968(**a**) in relation to England and Wales respectively hereby make the following Order :—

1. The provisions of the Town and Country Planning Act 1968 (hereinafter referred to as "the Act") specified in the first column of Schedule 1 hereto (which relate to the matters specified in the second column of the said Schedule) shall come into operation in the whole of England and Wales on 6th December 1968.

2. The transitional provisions contained in Schedule 2 to this Order shall have effect in connection with the provisions brought into force by this Order.

3. This Order may be cited as the Town and Country Planning Act 1968 (Commencement No. 1) Order 1968.

SCHEDULE 1

Provisions coming into operation on 6th December 1968.

Provisions of the Act	*Subject matter of provisions*
Section 39	Restriction on exercise by public authorities of power of disposing of land.
Section 61	Constitution of Planning Inquiry Commissions.
Section 62	References to a Planning Inquiry Commission.
Section 63	Procedure on reference to a Planning Inquiry Commission.
Section 69	New provision as to what is "operational land" of statutory undertakers.

(**a**) 1968 c. 72.

Provisions of the Act	_Subject matter of provisions_
Section 70	Planning applications and appeals by statutory undertakers.
Section 71	Restrictions on entitlement of statutory undertakers to compensation for adverse planning decisions.
Section 72	Modifications of section 164 of the Town and Country Planning Act 1962(a) (hereinafter referred to as "the principal Act").
Section 73	Notice for same purposes as section 164 but given by statutory undertakers to developing authority.
Section 74	Expansion of building below ground to constitute development.
Section 75	Modifications of transitory exemptions based on pre-1948 use.
Section 79	Reference to Minister of application for approval under outline planning permission.
Section 82	Notice by Minister to planning authority when exercising default powers.
Section 98	Grants for research etc.
Section 99	Exchequer contributions in connection with town development.
Section 100	Agreements of Crown Estate Commissioners.
Section 101	Increase of certain penalties under the principal Act.
Section 102	Offences by corporations.
Section 103	Expenses.
Section 104	Interpretation.
Section 105	Commencement.
Section 106	Adaptation, amendment and modification of enactments.
Section 107	Transitional provisions and savings.
Section 108	Repeals.

(a) 1962 c. 38.

Provisions of the Act	Subject matter of provisions
Section 109 (except so far as it relates to amendments to section 24(9) of the Industrial Development Act 1966**(a)** and section 8(3) of the Civic Amenities Act 1967**(b)**).	Short title, citation and extent.
Schedule 6	Construction of references in section 62 and 63 to "the responsible Minister or Ministers".
Schedule 8	Increase of penalties under the principal Act.
In Schedule 9 paragraph 18	Power to define areas of special advertisement control by reference to the provisions of a development plan to cease to have effect.
In Schedule 9 paragraph 19	Approval of the Minister to agreements under section 37 of the principal Act to be dispensed with.
In Schedule 9 paragraph 30	Substitution of 1st August 1948 for previous provision as to dates of display of advertisement qualifying for compensation under section 126 of the principal Act.
In Schedule 9 paragraph 34	Alteration of reference to section 160(1) of the principal Act in section 160(2).
In Schedule 9 paragraph 43	Application of section 196 of the principal Act (expenses of county councils) to the provisions of the Act.
In Schedule 9 paragraph 44	Application of section 197(1) of the principal Act (power to modify that Act in relation to minerals) to the provisions of the Act.
In Schedule 9 paragraph 45(*a*)	Inclusion of the Greater London development plan as a plan which may contain proposals relating to the use of Crown land.
In Schedule 9 paragraph 46	Application of section 203(1) of the principal Act (power to apply that Act to Isles of Scilly) to the provisions of the Act.
In Schedule 9 paragraph 47	Power to apply sections 69 to 71 of the Act to the National Coal Board.

(a) 1966 c. 34.　　　　**(b)** 1967 c. 69.

2d

Provisions of the Act	*Subject matter of provisions*
In Schedule 9 paragraph 48(*a*)	Provision as to service of notices in respect of land which is ecclesiastical property.
In Schedule 9 paragraph 51	Power to require information as to interests in land in connection with an order or notice under the Act.
In Schedule 9 paragraph 52(*a*) and (*b*)	Provisions as to regulations prescribing forms, and orders under the Act.
In Schedule 9 paragraph 53(*a*)	Insertion in the principal Act of definition of the Act ("the Act of 1968").
In Schedule 9 paragraph 58 (except so far as it relates to applications under Part V of the Act for listed building consent).	Provision as to local planning authorities in Greater London for the purposes of the Act.
In Schedule 9 paragraph 59 (except so far as it relates to Part II of the Act).	Provision for cases where the Greater London Council is the local planning authority.
In Schedule 10 paragraph 1	Approval of Minister required to proposals for alteration or additions to a development plan under existing legislation.
In Schedule 10 paragraph 8	Meaning of reference to "development plan" in relation to Greater London.
In Schedule 10 paragraph 9	Provision for case where repeal of existing provisions as to development plans comes into operation on different days.
In Schedule 10 paragraph 21	Saving for existing regulations under section 204(1) of the principal Act.
In Schedule 11, the entries relating to the Town and Country Planning Act 1959(**a**), section 26(5)(*b*); and the principal Act, sections 13(6) and (10), 34(4), 37(1), 159(2), 160(1), 161(2), 162(2), 163(3)(*b*), 165(3), 200(2) and 203(1).	Repeals consequential on the bringing into operation of the above-mentioned provisions.

(**a**) 1959 c. 53.

SCHEDULE 2

Transitional provisions

The amendment of section 24 of the London Government Act 1963(**a**) effected by paragraph 58 of Schedule 9 to the Act shall be subject to the provisions of sections 25 to 27 of the said Act of 1963 for so long as those sections remain in force.

Given under the official seal of the Minister of Housing and Local Government on 29th November 1968.

(L.S.)   *Anthony Greenwood,*

Minister of Housing and Local Government.

Eirene White,

Minister of State. Welsh Office.

29th November 1968.

EXPLANATORY NOTE

(This Note is not part of the Order.)

This Order brings into force for the whole of England and Wales certain provisions of the Town and Country Planning Act 1968 which are set out in Schedule 1 to the Order, subject to the transitional provisions contained in Schedule 2.

(**a**) 1963 c. 33.

STATUTORY INSTRUMENTS

1968 No. 1909 (C.26)

TOWN AND COUNTRY PLANNING, ENGLAND AND WALES

The Town and Country Planning Act 1968 (Commencement No. 2) Order 1968

Made - - - - 29th November 1968

The Minister of Housing and Local Government and the Secretary of State in exercise of the power conferred on each of them by section 105 of the Town and Country Planning Act 1968(a) in relation to England and Wales respectively hereby make the following Order: —

1. The provisions of the Town and Country Planning Act 1968 (hereinafter referred to as " the Act ") specified in the first column of Schedule 1 hereto (which relate to the matters specified in the second column of the said Schedule) shall come into operation in the whole of England and Wales on 1st January 1969.

2. The transitional provisions contained in Schedule 2 to this Order shall have effect in connection with the provisions brought into force by this Order.

3. This Order may be cited as the Town and Country Planning Act 1968 (Commencement No. 2) Order 1968.

SCHEDULE 1

PROVISIONS COMING INTO OPERATION ON 1ST JANUARY 1969.

Provisions of the Act	*Subject matter of provisions*
Part III	Appeals.
Part V	Buildings of architectural or historic interest.
Schedule 5	Control of works for demolition, alteration or extension of listed buildings.
In Schedule 9 paragraph 10	Modification of Public Health Act 1961(b) as to attachment of street lamps to listed buildings.

(a) 1968 c. 72.   (b) 1961 c. 64.

Provisions of the Act	Subject matter of provisions
In Schedule 9 paragraph 12 so far as it relates to functions under Part V of the Act	Extension of provision (in section 3 of the Town and Country Planning Act 1962 (a) hereinafter referred to as the principal Act) for delegation of functions of local planning authorities, to functions under Part V of the Act.
In Schedule 9 paragraph 17	Duty of Minister to notify listing, or deletion from the list, of a building to be transferred to local authorities.
In Schedule 9 paragraph 22 so far as it relates to Part IV of Schedule 5 to the Act	Extension to listed building enforcement appeals of certain supplementary provisions as to enforcement appeals in section 64 of the principal Act.
In Schedule 9 paragraph 23 so far as it relates to Part IV of Schedule 5 to the Act	Extension of provision (in section 65 of the principal Act) for recovery of expenses of enforcement to listed building enforcement notices.
In Schedule 9 paragraph 25	Power in section 71 of the principal Act to acquire land by agreement extended to buildings appearing to be of special architectural or historic interest and land required for preserving the building etc.
In Schedule 9 paragraph 31 so far as it relates to Part V of the Act	Extension of provision (in section 127 of the principal Act) as to compensation for depreciation in value of land to compensation under Part V of the Act.
In Schedule 9 paragraph 32 so far as it relates to Part V of the Act	Extension of provision (in section 128 of the principal Act) as to determination of claims for compensation to claims under Part V of the Act.
In Schedule 9 paragraph 35(c), and paragraph 35(d) so far as it relates to listed building purchase notices and to the following decisions:— (k) any decision of the Minister on an application referred to him under paragraph 3 of Schedule 5 to the Act, being an application for listed building consent for any works :	Extension of section 176(2) and (3) of the principal Act (orders and actions of the Minister which are the subject of special provisions as to challenge) to orders and decisions about listed buildings.

(a) 1962 c. 38.

Provisions of the Act	*Subject matter of provisions*
(*l*) any decision of the Minister on an appeal to him under paragraph 7 of that Schedule; (*m*) any decision of the Minister under paragraph 18(5)(*a*) of that Schedule to grant listed building consent for any works or under paragraph 18(5)(*b*) of that Schedule to grant planning permission in respect of any works	
In Schedule 9 paragraph 36 so far as it relates to listed building enforcement notices	Extension of provisions of section 177 of the principal Act as to validity of enforcement notices to listed building enforcement notices.
In Schedule 9 paragraph 39 so far as it relates to appeals under Part IV of Schedule 5 to the Act.	Extension of section 180 of the principal Act (appeals to High Court relating to enforcement notices) to listed building enforcement notices.
In Schedule 9 paragraph 41 so far as it relates to Part III or V of the Act.	Extension of power in section 188 of the principal Act (for Ministers to make contributions towards compensation paid by local authorities) to decisions or orders under Part III or V of the Act.
In Schedule 9 paragraph 42 so far as it relates to Part V of, or Schedule 5 to, the Act.	Extension of power in section 189 of the principal Act (for local authorities or statutory undertakers to make contributions towards expenses incurred by other authorities) to expenses in performing functions in relation to listed buildings.
In Schedule 9 paragraph 45(*b*) in relation to the references to sections 30 and 31 of the principal Act and section 44 of the Act; paragraph 45(*c*) so far as it relates to enforcement notices under section 44 of the Act; and paragraph 45(*d*).	Provisions as to service of listed building enforcement notices and purchase notices in respect of Crown land.
In Schedule 9 paragraph 48(*b*) so far as it relates to section 49 of the Act.	Extension of provision (in section 205(3) of the principal Act) as to payment of compensation in respect of ecclesiastical property, to compensation under section 49 of the Act.

Provisions of the Act.	Subject matter of provisions.
In Schedule 9 paragraph 49 so far as it relates to enforcement notices under section 44 of the Act (listed building enforcement notices).	Default powers of the Minister under section 207 of the principal Act to apply to listed building enforcement notices.
In Schedule 9 paragraph 50 so far as it relates to listed buildings and buildings proposed to be listed.	Supplementary rights of entry in connection with listed buildings.
In Schedule 9 paragraph 58 so far as it relates to applications under Part V of the Act for listed building consent.	Provision as to local planning authorities in Greater London for the purposes of the Act.
In Schedule 9 paragraph 60	Provision as to functions of the Greater London Council in respect of listed buildings.
In Schedule 9 paragraph 68	Exemption from rating in respect of buildings which are the subject of a building preservation notice or are listed buildings.
In Schedule 9 paragraphs 69 to 71 and 74	Amendments of the Civic Amenities Act 1967(a) consequential on the provisions of the Act relating to listed buildings.
In Schedule 10 paragraphs 18 to 20	Transitional provisions in relation to buildings of architectural or historic interest.
In Schedule 11 the entries relating to the Housing Act 1957(b); the Local Authorities (Historic Buildings) Act 1962(c); the principal Act sections 23(3), 30, 31, 33, 52 to 55, 62(2) and (4), 64(2)(*b*), 125(1) and (2) and 199(2)(*b*); the London Government Act 1963(d) section 28(2) and (3); and the Civic Amenities Act 1967 section 1(6), 2, 6(2), 7, 9 and 10.	Repeals incidental to or consequential on the bringing into operation of the above-mentioned provisions.

SCHEDULE 2

TRANSITIONAL PROVISIONS

1. The bringing into operation of the amendments, made in paragraph 36 of Schedule 9 to the Act, of section 177 of the principal Act so far as they relate to listed building enforcement notices shall not prejudice the continued operation of subsections (1) to (3) of the said section.

(a) 1967 c. 69.   (b) 1957 c. 56.   (c) 1962 c. 36.   (d) 1963 c. 33.

2. The bringing into operation of the amendments, made in paragraph 39 of Schedule 9 to the Act, of section 180 of the principal Act so far as they relate to listed building enforcement notices shall not prejudice the continued operation of subsections (1) to (3) of the said section.

Given under the official seal of the Minister of Housing and Local Government on 29th November 1968.

(L.S.)

Anthony Greenwood,
Minister of Housing and Local Government.

Eirene White,
Minister of State,
Welsh Office.

29th November 1968.

EXPLANATORY NOTE

(This Note is not part of the Order.)

This Order brings into force for the whole of England and Wales provisions of the Town and Country Planning Act 1968 relating to appeals and to buildings of architectural or historic interest which are set out in Schedule 1 to the Order, subject to the transitional provisions contained in Schedule 2.

STATUTORY INSTRUMENTS

1968 No. 1910

TOWN AND COUNTRY PLANNING, ENGLAND AND WALES

The Town and Country Planning (Listed Buildings) Regulations 1968

Made - - - - - -	*29th November* 1968
Laid before Parliament	*6th December* 1968
Coming into Operation	*1st January* 1969

ARRANGEMENT OF REGULATIONS

1. Citation and commencement.
2. Interpretation.
3. Applications for listed building consent.
4. Advertisement of applications.
5. Certificates to accompany applications and appeals.
6. Appeals.
7. Claims for compensation and listed building purchase notices.
8. Advertisement of unopposed revocation or modification order.
9. Application of the Public Health Act 1936 to listed building enforcement notices.
10. Application of listed building control to buildings of local planning authorities.
11. Form of notice that a building has become, or ceased to be, listed.

SCHEDULES

Schedule 1—Notifications to be sent to applicants.

Schedule 2—Certificates to accompany applications and appeals; and related notices.

Schedule 3—Notice that a building has become, or ceased to be, listed.

The Minister of Housing and Local Government, in exercise of the powers conferred on him by sections 49 and 217 of the Town and Country Planning Act 1962(a) and sections 41, 42, 43, 46, 49, 55 and 104 of, and Schedule 5 to, the Town and Country Planning Act 1968(b) and of all other powers enabling him in that behalf, hereby makes the following regulations:—

Citation and commencement

1. These regulations may be cited as the Town and Country Planning (Listed Buildings) Regulations 1968 and shall come into operation on 1st January 1969.

(a) 1962 c. 38.   (b) 1968 c. 72.

Interpretation

2.—(1) In these regulations, unless the context otherwise requires—

"the Act of 1962" means the Town and Country Planning Act 1962;

"the Act of 1968" means the Town and Country Planning Act 1968;

"Greater London" has the same meaning as in the London Government Act 1963(**a**);

"local planning authority" means the council of a county, county borough, or London borough, and in regulations 7, 9 and 10 includes the Greater London Council;

"the Minister", as respects Wales and Monmouthshire, means the Secretary of State, and otherwise means the Minister of Housing and Local Government.

(2) The Interpretation Act 1889(**b**) shall apply for the interpretation of these regulations as it applies for the interpretation of an Act of Parliament.

Applications for listed building consent

3.—(1) An application to a local planning authority for listed building consent shall be made on a form issued by the local planning authority and obtainable from that authority or from the council with whom the application is to be lodged, and shall include the particulars required by that form to be supplied, and be accompanied by a plan sufficient to identify the building to which it relates and such other plans and drawings as are necessary to describe the works which are the subject of the application, together with two further copies of the form and plans and drawings.

(2) Any application made under this regulation shall be lodged:—

    (i) where the building in respect of which the application is made is in Greater London, with the council of the London borough in which the building is situated;

    (ii) where the building is not in Greater London, with the county borough council or the county district council for the area in which the building is situated,

and the authority with whom the application is lodged shall, where necessary, transmit it to the local planning authority to whom it is made.

(3) On receipt of any such application the local planning authority shall send to the applicant an acknowledgement thereof in the terms (or substantially in the terms) set out in Part I of Schedule 1 hereto.

(4) The period within which the local planning authority shall give notice to an applicant of their decision or of the reference of an application to the Minister shall be two months from the date of receipt of the application by the authority or such extended period as may at any time be agreed upon in writing between the applicant and the local planning authority (except where the applicant has already given notice of appeal to the Minister).

(5) Every such notice shall be in writing and where the local planning authority decide to grant listed buiding consent subject to conditions or to refuse it, they shall state their reasons in writing and send with the decision a notification in the terms (or substantially in the terms) set out in Part II of Schedule 1 hereto.

Advertisement of applications

4.—(1) Subject to the provisions of this regulation, where an application for listed building consent is made to a local planning authority in respect of any building the authority shall

---

        (**a**) 1963 c. 33.   (**b**) 1889 c. 63.

(a) publish in a local newspaper circulating in the locality in which the building is situated a notice indicating the nature of the works which are the subject of the application and naming a place within the locality where a copy of the application, and of all plans and other documents submitted with it, will be open to inspection by the public at all reasonable hours during the period of 21 days beginning with the date of publication of the notice; and

(b) for not less than 7 days display on or near the said building a notice containing the same particulars as are required to be contained in the notice to be published in accordance with sub-paragraph (a) above.

(2) An application for listed building consent shall not be determined by the local planning authority before both of the following periods have elapsed, namely:—

(a) the period of 21 days referred to in sub-paragraph (a) of paragraph (1) above; and

(b) the period of 21 days beginning with the date on which the notice required by sub-paragraph (b) of the said paragraph (1) was first displayed;

and in determining the application the authority shall take into account any representations relating to the application which are received by them before both those periods have elapsed.

(3) The preceding paragraphs of this regulation shall not apply to any application for consent to carry out works affecting only the interior of a Grade II building, namely a building which when first notified to the authority by the Minister as a building of architectural or historic interest was classified as a building of Grade II and not of Grade II*.

Certificates to accompany applications and appeals

5.—(1) A local planning authority shall not entertain an application for listed building consent unless it is accompanied by one or other of the following certificates signed by or on behalf of the applicant, that is to say—

(a) a certificate stating that, in respect of every part of the land to which the application relates, the applicant either is the estate owner in respect of the fee simple or is entitled to a tenancy thereof;

(b) a certificate stating that the applicant has given the requisite notice of the application to all the persons (other than the applicant) who, at the beginning of the period of 21 days ending with the date of the application, were owners of any of the land to which the application relates, and setting out the names of those persons, the addresses at which notice of the application was given to them respectively, and the date of service of each such notice;

(c) a certificate stating that the applicant is unable to issue a certificate in accordance with either of the preceding sub-paragraphs, that he has given the requisite notice of the application to such one or more of the persons mentioned in the last preceding sub-paragraph as are specified in the certificate (setting our their names, the addresses at which notice of the application was given to them respectively, and the date of service of each such notice) and that he does not know the names and addresses of the remainder of those persons;

(d) a certificate stating that the applicant is unable to issue a certificate in accordance with sub-paragraph (a) above and that he does not know the names and addresses of any of the persons mentioned in sub-paragraph (b) above.

(2) Any such certificate as is mentioned in sub-paragraph (*c*) or sub-paragraph (*d*) of paragraph (1) above shall also contain a statement that the requisite notice of the application, as set out in the certificate, has on a date specified in the certificate (being a date not earlier than the beginning of the period mentioned in sub-paragraph (*b*) of paragraph (1) above) been published in a local newspaper circulating in the locality in which the land in question is situated.

(3) Where an application for listed building consent is accompanied by such a certificate as is mentioned in sub-paragraph (*b*), sub-paragraph (*c*), or sub-paragraph (*d*) of paragraph (1) above, the local planning authority shall not determine the application before the end of the period of 21 days beginning with the date appearing from the certificate to be the latest of the dates of service of notices as mentioned in the certificate, or the date of publication of a notice as therein mentioned, whichever is the later.

(4) Where an application for listed building consent is accompanied by such a certificate as is mentioned in sub-paragraph (*b*), sub-paragraph (*c*), or sub-paragraph (*d*) of paragraph (1) above, the local planning authority—

(*a*) in determining the application, shall take into account any representations relating thereto which are made to them, before the end of the period mentioned in paragraph (3) above, by any person who satisfies them that he is an owner of any land to which the application relates, and

(*b*) shall give notice of their decision to every person who has made representations which they were required to take into account in accordance with the preceding sub-paragraph.

(5) The provisions of paragraphs (1) to (4) of this regulation shall apply, with any necessary modifications, in relation to an appeal to the Minister under paragraph 7 or paragraph 8 of Schedule 5 to the Act of 1968 as they apply in relation to an application for listed building consent which falls to be determined by the local planning authority.

(6) Certificates issued for the purposes of this regulation shall be in the forms set out in Part I of Schedule 2 hereto.

(7) The requisite notices for the purposes of the provisions of this regulation in relation to applications shall be in the forms set out in Part II of Schedule 2 hereto.

(8) The requisite notices for the purposes of the provisions of this regulation in relation to appeals shall be in the forms set out in Part III of Schedule 2 hereto.

Appeals

6.—(1) Any person who desires to appeal—

(*a*) against a decision of a local planning authority refusing listed building consent or granting consent subject to conditions, or

(*b*) on the failure by a local planning authority to give notice of their decision or of the reference of the application to the Minister

shall give notice of appeal to the Minister within six months of receipt of notice of the decision or of the expiry of the appropriate period allowed under regulation 3(4) above, as the case may be, or such longer period as the Minister may at any time allow.

(2) Such a person shall also furnish to the Minister a copy of the following documents:—

(i) the application made to the local planning authority;

   (ii) all relevant plans, drawings, particulars and documents submitted with the application, including a copy of the certificate given in accordance with regulation 5;

   (iii) the notice of the decision, if any;

   (iv) all other relevant correspondence with the local planning authority.

Claims for compensation and listed building purchase notices

7.—(1) A claim for compensation made to a local planning authority under section 43(2) or section 49(3) of or paragraph 11 of the Schedule 5 to the Act of 1968, or a listed building purchase notice served on the council of a county borough, county district or London borough under section 42(1) of that Act, shall be in writing and shall be served on that authority or council by delivering it at the offices of the authority or council addressed to the clerk thereof, or by sending it so addressed by prepaid post.

(2) The time within any such claim or notice as is mentioned in paragraph (1) above shall be served shall be—

   (*a*) in the case of a claim for compensation, 6 months; and

   (*b*) in the case of a listed building purchase notice, 12 months

from the date of the decision in respect of which the claim or notice is made or given, or such longer period as the Minister may allow in any particular case.

Advertisement of unopposed revocation or modification order

8. Where by virtue of the provisions of paragraph 12(2) of Schdule 5 to the Act of 1968 the making of an order under paragraph 9 of that Schedule in respect of works to a building is required to be advertised, the local planning authority shall publish in a local newspaper circulating in the area in which the building is situated an advertisement stating that the order has been made and specifying the periods required by the said paragraph 12(2) to be specified.

Application of the Public Health Act 1936 to listed building enforcement notices

9. The provisions of sections 276, 289, 292 and 294 of the Public Health Act 1936(**a**) shall apply in relation to steps required to be taken by a listed building enforcement notice, as if—

   (*a*) references to a local authority were references to a local planning authority;

   (*b*) references (in whatever form) to the execution of works under the said Act of 1936 were references to the taking of steps required to be taken under the notice;

   (*c*) references in the said section 289 to the occupier were references to a person having an interest in the premises other than the owner; and

   (*d*) the reference in the said section 294 to "expenses under this Act" were a reference to expenses incurred in the taking of such steps as aforesaid.

Application of listed building control to buildings of local planning authorities

10.—(1) In relation to buildings of local planning authorities which are listed, and to the execution of works for their demolition, alteration or extension, the provisions of Part V of the Act of 1968 shall have effect subject to the exceptions and modifications prescribed in this regulation.

(2) Where a local planning authority require listed building consent for the execution of works for the demolition, alteration or extension of any building

_____

(**a**) 1936 c. 49.

belonging to them, the authority shall make an application to the Minister for that consent.

(3) Any such application shall be made in the form of an application to the local planning authority, and shall be deemed to have been referred to the Minister under paragraph 3 of Schedule 5 to the Act of 1968 and the provisions of the said paragraph shall apply to the determination of the application by the Minister.

(4) In relation to a listed building belonging to a local planning authority, the Minister may serve any notice authorised to be served by a local planning authority in relation to a listed building.

(5) This regulation shall not apply to a council to which the functions of a local planning authority have been delegated, but any such council shall, notwithstanding that delegation, apply to the local planning authority for any consent referred to in this regulation as if the delegation to that council had not been made.

Form of notice that a building has become, or ceased to be, listed

11. The forms set out in Schedule 3 hereto (or forms substantially to the like effect) are the prescribed forms of notice for the purposes of subsection (4) of section 32 of the Act of 1962.

Regulation 3   SCHEDULE 1

PART I

Notification to be sent to applicant on receipt of his application

Your application dated [*insert date*] has been received and, if on [*insert date of expiry of the appropriate period under regulation* 3(4)] you have not been given notice by the local planning authority of their decision, you are entitled, unless the application has already been referred by the authority to the [Minister of Housing and Local Government] [Secretary of State for Wales], to appeal to the [Minister] [Secretary of State] in accordance with paragraphs 7 and 8 of Schedule 5 to the Town and Country Planning Act 1968 by notice served within six months from that date. You may, however, by agreement in writing with the local planning authority, extend the period within which the decision of the authority is to be given.

PART II

Notification to be sent to applicant on refusal of listed building consent or grant of consent subject to conditions

1. If the applicant is aggrieved by the decision of the local planning authority to refuse listed building consent for the proposed works, or to grant consent subject to conditions, he may, by notice served within six months of receipt of this notice, appeal to the [Minister of Housing and Local Government] [Secretary of State for Wales] in accordance with paragraph 7 of Schedule 5 to the Town and Country Planning Act 1968. The [Minister] [Secretary of State] has power to allow a longer period for the giving of a notice of appeal and he will exercise his power in cases where he is satisfied that the applicant has deferred the giving of notice because negotiations with the local planning authority in regard to the proposed works are in progress.

2. If listed building consent is refused, or granted subject to conditions, whether by the local planning authority or by the [Minister of Housing and

Local Government] [Secretary of State for Wales], and the owner of the land claims that the land has become incapable of reasonably beneficial use in its existing state and cannot be rendered capable of reasonably beneficial use by the carrying out of any works which have been or would be permitted, he may serve on the council of the county borough, county district, or London borough in which the land is situated (or, where appropriate, on the Common Council of the City of London) a listed building purchase notice requiring that council to purchase his interest in the land in accordance with the provisions of Part V of the Town and Country Planning Act 1968.

3. In certain circumstances, a claim may be made against the local planning authority for compensation, where permission is refused or granted subject to conditions by the [Minister] [Secretary of State] on appeal or on a reference of the application to him. The circumstances in which such compensation is payable are set out in section 43 of the Town and Country Planning Act 1968.

SCHEDULE 2   Regulation 5

PART I

TOWN AND COUNTRY PLANNING ACT 1968

Certificate under Schedule 5, paragraph 2

Certificate A*

I hereby certify that:

[I am] [The applicant is] [The appellant is]* [the estate owner in respect of the fee simple] [entitled to a tenancy]* of every part of the land(a) to which the accompanying [application] [appeal]* dated   relates.

or

Certificate B*

I hereby certify that:

[I have] [The applicant has] [The appellant has]* given the requisite notice to all the persons who, 20 days before the date of the accompanying [application] [appeal]* were owners of any of the land(a) to which the [application] [appeal] relates, viz.:—

Name of owner   *Address*   *Date of service of notice*

or

Certificate C*

I hereby certify that:

1. [I am] [The applicant is] [The appellant is]* unable to issue a certificate in accordance with either sub-paragraph (*a*) or sub-paragraph (*b*) of regulation 5(1) of the Town and Country Planning (Listed Buildings) Regulations 1968 in respect of the accompanying [application] [appeal]* dated

2. [I have] [The applicant has] [The appellant has]* given the requisite notice to the following persons who, 20 days before the date of the [application]

*Delete where inappropriate

[appeal]*, were owners of the land(**a**), or part thereof, to which the [application] [appeal]* relates, viz.:—

Name of owner	Address	Date of service of notice

3. [I do not] [The applicant does not] [The appellant does not]* know the names and addresses of the other owners of the land or part thereof.

4. Notice of the [application] [appeal]* as set out below has been published in the   (**b**) on   (**c**).

Copy of notice as published

or

Certificate D*

I hereby certify that:

1. [I am] [The applicant is] [The appellant is]* unable to issue a certificate in accordance with sub-paragraph (*a*) of regulation 5(1) of the Town and Country Planning (Listed Buildings) Regulations 1968 in respect of the accompanying [application] [appeal]* dated   and [I do not] [he does not]* know the names and addresses of any of the owners of any of the land (**a**) to which the [application] [appeal]* relates.

2. Notice of the [application] [appeal]* as set out below has been published in the   (**b**) on   (**c**).

Copy of notice as published

Signed ....

[*On behalf of* ....]*

Date   ....

Notes

(**a**) For the purposes of this certificate "land" includes a building or buildings.

(**b**) Insert name of a local newspaper circulating in the locality in which the land is situated.

(**c**) Insert date of publication (which must not be earlier than 20 days before the application or appeal).

PART II
TOWN AND COUNTRY PLANNING ACT 1968
Notice under Schedule 5, paragraph 2, of application for listed building consent

[*Notice for service on individuals*]

Proposal to carry out works for [demolishing] [altering] [extending]*
(**a**)

TAKE NOTICE that application is being made to the
(**b**) council by   (**c**) for listed building
consent to   (**d**).

*Delete where inappropriate

If you should wish to make representations about the application, you should make them in writing, within 20 days of the date of service of this notice upon you, to the [Town Clerk] [Clerk of the Council]* at
(e).

Signed ....

[*On behalf of* ....]*

Date ....

TOWN AND COUNTRY PLANNING ACT 1968

*Notice under Schedule 5, paragraph 2, of application for
listed building consent*

[*Notice for publication in local newspaper*]

Proposal to carry out works for [demolishing] [altering] [extending]*
(a).

Notice is hereby given that application is being made to the
(b) council by **(c)**
for listed building consent to
(d).

Any owner of the land or building(s) who wishes to make representations to the council about the application should make them in writing, within 20 days of the date of publication of this notice, to the [Town Clerk] [Clerk of the Council]* at **(e).**

Signed ....

[*On behalf of* ....]*

Date ....

Notes

(a) Insert name, address, or location, of building with sufficient precision to ensure identification of it.

(b) Insert name of council.

(c) Insert name of applicant.

(d) Insert description of proposed works and name, address, or location, of building.

(e) Insert address of council.

PART III

TOWN AND COUNTRY PLANNING ACT 1968

*Notice under Schedule 5, paragraph 7, of appeal against
refusal, etc., of listed building consent*

[*Notice for service on individuals*]

Proposal to carry out works for [demolishing] [altering] [extending]*
(a).

---

* Delete where inappropriate

TAKE NOTICE that an appeal is being made to [the Minister of Housing and Local Government, Whitehall, London, S.W.1.] [the Secretary of State for Wales, Welsh Office, Summit House, Windsor Place, Cardiff]* by   **(b)**
against the decision of   **(c)** council

or

on the failure of the   **(c)** council to give a decision
on an application to   **(d)**.

If you should wish to make representations to [the Minister] [the Secretary of State]* about the appeal you should make them in writing, within 20 days of the date of service of this notice, to [the Secretary, Ministry of Housing and Local Government] [the Secretary, Welsh Office]* at the above address.

Signed ....

[On behalf of ....)]*

Date ....

TOWN AND COUNTRY PLANNING ACT 1968

Notice under Schedule 5, paragraph 7, of appeal against refusal, etc., of listed building consent

[Notice for publication in local newspaper]

Proposal to carry out works for [demolishing] [altering] [extending]*
(a).

Notice is hereby given that an appeal is being made to [the Minister of Housing and Local Government, Whitehall, London, S.W.1.] [the Secretary of State, Welsh Office, Summit House, Windsor Place, Cardiff]* by
(b)
against the decision of the   **(c)** council

or

on the failure of the   **(c)** council to give a decision
on an application to
(d).

Any owner of the land who wishes to make representations to [the Minister] [the Secretary of State]* about the appeal should make them in writing, within 20 days of the date of publication of this notice, to [the Secretary, Ministry of Housing and Local Government] [the Secretary, Welsh Office]* at the above address.

Signed ....

[On behalf of ....)]*

Date ....

Notes

(a) Insert name, address, or location, of building with sufficient precision to ensure identification of it.

(b) Insert name of appellant.

(c) Insert name of council.

(d) Insert description of proposed works and name, address, or location, of building.

Delete where inappropriate

SCHEDULE 3 Regulation 11

Notice that a building has become listed

IMPORTANT—This communication affects YOUR PROPERTY

TOWN AND COUNTRY PLANNING ACTS 1962 TO 1968

CIVIC AMENITIES ACT 1967

BUILDINGS OF SPECIAL ARCHITECTURAL OR
HISTORIC INTEREST

To:

NOTICE IS HEREBY GIVEN that the building known as

situated in

has been included in the list of buildings of special architectural or historic interest in that area, compiled by the [Minister of Housing and Local Government] [Secretary of State for Wales] under section 32 of the Town and Country Planning Act 1962

on 19

Dated 19 [Town Clerk]

[Clerk of the Council]

Explanatory Note

Listing of Buildings of Special Architectural or Historic Interest

The above notice is addressed to you as owner or occupier of the building named, which has been included in one of the lists of buildings of special architectural or historic interest prepared under section 32 of the Town and Country Planning Act 1962 by the [Minister of Housing and Local Government] [Secretary of State for Wales]. The lists are compiled by the [Minister] [Secretary of State] as a statutory duty, on the advice of an expert committee of architects and historians which advises him on these matters.

This notice does not call for any action on your part unless you propose at any time to demolish the building or to do any works (either to the exterior or to the interior) which would affect its character. In that event you will need to seek "listed building consent", that is to say, the consent of the local planning authority (the   Council) to the work you wish to do.

Certain buildings are exempt from this requirement, notably ecclesiastical buildings in use for the time being for ecclesiastical purposes.

Works which are urgently necessary in the interests of safety or of health, or to preserve the building, may be carried out at any time without prior consent provided that you notify the local planning authority in writing, as soon as reasonably practicable, of the need for the works.

There is no right of appeal as such against the listing of a building but if the local planning authority should refuse consent for the carrying out of any proposed works, section 41(6) of the Town and Country Planning Act 1968 provides a right of appeal against the refusal to the [Minister of Housing and Local Government] [Secretary of State for Wales]. You are not precluded at any time from writing to the [Minister] [Secretary of State] claiming that the building should cease to be listed, on the ground that it is not in fact of special architectural or historic interest; and any such claim, with the evidence supporting it, will be carefully considered.

A fuller explanation of the consequences of the listing of a building is enclosed with this notice. If at any time you propose to take any action which may affect the character of your building, you would be well advised to refer to the provisions of the Town and Country Planning Act 1968, Part V and Schedule 5, and of the Town and Country Planning (Listed Buildings) Regulations 1968.

Notice that a building has ceased to be listed

IMPORTANT—This communication affects YOUR PROPERTY

TOWN AND COUNTRY PLANNING ACTS 1962 TO 1968

CIVIC AMENITIES ACT 1967

BUILDINGS OF SPECIAL ARCHITECTURAL OR HISTORICAL INTEREST

To:

NOTICE IS HEREBY GIVEN that the building known as

situated in

has, by an amendment made by the [Minister of Housing and Local Government] [Secretary of State for Wales] under section 32(1) of the Town and Country Planning Act 1962 on   19 , been excluded from the list of buildings of special architectural or historic interest in that area compiled by the [Minister] [Secretary of State] on   19 .

Date: [Town Clerk] [Clerk of the Council]

Explanatory Note

The building referred to in the above notice has been excluded from the list because*

*Insert reason for exclusion.

Given under the official seal of the Minister of Housing and Local Government on 29th November 1968.

Anthony Greenwood,
(L.S.)   Minister of Housing
and Local Government.

EXPLANATORY NOTE

(This Note is not part of the Regulations.)

These regulations prescribe the manner in which applications for listed building consent under Part V of the Town and Country Planning Act 1968 are to be made and advertised, and the manner in which appeals may be made by persons aggrieved by decisions of local planning authorities under that part of the Act.

The regulations also deal with the making of claims for compensation arising from the application of listed building control, the serving of listed building purchase notices, the advertising of unopposed orders revoking or modifying listed building consents, and the execution of works under listed building enforcement procedure. Provision is made for applying Part V of the Act in relation to works affecting listed buildings belonging to local planning authorities. Forms of notices are prescribed for notifying the owner and occupier of a building when it has become listed, or has ceased to be listed.

STATUTORY INSTRUMENTS

1968 No. 1911

TOWN AND COUNTRY PLANNING, ENGLAND AND WALES

The Town and Country Planning (Planning Inquiry Commissions) Regulations 1968

Made - - -	*29th November* 1968
Laid before Parliament	*9th December* 1968
Coming into Operation	11*th December* 1968

The Minister of Housing and Local Government, in exercise of the powers conferred on him by sections 63(2) and 104 of the Town and Country Planning Act 1968(**a**) and of all other powers enabling him in that behalf hereby makes the following regulations:—

1.—(1) These regulations may be cited as the Town and Country Planning (Planning Inquiry Commissions) Regulations 1968 and shall come into operation on 11th December 1968.

(2) The Interpretation Act 1889(**b**) shall apply to the interpretation of these regulations as it applies to the interpretation of an Act of Parliament.

2. Where a reference is made to a Planning Inquiry Commission in relation to any proposed development, the notice of the making thereof required to be published in accordance with section 63(2) of the Town and Country Planning Act 1968 shall be published in the London Gazette and in at least one newspaper circulating in the locality, or in each locality, where there are more than one, in which it is proposed that the relevant development shall be carried out.

Given under the official seal of the Minister of Housing and Local Government on 29th November 1968.

(L.S.)

Anthony Greenwood,
Minister of Housing and
Local Government.

(**a**) 1968 c. 72.   (**b**) 1889 c. 63.

EXPLANATORY NOTE

(*This Note is not part of the Regulations.*)

These regulations prescribe the manner in which notice is to be published of the making of a reference to a Planning Inquiry Commission constituted under Part VI of the Town and Country Planning Act 1968.

STATUTORY INSTRUMENTS

1968 No. 1913 (S. 169)

PUBLIC HEALTH, SCOTLAND

The Public Health (Ships) (Scotland) Amendment Regulations 1968

Made - - -	*25th November* 1968
Laid before Parliament	*5th December* 1968
Coming into Operation	*6th December* 1968

In exercise of the powers conferred on me by section 1 of the Public Health (Scotland) Act 1945 **(a),** as extended by section 62 of the Health Services and Public Health Act 1968 **(b),** and of all other powers enabling me in that behalf, I hereby make the following regulations:—

1.—(1) These regulations may be cited as the Public Health (Ships) (Scotland) Amendment Regulations 1968, and shall come into operation on 6th December 1968.

(2) The Interpretation Act 1889 **(c)** shall apply for the interpretation of these regulations as it applies for the interpretation of an Act of Parliament.

2. For the definition of "ship" in regulation 2 (1) of the Public Health (Ships) (Scotland) Regulations 1966 **(d)** there shall be substituted the following definition:

" "ship" has the same meaning as the expression "vessel" bears for the purposes of the Public Health (Scotland) Act 1945 and accordingly includes:

(*a*) any ship or boat;

(*b*) any other description of vessel used in navigation;

(*c*) any hover vehicle, that is to say, any vehicle designed to be supported on a cushion of air;".

William Ross,
One of Her Majesty's Principal
Secretaries of State.

St. Andrew's House,
Edinburgh, 1.
25th November 1968.

EXPLANATORY NOTE

(This Note is not part of the Regulations.)

These Regulations extend the definition of "ship" in the Public Health (Ships) (Scotland) Regulations 1966 to include hover vehicles, to which those Regulations will accordingly now apply.

(a) 9 & 10 Geo. 6. c. 15.	(b) 1968 c. 46.
(c) 1889 c. 63.	(d) S.I. 1966/1570 (1966 III, p. 4822).

STATUTORY INSTRUMENTS

1968 No. 1914

EDUCATION, ENGLAND AND WALES

The Teachers' Superannuation (Family Benefits) (Amending) Regulations 1968

Made - - -	*29th November* 1968
Laid before Parliament	*9th December* 1968
Coming into Operation	*10th December* 1968

The Secretary of State for Education and Science, with the consent of the Minister for the Civil Service and after consultation with representatives of local education authorities and of teachers appearing to him to be likely to be affected, in exercise of the powers conferred upon him by section 7 of the Teachers' Superannuation Act 1967(**a**) as amended by the Minister for the Civil Service Order 1968(**b**) hereby makes the following Regulations :—

1.—(1) These Regulations may be cited as the Teachers' Superannuation (Family Benefits) (Amending) Regulations 1968 and shall come into operation on 10th December 1968.

(2) The Teachers' Superannuation (Family Benefits) Regulations 1966 and 1967(**c**) and these Regulations may be cited together as the Teachers' Superannuation (Family Benefits) Regulations 1966 to 1968.

2.—(1) In these Regulations the expression "the principal Regulations" means the Teachers' Superannuation (Family Benefits) Regulations 1966 as amended by the Teachers' Superannuation (Family Benefits) (Amending) Regulations 1967.

(2) The Interpretation Act 1889(**d**) shall apply for the interpretation of these Regulations as it applies for the interpretation of an Act of Parliament.

3. Except as in these Regulations expressly provided, the amendment of the principal Regulations by these Regulations shall not—

(*a*) affect the previous operation of the principal Regulations or anything duly done or suffered under those Regulations ; or

(*b*) affect any right, obligation or liability acquired, accrued or incurred under the principal Regulations before the coming into operation of these Regulations.

4. In regulation 11 of the principal Regulations (which relates to expenses of the Board of Management) for paragraph (1) there shall be substituted the following paragraph—

"(1) The Board shall, in such manner and for such period as the Secretary of State may from time to time require, prepare estimates of its administrative expenses, including expenses incurred in connection with investments other than those which under regulation 17(2) are to be debited to the Investment Account, and shall submit such estimates for the approval of the Secretary of State."

(**a**) 1967 c. 12.　　　(**b**) S.I. 1968/1656 (1968 III, p.4485).
(**c**) S.I. 1966/357, 1967/1856 (1966 I, p.813; 1967 III, p.4975).　　(**d**) 1889 c. 63.

5. Regulation 13 of the principal Regulations (which relates to the appointment and removal of a trustee or trustees) is hereby revoked.

6. In regulation 17 of the principal Regulations (which relates to the Investment Account) for sub-paragraph (*c*) of paragraph (2) there shall be substituted the following sub-paragraph :—

"(*c*) any expenses incurred in connection with any investment or proposed investment by way of—

(i) brokerage, commission and professional fees ; and

(ii) stamp duty on any contract, transfer and other assurance."

7. For regulation 18 of the principal Regulations there shall be substituted the following regulation :—

"Investments

18.—(1) Subject as hereafter in this regulation provided, the Board shall invest any property for the time being held for the purposes of the Investment Account and not needed as a balance for working purposes, whether at the time in a state of investment or not, in accordance with the provisions of this regulation, and may also from time to time vary any investments so made.

(2) The property held for the purposes of the Investment Account on 10th December 1968 shall, as soon as may be thereafter, be divided into two parts (hereafter in this regulation referred to as the narrower-range part and the wider-range part) in such manner that the value at cost of the wider-range part shall as nearly as possible be three times that of the narrower-range part.

(3) When the division required by paragraph (2) above has been made no transfer shall be made from one part to the other unless either—

(*a*) the transfer is authorised or required by the following provisions of this regulation ; or

(*b*) a compensating transfer is made at the same time.

(4) When any property accrues to the Investment Account after the division required by paragraph (2) above has been made, then—

(*a*) if, not being dividends or interest in respect of investments, it accrues in respect of property comprised in either the narrower-range part or the wider-range part, it shall be treated as belonging to that part ; and

(*b*) in any other case, by apportionment of the accruing property or the transfer of property from one part to the other, or both, the value of the wider-range part shall be increased by an amount equal to three-quarters of the value of the accruing property and of the narrower-range part by an amount equal to one-quarter of that value.

(5) Property belonging to the narrower-range part shall be invested only in investments for the time being falling within Part I or Part II of the First Schedule to the Act of 1961 and any property invested in any other manner which is or becomes comprised in the narrower-range part shall either be transferred to the wider-range part, with a compensating transfer, or be re-invested in such investments as aforesaid as soon as may be.

(6) Subject as hereafter in this regulation provided, property belonging to the wider-range part shall be invested in—

(*a*) investments for the time being falling within Part I, Part II or Part III of the First Schedule to the Act of 1961 ;

(*b*) the acquisition, development or management (whether in association with any other person or not) of land situated in the United Kingdom or any interest in such land ;

(*c*) fixed interest securities issued by the government of any country outside the United Kingdom or by a public, municipal or local authority or a publicly controlled or nationalised industry or undertaking in such a country ; or

(*d*) the stocks, shares, debentures or other securities issued in the United Kingdom or elsewhere by a company incorporated outside the United Kingdom.

(7) No investment shall be made in pursuance of sub-paragraphs (*c*) and (*d*) of paragraph (6) above if it would result in more than one-tenth of the total value at cost of the property held for the purposes of the Investment Account being invested in securities the price of which is not quoted on a recognised stock exchange within the meaning of the Prevention of Fraud (Investments) Act 1958(**a**) or the Belfast stock exchange.

(8) In relation to investments made in pursuance of paragraph (5) above and sub-paragraph (*a*) of paragraph (6) above—

(*a*) paragraphs 1, 2 and 3 of Part IV of Schedule 1 to the Act of 1961 shall not apply ; and

(*b*) paragraphs 4, 5, 6 and 7 of that Part shall apply.

(9) If for the purposes of paragraph (4) above the Board obtains, from a person reasonably believed by the Board to be qualified to make it and whether made in the course of his employment as an officer or servant or not, a valuation in writing of any property, the valuation shall be conclusive in determining whether any transfer or apportionment of property made under paragraph (4) above has been duly made.

(10) When property falls to be taken out of the Investment Account nothing in this regulation shall restrict the discretion of the Board as to the choice of property to be taken out.

(11) For the purposes of this regulation the Board may make such arrangements as they think fit for the management of investments, including the employment of an investment manager, and for obtaining proper advice in relation to investments.

(12) In this regulation—

"the Act of 1961" means the Trustee Investments Act 1961(**b**) ;

"compensating transfer", in relation to any property transferred between the narrower-range part and the wider-range part, means a transfer in the opposite direction of property of equal value ;

"proper advice" means the advice of a person who is reasonably believed by the Board to be qualified by his ability in, and practical experience of, investment matters notwithstanding that he may give it in the course of his employment as an officer or servant ;

"property" includes real and personal property of any description, including money and things in action, but does not include an interest in expectancy."

8. Regulation 36 of the principal Regulations (which relates to the payment of additional contributions on death) is hereby revoked.

(**a**) 1958 c. 45.   (**b**) 1961 c. 62.

9. In regulation 46 of the principal Regulations (which relates to the amount of a widow's pension) for paragraph (1) there shall be substituted the following paragraph :—

"(1) Subject as in regulation 54 provided, the annual amount of a widow's pension shall be determined in accordance with the provisions of the following paragraphs of this regulation, except that it shall be not less than—

(a) £125 in the case of a widow whose husband, on or after 10th December 1968, ceased to be employed in reckonable service or class A external service or died while so employed ; or

(b) £115 in any other case."

10. For regulation 49 of the principal Regulations there shall be substituted the following regulation :—

"Amount of Short Service Widow's Pension

49. Subject as in regulation 54 provided, the annual amount of a short service widow's pension shall be the amount which, opposite to the number in column (1) of the following Table of the years of service counting for benefit of her husband, is specified—

(a) in column (2) thereof, in the case of a widow whose husband, on or after 10th December 1968, ceased to be employed in reckonable service or class A external service or died while so employed ; or

(b) in column (3) thereof, in any other case :—

TABLE

(1) Years of Service	(2) Annual Amount	(3) Annual Amount
3	£ 63	£ 58
4	£ 71	£ 66
5	£ 80	£ 74
6	£ 89	£ 82
7	£ 98	£ 90
8	£107	£ 98
9	£116	£106

11. In regulation 52 of the principal Regulations (which relates to the amount of a children's pension) for paragraphs (1) and (2) there shall be substituted the following paragraphs :—

"(1) Subject as hereafter in this regulation and in regulation 54 provided, the annual amount of a children's pension shall be the amount which, opposite to the number of eligible children in respect of whom it is for the time being payable specified in column (1) of the following Table, is specified—

(a) under letter A in column (2) or column (3) thereof, whichever column shall for the time being be appropriate, where the pension is payable to or for the benefit of a child or children of a contributor who, on or after 10th December 1968, ceased to be employed in reckonable service or class A external service or died while so employed ; or

(b) under letter B in column (2) or (3) thereof, whichever column shall for the time being be appropriate, in any other case : —

TABLE

(1) Number of Eligible Children	(2) Annual Amount of Pension where there is a Surviving Widow of the Contributor or Deceased Teacher		(3) Annual Amount of Pension where there is not a Surviving Widow of the Contributor or Deceased Teacher	
	A	B	A	B
1	£ 65	£ 60	£ 95	£ 85
2	£120	£110	£180	£165
3	£175	£160	£265	£245
4 or more	£230	£210	£355	£325

(2) Where the eligible child or eligible children to or for whose benefit a children's pension is payable is or include an incapacitated child who has attained the age of sixteen the annual amount of the pension shall be the aggregate of the following two amounts :—

(a) the amount for the time being payable under paragraph (1) above in respect of four or more eligible children ; and

(b) the amount, if any, for the time being payable under paragraph (1) above in respect of not more than three other eligible children."

12. In regulation 57 of the principal Regulations (which relates to the nomination of dependants by teachers for the purposes of the Teachers' Dependants' Pension Scheme) the proviso to paragraph (5) shall be amended as follows :—

(a) for the amount of £210 specified in sub-paragraph (a)(iii) there shall be substituted the amount of £230 ; and

(b) for the amount of £320 specified in sub-paragraph (b)(ii) there shall be substituted the amount of £350.

Given under the Official Seal of the Secretary of State for Education and Science on 27th November 1968.

(L.S.)

Edward Short,
Secretary of State for Education
and Science.

Consent of the Minister for the Civil Service given under his Official Seal on 29th November 1968.

(L.S.)

J. E. Herbecq,
Authorised by the Minister
for the Civil Service.

EXPLANATORY NOTE

(This Note is not part of the Regulations.)

These Regulations amend the Teachers' Superannuation (Family Benefits) Regulations 1966 and 1967 with respect to the management and investment of the Teachers' Family Benefits Fund. The previous requirement that not more than one half of the total value of the Fund should be invested in preference, preferred or ordinary stocks or shares is replaced by provision for the division of the Fund's investments into wider-range and narrower-range parts in the proportions, respectively, of three to one and for limited investment in real property. Provision for the Board of Management to employ an investment manager and to make arrangements for obtaining investment advice replaces the provision previously made for appointment of a trustee or trustees, and there are consequential amendments of the regulations which deal with the expenses of administration payable by the Secretary of State.

New rates are laid down for the minimum widow's pension and for the flat-rate children's and short service widows' pensions in respect of contributors who die in reckonable service or who retire after the Regulations come into operation.

STATUTORY   INSTRUMENTS

1968 No. 1919 (L.19)

MAGISTRATES' COURTS

PROCEDURE

The Magistrates' Courts (Forms) Rules 1968

Made - - - -	*27th November* 1968
Laid before Parliament	*17th December* 1968
Coming into Operation	*1st March* 1969

I, Gerald, Baron Gardiner, Lord High Chancellor of Great Britain, in exercise of the power conferred on me by section 15 of the Justices of the Peace Act 1949(a), as extended by section 122 of the Magistrates' Courts Act 1952(b), do hereby, after consultation with the Rule Committee appointed under the said section 15, make the following Rules : —

1.—(1) The forms contained in the Schedule to these Rules or forms to the like effect may be used, with such variation as the circumstances may require, in connection with proceedings in magistrates' courts.

(2) Where a requirement is imposed by or under any Act for the use of a form prescribed by rules made under section 15 of the Justices of the Peace Act 1949, and an appropriate form is contained in the Schedule to these Rules, that form or a form to the like effect shall be used.

2. These Rules may be cited as the Magistrates' Courts (Forms) Rules 1968 and shall come into operation on 1st March 1969.

Dated 27th November 1968.

Gardiner, C.

SCHEDULE

FORMS

TABLE OF CONTENTS

CRIMINAL PROCEDURE

Forms Common to Inquiry by Examining Justices and Summary Trial

(a) 1949 c. 101.   (b) 1952 c. 55.

Inquiry by Examining Justices

11. Certificate of authentication of depositions and statements of witnesses and list of witnesses.
12. Statement of accused.
13. Warrant of commitment in custody for trial.
14. Order committing corporation for trial.
15. Notice to governor of prison of person committed on bail for trial.
16. Notice on committal for trial of person subject to transfer direction under s. 73 of Mental Health Act 1959.
17. Witness order.
18. Notice to witness that a witness order is to be treated as a conditional order.
19. Notice directing witness to appear at a court other than that specified in his witness order.
20. Notice to witness subject to conditional witness order that accused has been committed for trial to some other court.
21. Notice to witness that accused has not been committed for trial.
22. Notice requiring attendance of witness subject to conditional witness order.
23. Notice of provisions of s. 11 of Criminal Justice Act 1967.
24. Certificate in respect of alibi warning.
25. List of exhibits.
26. Warrant to arrest person indicted.
27. Warrant of commitment of person indicted.
28. Warrant of commitment of person indicted who is already in custody.

Summary Trial

29. Notice to defendant: plea of guilty in absence.
30. Statement of facts.
31. Notice of intention to cite previous convictions.
32. Warrant for arrest of defendant on failure to appear before evidence has been received.
33. Warrant for arrest on failure to appear after evidence has been received where defendant at large otherwise than on bail.
34. Commitment on remand after conviction or for medical examination.
35. Hospital order.
36. Guardianship order.
37. Order of dismissal of information.
38. Order for absolute discharge.
39. Conviction: imprisonment.
40. Conviction: fine.
41. Commitment to Sessions: borstal case.
42. Commitment to Sessions for sentence.
43. Commitment to Sessions for restriction order.
44. Commitment to Sessions for restriction order or sentence.
45. Order of admission to hospital pending restriction order.
46. Commitment: sentence of imprisonment.
47. Commitment to detention centre: offence.
48. Order of return to borstal.

Enforcement of Fines

49. Notice of fine.
50. Distress warrant.
51. Return of insufficient distress.
52. Account of charges incurred on distress warrant.
53. Commitment on occasion of conviction.
54. Commitment on occasion subsequent to conviction where imprisonment fixed by magistrates' court at time of conviction.
55. Summons to defaulter: fine.
56. Warrant for arrest of defaulter: fine.
57. Commitment where imprisonment not imposed by magistrates' court on occasion of conviction.

PROBATION AND CONDITIONAL DISCHARGE

SUSPENDED SENTENCES

CRIMINAL PROCEDURE

FORMS COMMON TO INQUIRY BY EXAMINING JUSTICES AND SUMMARY TRIAL

1

*Information (M.C. Act 1952, s. 1 ; M.C. Rules 1968, r. 1.)

In the [county of   . Petty Sessional Division of   ].

The information of C.D., of   , who [upon oath [*or* affirmation]] states that A.B., of   , on the   day of   , 19   , at   , in the [county] aforesaid [*or* of   ], (*stating particulars of offence*).

Taken [and sworn [*or* affirmed]] before me this   day of   , 19   .

J.P.,

Justice of the Peace for the [county] first above mentioned.

* Where the information is substantiated on oath any sworn statement forming part of the information may conveniently be taken in the form of a deposition.

2

Summons to defendant (M.C. Act 1952, s. 1 ; M.C. Rules 1968, r. 81.)

In the [county of   . Petty Sessional Division of   ].

To A.B., of   .

Information has this day been [*or* was on the   day of   , 19   ,] laid before me, the undersigned [*or state name*] Justice of the Peace, by   that you on the   day of   , 19   , at   in the [county] aforesaid [*or* of   ], (*state shortly particulars of offence*):

You are therefore hereby summoned to appear on   day the day of   , 19   , at the hour of   in the   noon, before the Magistrates' Court sitting at   , to answer to the said information.

Dated the   day of   , 19   .

J.P.,

Justice of the Peace for the [county] first above mentioned.

[*or* This summons was issued by the above named justice of the peace.

J.C.,

Clerk of the Magistrates' Court sitting at   .]

3

Warrant for arrest of defendant in first instance (M.C. Act 1952, ss. 1, 93 ; C.J. Act 1967, s. 24 ; M.C. Rules 1968, rr. 78, 79.)

In the [county of   . Petty Sessional Division of   ].
To each and all of the constables of   [*or* To X.Y. of   ].

Information on oath [*or* affirmation] has this day been laid before me, the undersigned Justice of the Peace, by   that A.B. (hereinafter called the defendant) on the   day of   , 19   , at   , in the [county] aforesaid [*or* of   ], (*state shortly particulars of offence*) being an offence punishable with imprisonment [*or* being an indictable offence] [*or* and that the address of the defendant is not sufficiently established for a summons to be served on him]:

You are hereby commanded to bring the defendant before the Magistrates' Court sitting at   , or a justice of the peace of the petty sessional division in which the court is situate, forthwith.

Dated the   day of   , 19   .

                            J.P.,
Justice of the Peace for the [county] first above mentioned.

(Endorsement where bail is allowed)

It is directed that the defendant on arrest be released on bail on entering into a recognizance in the sum of   , with   suret in the sum of   [each], for his/her appearance before the Magistrates' Court sitting at   , at the hour of   in the   noon of the next day upon which the Court is open [*or* on the   day of   , 19   ]. [The defendant's recognizance shall be subject to the following condition[s] (*specify*)].

                            J.P.,
Justice of the Peace for the [county] first above mentioned.

4

Commitment on remand (M.C. Act 1952, ss. 6, 14, 105 ; C.J. Act 1967, s. 18 ; M.C. Rules 1968, rr. 77, 78, 80.)

In the [county of   . Petty Sessional Division of   ].
To each and all of the constables of   [*or* To X.Y. of   ]
and to the Governor of Her Majesty's prison [*or* the remand centre] at

[*or* To   constable[s] of   .]

A.B. (hereinafter called the defendant) appeared this day before the Magistrates' Court sitting at   , charged with (*state shortly particulars of offence*):

And the court decided to adjourn the hearing and remand the defendant:

You, the said constables [*or* X.Y.], are hereby commanded to convey the defendant, to the said prison [*or* remand centre] and there deliver him/her to the Governor thereof, together with this warrant ; and you, the said Governor, to receive him/her into your custody and, unless he/she shall have been bailed in the meantime, to keep him/her until the   day of   , 19   , and on that day to convey him/her at the hour of   in the   noon before the [said] Magistrates' Court [sitting at   ] to be further dealt with according to law, unless you, the said Governor, shall be otherwise ordered in the meantime.

[*or* You, the said constable[s] are hereby commanded to receive the defendant into your custody and, unless he/she shall have been bailed in the meantime, to keep him/her until the   day of   , 19   , and on that day to convey him/her at the hour of   in the   noon before the [said] Magistrates' Court [sitting at   ] to be further dealt with according to law, unless you shall be otherwise ordered in the meantime.]

Dated the day of , 19 .

J.P.,

Justice of the Peace for the [county] aforesaid.

[*or* By order of the Court,

J.C.,

Clerk of the Court.]

(Endorsement where bail is allowed)

The Court hereby certifies that the defendant may be bailed by recognizance, in the sum of , with suret in the sum of [each], to appear before the Magistrates' Court sitting at , on the day of , 19 , at the hour of in the noon [, and at every time and place to which during the course of the proceedings against the defendant the hearing may be from time to time adjourned], and that the defendant has [not] entered into his/her recognizance. [The defendant's recognizance shall be subject to the following condition[s] *(specify)*].

J.P.,

Justice of the Peace for the [county] aforesaid.

[*or* By order of the Court,

J.C.,

Clerk of the Court.]

5

Commitment on further remand of person in custody unable to appear through illness or accident (M.C. Act 1952, s. 106 ; C.J. Act 1967, s. 18 ; M.C. Rules 1968, rr. 77, 78, 80.)

In the [county of . Petty Sessional Division of].

To the Governor of Her Majesty's prison [*or* the remand centre] at
.

A.B. (hereinafter called the defendant) was on the day of , 19 , committed to your custody under a warrant of commitment by the Magistrates' Court sitting at , on remand until this day, the defendant being accused [*or* convicted] of the offence set forth in the said warrant:

And the said Court is now satisfied that by reason of illness [*or* accident] the defendant is unable to appear personally before the Court:

You are therefore hereby commanded to keep the defendant until the day of , 19 , unless he/she shall have been bailed in the meantime, and on that day to convey him/her at the hour of in the noon, before the [said] Magistrates' Court [sitting at ,] to be further dealt with according to law, unless you shall be otherwise ordered in the meantime.

Dated the day of , 19 .

J.P.,

Justice of the Peace for the [county] aforesaid.

[*or* By order of the Court,

J.C.,

Clerk of the Court.]

(Endorsement where bail is allowed)

The Court hereby certifies that the defendant may be bailed by recognizance, in the sum of   , with   suret   in the sum of [each], to appear before the Magistrates' Court sitting at   , on the day of   , 19   , at the hour of   in the   noon [, and at every time and place to which during the course of the proceedings against the defendant the hearing may be from time to time adjourned], and that the defendant has [not] entered into his/her recognizance.   [The defendant's recognizance shall be subject to the following condition[s] *(specify)*].

J.P.,

Justice of the Peace for the [county] aforesaid.

[*or* By order of the Court,

J.C.,

Clerk of the Court.]

6

Order for taking finger-prints and palm-prints of defendant
(M.C. Act 1952, s. 40 ; C.J. Act 1967, s. 33.)

In the [county of   .   Petty Sessional Division of   ].
Before the Magistrates' Court sitting at   .

A.B. (hereinafter called the defendant) having on the   day of   , 19   , been taken into custody is this day charged that he/she on the   day of   , 19   , at   , in the [county] aforesaid, did *(state shortly particulars of offence)*:

[*or* A.B. (hereinafter called the defendant) appearing before this Court in answer to a summons for *(state shortly particulars of offence)* being an offence punishable with imprisonment:]

And application being made to the Court in that behalf by *(insert name and rank)* of the   Police Force:

And it appearing to the Court that the defendant is not less than fourteen years of age:

It is ordered that the finger-prints and palm-prints of the defendant be taken by a constable.

Dated the   day of   , 19   .

J.P.,

Justice of the Peace for the [county] aforesaid.

[*or* By order of the Court,

J.C.,

Clerk of the Court.]

7

Warrant for arrest of defendant on failure to surrender to bail (M.C. Act 1952,
ss. 93, 97 ; M.C. Rules 1968, rr. 78, 79.)

In the [county of   .   Petty Sessional Division of   ].

To each and all of the constables of   [*or* To X.Y. of   ].

A.B. (hereinafter called the defendant) was on the   day of   , 19   , charged before [*or* convicted by] the Magistrates' Court sitting at   , [*or* was charged at the   Police Station] *(state shortly particulars of offence)*:

And [, the hearing of the case being adjourned,] the defendant was released [in pursuance of section 38 [*or* 93] of the Magistrates' Courts Act 1952,] upon a recognizance conditioned for his/her appearance this day, at the hour of   in the   noon, before the Magistrates' Court sitting at   :

And, in breach of the said recognizance, the defendant has this day failed to appear:

You are hereby commanded to bring the defendant before the Magistrates' Court sitting at   , or a justice of the peace of the petty sessional division in which the court is situate, forthwith.

Dated the   day of   , 19   .

J.P.,

Justice of the Peace for the [county] aforesaid.

[*or* By order of the Court,

J.C.,

Clerk of the Court.]

(*Endorsement where bail is allowed*)

It is directed that the defendant on arrest be released on bail on entering into a recognizance in the sum of   , with   suret   in the sum of [each], for his/her appearance before the Magistrates' Court sitting at   , at the hour of   in the   noon of the next day upon which the Court is open [*or* on the   day of   , 19   ]. [The defendant's recognizance shall be subject to the following condition[s] (*specify*)].

J.P.,

Justice of the Peace for the [county] aforesaid.

[*or* By order of the Court,

J.C.,

Clerk of the Court.]

8

Statement of witness
(*C.J. Act* 1967, *ss.* 2, 9 ; *M.C. Rules* 1968, *r.* 58.)

STATEMENT OF (*name of witness*)

Age of witness (*if over* 21 *enter* " *over* 21 ")
Occupation of witness

Address

This statement [, consisting of   pages each signed by me,] is true to the best of my knowledge and belief and I make it knowing that, if it is tendered in evidence, I shall be liable to prosecution if I have wilfully stated in it anything which I know to be false or do not believe to be true.

Dated the   day of   , 19   .   A.B.

[A.B. being unable to read the above statement I, C.D. of   , read it to him before he signed it.

Dated the   day of   , 19   .   C.D.]

NOTE. Wherever possible statements should be on foolscap paper. If statements are typed double spacing should be used. One side only of the paper should be used ; a space should be left at the top of the first page for headings to be entered by the clerk of the court ; and each page should have a wide margin on the left.

9

Notice to defendant : proof by written statement
(C.J. Act 1967, ss. 2, 9 ; M.C. Rules 1968, r. 58.)

To A.B., of   .

On the   day of   , 19   , the Magistrates' Court sitting at   will hear evidence relating to the following charge[s] against you.

This offence [*or* these offences] may only be tried before a jury [*or* may be tried before a jury or by the Magistrates' Court] [*or* may be tried by the Magistrates' Court].

Written statements have been made by the witnesses named below and copies of their statements are enclosed. Each of these statements will be tendered in evidence before the magistrates unless you want the witness to give oral evidence. If you want any of these witnesses to give oral evidence you should inform me as soon as possible. If [*you do not do so within 7 days of receiving this notice and the offence[s] is/are tried by the Magistrates' Court you will lose your right to prevent the statement being tendered in evidence and you will be able to require the attendance of the witness only with the leave of the Court. If the offence[s] is/are not tried by the Magistrates' Court this time limit will not apply but if] you have not informed me that you want the witness to attend he will not be present when you appear before the magistrates and delay and expense will be caused if he has then to be called.

[†A [prepaid] reply form [and prepaid envelope] is/are enclosed and it will help to save time and expense if you reply whether or not you wish any of these witnesses to give oral evidence.

If you intend to consult a solicitor about your case you should do so at once and hand this notice and the statements to him so that he may deal with them.]

Names of witnesses whose statements are enclosed—

Address any reply to : —

                                        (Signed) ....
                                        [On behalf of the Prosecutor.]

---

* Omit if offence cannot be tried by magistrates' court.
† Omit if documents are sent to defendant's solicitor.

10

Warrant for arrest of defendant on failure to appear to summons or issued before return date thereof (M.C. Act 1952, ss. 1, 93 ; M.C. Rules 1968, rr. 78, 79.)

In the [county of   . Petty Sessional Division of
              ].

To each and all of the constables of   [*or* To X.Y. of
              ].

Information [on oath [*or* affirmation]] has this day been [*or* was on the   day of   , 19   ,] laid before me, the undersigned Justice of the Peace, by   that A.B. (hereinafter called the defendant) on the   day of   , 19   , at   in the [county] aforesaid [*or* of   ], (*state shortly particulars of offence*):

[And the said information having been this day substantiated on oath before me :]

You are hereby commanded to bring the defendant before the Magistrates' Court sitting at   , or a justice of the peace of the petty sessional division in which the court is situate, forthwith.

        Dated the   day of   , 19   .

                            J.P.,
Justice of the Peace for the [county] first above mentioned.

(Endorsement where bail is allowed)

It is directed that the defendant on arrest be released on bail on entering into a recognizance in the sum of   , with   suret   in the sum of   [each], for his/her appearance before the Magistrates' Court sitting at   , at the hour of   in the   noon of the next day upon which the Court is open [*or* on the   day of   , 19   ]. [The defendant's recognizance shall be subject to the following condition[s] (*specify*)].

J.P.,

Justice of the Peace for the [county] first above mentioned.

INQUIRY BY EXAMINING JUSTICES

11

Certificate of authentication of depositions and statements of witnesses and list of witnesses (C.J. Act 1925, s. 13 ; M.C. Act 1952, ss. 4, 78 ; C.J. Act 1967, s. 7 ; M.C. Rules 1968, rr. 4, 10.)

In the [county of   . Petty Sessional Division of   ].

Before the Magistrates' Court sitting as Examining Justices at   , A.B. having been committed for trial to the next Court of Assize [*or* Quarter Sessions] for the [county] of   to be held at charged with the offence[s] specified in Schedule 1 hereto.

[I hereby certify that the (*state number*) depositions of the witnesses whose names are listed in Part I of Schedule 2 hereto were taken and sworn before me in the presence and hearing of the said A.B. on the   day of   , 19 , [and the   day of   , 19 ,] and that he/she or his/her counsel or solicitor had full opportunity of cross-examining each of the witnesses called for the prosecution.]

[I hereby [further] certify that the (*state number*) statements purporting to be signed by the persons whose names are listed in Part II of Schedule 2 hereto were tendered in evidence under section 2 of the Criminal Justice Act 1967 in the said proceedings.]

Dated the   day of   , 19   .

J.P.,

Justice of the Peace for the [county] aforesaid.
An Examining Justice.

SCHEDULE 1

(Specify charge(s) on which accused was committed.)

SCHEDULE 2

PART I

Depositions

Name of witness	Address	Occupation	Witness order (*w*) Conditional witness order or direction given that witness order be treated as conditional order(*c*)	If notice given requiring attendance at trial of witness subject to conditional order give date of notice	Page No.

PART II
Written statements

Name of witness	Address	Occupation	Witness order (w) Conditional witness order or direction given that witness order be treated as conditional order(c)	If notice given requiring attendance at trial of witness subject to conditional order give date of notice	Page No.

12
Statement of accused (M.C. Rules 1968, r. 4.)

In the [county of   . Petty Sessional Division of   ].

Before the Magistrates' Court sitting as Examining Justices at .

A.B. (hereinafter called the accused) stands charged this day with the offence hereinbefore particularly set out:

And the witnesses for the prosecution having each been examined in the presence of the accused or their written statements tendered in evidence:

And the said charge being read and its nature explained in ordinary language to the accused:

The accused was then addressed by the Court in accordance with Rule 4 of the Magistrates' Courts Rules 1968, as follows:—

"You will have an opportunity to give evidence on oath before us [me] and to call witnesses. But first I am going to ask you whether you wish to say anything in answer to the charge. You need not say anything unless you wish to do so. Anything you say will be taken down and may be given in evidence at your trial. You should take no notice of any promise or threat which any person may have made to persuade you to say anything."

and asked whether he wished to say anything in answer to the charge.

[or The accused, being represented by counsel or a solicitor, was asked whether he wished to say anything in answer to the charge.]

Whereupon the accused said as follows:—[or made no reply:]

[And the above statement of the accused has been read over to him/her; and the accused has been told that he/she may sign it if he/she wishes:]

And the accused has been given an opportunity to give evidence himself/herself and to call witnesses.

Taken before me this   day of   , 19 .

J.P.,
Justice of the Peace for the [county] aforesaid.
An Examining Justice.

13

Warrant of commitment in custody for trial (M.C. Act 1952, ss. 7, 26 ;
M.C. Rules 1968, rr. 73, 77, 78, 80.)

In the [county of   . Petty Sessional Division of   ].

To each and all of the constables of   [*or* To X.Y. of   ] and
to the Governor of Her Majesty's prison [*or* the remand centre] at

.

A.B. (hereinafter called the accused) having been charged this day before the
Magistrates' Court sitting as Examining Justices at   with (*state shortly*
particulars of offence):

And the said Court after inquiry into the said offence having committed the
accused for trial at the next Court of Assize [*or* Quarter Sessions] for the
[county] of   to be held at   :

You, the said constables [*or* X.Y.] are hereby commanded to convey the
accused to the said prison [*or* remand centre] and there deliver him/her to the
Governor thereof, together with this warrant ; and you, the said Governor, to
receive him/her into your custody and keep him/her until he/she shall be delivered
in due course of law.

Dated the   day of   , 19 .

J.P.,

Justice of the Peace for the [county] first above mentioned.

[*or* By order of the Court,

J.C.,

Clerk of the Court.]

(*Endorsement where bail is allowed*)

The Court hereby certifies that the accused may be bailed by recognizance
in the sum of   , with   suret   in   [each], to
appear before the next Court of Assize [*or* Quarter Sessions] for the
[county] of   to be held at   , to take his/her trial upon
any indictment preferred against him/her, [and, subject to the condition for
his/her said appearance, to undergo medical examination by a duly qualified
medical practitioner at (*insert name and address of institution or place*) [and
to reside, for the purpose of undergoing the said examination, at the said
institution [place] from the   day of   , 19 , to the
day of   , 19 , [*or* until he/she appears to take his/her trial as
aforesaid,]]] and that the defendant has [not] entered into his/her recognizance.
[The accused's recognizance shall be subject to the following [additional]
condition[s] (*specify*)].

J.P.,

Justice of the Peace for the [county] first above mentioned.

[*or* By order of the Court,

J.C.,

Clerk of the Court.]

14

Order committing corporation for trial (M.C. Act 1952, s. 7, Sch. 2.)

In the [county of   . Petty Sessional Division of   ].

To C.D., of   .

A.B. and Company, Limited (hereinafter called the accused corporation) were
this day charged before the Magistrates' Court sitting as Examining Justices
at   with (*state shortly particulars of offence*):

And the said Court after inquiry into the said offence having determined to commit the accused corporation for trial [and you, the said C.D., having this day been bound over to prosecute the accused corporation] at the next Court of Assize [or Quarter Sessions] for the [county] of   to be held at   :

You, the said C.D., are hereby empowered, as prosecutor, to prefer at the said Court of Assize [or Quarter Sessions] a bill of indictment in respect of the said offence.

Dated the   day of   , 19 .

J.P.,
Justice of the Peace for the [county] first above mentioned.

[or By order of the Court,

J.C.,
Clerk of the Court.]

15

Notice to governor of prison of person committed on bail for trial
(M.C. Rules 1968, r. 8.)

In the [county of   . Petty Sessional Division of   ].

To the Governor of Her Majesty's prison [or the remand centre] at   .

The undermentioned person has been committed on bail for trial at the next Court of Assize [or Quarter Sessions] for the [county] of   to be held at   .

Name, age, address and occupation of accused	
Charge	
Committing Court	

Bailed this   day of   , 19 .

J.C.,
Clerk of the Court.

16

Notice on committal for trial of person subject to transfer direction under s. 73
of Mental Health Act 1959 (M.C. Rules 1968, r. 9.)

In the [county of   . Petty Sessional Division of   ].

To the Governor of Her Majesty's prison at   and to the Managers of the   Hospital at   .

The undermentioned person, being subject to a transfer direction under section 73 of the Mental Health Act 1959, and detained at the above mentioned hospital, was this day committed in custody for trial at the next Court of Assize [or Quarter Sessions] for the [county] of   to be held at

Name, age, address and occupation of accused	
Charge	
Committing Court	

Dated this   day of   , 19   .

J.C.,

Clerk of the Court.

17

Witness order (C.P. (A. of W.) Act 1965, s. 1(1); M.C. Rules 1968, r. 5(1).)

In the [county of   . Petty Sessional Division of   ].

To C.D., of   .

You are hereby ordered [if notice is later given to you to that effect]* to attend and give evidence at the trial of A.B. before the next Court of Assize [*or* Quarter Sessions] for the [county] of   to be held at

or, if you are so directed, at such other Court as may be notified to you.

Dated the   day of   , 19   .

J.P.,

Justice of the Peace for the [county] of

[*or* By order of the Court,

J.C.,

Clerk of the Magistrates' Court sitting at   .]

NOTE.—Under section 3(1) of the Criminal Procedure (Attendance of Witnesses) Act 1965, a person who disobeys a witness order without just excuse may be punished with imprisonment not exceeding 3 months and a fine.

* Delete unless the order is a conditional order.

18

Notice to witness that a witness order is to be treated as a conditional order
(C.P. (A. of W.) Act 1965, s. 1(2)(b); M.C. Rules 1968, r. 5(2).)

Whereas you, C.D., of   , were on the   day of   , 19   , ordered to attend at the next Court of Assize [*or* Quarter Sessions] for the [county] of   , or at such other Court as you should be directed, and there to give evidence at the trial of A.B.:

And whereas the Examining Justices have [since committed the said A.B. for trial at the next Court of Assize [*or* Quarter Sessions] for the [county] of   , to be held at   , and have] directed that that order be treated as a conditional order:

THIS IS TO GIVE YOU NOTICE that you are NOT required to attend the Court of Trial unless you subsequently receive notice directing you to appear thereat.

Dated the   day of   , 19   .

J.P.,

Justice of the Peace for the [county] of

[*or* J.C.,

Clerk of the Magistrates' Court sitting at   .]

19

Notice directing witness to appear at a court other than that specified in his witness order (M.C. Rules 1968, r. 5(3).)

Whereas you, C.D., of   , were on the   day of   , 19 , ordered to attend at the next Court of Assize [*or* Quarter Sessions] for the [county] of   , to be held at
or at such other Court as you should be directed, to give evidence on the trial of A.B.:

THIS IS TO GIVE YOU NOTICE that you are no longer required to attend the above mentioned Court at   but you are hereby directed and required to attend at the next Court of Assize [*or* Quarter Sessions] for the [county] of   , to be held at   .

Dated the   day of   , 19 .

J.P.,
Justice of the Peace for the [county] of   .
[*or* J.C.,
Clerk of the Magistrates' Court sitting at   .]

20

Notice to witness subject to conditional witness order that accused has been committed for trial to some other court (M.C. Rules 1968, r. 5(3).)

Whereas you, C.D., of   , were on the   day of   , 19   , ordered to attend, upon notice being given to you, at the next Court of Assize [*or* Quarter Sessions] for the [county] of   ,
to be held at   , or at such other Court as you should be directed, to give evidence on the trial of A.B. (hereinafter called the accused):

And whereas the accused has since been committed for trial at the next Court of Assize [*or* Quarter Sessions] for the [county] of   , to be held at   :

THIS IS TO GIVE YOU NOTICE that you will NOT be required to attend at the first above mentioned Court, but that you may receive notice to attend at the Court to which the accused has been committed for trial. You are NOT however required to attend the Court of Trial unless you subsequently receive notice directing you to attend thereat.

Dated the   day of   , 19 .

J.P.,
Justice of the Peace for the [county] of   .
[*or* J.C.,
Clerk of the Magistrates' Court sitting at   .]

21

Notice to witness that accused has not been committed for trial (M.C. Rules 1968, r. 5(4).)

Whereas you, C.D., of   , were on the   day of   , 19   , ordered to attend [upon notice being given to you] at the next Court of Assize [*or* Quarter Sessions] for the [county] of   ,
to be held at   , to give evidence upon the trial of A.B.:

THIS IS TO GIVE YOU NOTICE that the Court has determined not to commit the said A.B. for trial and that consequently you are NOT required to attend at the said Court for the purpose aforesaid.

Dated the   day of   , 19 .

J.P.,
Justice of the Peace for the [county] of
[or J.C.,
Clerk of the Magistrates' Court sitting at   .]

22

Notice requiring attendance of witness subject to conditional witness order
(M.C. Rules 1968, r. 6(1).)

Whereas you, C.D., of   , were by a witness order dated the   day of   , 19 , ordered to attend* upon notice being given to you at the Court specified in the order and there to give evidence at the trial of A.B. :

[*Or (where the Court has directed that the witness order be treated as a conditional order insert instead after asterisk*) at the next Court of Assize [or Quarter Sessions] for the [county] of   , or at such other Court as you should be directed, to give evidence at the trial of A.B. ; and whereas notice was subsequently given to you that you would not be required to attend the trial unless you received notice :]*

THIS IS TO GIVE YOU NOTICE that you ARE required to attend at the next Court of Assize [or Quarter Sessions] for the [county] of   , to be held at   , and there to give evidence accordingly.

Dated the   day of   , 19 .

J.C.,
Clerk of the Magistrates' Court sitting at   .

NOTE.—Under section 3(1) of the Criminal Procedure (Attendance of Witnesses) Act 1965, a person who disobeys a witness order without just excuse may be punished with imprisonment not exceeding 3 months and a fine.

23

Notice of provisions of s. 11 of Criminal Justice Act 1967
(C.J. Act 1967, s. 11 ; M.C. Rules 1968, rr. 3(5), 4(13).)

PARTICULARS OF ALIBI

In the [county of   . Petty Sessional Division of   ].

To A.B., of   .

If you wish to raise an alibi defence at your trial you should read this notice carefully and if you intend to consult a solicitor you should show it to him at once.

Section 11 of the Criminal Justice Act 1967 provides that a defendant who is tried before a jury shall not (without the leave of the court) give evidence himself, or call witnesses in support, of an alibi unless he has given particulars of the alibi and of the witnesses as required by that section. To comply with section 11 the defendant must—

1. give notice of the particulars in the magistrates' court (the time for doing this has passed in your case) or *to the solicitor for the prosecution before the end of the period of seven days from the end of the proceedings in the magistrates' court ; and*

2. include in the notice particulars of the alibi and the name and address of any witness whom he proposes to call in support of the alibi.

If the defendant is unable to give the name and address of a witness in the notice, he must include in it any information in his possession which might help to find the witness and must take all reasonable steps to enable the name and address to be discovered. If the name or address of a witness was not included in the notice but the defendant subsequently discovers the name or address or other information which might help to find the witness, he must immediately give notice to the solicitor for the prosecution of the name, address or other information. If the defendant is notified by or on behalf of the prosecutor that a witness has not been traced by the name or at the address given by the defendant, he must forthwith give notice to the solicitor for the prosecution of any information then in his possession or subsequently received by him which might help to find the witness.

Any notice required to be given by the defendant to the solicitor for the prosecution as mentioned above must be in writing and delivered to the solicitor or left at his office or sent in a registered letter or by the recorded delivery service addressed to him at his office.

" Evidence in support of an alibi " means " evidence tending to show that by reason of the presence of the defendant at a particular place or in a particular area at a particular time he was not, or was unlikely to have been, at the place where the offence is alleged to have been committed at the time of its alleged commission ".

The name and address of the solicitor for the prosecution in your case is   .

J.C.,

Clerk of the Magistrates' Court sitting at   .

24

Certificate in respect of alibi warning (C.J. Act 1967, s. 11 ; M.C. Rules 1968, rr. 3(4), 4(9), 10(2)(i).)

In the [county of   . Petty Sessional Division of   ].

I hereby certify that A.B. (who on the   day of   , 19 , was committed by the Magistrates' Court sitting at   for trial at the next Court of Assize [*or* Quarter Sessions] for the [county] of   ) was [not] informed by the Court of the requirements of section 11 of the Criminal Justice Act 1967 and that he gave to the Court no [*or* the following] particulars of an alibi :—

Dated the   day of   , 19 .

J.C.,

Clerk of the Court.

25

List of exhibits (M.C. Rules 1968, r. 10(2)(g).)

R.v.

Number on exhibit	Short description of exhibit	Produced by prosecution (P) or defence (D)	Name and address of person retaining exhibit where exhibit is not sent to court of trial
1.			
2.			

J.C.,

Clerk to committing Justice[s].

26

Warrant to arrest person indicted (*M.C. Act* 1952, *s.* 12 ; *M.C. Rules* 1968, *rr.* 78, 79.)

In the [county of   .   Petty Sessional Division of   ].
To each and all of the constables of   [*or* To X.Y. of
                          ].

There having been produced to me, the undersigned Justice of the Peace, a certificate signed by C.D., Clerk of Assize of the   Circuit [*or* Clerk of the Peace for the [county] of   ] that on the day of   , 19   , at the Court of Assize [*or* Quarter Sessions] for the [county] of   , held at   , a bill of indictment was signed against A.B. (*state shortly particulars as in certificate*):

You are hereby commanded to bring the said A.B. before the Magistrates' Court sitting at   , or a justice of the peace of the petty sessional division in which the court is situate, forthwith.

Dated the   day of   , 19   .

J.P.,

Justice of the Peace for the [county] first above mentioned.

27

Warrant of commitment of person indicted (*M.C. Act* 1952, *s.* 12 ; *M.C. Rules* 1968, *rr.* 77, 78, 80.)

In the [county of   .   Petty Sessional Division of   ].

To each and all of the constables of   [*or* To X.Y. of   ] and to the Governor of Her Majesty's prison [*or* the remand centre] at

A.B. (hereinafter called the defendant) has been brought this day before the Magistrates' Court sitting at   , by virtue of a warrant issued on production of a certificate signed by C.D., Clerk of Assize of the   Circuit [*or* Clerk of the Peace for the [county] of   ] that on the   day of   , 19   , at the Court of Assize [*or* Quarter Sessions] for the [county] of   , held at   , a bill of indictment was signed against the defendant:

And, it being proved on oath to the satisfaction of the said Magistrates' Court that the defendant is the person named in the said indictment, the Court has committed the defendant for trial at the next Court of Assize [*or* Quarter Sessions] for the [county] of   , to be held at   :

You, the said constables [*or* X.Y.], are hereby commanded to convey the defendant to the said prison [*or* remand centre] and there deliver him/her to the Governor thereof, together with this warrant ; and you, the said Governor, to receive him/her into your custody and keep him/her until he/she shall be delivered in due course of law.

Dated this   day of   , 19   .

J.P.,

Justice of the Peace for the [county] first above mentioned.

[*or* By order of the Court,

J.C.,

Clerk of the Court.]

(*Endorsement where bail is allowed*)

The Court hereby certifies that the defendant may be bailed by recognizance in the sum of   , with   suret   in the sum of [each], to appear before the next Court of Assize [*or* Quarter Sessions] for the [county] of   , to be held at   , and take his/her trial upon the indictment which stands preferred against him/her, and that the defendant has [not] entered into his/her recognizance. [The defendant's recognizance shall be subject to the following condition[s] (*specify*)].

J.P.,

Justice of the Peace for the [county] first above mentioned.
[*or* By order of the Court,

J.C.,
Clerk of the Court.]

28

Warrant of commitment of person indicted who is already in custody (*M.C. Act 1952, s. 12 ; M.C. Rules 1968, rr. 77, 78, 80.*)

In the [county of   . Petty Sessional Division of   ].

To each and all of the constables of   and to the Governor of Her Majesty's prison at   [*or* Warden in charge of   ].

There having been produced to me, the undersigned Justice of the Peace, a certificate signed by C.D., Clerk of Assize of the   Circuit [*or* Clerk of the Peace for the [county] of   ] that on the   day of   , 19   , at the Court of Assize [*or* Quarter Sessions] for the [county] of   , held at   , a bill of indictment was signed against A.B. (hereinafter called the defendant) (*state shortly particulars as in certificate*):

And, it having been proved on oath [*or* affirmation] to my satisfaction that the defendant is detained in the said   (*insert description of place of detention*), I have this day committed him/her for trial at the next Court of Assize [*or* Quarter Sessions] for the [county] of   , to be held at   .

You, the said Governor [*or* Warden], are hereby required to keep the defendant in your custody until he/she be tried upon the said indictment or until he/she shall otherwise be removed or discharged out of your custody in due course of law.

Dated the   day of   , 19   .

J.P.,

Justice of the Peace for the [county] first above mentioned.
[*or* By order of the Court,

J.C.,
Clerk of the Court.]

(*Endorsement where bail is allowed*)

It is hereby certified that the defendant, if no longer held for any other cause, may be bailed by recognizance in the sum of   , with suret   in the sum of   [each], to appear before the next Court of Assize [*or* Quarter Sessions] for the [county] of   , to be held at   , and take his/her trial upon the indictment which stands preferred against him/her, and that the defendant has [not] entered into his/her recognizance. [The defendant's recognizance shall be subject to the following condition[s] (*specify*)].

J.P.,

Justice of the Peace for the [county] first above mentioned.
[*or* By order of the Court,

J.C.,
Clerk of the Court.]

SUMMARY TRIAL

29

Notice to defendant : plea of guilty in absence

(*M.C. Act* 1957, *s.* 1(1)(*i*).)

In the [county of   . Petty Sessional Division of   ].

To A.B., of   .

PLEASE READ THIS NOTICE CAREFULLY

If you admit the offence[s] referred to in the summons[es] served herewith and do not wish to appear before the Court, it is open to you under section 1 of the Magistrates' Courts Act 1957, to inform the Clerk of the Court in writing that you wish to plead guilty to the charge[s] without appearing. If you decide to do this, you should write to the Clerk in time for him to receive your reply at least three days before the date fixed for the hearing in order to avoid the unnecessary attendance of witnesses. In writing to the Clerk you should mention any mitigating circumstances which you wish to have put before the Court. A form which you can use for writing to the Clerk is enclosed.

If you send in a written plea of guilty, the enclosed Statement[s] of Facts and your statement in mitigation will be read out in open Court before the Court decides whether to accept your plea and hear and dispose of the case in your absence. Unless the Court adjourns the case after accepting your plea and before sentencing you (in which case you will be informed of the time and place of the adjourned hearing so that you may appear) the prosecution will not be permitted to make any statement with respect to any facts relating to the offence[s] other than the Statement[s] of Facts.

If you send in a written plea of guilty but the Court decides not to accept the plea, the hearing will be adjourned and you will be informed of the time and place of the adjourned hearing. The case will then be heard as if you had not sent in a written plea of guilty.

* [A notice from the Department of Health and Social Security claiming certain contributions is also served herewith. If, in addition to pleading guilty to the charge[s] referred to in the summons[es], you wish to admit failing to pay the contributions specified in the notice or any of them, it is open to you so to inform the Clerk in writing. If you use the enclosed form to plead guilty, you may use it also to admit failing to pay the contributions specified in the notice.]

If you send in a written plea of guilty you may, if you wish, withdraw it by informing the Clerk of the withdrawal at any time before the hearing.

Neither this notice nor any reply you may send limits your right to appear before the Court at the time fixed for the hearing, either in person or by counsel or a solicitor, and then to plead guilty or not guilty as you may desire ; if after sending in a written plea of guilty you do so appear, or if you inform the Clerk before the hearing of the withdrawal of your written plea, the case will be heard as if you had not sent it in. If after sending in a written plea of guilty you wish to appear and plead not guilty you will avoid delay and expense by informing the Clerk immediately of your change of intention: unless you do inform the Clerk in good time there will have to be an adjournment to allow the prosecution to bring their witnesses to Court.

NOTES

1. If you want any more information you may get in touch with the Clerk of the Court.

2. If you intend to consult a solicitor you would be well advised to do so before taking any action in response to this notice.

3. Address any letter to

     The Clerk of the   Magistrates' Court

         (*set out address*)

---

* To be inserted only in cases to which it applies.

30

Statement of facts
(*M.C. Act* 1957, *s.* 1(1)(ii).)

To A.B., of   (*state age and occupation if known*).

If you inform the Clerk of the Court that you wish to plead guilty to the charge of   , set out in the summons served herewith, without appearing before the Court and the Court proceeds to hear and dispose of the case in your absence under section 1 of the Magistrates' Courts Act 1957, the following Statement of Facts will be read out in open Court before the Court decides whether to accept your plea. If your plea of guilty is accepted the Court will not, unless it adjourns the case after convicting you and before sentencing you, permit any other statement to be made by or on behalf of the prosecutor with respect to any facts relating to the charge.

Statement of Facts

Signed..
[On behalf of the Prosecutor.]

31

Notice of intention to cite previous convictions
(*M.C. Act* 1957, *s.* 3.)

To A.B., of   .

You are hereby given notice that if, but only if, you are convicted of [any of] the offence[s] of   in respect of which you are summoned to appear before the   Magistrates' Court on the   day of   , 19   , the under-mentioned convictions which are recorded against you will be brought to the notice of the Court; and if you are not present in person before the Court, the Court may take account of any such previous conviction as if you had appeared and admitted it.

Date of conviction	Court	Offence	Sentence

Signed....................................
[For Chief Constable.]

If you do not intend to appear in person at the hearing and you dispute any of the above convictions, or any of the details in connection with them, you should immediately notify [the Chief Constable of   ] at (*state address*) so that further inquiries can be made.

Nothing in this notice limits in any way your right to appear in person on the date fixed for the hearing and to dispute any conviction alleged against you.

32

Warrant for arrest of defendant on failure to appear before evidence has been received (M.C. Act 1952, ss. 15, 93 ; C.J. Act 1967, s. 24 ; M.C. Rules 1968, rr. 78, 79.)

In the [county of   . Petty Sessional Division of   ].

To each and all of the constables of   [or To X.Y. of   ].

Information [on oath [or affirmation]] was laid on the   day of   , 19   , by   that A.B. (hereinafter called the defendant) on the   day of   , 19   , at   in the [county] aforesaid [or of   ], (*state shortly particulars of offence*) being an offence punishable with imprisonment:

And the defendant was thereupon summoned to appear before the Magistrates' Court sitting at   this day [or on the   day of   , 19   ,] to answer to the said information:

And the defendant having this day failed to appear in answer to the said summons [or at the time fixed for the adjourned trial of the said information], and no evidence having been received:

[And the said information having been substantiated on oath [or affirmation]:]

And oath [or affirmation [or declaration]] having been made [or it having been certified] that the summons was duly served on the defendant [or the defendant having appeared on a previous occasion]:

You are hereby commanded to bring the defendant before the Magistrates' Court sitting at   , or a justice of the peace of the petty sessional division in which the court is situate, forthwith.

Dated the   day of   , 19   .

J.P.,

Justice of the Peace for the [county] first above mentioned.

[or By order of the Court,

J.C.,

Clerk of the Court.]

(*Endorsement where bail is allowed*)

It is directed that the defendant on arrest be released on bail on entering into a recognizance in the sum of   , with   suret   in the sum of   [each], for his/her appearance before the Magistrates' Court sitting at   , at the hour of   in the   noon of the next day upon which the Court is open [or on the   day of   , 19   ]. [The defendant's recognizance shall be subject to the following condition[s] (*specify*)].

J.P.,

Justice of the Peace for the [county] first above mentioned.

[or By order of the Court,

J.C.,

Clerk of the Court.]

33

Warrant for arrest on failure to appear after evidence has been received where defendant at large otherwise than on bail (M.C. Act 1952, ss. 15, 93 ; C.J. Act 1967, s. 24 ; M.C. Rules 1968, rr. 78, 79.)

In the [county of   . Petty Sessional Division of   ].

To each and all of the constables of   [or To X.Y. of   ].

Information [on oath [or affirmation]] was laid on the   day of   , 19   , by   that A.B. (hereinafter called the defendant) on the   day of   , 19   , at   in the [county] aforesaid [or of   ], (*state shortly particulars of offence*) [being an offence punishable with imprisonment]:

And the defendant was thereupon summoned to appear before the Magistrates' Court sitting at   this day [*or* on the   day of   , 19   ,] to answer to the said information:

And the defendant having this day failed to appear in answer to the said summons [*or* at the time fixed for the adjourned trial of the said information], and evidence having been received, the Court is of opinion that it is undesirable, by reason of the gravity of the offence, to continue the trial in the absence of the defendant [the Court, having convicted the defendant, proposes to impose a disqualification on him]:

[And the said information having been substantiated on oath [*or* affirmation]:]

And oath [*or* affirmation [*or* declaration]] having been made [*or* it having been certified] that the summons was duly served on the defendant [*or* the defendant having appeared on a previous occasion]:

You are hereby commanded to bring the defendant before the Magistrates' Court sitting at   , or a justice of the peace of the petty sessional division in which the court is situate, forthwith.

Dated the   day of   , 19 .

J.P.,

Justice of the Peace for the [county] first above mentioned.

[*or* By order of the Court,

J.C.,

Clerk of the Court.]

(*Endorsement where bail is allowed*)

It is directed that the defendant on arrest be released on bail on entering into a recognizance in the sum of   , with   suret   in the sum of   [each], for his/her appearance before the Magistrates' Court sitting at   , at the hour of   in the   noon of the next day upon which the Court is open [*or* on the   day of   , 19]. [The defendant's recognizance shall be subject to the following condition[s] (*specify*)].

J.P.,

Justice of the Peace for the [county] first above mentioned.

[*or* By order of the Court,

J.C.,

Clerk of the Court.]

34

Commitment on remand after conviction or for medical examination (*M.C. Act 1952, ss. 14(3), 26, 28, 105 ; C.J. Act 1961, ss. 4(4), 12(4) ; C.I. Act 1962, s. 8(2) ; C.J. Act 1967, s. 18 ; M.C. Rules 1968, rr. 23, 77, 78, 80.*)

In the [county of   .   Petty Sessional Division of   ].

To each and all of the constables of   [*or* To X.Y. of   ] and to the Governor of Her Majesty's prison [*or* the remand centre] at

A.B. (hereinafter called the defendant) appeared this day before the Magistrates' Court sitting at   , charged with (*state shortly particulars of offence*):

And, the defendant [, having consented to be tried summarily and] having been convicted of the said offence, the Court decided to adjourn the hearing and remand the defendant for the purpose of enabling inquiries to be made [and] [*or* of determining the most suitable method of dealing with the case] [and] [*or* for the purpose of enabling a notice to be given to the defendant under section 8(1) of the Commonwealth Immigrants Act 1962] [*or* for the purpose of enabling a period of seven days to elapse from the date on which a notice under section 8(1) of the Commonwealth Immigrants Act 1962 had been given to the defendant] [*or* for the purpose of enabling the Secretary of State to make a report on the defendant under section 4(4) [*or* 12(3)] of the Criminal Justice Act 1961]:

[*or* And, the said offence being punishable with imprisonment, the Court, being satisfied that the defendant did the act or made the omission charged but, being of opinion that an inquiry ought to be made into his/her physical [and] [*or* mental] condition before the method of dealing with him/her was determined, decided to adjourn the hearing and remand the defendant:]

You, the said constables [*or* X.Y.], are hereby commanded to convey the defendant to the said prison [*or* remand centre] and there deliver him/her to the Governor thereof, together with this warrant; and you, the said Governor, to receive him/her into your custody and, [unless he/she shall have been bailed in the meantime, or] unless you, the said Governor shall be otherwise ordered in the meantime, to keep him/her until the   day of   , 19 :

And you, the said Governor, are hereby requested [to arrange for an inquiry to be made into the defendant's physical [and] [*or* mental] condition by a duly qualified medical practitioner [*or* by two duly qualified medical practitioners, of whom one is approved for the purposes of section 28 of the Mental Health Act 1959, by a local health authority as having special experience in the diagnosis or treatment of mental disorders], who shall report thereon to the Court.

And you, the said Governor, are further commanded to convey the defendant on the said   day of   , 19 , at the hour of in the   noon before the Court to be further dealt with according to law.

Dated the   day of   , 19 .

J.P.,
Justice of the Peace for the [county] aforesaid.
[*or* By order of the Court,
J.C.,
Clerk of the Court.]

(*Endorsement where bail is allowed*)

The Court hereby certifies that the defendant may be bailed by recognizance, in the sum of   , with   suret   in the sum of [each], to appear before the Magistrates' Court sitting at   , on the   day of   , 19 , at the hour of   in the   noon [and, subject to the condition for his/her said appearance, to undergo medical examination by a duly qualified medical practitioner [*or* by two duly qualified medical practitioners, of whom one is approved for the purposes of section 28 of the Mental Health Act 1959,] and for the purpose attend at (*insert name and address of institution or place or name and address of doctor*), [and comply with any directions given to him/her for that purpose by   ] [and reside there until the expiration of   from the date of admission or until earlier discharge.]]

And that the defendant has [not] entered into his/her recognizance. [The defendant's recognizance shall be subject to the following [additional] condition[s] (*specify*)].

J.P.,
Justice of the Peace for the [county] aforesaid.
[*or* By order of the Court,
J.C.,
Clerk of the Court.]

35

Hospital order (M.H. Act 1959, s. 60 ; M.C. Rules 1968, r. 27.)

In the [county of   . Petty Sessional Division of   ].
Before the Magistrates' Court sitting at   .

A.B. is this day charged with (*state shortly particulars of offence*), being an offence punishable on summary conviction with imprisonment:

And the Court has convicted A.B. of the said offence [*or* is satisfied that A.B. did the act or made the omission charged]:

And the Court has heard [*or* considered] the [written] evidence of two medical practitioners, namely (*insert names and addresses*), [each] of whom [the first mentioned] is approved for the purposes of section 28 of the Mental Health Act 1959, by a local health authority as having special experience in the diagnosis or treatment of mental disorders, and each of the said practitioners has described the said A.B. as suffering from mental illness [*or* psychopathic disorder *or* subnormality *or* severe subnormality]:

And the Court is satisfied that he/she is suffering from the following form(s) of mental disorder within the meaning of the Mental Health Act 1959, namely mental illness [*or* psychopathic disorder *or* subnormality *or* severe subnormality], and that the disorder is of a nature or degree which warrants his/her detention in a hospital for medical treatment and is satisfied that arrangements have been made for his/her admission to the hospital hereinafter specified within twenty-eight days of this date and that the most suitable method of disposing of the case is by means of a hospital order:

It is ordered that the said A.B. be admitted to and detained in (*insert name and address of hospital*):

[And that he/she be conveyed to the said hospital by E.F.]:

[And it is directed that pending admission to the said hospital within the said period of twenty-eight days the said A.B. shall be detained in a place of safety, namely   ] [and shall be conveyed thither by E.F.].

     Dated the   day of   , 19   .

                J.P.,

       Justice of the Peace for the [county] first above mentioned.

       [*or* By order of the Court,

                J.C.,

           Clerk of the Court.]

36

Guardianship order (*M.H. Act* 1959, *s.* 60 ; *M.C. Rules* 1968, *r.* 27.)

In the [county of   . Petty Sessional Division of   ].

Before the Magistrates' Court sitting at   .

A.B. is this day charged with (*state shortly particulars of offence*), being an offence punishable on summary conviction with imprisonment:

And the Court has convicted A.B. of the said offence [*or* is satisfied that A.B. did the act or made the omission charged]:

And the Court has heard [*or* considered] the [written] evidence of two medical practitioners, namely (*insert names and addresses*), [each] of whom [the first mentioned] is approved for the purposes of section 28 of the Mental Health Act 1959, by a local health authority as having special experience in the diagnosis or treatment of mental disorders, and each of the said practitioners has described the said A.B. as suffering from mental illness [*or* psychopathic disorder *or* subnormality *or* severe subnormality]:

And the Court is satisfied that he/she is suffering from the following form(s) of mental disorder within the meaning of the Mental Health Act 1959, namely mental illness [*or* psychopathic disorder *or* subnormality *or* severe subnormality], and that the disorder is of a nature or degree which warrants his/her reception into guardianship under that Act and is satisfied that the authority [*or* person] hereinafter specified is willing to receive him/her into guardianship and that the most suitable method of disposing of the case is by means of a guardianship order:

It is ordered that the said A.B. be placed under guardianship of a local health authority, namely the   County [Borough] Council [*or* of C.D. being a person approved by a local health authority, namely the   County [Borough] Council].

Dated the   day of   , 19   .

J.P.,

Justice of the Peace for the [county] first above mentioned.

[or By order of the Court,

J.C.,

Clerk of the Court.]

37

Order of dismissal of information (M.C. Act 1952, s. 13.)

In the [county of   .   Petty Sessional Division of   ].

Before the Magistrates' Court sitting at   .

Information having been laid by C.D., of   , that A.B., of   ,
(hereinafter called the defendant) on the   day of   , 19   ,
at   , in the [county] aforesaid [or of   ], did (*state
shortly particulars of offence*):

[And the defendant having consented to be tried summarily:]

It is adjudged that the said information be dismissed.

[And it is ordered that the said C.D. pay to the defendant the sum of
for costs [by weekly [or monthly] instalments of   , the first instalment to be paid] forthwith [or not later than the   day of   , 19   .]]

Dated the   day of   , 19   .

J.P.,

Justice of the Peace for the [county] first above mentioned.

[or By order of the Court,

J.C.,

Clerk of the Court.]

38

Order for absolute discharge (C.J. Act 1948, s. 7.)

In the [county of   .   Petty Sessional Division
of   ].

Before the Magistrates' Court sitting at   .

A.B. (hereinafter called the defendant) [, having consented to be tried
summarily,] is this day convicted (*state shortly particulars of offence*):

And the Court is of opinion having regard to the circumstances, including the
nature of the offence and the character of the defendant, that it is inexpedient
to inflict punishment and that a probation order is not appropriate:

It is ordered that the defendant be discharged absolutely.

[And it is ordered that the defendant pay   [as damages for injury
suffered by [or compensation for loss incurred by]   and   ]
for costs, [by weekly [or monthly] instalments of   [or by a first instalment of   and subsequent weekly [monthly] instalments of   ,],
the first instalment of] the said sum[s] to be paid forthwith [or not later than
the   day of   , 19   ].]

Dated the   day of   , 19   .

J.P.,

Justice of the Peace for the [county] aforesaid.

[or By order of the Court,

J.C.,

Clerk of the Court.]

39

Conviction: imprisonment (M.C. Act 1952, s. 13; C.J. Act 1967, s. 39; M.C. Rules 1968, r. 15.)

In the [county of   . Petty Sessional Division of   ].

Before the Magistrates' Court sitting at   .

A.B. (hereinafter called the defendant) [, having consented to be tried summarily,] is this day convicted (*state shortly particulars of offence*):

[*And the Court is of opinion that no method of dealing with the defendant other than the imposition of imprisonment, is appropriate because (*stating reason*):]

[†And the Court is not required to suspend this sentence because paragraph of section 39(3) of the Criminal Justice Act 1967 applies:]

And it is adjudged that the defendant for his/her offence be imprisoned in Her Majesty's prison at   for (*state period*).

[And it is ordered that the defendant pay the sum of   [for compensation and   ] for costs [by weekly [*or* monthly] instalments of   , the first instalment of] the said sum[s] to be paid forthwith [*or* not later than the   day of   , 19   ]:]

[And in default of payment it is ordered that the defendant be imprisoned in the said prison for (*state period*) commencing at the termination of the imprisonment before adjudged, unless the said sum[s] be sooner paid.]

Dated the   day of   , 19   .

J.P.,

Justice of the Peace for the [county] aforesaid.

[*or* By order of the Court,

J.C.,

Clerk of the Court.]

---

* Delete if defendant appears to have attained the age of 21 years and is not a first offender within the meaning of the First Offenders Act 1958.
† Delete if sentence is for more than 6 months in respect of one offence.

40

Conviction: fine (M.C. Act 1952, s. 13; M.C. Rules 1968, r. 15.)

In the [county of   . Petty Sessional Division of   ].
Before the Magistrates' Court sitting at   .

A.B. (hereinafter called the defendant) [, having consented to be tried summarily,] is this day convicted (*state shortly particulars of offence*):

And it is adjudged that the defendant for his/her said offence pay a fine of   [and   for compensation] [and   for costs,] [by weekly [*or* monthly] instalments of   , the first instalment of] the said sum[s] to be paid forthwith [*or* not later than the   day of   , 19   ]:

[And in default of payment it is adjudged that the defendant be imprisoned in Her Majesty's prison at   for (*state period*) unless the said sum[s] be sooner paid.]

Dated the   day of   , 19   .
J.P.,

Justice of the Peace for the [county] aforesaid.

[*or* By order of the Court,

J.C.,

Clerk of the Court.]

41

Commitment to Sessions: borstal case (*M.C. Act* 1952, *s.* 28; *C.J. Act* 1948, *s.* 20; *C.J. Act* 1961, *s.* 1; *M.C. Rules* 1968, *rr.* 77, 78, 80.)

In the [county of   . Petty Sessional Division of   ].

To each and all of the constables of   [*or* To X.Y. of   ] and to the Governor of the remand centre at   [*or* Her Majesty's prison at   ].

A.B. (hereinafter called the defendant) [, having consented to be tried summarily,] was this day [*or* on the   day of   , 19 ,] convicted by the Magistrates' Court sitting at   , (*state shortly particulars of offence*):

And it appeared to the Court that on the day of his/her said conviction the defendant was not less than fifteen and under twenty-one years of age:

And the Court is of opinion, having regard to the circumstances of the offence and taking into account the defendant's character and previous conduct, that it is expedient that he/she should be detained for training for not less than six months [and, he/she being then under seventeen years of age, that no other method of dealing with him/her is appropriate]:

And it was this day adjudged that the defendant should be committed in custody to Quarter Sessions for sentence in accordance with the provisions of section 20 of the Criminal Justice Act 1948:

You, the said constables [*or* X.Y.], are hereby commanded to convey the defendant to the said remand centre [*or* prison] and there deliver him/her to the Governor thereof, together with this warrant; and you, the said Governor, to receive the defendant into your custody and, unless he/she shall have been bailed in the meantime, keep him/her until the next Quarter Sessions for the said [county] and to have him/her there, together with this warrant, there to be dealt with according to law.

Dated the   day of   , 19 .

J.P.,

Justice of the Peace for the [county] aforesaid.

[*or* By order of the Court,

J.C.,

Clerk of the Court.]

(*Endorsement where bail is allowed*)

The Court hereby certifies that the defendant may be bailed by recognizance in the sum of   , with   suret   in the sum of   [each], to appear before the next Quarter Sessions for the said [county], and that the defendant has [not] entered into his/her recognizance. [The defendant's recognizance shall be subject to the following condition[s] (*specify*)].

J.P.,

Justice of the Peace for the [county] aforesaid.

[*or* By order of the Court,

J.C.,

Clerk of the Court.]

42

Commitment to Sessions for sentence (*M.C. Act* 1952, *s.* 29; *C.J. Act* 1948, *s.* 29; *M.C. Rules* 1968, *rr.* 77, 78, 80.)

In the [county of   . Petty Sessional Division of   ].

To each and all of the constables of   [*or* To X.Y. of   ] and to the Governor of Her Majesty's prison [*or* the remand centre] at   .

A.B. (hereinafter called the defendant) having consented to be tried summarily under section 19 of the Magistrates' Courts Act 1952, [or, having been tried summarily under section 18(3) of the Magistrates' Courts Act 1952,] was this day [or on the   day of   , 19 ,] convicted by the Magistrates' Court sitting at   , (state shortly particulars of offence):

And it appeared to the Court that on the day of his/her said conviction the defendant was not less than seventeen years of age:

And the Court, on obtaining information as to the character and antecedents of the defendant, was of opinion that they were such that greater punishment should be inflicted in respect of the offence than the Court had power to inflict:

And it was this day adjudged that the defendant should be committed in custody to Quarter Sessions for sentence in accordance with the provisions of section 29 of the Criminal Justice Act 1948:

You, the said constables [or X.Y.], are hereby commanded to convey the defendant to the said prison [or remand centre] and there deliver him/her to the Governor thereof, together with this warrant; and you, the said Governor, to receive the defendant into your custody and, unless he/she shall have been bailed in the meantime, keep him/her until the next Quarter Sessions for the said [county] and to have him/her there, together with this warrant, there to be dealt with according to law.

Dated the   day of   , 19 .

J.P.,

Justice of the Peace for the [county] aforesaid.

[or By order of the Court,

J.C.,

Clerk of the Court.]

(Endorsement where bail is allowed)

The Court hereby certifies that the defendant may be bailed by recognizance in the sum of   , with   suret   in the sum of   [each], to appear before the next Quarter Sessions for the said [county], and that the defendant has [not] entered into his/her recognizance. [The defendant's recognizance shall be subject to the following condition[s] (specify)].

J.P.,

Justice of the Peace for the [county] aforesaid.

[or By order of the Court,

J.C.,

Clerk of the Court.]

43

Commitment to Sessions for restriction order (M.H. Act 1959, s. 67(1).)

In the [county of   . Petty Sessional Division of   ].

To each and all of the constables of   [or To X.Y. of   ] and to the Governor of Her Majesty's prison [or the remand centre] at   .

A.B. (hereinafter called the defendant) [, having consented to be tried summarily,] was this day [or on the   day of   , 19 ,] convicted by the Magistrates' Court sitting at   , (state shortly particulars of offence), being an offence punishable on summary conviction with imprisonment:

And it appeared to the Court that on the day of his/her said conviction the defendant was not less than fourteen years of age:

And the conditions which, under section 60(1) of the Mental Health Act 1959, are required to be satisfied for the making of a hospital order are satisfied in respect of the defendant:

And it appeared to the Court, having regard to the nature of the offence, the antecedents of the defendant and the risk of his/her committing further offences if set at large, that if a hospital order is made an order restricting the discharge of the defendant should also be made:

And it was this day adjudged that the defendant should be committed in custody to Quarter Sessions under the provisions of section 67(1) of the Mental Health Act 1959, to be dealt with in respect of the offence:

You, the said constables [*or* X.Y.], are hereby commanded to convey the defendant to the said prison [*or* remand centre] and there deliver him/her to the Governor thereof, together with this warrant; and you, the said Governor, to receive the defendant into your custody and to keep him/her until the next Quarter Sessions for the said [county] and to have him/her there, together with this warrant, there to be dealt with according to law.

Dated the   day of   , 19   .

J.P.,

Justice of the Peace for the [county] aforesaid.

[*or* By order of the Court,

J.C.,

Clerk of the Court.]

44

Commitment to Sessions for restriction order or sentence (M.H. Act 1959, s. 67(4).)

In the [county of   . Petty Sessional Division of   ].

To each and all of the constables of   [*or* To X.Y. of   ] and to the Governor of Her Majesty's prison at   .

A.B. (hereinafter called the defendant) [, having consented to be tried summarily,] was this day [*or* on the   day of   , 19   ,] convicted by the Magistrates' Court sitting at   (*state shortly particulars of offence*):

And it appeared to the Court that on the day of his/her said conviction the defendant was not less than seventeen years of age:

And the conditions which, under section 60(1) of the Mental Health Act 1959, are required to be satisfied for the making of a hospital order are satisfied in respect of the defendant:

And it appeared to the Court, having regard to the nature of the offence, the antecedents of the defendant and the risk of his/her committing further offences if set at large, that if a hospital order is made an order restricting the discharge of the defendant should also be made:

And the Court, on obtaining information as to the character and antecedents of the defendant, was of opinion that they were such that greater punishment should be inflicted in respect of the offence than the Court had power to inflict unless a hospital order is made in the case of the defendant with an order restricting his/her discharge:

And it was this day adjudged that the defendant should be committed in custody to Quarter Sessions under section 29 of the Magistrates' Courts Act 1952, as modified by section 67(4) of the Mental Health Act 1959, for sentence in accordance with the provisions of section 29 of the Criminal Justice Act 1948:

You, the said constables [*or* X.Y.], are hereby commanded to convey the defendant to Her Majesty's prison aforesaid and there deliver him/her to the Governor thereof, together with this warrant; and you, the Governor of the said prison, to receive the defendant into your custody and keep him/her until the next Quarter Sessions for the said [county] and to have him/her there, together with this warrant, there to be dealt with according to law.

Dated the   day of   , 19   .

J.P.,

Justice of the Peace for the [county] aforesaid.

[*or* By order of the Court,

J.C.,

Clerk of the Court.]

45

Order of admission to hospital pending restriction order
(M.H. Act 1959, s. 68.)

In the [county of   .   Petty Sessional Division of   ].
To the Managers of the   Hospital at   .

A.B. (hereinafter called the defendant) [, having consented to be tried sum-marily,] was this day [or on the   day of   , 19   ,] convicted by the Magistrates' Court sitting at   *(state shortly particulars of offence)* being an offence punishable on summary conviction with imprison-ment:

And it appeared to the Court that on the day of his/her said conviction the defendant was not less than fourteen years of age:

And the conditions which, under section 60 of the Mental Health Act 1959, are required to be satisfied for the making of a hospital order are satisfied in respect of the defendant:

And it appeared to the Court, having regard to the nature of the offence, the antecedents of the defendant and the risk of his/her committing further offences if set at large, that if a hospital order is made an order restricting his/her discharge should also be made:

And the Court has committed the defendant to Quarter Sessions under section 67(1) of the Mental Health Act 1959, to be dealt with in respect of the offence:

The Court being satisfied that arrangements have been made for the admission of the defendant to the hospital hereinafter specified:

It was this day directed that the defendant be admitted to the Hospital at   and be detained there until Quarter Sessions has disposed of the case:

And it was directed that C.D. [or you, the said Managers,] should produce the defendant from the said hospital to attend the next Quarter Sessions for the said [county] on the day and at the time to be notified by the Clerk of the Peace.

Dated the   day of   , 19   .

J.P.,
Justice of the Peace for the [county] aforesaid.
[or By order of the Court,

J.C.,
Clerk of the Court.]

46

Commitment : sentence of imprisonment (M.C. Rules 1968, rr. 77, 78, 80.)

In the [county of   .   Petty Sessional Division of   ].

To each and all of the constables of   [or To X.Y. of   ] and to the Governor of Her Majesty's prison at   .

A.B. (hereinafter called the defendant) [, having consented to be tried sum-marily,] is this day [or was on the   day of   , 19   ,] convicted by the Magistrates' Court sitting at   , *(state shortly particulars of offence)*:

[*And the Court is of opinion that no method of dealing with the defendant, other than the imposition of imprisonment, is appropriate because *(stating reason)*:]

[†And the Court is not required to suspend the sentence because paragraph of section 39(3) of the Criminal Justice Act 1967 applies:]

It is adjudged that the defendant for his/her offence be imprisoned in Her Majesty's prison aforesaid, for (*state period*).

You, the said constables [*or* X.Y.], are hereby commanded to convey the defendant to the said prison and there deliver him/her to the Governor thereof, together with this warrant ; and you, the Governor of the said prison, to receive the defendant into your custody, and keep him/her for (*state period*).

Dated the   day of   , 19 .

J.P.,

Justice of the Peace for the [county] aforesaid.

[*or* By order of the Court,

J.C.,

Clerk of the Court.]

* Delete if defendant appears to have attained the age of 21 years and is not a first offender within the meaning of the First Offenders Act 1958.
† Delete if sentence is for more than 6 months in respect of one offence.

47

Commitment to detention centre : offence (C.J. Act 1961, s. 4 ; M.C. Rules 1968, rr. 77, 78, 80.)

In the [county of   .   Petty Sessional Division of   ].

To each and all of the constables of   [*or* to X.Y. of   ] and to the Warden of the detention centre at   .

A.B. (hereinafter called the defendant) who appears to the Court to have attained the age of seventeen years and to be under the age of twenty-one years, is this day [*or* was on the   day of   , 19 ,] [, having consented to be tried summarily,] convicted by the Magistrates' Court sitting at   of   (*state shortly particulars of offence*), being an offence for which the Court has or would but for the statutory restrictions upon the imprisonment of young offenders have power to impose imprisonment on him/her in that he/she on the   day of   , 19 , did (*state shortly particulars of offence*):

And the Court having been notified by the Secretary of State that the detention centre specified herein is available for the reception from the Court of persons of his/her class or description :

[And, the defendant being a person who is serving/has served a sentence of imprisonment of not less than six months [*or* of borstal training], the Court finds that there are special circumstances which warrant the making of this order in his/her case and has considered a report in respect of the defendant by or on behalf of the Secretary of State :]

[And the maximum term of imprisonment for which the Court could (or could but for any such restriction) pass sentence in his/her case exceeds three months :]

It is ordered that the defendant be detained in the detention centre aforesaid for [three] months :

You, the said constables [*or* X.Y.], are hereby commanded to convey the defendant to the said detention centre, and there deliver him/her to the Warden thereof, together with this warrant ; and you, the Warden of the said detention centre, to receive the defendant into your custody and keep him/her for months

Dated the   day of   , 19 .

J.P.,

Justice of the Peace for the [county] aforesaid.

[*or* By order of the Court,

J.C.,

Clerk of the Court.]

48

Order of return to borstal (C.J. Act 1961, s. 12.)

In the [county of   . Petty Sessional
Division of   ].

Before the Magistrates' [*or* Juvenile] Court sitting at   .

To each and all of the constables of   [*or* to X.Y. of
                    ] and to the Governor of Her Majesty's prison at   .

A.B. (hereinafter called the defendant) [, having consented to be tried summarily,] is this day [*or* was on the   day of   , 19 ,] convicted (*state shortly particulars of offence*), which offence is punishable on summary conviction in the case of an adult with imprisonment:

And the defendant having been sentenced to borstal training is under supervision after his/her release from a borstal institution [*or* and, having become unlawfully at large from a borstal institution, has not returned or been returned thereto]:

The Court having considered the Secretary of State's report on his/her response to the training already undergone:

It is ordered that the defendant for his/her offence be returned to a borstal institution:

You, the said constables [*or* X.Y.], are hereby commanded to convey the defendant to the said prison and there deliver him/her to the Governor thereof, together with this order ; and you, the Governor of the said prison, to receive the defendant into your custody and keep him/her until he/she shall be duly transferred to one of Her Majesty's borstal institutions there to be detained in accordance with section 12 (2) of the Criminal Justice Act 1961.

Dated the   day of   , 19 .

J.P.,

Justice of the Peace for the [county] aforesaid.
[*or* By order of the Court,

J.C.,
Clerk of the Court.]

ENFORCEMENT OF FINES

49

Notice of fine (M.C. Rules 1968, r. 38.)

In the [county of   . Petty Sessional Division of   ].

To A.B., of   .

ADJUDICATION			
	£	s.	d.
Fine ...			
Compensation			
Costs ...			
Total ...			

You were this day [*or* on the   day of   , 19   ,] convicted by [*or* before] the Magistrates' Court [*or* Court of Assize *or* Quarter Sessions for the [county] of   ] sitting at   , (*state shortly particulars of offence*) and were ordered to pay the sum of   as shown in the margin hereof ; the sum to be paid forthwith [*or* on or before

day the   day of   , 19   ] [*or* by weekly
[*or* monthly] instalments of   , the first instalment to be paid on
or before   day the   day of   , 19   ] [and
this Court is required under section 47(3) of the Criminal Justice Act 1967
to enforce payment].

[And the Court of Assize [*or* Quarter Sessions] fixed the term of imprisonment
in default as   months.]

Payment should be made either by post to me, the Clerk of the Court at (*insert
address*) or made personally at (*insert the address and also days and hours when
payment can be made*).

Failure to pay forthwith [*or* on or before the appointed day[s]] will render you
liable to [*imprisonment for (*state period*)] [arrest] or your money and goods
liable to distraint without further notice [, unless you have applied for and
been granted before that day further time for payment. Application for the
grant of further time may be made either in person to the Court or by letter
addressed to me, the Clerk of the Court at (*insert address*) and stating fully
the grounds on which the application is made].

Dated the   day of   , 19   .

J.C.,

Clerk of the Court.

NOTE.—Any communication sent by post must be properly stamped.   Cash should not
be sent in unregistered envelopes.

---

* Delete unless magistrates' court on occasion of conviction has, under s. 65(2) of the
Magistrates' Courts Act 1952, fixed a term of imprisonment in default and postponed the
issue of the warrant of commitment.

50

*Distress warrant (M.C. Act 1952, ss. 64, 66 ; C.J. Act 1967, s. 47 ; M.C. Rules
1968, rr. 44, 78.)*

In the county of   . Petty Sessional Division of   ].

To each and all of the constables of   [*or* To X.Y. of
].

A.B. (hereinafter called the defendant) was on the   day of   ,
19   , convicted by [*or* before] the Magistrates' Court [*or* Court of Assize
or Quarter Sessions for the [county] of   ] sitting at
(*state shortly particulars of offence*):

And it was adjudged that the defendant for the said offence be imprisoned for
(*state period*) and [*or* pay a fine of   and] pay   [for compensation and   ] for costs, [by weekly [*or* monthly] instalments, the
first instalment of] the said sum[s] to be paid forthwith [*or* not later than
the   day of   , 19   ]:

And [a notice of fine having been served on the defendant and] default having
been made in payment:

You are hereby commanded forthwith to make distress of the money and goods
of the defendant (except the wearing apparel and bedding of him/her and his/her
family, and, to the value of fifty pounds, the tools and implements of his/her
trade) ; and if the sum stated at the foot of this warrant, together with the
reasonable costs and charges of the making and keeping of the said distress,
be not paid, then not earlier than the [sixth] day after the making of such

distress, unless the defendant consents in writing to an earlier sale, to sell the said goods, and pay the proceeds of the said distress to the Clerk of the said Court, and if no such distress can be found, to certify the same to the Court.

Dated the   day of   , 19 .

J.P.,
Justice of the Peace for the [county] aforesaid.
[*or* By order of the Court,

J.C.,
Clerk of the Court.]

	£	s.	d.
Amount adjudged			
Paid			
Amount to be levied			

51
Return of insufficient distress (M.C. Act 1952, s. 64(2).)

(*Endorsement*)

I,   , [constable of the   ] of   ,
hereby certify that, by virtue of this warrant, I have made diligent search for the money and goods of the above named A.B., and that I can find no [sufficient] money or goods of him/her whereon the sums specified in this warrant can be levied.

Dated the   day of   , 19 .

X.Y.

52
Account of charges incurred on distress warrant (M.C. Rules 1968, r. 44(10).)

Charges incurred on distress warrant upon the money and goods of   dated the   day of   , 19 .

I,   of   , being the constable [*or* person] charged with the execution of the said warrant of distress, hereby declare that the following is a true account of the costs and charges incurred in respect of the execution of the said warrant:—

	£	s.	d.
Total... ...			

Dated the   day of   , 19 .

X.Y.

53

Commitment on occasion of conviction (M.C. Act 1952, ss. 64, 107; C.J. Act 1967, s. 44; M.C. Rules 1968, rr. 77, 78, 80.)

In the [county of . Petty Sessional Division of].

To each and all of the constables of [*or* To X.Y.
of] and to the Governor of Her Majesty's prison
at .

A.B. (hereinafter called the defendant) [, having consented to be tried summarily,] was this day convicted by the Magistrates' Court sitting at
(*state shortly particulars of offence*), and was adjudged to pay a fine of
[, and for compensation] [and for costs,] forthwith:

[* And the Court was of opinion that no method of dealing with the defendant in the event of a default in payment, other than the imposition of imprisonment, was appropriate because (*stating reason*):]

ADJUDICATION

	£	s.	d.
Fine ...			
Compensation			
Costs ...			
Total ...			

Imprisonment
in default

PART PAYMENTS
RECEIVED

	£	s.	d.
Balance			
payable			

Balance of
imprisonment

And in default of payment it was ordered that the defendant be imprisoned for (*state period*) and that his/her committal take place forthwith for the reason that—

the said offence is punishable with imprisonment and he/she appeared to the Court to have sufficient means to pay the sum[s] forthwith:

or it appeared to the Court that he/she is unlikely to remain long enough at a place of abode in the United Kingdom to enable payment of the sum[s] to be enforced by other methods:

or he/she is already serving a term of imprisonment:

or the court had on the occasion of this conviction sentenced him/her to immediate imprisonment:

And the defendant having [paid in part payment, but having] made default in payment [of a balance of]:

You, the said constables [*or* X.Y.], are hereby commanded to convey the defendant to the said prison, and there deliver him/her to the Governor thereof, together with this warrant; and you, the Governor of the said prison, to receive the defendant into your custody and keep him/her for (*state period*) [to commence at the expiration of the term of imprisonment (*give particulars*)] unless the said sum[s] [*or* balance] be sooner paid.

Dated the day of , 19 .

J.P.,
Justice of the Peace for the [county] aforesaid.
[*or* By order of the Court,

J.C.,
Clerk of the Court.]

(*Endorsement of payments*)

PAYMENTS RECEIVED BY PERSONS HAVING CUSTODY OF THE DEFENDANT

Date of Receipt	£	s.	d.	Signature

* Delete if defendant appears to have attained the age of 21 years.

54

Commitment on occasion subsequent to conviction where imprisonment fixed by magistrates' court at time of conviction (M.C. Act 1952, ss. 64, 65(2), 67, 71, 107 ; C.J. Act. 1967, s. 44 ; M.C. Rules 1968, rr. 77, 78, 80.)

In the [county of   . Petty Sessional Division of   ].

To each and all of the constables of   [*or* To X.Y.
of   ] and to the Governor of Her Majesty's prison
at   .

ADJUDICATION	£	s.	d.
Fine ...			
Compensation			
Costs ...			
Total ...			

Imprisonment
in default

PART PAYMENTS RECEIVED	£	s.	d.
Balance payable			

Balance of
imprisonment

A.B. (hereinafter called the defendant) [, having consented to be tried summarily,] was on the   day of   , 19 , convicted by the Magistrates' Court sitting at   , (*state shortly particulars of offence*), and was adjudged to pay a fine of [, and   for compensation] [and for costs,] [by weekly [*or* monthly] instalments of   , the first instalment of] the said sum[s] to be paid not later than the day of   , 19   :
[*And the Court was of opinion that no method of dealing with the defendant in the event of a default in payment, other than the imposition of imprisonment, was appropriate because (*stating reason*):]
And it was ordered that in default of payment the defendant be imprisoned for (*state period*), the Court having power to fix the term of imprisonment and postpone the issue of the warrant of commitment for the reason that—

the said offence is punishable with imprisonment and he/she appeared to the Court to have sufficient means to pay the sum[s] forthwith:

or it appeared to the Court that he/she was unlikely to remain long enough at a place of abode in the United Kingdom to enable payment of the sum[s] to be enforced by other methods:

And a notice of fine having been served on the defendant:

[†And the defendant having been placed under supervision [*or* this Court is satisfied that it is undesirable [*or* impracticable] to place the defendant under supervision on the grounds that (*stating grounds*)] :]

[‡And [§ it not being practicable to obtain] a report as to the defendant's conduct and means by the person under whose supervision he/she was placed [§ having been duly considered] :]

And the defendant having [paid   in part payment, but having] made default in payment [of a balance of   ] :

You, the said constables [*or* X.Y.], are hereby commanded to take the defendant and convey him/her to the said prison, and there deliver him/her to the Governor thereof, together with this warrant ; and you, the Governor of the said prison, to receive the defendant into your custody and keep him/her for (*state period*) [to commence at the expiration of the term of imprisonment (*give particulars*)] unless the said sum[s] [*or* balance] be sooner paid.

Dated the   day of   , 19 .

J.P.,

Justice of the Peace for the [county] first above mentioned.

[*or* By order of the Court,

J.C.,

Clerk of the Court.]

(*Endorsement of payments*)

PAYMENTS RECEIVED BY PERSONS HAVING CUSTODY OF THE DEFENDANT

Date of Receipt	£	s.	d.	Signature

* Delete if defendant appears to have attained the age of 21 years.
† Delete if defendant appears to have attained the age of 21 years and has not been placed under supervision.
‡ Delete if defendant has not been placed under supervision.
§ Delete whichever is inappropriate where defendant has been placed under supervision.

55

Summons to defaulter : fine (M.C. Act 1952, s. 70 ; C.J. Act 1967, ss. 44, 47 ; M.C. Rules 1968, r. 81.)

In the [county of   . Petty Sessional Division of   ].

To A.B., of   .

	£	s.	d.
Fine ...			
Compensation			
Costs ...			
Total ...			
Part Payments			
Balance ...			

On the   day of   , 19 , you were adjudged by the Magistrates' Court [or Court of Assize or Quarter Sessions for the [county] of   ] sitting at   , to pay the sum[s] shown in the margin hereof and you have failed to pay the said sum[s] [or the balance of   ]:

You are therefore hereby summoned to appear before the Magistrates' Court sitting at   , on   day the   day of   , 19 , at the hour of   in the   noon, unless the said sum[s] [or balance] be sooner paid, for inquiry to be made as to your means.

Dated the   day of   , 19 .

J.P.,

Justice of the Peace for the [county] first above mentioned.

[or Issued by   , Justice of the Peace.

J.C.,

Clerk of the Magistrates' Court.]

NOTE.—The object of the inquiry as to your means is to enable the Court to decide whether or not to commit you to prison for default in payment. If, not having paid, you fail to appear personally in obedience to this summons, you will render yourself liable to arrest without further notice. Payment may be made either by post to the Clerk of the Court at (insert address) or made personally at (insert address and also days and hours when payment can be made).

Any communication sent by post should be properly stamped. Cash should not be sent in unregistered envelopes.

56

Warrant for arrest of defaulter : fine (M.C. Act 1952, s. 70 ; C.J. Act 1967, ss. 44, 47 ; M.C. Rules 1968, rr. 78, 79.)

In the [county of   . Petty Sessional Division of   ].
To each and all of the constables of   [or To X.Y. of   ].

A.B. (hereinafter called the defendant) was on the   day of   , 19 , adjudged by the Magistrates' Court [or Court of Assize or Quarter Sessions for the [county] of   ] sitting at   , to pay a fine of   [, and   for compensation,] [and for costs]:

And the defendant has [paid   in part payment, but has] made default in payment [of a balance of   ]:

You are hereby commanded to bring the defendant before the Magistrates' Court sitting at   , or a justice of the peace of the petty sessional division in which the court is situate, forthwith.

Dated the   day of   , 19 .

J.P.,

Justice of the Peace for the [county] first above mentioned.

(Endorsement where bail is allowed)

It is directed that the defendant on arrest be released on bail on entering into a recognizance in the sum of   , with   suret   in the sum of   [each], for his/her appearance, unless the sum[s] [or balance] specified in this warrant

be sooner paid, before the Magistrates' Court sitting at   ,
at the hour of   in the   noon of the next day upon which such Court
is open [*or* on the   day of   , 19]. [The defendant's recognizance
shall be subject to the following condition[s] (*specify*)].

J.P.,

Justice of the Peace for the [county] first above mentioned.

PAYMENTS RECEIVED BY THE PERSON HOLDING THIS WARRANT

Date of Receipt	£	s.	d.	Signature

57

*Commitment where imprisonment not imposed by magistrates' court on occasion
of conviction* (*M.C. Act* 1952, *ss.* 64, 65(2), 67, 71, 107 ; *C.J. Act* 1967,
ss. 44, 47 ; *M.C. Rules* 1968, *rr.* 77, 78, 80.)

In the [county of   .   Petty Sessional Division of   ].
To each and all of the constables of   [*or* To X.Y. of   ]
and to the Governor of Her Majesty's prison at   .

	£	s.	d.
Fine ...			
Compensation			
Costs ...			
Total ...			
Part Payments			
Balance ...			
Imprisonment in default			

PART PAYMENTS RECEIVED
SINCE IMPRISONMENT
IMPOSED

	£	s.	d.
Amount unpaid			
Enforcement costs and charges payable ...			
Balance of imprisonment			

A.B. (hereinafter called the defendant) was
on the   day of   , 19 ,
convicted by [*or* before] the Magistrates' Court
[*or* Court of Assize *or* Quarter Sessions for
the [county] of   ] sitting at
     , (*state shortly particulars of
offence*), and was adjudged to pay a fine of
[, and   for compensation,] [and
     for costs,] [by weekly [*or* monthly]
instalments of   , the first instalment of]
the said sum[s] to be paid not later than the
     day of   , 19 , [and the
term of imprisonment in default fixed by the
said Court of Assize *or* Quarter Sessions was
[months]]:
   And the defendant having [paid
in part payment, but having] made default in
payment [of a balance of   ]:
   And a notice of fine having been served on
the defendant [, the constables aforesaid were
authorised by warrant dated the   day
of   , 19 , to levy the sum of
     by distress:
   And it appearing that no sufficient distress
whereon to levy the said sum could be found
[and that a balance of
is due]]:
   [And inquiry as to the means of the defendant
having subsequently to the conviction been
made by the competent Court in his/her
presence:]

[* And the defendant having been placed under supervision [*or* this Court is satisfied that it is undesirable [*or* impracticable] to place the defendant under supervision on the grounds that (*stating grounds*)] :]

[† And [‡ it not being practicable to obtain] a report as to the defendant's conduct and means by the person under whose supervision he/she was placed [‡ having been duly considered] :]

And this Court has considered or tried all other methods of enforcing payment and it appears to this Court that they are inappropriate or unsuccessful : [*or* And the said offence is punishable with imprisonment and the defendant appears to this Court to have sufficient means to pay the said sum[s] [*or* balance] forthwith :]

[*or* And the defendant being in prison :]

[§ And this Court is [*or* was] of opinion that no method of dealing with the defendant in respect of the said default, other than the imposition of imprisonment, is [*or* was] appropriate because (*stating reason*) :]

It is this day [*or* was on the   day of   , 19   ,] ordered that the defendant be imprisoned in Her Majesty's prison aforesaid and there kept for (*state period*) unless the said sum[s] [*or* balance] [and any costs and charges of the said distress] be sooner paid :

[And the defendant has since paid   in [further] part payment, leaving a balance of   now due :]

You, the said constables [*or* X.Y.], are hereby commanded to take the defendant and convey him/her to the said prison, and there deliver him/her to the Governor thereof, together with this warrant ; and you, the Governor of the said prison, to receive the defendant into your custody and keep him/her for (*state period*) [to commence at the expiration of the term of imprisonment (*give particulars*)], unless the amount outstanding be sooner paid.

Dated the   day of   , 19   .

J.P.,

Justice of the Peace for the [county] first above mentioned.

[*or* By order of the Court,

J.C.,

Clerk of the Court.]

(*Endorsement of payments*)

PAYMENTS RECEIVED BY PERSONS HAVING CUSTODY OF THE DEFENDANT

Date of Receipt	£	s.	d.	Signature

* Delete if defendant appears to have attained the age of 21 years and has not been placed under supervision.

† Delete if defendant has not been placed under supervision.

‡ Delete whichever is inappropriate where defendant has been placed under supervision

§ Delete if defendant appears to have attained the age of 21 years.

58

Commitment to detention centre : non-payment of fine : defaulter already detained in detention centre (C.J. Act 1961, s. 6.)

In the [county of   . Petty Sessional Division of   ].

To each and all of the constables of   [*or* To X.Y. of   ]
and to the Warden of the detention centre at   .

Before the Magistrates' Court sitting at   .

	£	s.	d.
Fine ...			
Compensation			
Costs ...			
Total ...			
Part Payments			
Balance ...			

Detention
in default

A.B. (hereinafter called the defendant) who appears to the Court to have attained the age of seventeen years and to be under the age of twenty-one years was on the   day of   , 19   , convicted by [*or* before] the Magistrates' Court [*or* Court of Assize *or* Quarter Sessions for the [county] of   ] sitting at   , (*state shortly particulars of offence*), and was adjudged to pay a fine of   [, and for compensation,] [and   for costs,] [by weekly [*or* monthly] instalments of   , the first instalment of] the said sum[s] to be paid not later than the   day of   , 19   [and the term of imprisonment in default fixed by the said Court of Assize *or* Quarter Sessions was   [months]] :

And a notice of fine having been served on the defendant and inquiry as to his/her means having subsequently been made by the competent Court in his/her presence :

And the defendant having [paid   in part payment, but having] made default in payment [of a balance of   ] :

And the defendant has been placed under supervision [*or* this Court is satisfied that it is undesirable [*or* impracticable] to place the defendant under supervision on the grounds that (*stating grounds*)] :

[And [it not being practicable to obtain] a report as to the defendant's conduct and means by the person under whose supervision he/she was placed [having been duly considered] :]

And the defendant is at present detained in a detention centre under a previous sentence or warrant :

It is ordered that the defendant be detained in the detention centre at   for (*state period*) unless the said sum[s] [*or* balance] be sooner paid :

You, the said constables [*or* X.Y.], are hereby commanded to take the defendant and convey him/her to the said detention centre, and there deliver him/her to the Warden thereof, together with this warrant ; and you, the Warden of the said detention centre, to receive the defendant into your custody and keep him/her for the said period unless the said sum[s] [*or* balance] be sooner paid.

Dated the   day of   , 19   .

J.P.,

Justice of the Peace for the [county] first above mentioned.

[*or* By order of the Court,

J.C.,

Clerk of the Court.]

(*Endorsement of payments*)

PAYMENTS RECEIVED BY PERSONS HAVING CUSTODY OF THE DEFENDANT

Date of Receipt	£	s.	d.	Signature

59

Endorsement on warrant of commitment in default : defaulter in detention centre
(C.J. Act 1961, s. 6(3).)

It has been made to appear to me that the aforementioned defendant is at present detained in the detention centre at . Accordingly I amend this warrant committing him/her to prison by substituting that detention centre for the prison named [and by reducing the term of imprisonment specified therein to six months].

Dated the day of , 19 .

J.P.,
Justice of the Peace for .

60

Warrant for detention in police cells, etc. (M.C. Act 1952, s. 109 ;
M.C. Rules 1968, rr. 77, 78, 80.)

In the [county of . Petty Sessional Division of].
To each and all of the constables of
and to the Police Officer in charge of .

A.B. (hereinafter called the defendant) is this day [*or* was on the day of , 19 ,] convicted by the Magistrates' Court sitting at , (*state shortly particulars of offence*), and was adjudged to pay a fine of [, and for compensation,] [and for costs]:

(*Here follow the appropriate form of commitment to prison for non-payment of fine substituting for any reference to imprisonment a reference to detention in certified police cells, etc.*)

61

Warrant for detention in police station (M.C. Act 1952,
s. 111 ; M.C. Rules 1968, rr. 78, 80.)

In the [county of   . Petty Sessional Division of   ].

To each and all of the constables of
and to all whom it may concern.

	£	s.	d.
Fine ...			
Compensation			
Costs ...			
Total ...			
Part Payments			
Balance ...			

A.B. (hereinafter called the defendant) is this day [or was on the   day of   , 19   ,] convicted by the Magistrates' Court sitting at   , (*state shortly particulars of offence*), and was adjudged to pay a fine of   [, and   for compensation,] [and   for costs]:

And it is this day ordered that in default of payment of the said sum[s] the defendant be detained in a police station in accordance with section 111 of the Magistrates' Courts Act 1952:

And the defendant having [paid   in part payment, but having] made default in payment [of a balance of   ]:

You, the said constables and any other constables, are hereby commanded unless the said sum[s] [or balance] be sooner paid, to take the defendant, and convey him to a convenient police station and to detain him therein until eight o'clock in the morning of the day following that on which he is arrested under this warrant, or, if he is arrested under this warrant between midnight and eight o'clock in the morning, until eight o'clock in the morning of the day on which he is arrested, provided that the officer in charge of the police station in which the defendant is detained in pursuance of this warrant is authorised to discharge him at any time within four hours before eight o'clock in the morning if the said officer thinks it expedient to do so in order to enable him to go to his work or for any other reason appearing to the said officer to be sufficient.

Dated the   day of   , 19   .

J.P.,

Justice of the Peace for the [county] aforesaid.

[or By order of the Court,

J.C.,
Clerk of the Court.]

(*Endorsement of payments*)

PAYMENTS RECEIVED BY PERSONS HAVING CUSTODY OF THE DEFENDANT

Date of Receipt	£	s.	d.	Signature

62

Transfer of fine order (M.C. Act 1952, *s.* 72 ; *C.J. Act* 1967, *s.* 47 ;
M.C. Rules 1968, *r.* 47.)

In the [county of   . Petty Sessional Division of   ].

	£	s.	d.
Fine ...			
Compensation			
Costs ...			
Total ...			
Part Payments			
Balance ...			

A.B. (hereinafter called the defendant) was this day [*or* on the   day of   , 19 ,] convicted by [*or* before] the Magistrates' Court [*or* Court of Assize *or* Quarter Sessions for the [county] of   ] sitting at   , (*state shortly particulars of offence*), and was adjudged to pay a fine of   [, and for compensation,] [and   for costs,] [by weekly [*or* monthly] instalments of   , the first instalment of] the said sum[s] to be paid forthwith [*or* not later than the   day of   , 19 ,] [and the Magistrates' Court for this [Petty Sessional Division] is the court required under section 47(3) of the Criminal Justice Act 1967 to enforce payment of the said sum]:

[And the said Court of Assize *or* Quarter Sessions fixed the term of imprisonment in default as   [months]:]

And the defendant has [paid   in part payment, but has] made default in payment [of a balance of   ]:

[And the time for payment has not yet expired:]

And it appears that the defendant is residing at (*state address*) in the [Petty Sessional Division] hereinafter mentioned:

A transfer of fine order is hereby made in pursuance of section 72 of the Magistrates' Courts Act 1952, transferring to a Magistrates' Court acting for the [Petty Sessional Division] of   in the county of   ,] and to the clerk of the said Court, all the functions referred to in the said section with respect to the said sum[s]] [*or* balance].

Dated the   day of   , 19   .

J.P.,
Justice of the Peace for the [county] first above mentioned.
[*or* By order of the Court,

J.C.,
Clerk of the Court.]

*[Steps taken to recover the sum:—

Other information likely to assist court in enforcing payment:—   ]

---

* To be entered on copy sent to the clerk of the court having jurisdiction under the order.

63

Transfer of fine order to Scotland (M.C. Act 1952, s. 72A ;
C.J. Act 1967, ss. 47, 48 ; M.C. Rules 1968, r. 47.)

In the [county of　　　　　　.　Petty Sessional Division of　　　　　　].

	£	s.	d.
Fine　...			
Compensation			
Costs　...			
Total　...			
Part Payments			
Balance　...			

A.B. (hereinafter called the defendant) was
this day [*or* on the　　　　　　day of　　　　　　,
19　　,] convicted by [*or* before] the Magistrates' Court [*or* Court of Assize *or* Quarter
Sessions for the [county] of　　　　　　]
sitting at　　　　　　, (*state shortly*
particulars of offence), and was adjudged to pay
a fine of　　　　　　[, and
for compensation,] [and　　　　　　for costs,]
[by weekly [*or* monthly] instalments of　　　　,
the first instalment of] the said sum[s] to be

paid forthwith [*or* not later than the　　　　　　day of　　　　　　, 19　　]
[and the Magistrates' Court for this [Petty Sessional Division] is the court
required under section 47(3) of the Criminal Justice Act 1967 to enforce payment
of the said sum]:

[And the said Court of Assize *or* Quarter Sessions fixed the term of imprisonment in default as　　　　　　[months]:]

And the defendant has [paid　　　　　　in part payment, but has] made
default in payment [of a balance of　　　　　　]:

[And the time for payment has not yet expired:]

And it appears that the defendant is residing at (*state address*) within the
jurisdiction of the court of summary jurisdiction in Scotland hereinafter
mentioned :

[And no term of imprisonment has been fixed in the event of a future default
in paying the sum[s] in question:]

A transfer of fine order is hereby made in pursuance of section 72A of the
Magistrates' Courts Act 1952 [as read with section 48 of the Criminal Justice Act
1967], transferring to the　　　　　　Court sitting at　　　　　　the
enforcement of payment of the said sum[s] [*or* balance].

Dated the　　　　　　day of　　　　　　, 19　　.

J.P.,
Justice of the Peace for the [county] first above mentioned.
[*or* By order of the Court,

J.C.,
Clerk of the Court.]

*[Steps taken to recover the sum:—

Other information likely to assist court in enforcing payment:—　　　　　　]

---

* To be entered on copy sent to the clerk of the court having jurisdiction under the order.

64

Further transfer of fine order (M.C. Act 1952, ss. 72(3), 72A, 72B ;
C.J. Act 1967, s. 47 ; M.C. Rules 1968, r. 47.)

In the [county of   . Petty Sessional Division of   ].

	£	s.	d.
Fine ...			
Compensation			
Costs ...			
Total ...			
Part Payments			
Balance ...			

A.B. (hereinafter called the defendant) was on the   day of   ,
19 , adjudged to pay a fine of
[, and   for compensation,] [and
for costs,] by the Magistrates' Court [*or* Court
of Assize *or* Quarter Sessions for the [county]
of   ] sitting at
[*or* the   Court at
in Scotland [and the Magistrates' Court for the
[Petty Sessional Division of
in the county of   ] was the

Court required under section 47(3) of the Criminal Justice Act 1967 to enforce payment of the said sum]:

[And the said Court of Assize *or* Quarter Sessions fixed the term of imprisonment in default as   [months]:]

By virtue of a transfer of fine order dated the   day of   , 19 ,
the enforcement of payment of the said sum[s] has been transferred to a court acting for this petty sessions area:

And the defendant has [paid   in part payment, but has] made default in payment [of a balance of   ]:

[And the time for payment has not yet expired:]

And it appears that the defendant is residing at (*state address*) in the [Petty Sessional Division] [*or* within the jurisdiction of the court of summary jurisdiction] hereinafter mentioned:

A further transfer of fine order is hereby made in pursuance of section 72(3) [*or* 72A] [as applied by section 72B] of the Magistrates' Courts Act 1952, transferring to a Magistrates' Court acting for the [Petty Sessional Division of   in the county of   ] [*or* to the Court at   in Scotland] the enforcement of payment of the said sums[s] [*or* balance].

Dated the   day of   , 19 .

J.P.,
Justice of the Peace for the [county] first above mentioned.

[*or* By order of the Court,

J.C.,
Clerk of the Magistrates' Court sitting at   .]

*[Steps taken to recover the sum:—

Other information likely to assist court in enforcing payment:—   ]

---

* To be entered on copy sent to the clerk of the court having jurisdiction under the order.

65

Notice of transfer of fine order (M.C. Rules 1968, r. 47.)

In the [county of . Petty Sessional Division of].
To A.B., of .

	£	s.	d.	
Fine ...				On the day of , 19 , you were adjudged by the Magistrates' Court [or Court of Assize or Quarter Sessions for the [county] of] sitting at [or by a court of summary jurisdiction in Scotland, namely the Court at ,] to pay the sum[s] shown in the margin hereof [in instalments of] and the said sum[s] [or the balance of] remains unpaid: You are hereby given notice that in consequence of a transfer of fine order made on the
Compensation				
Costs ...				
Total ...				
Part Payments				
Balance ...				

day of , 19 , the enforcement of payment of the said sum[s] [or balance] has become a matter for the Magistrates' Court acting for this [Petty Sessional Division].

Payment of the said sum[s] [or balance] should therefore be made forthwith [or before the day of , 19 ,] either by post to me (*insert name*), the Clerk of the Court at (*insert address*), or made personally at (*insert address and also days and hours when payment can be made*).

If you cannot pay, you should at once make an application for [further] time to be granted and the application may be made either in person to this Court at (*insert address*) or by letter addressed to me and stating fully the grounds on which the application is made.

Dated the day of , 19

J.C.,

Clerk of the Court.

NOTE—Any communication sent by post must be properly stamped. Cash should not be sent in unregistered envelopes.

66

Notice of order of supervision : fine (M.C. Rules 1968, r. 46.)

In the [county of . Petty Sessional Division of].
To A.B., of

	£	s.	d.	
Fine ...				You were this day [or on the day of , 19 ,] adjudged by the Magistrates' Court [or Court of Assize or Quarter Sessions for the [county] of] sitting at , to pay the sum[s] shown in the margin hereof [and you have failed to pay the said sum[s] [or the balance of]]. You are hereby given notice that you were this day [or on the day of , 19 ,] by order of this Court placed under the supervision of until the said
Compensation				
Costs ...				
Total ...				
Part Payments				
Balance ...				

sum[s] [or balance] be paid or further order be made [and that the said sum[s] [or balance] is/are to be paid by weekly [or monthly] instalments of , the first instalment to be paid forthwith].

Dated the day of , 19 .

J.C.,

Clerk of the Court.

67

Authority for clerk of magistrates' court to enforce payment of fine in High Court or County Court (C.J. Act 1967, s. 45.)

In the [county of   . Petty Sessional Division of   ].

	£	s.	d.
Fine ...			
Compensation			
Costs ...			
Total ...			
Part Payments			
Balance ...			

A.B. (hereinafter called the defendant) was on the   day of   , 19 , convicted by [*or* before] the Magistrates' Court [*or* Court of Assize *or* Quarter Sessions for the [county] of   ] sitting at   , (*state shortly particulars of offence*) and was adjudged to pay a fine of   [, and   for compensation,] [and   for costs,] [by weekly [*or* monthly] instalments of   , the first instalment of] the said sum[s] to be paid forthwith [*or* not later than the   day of   , 19] [and the Magistrates' Court for this [Petty Sessional Division] is the court required under section 47(3) of the Criminal Justice Act 1967 to enforce payment of the said sum]:

And the defendant has [paid   in part payment, but has] made default in payment [of a balance of   ]:

This Court having inquired into the defendant's means hereby authorises the Clerk of the Court to take the undermentioned proceedings in the High Court [County Court] for the recovery of the said sum[s] [*or* balance].

Nature of proceedings: —

Dated the   day of   , 19 .

J.P.,
Justice of the Peace for the [county] aforesaid.

PROBATION AND CONDITIONAL DISCHARGE

68

Probation order (C.J. Act 1948, s. 3.)

In the [county of   . Petty Sessional Division of   ].

Before the Magistrates' Court sitting at   .

A.B. (hereinafter called the defendant) [, having consented to be tried summarily,] is this day convicted (*state shortly particulars of offence*):

And the Court is of opinion, having regard to the circumstances including the nature of the offence and the character of the defendant, that it is expedient to make a probation order:

And the Court has explained to the defendant the effect of this order (including the additional requirements specified below) and that if he/she fails to comply therewith or commits another offence he/she will be liable to be sentenced for the offence in respect of which this order is made, and the defendant has expressed his/her willingness to comply with the requirements of this order:

It is therefore ordered that the defendant, who resides [*or* will reside] at (*state address*) in the [Petty Sessional Division] of   , be required for the period of   [years] from the date of this order to be under the supervision of a probation officer appointed for or assigned to that [Division];

and it is further ordered that the defendant shall during the said period comply with the following additional requirements: —

*1. *That he/she shall be of good behaviour and lead an industrious life;*

2. *That he/she shall inform the probation officer at once of any change of his/her residence or employment;*

3. *That he/she shall keep in touch with the probation officer in accordance with such instructions as may from time to time be given by the probation officer; and, in particular, that he/she shall, if the probation officer so requires, receive visits from the probation officer at his/her home;*

4. (*Here will follow any other requirements relating to residence, etc.*).

[And it is ordered that the defendant pay   [as damages for injury suffered by [*or* compensation for loss incurred by]   and   ] for costs, [by weekly [*or* monthly] instalments of   , the first instalment of] the said sum[s] to be paid forthwith [*or* not later than the   day of   , 19   ].]

Dated the   day of   , 19   .

J.P.,

Justice of the Peace for the [county] first above mentioned.

[*or* By order of the Court,

J.C.,

Clerk of the Court.]

* These are specimens of additional requirements which are commonly inserted and are not part of the prescribed form.

69

Order for conditional discharge (C.J. Act 1948, *s.* 7.)

In the [county of   . Petty Sessional Division of   ].

Before the Magistrates' Court sitting at   .

A.B. (hereinafter called the defendant) [, having consented to be tried summarily,] is this day convicted (*state shortly particulars of offence*):

And the Court is of opinion, having regard to the circumstances including the nature of the offence and the character of the defendant, that it is inexpedient to inflict punishment and that a probation order is not appropriate:

It is ordered that the defendant be discharged subject to the condition that he/she commits no offence during the period of   years from the date of this order.

[And it is ordered that the defendant pay   [as damages for injury suffered by [*or* compensation for loss incurred by]   and   ] for costs, [by weekly [*or* monthly] instalments of   , the first instalment of] the said sum[s] to be paid forthwith [*or* not later than the   day of   , 19   ].]

Dated the   day of   , 19   .

J.P.,

Justice of the Peace for the [county] first above mentioned.

[*or* By order of the Court,

J.C.,

Clerk of the Court.]

70

*Summons to probationer on application to amend probation order
(C.J. Act 1948, Sch. 1.)*

In the [county of . Petty Sessional Division of].

To A.B., of .

You are hereby summoned to appear on day the day
of , 19 , at the hour of in the noon,
before the Magistrates' Court sitting at , on the hearing of an
application by to amend the probation order made in your case
on the day of , 19 , by the [said] Magistrates'
Court [or Court of Assize or Quarter Sessions for the [county] of]
sitting at .

Dated the day of , 19 .

J.P.,
Justice of the Peace for the [county] first above mentioned.

[or Issued by , Justice of the Peace.

J.C.,
Clerk of the Magistrates' Court.]

71

Order amending probation order (C.J. Act 1948, Sch. 1.)

In the [county of . Petty Sessional Division of].

Before the Magistrates' Court sitting at .

This Court [or the Magistrates' Court [or Court of Assize or Quarter Sessions
for the [county] of] sitting at
,] having on the day of ,
19 , made a probation order which [, as subsequently amended by the
competent Court,] required A.B. now of (*insert present address of probationer*)
for a period of [years] from the date thereof to be under the
supervision of a probation officer appointed for or assigned to the [Petty
Sessional Division] of and further required him/her to (*set
out any requirement which is amended*):

Upon the application of the Court hereby amends
the said probation order as follows :—(*set out details of amendment*).

Dated the day of , 19 .

J.P.,
Justice of the Peace for the [county] first above mentioned.

[or By order of the Court,

J.C.,
Clerk of the Court.]

72

*Order discharging probation order (C.J. Act 1948, Sch. 1 ;
C.J. Act 1967, s. 54(1).)*

In the [county of   . Petty Sessional Division of   ].
Before the Magistrates' Court sitting at   .

This Court [*or* The Magistrates' Court [*or* Court of Assize *or* Quarter Sessions
for the [county] of   ] sitting at   ] having on the
day of   , 19   , made a probation order which [, as subsequently
amended by the competent Court,] required A.B. for a period of   [years]
from the date thereof to be under the supervision of a probation officer appointed
for or assigned to this Petty Sessions Area :

[And the said probation order does not contain a direction reserving the power
of discharge to the Court of Assize [*or* Quarter Sessions]:]

Upon the application of   the Court hereby discharges the said
probation order.

Dated the   day of   , 19

J.P.,

Justice of the Peace for the [county] first above mentioned.

[*or* By order of the Court,

J.C.,
Clerk of the Court.]

73

*Order substituting conditional discharge for probation (C.J. Act 1948, Sch. 1 ;
C.J. Act 1967, s. 53.)*

In the [county of   . Petty Sessional Division of   ].
Before the Magistrates' Court sitting at   .

This Court [*or* the Magistrates' Court [*or* Court of Assize *or* Quarter Sessions
for the [county] of   ] sitting at   ] having on the
day of   , 19   , made a probation order which [, as
subsequently amended by the competent Court,] required A.B. for a period of
          [years] from the date thereof to be under the supervision of a probation
officer appointed for or assigned to this Petty Sessions Area :

[And the said probation order does not contain a direction reserving the power
of discharge to the Court of Assize [*or* Quarter Sessions]:]

Upon the application of   the Court hereby makes, in substitution for the said probation order, an order discharging the said A.B. in respect
of his original offence, subject to the condition that he commits no offence
between the making of this order and the expiration of the said period of   years
from the date of the said probation order.

Dated the   day of   , 19   .

J.P.,

Justice of the Peace for the [county] first above mentioned.

[*or* By order of the Court,

J.C.,
Clerk of the Court.]

74

*Information for breach of requirement of probation order (C.J. Act 1948, s. 6 ;
M.C. Rules 1968, r. 1.)*

In the [county of   . Petty Sessional Division of   ].
The information of   , who [upon oath [*or* affirmation]]
states : —

A.B. was on the   day of   , 19   , convicted by [*or* before]
the Magistrates' Court [*or* Court of Assize *or* Quarter Sessions for the [county]
of   ] sitting at   , (*stating shortly
particulars of offence*), and on the said date [*or* on the   day of
, 19   ,] the said Court made a probation order which [, as subsequently amended by the competent Court,] required the said A.B. for the
period of   [years] from the date thereof to be under the supervision
of a probation officer appointed for or assigned to the [Petty Sessional Division]
of   and further required the said A.B. to (*set out requirement which
is contravened*) :

And the said A.B. did on the   day of   , 19   , fail to comply
with the last mentioned requirement [inasmuch as he/she (*state shortly particulars
of breach*)].

Taken [and sworn [*or* affirmed]] before me,

J.P.,

Justice of the Peace for the [county] first above mentioned.

75

*Summons for breach of requirement of probation order (C.J. Act 1948, s. 6 ;
M.C. Rules 1968, r. 81.)*

In the [county of   . Petty Sessional Division of   ].
To A.B., of   .

Information has this day been laid before me, the undersigned [*or state name*]
Justice of the Peace, by   that you on the   day of   ,
19   , were convicted by [*or* before] the Magistrates' Court [*or* Court of Assize
or Quarter Sessions for the [county] of   ] sitting at   , (*state
shortly particulars of offence*), and that on the said date [*or* on the
day of   , 19   ,] the said Court made a probation order which [as
subsequently amended by the competent Court,] required you for the period
of   [years] from the date thereof to be under the supervision
of a probation officer appointed for or assigned to the [Petty Sessional Division]
of   and further required you to (*set out
requirement which is contravened*) ; and by the said information it is further
alleged that you did on the   day of   , 19   , fail to comply
with the last mentioned requirement of the said order inasmuch as (*state shortly
particulars of breach*) :

You are therefore hereby summoned to appear on   day the   day
of   , 19   , at the hour of   in the   noon, before the
Magistrates' Court sitting at   , to answer to the said
information.

Dated the   day of   , 19   .

J.P.,

Justice of the Peace for the [county] first above mentioned.

[*or* This summons was issued by the above named Justice of the Peace.

J.C.,

Clerk of the Magistrates' Court sitting at   .]

76

Warrant for breach of requirement of probation order (C.J. Act 1948, s. 6;
M.C. Act 1952, s. 93; M.C. Rules 1968, rr. 78, 79.)

In the [county of   . Petty Sessional Division of   ].

To each and all of the constables of   [or To X.Y. of   ].

Information on oath [*or* affirmation] has this day been laid before me, the
undersigned Justice of the Peace, by   that A.B. (hereinafter
called the defendant) was on the   day of   , 19 ,
convicted by [*or* before] the Magistrates' Court [*or* Court of Assize *or* Quarter
Sessions for the [county] of   ] sitting at   , (*state shortly*
particulars of offence), and that on the said date [*or* on the   day
of   , 19 ,] the said Court made a probation order which [, as
subsequently amended by the competent Court,] required the defendant for
the period of   [years] from the date thereof to be under
the supervision of a probation officer appointed for or assigned to the [Petty
Sessional Division] of   and further required the defendant
(*set out requirement which is contravened*): and by the said information it is
further alleged that the defendant did on the   day of   ,
19 , fail to comply with the last mentioned requirement of the said order
inasmuch as (*state shortly particulars of breach*).

You are hereby commanded to bring the said defendant forthwith before
the Magistrates' Court sitting at   , or a justice of the peace of the
petty sessional division in which the court is situate, to answer to the said
information.

Dated the   day of   , 19 .

J.P.,

Justice of the Peace for the [county] first above mentioned.

(*Endorsement where bail is allowed*)

It is directed that the defendant on arrest be released on bail on entering into
a recognizance in the sum of   , with   suret   in the sum of
[each], for his/her appearance before the Magistrates' Court sitting at
                    , at the hour of   in the   noon of the next day upon which
the said Court is open [*or* on the   day of   , 19]. [The
defendant's recognizance shall be subject to the following condition[s] (*specify*)].

J.P.,

Justice of the Peace for the [county] first above mentioned.

77

Remand of probationer to Assizes or Sessions on breach of requirement of
probation order (C.J. Act 1948, s. 6; M.C. Rules 1968, rr. 77, 78, 80.)

In the [county of   . Petty Sessional Division of   ].

To each and all of the constables of   [or To X.Y. of   ],
and to the Governor of Her Majesty's prison [*or* the remand centre] at   .

A.B. (hereinafter called the defendant) has this day appeared [*or* been brought]
before the Magistrates' Court sitting at   , charged with having
failed to comply with the following requirement of a probation order made
on the   day of   , 19 , in his/her case by the Court
of Assize [*or* Quarter Sessions] for the [county] of   sitting at
                    , [as subsequently amended by the competent Court,] namely,
(*set out requirement which is contravened*):

And the said failure has been proved to the satisfaction of this Court and it appears necessary to remand the defendant until he/she can be brought before the said Court of Assize [or Quarter Sessions]:

You, the said constables [or X.Y.], are hereby commanded to convey the defendant to the said prison [or remand centre], and there to deliver him/her to the Governor thereof, together with this warrant ; and you, the said Governor, to receive him/her into your custody, and, unless he/she shall have been bailed in the meantime, keep him/her until the next Court of Assize [or Quarter Sessions] at   , and then to convey him/her before the said Court to be further dealt with according to law.

Dated the   day of   , 19 .

J.P.,

Justice of the Peace for the [county] first above mentioned.

[or By order of the Court,

J.C.,

Clerk of the Court.]

(Endorsement where bail is allowed)

The Court hereby certifies that the defendant may be bailed by recognizance in   , with   suret   in the sum of   [each], to appear before the Court of Assize [or Quarter Sessions] above mentioned and that the defendant has [not] entered into his/her recognizance. [The defendant's recognizance shall be subject to the following condition[s] (specify)].

J.P.,

Justice of the Peace for the [county] first above mentioned.

[or By order of the Court,

J.C.,

Clerk of the Court.]

78

Certificate that probationer has failed to comply with requirement of probation order (C.J. Act 1948, s. 6(4)(a).)

In the [county of   .   Petty Sessional Division of   ].

To the Court of Assize [or Quarter Sessions] for the [county] of

A.B. (hereinafter called the defendant) has this day appeared [or been brought] before the Magistrates' Court sitting at   , charged with having failed to comply with the hereinafter mentioned requirement of a probation order made in his/her case on the   day of   , 19 , by the Court of Assize [or Quarter Sessions] for the [county] of   sitting at   [, and subsequently amended by the competent Court]:

Having heard the evidence relating to the said charge, it is this day adjudged and hereby certified that the defendant has failed to comply with the requirement of the said order that he/she should (*set out requirement which is contravened*) inasmuch as (*set out full particulars of the circumstances*).

Dated the   day of   , 19 .

J.P.,

Justice of the Peace for the [county] first above mentioned.

79

Order on failure to comply with requirement of probation order (*C.J. Act 1948, s. 6.*)

In the [county of . Petty Sessional Division of].

Before the Magistrates' Court sitting at .

A.B. (hereinafter called the defendant) was on the day of , 19 , convicted by the Magistrates' Court sitting at , (*state shortly particulars of offence*), and on the said date [*or* on the day of , 19 ,] the said Court made a probation order which [, as subsequently amended by the competent Court,] required him/her for the period of [years] from the date thereof to be under the supervision of a probation officer appointed for or assigned to the [Petty Sessional Division] of and further required him/her (*set out requirement which is contravened*):

And the defendant has this day appeared [*or* been brought] before the [said] Magistrates' Court sitting at , and the Court was satisfied that he/she had failed to comply with the last mentioned requirement of the said order inasmuch as (*state shortly particulars of breach*):

It is adjudged that the defendant in respect of his failure to comply with the said requirement pay a fine of (*as in form of conviction where fine imposed*) [(*or, where defendant is dealt with for original offence*) for the said offence in respect of which the said probation order was made (*as in appropriate form of conviction*)].

Dated the day of , 19 .

J.P.,

Justice of the Peace for the [county] first above mentioned.

[*or* By order of the Court,

J.C.,

Clerk of the Court.]

80

Commitment on failure to comply with requirement of probation order (*C.J. Act 1948, s. 6; M.C. Rules 1968, rr. 77, 78, 80.*)

In the [county of . Petty Sessional Division of].

To each and all of the constables of [*or* To X.Y. of] and to the Governor of Her Majesty's prison at [*or* to the Police Officer in charge of].

A.B. (hereinafter called the defendant) was on the day of , 19 , convicted by [*or* before] the Magistrates' Court [*or* Court of Assize *or* Quarter Sessions for the [county] of] sitting at , (*state shortly particulars of offence*), and on the said date [*or* on the day of , 19 ,] the said Court made a probation order which [, as subsequently amended by the competent Court,] required him/her for the period of [years] from the date thereof to be under the supervision of a probation officer appointed for or assigned to the [Petty Sessional Division] of and further required him/her (*set out requirement which is contravened*):

And the defendant has this day appeared [*or* been brought] before the Magistrates' Court sitting at , and the Court was satisfied that he/she had failed to comply with the last mentioned requirement of the said order inasmuch as (*state shortly particulars of breach*) and it was adjudged that the defendant (*as in previous form*).

(*Here follow the appropriate form of commitment contained in this Schedule.*)

81

Information on commission of further offence during probation period or period of conditional discharge (C.J. Act 1948, s. 8 ; M.C. Rules 1968, r. 1.)

In the [county of   Petty Sessional Division
of   ].

The information of   who [upon oath [*or* affirmation]]
states: —

A.B. was on the   day of   , 19 , convicted by [*or* before] the Magistrates' Court [*or* Court of Assize *or* Quarter Sessions for the [county] of   ] sitting at   , *(state shortly particulars of offence)*, and on the said date [*or* on the   day of   , 19 ,] the said Court made a probation order which [, as subsequently amended by the competent Court,] required him/her for the period of   [years] from the date thereof to be under the supervision of a probation officer appointed for or assigned to the [Petty Sessional Division] of   [*or* an order discharging him/her subject to the condition that he/she should commit no offence during the period of   years from the date thereof]:

And the said A.B. was on the   day of   , 19 , convicted by [*or* before] the Magistrates' Court [*or* Court of Assize *or* Quarter Sessions for the [county] of   ] sitting at   , of a further offence, namely, *(state shortly particulars of offence)*, committed by him/her on the   day of   , 19 , during the said period, and was sentenced [*or* ordered] to

Taken [and sworn [*or* affirmed]] before me,

J.P.,
Justice of the Peace for the [county] first above mentioned.

82

Summons on commission of further offence during probation period or period of conditional discharge (C.J. Act 1948, s. 8 ; M.C. Rules 1968, r. 81.)

In the [county of   Petty Sessional Division
of   ].

To A.B., of

Information has this day been laid before me, the undersigned [*or state name*] Justice of the Peace, by   that you on the   day of   , 19 , were convicted by [*or* before] the Magistrates' Court [*or* Court of Assize *or* Quarter Sessions for the [county] of   ] sitting at   , *(state shortly particulars of offence)*, and that on the said date [*or* on the day of   , 19 ,] the said Court made a probation order which [, as subsequently amended by the competent Court,] required you for the period of   [years] from the date thereof to be under the supervision of a probation officer appointed for or assigned to the [Petty Sessional Division] of   [*or* an order discharging you subject to the condition that you should commit no offence during the period of   years from the date thereof] ; and by the said information it is further alleged that you were on the   day of   , 19 , convicted by [*or* before] the Magistrates' Court [*or* Court of Assize *or* Quarter Sessions for the [county] of   ] sitting at   , of a further offence, namely, *(state shortly particulars of offence)*, committed by you on the   day of   , 19 , during the said period, and that you were sentenced [*or* ordered] to   :

You are therefore hereby summoned to appear on   day the day of   , 19 , at the hour of   in the   noon, before the Magistrates' Court [*or* Court of Assize *or* Quarter Sessions for the [county] of   ] sitting at   , to answer the said information.

Dated the   day of   , 19   .

J.P.,

Justice of the Peace for the [county] first above mentioned.

[*or* This summons was issued by the above named Justice of the Peace.

J.C.,

Clerk of the Magistrates' Court sitting at   .]

83

Warrant on commission of further offence during probation period or period of conditional discharge (C.J. Act 1948, s. 8; M.C. Act 1952, s. 93; M.C. Rules 1968, rr. 77, 78, 80.)

In the [county of   . Petty Sessional Division of   ].

To each and all of the constables of   [*or* To X.Y. of   ].

Information on oath [*or* affirmation] has this day been laid before me, the undersigned Justice of the Peace, by   that A.B. (hereinafter called the defendant) was on the   day of   , 19   , convicted by [*or* before] the Magistrates' Court [*or* Court of Assize *or* Quarter Sessions for the [county] of   ] sitting at   , (*state shortly particulars of offence*), and on the said date [*or* on the   day of   , 19   ,] the said Court made a probation order which [, as subsequently amended by the competent Court,] required the defendant for the period of [years] from the date thereof to be under the supervision of a probation officer appointed for or assigned to the [Petty Sessional Division] of [*or* an order discharging the defendant subject to the condition that he/she should commit no offence during the period of   years from the date thereof] ; and by the said information it is further alleged that the defendant was on the   day of   , 19   , convicted by [*or* before] the Magistrates' Court [*or* Court of Assize *or* Quarter Sessions for the [county] of   ] sitting at   , of a further offence, namely, (*state shortly particulars of offence*), committed by him/her on the   day of   , 19   , during the said period, and was sentenced [*or* ordered] to   :

You are hereby commanded to bring the defendant forthwith before the Magistrates' Court [*or* Court of Assize *or* Quarter Sessions for the [county] of   ] sitting at   , or a justice of the peace of the petty sessional division in which the court is situate, to answer to the said information.

Dated the   day of   , 19   .

J.P.,

Justice of the Peace for the [county] first above mentioned.

(*Endorsement where warrant requires the defendant to be brought before a Magistrates' Court and bail is allowed*)

It is directed that the defendant on arrest be released on bail on entering into a recognizance in the sum of   , with   suret   in the sum of   [each], for his/her appearance before the Magistrates' Court sitting at   , at the hour of   in the   noon of the next day upon which the Court is open [*or* on the   day of   , 19   ]. [The defendant's recognizance shall be subject to the following condition[s] (*specify*)].

J.P.,

Justice of the Peace for the [county] first above mentioned.

84

Remand to Assizes or Sessions on commission of further offence by probationer or person in whose case an order for conditional discharge has been made (*C.J. Act* 1948, *s.* 8 ; *M.C. Rules* 1968, *rr.* 77, 78, 80.)

In the [county of   . Petty Sessional Division of   ].

To each and all of the constables of   [*or* To **X.Y.** of   ] and to the Governor of Her Majesty's prison [*or* the remand centre] at   .

A.B. (hereinafter called the defendant) has this day been brought before the Magistrates' Court sitting at   , on an information alleging that he/she has been convicted of a further offence committed during the currency of a probation order [*or* order for conditional discharge] made in his/her case on the   day of   , 19   , by the Court of Assize [*or* Quarter Sessions] for the [county] of   sitting at   [, and as subsequently amended by the competent Court,] :

[*or* has this day been convicted by the Magistrates' Court sitting at (*state shortly particulars of offence*) [and sentenced [*or* ordered] to   ], and it appears to the Court that on the date when the said offence was committed, namely, the   day of   , 19   , there was in force a probation order [*or* order for conditional discharge] made in his/her case on the   day of   , 19   , by the Court of Assize [*or* Quarter Sessions] for the [county] of   sitting at   :]

And it appears necessary to remand the defendant until he/she can be brought before the said Court of Assize [*or* Quarter Sessions] :

You, the said constables [*or* X.Y.], are hereby commanded to convey the defendant to the said prison [*or* remand centre] and there to deliver him/her to the Governor thereof, together with this warrant ; and you, the said Governor, to receive him/her into your custody and, unless he/she shall have been bailed in the meantime, keep him/her until the next Court of Assize [*or* Quarter Sessions] at   , and then convey him/her before the said Court at the hour of   in the   noon, to be there dealt with according to law.

          Dated the   day of   , 19   .

                                             J.P.,
          Justice of the Peace for the [county] first above mentioned.

          [*or* By order of the Court,

                                             J.C.,
                                             Clerk of the Court.]

(*Endorsement where bail is allowed*)

The Court hereby certifies that the defendant may be bailed by recognizance in the sum of   , with   suret   in the sum of   [each], to appear before the Court of Assize [*or* Quarter Sessions] above mentioned, at the hour and on the day above mentioned, and that the defendant has [not] entered into his/her recognizance. [The defendant's recognizance shall be subject to the following condition[s] (*specify*)].

                                             J.P.,
          Justice of the Peace for the [county] first above mentioned.

          [*or* By order of the Court,

                                             J.C.,
                                             Clerk of the Court.]

85

*Order in respect of original offence on commission of further offence during
probation period or period of conditional discharge (C.J. Act 1948, s. 8.)*

In the [county of   . Petty Sessional Division of   ].
Before the Magistrates' Court sitting at   .

A.B. (hereinafter called the defendant) was on the   day of   ,
19   , convicted by the Magistrates' Court sitting at   , (*state
shortly particulars of offence*), and on the said date [*or* on the   day of
                    , 19   ,] the said Court made a probation order which [, as subse-
quently amended by the competent Court,] required him/her for the period of
                    [years] from the date thereof to be under the supervision of a proba-
tion officer appointed for or assigned to the [Petty Sessional Division] of
[*or* an order discharging him/her subject to the condition that he/she should
commit no further offence during the period of   years from the date
thereof]:

And the defendant has this day appeared [*or* been brought] before the said [*or*
first mentioned] Court and the Court was satisfied that the defendant had on
the   day of   , 19   , been convicted by [*or* before] the
Magistrates' Court [*or* Court of Assize *or* Quarter Sessions for the [county] of
                    ] sitting at   , of a further offence,
namely, (*state shortly particulars of offence*), committed by him/her on the
day of   , 19   , during the said period:

[(*or*) And the defendant has this day been convicted by the first mentioned
Court of a further offence, namely, (*state shortly particulars of offence*), and the
Court was satisfied that the said offence was committed by him/her on the
                    day of   , 19   , during the said period:

And the Court was satisfied that the consent of the Court by which the said
order was made [*or* the   supervising Court] had in accordance
with section 8(7) of the Criminal Justice Act 1948 been duly given:]

It is adjudged that the defendant for the offence in respect of which the said
order is made (*as in appropriate form of conviction*).

Dated the   day of   , 19   .

J.P.,

Justice of the Peace for the [county] first above mentioned.
[*or* By order of the Court,

J.C.,

Clerk of the Court.]

86

*Commitment on commission of further offence during probation period or period
of conditional discharge (C.J. Act 1948, s. 8 ; M.C. Rules 1968, rr. 77, 78, 80.)*

In the [county of   . Petty Sessional Division of   ].
To each and all of the constables of   [*or* to X.Y. of   ]
and to the Governor of Her Majesty's prison at   .

A.B. (hereinafter called the defendant) was on the   day of   ,
19   , convicted by the Magistrates' Court sitting at   , (*state shortly
particulars of offence*), and on the said date [*or* on the   day of   ,
19   ,] the said Court made a probation order which [, as subsequently amended
by the competent Court,] required him/her for the period of   [years]
from the date thereof to be under the supervision of a probation officer appointed

for or assigned to the [Petty Sessional Division] of   [*or* an order discharging him/her subject to the condition that he/she should commit no further offence during the period of   years from the date thereof]:

And the defendant has this day appeared [*or* been brought] before the said [*or* first mentioned] Court and the Court was satisfied that the defendant had on the   day of   , 19   , been convicted by [*or* before] the Magistrates' Court [*or* Court of Assize *or* Quarter Sessions for the [county] of   ] sitting at   , of a further offence, namely, (*state shortly particulars of offence*), committed by him/her on the   day of , 19   , during the said period:

[(*or*) And the defendant has this day been convicted by the first mentioned Court of a further offence, namely, (*state shortly particulars of offence*), and the Court was satisfied that the said offence was committed by him/her on the   day of   , 19   , during the said period:

And the Court was satisfied that the consent of the Court by which the said order was made [*or* the supervising Court] had in accordance with section 8(7) of the Criminal Justice Act 1948 been duly given:]

And it was adjudged that the defendant for the offence in respect of which the said order was made (*as in previous form*).

(*Here follow the appropriate form of commitment contained in this Schedule.*)

SUSPENDED SENTENCES

87

Conviction: suspended sentence (M.C. Act, 1952, s. 13; C.J. Act 1967, s. 39; M.C. Rules 1968, r. 15.)

In the [county of   .   Petty Sessional Division of   ].

Before the Magistrates' Court sitting at   .

A.B. (hereinafter called the defendant) [, having consented to be tried summarily,] is this day convicted (*state shortly particulars of offence*):

And the Court sentences the defendant to imprisonment for (*state period*):

And it is ordered that the said sentence of imprisonment shall not take effect unless during the period of   years from today the defendant commits in Great Britain another offence punishable with imprisonment and thereafter an order is made under section 40 of the Criminal Justice Act 1967 that the sentence shall take effect:

[And it is ordered that the defendant pay the sum of   [for compensation and   ] for costs [by weekly [*or* monthly] instalments of   , the first instalment of] the said sum[s] to be paid forthwith [*or* not later than the day of   , 19   ].]

Dated the   day of   , 19   .

J.P.,

Justice of the Peace for the [county] aforesaid.

[*or* By order of the Court,

J.C.,

Clerk of the Court.]

88

Information on commission of further offence during operational period of suspended sentence (C.J. Act 1967, s. 42 ; M.C. Rules 1968, r. 1.)

In the [county of   . Petty Sessional Division of   ].
The information of   who [upon oath [*or* affirmation]] states: —
A.B. (hereinafter called the defendant) was on the   day of   ,
19   , convicted by the Magistrates' Court sitting at   , *(state*
shortly particulars of offence), and on the said date [*or* on the   day of
     , 19   ,] the said Court sentenced him/her to imprisonment for
(*state period*) but made an order which [, as subsequently varied by the
competent court,] provided that the sentence should not take effect unless during
the period beginning on the date of the order and ending on the   day
of   , 19   , he/she committed in Great Britain another offence
punishable with imprisonment:
And the defendant was on the   day of   , 19   , convicted by
[*or* before] the Magistrates' Court [*or* Court of Assize *or* Quarter Sessions for the
[county] of   ] sitting at   , of (*state shortly particulars of*
offence), being an offence punishable with imprisonment committed by him/her
on the   day of   , 19   , during the said period, and was
sentenced [*or* ordered] to   .

Taken [and sworn [or affirmed]] before me,
J.P.,
Justice of the Peace for the [county] first above mentioned.

89

Summons on commission of further offence during operational period of suspended sentence (C.J. Act 1967, s. 42 ; M.C. Rules 1968, r. 81.)

In the [county of   . Petty Sessional Division of   ].
To A.B., of   .
Information has this day been laid before me, the undersigned [*or* state name]
Justice of the Peace, by   that you on the   day of   ,
19   , were convicted by the Magistrates' Court sitting at   ,
(*state shortly particulars of offence*), and that on the said date [*or* on the
day of   , 19   ,] the said Court sentenced you to imprisonment for
(*state period*) but made an order which [, as subsequently varied by the
competent court,] provided that the sentence should not take effect unless during
the period beginning on the date of the order and ending on the   day
of   , 19   , you committed in Great Britain another offence punishable with imprisonment:
And by the said information it is further alleged that you were on the
day of   , 19   , convicted by [*or* before] the Magistrates' Court [*or*
Court of Assize *or* Quarter Sessions for the [county] of   ] sitting
at   , of (*state shortly particulars of offence*), being an offence
punishable with imprisonment committed by you on the   day of
     , 19   , during the said period, and that you were sentenced [*or*
ordered] to   :
You are therefore hereby summoned to appear on   day the
day of   , 19   , at the hour of   in the   noon,
before the Magistrates' Court sitting at   , to answer to the said
information.

Dated the   day of   , 19   .

J.P.,
Justice of the Peace for the [county] first above mentioned.

[*or* This summons was issued by the above named Justice of the Peace.

J.C.,
Clerk of the Magistrates' Court sitting at   .]

90

Warrant on commission of further offence during operational period of suspended sentence (C.J. Act 1967, s. 42 ; M.C. Act 1952, s. 93 ; M.C. Rules 1968, rr. 77, 78, 80.)

In the [county of . Petty Sessional Division of].
To each and all of the constables of [*or* To X.Y. of].

Information on oath [*or* affirmation] has this day been laid before me, the undersigned Justice of the Peace, by that A.B. (hereinafter called the defendant) was on the day of , 19 , convicted by the Magistrates' Court sitting at , (*state shortly particulars of offence*), and that on the said date [*or* on the day of , 19 ,] the said Court sentenced the defendant to imprisonment for (*state period*) but made an order which [, as subsequently varied by the competent court,] provided that the sentence should not take effect unless during the period beginning on the date of the order and ending on the day of , 19 , the defendant committed in Great Britain another offence punishable with imprisonment :

And by the said information it is further alleged that the defendant was on the day of , 19 , convicted by [*or* before] the Magistrates' Court [*or* Court of Assize *or* Quarter Sessions for the [county] of] sitting at , of (*state shortly particulars of offence*), being an offence punishable with imprisonment committed by him/her on the day of , 19 , during the said period, and that the defendant was sentenced [*or* ordered] to :

You are hereby commanded to bring the defendant forthwith before the Magistrates' Court sitting at , or a justice of the peace of the petty sessional division in which the court is situate, to answer to the said information.

Dated the day of , 19 .

J.P.,
Justice of the Peace for the [county] first above mentioned.

(*Endorsement where bail is allowed*)

It is directed that the defendant on arrest be released on bail on entering into a recognizance in the sum of , with suret in the sum of [each], for his/her appearance before the Magistrates' Court sitting at , at the hour of in the noon of the next day upon which the Court is open [*or* on the day of , 19]. [The defendant's recognizance shall be subject to the following condition[s] (*specify*)].

J.P.,
Justice of the Peace for the [county] first above mentioned.

91

Commitment to Assizes or Sessions on commission of further offence during operational period of suspended sentence (C.J. Act 1967, ss. 41(2), (3), 42(5) ; M.C. Rules 1968, rr. 77, 78, 80.)

In the [county of . Petty Sessional Division of].
To each and all of the constables of [*or* To X.Y. of] and to the Governor of Her Majesty's prison [*or* the remand centre] at .

A.B. (hereinafter called the defendant) has this day been brought before the Magistrates' Court sitting at , on an information alleging that he has been convicted of an offence punishable with imprisonment committed

during the operational period of a suspended sentence made in his/her case
on the   day of   , 19 , by the Court of Assize [*or* Quarter
Sessions] for the [county] of   sitting at   [and subsequently
varied by the competent court]:

[*or* has this day been convicted by the Magistrates' Court sitting at   ,
of an offence punishable with imprisonment, namely (*state shortly particulars
of offence*), [and sentenced [*or* ordered] to   ], and it appears to
the Court that the date on which the said offence was committed, namely
the   day of   , 19 , fell within the operational
period of a suspended sentence made in his/her case on the   day of
              , 19 , by the Court of Assize [*or* Quarter Sessions] for the [county]
of   sitting at   [and subsequently varied by the
competent court]:]

  And it was this day ordered that the defendant should be committed in
custody to the next Court of Assize [*or* Quarter Sessions] for the [county] of
              in accordance with the provisions of section 42(5) [*or*
41(2)] of the Criminal Justice Act 1967:

  You, the said constables [*or* X.Y.], are hereby commanded to convey the
defendant to the said prison [*or* remand centre] and there to deliver him/her to
the Governor thereof, together with this warrant; and you, the said Governor,
to receive him/her into your custody and, unless he/she shall have been bailed
in the meantime, keep him/her until the next Court of Assize [*or* Quarter
Sessions] for the [county] of   sitting at   ,
and then convey him/her before the said Court to be there dealt with according
to law.

      Dated the   day of   , 19 .

                                      J.P.,

              Justice of the Peace for the [county] first above mentioned.
              [*or* By order of the Court,

                                      J.C.,
                                Clerk of the Court.]

(*Endorsement where bail is allowed*)

  The Court hereby certifies that the defendant may be bailed by recognizance
in the sum of   , with   suret   in the sum of
              [each], to appear before the Court of Assize [*or* Quarter Sessions]
above mentioned and that the defendant has [not] entered into his/her
recognizance. [The defendant's recognizance shall be subject to the following
condition[s] (*specify*)].

                                      J.P.,
              Justice of the Peace for the [county] first above mentioned.
              [*or* By order of the Court,

                                      J.C.,
                                Clerk of the Court.]

                            92

Order that suspended sentence shall take effect (C.J. Act 1967, s. 40(1)(a) and (b).)

  In the [county of   Petty Sessional Division of   ].

  Before the Magistrates' Court sitting at   .

  A.B. (hereinafter called the defendant) was on the   day of   ,
19 , convicted by the Magistrates' Court sitting at   , (*state
shortly particulars of offence*) and on the said date [*or* on the   day of
              , 19 ,] the said Court sentenced the defendant to imprisonment for
(*state period*) but made an order which [, as subsequently varied by the
competent court,] provided that the sentence should not take effect unless during

the period beginning on the date of the order and ending on the   day of , 19 , he/she committed in Great Britain another offence punishable with imprisonment :

And the defendant has this day appeared [or been brought] before the said [or first mentioned] Court and the Court was satisfied that the defendant had on the day of , 19 , been convicted by [or before] the Magistrates' Court [or Court of Assize or Quarter Sessions for the [county] of] sitting at , of a further offence, namely, (state shortly particulars of offence), being an offence punishable with imprisonment committed by him/her on the day of , 19 , during the said period :

[or And the defendant has this day been convicted by the said [or first mentioned] Court of (state shortly particulars of offence), being an offence punishable with imprisonment and the Court was satisfied that the said offence was committed by him/her on the day of , 19 , during the said period :]

It is ordered that the said suspended sentence take effect [with the substitution of a term of imprisonment of for the original term].

Dated the day of , 19 .

J.P.,

Justice of the Peace for the [county] first above mentioned.

[or By order of the Court,

J.C.,

Clerk of the Court.]

93

Commitment on commission of further offence during operational period of suspended sentence (C.J. Act 1967, s. 40 ; C.J. Act 1961, s. 4 ; M.C. Rules 1968, rr. 77, 78, 80.)

In the [county of . Petty Sessional Division of].

Before the Magistrates' Court sitting at .

To each and all of the constables of [or To X.Y. of] and to the Governor of Her Majesty's prison at [or Warden of the detention centre at].

A.B. (hereinafter called the defendant) was on the day of , 19 , convicted by the Magistrates' Court sitting at , (state shortly particulars of offence), and on the said date [or on the day of , 19 ,] the said Court sentenced the defendant to imprisonment for (state period) but made an order which [, as subsequently varied by the competent court,] provided that the sentence should not take effect unless during the period beginning on the date of the order and ending on the day of , 19 , he/she committed in Great Britain another offence punishable with imprisonment:

And the defendant has this day appeared [or been brought] before this Court and the Court was satisfied that the defendant had on the day of , 19 , been convicted by [or before] the Magistrates' Court [or Court of Assize or Quarter Sessions for the [county] of] sitting at , of a further offence, namely, (state shortly particulars of offence), being an offence punishable with imprisonment committed by him/her on the day of , 19 , during the said period :

[or And the defendant has this day been convicted by this Court of (state shortly particulars of offence), being an offence punishable with imprisonment and the Court was satisfied that the said offence was committed by him/her on the day of , 19 , during the said period:]

It is ordered that the said suspended sentence take effect [with the substitution of a term of imprisonment of for the original term:]

[*or* And the defendant appears to the Court to be under the age of twenty-one years, having been born, so far as has been ascertained, on the   day of   , 19   :

And the Court having been notified by the Secretary of State that the detention centre specified herein is available for the reception from the Court of persons of his/her class or description:

It is ordered that the said suspended sentence take effect [with the substitution of the term of   for the original term], and it is directed that the defendant serve the said sentence in the said detention centre:]

You, the said constables [*or* X.Y.] are hereby commanded to convey the defendant to the said prison [*or* detention centre] and there deliver him/her to the Governor [*or* Warden] thereof, together with this warrant; and you, the Governor of the said prison [*or* Warden of the said detention centre], to receive the defendant into your custody and keep him/her for   years/months [to commence at the expiration of the term of imprisonment (*give particulars*)].

Dated the   day of   , 19   .

J.P.,

Justice of the Peace for the [county] first above mentioned.
[*or* By order of the Court,

J.C.,

Clerk of the Court.]

94

Order varying suspended sentence (C.J. Act 1967, s. 40(1)(c).)

In the [county of   . Petty Sessional Division of   ].

Before the Magistrates' Court sitting at   .

A.B. (hereinafter called the defendant) was on the   day of   , 19   , convicted by the Magistrates' Court sitting at   , (*state shortly particulars of offence*) and on the said date [*or* on the   day of   , 19   ,] the said Court sentenced the defendant to imprisonment for (*state period*) but ordered that the sentence should not take effect unless during the period of   years from the date of the order the defendant committed in Great Britain another offence punishable with imprisonment:

And the defendant has this day appeared [*or* been brought] before the said [*or* first mentioned] Court and the Court was satisfied that the defendant had on the   day of   , 19   , been convicted by [*or* before] the Magistrates' Court [*or* Court of Assize *or* Quarter Sessions for the [county] of   ] sitting at   , of a further offence, namely, (*state shortly particulars of offence*), being an offence punishable with imprisonment committed by him/her on the   day of   , 19   , during the said period:

[*or* And the defendant has this day been convicted by the said [*or* first mentioned] Court of (*state shortly particulars of offence*), being an offence punishable with imprisonment and the Court was satisfied that the said offence was committed by him/her on the   day of   , 19   , during the said period:]

It is ordered that the said order suspending the said sentence of imprisonment be varied by substituting for the said period a period expiring   years from today.

Dated the   day of   , 19   .

J.P.,

Justice of the Peace for the [county] first above mentioned.
[*or* By order of the Court,

J.C.,

Clerk of the Court.]

95

Commitment to higher court: summary offence, etc. (*C.J. Act* 1967, *s.* 56 ; *M.C. Rules* 1968, *rr.* 77, 78, 80.)

In the [county of   . Petty Sessional Division of   ].

Before the Magistrates' Court sitting at   .

To each and all of the constables of   [*or* To X.Y. of   ] and to the Governor of Her Majesty's prison [*or* the remand centre] at   .

A.B. (hereinafter called the defendant) [, having consented to be tried summarily,] was this day [*or* on the   day of   , 19   ,] convicted by this Court (*state shortly particulars of offence*) :

[*or* A.B. (hereinafter called the defendant) was on the   day of   , 19   , convicted by this Court [*or* the Magistrates' Court sitting at   ], (*state shortly particulars of offence*) and on the said date [*or* on the   day of   , 19   ,] the Court sentenced the defendant to imprisonment for (*state period*) but made an order which [, as subsequently amended by the competent court,] provided that the sentence should not take effect unless during the period beginning on the date of the order and ending on the   day of   , 19   , he/she committed in Great Britain another offence punishable with imprisonment:

And [this Court was satisfied that] the defendant was this day [*or* on the   day of   , 19   ,] convicted by this Court [*or* the Magistrates' Court sitting at   ] of a further offence, namely, (*state shortly particulars of offence*), being an offence punishable with imprisonment committed by him/her on the   day of   , 19   , during the said period:]

And this Court has committed the defendant to the next Court of Assize [*or* Quarter Sessions] for the [county] of   to be held at   under the Vagrancy Act 1824 [*or* section 8(4) of the Criminal Justice Act 1948] [*or* section 28 [*or* 29] of the Magistrates' Courts Act 1952] [*or* section 41(2) [*or* 62(6)] of the Criminal Justice Act 1967]:

And it was this day adjudged that the defendant should be committed in custody under section 56 of the Criminal Justice Act 1967 to the said Court of Assize [*or* Quarter Sessions] to be dealt with in respect of the said offence [*or* suspended sentence]:

You, the said constables [*or* X.Y.], are hereby commanded to convey the defendant to the said prison [*or* remand centre] and there deliver him/her to the Governor thereof, together with this warrant: and you, the said Governor, to receive the defendant into your custody and, unless he/she shall have been bailed in the meantime, keep him/her until the next Court of Assize [*or* Quarter Sessions] for the said [county] and to have him/her there, together with this warrant, there to be dealt with according to law.

Dated the   day of   , 19   .

J.P.,

Justice of the Peace for the [county] aforesaid.

[*or* By order of the Court,

J.C.,

Clerk of the Court.]

(Endorsement where bail is allowed)

The Court hereby certifies that the defendant may be bailed by recognizance in the sum of   , with   suret   in the sum of   [each], to appear before the next Court of Assize [*or* Quarter Sessions] for the said [county], and that the defendant has [not] entered into his/her recognizance. [The defendant's recognizance shall be subject to the following condition[s] (*specify*)].

J.P.,

Justice of the Peace for the [county] aforesaid.

[*or* By order of the Court,

J.C.,

Clerk of the Court.]

96

Notice to governor of prison of person committed on bail to higher court otherwise than for trial (M.C. Rules 1968, r. 16(3).)

In the [county of   .   Petty Sessional Division of   ].

To the Governor of Her Majesty's prison [*or* the remand centre] at   .

The undermentioned person has been committed on bail to the next Court of Assize [*or* Quarter Sessions] for the [county] of   to be held at   .

Name, age, address and occupation of person committed	
Enactment under which he/she is committed and brief particulars of offence or other circumstance giving rise to committal	
Committing court	

Bailed this   day of   , 19 .

J.C.,

Clerk of the Court.

97

Order of removal from approved school to borstal (C.J. Act 1961, s. 16(2).)

In the [county of   .   Petty Sessional Division of   ].

Before the Magistrates' [*or* Juvenile] Court sitting at   .

To each and all of the constables of   [*or* To X.Y. of   ], and to the Governor of the borstal institution at   :

A.B. (hereinafter called the defendant) who appears to the Court to have attained the age of fifteen years [and to be under the age of seventeen years],

having been born, so far as has been ascertained, on the   day of   ,
19   , has, with the consent of the Secretary of State, been brought before
the Court by the Managers of the approved school at   ,
where the defendant is detained as an offender within the meaning of section
16(5) of the Criminal Justice Act 1961:

The Court, having regard to the defendant's conduct while in that school
[and] [or in the   approved school], is satisfied that his/her
continued detention in an approved school would be ineffective for the purposes
of his/her own reformation [and] [or would be detrimental to the training or
welfare of other persons therein] and is of opinion that it is in his/her interests
that he/she should receive training in a borstal institution:

It is ordered that the defendant be removed to the borstal institution at
     :

You, the said constables [or X.Y.], are hereby commanded to convey the
defendant to the said borstal institution and there deliver him/her to the Governor
thereof, together with this order; and you, the Governor of the said borstal
institution, to receive the defendant into your custody and keep him/her in
accordance with the provisions of section 16(3) of the Criminal Justice Act
1961.

Dated the   day of   , 19   .

             J.P.,
      Justice of the Peace for the [county] aforesaid.
      [or By order of the Court,

                J.C.,
           Clerk of the Court.]

98

*Interim order on application for removal from approved school to
borstal (C.J. Act 1961, s. 17(2).)*

In the [county of   . Petty Sessional
Division of   ].

Before the Magistrates' [or Juvenile] Court sitting at   .

[To each and all of the constables of   [or To X.Y. of   ]:]

To the Managers of the approved school [or Governor of the remand centre
or Superintendent of the remand home] at   .

A.B. (hereinafter called the defendant) who appears to the Court to have
attained the age of fifteen years [and to be under the age of seventeen years],
having been born, so far as has been ascertained, on the   day of   ,
19   , has, with the consent of the Secretary of State, been brought before the
Court by the Managers of the approved school at   ,
where the defendant is detained as an offender within the meaning of section
16(5) of the Criminal Justice Act 1961:

The Court not being in a position to decide whether to make an order under
the said section 16 in his/her case:

[And the Court having been informed that arrangements have been made for
the reception of the defendant in (*state name of institution*):]

[You, the Managers of the said approved school [or Governor of the said
remand centre or Superintendent of the said remand home] at
     are hereby commanded to detain the defendant for a period of
[twenty-one] days from the   day of   19   , unless
sooner dealt with according to law:]

[You, the said constables [or X.Y.], are hereby commanded to convey the defendant to the approved school [or remand centre or remand home] at
                              , and there deliver him/her to the Managers [or Governor or Superintendent] thereof together with this order:

And you, the Managers [or Governor or Superintendent] of the said approved school [or remand centre or remand home] to receive him/her into your custody and keep him/her for a period of [twenty-one] days from the   day of
                      , 19   , unless sooner dealt with according to law:]

[You, the said constables, are hereby commanded to convey the defendant to the police station at   and there deliver him/her to the Officer in charge of the said police station together with this order; and you, the said Officer, to receive him/her into your custody and keep him/her for a period of forty-eight hours unless sooner dealt with according to law, pending his/her further removal pursuant to an endorsement of this order:]

And unless otherwise sooner ordered you, the said constables [or Managers or Governor or Superintendent or X.Y.], are further commanded to convey [or to arrange for the conveyance of] the defendant on the   day of   , 19   , at the hour of   in the   noon before the Court to be further dealt with according to law.

    Dated the   day of   , 19   .

                        J.P.,
           Justice of the Peace for the [county] aforesaid.
           [or By order of the Court,

                        J.C.,
                  Clerk of the Court.]

(Endorsement for variation and extension of interim order)

The Court has been informed that arrangements have been made for the reception of the defendant in (*state name of institution*):

[And the Court is still not in a position to decide whether to make an order under section 16 of the Criminal Justice Act 1961 in his/her case:]

[And the Court is satisfied that by reason of illness [or accident] the defendant is unable to appear personally before the Court:]

[You, the said constables, are hereby commanded to convey the defendant to the approved school [or remand centre or remand home] at   , and there deliver him/her to the Managers [or Governor or Superintendent] thereof together with this order and endorsement:]

And you, the Managers [or Governor or Superintendent] are commanded to [receive the defendant into your custody and] keep the defendant until the day of   , 19   , unless sooner dealt with according to law; and unless otherwise sooner ordered you, the said constables [or Managers or Governor or Superintendent or X.Y.] are further commanded to convey [or to arrange for the conveyance of] the defendant on that day at the hour of in the   noon before the Court to be further dealt with according to law.

    Dated the   day of   , 19   .

                        J.P.,
            Justice of the Peace for the [county] aforesaid.
           [or By order of the Court,

                        J.C.,
                  Clerk of the Court.]

CIVIL PROCEDURE

ORDERS OTHER THAN CIVIL DEBT

99

Complaint (M.C. Act 1952, ss. 43, 44 ; M.C. Rules 1968, r. 1.)

In the [county of . Petty Sessional Division of].

The complaint of C.D., of , who [upon oath [*or* affirmation]] states that A.B. of , on the
day of , 19 , at , in the [Petty Sessional Division] aforesaid [*or* in the [county] aforesaid [*or* of]], (*stating grounds of complaint*).

Taken [and sworn [*or* affirmed]] before me this day of , 19 .

J.P.,

Justice of the Peace for the [county] first above mentioned.

100

Summons to defendant (M.C. Act 1952, ss. 43, 44 ; M.C. Rules 1968, r. 81.)

In the [county of . Petty Sessional Division of].

To A.B., of .

Complaint has this day been [*or* was on the day of , 19 ,] made to me, the undersigned [*or state name*] Justice of the Peace, by that you on the day of , 19 , at , in the [Petty Sessional Division] aforesaid [*or* in the [county] aforesaid [*or* of]], (*state shortly grounds of complaint*):

You are therefore hereby summoned to appear on day the day of , 19 , at the hour of in the noon, before the Magistrates' Court sitting at , to answer to the said complaint.

Dated the day of , 19 .

J.P.,

Justice of the Peace for the [county] first above mentioned.

[*or* This summons was issued by the above named Justice of the Peace.

J.C.,

Clerk of the Magistrates' Court sitting at .]

101

Domestic proceedings: report by probation officer of attempted conciliation (M.C. Act 1952, s. 59.)

To the Magistrates' Court sitting at

1. Name and age—
   (a) of complainant..
   (b) of defendant..

2. Address—
   (a) of complainant..
   (b) of defendant..

3. Date of the marriage..

4. Age and sex of any children under 16 years of age and where living......
   ....

5. Allegations made by the complainant..

6. Defendant's answer to complainant's allegations and any counter allegations made by the defendant..

7. Complainant's answer to defendant's counter allegations..

8. Names and addresses of persons furnished as being able to give material evidence by—
   (a) the complainant..
   (b) the defendant..

Dated the   day of   , 19 .

G.H.,
Probation Officer.

102

Order of dismissal of complaint (M.C. Act 1952, s. 45.)

In the [county of   . Petty Sessional Division of   ].

Before the Magistrates' Court sitting at   .

Complaint having been made by C.D., of   , that A.B., of   , (hereinafter called the defendant) on the   day of   , 19 , at   , in the [Petty Sessional Division] aforesaid [*or* in the [county] aforesaid [*or* of   ]], did (*state shortly grounds of complaint*):

It is this day adjudged that the said complaint be dismissed.

[And it is ordered that the complainant pay to the defendant the sum of   for costs [by weekly [*or* monthly] instalments of   , the first instalment to be paid] forthwith [*or* not later than the   day of   , 19   ]:]

Dated the   day of   , 19   .

Justice of the Peace for the [county] first above mentioned.
[*or* By order of the Court,

J.C.,
Clerk of the Court.]

103
Order on complaint (M.C. Act 1952, s. 45.)

In the [county of　　　　　　　.　Petty Sessional Division of　　　　　　　].

Before the Magistrates' Court sitting at　　　　　　　.

Complaint having been made by C.D. of　　　　　　　, that A.B.
of　　　　　　　, (hereinafter called the defendant) on the
day of　　　　　　　, 19　, at　　　　　　　in the [Petty Sessional
Division] aforesaid [*or* in the [county] aforesaid [*or* of　　　　　　　]], did
(*state shortly grounds of complaint*):

It is this day adjudged that the said complaint is true and it is ordered that
(*state adjudication*).

Dated the　　　　　　　day of　　　　　　　, 19　.

J.P.,

Justice of the Peace for the [county] first above mentioned.

[*or* By order of the Court,

J.C.,

Clerk of the Court.]

104
Summons to defaulter : rate (G.R. Act 1967, s. 104 ;
M.C. Rules 1968, r. 81.)

In the [county of　　　　　　　.　Petty Sessional Division of　　　　　　　].

To A.B., of　　　　　　　.

On the　　　　　　　day of　　　　　　　, 19　, you were summoned to appear
on the　　　　　　　day of　　　　　　　, 19　, before the Magistrates' Court sitting
at　　　　　　　, to show cause why a distress warrant should not be issued
in respect of the sum of　　　　　　　due from you in payment of the
rate levied by the　　　　　　　Council of　　　　　　　for the
　　　　　　　months ended the　　　　　　　day of　　　　　　　, 19　.

A distress warrant was subsequently issued for the recovery of the said sum
and the sum of　　　　　　　for costs incurred in obtaining that warrant, but no
sufficient distress whereon to levy the said sums, could be found.

And the further sum of　　　　　　　, being the costs attending the said distress,
is due from you.

You have [paid　　　　　　　in part payment, but have] made default in payment
[of a balance of　　　　　　　].

And the said Council has applied to the said Court for a warrant for your
committal to prison in respect of the said sums [*or* balance].

You are therefore hereby summoned to appear, unless the said sums [*or* balance]
be sooner paid, on　　　　　　　day the　　　　　　　day of　　　　　　　, 19　, at the
hour of　　　　　　　in the　　　　　　　noon, before the Magistrates' Court sitting at
　　　　　　　, for inquiry to be made as to your conduct and means.

Dated the　　　　　　　day of　　　　　　　, 19　.

J.P.,

Justice of the Peace for the [county] aforesaid.

[*or* Issued by　　　　　　　, Justice of the Peace.

J.C.,

Clerk of the Magistrates' Court.]

NOTE.—The object of the inquiry as to your means is to enable the Court to
decide whether or not to commit you to prison for default in payment. If, not
having paid, you fail to appear personally in obedience to this summons you
will render yourself liable to arrest without further notice.

105

Warrant for arrest of defaulter : rate (M.C. Act 1952, s. 93 ;
G.R. Act 1967, s. 104 ; M.C. Rules 1968, rr. 78, 79.)

In the [county of   .   Petty Sessional Division of   ].

To each and all of the constables of   [*or* To X.Y. of   ].

A.B. (hereinafter called the defendant) was on the   day of   ,
19   , summoned to appear before the Magistrates' Court sitting at   ,
to show cause why a distress warrant should not be issued in respect of the
sum of   due from him/her in payment of the rate levied by
the   Council of   for the   months ended the
          day of   , 19   :

And a distress warrant was subsequently issued for the recovery of the said sum
and the sum of   for costs incurred in obtaining that warrant, but no
sufficient distress whereon to levy the said sums could be found.

And the further sum of   , being the costs attending the said distress,
is due from the defendant:

And the defendant has [paid   in part payment, but has] made default
in payment [of a balance of   ]:

And the said Council has applied to the said Court for a warrant for the
commitment of the defendant to prison in respect of the said sums [*or* balance]:

You are hereby commanded to bring the defendant before the Magistrates'
Court sitting at   , or a justice of the peace of the petty sessional
division in which the court is situate, forthwith.

Dated the   day of   , 19   .

J.P.,

Justice of the Peace for the [county] aforesaid.

(Endorsement where bail is allowed)

It is directed that the defendant on arrest be released on bail on entering into
a recognizance in the sum of   , with   suret   in the sum of
          [each], for his/her appearance, unless the sum[s] [*or* balance] specified
in this warrant be sooner paid, before the Magistrates' Court sitting at
          , at the hour of   in the   noon of the next day upon which
the said Court is open [*or* on the   day of   , 19   ].

J.P.,

Justice of the Peace for the [county] aforesaid.

(Endorsement of payments)

PAYMENTS RECEIVED BY THE PERSON HOLDING THIS WARRANT

Date of Receipt	£	s.	d.	Signature

CIVIL DEBT

106

Complaint : civil debt (M.C. Act 1952, *s.* 50 ; *M.C. Rules* 1968, *r.* 1.)

In the [county of   . Petty Sessional Division of   ].

The complaint of C.D., of   , who states that A.B. (*stating grounds of complaint*) and claims from the said A.B. [the sum of   ,] being money recoverable summarily as a civil debt.

Taken before me the   day of   , 19   .

                      J.P.,

Justice of the Peace for the [county] aforesaid.

107

Summons to defendant : civil debt (M.C. Act 1952, *s.* 43 ; *M.C. Rules* 1968, *r.* 81.)

In the [county of   . Petty Sessional Division of   ].

To A.B., of   .

Complaint has this day been made to me, the undersigned [*or state name*] Justice of the Peace, by C.D., of   , (hereinafter called the complainant) that (*state shortly grounds of complaint*) and claiming from you [the sum of   ], being money recoverable summarily as a civil debt :

Particulars of the complainant's claim are given on the reverse of [*or* are annexed to] this summons:

You are therefore hereby summoned to appear on   day the day of   , 19   , at the hour of   in the   noon, before the Magistrates' Court sitting at   , to answer to the said complaint.

Dated the   day of   , 19   .

                      J.P.,

Justice of the Peace for the [county] aforesaid.

[*or* This summons was issued by the above named Justice of the Peace.

                      J.C.,

Clerk of the Magistrates' Court sitting at   .]

108

Order : civil debt (M.C. Act 1952, s. 50.)

In the [county of   . Petty Sessional Division of   ].

Before the Magistrates' Court sitting at   .

It is this day adjudged that A.B., of   , pay to C.D., of
, the sum of [, being an amount recoverable
summarily as a civil debt, and]   for costs [, by weekly [*or* monthly]
instalments of   , the first instalment of] the said sum[s] to be paid forthwith [*or* not later than the   day of   , 19   ] ; [and it is
ordered that in default of payment the sum due thereunder be levied by distress
and sale of the goods of the said A.B.].

Dated the   day of   , 19

J.P.,
Justice of the Peace for the [county] aforesaid.
[*or* By order of the Court,

J.C.,
Clerk of the Court.]

109

Complaint to enforce order : civil debt (M.C. Act 1952, s. 73 ; M.C. Rules 1968,
r. 1.)

In the [county of   . Petty Sessional Division of   ].

The complaint of C.D., of   , who states that on the
day of   , 19   , A.B. (hereinafter called the debtor) was ordered by
the Magistrates' Court [*or* Court of Assize *or* Quarter Sessions for the [county]
of   ] sitting at   , to pay to the
complainant the sum of   (enforceable summarily as a civil debt),
particulars of which are given below, [by weekly [*or* monthly] instalments of
, the first instalment to be paid] forthwith [*or* not later than the
day of   , 19   ] ; and the complainant further states that
the debtor has made default in payment of the sum ordered to be paid [, by reason
of his refusal or neglect to pay the instalments thereof], particulars of which
are given below.

	£	s.	d.
Amount of order and costs			
Costs of distress, if any			
Amount paid			
Total sum outstanding			
	£	s.	d.
Amount of default in instalments due to date			

Taken before me the   day of   , 19   .

J.P.,
Justice of the Peace for the [county] aforesaid.

110

Judgment summons (M.C. Act 1952, s. 73 ; M.C. Rules 1968, rr. 48, 81.)

In the [county of   . Petty Sessional Division of   ].
To A.B., of   .

Complaint has this day been made to me, the undersigned Justice of the Peace, by C.D., of   , (hereinafter called the complainant) that on the   day of   , 19   , you were ordered by the Magistrates' Court [or Court of Assize or Quarter Sessions for the [county] of   ] sitting at   , to pay to the complainant the sum of   , (enforceable summarily as a civil debt), particulars of which are given below, [by weekly [or monthly] instalments of   , the first instalment to be paid] forthwith [or not later than the   day of   , 19   ] ; and that you have made default in payment of the said sum [, by reason of your refusal or neglect to pay the instalments thereof], particulars of which are given below:

You are therefore hereby summoned to appear on   day the   day of   , 19   , at the hour of   in the   noon, before the Magistrates' Court sitting at   , to answer to the said complaint and to be examined as to the means which you have or have had since the said order was made to pay the said sum or the undermentioned instalments thereof, and to show cause why you should not be committed to prison pursuant to section 73 of the Magistrates' Courts Act 1952, in default of payment.

Dated the   day of   , 19   .

                                                              J.P.,
                              Justice of the Peace for the [county] aforesaid.

Particulars

	£	s.	d.
Amount of order and costs			
Costs of distress, if any			
Amount paid			
Total sum outstanding			
	£	s.	d.
Amount of default in instalments due to date			
Costs of this summons			
Amount upon the payment of which, before the date fixed by this summons for your appearance, no further proceedings will be taken unless you default in payment of a further instalment			

111

Distress warrant : civil debt (M.C. Act 1952, s. 64 ; M.C. Rules 1968, rr. 43, 44.)

In the [county of   . Petty Sessional Division of   ].

To each and all of the constables of [or To X.Y. of   ].

On the   day of   , 19   , it was ordered by the Magistrates' Court [or Court of Assize or Quarter Sessions for the [county] of

] sitting at , that A.B. (hereinafter called the debtor) pay to C.D., of , the sum of [, being an amount recoverable summarily as a civil debt, and] for costs, [the said order being made in the presence of the debtor] ; and [on the day of , 19 ,] it was [further] ordered [by the Magistrates' Court sitting at ,] that in default of payment the sums due thereunder should be levied by distress and sale of the debtor's goods:

[And the debtor having been served with a copy of a minute of the first mentioned order:]

And default having been made in payment, you are hereby commanded forthwith to make distress of the money and goods of the debtor (except the wearing apparel and bedding of him/her and his/her family and, to the value of fifty pounds, the tools and implements of his/her trade) ; and if the sum stated at the foot of this warrant to be levied, together with the reasonable charges of the making and keeping of the said distress, be not paid, then not earlier than the [sixth] day after the making of such distress, unless the debtor consents in writing to an earlier sale, to sell the said goods by you distrained and pay the money arising thereby to the Clerk of the Magistrates' Court sitting at and if no such distress can be found to certify the same to the Court.

Dated the day of , 19 .

J.P.,

Justice of the Peace for the [county] first above mentioned.

[or By order of the Court,

J.C.,

Clerk of the Court.

	£	s.	d.
Amount ordered to be paid			
Amount paid			
Amount remaining due			
Cost of issuing this warrant			
Total amount to be levied			

112

Commitment : civil debt (M.C. Act 1952, *ss.* 64, 71, 73, 107 ; *M.C. Rules* 1968, *rr.* 77, 78, 80.)

In the [county of . Petty Sessional Division of].

To each and all of the constables of [or To X.Y. of] and to the Governor of Her Majesty's prison at [or the Police Officer in charge of].

On the day of , 19 , it was ordered by the Magistrates' Court [or Court of Assize *or* Quarter Sessions for the [county] of] sitting at , that A.B. (hereinafter called the debtor) should pay to C.D., of   , the sum of [, being an amount recoverable summarily as a civil debt, and]   for costs:

And the debtor has made default in payment of the sum ordered to be paid and has been summoned for an examination as to his/her means:

And it being proved to the satisfaction of the Court that the debtor has [or has had, since the date of the said order,] the means to pay the sum [now] due and payable and refuses or neglects [or has refused or neglected] to pay the said sum:

[And the constables aforesaid having been authorised by warrant dated the   day of   , 19   , to levy the sum of   by distress and it appearing that no sufficient distress whereon to levy the said sum could be found [and that a balance of   is due]:]

It is ordered that the debtor be committed to prison [or detained in police custody] for (state period), unless he/she sooner pays the [balance of the] sum ordered to be paid [, together with the costs of enforcement], as set out below:

You, the said constables [or X.Y.], are hereby required to take the debtor and convey him/her to the Governor of Her Majesty's prison [or the Police Officer in charge of   ] at   ; and you, the said Governor [or Police Officer], to receive the debtor into your custody and keep him/her for (state period) from his/her arrest under this order, or until he/she be sooner discharged in due course of law.

Dated the   day of   , 19   .

J.P.,
Justice of the Peace for the [county] first above mentioned.
[or By order of the Court,

J.C.,
Clerk of the Court.]

	£	s.	d.
Sum [or balance] payable under order			
Enforcement costs payable			
Total sum payable by debtor			

(*Endorsement of payments*)

PAYMENTS RECEIVED BY PERSONS HAVING CUSTODY OF THE DEBTOR

Date of Receipt	£	s.	d.	Signature

PERIODICAL PAYMENTS: VARIATION, ETC.

113

*Complaint to vary, etc., order for periodical payments (M.C. Act 1952, s. 53 ;
M.C. Rules 1968, rr. 1, 34.)*

In the [county of   . Petty Sessional Division of   ].

The complaint of C.D., of   , (hereinafter called the complainant)
who [upon oath [*or* affirmation]] states that by an order made on the
day of   , 19   , under the   Act, by the Magistrates'
Court sitting at   , in the county aforesaid [*or* of   ], A.B.
(hereinafter called the defendant) of (*insert last known address and description
of defendant*) was ordered (*state shortly terms of the original order, and mention
any subsequent order and effect thereof*).

And the complainant now applies for the said order to be revived [*or* revoked
[*or* varied by an order requiring   ]] on the ground that   .
[The nature of the evidence that the complainant proposes to adduce at the
hearing of this complaint is as follows: —   . The names and
addresses of the complainant's witnesses are   .]

Taken [and sworn [*or* affirmed]] before me this   day of   ,
19   .

                 J.P.,

Justice of the Peace for the [county] first above mentioned.

114

*Summons to vary, etc., order for periodical payments (M.C. Act 1952, ss. 43, 53 ;
M.C. Rules 1968, rr. 34, 81.)*

In the [county of   . Petty Sessional Division of   ].

To A.B., of   .

Complaint has this day been [*or* was on the   day of   ,
19   ,] made before a Justice of the Peace acting for the [Petty Sessional Division
of   ] by C.D., of   , (hereinafter called the
complainant) who states that by an order made on the   day of
     , 19   , under the   Act, by this Court [*or* the
Magistrates' Court sitting at   , in the [county] of   ,]
you were [*or* he/she was] ordered (*state shortly terms of the original order,
and mention any subsequent order and effect thereof*):

And the complainant now applies for the said order to be revived [*or* revoked]
[*or* varied by an order requiring   ] on the ground that   .

And the complainant has furnished me with written particulars in accordance
with Rule 34 of the Magistrates' Courts Rules 1968 [*or* it appears to me, the
undersigned [*or* state name] Justice of the Peace, that your last address known to
the complainant is within the [Petty Sessional Division] aforesaid] [*or* the said
complaint has been transferred to this petty sessions area under Rule 34 of the
Magistrates' Courts Rules 1968].

You are therefore hereby summoned to appear on   day the
day of   , 19   , at the hour of   in the   noon, before
the Magistrates' Court sitting at   , to answer to the said
complaint.

Dated the   day of   , 19   .

                 J.P.,

Justice of the Peace for the [county] first above mentioned.

[*or* This summons was issued by the above named Justice of the Peace.

                 J.C.,

Clerk of the Magistrates' Court sitting at   .]

115

Order varying, etc., order for periodical payments (M.C. Act 1952, s. 53.)

In the [county of   . Petty Sessional Division of   ].
Before the Magistrates' Court sitting at   .

Complaint has been made by C.D., of   , (hereinafter called the complainant) who states that by an order made on the   day of   , 19   , under the   Act, by this Court [*or* the Magistrates' Court sitting at   , in the [county of   ,] A.B. (hereinafter called the defendant) [*or* he/she] was ordered (*state shortly terms of the original order, and mention any subsequent order and effect thereof*):

And the complainant has applied for the said order to be revived [*or* revoked] [*or* varied by an order requiring   ] on the ground that   :

And the said complaint has been sent to the Clerk of this Court in pursuance of Rule 34 of the Magistrates' Courts Rules 1968:

It is this day adjudged that the said order be forthwith revived [*or* revoked] [*or* varied as follows: —   ].

Dated the   day of   , 19   .

J.P.,

Justice of the Peace for the [county] first above mentioned.
[*or* By order of the Court,

J.C.,

Clerk of the Court.]

RECOGNIZANCES

116

Order of recognizance to keep the peace, etc. (M.C. Act 1952, s. 91.)

In the [county of   . Petty Sessional Division of   ].
Before the Magistrates' Court sitting at   .

Complaint having been made by C.D. that A.B. (hereinafter called the defendant) did (*state shortly grounds of complaint*):

It is adjudged that the said complaint is true, and it is ordered that the defendant do forthwith enter into a recognizance in the sum of   , with   suret   in the sum of   [each], to keep the peace and be of good behaviour towards Her Majesty and all Her liege people, and especially towards the said C.D., for the period of   from the date of this order:

And it is adjudged that if the defendant fail to comply with this order he/she be imprisoned in Her Majesty's prison at   for (*state period*), unless he/she sooner complies with this order.

[And it is ordered that the defendant pay to the said C.D. the sum of   for costs [by weekly [*or* monthly] instalments of   , the first instalment to be paid] forthwith [*or* not later than the   day of   , 19   ].]

Dated the   day of   , 19   .

J.P.,

Justice of the Peace for the [county] aforesaid.
[*or* By order of the Court,

J.C.,

Clerk of the Court.]

117

Summons to vary sureties, etc. (M.C. Act 1952, *s.* 94 ; *M.C. Rules* 1968, *rr.* 70, 81.)

In the [county of   .   Petty Sessional Division of   ].

To C.D., of   .

Application having been duly made in that behalf, you are hereby summoned
to appear on   day the   day of   , 19 , at
the hour of   in the   noon, before the Magistrates' Court
sitting at   , to show cause why the order made on the
day of   , 19 , by the said Court requiring A.B., of
to find   suret   should not be varied or otherwise dealt with.

Dated the   day of   , 19 .

                                                J.P.,
                              Justice of the Peace for the [county] aforesaid.

[*or* Issued by   , Justice of the Peace.

                                                J.C.,
                                    Clerk of the Magistrates' Court.]

118

Order varying order for sureties (M.C. Act 1952, *s.* 94 ; *M.C. Rules* 1968, *r.* 70.)

In the [county of   .   Petty Sessional Division of   ].

Before the Magistrates' Court sitting at   .

A.B. (hereinafter called the defendant) having, under a warrant of commitment
dated the   day of   , 19 , issued by this Court, been
committed to prison for default in finding   suret   in the sum
of   [each] :

And application having been duly made in that behalf, it is this day ordered
that the amount in which the suret   of the defendant [are] to be bound
be reduced to [*or* that the obligation of the defendant to find [a] suret   be
dispensed with].

Dated the   day of   , 19 .

                                                J.P.,
                              Justice of the Peace for the [county] aforesaid.
                              [*or* By order of the Court,

                                                J.C.,
                                        Clerk of the Court.]

119

Recognizance : general (M.C. Act 1952, ss. 7, 14, 26, 89, 91 ; C.J. Act 1967, ss. 20, 21, 41, 62 ; M.C. Rules 1968, rr. 69, 72.)

In the [county of   .   Petty Sessional Division of   ].

Recognizance of principal

I acknowledge that I owe to our Sovereign Lady the Queen the sum of
, payment thereof to be enforced against me by due process of
law if I fail to comply with any of the conditions endorsed hereon.

> (Signed)   A.B. of   .
> Taken before me the   day of   , 19 .

J.P.,

Justice of the Peace for the [county] aforesaid.

[*or* J.C.,

Clerk of the Magistrates' Court sitting at   .]

[*or* E.F.,

[Inspector] of the   Police.]

Recognizance of surety

I/We acknowledge that I/we owe to our Sovereign Lady the Queen the sum
of   [each], payment thereof to be enforced [severally] against me/us
by due process of law if the above mentioned principal fails to comply with the
condition[s] endorsed hereon [other than the condition[s] requiring him to   ].

> (Signed)   G.H. of   .
>   J.K. of   .

Taken before me the   day of   , 19 .

J.P.,

Justice of the Peace for the [county] aforesaid.

[*or* J.C.,

Clerk of the Magistrates' Court sitting at   .]

[*or* E.F.,

[Inspector] of the   Police.]

(*Endorsement*)

Condition[s]

The condition[s] of this recognizance is [are] that if the principal—
appears before the Magistrates' Court sitting at   , on   day
the   day of   , 19   , at the hour of   in the
noon [and appears at every time and place to which during the course of the
proceedings against the principal the hearing may be from time to time adjourned,
unless the Court otherwise orders in the meantime,] to answer to the charge
made against him/her by   ,

[*or* appears before the next Court of Assize [*or* Quarter Sessions] for the
[county] of   to be held at   , and there
surrenders himself/herself into custody [and takes his/her trial upon any indictment preferred against him/her],]

[and, subject to the condition for his/her said appearance, undergoes medical
examination by a [*or* two] duly qualified medical practitioner[s] [, of whom one
is approved for the purposes of section 28 of the Mental Health Act 1959,] and

for the purpose attends at (*insert name and address of institution or place or name and address of doctor*) and complies with any directions given to him/her for that purpose by   [and resides there until the expiration of
from the date of admission or until earlier discharge],]

[and, subject to the condition for his/her appearance, (*state any special conditions of bail*),]

[or keeps the peace and is of good behaviour towards Her Majesty and all Her liege people, and especially towards   for the period of
from the date of this recognizance,]

[or appears on such date and at such time and place as may be notified to him/her by the Clerk of the Peace at the hearing of his/her appeal to Quarter Sessions for the [county] aforesaid from a decision of the Magistrates' Court sitting at   , dated the   day of   , 19   , whereby the principal was convicted (*state shortly particulars of offence*) [or was sentenced *or* ordered   ].]

[or prosecutes without delay his/her appeal to the High Court of Justice from a conviction [or order] of the Magistrates' Court sitting at   , dated the   day of   , 19   , whereby the principal was convicted (*state shortly particulars of offence*) [or was ordered   ], and submits to the judgment of the High Court and pays such costs as may be awarded by the High Court [*and, unless the determination appealed against is reversed, appears before the said Magistrates' Court within ten days after the said judgment is given],]

[or (*where prosecutor is appealing*) prosecutes without delay his/her appeal to the High Court of Justice from a determination of the Magistrates' Court sitting at   on the   day of   , 19   , whereby the said Magistrates' Court dismissed an information laid by the principal alleging that X.Y. had (*state shortly particulars of offence*) [or (*state other determination appealed against*)], and pays such costs as may be awarded by the High Court,]

then this recognizance shall be void, but otherwise shall remain in full force.

---

* Delete if the principal is not to be released on bail pending the appeal to the High Court.

120

Notice of recognizance to principal and sureties

In the [county of   . Petty Sessional Division of   ].

Take notice that you, A.B., are bound in the sum of   as principal, and you, G.H. [and J.K.], in the sum of   [each] as suret   , that you, the said principal, appear before the Magistrates' Court sitting at   , on   day the   day of   , 19   , at the hour of   in the   noon, to answer the charge made against you (*or as the case may be*), and unless you, the said principal, appear accordingly, payment of the said sums will forthwith be enforced by due process of law severally against you, the said principal, and you, the said suret   .

Dated the   day of   , 19   .

J.P.,
Justice of the Peace for the [county] aforesaid.
[or J.C.,
Clerk of the Magistrates' Court sitting at   .]

121

*Recognizance of witness and surety (C.P. (A. of W.) Ac*t 1965, *s.* 5 ; *M.C. Rules 1968, r.* 75.)

In the [county of   . Petty Sessional Division of   ].

The undermentioned persons each acknowledge that they owe to our Sovereign Lady the Queen the following sums, namely:

C.D. of   , as principal, the sum of   , and of   , [and   of   ] as suret   the sum of [each], payment thereof to be enforced severally against them by due process of law if the principal fails to comply with the condition endorsed hereon.

(Signed) C.D.
X.Y.

Taken before me this   day of   , 19   .

J.P.,
Justice of the Peace for the [county] aforesaid.
[*or* J.C.,
Clerk of the Magistrates' Court sitting at   .]
[*or* E.F.,
Officer in charge of the   Police Station.]

(Endorsement)

Condition

The condition of this recognizance is that whereas a warrant was issued by   to arrest the said C.D. and bring him before the Court of Assize [*or* Quarter Sessions] for the [county] of   and the said C.D. having been arrested in pursuance of the warrant was brought before the   Magistrates' Court [*or* taken to the Police Station] under section 5 of the Criminal Procedure (Attendance of Witnesses) Act 1965:

If therefore the said C.D. appears at the Court of Assize [*or* Quarter Sessions] for the [county] of   at such time as he/she may be directed,

then this recognizance shall be void, but otherwise shall remain in full force.

122

Notice of recognizance to witness (C.P. (A. of W.) Act 1965, *s.* 5 ; *M.C. Rules 1968, r.* 75.)

TAKE NOTICE that you, C.D., of   , are bound by a recognizance in the sum of   to appear at the Court of Assize [*or* Quarter Sessions] for the [county] of   to be held at   ; and unless you appear accordingly, and unless you comply with the requirements of any direction you may receive in relation thereto, the said recognizance will be forthwith enforced against you.

Dated the   day of   , 19   .

J.C.,
Clerk of the Magistrates' Court sitting at   .
[*or* E.F.,
Officer in charge of the   Police Station.]

123

Certificate of amount and conditions of recognizance (M.C. Rules 1968,
rr. 72, 73.)

In the [county of   .   Petty Sessional Division of   ].

A.B. (hereinafter called the defendant) was on the   day of   ,
19   , committed by the Magistrates' Court sitting at   , to Her
Majesty's prison at   , charged with [*or* convicted of [*or* on the
complaint of   ]] (*state shortly particulars of offence or
complaint*):

[And the defendant having given notice of appeal [*or* applied for a case to be
stated]:]

I hereby certify that the said Court has consented to the defendant being bailed
by recognizance, himself/herself in the sum of   , [*or* has fixed
the amount of the recognizance to be entered into by the defendant at the sum
of   ,] with   suret   in the sum of
[each], conditioned as follows†

(Specify conditions)

And I hereby further certify that, on the said recognizance[s] being entered
into, the defendant is to be released from custody, if he/she be held for no
other cause.

Dated the   day of   , 19   .

J.C.,
Clerk of the Court.

---

† If under s. 21(2) of the Criminal Justice Act 1967 the defendant is not required to find
sureties in respect of one or more of the conditions specified this should be indicated.

124

Certificate of ability of surety to pay (M.C. Rules 1968, r. 73.)

In the [county of   .   Petty Sessional Division of   ].

To the Governor of Her Majesty's prison at   .

A.B., being now in your custody under a warrant of the Magistrates' Court
sitting at   , in the [county] of   , dated
the   day of   , 19   :

I hereby certify that the bearer of this certificate, G.H. of
in the [county] of   (*description*), whose signature is in the
margin hereof, has offered himself/herself as surety for the above-named prisoner,
and has satisfied me [*or* the Magistrates' Court sitting at   ,]
of his/her ability to pay the sum of   in the event of the recognizance
[for the appearance of the said A.B. before the   sitting at
     ,] referred to in the said warrant [*or* in the certificate
hereto attached] becoming forfeited.

Dated the   day of   , 19

J.C.,
Clerk of the Magistrates' Court sitting at

Signature of Surety

125

Notice of recognizance having been entered into (M.C. Rules 1968, r. 73.)

In the [county of　　　　　　.　Petty Sessional Division of　　　　　　　].

To the Governor of Her Majesty's prison at　　　　　　.

A.B., being now in your custody under a warrant of the Magistrates' Court sitting at　　　　　　, in the [county] of　　　　　　, dated the　　　　　　day of　　　　　　, 19　　:

I hereby give notice that　　　　suret　　　　referred to in the said warrant [*or* in the certificate from the Clerk of the said Court hereto attached] [have] duly entered into a recognizance [each] in the sum of　　　　　　before the said Court [*or* the Magistrates' Court sitting at　　　　　　, [*or* before me]].

Dated the　　　　　　day of　　　　　　, 19

J.P.,

Justice of the Peace for the [county] of　　　　　　.

[*or* J.C.,

Clerk of the Magistrates' Court sitting at　　　　　　.]

[*or* E.F.,

[Inspector] of the　　　　　　Police.]

126

Notice of enlargement of recognizance (M.C. Act 1952, s. 106 ; M.C. Rules 1968, r. 71.)

In the [county of　　　　　　.　Petty Sessional Division of　　　　　　].

Before the Magistrates' Court sitting at　　　　　　.

Take notice that by reason of the enlargement by this Court of the recognizance entered into by you on the　　　　　　day of　　　　　　, 19　　, you, A.B., are bound in the sum of　　　　　　as principal, and you, G.H. [and J.K.], in the sum of　　　　[each] as suret　　　　, that you, the said principal, appear on the　　　　　　day of　　　　　　, 19　　, at the hour of　　　　in the noon, before the Magistrates' Court sitting at　　　　　　, to answer to the charge made against you, and unless you, the said principal, appear accordingly, payment of the said sums will forthwith be enforced by due process of law severally against you, the said principal, and you, the said suret　　.

Dated the　　　　　　day of　　　　　　, 19　　.

J.P.,

Justice of the Peace for the [county] aforesaid.

[*or* J.C.,

Clerk of the Court.]

127

Complaint for forfeiture of recognizance to keep the peace, etc. (M.C. Act 1952, s. 96(2) ; M.C. Rules 1968, r. 1.)

In the [county of　　　　　　.　Petty Sessional Division of　　　　　　].

The complaint of C.D., who [upon oath [*or* affirmation]] states that A.B. (*stating particulars of recognizance and breach of condition*).

Taken [and sworn [*or* affirmed]] before me this　　　　　　day of　　 19　　.

J.P.,

Justice of the Peace for the [county] aforesaid.

128

Summons for forfeiture of recognizance (M.C. Act 1952, s. 96 ;
M.C. Rules 1968, r. 81.)

In the [county of . Petty Sessional Division of].

To A.B., of .

[Complaint has this day been made before me, the undersigned [*or state name*] Justice of the Peace, by that (*state shortly grounds of complaint*) :]

You are therefore hereby summoned to appear on day the day of , 19 , at the hour of in the noon, before the Magistrates' Court sitting at
to show cause why the recognizance entered into on the day of , 19 , whereby you are bound to pay the sum of should not be forfeited.

Dated the day of , 19 .

J.P.,

Justice of the Peace for the [county] aforesaid.

[*or* This summons was issued by the above named Justice of the Peace.

J.C.,

Clerk of the Magistrates' Court sitting at .]

129

Notice of forfeiture of recognizance (M.C. Act 1952, s. 96 ;
M.C. Rules 1968, r. 38.)

In the [county of . Petty Sessional Division of].

Before the Magistrates' Court sitting at .

To A.B., of .

Take notice that [on the complaint of C.D.] this Court has this day adjudged that the recognizance entered into by you on the day of , 19 , be forfeited and that you pay the sum of [and for costs] [by instalments of for every days, the first instalment of] the said sum[s] to be paid forthwith [*or* not later than the day of , 19].

Failure to pay forthwith [*or* on or before the appointed day[s]] will render you liable to [*imprisonment for (*state period*)] [*or* arrest] *or* your money and goods liable to distraint without further notice [unless you shall have been granted further time for payment. Application for the grant of further time may be made either in person to the Court or by letter addressed to me, the Clerk of the Court at (*insert address*) and stating fully the grounds on which the application is made].

Dated the day of , 19 .

J.C.,

Clerk of the Court.

NOTE.—Any communication sent by post must be properly stamped.

* Delete unless magistrates' court has, under s. 65(2) of the Magistrates' Courts Act 1952, fixed a term of imprisonment in default and postponed the issue of the warrant of commitment.

130

Distress warrant: forfeited recognizance (M.C. Act 1952, ss. 64, 96 ;
M.C. Rules 1968, rr. 38, 78.)

In the [county of   . Petty Sessional Division of   ].
To each and all of the constables of   [*or* To X.Y. of   ].
A.B. was by his/her recognizance entered into on the   day of
                    , 19   , bound in the sum of   :

And the condition of the said recognizance having been broken, it was on
the   day of   , 19   , adjudged by the Magistrates' Court
sitting at   , that the said recognizance should be forfeited and
that he/she should pay the said sum [*or* the sum of   ] [, and the further
sum of   for costs,] [by weekly [*or* monthly] instalments of   ,
the first instalment of] the said sum[s] to be paid forthwith [*or* on the
day of   , 19   ]:

And notice of the said forfeiture having been served on the defendant and
default having been made in payment :

You are hereby commanded forthwith to make distress of the money and
goods of the said A.B. (except the wearing apparel and bedding of him/her and
his/her family, and, to the value of fifty pounds, the tools and implements of
his/her trade) ; and if the sum stated at the foot of this warrant, together with
the reasonable costs and charges of the making and keeping of the said distress,
be not paid, then not earlier than the [sixth] day after the making of such
distress, unless the said A.B. consents in writing to an earlier sale, to sell the said
goods, and pay the proceeds of the said distress to the Clerk of the said Court,
and if no such distress can be found, to certify the same to the Court.

Dated the   day of   , 19   .

J.P.,
Justice of the Peace for the [county] aforesaid.
[*or* By order of the Court,

J.C.,
Clerk of the Court.]

	£	s.	d.
Amount due under adjudication			
Paid			
Remaining due			
Cost of issuing this warrant			
Amount to be levied			

131

Commitment : forfeited recognizance (M.C. Act 1952, s. 96 ;
M.C. Rules 1968, rr. 38, 77, 78, 80.)

In the [county of   . Petty Sessional Division of   ].
To each and all of the constables of   [*or* To X.Y. of   ]
and to the Governor of Her Majesty's prison at   .
A.B. was by his/her recognizance entered into on the   day of
                    , 19   , bound in the sum of   :

And the condition of the said recognizance having been broken, it was on the   day of   , 19   , adjudged by the Magistrates' Court sitting at   , that the said recognizance should be forfeited and that he/she should pay the said sum [*or* the sum of   ] [, and the further sum of   for costs,] [by weekly [*or* monthly] instalments of   , the first instalment of] the said sum[s] to be paid forthwith [*or* on the   day of   , 19   ]:

(*Here follow the appropriate form of commitment for non-payment of fine substituting for any reference to conviction or fine a reference to the adjudication forfeiting the recognizance.*)

GENERAL

132

Summons to witness (*M.C. Act* 1952, *s.* 77 ; *M.C. Rules* 1968, *r.* 81.)

In the [county of   . Petty Sessional Division of   ].

To E.F., of   .

Information [*or* complaint] has been laid [*or* made] by   that A.B. (*state shortly particulars of offence or complaint*):

And I, the undersigned [*or state name*] Justice of the Peace, being satisfied that you are likely to be able to [give material evidence] [and] [produce the undermentioned document[s] or thing[s] likely to be material evidence] therein and that you will not voluntarily attend for that purpose:

You are therefore hereby summoned to appear on   day the   day of   , 19   , at the hour of   in the   noon, before the Magistrates' Court sitting at   , to [give evidence therein] [and] [produce the following document[s] or thing[s] : —   ].

Dated the   day of   , 19   .

J.P.,

Justice of the Peace for the [county] first above mentioned.

[*or* This summons was issued by the above named Justice of the Peace.

J.C.,

Clerk of the Magistrates' Court sitting at   .]

133

Warrant for arrest of witness on failure to appear to summons (*M.C. Act* 1952, *ss.* 77, 93 ; *M.C. Rules* 1968, *rr.* 78, 79.)

In the [county of   . Petty Sessional Division of   ].

To each and all of the constables of   [*or* To X.Y. of   ].

E.F. (hereinafter called the witness) was summoned to appear on   day the   day of   , 19   , at the hour of   in the   noon, before the Magistrates' Court sitting at   , on the hearing of an information [*or* complaint] against A.B., to [give evidence therein] [and] [produce the following document[s] or thing[s] : —   ].

And the witness has failed to attend in answer to the said summons and it appears to the Court that there is no just excuse for the failure:

And it is proved to the satisfaction of the Court by evidence on oath [*or* affirmation] that the witness is likely to be able to [give material evidence] [and] [produce the document[s] or thing[s] aforesaid] on the said hearing, and [and it is further proved by declaration [or certificate]] that he/she has been duly served with the said summons and has been paid [or had tendered to him/her] a reasonable sum for his/her costs and expenses in that behalf.

You are hereby commanded to bring the witness before the Magistrates' Court sitting at   , or a justice of the peace of the petty sessional division in which the court is situate, forthwith.

Dated the   day of   , 19   .

J.P.,

Justice of the Peace for the [county] aforesaid.
[or By order of the Court,

J.C.,
Clerk of the Court.]

(Endorsement where bail is allowed)

It is directed that the witness on arrest be released on bail on entering into a recognizance in the sum of   , with   suret   in the sum of   [each], for his/her appearance for the purpose above mentioned before the Magistrates' Court sitting at   , at the hour of   in the   noon of the next day upon which such Court is open [or on the   day of   , 19   ]. [The witness's recognizance shall be subject to the following condition[s] *(specify)*].

J.P.,

Justice of the Peace for the [county] aforesaid.
[or By order of the Court,

J.C.,
Clerk of the Court.]

134

Warrant for arrest of witness in first instance (M.C. Act 1952, ss. 77, 93 ; M.C. Rules 1968, rr. 78, 79.)

In the [county of   . Petty Sessional Division of   ].
To each and all of the constables of   [or To X.Y. of   ].
Information has been laid by   that A.B. (*state shortly particulars of offence*):

And I, the undersigned Justice of the Peace, being satisfied by evidence on oath [or affirmation] that E.F. (hereinafter called the witness) is likely to be able to [give material evidence therein] [and] [produce the undermentioned document[s] or thing[s] likely to be material evidence therein,] and that he/she will not voluntarily attend for that purpose and that it is probable that a summons would not procure his/her attendance:

You are hereby commanded to bring the witness before the Magistrates' Court sitting at   , or a justice of the peace of the petty sessional division in which the court is situate, forthwith.

Dated the   day of   , 19   .

J.P.,

Justice of the Peace for the [county] first above mentioned.

(Endorsement where bail is allowed)

It is directed that the witness on arrest be released on bail on entering into a recognizance in the sum of   , with   suret   in the sum of   [each], for his/her appearance for the purpose above mentioned before the Magistrates' Court sitting at   , at the hour of   in the   noon of the next day upon which the court is open [or on the   day of   , 19   ]. [The witness's recognizance shall be subject to the following condition[s] *(specify)*].

J.P.,

Justice of the Peace for the [county] first above mentioned.

135

Commitment of witness (M.C. Act 1952, ss. 77, 109 ; M.C. Rules 1968,
rr. 77, 78, 80.)

In the [county of   . Petty Sessional Division of   ].

To each and all of the constables of   [*or* To X.Y. of   ]
and to the Governor of Her Majesty's prison at   [*or* to the
Police Officer in charge of   ].

E.F. (hereinafter called the witness) having this day appeared [*or* been brought]
before the Magistrates' Court sitting at   , as a witness on the
hearing of an information [*or* complaint] against A.B., refused without just
excuse to be sworn [*or* to affirm] [*or* to give evidence] [*or* to produce the following document[s] or thing[s] : —   ].

You, the said constables [*or* X.Y.], are hereby commanded to take the witness
and convey him/her to the said prison [*or*   ], and there deliver him/her
to the Governor thereof [*or* Police Officer in charge], together with this warrant ;
and you, the Governor of the said prison [*or* the Police Officer in charge of the
said   ] to receive the witness into your custody, and keep him/her
for (*state period*), unless he/she in the meantime consents to give evidence [*or*
to produce the document[s] or thing[s] aforesaid].

Dated the   day of   , 19   .

J.P.,

Justice of the Peace for the [county] aforesaid.
[*or* By order of the Court,

J.C.,

Clerk of the Court.]

136

Commitment of witness after failure to attend trial or after High Court warrant
(C.P. (A. of W.) Act 1965, s. 5.)

In the [county of   . Petty Sessional Division of   ].

To each and all of the constables of   [*or* To X.Y. of   ]
and to the Governor of Her Majesty's prison at   .

C.D. (hereinafter called the witness) being required by a witness order/
summons under the Criminal Procedure (Attendance of Witnesses) Act 1965 to
attend the trial on indictment of A.B. was ordered to be arrested and brought
before the Court of Trial by a warrant of Mr. Justice   under
section 4(1) of that Act dated the   day of   , 19   ,
[*or* failed to do so and a warrant for the arrest of the witness was issued under
section 4(2) of that Act by the Court of Assize [*or* Quarter Sessions] sitting at
on the   day of   , 19   , [endorsed
under section 5(3) of that Act with the opinion of the Court that the evidence
of the witness could be dispensed with but that consideration should be given to
dealing with him for the disobedience under section 3 thereof]] :

The witness having been brought before this Court in pursuance of section
5(1) of that Act :

You, the said constables [or X.Y.], are hereby commanded to convey the witness to the said prison and there deliver him/her to the Governor thereof, together with this warrant ; and you, the Governor of the said prison, to receive the witness into your custody and to keep the witness in custody until he/she can be brought before the Court of Trial [or (in a case where the warrant was endorsed as mentioned above and the magistrates' court is not satisfied that that Court will be held within 7 days of the committal) until he/she can be brought before a Judge of the High Court or a Commissioner of Assize.]

Dated the   day of   , 19   .

                                             J.P.,

                    Justice of the Peace for the [county] first above mentioned.

                    [or By order of the Court,

                                             J.C.,

                    Clerk of the Magistrates' Court sitting at   .]

(*Endorsement where bail is allowed*)

The Court hereby certifies that the witness may be bailed by recognizance in the sum of   , with   suret   in the sum of [each], to appear at the Court of Assize [or Quarter Sessions] for the [county] of   , at such time as he/she may be directed, and that the witness has [not] entered into his/her recognizance. [The witness's recognizance shall be subject to the following condition[s] (*specify*)].

                                             J.P.,

                    Justice of the Peace for the [county] first above mentioned.

                    [or By order of the Court,

                                             J.C.,

                                         Clerk of the Court.]

137

Warrant for temporary removal from approved school (C.J. Act 1961, s. 15(1).)

In the [county of   . Petty Sessional Division of   ].

To each and all of the constables of   [or To X.Y. of   ].

[And to the Managers of the approved school at   .]

[And to the Governor of the remand centre at   .]

[And to the Superintendent of the remand home at   .]

[And to the Officer in charge of the police station at   .]

Information on oath [or affirmation] has this day been [or was on the day of   , 19   .] laid before me, the undersigned Justice of the Peace (not being one of the Managers of the approved school at   ) by   , on behalf of the Managers of the said approved school, that A.B. (hereinafter called the defendant) who is detained in that school is unruly or subversive there:

And it appears to me that the defendant has attained the age of fifteen years, having been born, so far as has been ascertained, on the day of , 19 :

And it appears to me that the defendant is so seriously unruly [and] [or subversive] that it is necessary for maintaining the discipline of the school that he/she should forthwith be removed therefrom pending inquiry as to the best means of dealing with him/her:

[And I have been informed that arrangements have been made for the reception of the defendant in (*state name of institution*):]

You, the said constables [*or* X.Y.], are hereby commanded to convey the defendant to the approved school [*or* remand centre *or* remand home] at , and there deliver him/her to the Managers [*or* Governor *or* Superintendent] thereof together with this warrant; and you, the Managers [*or* Governor *or* Superintendent], to receive him/her into your custody and keep him/her for a period of twenty-eight days unless sooner dealt with according to law [*or* the police station at and there deliver him/her to the Officer in charge of the said police station together with this warrant; and you, the said Officer, to receive him/her into your custody and keep him/her for a period of forty-eight hours unless sooner dealt with according to law pending his/her further removal pursuant to an endorsement of this warrant]:

And if at the expiration of the said period of twenty-eight days [*or* forty-eight hours], the defendant has not been otherwise dealt with according to law, you, the Managers [*or* Governor *or* Superintendent of the last-mentioned institution *or* Officer in charge of the said police station] are further commanded to arrange for the conveyance of the defendant forthwith to the approved school at (*insert name of approved school from which defendant was removed*).

Dated the day of , 19 .

J.P.,
Justice of the Peace for the [county] aforesaid.

(*Endorsement after removal to police station*)

I have been informed that arrangements have been made for the reception of the defendant in (*state name of institution*):

You, the said constables, are hereby commanded to convey the defendant to the approved school [*or* remand centre *or* remand home] at , and there deliver him/her to the Managers [*or* Governor *or* Superintendent] thereof together with this warrant and endorsement:

And you, the Managers [*or* Governor *or* Superintendent] to receive him/her into your custody and keep him/her for a period of twenty-eight days unless sooner dealt with according to law:

And if at the expiration of the said period of twenty-eight days the defendant has not been otherwise dealt with according to law, you, the Managers [*or* Governor *or* Superintendent] are further commanded to arrange for the conveyance of the defendant forthwith to the approved school at (*insert name of school from which defendant was removed*).

Dated the day of , 19 .

J.P.,
Justice of the Peace for the [county] aforesaid.

138
Warrant for further removal after temporary removal from approved school
(C.J. Act 1961, s. 15(4).)

In the [county of   . Petty Sessional
Division of   ].

To each and all of the constables of
[*or* To X.Y. of   ] and to the Managers of the approved school [*or*
Governor of the remand centre *or* Superintendent of the remand home] at
                    :

A.B. (hereinafter called the defendant) has been removed from the approved
school at   to the approved school [*or* remand centre
or remand home] at   in pursuance of a warrant under
section 15(1) of the Criminal Justice Act 1961:

And I have been informed that arrangements have been made for the reception
of the defendant in (*state name of institution*):

You, the said constables [*or* X.Y.], are hereby commanded to convey the
defendant to the approved school [*or* remand centre *or* remand home] at
and there deliver him/her to the Managers [*or* Governor *or* Superintendent]
thereof together with this warrant; and you, the Managers [*or* Governor *or*
Superintendent], to receive him/her into your custody and keep him/her for the
remainder of the period of twenty-eight days commencing with the   day
of   , 19   , unless sooner dealt with according to law:

And if at the expiration of the said period of twenty-eight days the defendant
has not been otherwise dealt with according to law, you, the Managers [*or*
Governor *or* Superintendent] are further commanded to arrange for the conveyance of the defendant forthwith to the approved school at (*insert name of
approved school from which defendant was first removed*).

Dated the   day of   , 19   .

                                        J.P.,
                        Justice of the Peace for the [county] aforesaid.

139
Order to bring up prisoner before expiration of period of remand or in
connection with recognizance (M.C. Act 1952, ss. 91, 94, 105.)

In the [county of   . Petty Sessional Division of   ].

To the Governor of Her Majesty's prison at   [*or* to the Police
Officer in charge of   ].

A.B. was committed to your custody under a warrant of commitment dated
the   day of   , 19   , on remand until the
day of   , 19   , [*or* (*state other circumstances of commitment*)]:

[And it appears expedient to continue the hearing of the charge against the
said A.B. before the expiration of the period of remand:]

You are hereby ordered to bring the said A.B. on the   day
of   , 19   , at the hour of   in the   noon,
before the Magistrates' Court sitting at   , to be further dealt with
according to law [*or* that he/she may enter into a recognizance with
suret   conditioned to keep the peace] [*or* that he/she may make an application under section 94 of the Magistrates' Courts Act 1952] [, and may
thereupon be released from your custody unless the Court shall otherwise order].

Dated the   day of   , 19   .

                                        J.P.,
                        Justice of the Peace for the [county] aforesaid.
                        [*or* By order of the court,

                                        J.C.,
                                Clerk of the Court.]

140

Declaration of service (M.C. Rules 1968, r. 55.)

I, X.Y., of   , hereby solemnly declare that
I did on the   day of   , 19   , serve A.B., of
                   , with the summons (*or other document, as the case may be*),
of which a true copy is now shown to me and marked A, by delivering the said
summons to him/her [*or* by leaving the said summons for him/her with
                   at   , being the said A.B.'s last [*or*
usual] place of abode].

X.Y.

Declared before me the   day of   , 19   .

J.P.,
Justice of the Peace for the [county] of   .
(*Or other description*)

141

Declaration as to handwriting and seal (M.C. Rules 1968, r. 55.)

I, X.Y., of   , hereby solemnly declare that
the signature   to the document now produced and
shown to me, and marked A, is in the handwriting of
of   [and that the seal on the said document is the seal
of   ].

X.Y.

Declared before me the   day of   , 19   .

J.P.,
Justice of the Peace for the [county] of   .
(*Or other description*)

142

Certificate of service (M.C. Rules 1968, r. 55.)

(*Endorsement*)

I, X.Y., of   , hereby certify that on the   day of
                   , 19   , I served A.B., of   , with the summons (*or
other documents, as the case may be*), of which this is a true copy, by delivering
the said summons to him/her personally [together with the sum of
for costs and expenses] [*or* and that I tendered to him/her the sum of
for costs and expenses].

[*or* by leaving the said summons for him/her [, together with the sum of
                   for costs and expenses,] with   at   being
the said A.B.'s last known [*or* usual] place of abode [*or* business]].

Dated the   day of   , 19   .

X.Y.

143

Certificate of service by post (M.C. Rules 1968, rr. 55, 82(6).)

(Endorsement)

I, X.Y., of   , hereby certify that I served A.B. with the summons *(or other document, as the case may be)*, of which this is a true copy, by sending the said summons by post [*or* by the recorded delivery service] to him/her in a prepaid [registered] letter posted by me at the Post Office situate at   at   o'clock in the   noon on the   day of   , 19   , and addressed to A.B. at   , being his/her last known [*or* usual] place of abode [*or* address given by him/her for the purpose of service].

Dated the   day of   , 19   .

                                         X.Y.

144

Certificate of clerk of magistrates' court of non-payment of sums adjudged (M.C. Act 1952, s. 79.)

I hereby certify that the payments due to me, on behalf of C.D., from A.B. under an order made by the Magistrates' Court sitting at on the   day of   , 19   , under the *(state the Act under which the order was made)* have not been made to me in full, and that there is now in arrear the sum of   [in respect of periodical payments [*or* instalments] due up to and including the   day of   , 19   ].

Dated the   day of   , 19   .

                                   J.C.,
Clerk of the Magistrates' Court sitting at   .

145

Declaration as to non-payment of sums adjudged (M.C. Act 1952, s. 79.)

I, G.L., of   , do solemnly and sincerely declare that the payments due to me from A.B., under an order made by the Magistrates' Court sitting at   , on the   day of   , 19   , under *(state the Act under which the order was made)* have not been made to me in full, and that there is now in arrear the sum of   [in respect of periodical payments [*or* instalments] due up to and including the   day of   , 19   ].

And I make this solemn declaration, conscientiously believing the same to be true, by virtue of the provisions of the Statutory Declarations Act 1835.

                                   G.L.

Declared at   , the   day of   , 19   , before me,

                                   J.P.,
Justice of the Peace for the [county] of   .
(Or other description)

146

Register (M.C. Rules 1968, r. 54.)

In the [county of   .   Petty Sessional Division of   ].
Register of the Magistrates' Court sitting at   .
     The   day of   , 19   .

*Number	Name of informant or com- plainant	Name of defen- dant. Age, if known	Nature of offence or matter of com- plaint	Date of offence or matter of com- plaint	Plea or consent to order	Minute of adjudi- cation	Time allowed for pay- ment and instal- ments
(1)	(2)	(3)	(4)	(5)	(6)	(7)	(8)

(Signature)...

Justice of the Peace for the [county] of   .
A Justice adjudicating.

[*or* Clerk of the Court present during these proceedings.]

* Where separate registers are kept for criminal and civil proceedings these headings will be modified accordingly.

147

Extract from register proving proceeding of a magistrates' court
(M.C. Rules 1968, r. 56.)

In the [county of   .   Petty Sessional Division of   ].

Memorandum of a conviction [*or* order] (*or other proceeding*) entered in the Register of the Magistrates' Court sitting at   , the
day of   , 19   .

Name of informant or of com- plainant	Name of defendant. Age, if known	Nature of offence or matter of complaint	Date of offence or matter of complaint	Plea or consent to order	Minute of adjudica- tion	Time allowed for pay- ment and instal- ments

I certify the above extract to be a true copy.

     J.C.,

Clerk of the said Magistrates' Court.

Dated the   day of   , 19   .

148

Case stated (M.C. Act 1952, s. 87 ; M.C. Rules 1968, rr. 66, 68.)

In the High Court of Justice
Queen's Bench Division

Between A.B., Appellant

and

C.D., Respondent.

Case stated by Justices for the [county of , acting in and for
the Petty Sessional Division of], in respect of their
adjudication as a Magistrates' Court sitting at .

CASE

1. On the day of , 19 , an information [*or* complaint] was preferred by the appellant [*or* respondent] against the respondent [*or* appellant] that he/she (*state shortly particulars of information or complaint and refer to any relevant statutes*).

2. We heard the said information [*or* complaint] on the day of , 19 , and found the following facts:—(*set out in separate lettered paragraphs*).

*[The following is a short statement of the evidence:—(*set out so as to show relevant evidence given by each witness*)].

†3. It was contended by the appellant that

†4. It was contended by the respondent that

5. We were referred to the following cases

6. We were of opinion that (*state grounds of decision*) and accordingly (*state decision including any sentence or order*).

QUESTION

7. The question for the opinion of the High Court is

Dated the day of , 19 .

E.F.,
G.H.,

Justices of the Peace for the [county] aforesaid [on behalf of all the Justices adjudicating].

---

* Insert only if the opinion of the High Court is sought whether there was evidence upon which the Magistrates' Court could come to its decision.
† Only a brief summary should be given.

EXPLANATORY NOTE

(This Note is not part of the Rules.)

The Schedule to these Rules prescribes forms for use in magistrates' courts. With few exceptions, the forms are those hitherto contained in a number of statutory instruments now revoked by the Magistrates' Courts Rules 1968. The only substantial change is that certain forms may be signed by a justice's clerk instead of by a justice.

STATUTORY INSTRUMENTS

1968 No. 1920 (L.20)

MAGISTRATES' COURTS

PROCEDURE

The Magistrates' Courts Rules 1968

Made -   -   -   -   *27th November* 1968

Laid before Parliament   *17th December* 1968

Coming into Operation   *1st March* 1969

ARRANGEMENT OF RULES

I, Gerald, Baron Gardiner, Lord High Chancellor of Great Britain, in
exercise of the power conferred upon me by section 15 of the Justices of the
Peace Act 1949(a), as extended by section 122 of the Magistrates' Courts
Act 1952(b), do hereby, after consultation with the Rule Committee
appointed under the said section 15, make the following Rules:—

INFORMATION AND COMPLAINT

Information and complaint

1.—(1) An information may be laid or complaint made by the prosecutor
or complainant in person or by his counsel or solicitor or other person
authorised in that behalf.

(2) Subject to any provision of the Act and any other enactment, an
information or complaint need not be in writing or on oath.

(3) It shall not be necessary in an information or complaint to specify or
negative an exception, exemption, proviso, excuse or qualification, whether or
not it accompanies the description of the offence or matter of complaint
contained in the enactment creating the offence or on which the complaint is
founded.

(a) 1949 c. 101.   (b) 1952 c. 55.

PROCEEDINGS PRELIMINARY TO TRIAL ON INDICTMENT

Restrictions on reports of committal proceedings

2.—(1) A magistrates' court acting as examining justices shall before admitting in evidence any written statement or taking depositions of witnesses in accordance with Rule 4 of these Rules explain to the accused the restrictions on reports of committal proceedings imposed by section 3 of the Criminal Justice Act 1967(**a**) and inform him of his right to apply to the court for an order removing those restrictions.

(2) Where a magistrates' court has made an order under section 3(2) of the Criminal Justice Act 1967 removing restrictions on the reports of committal proceedings, such order shall be entered in the register.

(3) Where the court adjourns any such proceedings to another day, the court shall, at the beginning of any adjourned hearing, state that the order has been made.

Committal for trial without consideration of evidence

3.—(1) This Rule applies to committal proceedings where the accused is represented by counsel or a solicitor and where the court has been informed that all the evidence for the prosecution is in the form of written statements copies of which have been given to the accused.

(2) A magistrates' court inquiring into an offence in committal proceedings to which this Rule applies shall cause the charge to be written down, if this has not already been done, and read to the accused and shall then ascertain whether he wishes to—

    (*a*) object to any of the prosecution statements being tendered in evidence;

    (*b*) give evidence himself or call witnesses; or

    (*c*) submit that the prosecution statements disclose insufficient evidence to put him on trial by jury for the offence with which he is charged.

(3) If the court is satisfied that the accused or, as the case may be, each of the accused does not wish to take any of the steps mentioned in sub-paragraphs (*a*), (*b*) and (*c*) of the last foregoing paragraph and determines, after receiving any written statements tendered by the prosecution and the defence under section 2 of the Criminal Justice Act 1967, to commit the accused for trial without consideration of the evidence, the court shall proceed in accordance with the next following paragraph and in any other case shall proceed in accordance with Rule 4 of these Rules.

(4) The court shall then say to the accused—

"You will be committed for trial by jury but I must warn you that at that trial you may not be permitted to give evidence of an alibi or to call witnesses in support of an alibi unless you have earlier given particulars of the alibi and of the witnesses. You may give those particulars now to this court or at any time in the next seven days to the solicitor for the prosecution.",

or words to that effect:

Provided that the court shall not be required to give this warning in any case where it appears to the court that, having regard to the nature of the offence with which the accused is charged, it is unnecessary to do so.

(**a**) 1967 c. 80.

(5) Where the court has given to the accused the warning required by the last foregoing paragraph the clerk of the court shall give to him written notice of the provisions of section 11 of the Criminal Justice Act 1967 about giving notice of particulars of alibi to the solicitor for the prosecution and the solicitor's name and address shall be stated in the notice.

Taking depositions of witnesses and statement of accused

4.—(1) This Rule does not apply to committal proceedings where under section 1 of the Criminal Justice Act 1967 a magistrates' court commits a person for trial without consideration of the evidence.

(2) A magistrates' court inquiring into an offence as examining justices shall cause the evidence of each witness, including the evidence of the accused, but not including any witness of his merely to his character, to be put into writing; and as soon as may be after the examination of such a witness shall cause his deposition to be read to him in the presence and hearing of the accused, and shall require the witness to sign the deposition.

(3) The depositions shall be authenticated by a certificate signed by one of the examining justices.

(4) Before a statement made in writing by or taken in writing from a child is received in evidence under section 27(1) of the Children and Young Persons Act 1963(a) the court shall cause the effect of that subsection to be explained to the accused in ordinary language and, if the defence does not object to the application of that subsection, shall inform him that he may ask questions about the circumstances in which the statement was made or taken.

(5) Any such statement as aforesaid which is received in evidence shall be made an exhibit.

(6) After the evidence for the prosecution (including any statements tendered under section 2 of the Criminal Justice Act 1967) has been given and after hearing any submission, if any is made, the court shall, unless it then decides not to commit for trial, cause the charge to be written down, if this has not already been done, and read to the accused, and shall explain it to him in ordinary language.

(7) The court shall then ask the accused whether he wishes to say anything in answer to the charge and, if he is not represented by counsel or a solicitor, shall before asking the question say to him—

"You will have an opportunity to give evidence on oath before us and to call witnesses. But first I am going to ask you whether you wish to say anything in answer to the charge. You need not say anything unless you wish to do so. Anything you say will be taken down and may be given in evidence at your trial. You should take no notice of any promise or threat which any person may have made to persuade you to say anything.",

or words to that effect.

(8) Whatever the accused says in answer to the charge shall be put into writing, read over to him and signed by one of the examining justices and also, if the accused wishes, by him.

(9) The court shall then say to the accused—

"I must warn you that if this court should commit you for trial you may not be permitted at that trial to give evidence of an alibi or to call witnesses in support of an alibi unless you have earlier given particulars of the alibi

(a) 1963 c. 37.

and of the witnesses. You may give those particulars now to this court or to the solicitor for the prosecution not later than seven days from the end of these committal proceedings.",

or words to that effect and, if it appears to the court that the accused may not understand the meaning of the term "alibi", the court shall explain it to him:

Provided that the court shall not be required to give this warning in any case where it appears to the court that, having regard to the nature of the offence with which the accused is charged, it is unnecessary to do so.

(10) After complying with the requirements of this Rule relating to the statement of the accused, and whether or not he has made a statement in answer to the charge, the court shall give him an opportunity to give evidence himself and to call witnesses.

(11) Where the accused is represented by counsel or a solicitor, his counsel or solicitor shall be heard on his behalf, either before or after the evidence for the defence is taken, at his discretion, and may, if the accused gives evidence himself and calls witnesses, be heard on his behalf with the leave of the court both before and after the evidence is taken:

Provided that, where the court gives leave to counsel or the solicitor for the accused to be heard after, as well as before, the evidence is taken, counsel or the solicitor for the prosecution shall be entitled to be heard immediately before counsel or the solicitor for the accused is heard for the second time.

(12) Where the court determines to commit the accused for trial in respect of a charge which differs from that which was read to him in accordance with the provisions of paragraph (6) of this Rule, the court shall cause the new charge to be read to him.

(13) Where the court has given to the accused the warning required by paragraph (9) of this Rule the clerk of the court shall give to him written notice of the provisions of section 11 of the Criminal Justice Act 1967 about giving notice of particulars of alibi to the solicitor for the prosecution and the solicitor's name and address shall be stated in the notice.

Order for attendance of witness at court of trial

5.—(1) A witness order under section 1 of the Criminal Procedure (Attendance of Witnesses) Act 1965(a) shall be in the prescribed form and shall be served on the witness as soon as practicable after the accused has been committed for trial:

Provided that where, at the conclusion of the examination of a witness, the court determines that the witness order shall be a conditional order, the order shall be served on him immediately after the deposition has been signed.

(2) Where a court has directed under section 1(2)(b) of the said Act that a witness order shall be treated as a conditional order, it shall give notice to the witness in the prescribed form.

(3) If after a witness order has been made requiring a person to attend before any court of assize or quarter sessions the magistrates' court commits the accused for trial before some other court of assize or quarter sessions, the committing court shall forthwith give the witness notice of the court at which he is required to attend.

(4) If a witness order has been made as aforesaid and the court determines not to commit the accused for trial, it shall give notice to the witness that he is no longer required to attend.

(a) 1965 c. 69.

(5) A notice given under this Rule shall be in writing and signed by one of the justices composing the court or the clerk of the court.

(6) A witness order under section 1 of the Criminal Procedure (Attendance of Witnesses) Act 1965 and a notice given under this Rule shall be served by delivering it to the witness or by leaving it for him with some person at his last known or usual place of abode or by sending it by post in a registered letter or by recorded delivery service addressed to him at his last known or usual place of abode.

Procuring attendance at trial of witness subject to conditional order

6.—(1) Where in pursuance of section 1(2) of the Criminal Procedure (Attendance of Witnesses) Act 1965 a conditional witness order has been made, or a direction has been given that a witness order be treated as a conditional order, then if the prosecutor or the person committed for trial gives notice, at any time before the opening of the assizes or quarter sessions at which that person is to be tried, to the clerk of the magistrates' court that committed him, or at any time thereafter to the clerk of assize or the clerk of the peace, as the case may be, that he wishes the witness to attend at the trial, the clerk to whom the notice is given (in this Rule referred to as "the notifying clerk") shall forthwith give notice in writing to the witness that he is required to attend in pursuance of the witness order.

(2) A notice by the notifying clerk under the preceding paragraph shall be served by delivering it to the witness:

Provided that if time does not permit the notice to be served in that manner, the clerk may notify the witness in such manner as may be most expedient in the circumstances.

(3) Where the notifying clerk gives notice to a witness under the preceding provisions of this Rule at the instance of the prosecutor, the clerk shall inform the person committed for trial thereof; and, when he gives notice as aforesaid at the instance of the person committed for trial, he shall inform the prosecutor thereof.

Place of trial to be stated in warrant or recognizance

7. A magistrates' court committing any person for trial shall cause to be entered in the register and shall specify in the warrant of commitment, or, as the case may be, in the conditions of the recognizance on which he is committed on bail, the assizes or quarter sessions before which he is to be tried:

Provided that, if the person committed is a corporation, the court shall specify the said assizes or quarter sessions in the order made by the court under paragraph 1 of Schedule 2 to the Act instead of in the said warrant or conditions.

Notice to governor of prison of committal on bail

8.—(1) Where the accused is committed for trial on bail, the clerk of the court shall give notice thereof in writing to the governor of the prison to which persons of the sex of the person committed are committed by that court if committed in custody for trial and also, if the person committed is under 21, to the governor of the remand centre to which he would have been committed if the court had refused him bail.

(2) Where a corporation is committed for trial, the clerk of the court shall give notice thereof to the governor of the prison to which would be committed a man committed by that court in custody for trial.

Notices on committal of person subject to transfer direction

9. Where a transfer direction has been given by the Secretary of State under section 73 of the Mental Health Act 1959(**a**) in respect of a person remanded in custody by a magistrates' court and, before the direction ceases to have effect, that person is committed for trial, the clerk of the court shall give notice in the prescribed form—

(*a*) to the governor of the prison to which persons of the sex of that person are committed by that court if committed in custody for trial; and

(*b*) to the managers of the hospital where he is detained.

Documents and exhibits to be retained and sent to court of trial

10.—(1) A magistrates' court that commits a person for trial shall, unless there are reasons for not doing so, retain any documents and articles produced by a witness who is subject to a conditional witness order or in whose case the court has directed that a witness order be treated as a conditional order.

(2) As soon as practicable after the committal of any person for trial, and in any case before the first day of sitting of the court to which he is committed, the clerk of the magistrates' court that committed him shall, subject to the provisions of section 5 of the Prosecution of Offences Act 1879(**b**) (which relates to the sending of documents and things to the Director of Public Prosecutions), send to the proper officer of the court of trial—

(*a*) the information, if it is in writing;

(*b*) the depositions and written statements tendered in evidence, together with a certificate authenticating the depositions and statements, and any admission of facts made for the purposes of the committal proceedings under section 10 of the Criminal Justice Act 1967 and not withdrawn;

(*c*) all statements made by the accused before the magistrates court;

(*d*) a list of the names, addresses and occupations of the witnesses in respect of whom witness orders have been made;

(*e*) if the accused is committed for trial on bail, the recognizance of the accused;

(*f*) any recognizance entered into by any person as surety for the accused;

(*g*) a list of the documents and articles produced in evidence before the justices or treated as so produced;

(*h*) such of the documents and articles referred to in the last preceding sub-paragraph as have been retained by the justices;

(*i*) a certificate showing whether the accused was informed at the committal proceedings of the requirements of section 11 of the Criminal Justice Act 1967 (notice of alibi) and a record of any particulars given by him to the magistrates' court under that section;

(*j*) if the committal was under section 1 of the Criminal Justice Act 1967 (committal for trial without consideration of the evidence), a statement to that effect;

(*k*) if the magistrates' court has made an order under section 3(2) of the Criminal Justice Act 1967 (removal of restrictions on reports of committal proceedings), a statement to that effect;

(*l*) the certificate of the examining justices as to costs of prosecution (Form B in the Schedule to the Costs in Criminal Cases Regulations 1908(**c**));

(a) 1959 c. 72. (b) 1879 c. 22.
(c) S.R. & O. 1908/1001 (Rev. V, p. 404: 1908 I, p. 234).

(*m*) if any person under 17 is concerned in the committal proceedings, a statement whether the magistrates' court has given a direction under section 39 of the Children and Young Persons Act 1933(a) (prohibition of publication of certain matter in newspapers).

(3) Paragraph (2) of this Rule shall apply to the committal of a person under section 12(2) or (3) of the Act as if sub-paragraphs (*b*) to (*d*) and (*g*) to (*m*) were omitted.

(4) The clerk shall, in compiling the list mentioned in paragraph (2)(*d*) of this Rule, indicate the names of the witnesses, if any, to whom he has given any such notice as is referred to in Rule 6(1) of these Rules and shall include in the list the date of any such notice.

(5) The clerk shall retain a copy of any list sent in pursuance of paragraph (2)(*d*) of this Rule.

(6) If after a list has been sent in pursuance of paragraph (2)(*d*) of this Rule to the proper officer of the court of trial the clerk of the magistrates' court gives any such notice as aforesaid, he shall send written particulars of the notice to the officer.

(7) In the application of this Rule in relation to any committal to the Central Criminal Court, in paragraph (2) for the words "before the first day of sitting of the court to which he is committed" there shall be substituted the words "within four days from the date of his committal (not counting Sundays, Good Friday, Christmas Day or bank holidays)".

(8) In the application of this Rule as aforesaid, the said period of four days may be extended for so long as the clerk of the Central Criminal Court directs, having regard to the length of any document mentioned in paragraph (2) of this Rule or any other relevant circumstance.

(9) Upon the committal of any person to the Central Criminal Court, the clerk of the magistrates' court that committed him shall forthwith in writing notify the clerk of the Central Criminal Court of that committal.

(10) In the application of this Rule in relation to any committal under section 14 of the Criminal Justice Administration Act 1962(b) to a court other than the Central Criminal Court, in paragraph (2) the words "and in any case before the first day of sitting of the court to which he is committed" shall be omitted.

Supply of copies of depositions and information to accused

11. The person having custody of the depositions on which any person has been committed for trial shall, as soon as is practicable after application is made to him by or on behalf of the accused, supply to the accused copies of the depositions, a copy of the list of witnesses mentioned in Rule 10(2)(*d*) of these Rules and, if the information is in writing, of the information.

SUMMARY TRIAL OF INFORMATION AND HEARING OF COMPLAINT

Information to be for one offence only

12.—(1) Subject to any Act passed after 2nd October 1848, a magistrates' court shall not proceed to the trial of an information that charges more than one offence.

(2) Nothing in this Rule shall prohibit two or more informations being set out in one document.

(a) 1933 c. 12. (b) 1962 c. 15.

Order of evidence and speeches: information

13.—(1) On the summary trial of an information, where the accused does not plead guilty, the prosecutor shall call the evidence for the prosecution, and before doing so may address the court.

(2) At the conclusion of the evidence for the prosecution, the accused may address the court, whether or not he afterwards makes an unsworn statement or calls evidence.

(3) At the conclusion of the evidence, if any, for the defence, the prosecutor may call evidence to rebut that evidence.

(4) At the conclusion of the evidence for the defence and any unsworn statement which the accused may make and the evidence, if any, in rebuttal, the accused may address the court if he has not already done so.

(5) Either party may, with the leave of the court, address the court a second time, but where the court grants leave to one party it shall not refuse leave to the other.

(6) Where both parties address the court twice the prosecutor shall address the court for the second time before the accused does so.

Order of evidence and speeches: complaint

14.—(1) On the hearing of a complaint, except where the court determines under section 45(3) of the Act to make the order with the consent of the defendant without hearing evidence, the complainant shall call his evidence, and before doing so may address the court.

(2) At the conclusion of the evidence for the complainant the defendant may address the court, whether or not he afterwards calls evidence.

(3) At the conclusion of the evidence, if any, for the defence, the complainant may call evidence to rebut that evidence.

(4) At the conclusion of the evidence for the defence and the evidence, if any, in rebuttal, the defendant may address the court if he has not already done so.

(5) Either party may, with the leave of the court, address the court a second time, but where the court grants leave to one party it shall not refuse leave to the other.

(6) Where the defendant obtains leave to address the court for a second time his second address shall be made before the second address, if any, of the complainant.

Form of conviction or order

15.—(1) A form of summary conviction or order made on complaint shall be drawn up if required for an appeal or other legal purpose, and if drawn up shall be in such one of the prescribed forms as is appropriate to the case.

(2) Where the conviction is of an offence that could not have been tried summarily without the consent of the accused, the conviction shall contain a statement that the accused consented to the summary trial.

Committals for sentence, etc.

16.—(1) Where a magistrates' court commits an offender to a court of assize or quarter sessions under the Vagrancy Act 1824(a), section 28 or 29 of the Act or section 41(2)(*a*), 56(1) or 62(6) of the Criminal Justice Act 1967 after convicting him of an offence, the clerk of the magistrates' court shall send to the proper officer of the court to which the offender is committed—

(*a*) a copy signed by the clerk of the magistrates' court of the minute or memorandum of the conviction entered in the register;

(*b*) a copy of any note of the evidence given at the trial of the offender, any written statement tendered in evidence and any deposition;

(*c*) such documents and articles produced in evidence before the court as have been retained by the court;

(*d*) any report relating to the offender considered by the court; and

(*e*) if the offender is committed on bail, his recognizance and any recognizance entered into by any person as his surety.

(2) Where a magistrates' court commits an offender to a court of assize or quarter sessions under the Vagrancy Act 1824, section 8(4) of the Criminal Justice Act 1948(b), section 28 or 29 of the Act or section 41(2), 56(1) or 62(6) of the Criminal Justice Act 1967 and the magistrates' court on that occasion imposes, under section 56(8) of the Criminal Justice Act 1967, an interim disqualification for holding or obtaining a licence under Part II of the Road Traffic Act 1960(c), the clerk of the magistrates' court shall give notice of the interim disqualification to the proper officer of the court to which the offender is committed.

(3) Where a magistrates' court commits a person on bail to a court of assize or quarter sessions under any of the enactments mentioned in paragraph (2) of this Rule or under section 6(3)(*b*) or 8(3)(*b*) of the Criminal Justice Act 1948 the clerk of the magistrates' court shall give notice thereof in writing to the governor of the prison to which persons of the sex of the person committed are committed by that court if committed in custody for trial and also, if the person committed is under 21, to the governor of the remand centre to which he would have been committed if the court had refused him bail.

Committal to quarter sessions for order restricting discharge, etc.

17. Where a magistrates' court commits an offender to a court of quarter sessions either—

(*a*) under section 67(1) of the Mental Health Act 1959 with a view to the making of a hospital order with an order restricting his discharge; or

(*b*) under section 29 of the Act, as modified by subsection (4) of the said section 67, with a view to the passing of a more severe sentence than the magistrates' court has power to inflict if such an order is not made,

the clerk of the court shall send to the clerk of the peace—

(i) the copies, documents and articles specified in Rule 16 of these Rules;

(ii) any written evidence about the offender given by a medical practitioner under section 60(1)(*a*) of the Mental Health Act 1959 or a copy of a note of any oral evidence so given;

(iii) the name and address of the hospital the managers of which have agreed to admit the offender if a hospital order is made; and

(iv) if the offender has been admitted to a hospital under section 68 of that Act, the name and address of that hospital.

(a) 1824 c. 83.   (b) 1948 c. 58.   (c) 1960 c. 16.

Duty of clerk receiving statutory declaration under s.24(3) of Criminal Justice Act 1967

18. Where the clerk of a magistrates' court receives a statutory declaration which complies with section 24(3) of the Criminal Justice Act 1967, he shall—

(*a*) note the receipt of the declaration in the register against the entry in respect of the trial of the information to which the declaration relates; and

(*b*) inform the prosecutor and, if the prosecutor is not a constable, the chief officer of police of the receipt of the declaration.

SUMMARY TRIAL OF INDICTABLE OFFENCE

Duty to recall witnesses who have given evidence before examining justices

19. Where under any provision of the Act a magistrates' court, having begun to inquire into an information as examining justices, proceeds to try the information summarily, then, unless the accused pleads guilty, the court shall recall for cross-examination any witnesses who have already given evidence, except any not required by the accused or the prosecutor to be recalled for that purpose.

Preservation of depositions where indictable offence is dealt with summarily

20. The clerk of the magistrates' court by which any person charged with an indictable offence has been tried summarily shall preserve for a period of three years such depositions as have been taken.

RIGHT TO CLAIM TRIAL BY JURY DEPENDING ON PREVIOUS CONVICTION

Inquiry into antecedents where right to claim trial by jury depends on previous conviction

21. Where the accused claims to be tried by a jury for an offence for which he is entitled to make the claim if he has been previously convicted of a like offence but not otherwise, the court shall, so far as practicable, restrict any inquiry it may make into his antecedents for the purpose of verifying his right to make the claim to matters necessary for determining whether he has a previous conviction giving him that right.

REMAND

Remand on bail for more than eight days where sureties have not entered into recognizances

22. Where the court, with a view to a person's being remanded on bail, under paragraph (*a*) of the proviso to section 105(4) of the Act, for a period exceeding eight days, has fixed the amount of the recognizances to be taken for that purpose but commits that person to custody because the recognizances of the sureties have not yet been taken, the warrant of commitment shall direct the governor or keeper of the prison or place to which he is committed to bring him before the court at the end of eight clear days or at such earlier time as may be specified in the warrant, unless in the meantime the sureties have entered into their recognizances.

Documents to be sent on remand for medical inquiry

23. On exercising the powers conferred by section 26 of the Act a court shall—

(*a*) where the accused is remanded in custody, send to the institution or place to which he is committed;

(*b*) where the accused is remanded on bail, send to the institution or place at which, or the person by whom, he is to be examined,

a statement of the reasons why the court is of opinion that an inquiry ought to be made into his physical or mental condition and of any information before the court about his physical or mental condition.

Notice of further remand in certain cases

24. Where a transfer direction has been given by the Secretary of State under section 73 of the Mental Health Act 1959 in respect of a person remanded in custody by a magistrates' court and the direction has not ceased to have effect, the clerk of the court shall give notice in writing to the managers of the hospital where he is detained of any further remand under section 105 of the Act.

CONDITIONAL DISCHARGE AND PROBATION

Notification of discharge, etc., of probation order or order for conditional discharge

25.—(1) Where a magistrates' court discharges a probation order which was not made by that court the clerk of the court shall give notice of the discharge to the clerk of the court by which the order was made.

(2) Where a magistrates' court deals with a person under section 6 or 8 of the Criminal Justice Act 1948 in relation to a probation order or order for conditional discharge which was not made by that court the clerk of the court shall give notice of the result of the proceedings to the clerk of the court by which the order was made.

(3) Where a magistrates' court makes an order under section 53 of the Criminal Justice Act 1967 substituting an order for conditional discharge for a probation order which was not made by that court the clerk of the court shall give notice of the substitution to the clerk of the court by which the probation order was made.

(4) The clerk of a magistrates' court receiving a notice under this Rule shall note the decision of the other court in the register against the entry in respect of the original order.

SUSPENDED SENTENCES

Entries in register in respect of suspended sentences

26.—(1) Where a magistrates' court passes a sentence of imprisonment for a term of not more than six months in respect of one offence and does not make an order under section 39(1) of the Criminal Justice Act 1967 suspending the sentence the court shall cause to be entered in the register and specified in the warrant of commitment the paragraph of section 39(3) of that Act which gives the court jurisdiction to pass the sentence without making such an order.

(2) Where under section 40 of the Criminal Justice Act 1967 a magistrates' court deals with a person in respect of a suspended sentence otherwise than by making an order under subsection (1) (a) of that section, the court shall cause to be entered in the register its reasons for its opinion that it would be unjust to make such an order.

(3) Where an offender is dealt with under the said section 40 in respect of a suspended sentence passed by a magistrates' court, the clerk of the court shall note this in the register against the original entry in respect of the suspended sentence, or where the suspended sentence was not passed by that court, shall notify the clerk of the court by which it was passed who shall note it in the register against the original entry in respect of the suspended sentence.

HOSPITAL ORDER

Documents to be sent under Mental Health Act 1959

27.—(1) The court by which a hospital order is made under section 60 or 61 of the Mental Health Act 1959 shall send to the hospital named in the order such information in the possession of the court as it considers likely to be of assistance in dealing with the patient to whom the order relates, and in particular such information about the mental condition, character and antecedents of the patient, and, in the case of an order made under the said section 60, about the nature of the offence.

(2) The court by which a guardianship order is made under the said section 60 or 61 shall send to the local health authority named therein as guardian or, as the case may be, the local health authority for the area in which the person so named resides, such information in the possession of the court as it considers likely to be of assistance in dealing with the patient to whom the order relates and in particular such information about the mental condition, character and antecedents of the patient, and, in the case of an order made under the said section 60, about the nature of the offence.

(3) The court by which an offender is ordered to be admitted to hospital under section 68 of the Mental Health Act 1959 shall send to the hospital such information in the possession of the court as it considers likely to assist in the treatment of the offender until his case is dealt with by quarter sessions.

ENDORSEMENT

Endorsement of driving licence

28. Where a magistrates' court convicts a person of an offence and, under section 7 of the Road Traffic Act 1962(a), orders that particulars of the conviction, and, if the court orders him to be disqualified, particulars of the disqualification, shall be endorsed on any licence held by him, the particulars to be endorsed shall include—

(a) the name of the petty sessions area for which the court is acting;

(b) the date of the conviction and the date on which sentence was passed (if different);

(c) particulars of the offence including the date on which it was committed;

(d) particulars of the sentence of the court (including the period of disqualification, if any) and of any order for costs.

(a) 1962 c. 59.

DEPOSITION OF PERSON DANGEROUSLY ILL

Deposition of person dangerously ill

29.—(1) Where a justice of the peace takes the deposition of a person under section 41 of the Act and the deposition relates to an offence with which a person has been charged, the justice shall give the person, whether prosecutor or accused, against whom it is proposed to use it reasonable notice of the intention to take the deposition, and shall give that person or his counsel or solicitor full opportunity of cross-examining the deponent.

(2) The justice shall sign the deposition and add to it a statement of his reason for taking it, the day when, and the place where, it was taken and the names of any persons present when it was taken.

(3) The justice shall send the deposition, with the statement—

(*a*) if it relates to an offence for which a person has been committed for trial, to the proper officer of the court for trial before which the accused has been committed;

(*b*) in any other case, to the clerk to the examining justices before whom proceedings are pending in respect of the offence, or, if no such proceedings are pending, to the clerk of the peace for the county or borough in which the deposition was taken.

APPEAL TO MAGISTRATES' COURT

Appeal to be by complaint

30. Where under any enactment an appeal lies to a magistrates' court against the decision or order of a local authority or other authority, or other body or person, the appeal shall be by way of complaint for an order.

AFFILIATION ORDERS

Time for hearing affiliation summons

31.—(1) The time at which a summons issued under section 1 of the Affiliation Proceedings Act 1957(**a**), shall require the defendant to appear shall be after the day on which the birth of the child is expected.

(2) If at the time when such a summons requires the defendant to appear before a magistrates' court the complainant has not been delivered of the child, or has been so recently delivered that she is unable to appear, the court shall adjourn the hearing until a time after the complainant has been delivered and when she is able to appear.

(3) The last preceding paragraph shall apply to the non-appearance of the complainant at the time fixed on any such adjournment as aforesaid as it applies to the time specified in the summons.

ORDERS FOR PERIODICAL PAYMENTS

Method of making periodical payments

32.—(1) A magistrates' court ordering periodical payments to be made through a clerk of a magistrates' court under section 52 of the Act shall notify both parties of the hours during which, and the place at which, payments are to be made and received.

(**a**) 1957 c. 55.

(2) A clerk of a magistrates' court may send by post any periodical payments to the person entitled to them at the request, and at the risk, of that person.

(3) If a person makes any periodical payments to a clerk of a magistrates' court otherwise than in person at the clerk's office, he shall do so at his own risk and expense.

Duty of clerk to notify arrears of weekly payments

33. Where an order under section 52(1) of the Act requires payment of any weekly sum to the clerk of a magistrates' court on behalf of any person and the payments are at any time in arrear to an amount equal to four times the sum payable weekly under the order, the clerk shall, unless it appears to him that it is unnecessary or inexpedient to do so, give to that person notice in writing stating the particulars of the arrears.

Revocation, variation, etc., of orders for periodical payment

34.—(1) This Rule shall apply to a complaint for the revocation, discharge, revival, alteration or variation of an affiliation order or order enforceable as an affiliation order, but shall not apply—

(*a*) where jurisdiction is confined by paragraph (*a*) of subsection (2) of section 88 of the Children and Young Persons Act 1933 to courts having jurisdiction in the place where the person liable is residing;

(*b*) where an order has been made under the proviso to subsection (4) of that section;

(*c*) to a contribution order;

(*d*) to a complaint for an order under section 26(4) of the Children Act 1948(a);

(*e*) to a complaint for an order under section 22(1) of the Maintenance Orders Act 1950(b);

(*f*) to a complaint for an order under section 5 of the Guardianship of Infants Act 1886(c).

(2) A complaint to which this Rule applies may be made to a justice of the peace acting for the same petty sessions area as the responsible court or to a justice of the peace acting for the petty sessions area where the complainant is for the time being.

(3) A justice of the peace shall not take action on a complaint to which this Rule applies unless either the complainant has furnished him with written particulars—

(*a*) of the nature of the evidence that the complainant proposes to adduce at the hearing of the complaint and the names and addresses and, if known to him, the occupations of his witnesses; and

(*b*) of the occupations of the complainant and defendant and the address of the complainant and last address of the defendant known to the complainant,

or the justice is acting for the same petty sessions area as the responsible court and it appears to him that the last address of the defendant known to the complainant is within that area.

(4) Where a complaint to which this Rule applies is made to a justice of the peace acting for the same petty sessions area as the responsible court, and it appears to him that either of the places stated in the said particulars as being the addresses of the complainant and defendant is within another petty sessions

---

(**a**) 1948 c. 43.　　　(**b**) 1950 c. 37.　　　(**c**) 1886 c. 27.

area, then, if the justice determines that the complaint could more conveniently be dealt with by a magistrates' court acting for that other petty sessions area, he shall cause the clerk of the responsible court to send by post to the clerk of that other court the complaint and the said particulars.

(5) Where the places stated in the said particulars as being the addresses of the complainant and the defendant appear to the justice to be outside the petty sessions area for which the justice is acting and in other and different petty sessions areas, the reference in the last preceding paragraph to another petty sessions area shall be construed as a reference to such one of those other areas aforesaid as appears to the justice convenient.

(6) On receipt by the clerk of a magistrates' court of a complaint and particulars under paragraph (4) of this Rule, he shall bring the complaint before the court, and the court shall issue a summons requiring the defendant to appear before it, and shall hear and determine the complaint.

(7) Where a complaint to which this Rule applies is made to a justice of the peace acting for a petty sessions area other than that for which the responsible court acts, the justice shall cause the clerk of the magistrates' court acting for that other petty sessions area to send the complaint and the said particulars by post to the clerk of the responsible court; and the clerk of the responsible court shall bring the complaint before the court; and thereupon paragraphs (4) to (6) of this Rule shall have effect as if the complaint had been made and the particulars furnished to a justice of the peace acting for the same petty sessions area as the responsible court.

(8) Notwithstanding the foregoing provisions of this Rule, a justice to whom a complaint is made may refer the complaint to the responsible court which may, in such case or when the complaint is brought before the court in accordance with paragraph (6) of this Rule, cause the complaint and particulars to be sent by post to the clerk of the court which made the original order and that clerk and that court shall proceed in accordance with the provisions of paragraph (6).

(9) In this Rule "responsible court" means—

(a) where payments under the order are made to the clerk of a magistrates' court, that court;

(b) where payments are not so made, the court which made the order.

Application for sums under affiliation order to be paid to person having custody of child

35. An application under section 5(3) of the Affiliation Proceedings Act 1957 shall be by complaint for an order.

Service of copy of order

36. Where a magistrates' court makes, revokes, discharges, revives, alters or varies an affiliation order or order enforceable as an affiliation order the court shall cause a copy of its order to be served on the defendant by delivering it to him or by sending it by post in a letter addressed to him at his last known or usual place of abode.

Remission of sums due under order

37.—(1) Before remitting the whole or any part of a sum due under an affiliation order or an order enforceable as an affiliation order under section 76 of the Act, the court shall, except save where it appears to it to be unnecessary or impracticable to do so, cause the person in whose favour the order is made to be notified of its intention and shall afford to such person a reasonable opportunity to make representations to the court, either orally at an adjourned hearing of the complaint for enforcement or in writing and such representations shall be considered by the court.

(2) Any written representations may be considered by the Court if they purport to be signed by or on behalf of the person in whose favour the order is made.

SATISFACTION, ENFORCEMENT AND APPLICATION OF PAYMENTS

Notice to defendant of fine or forfeited recognizance

38.—(1) Where under section 47(3) or 49 of the Criminal Justice Act 1967 or section 19(5) of the Coroners Act 1887(a) a magistrates' court is required to enforce payment of a fine imposed or recognizance forfeited by a court of assize or quarter sessions or by a coroner or where a magistrates' court allows time for payment of a sum adjudged to be paid by a summary conviction, or directs that the sum be paid by instalments, or where the offender is absent when a sum is adjudged to be paid by a summary conviction, the clerk of the court shall serve on the offender notice in writing stating the amount of the sum and, if it is to be paid by instalments, the amount of the instalments, the date on which the sum, or each of the instalments, is to be paid and the places and times at which payment may be made; and a warrant of distress or commitment shall not be issued until the preceding provisions of this Rule have been complied with.

(2) A notice under this Rule shall be served by delivering it to the offender or by sending it to him by post in a letter addressed to him at his last known or usual place of abode.

To whom payments are to be made

39.—(1) A person adjudged by the conviction or order of a magistrates' court to pay any sum shall, unless the court otherwise directs, pay that sum, or any instalment of that sum, to the clerk of the court.

(2) Where payment of any sum or instalment of any sum adjudged to be paid by the conviction or order of a magistrates' court is made to any person other than the clerk of the court, that person, unless he is the person to whom the court has directed payment to be made, shall, as soon as may be, account for and, if the clerk so requires, pay over the sum or instalment to the clerk of the court.

(3) Where payment of any sum adjudged to be paid by the conviction or order of a magistrates' court, or any instalment of such a sum, is directed to be made to the clerk of some other magistrates' court, the clerk of the court that adjudged the sum to be paid shall pay over any sums received by him on account of the said sum or instalment to the clerk of that other court.

Duty of clerk to give receipt

40. The clerk of a magistrates' court shall give or send a receipt to any person who makes a payment to him in pursuance of a conviction or order of a magistrates' court and who asks for a receipt.

(a) 1887 c. 71.

Relief of collecting officer

41.—(1) Where a magistrates' court has ordered periodical payments to be made through the clerk of a magistrates' court, then, if it is proved that the person on whose behalf the order was made has persistently received the payments direct from the person liable to make them, the court that made the order may by order vary it so as to require the payments to be made direct.

(2) An order under this Rule may be made—

(*a*) on complaint by the clerk through whom payments were ordered to be made; or

(*b*) on the hearing of a complaint to enforce the original order, if both parties are present.

Application for further time

42. An application under section 63(2) of the Act may, unless the court requires the applicant to attend, be made in writing.

Notice to defendant before enforcing order

43.—(1) A warrant of distress shall not be issued for failure to pay a sum enforceable as a civil debt unless the defendant has been previously served with a copy of the minute of the order, or the order was made in his presence and the warrant is issued on that occasion.

(2) A warrant of commitment shall not be issued for disobedience to an order of a magistrates' court other than an order to pay money unless the defendant has been previously served with a copy of the minute of the order, or the order was made in his presence and the warrant is issued on that occasion.

(3) A copy of the minute of the order shall be served under this Rule by delivering it to the defendant or by sending it to him by post in a letter addressed to him at his last known or usual place of abode.

Execution of distress warrant

44.—(1) A warrant of distress issued for the purpose of levying a sum adjudged to be paid by a summary conviction or order—

(*a*) shall name or otherwise describe the person against whom the distress is to be levied;

(*b*) shall be directed to the constables of the police area in which the warrant is issued or to a person named in the warrant and shall, subject to, and in accordance with, the provisions of this Rule, require them to levy the said sum by distress and sale of the goods belonging to the said person;

(*c*) may where it is directed to the constables of a police area, instead of being executed by any of those constables, be executed by any person under the direction of a constable.

(2) The warrant shall authorise the person charged with the execution of it to take as well any money as any goods of the person against whom the distress is levied; and any money so taken shall be treated as if it were the proceeds of the sale of goods taken under the warrant.

(3) The warrant shall require the person charged with execution to pay the sum to be levied to the clerk of the court that issued the warrant.

(4) There shall not be taken under the warrant the wearing apparel or bedding of any person or his family or the tools and implements of his trade; so however that if the tools and implements of his trade exceed in value fifty pounds it shall be lawful to take such of the tools and implements as will leave in that person's possession tools and implements of his trade to the value of fifty pounds.

(5) The distress levied under any such warrant as aforesaid shall be sold within such period beginning not earlier than the sixth day after the making of the distress as may be specified in the warrant, or if no period is specified in the warrant, within a period beginning on the sixth day and ending on the fourteenth day after the making of the distress:

Provided that with the consent in writing of the person against whom the distress is levied the distress may be sold before the beginning of the said period.

(6) The said distress shall be sold by public auction or in such other manner as the person against whom the distress is levied may in writing allow.

(7) Notwithstanding anything in the preceding provisions of this Rule, the said distress shall not be sold if the sum for which the warrant was issued and the charges of taking and keeping the distress have been paid.

(8) Subject to any direction to the contrary in the warrant, where the distress is levied on household goods, the goods shall not, without the consent in writing of the person against whom the distress is levied, be removed from the house until the day of sale; and so much of the goods shall be impounded as is in the opinion of the person executing the warrant sufficient to satisfy the distress, by affixing to the articles impounded a conspicuous mark.

(9) The constable or other person charged with the execution of any such warrant as aforesaid shall cause the distress to be sold, and may deduct out of the amount realised by the sale all costs and charges incurred in effecting the sale; and he shall return to the owner the balance, if any, after retaining the amount of the sum for which the warrant was issued and the proper costs and charges of the execution of the warrant.

(10) The constable or other person charged with the execution of any such warrant as aforesaid shall as soon as practicable send to the clerk of the court that issued it a written account of the costs and charges incurred in executing it; and the clerk shall allow the person against whom the distress was levied to inspect the account within one month after the levy of the distress at any reasonable time to be appointed by the court.

(11) If any person pays or tenders to the constable or other person charged with the execution of any such warrant as aforesaid the sum mentioned in the warrant, or produces a receipt for that sum given by the clerk of the court that issued the warrant, and also pays the amount of the costs and charges of the distress up to the time of the payment or tender or the production of the receipt, the constable or other person as aforesaid shall not execute the warrant, or shall cease to execute it, as the case may be.

Payment after imprisonment imposed

45.—(1) The persons authorised for the purposes of section 67(2) of the Act to receive a part payment are—

    (a) unless there has been issued a warrant of distress or commitment, the clerk of the court enforcing payment of the sum, or any person appointed under section 71 of the Act to supervise the offender;

(*b*) where the issue of a warrant of commitment has been suspended on conditions which provide for payment to be made to the clerk of some other magistrates' court, that clerk;

(*c*) any constable holding a warrant of distress or commitment or, where the warrant is directed to some other person, that person;

(*d*) the governor or keeper of the prison or place in which the defaulter is detained, or other person having lawful custody of the defaulter:

Provided that—

(i) the said governor or keeper shall not be required to accept any sum tendered in part payment under the said subsection (2) except on a week-day between nine o'clock in the morning and five o'clock in the afternoon; and

(ii) no person shall be required to receive in part payment under the said subsection (2) an amount which, or so much of an amount as, will not procure a reduction of the period for which the defaulter is committed or ordered to be detained.

(2) Where a person having custody of a defaulter receives payment of any sum he shall note receipt of the sum on the warrant of commitment.

(3) Where the clerk of a court other than the court enforcing payment of the sums receives payment of any sum he shall inform the clerk of the other court.

(4) Where a person appointed under section 71 of the Act to supervise an offender receives payment of any sum, he shall send it forthwith to the clerk of the court which appointed him.

(5) If the period of imprisonment imposed on any person in default of payment of a sum adjudged to be paid by a conviction or order of a magistrates' court, or for want of sufficient distress to satisfy such a sum, is reduced through part payments to less than five days, he may be committed either to a prison or to a place certified by the Secretary of State under section 109 of the Act, or, if he is already in prison, the Secretary of State may transfer him to a place so certified.

Order for supervision

46.—(1) Unless an order under section 71(1) of the Act is made in the offender's presence, the clerk of the court making the order shall deliver to the offender, or serve on him by post, notice in writing of the order.

(2) It shall be the duty of any person for the time being appointed under the said section to advise and befriend the offender with a view to inducing him to pay the sum adjudged to be paid and thereby avoid committal to custody and to give any information required by a magistrates' court about the offender's conduct and means.

Transfer of fine order

47.—(1) The clerk of a magistrates' court which has made a transfer of fine order under section 72 or 72A of the Act shall send to the clerk of the court having jurisdiction under the order a copy of the order with a statement of the offence and the steps, if any, taken to recover the sum adjudged to be paid, and with such further information as is available and is in the opinion of the first-mentioned clerk likely to assist the last-mentioned court.

(2) An additional copy of any second or subsequent transfer of fine order made under section 72 or 72A of the Act shall be sent by the clerk of the magistrates' court which made the order to the clerk of the convicting court in England and Wales or in Scotland, as the case may be.

(3) Where the clerk of a magistrates' court receives a copy of a transfer of fine order (whether made in England and Wales or in Scotland) specifying that court as the court by which payment of the sum in question is to be enforceable, he shall thereupon, if possible, deliver or send by post to the offender notice in writing in the prescribed form.

(4) If the said sum is paid, the clerk of the court on which jurisdiction is conferred by the order shall send it to the clerk of the convicting court; and if the said sum is not paid, the first-mentioned clerk shall inform the second-mentioned clerk of the manner in which the adjudication has been satisfied.

(5) Any reference in this Rule to a transfer of fine order made under section 72 or 72A of the Act shall include a reference to such an order made under that section as applied by section 72B thereof.

(6) Where it appears to the clerk of the court on which jurisdiction is conferred by the order that the sum or any balance thereof is irrecoverable, he shall so inform the clerk of the court which made the order or, in the case of a second or subsequent order, the clerk of the court which made the first order.

Civil debt: judgment summons

48.—(1) A summons issued on a complaint made for the purposes of section 73 of the Act (in these Rules referred to as a "judgment summons") shall be served on the judgment debtor personally:

Provided that if a justice of the peace is satisfied by evidence on oath that prompt personal service of the summons is impracticable, he may allow the summons to be served in such a way as he may think just.

(2) Unless the judgment debtor appears and consents to an immediate hearing, the court shall not hear the complaint unless the summons was served at least three clear days before the hearing.

(3) Service of a judgment summons outside the county or borough for which the justice issuing the summons acted may, without prejudice to any other provision of these Rules enabling service of a summons to be proved, be proved by affidavit.

Enforcement of affiliation orders, etc.

49.—(1) Subject to the following provisions of this Rule, a complaint for the enforcement of an affiliation order, or an order enforceable as an affiliation order, shall be heard by the court that made the order:

Provided that—

    (*a*) where the complainant is the person in whose favour the order was made and resides in a petty sessions area other than that for which that court acts, and payment is directed to be made to the complainant or to the clerk of a magistrates' court acting for that petty sessions area, the complaint may be heard by the last-mentioned court;

    (*b*) where the complainant is the clerk of a magistrates' court, the complaint may be heard by that court.

(2) Where a complaint is made to a justice of the peace for the enforcement of such an order as aforesaid and it appears to him that the defendant is for the time being in some petty sessions area other than that for which the justice is

acting and that the order may be more conveniently enforced by a magistrates' court acting for that area, the justice shall cause the clerk of the court to send the complaint by post to the clerk of a magistrates' court acting for that other petty sessions area, and for that purpose shall write down the complaint if this has not already been done.

(3) On receipt by the clerk of a magistrates' court of a complaint sent under the last preceding paragraph, he shall bring it before the court; and the court shall issue a summons or warrant for procuring the appearance of the defendant before it, and shall hear and determine the complaint.

(4) If, after a complaint has been sent to the clerk of a magistrates' court under this Rule, the clerk of the court to which the complaint was made receives any payment under the order, he shall forthwith send by post to the clerk to whom the complaint was sent a certificate of the amount of the payment and of the date when it was made.

(5) If, after a complaint has been sent as aforesaid, payment under the order is made, not to the clerk of the court to which the complaint was originally made, but to the person specified in the order, that person shall forthwith inform the clerk of the amount and date as aforesaid and the clerk shall forthwith send a certificate of the amount and date as required by the last preceding paragraph.

(6) A certificate under this Rule purporting to be signed by the clerk of the court to which the complaint was originally made shall be admissible as evidence on the hearing of the complaint that the amount specified in the certificate was paid on the date so specified.

(7) This Rule shall not apply—

(a) where jurisdiction is confined by section 88(2)(a) of the Children and Young Persons Act 1933, to courts having jurisdiction in the place where the person liable is residing;

(b) to a contribution order.

Notice of adjudication on complaint for enforcement of affiliation order, etc.

50. A magistrates' court shall give notice in writing to the complainant of its adjudication on a complaint for the enforcement of an affiliation order, or order enforceable as an affiliation order, unless the complainant is present or is the clerk of the court.

Notice of date of reception in custody and discharge

51.—(1) Where in proceedings to enforce an affiliation order, or an order enforceable as an affiliation order, the defendant is committed to custody, then on his discharge the governor or keeper of the prison or place of detention shall send to the clerk of the court that committed the defendant a certificate showing the dates of the defendant's reception and discharge; and that clerk shall, if the payments under the order are required to be made to the clerk of any other court, send the certificate to the last-mentioned clerk.

(2) Where a magistrates' court issues a warrant of commitment for a default in paying a sum adjudged to be paid by a summary conviction then on the discharge of the defaulter the governor or keeper of the prison or place of detention shall send to the clerk of the court a certificate showing the dates of the defaulter's reception and discharge.

Direction that money found on defaulter shall not be applied in satisfaction of debt

52. Where the defaulter is committed to, or ordered to be detained in, a prison or other place of detention, any direction given under section 68(2) of the Act shall be endorsed on the warrant of commitment.

Particulars of fine enforcement to be entered in register

53.—(1) Where the court on the occasion of convicting an offender of an offence issues a warrant of commitment for a default in paying a sum adjudged to be paid by the conviction or, having power to issue such a warrant, fixes a term of imprisonment under section 65(2) of the Act, the reasons for the court's action shall be entered in the register, or any separate record kept for the purpose of recording particulars of fine enforcement.

(2) There shall be entered in the register, or any such record particulars of any—

    (*a*) means inquiry under section 44 of the Criminal Justice Act 1967;

    (*b*) hearing under subsection (6) of the said section 44;

    (*c*) allowance of further time for the payment of a sum adjudged to be paid by a conviction;

    (*d*) direction that such a sum shall be paid by instalments;

    (*e*) distress for the enforcement of such a sum;

    (*f*) attachment of earnings order for the enforcement of such a sum;

    (*g*) order under the Act placing a person under supervision pending payment of such a sum;

    (*h*) order under subsection (10) of the said section 44 remitting the whole or any part of a fine;

    (*i*) order under section 96(4) of the Act remitting the whole or any part of any sum enforceable under that section (forfeiture of recognizance);

    (*j*) authority granted under section 45(3) of the Criminal Justice Act 1967 authorising the taking of proceedings in the High Court or county court for the recovery of any sum adjudged to be paid by a conviction;

    (*k*) transfer of fine order made by the court;

    (*l*) order transferring a fine to the court;

    (*m*) order under section 47(3) of the Criminal Justice Act 1967 specifying the court for the purpose of enforcing a fine imposed or a recognizance forfeited by a court of assize or quarter sessions; and

    (*n*) any fine imposed or recognizance forfeited by a coroner which has to be treated as imposed or forfeited by the court.

REGISTER

Register of convictions, etc.

54. (1) The clerk of every magistrates' court shall keep a register in which there shall be entered—

    (*a*) a minute or memorandum of every adjudication of the court;

    (*b*) a minute or memorandum of every other proceeding or thing required by these Rules or any other enactment to be so entered.

(2) The register shall be in the prescribed form, and entries in the register shall include, where relevant, such particulars as are provided for in the said form.

(3) On the summary trial of an information the accused's plea shall be entered in the register.

(4) Where a court tries any person summarily in any case in which he may be tried summarily only with his consent, the court shall cause his consent to be entered in the register.

(5) Where a person is charged before a magistrates' court with a summary offence for which he may claim to be tried by a jury, the court shall cause the entry in the register to show whether he was present and whether (if present) he claimed to be tried by a jury.

(6) Where a court has power under section 45(3) of the Act to make an order with the consent of the defendant without hearing evidence, the court shall cause any consent of the defendant to the making of the order to be entered in the register.

(7) The entry in the column of the register headed "Nature of Offence" shall show clearly, in case of conviction or dismissal, what is the offence of which the accused is convicted or, as the case may be, what is the offence charged in the information that is dismissed.

(8) An entry of a conviction in the register shall state the date of the offence.

(9) The entries shall be signed by one of the justices, or the justice, before whom the proceedings to which they relate took place, or by the clerk who was present when those proceedings took place:

Provided that, where the proceedings took place before a justice or justices sitting elsewhere than in a petty sessional court-house, the justice or, as the case may be, one of the justices may instead of signing an entry in the register, send to the clerk whose duty it is to keep the register a signed return of the proceedings containing the particulars required to be entered in the register; and the clerk shall enter the return in the register.

(10) Every register shall be open to inspection during reasonable hours by any justice of the peace, or any person authorised in that behalf by a justice of the peace or the Secretary of State.

EVIDENCE—GENERAL

Proof of service, handwriting, etc.

55.—(1) The service on any person of a summons, process, notice or document required or authorised to be served in any proceedings before a magistrates' court, and the handwriting or seal of a justice of the peace or other person on any warrant, summons, notice, process or documents issued or made in any such proceedings, may be proved in any legal proceedings by a document purporting to be a solemn declaration in the prescribed form made before a justice of the peace, commissioner for oaths, clerk of the peace, clerk of a magistrates' court or registrar of a county court.

(2) The service of any process or other document required or authorised to be served, the proper addressing, pre-paying and posting or registration for the purposes of service of a letter containing such a document, and the place, date and time of posting or registration of any such letter, may be proved in any proceedings before a magistrates' court by a document purporting to be a certificate signed by the person by whom the service was effected or the letter posted or registered.

(3) References in the last preceding paragraph to the service of any process shall, in their application to a witness summons, be construed as including references to the payment or tender to the witness of his costs and expenses.

(4) The last two preceding paragraphs shall apply to proceedings before a court of quarter sessions sitting to hear an appeal from a magistrates' court as they apply to proceedings before a magistrates' court.

Proof of proceedings

56. The register of a magistrates' court, or any document purporting to be an extract from the register and to be certified by the clerk as a true extract, shall be admissible in any legal proceedings as evidence of the proceedings of the court entered in the register.

Proof that affiliation, maintenance orders, etc., have not been revoked, etc.

57. A certificate purporting to be signed by the clerk of a magistrates' court, and stating that no minute or memorandum of an order revoking, discharging, reviving, altering or varying an affiliation order, or order enforceable as an affiliation order, made by the court is entered in the register of the court shall, in any proceedings relating to the enforcement of the order or the revocation, discharge, revival, alteration or variation of the order, be evidence that the order has not been revoked, discharged, revived, altered or varied.

EVIDENCE—CRIMINAL PROCEEDINGS

Written statements in committal proceedings or summary trial

58.—(1) Written statements to be tendered in evidence under section 2 or 9 of the Criminal Justice Act 1967 shall be in the prescribed form.

(2) When a copy of such a statement is given to or served on any party to the proceedings a copy of the statement and of any exhibit which accompanied it shall be given to the clerk of the magistrates' court as soon as practicable thereafter, and where a copy of any such statement is given or served by or on behalf of the prosecutor, the accused shall be given notice of his right to object to the statement being tendered in evidence.

(3) Where before a magistrates' court enquiring into an offence as examining justices the accused objects to a written statement being tendered in evidence and he has been given a copy of the statement but has not given notice of his intention to object to the statement being tendered in evidence, the court shall, if necessary, adjourn to enable the witness to be called.

(4) Where a written statement to be tendered in evidence under the said section 2 or 9 refers to any document or object as an exhibit, that document or object shall wherever possible be identified by means of a label or other mark of identification signed by the maker of the statement, and before a magistrates' court treats any document or object referred to as an exhibit in such a written statement as an exhibit produced and identified in court by the maker of the statement, the court shall be satisfied that the document or object is sufficiently described in the statement for it to be identified.

(5) If it appears to a magistrates' court that any part of a written statement is inadmissible there shall be written against that part "Treated as inadmissible, J.P., an Examining Justice" if the written statement is tendered in evidence under the said section 2, or "Ruled inadmissible, J.P., Justice of the Peace" if the written statement is tendered in evidence under the said section 9.

(6) Where a written statement is tendered in evidence under the said section 2 or 9 before a magistrates' court the name and address of the maker of the statement shall be read aloud unless the court otherwise directs.

(7) Where under subsection (5) of the said section 2 or subsection (6) of the said section 9 in any proceedings before a magistrates' court any part of a written statement has to be read aloud, or an account has to be given orally of so much of any written statement as is not read aloud, the statement shall be read or the account given by or on behalf of the party which has tendered the statement in evidence.

(8) Written statements tendered in evidence under the said section 2 before a magistrates' court acting as examining justices shall be authenticated by a certificate signed by one of the examining justices.

(9) A written statement tendered in evidence under the said section 2 or 9 before a magistrates' court and not sent to a court of assize or quarter sessions under Rule 10, 16 or 17 of these Rules shall be preserved for a period of three years by the clerk of the magistrates' court.

Proof by formal admission

59. Where under section 10 of the Criminal Justice Act 1967 a fact is admitted orally in court by or on behalf of the prosecutor or defendant for the purposes of the summary trial of an offence or proceedings before a magistrates' court acting as examining justices the court shall cause the admission to be written down and signed by or on behalf of the party making the admission.

Proof of previous convictions

60. Service on an accused person of a notice of intention to cite previous convictions under section 3 of the Magistrates' Courts Act 1957(a) may be effected by delivering it to him or by sending it by post in a registered letter or by recorded delivery service addressed to him at his last known or usual place of abode.

Clerk to have copies of documents sent to defendant under Magistrates' Courts Act 1957

61. Where the prosecutor sends to the accused the statement of facts referred to in section 1(1) of the Magistrates' Courts Act 1957 (plea of guilty in absence of accused), he shall send a copy of the statement to the clerk of the magistrates' court.

APPEAL TO QUARTER SESSIONS

Documents to be sent to quarter sessions

62.—(1) A clerk of a magistrates' court shall as soon as practicable send to the clerk of the peace any notice of appeal to quarter sessions given to the clerk of the court.

(2) The clerk of a magistrates' court shall send to the clerk of the peace, with the notice of appeal, a statement of the decision from which the appeal is brought and of the last known or usual place of abode of the parties to the appeal.

(3) Where any person, having given notice of appeal to quarter sessions, has for the purpose of his release from custody entered into a recognizance condi-

---

(a) 1957 c. 29.

tioned for his appearance at the hearing of the appeal, the clerk of the court from whose decision the appeal is brought shall before the day fixed for hearing the appeal send the recognizance to the clerk of the peace.

(4) Where any such recognizance has been entered into otherwise than before the magistrates' court from whose decision the appeal is brought, or the clerk of that court, the person who took the recognizance shall send it forthwith to that clerk.

(5) Where a notice of appeal is given in respect of a hospital order or guardianship order made under section 60 or 61 of the Mental Health Act 1959, the clerk of the magistrates' court from which the appeal is brought shall send with the notice to the clerk of the peace any written evidence considered by the court under paragraph (*a*) of subsection (1) of the said section 60.

(6) Where a notice of appeal is given in respect of an appeal against conviction by a magistrates' court the clerk of the court shall send with the notice to the clerk of the peace any admission of facts made for the purposes of the summary trial under section 10 of the Criminal Justice Act 1967.

Notices for purpose of appeal

63.—(1) A notice of appeal for the purposes of section 84 of the Act shall be in writing and signed by or on behalf of the appellant and shall state the general grounds of appeal.

(2) Any notice of appeal required by the Act to be given to any person may be sent by post in a registered letter or by recorded delivery service addressed to him at his last known or usual place of abode or, if he is the clerk of a court or an officer of the Crown or a local authority, at his office.

Abandonment of appeal

64.—(1) Service on any person of a notice under section 85 of the Act may be effected by delivering it to him or by sending it by post in a registered letter or by recorded delivery service addressed to him at his last known or usual place of abode or, if he is the clerk of a court or an officer of the Crown or a local authority, at his office.

(2) Where notice to abandon an appeal has been given by the appellant, any recognizance conditioned for the appearance of the appellant at the hearing of the appeal shall have effect as if conditioned for the appearance of the appellant before the court from whose decision the appeal was brought at a time and place to be notified to the appellant by the clerk of that court.

CASE STATED

Application to state case

65. An application under section 87(1) of the Act shall be made in writing and shall be delivered to the clerk of the magistrates' court whose decision is questioned, or sent to him by post.

Case stated by two justices on behalf of all

66. A case may be stated on behalf of the justices whose decision is questioned by any two or more of them.

Case to be stated within three months

67. The time within which justices shall state a case shall be three months after the application for the case to be stated.

Contents of case stated

68. A case stated by a magistrates' court shall state the facts found by the court and, unless one of the questions on which the opinion of the High Court is sought is whether there was evidence on which the magistrates' court could come to its decision, shall not contain a statement of the evidence.

RECOGNIZANCE

Recognizance to keep the peace, etc., taken by one court and discharged by another

69. Where a magistrates' court acting for any petty sessions area makes an order under section 92 of the Act discharging a recognizance entered into before a magistrates' court acting for any other petty sessions area, the clerk of the court that orders the recognizance to be discharged shall send a copy of the order of discharge to the clerk of the court acting for that other petty sessions area.

Application to vary order for sureties or dispense with them

70. Where a person has been committed to custody in default of finding sureties and the order to find sureties was made at the instance of another person, an application under section 94 of the Act shall be made by complaint against that other person.

Notice of enlargement of recognizances

71. If a magistrates' court before which any person is bound by a recognizance to appear enlarges the recognizance to a later time under section 106 of the Act in his absence, it shall give him and his sureties, if any, notice thereof.

Recognizances taken before person other than court which fixed them

72.—(1) Where a magistrates' court having jurisdiction to take a recognizance from any person has fixed the amount in which he and his sureties, if any, are to be bound, the recognizances may be entered into before any justice of the peace, or before the clerk of any magistrates' court, or before any police officer not below the rank of inspector, or before the officer in charge of any police station or, if the person to be bound is in a prison or other place of detention, before the governor or keeper of the prison or place.

(2) The clerk of a magistrates' court which has fixed the amount in which any person and his sureties, if any, are to be bound shall issue a certificate in the prescribed form showing the conditions of the recognizance and the amounts in which the principal and the sureties, if any, are to be bound; and a justice of the peace, clerk of a magistrates' court, police officer, governor of a prison or keeper of a place of detention, authorised to take a recognizance under this Rule shall not be required to take it without production of such a certificate as aforesaid.

(3) If any person proposed as a surety for a person committed to custody by a magistrates' court produces to the governor or keeper of the prison or other place of detention in which the person so committed is detained a certificate in the prescribed form signed by any of the justices composing the court or the clerk of the court and signed in the margin by the person proposed as surety, the governor or keeper shall take the recognizance of the person so proposed.

(4) Where the recognizance of any person committed to custody by a justice of the peace, or of that person's sureties, is taken under section 95 of the Act

and this Rule by any person other than the court which committed the first-mentioned person to custody, the person taking the recognizance shall send it to the clerk of that court:

Provided that if the person committed has been committed for trial before a court of assize or quarter sessions the person taking the recognizance shall send it to the proper officer of the court before which the first-mentioned person is to be tried.

Notice to governor of prison, etc., where release from custody is ordered

73. Where a magistrates' court has, with a view to the release on bail of a person in custody, fixed the amount in which he and his sureties, if any, shall be bound—

(*a*) the clerk of the court shall give notice thereof to the governor or keeper of the prison or place where that person is detained by sending him such a certificate as is mentioned in paragraph (2) of the last preceding Rule;

(*b*) any person taking the recognizance of a surety shall send notice thereof by post to the said governor or keeper in the prescribed form and shall give a copy of the notice to the surety.

Release when recognizances have been taken

74. Where a magistrates' court has, with a view to the release on bail of a person in custody for any cause, fixed the amount in which he and his sureties, if any, shall be bound, the governor or keeper of the prison or place where that person is detained, on receiving notice in accordance with these Rules that the amounts of the recognizances have been fixed and, where sureties are required, that the recognizances of the sureties have been taken, shall take the recognizance of that person, if this has not already been done, and, unless he is in custody for some other cause, release him.

Binding over witness under s. 5 of Criminal Procedure (Attendance of Witnesses) Act 1965

75.—(1) A recognizance entered into under section 5 of the Criminal Procedure (Attendance of Witnesses) Act 1965 shall be in the prescribed form and shall be acknowledged by the person entering into the recognizance and signed by the person before whom it is entered into.

(2) Where such a recognizance as aforesaid has been entered into, notice thereof shall be given forthwith to the person bound thereby.

(3) A recognizance taken as aforesaid shall be transmitted as soon as practicable to the proper officer of the court before which the person entering into the recognizance is required by it to appear.

Notification about witness to be sent to court of assize or quarter sessions

76. Where under section 5 of the Criminal Procedure (Attendance of Witnesses) Act 1965 a magistrates' court commits to custody or releases on bail a witness who has been arrested in pursuance of a warrant issued under section 4 of that Act, or the officer in charge of a police station releases such a witness on bail, the clerk of the court or the officer, as the case may be, shall forthwith notify the proper officer of the court of assize or quarter sessions before which the witness is required to be brought or to appear of the action taken in respect of him; or, in a case where the magistrates' court commits the witness in custody to be brought before a judge of the High Court or a commissioner of assize, the clerk of the magistrates' court shall forthwith notify the Master of the Crown Office of the action taken in respect of the witness.

WARRANT

Committal to custody to be by warrant

77. A justice of the peace shall not commit any person to a prison, detention centre, remand home, remand centre or place certified under section 109 of the Act or to the custody of a constable under section 105(5) of the Act except by a warrant of commitment.

Warrant to be signed

78. Except where signature by the clerk of a magistrates' court is permitted by Rule 93 of these Rules or by the Magistrates' Courts (Forms) Rules 1968(a), every warrant under the Act shall be signed by the justice issuing it.

Warrant of arrest

79.—(1) A warrant issued by a justice of the peace for the arrest of any person shall require the persons to whom it is directed, that is to say, the constables of the police area in which the warrant is issued, or any persons named in that behalf in the warrant, to arrest the person against whom the warrant is issued.

(2) The warrant shall name or otherwise describe the person for whose arrest it is issued, and shall contain a statement of the offence charged in the information or, as the case may be, the ground on which the warrant is issued.

Warrant of commitment

80.—(1) A warrant of commitment issued by a justice of the peace—

(a) shall name or otherwise describe the person committed;

(b) shall contain a statement of the offence with which the person committed is charged, or of which he has been convicted, or of any other ground on which he is committed;

(c) shall be directed to a person named in the warrant or to the constables of the police area in which the warrant is issued and to the governor or keeper of the prison or place of detention specified in the warrant, and shall require—

  (i) the named person or the constables to arrest the person committed, if he is at large, and convey him to that prison or place and deliver him with the warrant to the governor or keeper;

  (ii) the governor or keeper to keep in his custody the person committed until that person be delivered in due course of law, or until the happening of an event specified in the warrant, or for the period specified in the warrant, as the case may be.

(2) A warrant of commitment may be executed by conveying the person committed to any prison or place of detention in which he may lawfully be detained and delivering him there together with the warrant; and, so long as any person is detained in any such prison or place other than that specified in the warrant, the warrant shall have effect as if that other prison or place were the prison or place specified in it.

(a) S.I. 1968/1919 (1968 III, p. 5075).

(3) Notwithstanding the preceding provisions of this Rule, a warrant of commitment issued in pursuance of a valid conviction, or of a valid order requiring the person committed to do or abstain from doing anything, shall not, if it alleges that the person committed has been convicted, or ordered to do or abstain from doing that thing, be held void by reason of any defect in the warrant.

(4) The governor or keeper of the prison or place of detention at which any person is delivered in pursuance of a warrant of commitment shall give to the constable or other person making the delivery a receipt for that person.

(5) Notwithstanding the preceding provisions of this Rule, a warrant of a justice of the peace to commit to custody any person who to the justice's knowledge is already detained in a prison or other place of detention shall be delivered to the governor or keeper of the prison or place of detention in which that person is detained.

SUMMONS

Form of summons

81.—(1) A summons shall be signed by the justice issuing it or state his name and be authenticated by the signature of the clerk of a magistrates' court.

(2) A summons requiring a person to appear before a magistrates' court to answer to an information or complaint shall state shortly the matter of the information or complaint and shall state the time and place at which the defendant is required by the summons to appear.

(3) A single summons may be issued against a person in respect of several informations or complaints; but the summons shall state the matter of each information or complaint separately and shall have effect as several summonses, each issued in respect of one information or complaint.

Service of summons, etc.

82.—(1) Service of a summons issued by a justice of the peace on a person other than a corporation may be effected—

(a) by delivering it to the person to whom it is directed; or

(b) by leaving it for him with some person at his last known or usual place of abode; or

(c) by sending it by post in a registered letter or by recorded delivery service addressed to him at his last known or usual place of abode.

(2) If the person summoned fails to appear, service of a summons in manner authorised by sub-paragraph (b) or (c) of the preceding paragraph shall not be treated as proved unless it is proved that the summons came to his knowledge; and for that purpose any letter or other communication purporting to be written by him or on his behalf in such terms as reasonably to justify the inference that the summons came to his knowledge shall be admissible as evidence of that fact:

Provided that this paragraph shall not apply to any summons in respect of a summary offence which is not also an indictable offence.

(3) Service for the purposes of the Act of a summons or other document issued by a justice of the peace on a corporation may be effected by delivering it at, or sending it by post to, the registered office of the corporation, if that office is in England and Wales, or, if there is no registered office in England and Wales, any place in England and Wales where the corporation trades or conducts its business.

(4) Any summons or other document served in manner authorised by the preceding provisions of this Rule shall, for the purposes of any enactment other than the Act or these Rules requiring a summons or other document to be served in any particular manner, be deemed to have been as effectively served as if it had been served in that manner; and nothing in this Rule shall render invalid the service of a summons or other document in that manner.

(5) Sub-paragraph (c) of paragraph (1) of this Rule shall not authorise the service by post of—

(a) a summons requiring the attendance of any person to give evidence or produce a document or thing; or

(b) a summons issued under any enactment relating to the liability of members of the naval, military or air forces of the Crown for the maintenance of their wives and children, whether legitimate or illegitimate;

or authorise a summons to be served outside England and Wales.

(6) Where this Rule or any other of these Rules provides that a summons or other document may be sent by post to a person's last known or usual place of abode that Rule shall have effect as if it provided also for the summons or other document to be sent in the manner specified in the Rule to an address given by that person for that purpose.

(7) This Rule shall not apply to a judgment summons.

Form in which Offence may be stated in Documents

Statement of offence

83.—(1) Every information, summons, warrant or other document laid, issued or made for the purposes of, or in connection with, any proceedings before a magistrates' court for an offence shall be sufficient if it describes the specific offence with which the accused is charged, or of which he is convicted, in ordinary language avoiding as far as possible the use of technical terms and without necessarily stating all the elements of the offence, and gives such particulars as may be necessary for giving reasonable information of the nature of the charge.

(2) If the offence charged is one created by or under any Act, the description of the offence shall contain a reference to the section of the Act, or, as the case may be, the rule, order, regulation, byelaw or other instrument creating the offence.

Miscellaneous

Application for, and notice to be given of, order under s. 106 of Road Traffic Act 1960

84.—(1) An application under section 106 of the Road Traffic Act 1960 for an order removing a disqualification for holding or obtaining a licence shall be by complaint.

(2) The justice to whom the complaint is made shall issue a summons directed to the chief officer of police requiring him to appear before a magistrates' court acting for the petty sessions area for which the justice is acting to show cause why an order should not be made on the complaint.

(3) Where a magistrates' court makes an order under the said section 106 the court shall cause notice of the making of the order and a copy of the particulars of the order endorsed on the licence, if any, previously held by the

applicant for the order to be sent to the council of the county or county borough to which notice of the applicant's disqualification was sent.

Application for revocation of order under s.14 of Food and Drugs Act 1955

85.—(1) An application under section 14(4) of the Food and Drugs Act 1955(**a**) for the revocation of an order under that section disqualifying a person from using particular premises as catering premises shall be by complaint.

(2) The justice to whom the complaint is made shall issue a summons directed to the local authority upon whose application the disqualification order was made, requiring the local authority to show cause why the disqualification should not be revoked.

Application for substitution of conditional discharge for probation

86. An application to a magistrates' court under section 53 of the Criminal Justice Act 1967 for the substitution of an order of conditional discharge for a probation order shall be by complaint.

Application for alteration of maintenance agreement under s.24 of Matrimonial Causes Act 1965

87. An application to a magistrates' court under section 24 of the Matrimonial Causes Act 1965(**b**) for the alteration of a maintenance agreement shall be by complaint.

Application for summons to witness or warrant for his arrest

88.—(1) An application for the issue of a summons or warrant under section 77 of the Act may be made by the applicant in person or by his counsel or solicitor.

(2) An application for the issue of such a summons may be made by delivering or sending the application in writing to the clerk to the magistrates' court for submission to a justice of the peace.

Forms

89. Any requirement in these Rules that a document shall be in the prescribed form shall be construed as a requirement that the document shall be in the form prescribed in that behalf by rules made under section 15 of the Justices of the Peace Act 1949, or a form to like effect.

Saving for the Summary Jurisdiction (Children and Young Persons) Rules 1933

90. The provisions of these Rules shall have effect subject to the Summary Jurisdiction (Children and Young Persons) Rules 1933(**c**) as amended(**d**).

Application of other rules or instruments

91. Any reference in any rules or other instrument made under any enactment to a provision of the Magistrates' Courts Rules 1952(**e**) or the Magistrates' Courts (Forms) Rules 1952(**f**) shall be construed, where appropriate, as a reference to the corresponding provision of these Rules or the Magistrates' Courts (Forms) Rules 1968.

(**a**) 4 & 5 Eliz. 2. c. 16.   (**b**) 1965 c. 72.
(**c**) S.R. & O. 1933/819 (Rev. XI, p.573: 1933, p.959).
(**d**) The amending instruments are S.R. & O. 1938/1201 (Rev. XI, p. 613: 1938 I, p.1611); S.I. 1950/827, 1953/417, 1961/1421, 1962/1591, 1963/1262, 2120, 1967/1660 (1950 II, p. 887; 1953 I, p. 927; 1961 II, p. 2818; 1962 II, p. 1844; 1963 II, p. 2104; III, p. 4703; 1967 III, p. 4519).
(**e**) S.I. 1952/2190 (1952 II, p.1593).   (**f**) S.I. 1952/2191 (1952 II, p.1619).

Construction of references to registered post in rules made before 1961 *under Justices of the Peace Act* 1949

92. Any references in rules made before 13th February 1961 and made or having effect as if made under section 15 of the Justices of the Peace Act 1949 to registered post, a registered letter or the registration of a letter shall be construed as including a reference to the recorded delivery service, a letter sent by that service and the acceptance by an officer of the Post Office of a letter for recorded delivery, respectively.

Signature of forms prescribed by rules made under Justices of the Peace Act 1949

93.—(1) Subject to paragraph (2) of this Rule, where any form prescribed by rules made or having effect as if made under section 15 of the Justices of the Peace Act 1949 contains provision for signature by a justice of the peace only, the form shall have effect as if it contained provision in the alternative for signature by the clerk of a magistrates' court.

(2) This Rule shall not apply to any form of warrant, other than a warrant of commitment or of distress, or to any form prescribed in the Magistrates' Courts (Forms) Rules 1968.

Interpretation

94.—(1) In these Rules "the Act" means the Magistrates' Courts Act 1952, "contribution order" has the meaning assigned to it by section 87 of the Children and Young Persons Act 1933, "judgment summons" has the meaning assigned to it by Rule 47 and other expressions have the same meaning as in the Act.

(2) The Interpretation Act 1889(a) shall apply to the interpretation of these Rules as it applies to the interpretation of an Act of Parliament.

Revocation of previous Rules

95. The Rules mentioned in the Schedule to these Rules are hereby revoked.

Citation and commencement

96. These Rules may be cited as the Magistrates' Courts Rules 1968 and shall come into operation on 1st March 1969.

Dated 27th November 1968.

Gardiner, C.

(a) 1889 c. 63.

SCHEDULE   Rule 95

RULES REVOKED

Rules	References
The Magistrates' Courts Rules 1952	S.I. 1952/2190 (1952 II, p. 1593).
The Magistrates' Courts (Forms) Rules 1952	S.I. 1952/2191 (1952 II, p. 1619).
The Magistrates' Courts Rules 1957	S.I. 1957/1429 (1957 I, p. 1349).
The Magistrates' Courts Rules 1960	S.I. 1960/1431 (1960 II, p. 1867).
The Magistrates' Courts Rules 1961	S.I. 1961/169 (1961 I, p. 284).
The Magistrates' Courts (Forms) Rules 1962	S.I. 1962/1592 (1962 II, p. 1852).
The Magistrates' Courts (Forms) Rules 1963	S.I. 1963/1263 (1963 II, p. 2109).
The Magistrates' Courts Rules 1963	S.I. 1963/2121 (1963 III, p. 4719).
The Magistrates' Courts Rules 1964	S.I. 1964/168 (1964 I, p. 296).
The Magistrates' Courts (No. 2) Rules 1964	S.I. 1964/889 (1964 II, p. 1905).
The Magistrates' Courts (No. 3) Rules 1964	S.I. 1964/1842 (1964 III, p. 4007).
The Magistrates' Courts (Forms) Rules 1965	S.I. 1965/1601 (1965 II, p. 4608).
The Magistrates' Courts Rules 1965	S.I. 1965/1602 (1965 II, p. 4616).
The Magistrates' Courts Rules 1967	S.I. 1967/1661 (1967 III, p. 4521).

EXPLANATORY NOTE

(This Note is not part of the Rules.)

These Rules consolidate, with some amendments and additions, the various Rules relating to procedure in magistrates' courts contained in the Schedule. The most important amendments or additions are as follows.

In Rule 4(7) the caution addressed to an accused in committal proceedings has been simplified.

In Rules 13 and 14 the procedure relating to speeches by prosecutor and accused or defendant has been clarified and Rule 14 permits the complainant and defendant in civil proceedings to make a second speech with leave of the court. Where leave is granted to one, it is not to be refused to the other.

Rule 28 is new and provides for the matters to be included in the endorsement of a driving licence.

Rule 34 provides for applications for the revocation, variation, etc. of orders for periodical payments to be made to the court enforcing the order where that is not the court which made the original order, though the case may be referred to the original court in appropriate circumstances.

Rule 37 requires a court, before remitting any sums due under an order, to give an opportunity to the person in whose favour the order is made to make representations.

Rule 93 empowers justices' clerks to sign certain prescribed forms which hitherto could be signed only by a justice.

1968 No. 1921

DEFENCE

The Rules of Procedure (Air Force) (Second Amendment) Rules 1968

Made - - - -	*2nd December* 1968
Laid before Parliament	*10th December* 1968
Coming into Operation	*1st January* 1969

The Secretary of State in exercise of the powers conferred upon him by sections 103, 104, 105 and 106 of the Air Force Act 1955(a) and of all other powers enabling him in that behalf hereby makes the following Rules:—

Citation and Commencement

1. These Rules may be cited as the Rules of Procedure (Air Force) (Second Amendment) Rules 1968 and shall come into operation on the 1st January 1969.

Interpretation

2. The Interpretation Act 1889(b) shall apply to the interpretation of these Rules as it applies to an Act of Parliament.

Amendment to the Rules of Procedure (Air Force) 1956

3.—(1) The Rules of Procedure (Air Force) 1956(c), as amended (d), shall be further amended in accordance with the following provisions of this Rule.

(2) In Part (2) of the Second Schedule (Statements of Offences—Air Force Act 1955):—

(*a*) for the detail under Section 44(1)(*b*) there shall be substituted:—

"Handling stolen goods contrary to section 44(1)(*b*) of the Air Force Act, 1955"

(*b*) for the detail under Section 45(*b*) there shall be substituted:—

"Handling stolen goods contrary to section 45(*b*) of the Air Force Act, 1955".

(a) 1955 c. 19.   (b) 1889 c. 63.   (c) S.I. 1956/163 (1956 II, p. 2020).
(d) The relevant amending instruments are S.I. 1967/62, 1967/1466 (1967 I, p. 118; 1967 III, p. 4149).

(3) In Part (3) of the Second Schedule (Illustrations of Charge-Sheets) for Illustration (i) there shall be substituted the following:—

"CHARGE-SHEET

The accused, No 153 Leading Aircraftman John Smith of No 2 Squadron, Royal Air Force Station Andover, an airman of the regular air-force, is charged with:—

1st charge

STEALING PUBLIC PROPERTY CONTRARY TO SECTION 44(1)(a) OF THE AIR FORCE ACT 1955

in that he

at Uxbridge on 1st January, 1969 stole a pair of binoculars, public property.

2nd charge (alternative to the 1st charge)

HANDLING STOLEN GOODS CONTRARY TO SECTION 44(1)(b) OF THE AIR FORCE ACT, 1955

in that he

at Uxbridge on 1st January, 1969, knowing or believing a pair of binoculars, stolen public property, to be stolen, dishonestly received them.

Andover
7th January, 1969

A. B. JONES, Group Captain,
Commanding Royal Air Force Station,
Andover

To be tried by District Court-Martial

Leeds
9th January, 1969"

C. D. BROWN, Air Vice-Marshal
Commanding No 06 Group

Denis Healey,
One of Her Majesty's Principal
Secretaries of State.

Dated 2nd December 1968.

EXPLANATORY NOTE
(*This Note is not part of the Rules.*)

These Rules amend the Rules of Procedure (Air Force) 1956 to take account of the amendments to sections 44(1)(b) and 45(b) of the Air Force Act 1955 effected by the Theft Act 1968 in substituting in these sections references to handling stolen goods for the references to receiving stolen property.

STATUTORY INSTRUMENTS

1968 No. 1922 (C.27)

CLEAN AIR

The Clean Air Act 1968 (Commencement No. 1) Order 1968

Made - - - *2nd December* 1968

The Minister of Housing and Local Government, in exercise of the powers conferred on him by section 15(3) of the Clean Air Act 1968(a), and of all other powers enabling him in that behalf, hereby orders as follows:—

1. This order may be cited as the Clean Air Act 1968 (Commencement No. 1) Order 1968.

2. The appointed day for the coming into force of the provisions of the Clean Air Act 1968 specified in the Schedule to this order in their application to England and Wales shall be 1st April 1969.

SCHEDULE

Provisions of the Act	Subject matter of provisions
Section 2	Emission of grit and dust from furnaces.
Section 6	Height of chimneys.
Section 8	Power of appropriate Minister to require creation of smoke control areas.
Section 9	Acquisition and sale of unauthorised fuel in a smoke control area.
Section 10	Miscellaneous amendments of procedure for making orders with respect to smoke control areas.
Section 11	Relation of Clean Air Acts to, and amendment of, Alkali Act.
Section 12	Regulations.
Section 13	Interpretation.
Section 14(1) and paragraphs 1, 3, 4, 6, 7, 10 and 12 of Schedule 1, except so far as any of those paragraphs refer to sections 1 and 3 to 5	Adaptation and minor and consequential amendments of principal Act, and repeals.
Section 14(2) and Schedule 2	
Section 14(3)	
Section 15	Short title, citation, commencement and extent.

Given under the official seal of the Minister of Housing and Local Government on 2nd December 1968.

(L.S.)

Anthony Greenwood,

Minister of Housing and
Local Government.

(a) 1968 c. 62.

EXPLANATORY NOTE

(This Note is not part of the Order.)

This Order appoints 1st April 1969 as the appointed day for the coming into force of the provisions of the Clean Air Act 1968 listed in the schedule to the Order.

STATUTORY INSTRUMENTS

1968 No. 1925

FACTORIES

The Baking and Sausage Making (Christmas and New Year) Order 1968

Made	-	-	-	*2nd December* 1968
Coming into Operation			*11th December* 1968

The Secretary of State by virtue of her powers under section 117 of the Factories Act 1961(**a**) and of all other powers enabling her in that behalf, hereby makes the following special exemption order :—

1. This Order may be cited as the Baking and Sausage Making (Christmas and New Year) Order 1968 and shall come into operation on 11th December 1968.

2.—(1) The Interpretation Act 1889(**b**) shall apply to the interpretation of this Order as it applies to the interpretation of an Act of Parliament.

(2) In this Order "women" means women who have attained the age of eighteen.

3. The employment of women in England and Wales—

(*a*) on Saturdays, 21st and 28th December 1968, and on Sundays, 22nd and 29th December 1968, in the manufacture of meat pies, sausages or cooked meats, or in the pre-packing of bacon ; and

(*b*) on Saturdays, 14th and 21st December 1968, and on Sundays, 15th and 22nd December 1968, in the manufacture of bread or flour confectionery (including fruit pies but not biscuits),

or in work incidental or ancillary to such work, is hereby exempted from the provisions of section 86(*b*) of the Factories Act 1961 (so far as that paragraph prohibits the employment of women after one o'clock in the afternoon on Saturday) and from the provisions of section 93 of that Act (which relates to the prohibition of Sunday employment).

4. The employment of women in Scotland—

(*a*) on Saturdays, 21st and 28th December 1968, and on Sundays, 22nd and 29th December 1968, in the manufacture of meat pies, sausages or cooked meats, or in the pre-packing of bacon ; and

(*b*) on Sundays, 22nd and 29th December 1968, in the manufacture of bread or flour confectionery (including fruit pies but not biscuits),

---

(**a**) 1961 c. 34.   (**b**) 1889 c. 63.

or in work incidental or ancillary to such work, is hereby exempted from the provisions of the said section 86(*b*) (so far as that paragraph prohibits the employment of women after one o'clock in the afternoon on Saturday) and from the provisions of the said section 93.

Signed by order of the Secretary of State.

2nd December 1968.

K. Barnes,
Deputy Under Secretary of State,
Department of Employment and Productivity.

EXPLANATORY NOTE

(This Note is not part of the Order.)

This Order enables women who have attained the age of eighteen to be employed in England and Wales on the afternoons of Saturdays, 21st and 28th December 1968, and on Sundays, 22nd and 29th December 1968, in the manufacture of meat pies, sausages or cooked meats, or in the pre-packing of bacon, and on the afternoons of Saturdays, 14th and 21st December 1968, and on Sundays, 15th and 22nd December 1968, in the manufacture of bread or flour confectionery (including fruit pies but not biscuits).

The Order also enables women who have attained the age of eighteen to be employed in Scotland on the afternoons of Saturdays, 21st and 28th December 1968, and on Sundays, 22nd and 29th December 1968, in the manufacture of meat pies, sausages or cooked meats, or in the pre-packing of bacon, and on Sundays, 22nd and 29th December 1968, in the manufacture of bread or flour confectionery (including fruit pies but not biscuits).

STATUTORY INSTRUMENTS

1968 No. 1926

WAGES COUNCILS

The Wages Regulation (Ostrich and Fancy Feather and Artificial Flower) Order 1968

Made - - -	*2nd December* 1968
Coming into Operation	*1st January* 1969

Whereas the Secretary of State has received from the Ostrich and Fancy Feather and Artificial Flower Wages Council (Great Britain) the wages regulation proposals set out in the Schedule hereto ;

Now, therefore, the Secretary of State in exercise of her powers under section 11 of the Wages Councils Act 1959(**a**), and of all other powers enabling her in that behalf, hereby makes the following Order :—

1. This Order may be cited as the Wages Regulation (Ostrich and Fancy Feather and Artificial Flower) Order 1968.

2.—(1) In this Order the expression "the specified date" means the 1st January 1969, provided that where, as respects any worker who is paid wages at intervals not exceeding seven days, that date does not correspond with the beginning of the period for which the wages are paid, the expression "the specified date" means, as respects that worker, the beginning of the next such period following that date.

(2) The Interpretation Act 1889(**b**) shall apply to the interpretation of this Order as it applies to the interpretation of an Act of Parliament and as if this Order and the Orders hereby revoked were Acts of Parliament.

3. The wages regulation proposals set out in the Schedule hereto shall have effect as from the specified date and as from that date the Wages Regulation (Ostrich and Fancy Feather and Artificial Flower) Order 1966(**c**) as amended by the Wages Regulation (Ostrich and Fancy Feather and Artificial Flower) (Amendment) Order 1968(**d**) shall cease to have effect.

Signed by order of the Secretary of State.

2nd December 1968.

A. A. Jarratt,
Deputy Under Secretary of State,
Department of Employment and Productivity.

(**a**) 1959 c. 69. (**b**) 1889 c. 63.
(**c**) S.I. 1966/43 (1966 I, p.68). (**d**) S.I. 1968/4 (1968 I, p. 1).

Article 3   SCHEDULE

The following minimum remuneration shall be substituted for the statutory minimum remuneration set out in the Wages Regulation (Ostrich and Fancy Feather and Artificial Flower) Order 1966 (Order O.F. (36)), as amended by the Wages Regulation (Ostrich and Fancy Feather and Artificial Flower) (Amendment) Order 1968 (Order O.F. (39)).

STATUTORY MINIMUM REMUNERATION

PART I

GENERAL

1. The minimum remuneration payable to a worker to whom this Schedule applies for all work except work to which a minimum overtime rate applies under Part III is:—

    (1) in the case of a time worker, the hourly general minimum time rate payable to the worker under Part II of this Schedule;

    (2) in the case of a worker employed on piece work, piece rates each of which would yield, in the circumstances of the case, to an ordinary worker at least the same amount of money as the piece work basis time rate applicable to the worker under Part II of this Schedule.

PART II

GENERAL MINIMUM TIME RATES

FEMALE WORKERS

2. The general minimum time rates payable to female workers are as follows:—

    (1) Up to and including 31st December 1969

	Age of worker on first entering the trade						
	Under 15½ years	15½ and under 16 years	16 and under 16½ years	16½ and under 17 years	17 and under 17½ years	17½ and under 18 years	18 years or over
Aged—	Per hour s. d.	Per hour s. d.	Per hour s. d.	Per hour s. d.	Per hour s. d.	Per hour s. d.	Per hour s. d.
15 and under 15½ years	1 11¼	—	—	—	—	—	—
15½ „ „ 16 „	2 0¾	1 11¼	—	—	—	—	—
16 „ „ 16½ „	2 5¼	2 2¾	2 0¾	—	—	—	—
16½ „ „ 17 „	2 8½	2 8½	2 5¼	2 5¼	—	—	—
17 „ „ 17½ „	3 0	3 0	2 9½	2 9½	2 9½	—	—
17½ „ „ 18 „	3 3	3 3	3 1	2 11	2 11	2 9½	—
18 „ „ 18½ „	3 6	3 6	3 6	3 6	3 6	3 6	3 4½
18½ years or over	3 6	3 6	3 6	3 6	3 6	3 6	3 6

(2) On and after 1st January 1970

	Age of worker on first entering the trade						
	Under 15½ years	15½ and under 16 years	16 and under 16½ years	16½ and under 17 years	17 and under 17½ years	17½ and under 18 years	18 years or over
	Per hour s. d.	Per hour s. d.	Per hour s. d.	Per hour s. d.	Per hour s. d.	Per hour s. d.	Per hour s. d.
Aged—							
15 and under 15½ years	1 11¾	—	—	—	—	—	—
15½ " " 16 "	2 1¼	1 11¾	—	—	—	—	—
16 " " 16½ "	2 6	2 3½	2 1¼	—	—	—	—
16½ " " 17 "	2 9¼	2 9¼	2 6	2 6	—	—	—
17 " " 17½ "	3 0¾	3 0¾	2 10¼	2 10¼	2 10¼	—	—
17½ " " 18 "	3 4	3 4	3 2	2 11¾	2 11¾	2 10¼	—
18 " " 18½ "	3 7¼	3 7¼	3 7¼	3 7¼	3 7¼	3 7¼	3 5½
18½ years or over	3 7¼	3 7¼	3 7¼	3 7¼	3 7¼	3 7¼	3 7¼

MALE WORKERS

3. The general minimum time rates payable to male workers are as follows:—

Aged—	Up to and including 31st December 1969 Per hour s. d.	On and after 1st January 1970 Per hour s. d.
21 years or over	5 1½	5 3
20 and under 21 years	4 8	4 9¼
19 " " 20 "	4 1¼	4 2½
18 " " 19 "	3 8¾	3 9¾
17½ " " 18 "	3 6	3 7¼
17 " " 17½ "	3 4	3 5
16½ " " 17 "	3 0	3 0¾
16 " " 16½ "	2 9½	2 10¼
15½ " " 16 "	2 4¾	2 5½
under 15½ years	2 3¼	2 4

PIECE WORK BASIS TIME RATE

MALE OR FEMALE WORKERS

4. The piece work basis time rate applicable to all workers, male or female (including homeworkers), employed on piece work shall be a rate equal to the general minimum time rate which would be payable if the worker were a time worker, increased by 12½ per cent.

PART III

OVERTIME AND WAITING TIME

NORMAL NUMBER OF HOURS

5. Subject to the provisions of this Part of this Schedule the minimum overtime rates set out in paragraph 6 are payable to any worker in respect of any time worked:—

    (1) in excess of the hours following, that is to say:

        (a) (i) *in any week up to and including 31st December 1969*   ...   *41 hours*

            (ii) *in any week on and after 1st January 1970*   ...   ...   *40 hours*

(b) on any day other than a Saturday, Sunday or customary holiday—where the normal working hours exceed 8½ ... 9 hour

or

where the normal working hours are not more than 8½ ... 8½ hour~

or on and after 1st January 1970 where the normal working hours are not more than 8 ... ... *8 hours*

(2) on a Saturday, Sunday or customary holiday.

MINIMUM OVERTIME RATES

6. Minimum overtime rates are payable to any worker as follows:—

(1) on any day other than a Sunday or customary holiday—

    (a) for the first 2 hours of overtime worked ... ... time-and-a-quarter

    (b) for the next 2 hours ... ... time-and-a-half

    (c) thereafter ... ... double time

(2) on a Sunday or customary holiday—
for all time worked ... ... double time

(3)(a) *up to and including 31st December 1969*

in any week, exclusive of any time in respect of which any minimum overtime rate is payable under the foregoing provisions of this paragraph—

for all time worked in excess of *41 hours* ... time-and-a-quarter

(b) *on and after 1st January 1970*

in any week, exclusive of any time in respect of which any minimum overtime rate is payable under the foregoing provisions of this paragraph—

for all time worked in excess of 40 hours ... ... *time-and-a-quarter*

Provided that where it is the practice in a Jewish undertaking for the employer to require attendance on Sunday instead of Saturday the provisions of this paragraph shall apply as if in such provisions the word "Saturday" were substituted for "Sunday" except where such substitution is unlawful.

7. In this Part of this Schedule—

(1) the expression "customary holiday" means:—

    (a)   (i) in England and Wales—

Christmas Day (or, if Christmas Day falls on a Sunday, such week day as may be appointed by national proclamation, or, if none is so appointed, the next following Tuesday), Boxing Day, Good Friday, Easter Monday, Whit Monday and August Bank Holiday;

        (ii) in Scotland—

New Year's Day (or, if New Year's Day falls on a Sunday, the following Monday);

the local Spring holiday;

the local Autumn holiday; and

three other days (being days on which the worker normally works for the employer) in the course of a calendar year to be fixed by the employer and notified to the worker not less than three weeks before the holiday;

or (b) in the case of each of the said days (other than a day fixed by the employer in Scotland and notified to the worker as aforesaid) a day substituted therefor by the employer, being a day recognised by local custom as a day of holiday in substitution for the said day.

(2) The expressions "time-and-a-quarter", "time-and-a-half" and "double time" mean respectively:—

(*a*) in the case of a time worker, one and a quarter times, one and a half times and twice the hourly general minimum time rate otherwise applicable to the worker;

(*b*) in the case of a worker employed on piece work—

(i) a time rate equal respectively to one-quarter, one-half and the whole of the piece work basis time rate otherwise applicable to the worker, and, in addition thereto,

(ii) the piece rates otherwise applicable to the worker under paragraph 1(2).

WAITING TIME

8.—(1) A worker is entitled to payment of the minimum remuneration specified in this Schedule for all time during which he is present on the premises of his employer unless he is present thereon in any of the following circumstances:—

(*a*) without the employer's consent, express or implied;

(*b*) for some purpose unconnected with his work and other than that of waiting for work to be given to him to perform;

(*c*) by reason only of the fact that he is resident thereon;

(*d*) during normal meal times in a room or place in which no work is being done, and he is not waiting for work to be given to him to perform.

(2) The minimum remuneration payable under sub-paragraph (1) of this paragraph to a piece worker when not engaged on piece work is that which would be applicable if he were a time worker.

PART IV

INTERPRETATION

9. In this Schedule—

(1) the expression "homeworker" means a female worker who works in her own home or any other place not under the control or management of the employer.

(2) "the trade" means the ostrich and fancy feather and artificial flower trade.

PART V

APPLICABILITY OF STATUTORY MINIMUM REMUNERATION

10. This Schedule does not apply to male workers employed as dyers in the Feather Trade but save as aforesaid, this Schedule applies to workers in relation to whom the Ostrich and Fancy Feather and Artificial Flower Wages Council (Great Britain) operates, that is to say, workers employed in Great Britain in the Ostrich and Fancy Feather and Artificial Flower trade as specified in the Schedule to the Regulations made by the Minister of Labour, dated 3rd February 1921, with respect to the constitution and proceedings of the Trade Board for the Ostrich and Fancy Feather and Artificial Flower Trade (Great Britain)(a), which Schedule reads as follows:—

"The Ostrich and Fancy Feather and Artificial Flower Trade, that is to say:—

1. The preparation throughout of ostrich or fancy feathers from the natural condition to the finished feather product.

2. The making of artificial flowers, fruit, foliage, grasses, mosses, seeds or pods from paper, wax, textile materials, porcelain, glass, plaster, metal composition, rubber, leather, raffia, celiphane and similar materials.

3. The preservation of natural flowers, foliage, grasses, mosses, ferns, seeds or pods.

4. The making of hats of any of the articles specified in paragraphs 1, 2 and 3 above, when made in or in association with or in conjunction with any business or establishment or branch or department or workroom mainly engaged in any of the operations specified in those paragraphs.

5. The making of feather garments (including neckwear and muffs), feather trimmings for dresses, feather fans or feather mountings of any description, when made in or in association with or in conjunction with any business or establishment or branch or department or workroom mainly engaged in the preparation of ostrich or fancy feathers.

6. The cleaning, dyeing or renovating of any of the articles specified in paragraphs 1, 2 and 3 above, when carried on as a main business or in association with or in conjunction with any business or establishment or branch or department or workroom mainly engaged in any of the operations specified in these paragraphs.

Including:—

7. A. Any of the following and similar operations or processes known in the trade as:—

   (i) The sorting, stringing, washing, bleaching, dyeing, beating, scraping, laying-up, sewing, curling, finishing, sticking, twisting, mounting of ostrich or fancy feathers;

   (ii) Pattern-making, dyeing, stiffening, waterproofing, waxing, cutting, stamping, shading, veining, goffing, mould making, mounting, in connection with the manufacture of artificial flowers, fruits, foliage, grasses, mosses, seeds or pods;

   (iii) The dyeing, preserving, painting, varnishing or decorating of natural flowers, foliage, grasses, mosses, ferns, seeds or pods.

B. The making of any of the articles specified in paragraph 2 above by needle-work processes, when carried on in or in association with or in conjunction with a business or establishment or branch or department or workroom mainly engaged in any of the operations specified in that paragraph.

C. The making or mounting of any of the articles specified in paragraphs 1, 2 and 3 above for cakes or cracker ornaments, except when made or mounted in or in association with or in conjunction with an establishment or business or branch or department or workroom which is mainly engaged in the making of crackers.

D. The mounting (whether singly or in festoons or garlands) or assembling of any of the articles specified in paragraphs 1, 2 and 3 above for the purpose of decoration, when mounted or assembled in a business or establishment or branch or department or workroom mainly engaged in these operations.

E. The warehousing of, the packing of, and similar operations in regard to any of the articles specified in paragraphs 1 to 5 above when carried on in or in association with or in conjunction with a business or establishment or branch or department or workroom mainly engaged in any of the operations specified in paragraphs 1 to 6 above.

But excluding:—

8. A. The making of any of the articles mentioned in paragraph 2 above in a business or establishment or branch or department or workroom which is mainly engaged in the manufacture of the materials specified in that paragraph, and not of the articles therein specified.

B. The preparation, making or preservation of any of the articles specified in paragraphs 1, 2 and 3 above, when carried out in a business or establishment or branch or department or workroom mainly engaged in the manufacture of stationers' sundries.

C. The stiffening or preparation of textile materials for the making of any of the articles mentioned in paragraph 2 above, when carried on in a business or establishment or branch or department or workroom mainly engaged in the preparation of textile materials for other purposes.

D. The making of any of the articles specified in paragraph 2 above wholly from metal, or the mounting thereof when so made or the making or mounting of plaster flowers, fruits or foliage, except when made or mounted:—

    (i) For funeral tokens, wreaths or crosses.

    (ii) In association with, or in conjunction with the making of any of the articles specified in paragraph 2, from any of the materials specified therein.

    (iii) For cake or cracker ornaments as specifically mentioned in the operations and processes included in the trade.

E. The making from rubber of any of the articles mentioned in paragraph 2 above, or the mounting thereof when so made, where carried on in or in association with or in conjunction with a business or establishment or branch or department or workroom mainly engaged in the manufacture of other rubber articles.

F. All operations covered by the following orders:—

    (i) The Trade Boards (Sugar Confectionery and Food Preserving) Order, 1913**(a)**.

    (ii) The Trade Boards (Hat, Cap and Millinery) Order, 1919**(b)**.

    (iii) The Trade Boards (Women's Clothing) Order, 1919**(c)**.

    (iv) The Trade Boards (Toy) Order, 1920**(d)**."

EXPLANATORY NOTE

(This Note is not part of the Order.)

This Order, which has effect from 1st January 1969, sets out the statutory minimum remuneration payable in substitution for that fixed by the Wages Regulation (Ostrich and Fancy Feather and Artificial Flower) Order 1966 (Order O.F. (36)) as amended by the Wages Regulation (Ostrich and Fancy Feather and Artificial Flower) (Amendment) Order 1968 (Order O.F. (39)), which Orders are revoked.

New provisions are printed in italics.

(a) Confirmed by 3 & 4 Geo. 5. c. clxii.   (b) S.R. & O. 1919/1262 (1919 II, p. 515).
(c) S.R. & O. 1919/1263 (1919 II, p. 531).   (d) S.R. & O. 1920/470 (1920 II, p. 792).

STATUTORY INSTRUMENTS

1968 No. 1927

WAGES COUNCILS

The Wages Regulation (Ostrich and Fancy Feather and Artificial Flower) (Holidays) Order 1968

Made	-	-	-	*2nd December* 1968
Coming into Operation				*1st January* 1969

Whereas the Secretary of State has received from the Ostrich and Fancy Feather and Artificial Flower Wages Council (Great Britain) the wages regulation proposals set out in the Schedule hereto ;

Now, therefore, the Secretary of State in exercise of her powers under section 11 of the Wages Councils Act 1959(a), and of all other powers enabling her in that behalf, hereby makes the following Order :—

1. This Order may be cited as the Wages Regulation (Ostrich and Fancy Feather and Artificial Flower) (Holidays) Order 1968.

2.—(1) In this Order the expression "the specified date" means the 1st January 1969, provided that where, as respects any worker who is paid wages at intervals not exceeding seven days, that date does not correspond with the beginning of the period for which the wages are paid, the expression "the specified date" means, as respects that worker, the beginning of the next such period following that date.

(2) The Interpretation Act 1889(b) shall apply to the interpretation of this Order as it applies to the interpretation of an Act of Parliament and as if this Order and the Order hereby revoked were Acts of Parliament.

3. The wages regulation proposals set out in the Schedule hereto shall have effect as from the specified date and as from that date the Wages Regulation (Ostrich and Fancy Feather and Artificial Flower) (Holidays) Order 1966(c) shall cease to have effect.

Signed by order of the Secretary of State.
2nd December 1968.

A. A. Jarratt,

Deputy Under Secretary of State,
Department of Employment and Productivity.

(a) 1959 c. 69.   (b) 1889 c. 63.
(c) S.I. 1966/44 (1966 I, p. 75).

SCHEDULE   Article 3

The following provisions as to holidays and holiday remuneration shall be substituted for the provisions as to holidays and holiday remuneration set out in the Wages Regulation (Ostrich and Fancy Feather and Artificial Flower) (Holidays) Order 1966 (hereinafter referred to as "Order O.F.(37)").

PART I

APPLICATION

1.—(1) This Schedule applies to every worker (other than a homeworker) for whom statutory minimum remuneration has been fixed.

(2) For the purposes of this Schedule a homeworker is a worker who works in his own home or in any other place not under the control or management of the employer.

PART II

CUSTOMARY HOLIDAYS

2.—(1) An employer shall allow to every worker to whom this Schedule applies a holiday (hereinafter referred to as a "customary holiday") in each year on the days specified in the following sub-paragraph provided that the worker has been in his employment for a period of not less than two weeks immediately preceding the customary holiday and (unless excused by the employer or absent by reason of the proved illness of the worker) has worked for the employer throughout the last working day on which work was available to him immediately preceding the customary holiday.

(2) The said customary holidays are:—

  (a) (i) in England and Wales—

Christmas Day (or, if Christmas Day falls on a Sunday, such week day as may be appointed by national proclamation, or, if none is so appointed, the next following Tuesday), Boxing Day, Good Friday, Easter Monday, Whit Monday and August Bank Holiday.

   (ii) in Scotland—
New Year's Day (or, if New Year's Day falls on a Sunday, the following Monday);
the local Spring holiday;
the local Autumn holiday; and
three other days (being days on which the worker normally works for the employer) in the course of a calendar year to be fixed by the employer and notified to the worker not less than three weeks before the holiday;

  or (b) in the case of each of the said days (other than a day fixed by the employer in Scotland and notified to the worker as aforesaid) a day substituted by the employer therefor, being a day recognised by local custom as a day of holiday in substitution for the said day.

(3) Notwithstanding the preceding provisions of this paragraph, an employer may (except where in the case of a woman or young person such a requirement would be unlawful) require a worker who is otherwise entitled to any customary holiday under the foregoing provisions of this Schedule to work thereon and, in lieu of any holiday on which he so works, the employer shall allow to the worker a day's holiday (hereinafter referred to as a "holiday in lieu of a customary holiday") on a week day on which he would normally work for the employer, within the period of eight weeks next ensuing.

(4) A worker who is required to work on a customary holiday shall be paid:—

> (*a*) for all time worked thereon, the statutory minimum remuneration then appropriate to the worker for work on a customary holiday; and

> (*b*) in respect of the holiday in lieu of the customary holiday, holiday remuneration in accordance with paragraph 6.

PART III

ANNUAL HOLIDAY

3.—(1) Subject to the provisions of this paragraph and of paragraph 4, in addition to the holidays specified in Part II of this Schedule an employer shall, between 1st May 1969 and 30th September 1969 *and between 1st May 1970 and 30th September 1970* and in each succeeding year between 1st May and 30th September, allow a holiday (hereinafter referred to as an "annual holiday") to every worker in his employment to whom this Schedule applies who has been employed by him during the 12 months ended on 5th April immediately preceding the commencement of the holiday season for any of the periods of employment (calculated in accordance with the provisions of paragraph 10) specified below and the duration of the annual holiday shall, in the case of each such worker, be related to his period of employment during that 12 months as follows:—

Period of employment		Duration of annual holiday	
		1969	*1970 and each succeeding year*
At least 48 weeks		12 days	15 days
„ „ 45 „		11 „	14 „
„ „ 44 „		11 „	13 „
„ „ 42 „		10 „	13 „
„ „ 40 „		10 „	12 „
„ „ 39 „		9 „	12 „
„ „ 36 „		9 „	11 „
„ „ 33 „		8 „	10 „
„ „ 32 „		8 „	9 „
„ „ 30 „		7 „	9 „
„ „ 28 „		7 „	8 „
„ „ 27 „		6 „	8 „
„ „ 24 „		6 „	7 „
„ „ 21 „		5 „	6 „
„ „ 20 „		5 „	5 „
„ „ 18 „		4 „	5 „
„ „ 16 „		4 „	4 „
„ „ 15 „		3 „	4 „
„ „ 12 „		3 „	3 „
„ „ 8 „		2 „	2 „
„ „ 4 „		1 day	1 day

(2) Notwithstanding the provisions of the last foregoing sub-paragraph—

> (*a*) (i) the number of days of annual holiday which an employer is required to allow to a worker in respect of a period of employment during the 12 months ending on 5th April 1969 shall not exceed in the aggregate twice the number of days constituting the worker's normal working week, *plus two days;*

> (ii) the number of days of annual holiday which an employer is required to allow to a worker in respect of a period of employment during the 12 months ending on 5th April 1970 and during the 12 months ending on 5th April in any succeeding year shall not exceed in the aggregate *three times the number of days constituting the worker's normal working week;*

(3) In this Schedule the expression "holiday season" means in relation to the year 1969 the period commencing on 1st May 1969 and ending on 30th September 1969 and, in each succeeding year, the period commencing on 1st May and ending on 30th September of the same year.

4.—(1) *Subject to the provisions of this paragraph* an annual holiday shall be allowed on consecutive working days being days on which the worker is normally called upon to work for the employer, and days of annual holiday shall be treated as consecutive notwithstanding that a Sunday, a customary holiday on which the worker is not required to work for the employer or a holiday in lieu of a customary holiday intervenes.

(2) (a) Where the number of days of annual holiday for which a worker has qualified exceeds the number of days constituting his normal working week but does not exceed twice that number, the holiday may, by agreement between the employer and the worker or his representative, be allowed in two separate periods of consecutive working days; so, however, that when a holiday is so allowed, one of the periods shall consist of a number of such days not less than the number of days constituting the worker's normal working week;

(b) *Where the number of days of annual holiday for which a worker has qualified exceeds twice the number of days constituting his normal working week the holiday may be allowed as follows:—*

(i) *as to two periods of consecutive working days, each such period not being less than the period constituting the worker's normal working week, during the holiday season; and*

(ii) *as to any additional days, on working days which need not be consecutive, to be fixed by the employer after consultation with the worker, either during the holiday season or before the beginning of the next following holiday season.*

(3) *Where a day of holiday allowed to a worker under Part II of this Schedule immediately precedes a period of annual holiday or occurs during such a period then, notwithstanding the foregoing provisions of this paragraph, the duration of that period of annual holiday may be reduced by one day and in such a case one day of annual holiday may be allowed on any working day in the holiday season, or by agreement between the employer and the worker or his representative, on any working day before the beginning of the next following holiday season.*

(4) *Subject to the provisions of this paragraph, any day of annual holiday under this Schedule may be allowed on a day on which the worker is entitled to a day of holiday or to a half-holiday under any enactment other than the Wages Councils Act 1959.*

5. An employer shall give to a worker reasonable notice of the commencing date or dates and duration of the period or periods of his annual holiday. Such notice may be given individually to the worker or by the posting of a notice in the place where the worker is employed.

PART IV

HOLIDAY REMUNERATION

A—CUSTOMARY HOLIDAYS AND HOLIDAYS IN LIEU OF CUSTOMARY HOLIDAYS

6.—(1) For each day of holiday to which a worker is entitled under Part II of this Schedule he shall be paid by the employer as holiday remuneration whichever of the following amounts is the greater:—

(a) the appropriate proportion (as defined in paragraph 11) of the average weekly earnings of the worker during the 12 months ended on 5th April immediately preceding the holiday, such average weekly earnings to be determined by dividing, by the number of weeks of employment with the employer during the said period, the total remuneration paid to him by the employer during that period:

Provided that when Good Friday or Easter Monday in England and Wales or the local Spring holiday in Scotland (or days substituted therefor under the provisions of sub-paragraph (2) (*b*) of paragraph 2 or holidays in lieu of such customary holidays) fall after 5th April in any year, the holiday remuneration for any such holiday under this sub-paragraph shall be the appropriate proportion of the average weekly earnings of the worker during the 12 months ended on 5th April in the preceding calendar year; or

(*b*) the appropriate statutory minimum remuneration to which he would have been entitled as a time worker if the day had not been a day of holiday and he had been employed on work for which statutory minimum remuneration is payable for the time usually worked by him on that day of the week.

(2) Notwithstanding the provisions of sub-paragraph (1) of this paragraph, payment of the said holiday remuneration is subject to the condition that the worker (unless excused by the employer or absent by reason of the proved illness of, or accident to, the worker) presents himself for employment at the usual starting hour on the first working day following the holiday:

Provided that when two customary holidays occur on successive days (or so that no working day intervenes) the said condition shall apply only to the second customary holiday.

(3) Holiday remuneration in respect of any customary holiday shall be paid by the employer to the worker on the pay day on which the wages for the pay week including the holiday are paid.

(4) Holiday remuneration in respect of any holiday in lieu of a customary holiday shall be paid on the pay day on which the wages for the week including the holiday in lieu of a customary holiday are paid:

Provided that the said payment shall be made immediately upon the termination of the worker's employment if he ceases to be employed before being allowed such holiday in lieu of a customary holiday and in that case the condition specified in sub-paragraph (2) of this paragraph shall not apply.

B—ANNUAL HOLIDAY

7.—(1) Subject to the provisions of paragraph 8, a worker qualified to be allowed an annual holiday under this Schedule shall be paid as holiday remuneration by his employer in respect thereof, on the last pay day preceding such annual holiday, *whichever of the following sums is the greater:*—

(*a*) (i) in respect of the annual holiday to be allowed during the period of 12 months commencing on 1st May 1969 an amount equal to *twelve two-hundred-and-sixtieths* of the total remuneration paid by the employer to the worker in the 12 months ended on 5th April 1969;

(ii) in respect of the annual holiday to be allowed during the period of 12 months commencing on 1st May 1970 and during the period of 12 months commencing on 1st May in each succeeding year an amount equal to *three fifty-seconds* of the total remuneration paid by the employer to the worker in the 12 months ended on 5th April immediately preceding the holiday season; or

(*b*) one day's holiday pay (as defined in paragraph 11) in respect of each day of annual holiday.

(2) Where, under the provisions of paragraph 4, an annual holiday is allowed in more than one period the holiday remuneration shall be apportioned accordingly.

8. Where any accrued holiday remuneration has been paid by the employer to the worker (in accordance with the provisions of paragraph 9 of this Schedule or under Order O.F. (37)) in respect of employment during any of the periods referred to in that paragraph or that Order respectively, the amount of holiday remuneration payable by the employer in respect of any annual holiday for which the worker has qualified by reason of employment during the said period shall be

reduced by the amount of the said accrued holiday remuneration unless that remuneration has been deducted from a previous payment of holiday remuneration made under the provisions of this Schedule or of Order O.F. (37).

ACCRUED HOLIDAY REMUNERATION PAYABLE ON TERMINATION OF EMPLOYMENT

9. Where a worker ceases to be employed by an employer after the provisions of this Schedule become effective the employer shall, immediately on the termination of the employment, pay to the worker as accrued holiday remuneration:—

(1) in respect of employment in the 12 months up to the preceding *5th April*, a sum equal to the holiday remuneration to which the worker would have been entitled under the provisions of (*b*) of sub-paragraph (1) of paragraph 7 for any days of annual holiday for which he has qualified, except days of annual holiday which he has been allowed or has become entitled to be allowed before leaving the employment; and

(2) in respect of any employment since the said *5th April*, a sum equal to the holiday remuneration which would have been payable to him under the provisions of (*b*) of sub-paragraph (1) of paragraph 7 if he could have been allowed an annual holiday in respect of that employment at the time of leaving it.

(*3*) *Notwithstanding the provisions of sub-paragraphs (1) and (2) of this paragraph, the accrued holiday remuneration payable to a worker who has been employed by the employer for the whole of the 12 months ended on 5th April immediately preceding the termination of his employment shall be as follows:—*

    (*a*) *in respect of the 12 months ended on 5th April preceding the termination of his employment, whichever of the following amounts is the greater—*

        (*i*) *in respect of the 12 months ending on 5th April 1969 an amount equal to twelve two-hundred-and-sixtieths of the total remuneration as defined in paragraph 11 paid by the employer to the worker during that period; or*

        (*ii*) *the amount calculated in accordance with the provisions of sub-paragraph (1) of this paragraph; or*

        (*iii*) *in respect of the period of 12 months ending on 5th April 1970 or in respect of any subsequent period of 12 months ending on 5th April an amount equal to three fifty-seconds of the total remuneration as defined in paragraph 11 paid by the employer to the worker during any such period; or*

        (*iv*) *the amount calculated in accordance with the provisions of sub-paragraph (1) of this paragraph; and*

    (*b*) *in respect of any period of employment after such 5th April, the amount calculated in accordance with the provisions of sub-paragraph (2) of this paragraph.*

Part V

GENERAL

10. For the purposes of calculating any period of employment qualifying a worker for an annual holiday or for any accrued holiday remuneration under this Schedule, the worker shall be treated:—

(1) as if he were employed for a week in respect of any week in which—

    (*a*) he has worked for the employer for not less than 20 hours and has performed some work for which statutory minimum remuneration is payable;

> (b) he has been absent throughout the week by reason of the proved illness of, or accident to, the worker but not exceeding four weeks in the aggregate in the period of 12 months immediately preceding the commencement of the holiday season;
>
> (c) he has been suspended throughout the week owing to shortage of work but not exceeding six weeks in the aggregate in such period as aforesaid; and

(2) as if he were employed on any day of holiday allowed under the provisions of this Schedule or of Order O.F. (37), and for the purposes of the provisions of sub-paragraph (1) of this paragraph, a worker who is absent on such a holiday shall be treated as having worked thereon the number of hours ordinarily worked by him for the employer on that day of the week on work for which statutory minimum remuneration is payable.

11. In this Schedule, unless the context otherwise requires, the following expressions have the meanings hereby respectively assigned to them, that is to say:—

"appropriate proportion" means—

> where the worker's normal working week is five days   ...   one-fifth
> where the worker's normal working week is four days or less   one-quarter

"appropriate rate of statutory minimum remuneration" means—

> (a) in the case of a time worker, the rate or rates of statutory minimum remuneration applicable to the worker, and
>
> (b) in the case of a piece worker, the rate or rates of statutory minimum remuneration which would be applicable to the worker if he were a time worker.

"normal working week" means the number of days on which it has been usual for the worker to work in a week in the employment of the employer during the 12 months immediately preceding the commencement of the holiday season or, where under paragraph 9 accrued holiday remuneration is payable on the termination of the employment, during the 12 months immediately preceding the date of the termination of the employment:

Provided that—

> (i) part of a day shall count as a day;
>
> (ii) no account shall be taken of any week in which the worker did not perform any work for which statutory minimum remuneration has been fixed.

"one day's holiday pay" means the appropriate proportion (as defined in this paragraph) of the remuneration which the worker would be entitled to receive from his employer at the date of the annual holiday (or where the holiday is allowed in more than one period at the date of the first period) or at the termination of the employment, as the case may require, for one week's work if working his normal working week and the number of daily hours normally worked by him (exclusive of overtime) and if paid at the appropriate rate of statutory minimum remuneration for work for which statutory minimum remuneration is payable and at the same rate for any work for which such remuneration is not payable.

"statutory minimum remuneration" means minimum remuneration (other than holiday remuneration) fixed by a wages regulation order made by the Secretary of State to give effect to proposals submitted to her by the Wages Council.

"total remuneration" means any payments paid or payable to the worker under his contract of employment, for time worked or piece work done by him, holiday remuneration, any productivity, long service or other bonus payable to the worker on a weekly, fortnightly or monthly basis and merit payments so payable but does not include any other payments.

"week" in paragraphs 2, 3 and 10 means "pay week".

12. The provisions of this Schedule are without prejudice to any agreement for the allowance of any further holidays with pay or for the payment of additional holiday remuneration.

EXPLANATORY NOTE

(This Note is not part of the Order.)

This Order, which has effect from 1st January 1969, sets out the holidays which an employer is required to allow to workers and the remuneration payable to such workers for those holidays, in substitution for the holidays and holiday remuneration fixed by the Wages Regulation (Ostrich and Fancy Feather and Artificial Flower) (Holidays) Order 1966 (Order O.F. (37)), which Order is revoked.

New provisions are printed in italics.

STATUTORY INSTRUMENTS

1968 No. 1929

METROPOLITAN AND CITY POLICE DISTRICTS

CABS

The London Cab Order 1968

| *Made* | - | - | - | *4th December* 1968 |

| *Coming into Operation* | | *16th December* 1968 |

In pursuance of the powers conferred on me by section 9 of the Metropolitan Public Carriage Act 1869(a) and section 1 of the London Cab and Stage Carriage Act 1907(b) as extended by section 1 of the London Cab Act 1968(c), I hereby order as follows :—

1. For paragraph 40 of the London Cab Order 1934(d), as amended (e) (which prescribes the scale of fare payable for the hiring of a motor cab) there shall be substituted the following paragraph :—

'40. The fare payable for the hiring of a motor cab shall be according to the following scale :—

  (i) a hiring charge of one shilling, and

  (ii) in respect of any part of the hiring during which the cab travels at a speed exceeding 6 miles an hour, at the rate of 6d. for 450 yards or, if the fare shown on the meter is thirteen shillings or more, thereafter at the rate of 6d. for 225 yards, and

  (iii) in respect of any part of the hiring during which the cab is stationary or travels at a speed not exceeding 6 miles an hour, at the rate of 6d. for $2\frac{1}{2}$ minutes or, if the fare shown on the meter is thirteen shillings or more, thereafter at the rate of 6d. for $1\frac{1}{4}$ minutes:

Provided that—

  (*a*) in any case where the fare according to the foregoing scale is less than two shillings the fare payable shall be two shillings, and in any other case where the fare exceeds a multiple of 6d. by a sum which is less than 6d. the fare payable shall be the next higher multiple of 6d. ; and

  (*b*) where a motor cab is fitted with a taximeter which is not capable of recording automatically the fare payable according to the scale prescribed in this paragraph, the fare payable where the sum of ninety-nine shillings and sixpence has not already been recorded on the meter—

(a) 1869 c. 115.

(c) 1968 c. 7.

(b) 1907 c. 55.

(d) S.R. & O. 1934/1346 (Rev. XIV, p. 795: 1934 I, p. 1221).

(e) The relevant amending instrument is S.I. 1964/105 (1964 I, p.205).

(i) in the case of a fare shown on the meter not exceeding thirty-three shillings and sixpence shall, so long as a notice in terms of the notice set out in Schedule E to this Order is kept prominently displayed in the cab in such a manner as to be clearly legible by the hirer, be, as respects a fare shown on the meter and set out in a column of the notice entitled "Shown on Meter", the sum set out immediately thereunder in the column entitled "New Fare Charge", and otherwise shall be the fare shown on the meter,

(ii) in the case of a fare shown on the meter exceeding thirty-three shillings and sixpence but not exceeding ninety-nine shillings and sixpence shall, so long as a notice in the terms of the notice set out in Schedule E to this Order is available on request by the hirer from the driver of the motor cab, be, as respects a fare shown on the meter and set out in a column of the notice entitled "Shown on Meter", the sum set out immediately thereunder in the column entitled "New Fare Charge", and otherwise shall be the fare shown on the meter ;

(c) where the taximeter is capable of recording automatically the fare payable according to the scale prescribed in this paragraph, but is not capable of recording a total fare which exceeds ninety-nine shillings and sixpence, the fare payable shall be the fare shown on the meter (if any) and in addition five pounds shall become payable on each occasion when the meter has recorded ninety-nine shillings and sixpence and would record five pounds if it were capable of recording such a fare.'.

2. For Schedule E to the London Cab Order 1934, as amended **(a)**, there shall be substituted the Schedule set out in the Schedule to this Order.

3. In paragraph 41(1A) of the London Cab Order 1934, as amended **(b)** (which provides for an extra charge in respect of any hiring commencing or terminating between midnight and six in the morning) for the words "an extra charge of one shilling" there shall be substituted the words "an extra charge of one shilling and sixpence".

4. This Order may be cited as the London Cab Order 1968 and shall come into operation on 16th December 1968.

James Callaghan,
One of Her Majesty's Principal
Secretaries of State.

Home Office,
 Whitehall.
4th December 1968.

(a) The relevant amending instrument is S.I. 1964/105 (1964 I, p.205).

(b) The relevant amending instruments are S.I. 1951/1352, 1958/2148 (1951 I, p.1311; 1958 I, p.1503).

SCHEDULE

SCHEDULE E

INCREASE OF FARES

For all journeys beginning and ending within the Metropolitan and City Police Districts, the fare shown upon the taximeter, excluding extras, is (as authorised by the London Cab Order 1968 made by the Secretary of State) increased as shown in the table.

SHOWN ON METER	2/-	2/6	3/-	3/6	4/-	4/6	5/-	5/6	6/-	6/6	7/-	7/6	8/-	8/6
NEW FARE CHARGE	2/-	2/9	3/6	4/-	4/6	5/-	5/9	6/3	6/9	7/3	8/-	8/6	9/-	9/9

SHOWN ON METER	9/-	9/6	10/-	10/6	11/-	11/6	12/-	12/6	13/-	13/6	14/-	14/6	15/-	15/6
NEW FARE CHARGE	10/3	10/9	11/3	11/9	12/3	13/-	14/-	15/-	16/-	17/6	18/6	19/6	20/6	22/-

SHOWN ON METER	16/-	16/6	17/-	17/6	18/-	18/6	19/-	19/6	20/-	20/6	21/-	21/6	22/-	22/6
NEW FARE CHARGE	23/-	24/-	25/6	26/6	27/6	29/-	30/-	31/-	32/-	33/6	34/6	35/6	37/-	38/-

SHOWN ON METER	23/-	23/6	24/-	24/6	25/-	25/6	26/-	26/6	27/-	27/6	28/-	28/6	29/-	29/6
NEW FARE CHARGE	39/-	40/6	41/6	42/6	43/6	45/-	46/-	47/-	48/6	49/6	50/6	51/6	53/-	54/-

SHOWN ON METER	30/-	30/6	31/-	31/6	32/-	32/6	33/-	33/6	34/-	34/6	35/-	35/6	36/-	36/6
NEW FARE CHARGE	55/-	56/6	57/6	58/6	60/-	61/-	62/-	63/-	64/6	65/6	66/6	68/-	69/-	70/-

SHOWN ON METER	37/-	37/6	38/-	38/6	39/-	39/6	40/-	40/6	41/-	41/6	42/-	42/6	43/-	43/6
NEW FARE CHARGE	71/-	72/6	73/6	74/6	76/-	77/-	78/-	79/6	80/6	81/6	82/6	84/-	85/-	86/-

SHOWN ON METER	44/-	44/6	45/-	45/6	46/-	46/6	47/-	47/6	48/-	48/6	49/-	49/6	50/-	50/6
NEW FARE CHARGE	87/6	88/6	89/6	91/-	92/-	93/-	94/-	95/6	96/6	97/6	99/-	100/-	101/-	102/-

Shown on Meter	51/-	51/6	52/-	52/6	53/-	53/6	54/-	54/6	55/-	55/6	56/-	56/6	57/-	57/6
New Fare Charge	103/6	104/6	105/6	107/-	108/-	109/-	110/6	111/6	112/6	113/6	115/-	116/-	117/-	118/6

Shown on Meter	58/-	58/6	59/-	59/6	60/-	60/6	61/-	61/6	62/-	62/6	63/-	63/6	64/-	64/6
New Fare Charge	119/6	120/6	121/6	123/-	124/-	125/-	126/6	127/6	128/6	130/-	131/-	132/-	133/-	134/6

Shown on Meter	65/-	65/6	66/-	66/6	67/-	67/6	68/-	68/6	69/-	69/6	70/-	70/6	71/-	71/6
New Fare Charge	135/6	136/6	138/-	139/-	140/-	141/6	142/6	143/6	144/6	146/-	147/-	148/-	149/6	150/6

Shown on Meter	72/-	72/6	73/-	73/6	74/-	74/6	75/-	75/6	76/-	76/6	77/-	77/6	78/-	78/6
New Fare Charge	151/6	152/6	154/-	155/-	156/-	157/6	158/6	159/6	161/-	162/-	163/-	164/-	165/6	166/6

Shown on Meter	79/-	79/6	80/-	80/6	81/-	81/6	82/-	82/6	83/-	83/6	84/-	84/6	85/-	85/6
New Fare Charge	167/6	169/-	170/-	171/-	172/6	173/6	174/6	175/6	177/-	178/-	179/-	180/6	181/6	182/6

Shown on Meter	86/-	86/6	87/-	87/6	88/-	88/6	89/-	89/6	90/-	90/6	91/-	91/6	92/-	92/6
New Fare Charge	183/6	185/-	186/-	187/-	188/6	189/6	190/6	192/-	193/-	194/-	195/-	196/6	197/6	198/6

Shown on Meter	93/-	93/6	94/-	94/6	95/-	95/6	96/-	96/6	97/-	97/6	98/-	98/6	99/-	99/6
New Fare Charge	200/-	201/-	202/-	203/-	204/6	205/6	206/6	208/-	209/-	210/-	211/6	212/6	213/6	214/6

NOTES (1) The fare payable for journeys beginning and ending within the Metropolitan and City Police Districts and exceeding 6 miles, or one hour in duration, is no longer subject to agreement. After the sum of 11/- is shown on the taximeter the new fare is calculated at double the normal rate.

(2) The fare payable when an amount in excess of 33/6 is shown on the meter is contained in a table in possession of the driver who must produce it for inspection on request.

(3) The extra charge for each hiring commencing or terminating between midnight and six in the morning is increased to 1/6d. and this amount is to be recorded on the meter as an extra.

EXPLANATORY NOTE

(This Note is not part of the Order.)

This Order makes revised provision for the scale of fares payable for the hiring of a motor cab in the Metropolitan Police District and the City of London in respect of all journeys beginning and ending in London, as permitted under the London Cab Act 1968. The fares payable are increased and when the far exceeds 13/- the rate of increase is doubled in respect of the subsequent part of the journey. So long as a cab is not fitted with a meter capable of recording the new fares automatically, only the fare shown on the meter will be chargeable unless a notice in the terms set out in the Schedule is prominently displayed in the cab or is available at the request of the hirer in which case the increased fares shown in the notice will be chargeable.

1968 No. 1930

ROAD TRAFFIC

The Road Vehicles (Headlamps) Regulations 1968

Made - - - -	*4th December* 1968
Laid before Parliament	12th December 1968
Coming into Operation	1st January 1969

The Minister of Transport in exercise of his powers under section 15 of the Road Traffic Act 1962(a) and of all other enabling powers, and after consultation with representative organisations in accordance with the provisions of section 13 of the Road Transport Lighting Act 1957(b), as amended by section 264 of, and Schedule 17 to, the Road Traffic Act 1960(c) and as applied by section 15(5) of the said Act of 1962, hereby makes the following Regulations :—

Commencement and citation

1. These Regulations shall come into operation on the 1st January 1969 and may be cited as the Road Vehicles (Headlamps) Regulations 1968.

Interpretation

2.—(1) In these Regulations, any expression defined for the purposes of the Road Vehicles (Headlamps) Regulations 1967(d) has the same meaning as in those Regulations.

(2) The Interpretation Act 1889(e) shall apply for the interpretation of these Regulations as it applies for the interpretation of an Act of Parliament.

Vehicles to which Regulations apply

3. These Regulations apply to every motor vehicle to which the Road Vehicles (Headlamps) Regulations 1967 apply.

Requirements as to use of headlamps

4.—(1) This Regulation applies to every length of road, except that it does not apply to a length of road—

(*a*) on which there is provided a system of street lighting furnished by means of lamps placed not more than two hundred yards apart, and

(*b*) while such lamps are lit.

(2) When any motor vehicle to which these Regulations apply is in motion during the hours of darkness on a length of road to which this Regulation applies a matched pair of obligatory headlamps carried by the vehicle shall be kept lit :

Provided that this paragraph shall not apply—

(i) in conditions of fog or whilst snow is falling—

(*a*) before 1st January 1970 to a vehicle which carries one fog lamp if such lamp is kept lit ; or

(*b*) on or after 1st January 1970 to a vehicle which carries two permitted lamps, if both such permitted lamps are kept lit ;

(a) 10 & 11 Eliz. 2. c. 59. (b) 5 & 6 Eliz. 2. c. 51. (c) 8 & 9 Eliz. 2. c. 16.
(d) S.I. 1967/1933 (1967 III, p. 5382). (e) 52 & 53 Vict. c. 63.

(ii) to a public service vehicle first registered before 1st October 1969, or until 1st April 1970 to a road clearance vehicle (as defined in Regulation 3(1) of the 1964 Regulations) first registered before 1st January 1955, if one obligatory headlamp carried by the vehicle is kept lit ;

(iii) to a vehicle being drawn by another vehicle ; or

(iv) to a vehicle while being used to propel in front thereof a snow plough.

(3) In this Regulation " two permitted lamps " means two fog lamps or one fog lamp and one headlamp (not being an obligatory headlamp), being lamps which comply with the following conditions namely—

(a) the two lamps shall be fixed one on each side of the vertical plane passing through the longitudinal axis of the vehicle ;

(b) the centres of both lamps shall be at the same height above the ground ;

(c) the distances between the centre of each lamp and the vertical plane passing through the longitudinal axis of the vehicle shall be the same ; and

(d) each lamp shall be so positioned that in the case of a vehicle first registered before 1st January 1971 no part of the illuminated area of one lamp is less than 350 millimetres from any part of the illuminated area of the other lamp, and in the case of a vehicle first registered on or after 1st January 1971 the outermost part of the illuminated area of either lamp is not more than 400 millimetres from the outermost part of the vehicle on the side on which the lamp is placed.

Given under the Official Seal of the Minister of Transport the 4th December 1968.

(L.S.)

Richard Marsh,
Minister of Transport.

EXPLANATORY NOTE
(This Note is not part of the Regulations.)

These Regulations apply to motor vehicles which are required to carry two headlamps by the Road Vehicles (Headlamps) Regulations 1967, that is to say, most motor vehicles having four or more wheels.

The Regulations require that all such vehicles moving at night on roads (except roads lit by a system of street lighting where the lamps are not more than 200 yards apart) shall use a matched pair of headlamps. Certain public service and road clearance vehicles are permitted to use only one headlamp and a vehicle being towed and a snow plough are exempted from the obligation to use headlamps.

In fog or when snow is falling a foglamp may be used instead of headlamps until the 1st January 1970, and on or after that date two foglamps or a foglamp and a spotlamp may be used instead of headlamps if they satisfy certain conditions.

STATUTORY INSTRUMENTS

1968 No. 1933 (S.171)

LEGAL AID AND ADVICE, SCOTLAND

The Act of Adjournal (Criminal Legal Aid Fees Amendment) 1968

Made - - -	*29th November* 1968
Coming into Operation	*2nd January* 1969

ACT OF ADJOURNAL
Relative to Criminal Legal Aid Fees

AT EDINBURGH, the TWENTY NINTH day of NOVEMBER, Nineteen hundred and sixty eight years.

Present:

The Right Honourable
The Lord Justice-General ;
The Right Honourable
The Lord Justice-Clerk ;
The Honourable Lord Guthrie ;
The Honourable Lord Cameron ;
The Honourable Lord Johnston.

The Lord Justice-General, Lord Justice-Clerk and Lords Commissioners of Justiciary, by virtue of the powers conferred upon them by section 16 of the Legal Aid (Scotland) Act 1967(a), and of all other powers competent to them in that behalf, do hereby enact and declare as follows :

1. This Act of Adjournal may be cited as the Act of Adjournal (Criminal Legal Aid Fees Amendment) 1968 and shall come into operation on 2nd January 1969.

2. The Act of Adjournal (Criminal Legal Aid Fees) 1964(b) as amended by the Act of Adjournal (Criminal Legal Aid Fees Amendment) 1965(c) shall be further amended as follows :—

(a) By deleting sub-paragraph (1) of paragraph 3 and by substituting a new sub-paragraph (1) thereof as follows :—
"(1) There shall be allowed to the duty Solicitor representing accused persons in the sheriff court on rota in terms of Article 6 of the Scheme, fees on the following scales :—
(a) Attendance at the first session of a court for the day a sessional fee of (i) £5 for the first case and (ii) £1 for each additional case, subject to a maximum total fee of £10 for the session until its termination on

---

(a) 1967 c. 43. (b) S.I. 1964/1410 (1964 III, p. 3292).
(c) S.I. 1965/1788 (1965 III, p. 5461).

completion of business for the day or on adjournment by the court, whichever be the earlier ;

(b) Attendance at any other session of that court on the same day a sessional fee of (i) £5 for the first case and (ii) £1 for each additional case, subject to a maximum total fee of £7 for each such other session :

Provided that the fee according to the foregoing scale shall cover the appearance in court of the duty Solicitor on behalf of the accused as well as any interview or interviews with the accused or others whether such interview or interviews take place during the same or another session."

(b) By deleting sub-paragraph (2) of paragraph 12 and by substituting a new sub-paragraph (2) thereof as follows: —

"(2) Where the nominated Solicitor requires to instruct another Solicitor, whether an Edinburgh Solicitor in connection with an appeal or on a remit for sentence, or a Solicitor at the place of the prison or the court, or a local Solicitor for the purpose of local precognitions or enquiry, nevertheless only one account shall be rendered by the nominated Solicitor in accordance with this Act of Adjournal (payment of the other Solicitor being a matter for adjustment between the nominated Solicitor and the other Solicitor out of the fees payable hereunder) but in determining the sum to be allowed to the nominated Solicitor, account shall be taken also of the work carried out by that other Solicitor."

(c) By deleting paragraph 13 and by substituting a new paragraph 13 as follows: —

"**13.**—(1) The determination of the sum to be allowed to a Solicitor shall take into account all the relevant circumstances including the nature, importance, complexity or difficulty of the work and the time involved, including time necessarily spent at the court on any day in waiting for the case or for the appeal to be heard, where such time has not been occupied in waiting for or conducting another case, and shall include such amount as appears to represent fair remuneration for the work actually and reasonably done due regard being had to economy.

(2) It shall be competent immediately on conclusion of the trial for the Counsel or Solicitor who appeared for the accused to make oral application to the court for a certificate that the case has necessarily been one of exceptional length, complexity or difficulty. Such certificate may be granted or refused forthwith by the Court, or the Judge may adjourn the application for a hearing in Chambers. This hearing must take place within seven days of such adjournment. In the event of such an adjournment being ordered written grounds for such application must be lodged within two days of the adjournment being ordered, otherwise the application shall be refused. The Prosecutor may be represented at such hearing. If such a certificate shall be granted then any limitation contained in the foregoing paragraphs, or such of them as are referred to in such certificate, on the amount of any fee payable shall not apply and such fees shall be allowed, after taking into account all the relevant circumstances of the case, in respect of the work done as appears to represent fair remuneration according to the work actually and reasonably done due regard being had to economy."

(d) By deleting paragraph 15 and by substituting a new paragraph 15 as follows: —

"**15.**—(1) If any question or dispute arises as to the amount payable to any Solicitor or Counsel in respect of any remuneration payable for the representation of any person receiving legal aid in connection with any criminal proctedings in the High Court, including appeals, the matter shall be referred to the Auditor of the Court of Session for his decision as to what represents fair remuneration under and in terms of this Act of Adjournal: Provided that the Law Society and any other party to a reference to the Auditor under this sub-paragaph shall have the right to state written objections to the High Court in relation to the report of the Auditor under this sub-paragraph within seven days of the date of issue of such report and the Law Society and any such other party may be heard in Chambers thereon.

(2) If any question or dispute arises as to the amount payable to any Solicitor or Counsel in respect of any remuneration payable for the representation of any person receiving legal aid in connection with any criminal proceedings in the Sheriff Court, the matter shall be referred to the Auditor of the Sheriff Court for the district in which those proceedings took place for his decision as to what represents fair remuneration under and in terms of this Act of Adjournal: Provided that the Law Society and any other party to a reference to an Auditor under this sub-paragraph shall have the right to state written objections to the Sheriff in relation to the report of the Auditor under this sub-paragraph within seven days of the date of issue of such report and the Law Society and any such other party may be heard in Chambers thereon.

(3) A reference to an Auditor under this paragraph need not be joint but may be made at the instance either of the Solicitor concerned or of the Law Society and the Auditor concerned shall give reasonable notice to both of the diet of taxation."

And the Lords appoint this Act of Adjournal to be recorded in the Books of Adjournal, and to be published in the *Edinburgh Gazette.*

J. L. Clyde,
I.P.D.

EXPLANATORY NOTE
(This Note is not part of the Act of Adjournal.)

This Act of Adjournal amends the Act of Adjournal (Criminal Legal Aid Fees) 1964 by clarifying certain provisions relating to the fees of a duty Solicitor and of a nominated Solicitor, and by modifying the provisions relating to fees in exceptional cases. It also provides for the making of objections to the report of an Auditor of Court on the question of fair remuneration.

STATUTORY INSTRUMENTS

1968 No. 1934 (L.21)

MATRIMONIAL CAUSES
COUNTY COURTS

The Divorce County Courts (Amendment) Order 1968

Made - - - 3rd December 1968
Coming into Operation 1st January 1969

I, Gerald, Baron Gardiner, Lord High Chancellor of Great Britain, in exercise of the powers conferred on me by section 1(1) of the Matrimonial Causes Act 1967(**a**), and section 2 of the County Courts Act 1959(**b**), hereby make the following Order :—

1.—(1) This Order may be cited as the Divorce County Courts (Amendment) Order 1968, and shall come into operation on 1st January 1969.

(2) The Interpretation Act 1889(**c**) shall apply to the interpretation of this Order as it applies to the interpretation of an Act of Parliament.

2. The Divorce County Courts Order 1968(**d**), which designates certain courts as divorce county courts and courts of trial for undefended matrimonial causes, shall have effect subject to the provisions of this Order, and a reference in any of the following paragraphs to a schedule by number means the schedule so numbered in that Order.

3. The Guildford County Court shall be a court of trial for the purposes of section 1(1) of the Matrimonial Causes Act 1967, and accordingly that court shall be marked "T" in Schedule 1.

4. The following words shall be omitted from Schedule 1, namely :—

(*a*) "and Wigton" after "Carlisle";

(*b*) "and Horncastle" after "Lincoln";

(*c*) "and Oundle" after "Peterborough";

and the references to the Carlisle and Wigton County Court, the Lincoln and Horncastle County Court and the Peterborough and Oundle County Court shall be omitted from Schedule 2.

5. For the words "Newport and Ryde" in Schedule 1 there shall be substituted the words "Newport, Isle of Wight".

6. After the first entry in Schedule 2 there shall be inserted the following entry :—

Column 1	*Column* 2
"Norwich	Norwich"

Dated 3rd December 1968.

Gardiner, C.

(a) 1967 c. 56.   (b) 1959 c. 22.
(c) 1889 c. 63.   (d) S.I. 1968/314 (1968 I, p. 940).

EXPLANATORY NOTE
(This Note is not part of the Order.)

This Order amends the Divorce County Courts Order 1968 by adding Guildford to the list of county courts at which undefended matrimonial causes may be tried, and makes several minor amendments to take account of recent changes in the names and districts of county courts.

STATUTORY INSTRUMENTS

1968 No. 1935 (L.22)

BANKRUPTCY, ENGLAND

The Bankruptcy (Amendment) Rules 1968

Made	-	-	-	*3rd December* 1968
Laid before Parliament			*12th December* 1968
Coming into Operation			*1st January* 1969

I, Gerald, Baron Gardiner, Lord High Chancellor of Great Britain, with the concurrence of the President of the Board of Trade, in exercise of the powers conferred on me by section 132 of the Bankruptcy Act 1914(**a**), hereby make the following Rules :—

1. The form set out in the Schedule to these Rules shall be substituted for the form numbered 175 in Appendix I to the Bankruptcy Rules 1952(**b**), as amended (**c**).

2.—(1) These Rules may be cited as the Bankruptcy (Amendment) Rules 1968 and shall come into operation on 1st January 1969.

(2) The Interpretation Act 1889(**d**) shall apply to the interpretation of these Rules as it applies to the interpretation of an Act of Parliament.

Dated 2nd December 1968.

Gardiner, C.

I concur,
Dated 3rd December 1968.

Anthony Crosland,
President of the Board of Trade.

SCHEDULE

No. 175 (Rule 269)

NOTICE OF DIVIDEND

(Title)

Address
Date   19 .

(*a*) *Insert here* "first" *or* "second" *or* "final" *or as the case may be*.

NOTICE IS HEREBY GIVEN that a (a)   Dividend of   s.   d. in the £ has been declared in this matter, and that the same may be received at my office, as above, on   the   day of
19   or any subsequent weekday, except   , between the hours of   and

---

(a) 1914 c. 59.   (b) S.I. 1952/2113 (1952 I, p. 213).
(c) There are no relevant amendments.   (d) 1889 c. 63.

NOTE:

   (i) This form must be presented, or returned to, the Trustee when application for payment is made. Any bills of exchange, promissory notes or other negotiable instruments held by you must be produced.

   (ii) If you desire the dividend to be paid to some other person you should sign and lodge with the Trustee an authority in the prescribed form No. 176.

   (iii) If you do not desire to attend personally you must fill up, sign and return the form of authority below, when a dividend payable order will be delivered in accordance with the authority.

   (iv) Dividend payable orders lapse if not presented for payment within 3 months of the last day of the month of issue but will be re-issued after that period on application to the Board of Trade.

The fee payable on re-issue of a payable order is 2/6d. where the order is for £5 or less, and 5/- where the order exceeds £5.

To...........................   (Signed) *G. H., Trustee,*

AUTHORITY

Sir,

Please deliver to * $\dfrac{\text{me (us)}}{\text{the Bearer, Mr.}}$ by post, at my (our) risk   *Strike out words inapplicable

the Dividend Payable Order for

    pounds,   shillings and   pence

being the amount payable to * $\dfrac{\text{me}}{\text{us}}$ in respect of the dividend of

in the £ on * $\dfrac{\text{my}}{\text{our}}$ claim in this matter.

    £   :   :   .   *Creditor's signature*

To G. H., Trustee

           Date   19   .

(For use when payable order handed to creditor or representative)

Received Payable Order for £   :   :   Signed

                (Exempt from stamp duty)
           Date   19   .

EXPLANATORY NOTE

(This Note is not part of the Rules.)

These Rules substitute a new form of notice, to be sent to creditors by the Official Receiver or other trustee in bankruptcy, on the declaration of a dividend. The creditor will no longer be required to sign a receipt for the amount due when applying for payment.

STATUTORY INSTRUMENTS

1968 No. 1939

AGRICULTURE

The Price Stability of Imported Products (Rates of Levy No. 13) Order 1968

Made - - - - 5th December 1968

Coming into Operation 6th December 1968

The Minister of Agriculture, Fisheries and Food, in exercise of the powers conferred upon him by section 1(2), (4), (5), (6) and (7) of the Agriculture and Horticulture Act 1964(a) and of all other powers enabling him in that behalf, hereby makes the following order :—

1. This order may be cited as the Price Stability of Imported Products (Rates of Levy No. 13) Order 1968 ; and shall come into operation on 6th December 1968.

2.—(1) In this order—

" the Principal Order " means the Price Stability of Imported Products (Levy Arrangements) Order 1966(b), as amended by any subsequent order and if any such order is replaced by any subsequent order the expression shall be construed as a reference to such subsequent order ;

AND other expressions have the same meaning as in the Principal Order.

(2) The Interpretation Act 1889(c) shall apply to the interpretation of this order as it applies to the interpretation of an Act of Parliament and as if this order and the orders hereby revoked were Acts of Parliament.

3. In accordance with and subject to the provisions of Part II of the Principal Order (which provides for the charging of levies on imports of certain specified commodities)—

(a) the rate of general levy for such imports into the United Kingdom of any specified commodity as are described in column 2 of Part I of the Schedule to this order in relation to a tariff heading indicated in column 1 of that Part shall be the rate set forth in relation thereto in column 3 of that Part ;

(b) the rate of country levy for such imports into the United Kingdom of any specified commodity as are described in column 2 of Part II of the Schedule to this order in relation to a tariff heading indicated in column 1 of that Part shall be the rate set forth in relation thereto in column 3 of that Part.

4. The Price Stability of Imported Products (Rates of Levy No. 9) Order 1968(d) and the Price Stability of Imported Products (Rates of Levy No. 12) Order 1968(e) are hereby revoked.

In Witness whereof the Official Seal of the Minister of Agriculture, Fisheries and Food is hereunto affixed on 5th December 1968.

(L.S.)

R. J. E. Taylor,
Assistant Secretary.

(a) 1964 c. 28.   (b) S.I. 1966/936 (1966 II. p. 2271).   (c) 1889 c. 63.
(d) S.I. 1968/1617 (1968 III, p. 4440).   (e) S.I. 1968/1803 (1968 III, p. 4824).

SCHEDULE

PART I

1. Tariff Heading	2. Description of Imports	3. Rate of General Levy
		per ton £ s. d.
10.01	Imports of :— Denatured wheat	1 0 0
10.05	Maize (other than flat white maize and sweet corn on the cob)	10 0
11.02	Cereal meal— of maize	5 0 0

PART II

1. Tariff Heading	2. Description of Imports	3. Rate of Country Levy
		per ton £ s. d.
10.01	Imports of :— Denatured wheat which has been grown in and consigned to the United Kingdom from Belgium, the French Republic, the Kingdom of the Netherlands or the Kingdom of Sweden	1 0 0
10.05	Maize (other than flat white maize and sweet corn on the cob) which has been grown in and consigned to the United Kingdom from the United States of America	10 0
10.05	Maize (other than flat white maize and sweet corn on the cob) which has been grown in and consigned to the United Kingdom from the French Republic ..	5 0

EXPLANATORY NOTE

(This Note is not part of the Order.)

This order, which comes into operation on 6th December 1968, supersedes the Price Stability of Imported Products (Rates of Levy No. 12) Order 1968 and revokes the Price Stability of Imported Products (Rates of Levy No. 9) Order 1968. It :—

(a) reduces to 10s. per ton the general levy on imports of maize (other than flat white maize and sweet corn on the cob) ;

(b) reduces to 10s. per ton the country levy on imports of maize (other than flat white maize and sweet corn on the cob) which has been grown in and consigned to the United Kingdom from the United States of America ;

(c) reduces to £1 per ton the general levy on imports of denatured wheat ;

(d) reduces to £1 per ton the country levy on imports of denatured wheat which has been grown in and consigned to the United Kingdom from Belgium, France, the Netherlands or Sweden and removes the country levy on imports of denatured wheat grown in the United States of America;

(e) retains the £5 per ton general levy on imports of maize meal ; and

(f) retains the 5s. per ton country levy on imports of maize (other than flat white maize and sweet corn on the cob) which has been grown in and consigned to the United Kingdom from the French Republic.

STATUTORY INSTRUMENTS

1968 No. 1941 (C. 28) (S. 172)

CLEAN AIR

The Clean Air Act 1968 (Commencement No. 1) (Scotland) Order 1968

Made -   -   -   -   *4th December* 1968

In exercise of the powers conferred on me by section 15(3) of the Clean Air Act 1968(a), and of all other powers enabling me in that behalf, I hereby make the following order:—

1. This order may be cited as the Clean Air Act 1968 (Commencement No. 1) (Scotland) Order 1968.

2. The appointed day for the coming into operation of the provisions of the Clean Air Act 1968 specified in the schedule to this order in their application to Scotland shall be 1st April 1969.

William Ross,
One of Her Majesty's Principal
Secretaries of State.

St. Andrew's House,
   Edinburgh, 1.
4th December 1968.

(a) 1968 c. 62.

SCHEDULE

Provisions of the Act	Subject matter of provisions
Section 2	Emission of grit and dust from furnaces.
Section 6	Height of chimneys.
Section 8	Power of Secretary of State to require creation of smoke control areas.
Section 9	Acquisition and sale of unauthorised fuel in a smoke control area.
Section 10	Miscellaneous amendments of procedure for making orders with respect to smoke control areas.
Section 11	Relation of Clean Air Acts to, and amendment of, Alkali Act.
Section 12	Regulations.
Section 13	Interpretation.
Section 14(1) and paragraphs 1, 3, 4, 6, 7, 10 and 12 of schedule 1, except so far as any of those paragraphs refer to sections 1 and 3 to 5	Adaptation and minor and consequential amendments of principal Act, and repeals.
Section 14(2) and schedule 2	
Section 14(3)	
Section 15	Short title, citation, commencement and extent.

EXPLANATORY NOTE

(This Note is not part of the Order.)

This Order appoints 1st April 1969 as the appointed day for the coming into operation of the provisions of the Clean Air Act 1968 listed in the Schedule to the Order.

STATUTORY INSTRUMENTS

1968 No. 1944

EDUCATION, ENGLAND AND WALES

The Teachers' Superannuation Account (Rates of Interest) Regulations 1968

Made - - - -	*6th December* 1968
Laid before Parliament	*12th December* 1968
Coming into Operation	*13th December* 1968

The Secretary of State for Education and Science, with the consent of the Minister for the Civil Service and after consultation with representatives of local education authorities and of teachers appearing to him to be likely to be affected, in exercise of the powers conferred upon him by paragraph 3(1)(*d*) of Schedule 1 to the Teachers' Superannuation Act 1967(**a**) as amended by section 16 of the Superannuation (Miscellaneous Provisions) Act 1967(**b**), and the Minister for the Civil Service Order 1968(**c**), hereby makes the following Regulations:—

Citation and Commencement

1. These Regulations may be cited as the Teachers' Superannuation Account (Rates of Interest) Regulations 1968 and shall come into operation on 13th December 1968.

Interpretation

2.—(1) In these Regulations, unless the context otherwise requires—

"accounting period" means, in relation to the teachers' superannuation account, the period of twelve months beginning on 1st April in each year;

"the Secretary of State" means the Secretary of State for Education and Science;

"security" means a redeemable security issued by Her Majesty's Government in the United Kingdom;

"the teachers' superannuation account" means the account required to be kept under section 5(1) of the Teachers' Superannuation Act 1967.

(2) For the purposes of these Regulations—

(*a*) the price of a security shall be the price half-way between the highest and lowest prices shown in the quotations therefor in the Official Daily List of the London Stock Exchange for the relevant date or, if that Exchange is or was closed on that date, the latest previous date on which it is or was open; and

---

(**a**) 1967 c. 12.   (**b**) 1967 c. 28.
(**c**) S.I. 1968/1656 (1968 III, p. 4485).

(*b*) the rate of interest on an investment in a security shall be the rate equivalent to the gross annual yield therefrom expressed as a percentage of the sum deemed to be invested therein.

(3) The Interpretation Act 1889**(a)** shall apply for the interpretation of these Regulations as it applies for the interpretation of an Act of Parliament.

Rates of Interest

3.—(1) Subject as in regulations 4 and 5 provided, the sum representing interest which, pursuant to paragraph 3(1)(*d*) of Schedule 1 to the Teachers' Superannuation Act 1967 as amended by section 16 of the Superannuation (Miscellaneous Provisions) Act 1967, is to be treated as having been paid into the revenue of the teachers' superannuation account shall be calculated in accordance with the following provisions of this regulation.

(2) The rate of interest on each of the sums specified in column (1) of the following Table (being sums together making up the balance of revenue over expenditure remaining at the end of the accounting period beginning on 1st April 1960 and also forming part of the balance of revenue over expenditure remaining at the end of each subsequent accounting period) shall for the accounting period beginning on 1st April 1961 and for each subsequent accounting period be that specified opposite thereto in column (2):—

TABLE

(1) Sum	(2) Rate of Interest
£262,096,996	$3\frac{1}{2}\%$
£325,738,410	The rate of interest on an investment deemed to have been made on 1st April 1961 in Treasury $5\frac{1}{2}\%$ Stock, 2008—12
£24,621,617	The rate of interest on an investment deemed to have been made on 1st October 1956 in $3\frac{1}{2}\%$ Funding Stock, 1999—2004
£26,139,791	The rate of interest on an investment deemed to have been made on 1st October 1957 in $3\frac{1}{2}\%$ Funding Stock, 1999—2004
£25,410,238	The rate of interest on an investment deemed to have been made on 1st October 1958 in $3\frac{1}{2}\%$ Funding Stock, 1999—2004
£28,331,575	The rate of interest on an investment deemed to have been made on 1st October 1959 in $3\frac{1}{2}\%$ Funding Stock, 1999—2004
£30,006,685	The rate of interest on an investment deemed to have been made on 1st October 1960 in $3\frac{1}{2}\%$ Funding Stock, 1999—2004.

(a) 1889 c. 63.

(3) The rate of interest on the balance of revenue (exclusive of interest thereon) over expenditure during the accounting period beginning on 1st April 1961 and each subsequent accounting period shall for that period be one-half of the rate of interest on the investment of an amount equal to such balance deemed to have been made on 1st October in that period in a security selected by the Secretary of State after consultation with the Government Actuary.

(4) The rate of interest on any part of the balance of revenue over expenditure remaining at the end of any accounting period beginning on 1st April 1961 or subsequently, being a part which accrued during that period, shall for the next succeeding and each subsequent accounting period be the rate of interest on the investment deemed to have been made in accordance with paragraph (3) above in the accounting period in which such part accrued.

Redemption of Securities

4.—(1) Subject as in paragraph (3) below provided, on the date of redemption of a security in which an investment is deemed to have been made for the purposes of these regulations—

(a) the sum representing interest which, in accordance with regulation 3, is treated as having been paid into the revenue of the teachers' superannuation account in respect of that investment shall be increased by the amount by which the notional proceeds of the redemption thereof exceeds the sum deemed to have been invested therein or, as the case may be, reduced by the amount by which those proceeds fall short of that sum; and

(b) a sum equivalent to the sum deemed to have been invested therein shall be deemed to be re-invested in a security selected by the Secretary of State after consultation with the Government Actuary.

(2) The re-investment made in pursuance of paragraph (1)(b) above shall be deemed to be in substitution for the investment in the redeemed security and any rate of interest determined by reference to that investment shall be varied accordingly.

(3) The notional proceeds of redemption referred to in paragraph (1) above shall be the amount which would be received in respect of an investment on the redemption of the security in which it is deemed to have been made, less any capital gains tax deemed to be payable in accordance with regulation 5.

(4) For the purposes of this regulation the date of redemption of a security shall be the last date on which it may be redeemed in accordance with the terms on which it was issued.

Income Tax and Capital Gains Tax

5.—(1) In relation to any investment deemed to have been made for the purposes of these Regulations—

(a) income tax in respect of interest, and

(b) capital gains tax in respect of any capital gains accruing on the redemption of the security in which it was made shall be deemed to be payable to the same extent as they would be payable if the investment belonged to a superannuation fund approved for the purposes of section 379 of the Income Tax Act 1952(a) and providing benefits similar to those provided from the teachers' superannuation account.

(2) The rates of income tax and capital gains tax, if any, deemed to be payable in any year under paragraph (1) above shall be the rates of those taxes charged for that year under the relevant Finance Act.

(3) Any question arising under this regulation as to the extent to which income tax and capital gains tax shall be deemed to be payable under paragraph (1) above shall be decided by the Secretary of State and his decision thereon shall be final.

Given under the Official Seal of the Secretary of State for Education and Science on 4th December 1968.

(L.S.) *Shirley Williams,*
Minister of State for Education and Science.

Consent of the Minister for the Civil Service given under his Official Seal on 6th December 1968.

(L.S.) *J. E. Herbecq,*
Authorised by the Minister for the Civil Service.

(a) 1952 c. 10.

EXPLANATORY NOTE

(This Note is not part of the Regulations.)

The amount of interest added to the credit balance in the Teachers' Super-annuation Account has been calculated at $3\frac{1}{2}$ per cent. per annum since the account was started in 1926. Under these Regulations interest will continue at that rate on the part of the balance that accrued before 1st April 1956, but in respect of balances accruing subsequently it will be at rates determined by reference to the notional yield from investment in redeemable Government securities.

The Regulations have retrospective effect by virtue of section 16(1) of the Superannuation (Miscellaneous Provisions) Act 1967.

STATUTORY INSTRUMENTS

1968 No. 1945

NATIONAL HEALTH SERVICE, ENGLAND AND WALES

HOSPITAL AND SPECIALIST SERVICES

The National Health Service (Designation of London Teaching Hospitals) Amendment (No. 2) Order 1968

Made - - - -	*5th December* 1968
Coming into Operation	*16th December* 1968

The Secretary of State for Social Services, in exercise of his powers under sections 11 and 75 of the National Health Service Act 1946(**a**) and of all other powers enabling him in that behalf, and after consultation with the University of London, hereby orders as follows :—

1. This order may be cited as the National Health Service (Designation of London Teaching Hospitals) Amendment (No. 2) Order 1968 and shall come into operation on 16th December 1968.

2. The Interpretation Act 1889(**b**) shall apply to the interpretation of this order as it applies to the interpretation of an Act of Parliament.

3. In column 2 of the First Schedule to the National Health Service (Designation of London Teaching Hospitals) Order 1957(**c**) as amended(**d**) the words " The Jordan Hospital, Reigate, Surrey " shall be deleted.

4. Any officer employed immediately before 10th August 1968 at or for the purposes of the said Jordan Hospital who suffers loss of employment or loss or diminution of emoluments which is attributable to the closure of that hospital shall be entitled to have his case considered for the payment of compensation at the like rate and in the like manner and subject to the like conditions as if he had been entitled to claim compensation under the Local Government (Executive Councils) (Compensation) Regulations 1964(**e**) as amended(**f**) and those regulations (except regulations 3, 4 and 5 thereof) shall apply for this purpose as if they had been set out in this order with the modifications that—

(*a*) references to the " material date " shall be construed as references to 10th August 1968, and

(*b*) references to " any such provision as is mentioned in regulation 4 of these regulations " shall be construed as references to this order, and

---

(**a**) 1946 c. 81.
(**b**) 1889 c. 63.
(**c**) S.I. 1957/488 (1957 I, p. 1452).
(**d**) There is no amendment which relates to the subject matter of this order.
(**e**) S.I. 1964/1177 (1964 II, p. 2696).
(**f**) S.I. 1966/254 (1966 I, p. 653).

(c) at the end of regulation 7(1)(b) there shall be added the words " or 16th January 1969 whichever is the later.".

Given under the official seal of the Secretary of State for Social Services on 5th December 1968.

(L.S.) *J. Hauff,*

Assistant Under Secretary of State, Department of Health and Social Security.

EXPLANATORY NOTE

(This Note is not part of the Order.)

This Order deletes the Jordan Hospital, Reigate, Surrey, in consequence of the closing of that hospital, from the list of hospitals designated by the Secretary of State for Social Services as a teaching hospital under the name of University College Hospital. The Order also makes provision for compensation in certain cases to officers affected by the closure of the hospital.

STATUTORY INSTRUMENTS

1968 No. 1947

SHOPS AND OFFICES

The Offices, Shops and Railway Premises Act 1963 (Exemption No. 7) Order 1968

Made - - - *6th December* 1968

Coming into Operation *1st January* 1969

The Secretary of State—

(*a*) by virtue of her powers under section 45 of the Offices, Shops and Railway Premises Act 1963(**a**) (hereafter in this Order referred to as "the Act") and of all other powers enabling her in that behalf ; and

(*b*) after consulting, pursuant to section 45(4) of the Act, organisations appearing to her to be representative of workers concerned and employers concerned, respectively, and it appearing to her that there are no other persons concerned ;

hereby makes the following Order :—

1.—(1) This Order may be cited as the Offices, Shops and Railway Premises Act 1963 (Exemption No. 7) Order 1968 and shall come into operation on 1st January 1969.

(2) The Offices, Shops and Railway Premises Act 1963 (Exemption No. 3) Order 1965(**b**) is hereby revoked.

(3) The Interpretation Act 1889(**c**) shall apply to the interpretation of this Order as it applies to the interpretation of an Act of Parliament, and as if this Order and the Order hereby revoked were Acts of Parliament.

(4) For the purposes of this Order "building" includes structure.

2. The Secretary of State hereby exempts the class of premises specified in Article 3 of this Order from the requirements imposed by section 9 (which relates to sanitary conveniences) of the Act, subject to the conditions specified in Article 4 of this Order.

3. Article 2 of this Order applies to buildings in the case of which all the following circumstances exist, that is to say—

(*a*) that they consist of one room only ;

(*b*) that their floor area does not exceed one hundred square feet ;

(*c*) that they do not form part of a larger building and are unconnected with and separate from any other building ;

(**a**) 1963 c. 41.   (**b**) S.I. 1965/2046 (1965 III, p. 6068).

(**c**) 1889 c. 63.

(*d*) that members of the public are not permitted to enter therein ;

(*e*) that they are used solely or principally for the purpose of retail sales (including the sale to members of the public of food or drink for immediate consumption) ;

(*f*) that they are situated in a public park, garden, pleasure ground, ornamental enclosure or recreation ground, or in public grounds being or containing any place of historic, architectural, artistic or similar interest, or on a heath or common, or on or immediately adjacent to any public walk or promenade by sea, river or lake, or in a public open space similar to any of the foregoing, or on or in the immediate vicinity of a beach ; and

(*g*) that members of the public are admitted to the place where the building is situated for the purposes of recreation and are able to resort to the building without payment for admission to that place.

4. The conditions referred to in Article 2 of this Order are the following, that is to say—

(*a*) that suitable and conveniently accessible sanitary conveniences (whether or not they are sanitary conveniences available for use by all members of the public, or all members of the public of the same sex, and whether or not provided by a county council or local authority by virtue of powers contained in any enactment) shall be available for use by persons employed to work in any premises of the class to which Article 2 of this Order applies ;

(*b*) that the said sanitary conveniences shall be kept clean and properly maintained and that effective provision shall be made for lighting and ventilating them ;

(*c*) that the accommodation in which the said sanitary conveniences are situated shall be covered to an extent sufficient to ensure protection from the weather for persons using them ;

(*d*) that every such sanitary convenience (other than urinals) shall be enclosed to an extent sufficient to ensure privacy and be fitted with a suitable door and door fastening ;

(*e*) that every urinal shall be so placed or so screened as not to be visible outside the accommodation where the urinal is situated ;

(*f*) except in the case of sanitary conveniences which are not available for general use by members of the public and are not regularly available for use by more than five persons, that there shall be separate accommodation available for persons of each sex ; and

(*g*) that the occupier of any premises of the class to which Article 2 of this Order applies shall pay or discharge on behalf of the persons employed to work in those premises or shall refund to them any charge in respect of the use of the said sanitary conveniences.

Signed by order of the Secretary of State.
6th December 1968.

K. Barnes,
Deputy Under Secretary of State,
Department of Employment and Productivity.

EXPLANATORY NOTE

(This Note is not part of the Order.)

This Order continues without limit of time the exemption granted by the Offices, Shops and Railway Premises Act 1963 (Exemption No. 3) Order 1965 which was for a period of three years commencing with 1st January 1966. The Order exempts certain small buildings and structures used for retail sales and situated in certain public open spaces or on or near beaches from the requirements of section 9 of the Offices, Shops and Railway Premises Act 1963 as to sanitary conveniences for employed persons. The exemption is granted subject to conditions requiring that suitable public or other sanitary conveniences shall be available for use by persons employed to work in the exempted premises.

STATUTORY INSTRUMENTS

1968 No. 1948

CUSTOMS AND EXCISE

The Import Duties (Temporary Exemptions) (No. 6) Order 1968

Made - - - -	*9th December* 1968
Laid before the House of Commons - -	*13th December* 1968
Coming into Operation	*1st January* 1969

The Lords Commissioners of Her Majesty's Treasury, by virtue of the powers conferred on them by sections 3(6) and 13 of the Import Duties Act 1958(a), and of all other powers enabling them in that behalf, on the recommendation of the Board of Trade hereby make the following Order:—

1.—(1) Until the beginning of 1st January 1970 or, in the case of goods in relation to which an earlier day is specified in Schedule 1 to this Order, until the beginning of that day, any import duty which is for the time being chargeable on goods of a heading of the Customs Tariff 1959 specified in that Schedule shall not be chargeable in respect of goods of any description there specified in relation to that heading.

(2) In the said Schedule 1—

(*a*) a reference to I.U.P.A.C. numbering, in relation to a compound having a ring structure, is to be taken as a reference to the system of numbering such compounds specified in the rules of the International Union of Pure and Applied Chemistry;

(*b*) an item marked with an asterisk is an item not exempt from import duty at the date of this Order;

(*c*) an item marked with a dagger is an item appearing under a revised description, as compared with the corresponding description under which exemption from import duty was allowed at the date of this Order.

(3) Any entry in column 2 in the said Schedule 1 is to be taken to comprise all goods which would be classified under an entry in the same terms constituting a subheading (other than the final subheading) in the relevant heading in the Customs Tariff 1959.

(4) For the purposes of classification under the Customs Tariff 1959, in so far as that depends on the rate of duty, any goods to which paragraph (1) of this Article applies shall be treated as chargeable with the same duty as if this Order had not been made.

2. Until the beginning of 1st January 1970, goods of subheading 39.03(A)(2)(*b*) of the Customs Tariff 1959 (which comprises photographic, including cinematograph, film base of cellulose acetate) shall not be chargeable with import duty to an amount greater than 10 per cent. of their value.

(a) 1958 c. 6.

3. The Import Duties (Temporary Exemptions) Orders specified in Schedule 2 to this Order are hereby revoked.

4.—(1) This Order may be cited as the Import Duties (Temporary Exemptions) (No. 6) Order 1968.

(2) The Interpretation Act 1889(a) shall apply for the interpretation of this Order as applies for the interpretation of an Act of Parliament.

(3) This Order shall come into operation on 1st January 1969.

Walter Harrison,
B. K. O'Malley,
Two of the Lords Commissioners
of Her Majesty's Treasury.

9th December 1968.

(a) 1889 c. 63.

SCHEDULE 1

GOODS TEMPORARILY EXEMPT FROM IMPORT DUTY

Tariff heading	*Description*
05.15	Sand eels (ammodytes) (until 3rd July 1969)
12.01	Castor seed
15.17	Residues containing not less than 5 per cent. by weight and not more than 60 per cent. by weight of tocopherols
25.19	Magnesite, dead-burned, containing (a) not less than 94 per cent. by weight of magnesium compounds expressed as MgO (b) a total of not more than 1·0 per cent. by weight of aluminium compounds and iron compounds expressed as Al_2O_3 and Fe_2O_3 (c) a total of not less than 2·5 per cent. by weight and not more than 5·0 per cent. by weight of calcium compounds and silicon compounds expressed as CaO and SiO_2, and in which the weight of calcium compounds expressed as CaO is not less than 1·5 times the weight of silicon compounds expressed as SiO_2 (until 3rd July 1969)
27.07	Pyridine bases, having a basicity equivalent to not less than 7·0 millilitres and not more than 12·5 millilitres of 1·0 N sulphuric acid solution when estimated by method No. RB. 1–62 of " Standard Methods for Testing Tar and its Products " published by the Standardisation of Tar Products Test Committee
	Pyridine bases, of which, after drying, not less than 70 per cent. by volume distils between 140° and 250° centigrade at normal pressure
28.13	Hydrogen bromide, anhydrous
28.14	Arsenic trichloride
	Boron tribromide
	Boron trichloride
	Phosphorus pentabromide
	Phosphorus pentafluoride
	Silicon tetrachloride
	Sulphur tetrafluoride
	Thionyl chloride
28.15	Carbonyl sulphide
	*tetra*Phosphorus heptasulphide
	Phosphorus pentasulphide, containing less than 15 parts per million by weight of arsenic calculated as As_2O_3, and containing less than 35 parts per million by weight of iron calculated as Fe
28.17	Potassium hydroxide, pharmaceutical quality
28.18	Barium hydroxide containing not more than 0·035 per cent. by weight of sulphides calculated as BaS
	Barium oxide (until 6th March 1969)
	Magnesium oxide, dead-burned but not fused, of a purity not less than 96 per cent., which contains (a) not more than 0·05 per cent. by weight of boron compounds expressed as B_2O_3, (b) a total of not more than 0·5 per cent. by weight of aluminium compounds and iron compounds expressed as Al_2O_3 and Fe_2O_3, and (c) a total of not less than 1·0 per cent. by weight and not more than 3·5 per cent. by weight of calcium compounds and silicon compounds expressed as CaO and SiO_2, the weight of calcium compounds being not less than 1·5 times and not more than 2·5 times the weight of silicon compounds; and (d) of which not less than 35 per cent. by weight is retained by a sieve having a nominal width of aperture of $\frac{3}{16}$ inch and conforming to British Standard 410:1962 (until 3rd July 1969)

Tariff heading	*Description*
28.20	Aluminium oxide, not being artificial corundum, being in the form of spheres and containing by weight not more than $0 \cdot 06$ per cent. of acid soluble sulphates expressed as SO_3 and not more than $0 \cdot 005$ per cent. of sodium expressed as Na, and all of which passes a sieve having a nominal width of aperture of $4 \cdot 76$ millimetres and not less than 99 per cent. by weight of which is retained by a sieve having a nominal width of aperture of $1 \cdot 00$ millimetre (both sieves conforming to British Standard 410:1962)
28.23	γ-Ferric oxide
28.28	Beryllium hydroxide
	Beryllium oxide
	Hydroxylammonium chloride containing not more than $0 \cdot 0005$ per cent. by weight of heavy metals estimated as Pb
	Hydroxylammonium sulphate
28.29	Potassium fluorosilicate
	Sodium fluoride, which does not contain impurities equivalent to more than 5×10^{-9} grammes of U_3O_8 per gramme, and of which 1 gramme must not contain impurities capable of depressing the estimation of U_3O_8 by more than 1×10^{-8} grammes, when determined fluorimetrically
	Sodium fluorosilicate
	Tungsten hexafluoride
28.30	Beryllium chloride
	Ferric chloride, analytical reagent quality
	Ferrous chloride, analytical reagent quality
28.32	Ammonium perchlorate
	Calcium chlorate
	Sodium perchlorate
28.33	Barium bromide
28.35	Zinc sulphide
28.38	Beryllium sulphate
	Magnesium sulphate, anhydrous, containing not less than $0 \cdot 05$ per cent. by weight and not more than $1 \cdot 0$ per cent. by weight of potassium compounds calculated as K
	Mercuric sulphate
	Potassium hydrogen per*mono*sulphate
	Thallous sulphate
28.39	Barium nitrate containing not more than $0 \cdot 006$ per cent. by weight of heavy metals calculated as Pb
	Beryllium nitrate
	Potassium nitrite
28.40	*tetra*Potassium pyrophosphate
28.42	Magnesium carbonate, light, in rectangular blocks of a weight not less than 25 grammes and not more than 125 grammes and of a cubic capacity not less than 115 cubic centimetres
	Manganous carbonate
	Nickel carbonate, basic
	Potassium hydrogen carbonate
28.43	Potassium ferricyanide
	Sodium nitroprusside
28.44	Ammonium thiocyanate
	Potassium cyanate
	Sodium thiocyanate
28.46	Sodium metaborate tetrahydrate, $Na_2B_2O_4$, $4H_2O$

| Tariff heading | Description |

28.47   Bismuth aluminate containing not less than 52 per cent. by weight and not more than 55 per cent. by weight of bismuth calculated as Bi on the dry anhydrous salt
Calcium dichromate
Sodium antimonate
Sodium tungstate containing not more than 0·0003 per cent. by weight of arsenic compounds calculated as As and not more than 0·005 per cent. by weight of molybdenum compounds calculated as Mo

28.48   *tri*Aluminium sodium tetradecahydrogen octaorthophosphate
Dihydroxyaluminium sodium carbonate
Ferric sodium pyrophosphate

28.49   Pyruvic acid enol phosphate, barium silver salt
Silver protein, mild, which satisfies the requirements of the British Pharmaceutical Codex
Silver protein, which satisfies the requirements of the British Pharmaceutical Codex

28.50   All goods of this heading other than radium compounds, natural uranium and compounds thereof and nuclear reactor cartridges, spent or irradiated

28.51   Deuterium oxide
Lithium sulphate, of which the lithium is in the form of a stable isotope either of atomic weight 6 or of atomic weight 7, of a value not less than £1 per gramme
*di*Sodium tetraborate, of which the boron is in the form of a stable isotope either of atomic weight 10 or of atomic weight 11, of a value not less than £1 per gramme

28.52   Compounds of uranium depleted in uranium-235, the following:—
         Uranium hexafluoride
         Uranium tetrafluoride
Mixed rare earth compounds containing not less than 3·5 per cent. by weight and not more than 9·0 per cent. by weight of combined fluorine estimated as F, and not less than 0·5 per cent. by weight and not more than 4·0 per cent. by weight of barium compounds estimated as $BaSO_4$; and of which not less than 10 per cent. by weight is retained by a sieve having a nominal width of aperture of 45 microns and comforming to British Standard 410:1962
Samarium trioxide

28.57   Aluminium sodium hydride
Lithium borohydride
Silane

28.58   Cyanogen bromide
Lithamide
Trichlorosilane containing not more than 0·002 parts per million by weight of boron compounds calculated as B

29.01   Acenaphthylene
Allene
Azulene
1,2-Benzanthracene
1,2-Benzofluorene
2,3-Benzofluorene
Bicyclo[2,2,1]hepta-2,5-diene
*iso*Butane
†*n*-But-1-ene
*cis*But-2-ene
*trans*But-2-ene
But-2-ene, mixed isomers
*iso*Butylbenzene
But-1-yne

Tariff heading	Description
29.01	Chrysene
	*pseudo*Cumene
	trans-trans-trans-Cyclododeca-1,5,9-triene
	Cyclo-octa-1,3-diene
	Cyclo-octa-1,5-diene
	Cyclo-octene
	Cyclopentane
	p-Cymene
	Decahydronaphthalene
	†*n*-Decane
	†*n*-Dec-1-ene
	1,2:3,4-Dibenzanthracene
	9,10-Dihydroanthracene
	3,3'-Dimethylbiphenyl
	1,2-Dimethylcyclohexane
	1,6-Dimethylnaphthalene
	2,3-Dimethylnaphthalene
	2,6-Dimethylnaphthalene
	2,7-Dimethylnaphthalene
	2,2-Dimethylpropane
	†*n*-Docos-1-ene
	†*n*-Dodecane
	†*n*-Dodec-1-ene
	†*n*-Dodecylbenzene
	†*n*-Eicosane
	†*n*-Eicos-1-ene
	5-Ethylidenebicyclo[2,2,1]hept-2-ene
	Fluoranthene
	Fluorene
	†*n*-Hept-1-ene
	†*n*-Hept-2-ene
	†*n*-Hept-3-ene
	†*n*-Hept-1-yne
	†*n*-Hexadecane
	†*n*-Hexadec-1-ene
	Humulene
	Indane
	Isoprene
	Mesitylene
	2-Methylbut-2-ene
	3-Methylcholanthrene (I.U.P.A.C. numbering)
	1-Methylcycloheptene
	Methylcyclohexane
	4-Methylcyclohexene
	Methylcyclopentane
	1-Methylcyclopentene
	1-Methylnaphthalene
	2-Methylnaphthalene
	Methylnaphthalene, mixed isomers
	2-Methylpentane
	2-Methylpent-1-ene
	4-Methylpent-1-ene
	cis-4-Methylpent-2-ene
	Methylstyrene, mixed isomers
	Myrcene
	Naphthacene
	Nona-1,8-diyne
	†*n*-Nonane
	†*n*-Octadec-1-ene
	†*n*-Oct-1-ene
	†*n*-Oct-2-ene

Tariff heading	Description

29.01　†*n*-Oct-1-yne
　　　†*n*-Penta-1,3-diene
　　　Pentamethylbenzene
　　　†*n*-Pent-1-ene
　　　Perylene
　　　Phellandrene
　　　Phenylacetylene
　　　Picene
　　　Propyne
　　　Pyrene
　　　β-Santalene
　　　Squalane
　　　Squalene
　　　*trans*Stilbene
　　　m-Terphenyl
　　　p-Terphenyl
　　　†*n*-Tetracosane
　　　†*n*-Tetradecane
　　　†*n*-Tetradec-1-ene
　　　1,2,3,4-Tetrahydro-1,1,2,4,4,7-hexamethylnaphthalene
　　　1,2,3,4-Tetrahydronaphthalene
　　　4,5,9,10-Tetrahydropyrene (I.U.P.A.C. numbering)
　　　1,2,4,5-Tetramethylbenzene
　　　Tricyclo[5,2,1,0^{2,6}]decane
　　　†*n*-Tridecane
　　　2,2,4-Trimethylpentane
　　　†*n*-Undecane
　　　o-Xylene
　　　m-Xylene

29.02　Aldrin
　　　Allyl chloride
　　　Benzotrifluoride
　　　2-Bromobenzotrifluoride
　　　4-Bromobenzotrifluoride
　　　2-Bromobut-1-ene
　　　1-Bromo-3-chloro-2-methylpropane
　　　1-Bromo-3-chloropropane
　　　†4-Bromo-*n*-heptane
　　　†2-Bromo-*n*-hexane
　　　†3-Bromo-*n*-hexane
　　　2-Bromomesitylene
　　　2-Bromopropene
　　　Bromotrifluoroethylene
　　　Bromotrifluoromethane
　　　Carbon tetrafluoride
　　　Chlordane
　　　2-Chlorobenzotrifluoride
　　　3-Chlorobenzotrifluoride
　　　4-Chlorobenzotrifluoride
　　　*2-Chlorobuta-1,3-diene (until 6th March 1969)
　　　†1-Chloro-*n*-butane
　　　†1-Chloro-*n*-but-1-ene
　　　†3-Chloro-*n*-but-1-ene
　　　†1-Chloro-*n*-but-2-ene
　　　1-(Chloromethyl)naphthalene
　　　1-Chloronaphthalene
　　　†1-Chloro-*n*-octane
　　　Chloropentafluoroethane
　　　1-Chloroprop-1-ene
　　　3-Chloropropyne
　　　2-Chlorotoluene

Tariff heading	*Description*

29.02
    2-Chloro-*p*-xylene
Decachlorobicyclopenta-2,4-dienyl
1,4-Dibromobut-2-ene
2,3-Dibromobut-2-ene
Dibromodifluoromethane
1,2-Dibromoethane
Dibromomethane
1,2-Dibromo-2-methylpropane
1,1-Dibromoprop-1-ene
1,2-Dibromotetrafluoroethane
αα′-Dibromo-*m*-xylene
1,3-Dichlorobenzene
2,6-Dichlorobenzylidene chloride
2,3-Dichlorobuta-1,3-diene
1,4-Dichlorobutane
†1,3-Dichloro-*n*-but-2-ene
1,4-Dichlorobut-2-ene
1,1-Dichloro-2,2-di-(4-chlorophenyl)ethane
1,1-Dichloro-2,2-di-(4-ethylphenyl)ethane
1,2-Dichloroethylene
2,3-Dichlorohexafluorobut-2-ene
1,2-Dichlorohexafluorocyclopentene
1,1-Dichloroprop-1-ene
1,3-Dichloropropene
2,3-Dichloroprop-1-ene
2,6-Dichlorotoluene
3,4-Dichlorotoluene
2,5-Dichloro-*p*-xylene
1,1-Difluoroethane
1,1-Difluoroethylene
Diphenylchloromethane
Dodecachloropentacyclo[5,2,1,0^{2,6},0^{3,9},0^{5,8}]decane
1,6,7,8,9,14,15,16,17,17,18,18-Dodecachloropentacyclo-
    [12,2,1,1^{6,9},0^{2,13},0^{5,10}]octadeca-7,15-diene
Fluorobenzene
4-Fluorobenzotrifluoride
2-Fluoronaphthalene
Heptachlor
Heptafluoro-1-iodopropane
Hexabromobenzene
1,2,5,6,9,10-Hexabromocyclododecane
Hexachlorobuta-1,3-diene
1,2,3,4,5,6-Hexachlorocyclohexane, mixed isomers, of which either
    (*a*) the α-isomer content is not more than 50 per cent. by weight, or
    (*b*) the γ-isomer content is not less than 35 per cent. by weight pro-
    vided that, in a case where the γ-isomer content is not less than
    35 per cent. and not more than 40 per cent. by weight, not less than
    90 per cent. by weight of the material passes a sieve having a nominal
    width of aperture of 53 microns and conforming to British Standard
    410:1962
α-1,2,3,4,5,6-Hexachlorocyclohexane
γ-1,2,3,4,5,6-Hexachlorocyclohexane
Hexachlorocyclopentadiene
Hexafluoropropene
2-Iodobenzotrifluoride
Methallyl chloride
3-Methylbenzyl bromide
4-Methylbenzyl bromide
Octafluorocyclobutane
Pentachloroethane
1,1,2,2-Tetrabromoethane

Tariff heading   *Description*

29.02   1,2,4,5-Tetrachlorobenzene
          *1,1,2,2-Tetrachloroethane (until 6th March 1969)
          1,2,2,3-Tetrachloropropane
          2,3,5,6-Tetrachloro-*p*-xylene
          Tribromofluoromethane
          1,2,3-Tribromo-2-methylpropane
          1,2,3-Trichlorobenzene
          1,2,4-Trichlorobenzene
          Trichlorobenzene, mixed isomers, containing not less than 77·5 per
            cent. by weight of 1,2,4-trichlorobenzene
          Trifluoroiodomethane
          Vinyl fluoride

29.03   Benzene-1,3-disulphonic acid
          1-*tert*Butyl-3,4,5-trimethyl-2,6-dinitrobenzene
          Chloropicrin
          1,5-Dinitronaphthalene
          Ethanesulphonyl chloride
          1-Ethyl-2-nitrobenzene
          1-Fluoro-2-nitrobenzene
          Methanesulphonyl chloride
          2-Nitrobiphenyl
          4-Nitrobiphenyl
          Nitroethane
          Nitromethane
          1-Nitronaphthalene
          1-Nitropropane
          2-Nitropropane
          3-Nitro-*o*-xylene
          2-Nitro-*p*-xylene
          1,1,3,3,5-Pentamethyl-4,6-dinitroindane
          *di*Sodium benzene-1,3-disulphonate
          Sodium 2-bromoethanesulphonate
          Sodium 4-chlorobenzenesulphonate
          †Sodium 3-chloro-*n*-but-2-ene-1-sulphonate
          Sodium dibunate
          Sodium ethylenesulphonate
          Sodium styrenesulphonate, mixed isomers
          1,3,5-Trinitrobenzene

29.04   Adonitol
          Allyl alcohol
          †Amyl alcohol, containing not less than 58 per cent. by weight of
            n-pentan-1-ol and not more than 1 per cent. by weight of aldehydes
            or ketones calculated as $C_5H_{10}O$
          D-Arabitol
          3-Bromopropan-1-ol
          †*n*-Butane-1,3-diol
          Butane-1,4-diol
          †*n*-Butane-2,3-diol
          Butane-1,2,4-triol
          But-2-ene-1,4-diol
          †*n*-But-2-en-1-ol
          But-3-en-2-ol
          Butylchloral hydrate
          But-2-yne-1,4-diol
          But-3-yn-1-ol
          But-3-yn-2-ol
          4-Chlorobutan-1-ol
          2-Chloroethanol
          3-Chloropropane-1,2-diol

Tariff heading	Description
29.04	3-Chloropropan-1-ol

Decane-1,10-diol
1,6-Dibromo-1,6-dideoxymannitol
2,6-Dimethylheptan-4-ol
2,5-Dimethylhexane-2,5-diol
(±)-3,7-Dimethylnona-1,6-dien-3-ol
2,4-Dimethylnonan-4-ol
3,7-Dimethyloctan-3-ol
Dimethyloctanol, mixed 2,6,2- and 3,7,3- isomers
(−)-3,7-Dimethyloct-6-en-1-ol
3,7-Dimethyloct-6-en-1-yn-3-ol
3,6-Dimethyloct-4-yne-3,6-diol
2,4-Dimethylpentan-1-ol
2,2-Dimethylpropanediol
2,2-Dimethylpropanol
*meso*Erythritol
Ethchlorvynol
2-Ethylbutan-1-ol
2-Ethylhexane-1,3-diol
2-Ethyl-2-hydroxymethylpropanediol
2-Ethyl-4-methylpentan-1-ol
Farnesol
Glyoxal sodium bisulphite
†*n*-Heptan-1-ol
†*n*-Hept-1-en-4-ol
Hexadecyl alcohol, mixed isomers, which freezes at a temperature not higher than −40° centigrade
2*H*-Hexafluoropropan-2-ol
Hexane-1,6-diol
†*n*-Hexane-2,5-diol
Hexane-1,2,6-triol
Hexanetriol, mixed isomers
†*n*-Hexan-1-ol
†*n*-Hex-3-en-1-ol
7-Hydroxy-3,7-dimethyloctanal sodium bisulphite
2-Hydroxymethyl-2-methylpropanediol
2-Hydroxymethyl-2-nitropropanediol
Methallyl alcohol
3-Methylbutan-1-ol, of a purity not less than 90 per cent.
2-Methylbutan-2-ol
6-Methylhept-5-en-2-ol
3-Methylpentyn-3-ol
2-Methylpropan-2-ol containing not more than 0·007 per cent. by weight of unsaturated compounds calculated as butene
Nerolidol
1*H*,1*H*,5*H*-Octafluoropentan-1-ol
†2-*n*-Octyl-*n*-dodecan-1-ol
Pentane-1,5-diol
†*n*-Pentan-1-ol
Phytol
*iso*Phytol
Pinacol
Propane-1,3-diol
Prop-2-yn-1-ol
Succinaldehyde di(sodium bisulphite)
1*H*,1*H*,3*H*-Tetrafluoropropan-1-ol
3,7,11,15-Tetramethylhexadecane-1,2,3-triol
Tridecyl alcohol, mixed isomers (until 6th March 1969)
3,7,9-Trimethyldeca-1,6-dien-3-ol
2,2,4-Trimethylpentan-1-ol

Tariff heading	*Description*

29.04   †*n*-Undecan-1-ol
Xylitol

29.05   17α-Allyloestr-4-en-17*β*-ol
Borneol
*iso*Borneol
Dicyclopropylmethanol
Dihydrotachysterol
2,2-Di-(4-hydroxycyclohexyl)propane
1,4-Di(hydroxymethyl)cyclohexane
17α-Ethyloestr-4-en-17*β*-ol
Ethynodiol
Fenchyl alcohol
*meso*Inositol
Lynoestrenol
2-Methyl-4-phenylbutan-2-ol
3-Methyl-1-phenylpentan-3-ol
3-Nitrobenzyl alcohol
4-Nitrobenzyl alcohol
Nopol
1-Phenylethanol
α-Terpineol, having a freezing point not less than 20° centigrade
2,2,2-Trichlorodi-(4-chlorophenyl)ethanol
4,7,7-Trimethylbicyclo[4,1,0]hept-4-en-3-ylmethanol

29.06   2-Benzylphenol
2-*tert*Butyl-4-ethylphenol
2-*sec*Butylphenol (until 1st May 1969)
4-*sec*Butylphenol
2-*tert*Butylphenol
3,5-Di*tert*butyl-4-hydroxybiphenyl
†1,1-Di-(3-*tert*butyl-4-hydroxy-6-methylphenyl)-*n*-butane
2,6-Di*tert*butylphenol (until 3rd July 1969)
Di-(3,5-di*tert*butyl-4-hydroxyphenyl)methane
†2,3-Di-(3,4-dihydroxybenzyl)-*n*-butane
2,2′-Dihydroxybiphenyl
3,4-Dihydroxybiphenyl
1,3-Dihydroxynaphthalene
1,5-Dihydroxynaphthalene
2,3-Dihydroxynaphthalene
†3,4-Di-(4-hydroxyphenyl)-*n*-hexane-3,4-diol
Di-(1-methylbutyl)phenol, mixed isomers
2,4-Di*tert*pentylphenol
2,5-Di*tert*pentylquinol
2,6-Di*iso*propylphenol
2-Hydroxybiphenyl
4-Hydroxybiphenyl
Indan-5-ol
2-Methylquinol
1-Naphthol
†3-*n*-Pentadecylphenol
4-*tert*Pentylphenol
*iso*Propylcresol, mixed isomers
Salicyl alcohol
2,4,2′,4′-Tetrahydroxybiphenyl
Thymol
†1,1,3-Tri-(5-*tert*butyl-4-hydroxy-2-methylphenyl)-*n*-butane-toluene
    complex
2,4,6-Tri-(3,5-di*tert*butyl-4-hydroxybenzyl)mesitylene
2,3,5-Trimethylquinol
2,4-Xylenol
3,5-Xylenol

Tariff heading   *Description*

29.07   3-Bromophenol
               3-Chloro-4-hydroxybiphenyl
               3-Chlorophenol
               Chloro-5-*iso*propyl-*m*-cresol (−OH at 1), mixed isomers
               4-Chloro-3,5-xylenol (until 3rd July 1969)
               2,3-Dichlorophenol
               2,2-Di-(3,5-dichloro-4-hydroxyphenyl)propane
               6,7-Dihydroxynaphthalene-2-sulphonic acid
               2-Fluorophenol
               4-Fluorophenol
               Hexachlorophane
               5-Hydroxynaphthalene-1-sulphonic acid
               *di*Sodium 1,8-dihydroxynaphthalene-3,6-disulphonate
               2,4,5-Trichlorophenol (until 3rd July 1969)
               2-Trifluoromethylphenol
               3-Trifluoromethylphenol
               4-Trifluoromethylphenol

29.08   4-Allylanisole
               Allyl ethyl ether
               Anethole
               Batyl alcohol
               1-(2-Benzylphenoxy)propan-2-ol
               †*n*-Butyl vinyl ether
               *iso*Butyl vinyl ether
               Chloromethyl methyl ether
               †Di-*n*-butyldigol
               2,5-Di*tert*butylperoxy-2,5-dimethylhexane
               1,4-Di-(1-*tert*butylperoxy-1-methylethyl)benzene
               1,1-Di*tert*butylperoxy-3,3,5-trimethylcyclohexane
               Di-(2-chloroethyl) ether
               2,2-Di-(4,4-di*tert*butylperoxycyclohexyl)propane
               Di-(αα-dimethylbenzyl) peroxide
               1,2-Diethoxyethane
               Diethyldigol
               †Di-*n*-hexyl ether
               †2-[2,2-Di-(2-hydroxyethoxymethyl)-*n*-butoxy]ethanol
               1,2-Dimethoxyethane
               Dimethyldigol
               Dimethyl ether
               Dimethyltetragol
               Dimethyltrigol
               2,4-Dinitrophenetole
               1,4-Dioxan
               Di(phenoxyphenoxy)benzene, mixed isomers
               Di-(3-phenoxyphenyl) ether
               Di*iso*propylbenzene hydroperoxide, mixed 1,3- and 1,4- isomers
               Di-(2,3,3,3-tetrachloropropyl) ether
               Ethoxyacetylene
               2-Ethoxynaphthalene
               Ethyldigol, containing not more than 1 per cent. by weight of ethanediol
               13β-Ethyl-17α-ethynyl-3-methoxygona-2,5(10)-dien-17β-ol
               Ethyl vinyl ether
               †*n*-Hexyldigol
               p-Menthanyl hydroperoxide
               †3-Methoxy-*n*-butan-1-ol
               Methoxyflurane
               4-Methoxy-4-methylpentan-2-ol
               2-Methoxynaphthalene
               4-Methoxy-1-naphthol
               Methyl vinyl ether

Tariff heading   *Description*

29.08   Musk ambrette
4-Nitroanisole
4-Nitrophenetole
*iso*Pentyl 2-phenylethyl ether
2-Phenoxyethanol
Potassium guaiacolsulphonate
1,1,1-Trichlorodi-(4-methoxyphenyl)ethane
Trigol containing not more than 0·1 per cent. by weight of digol
1,2,3-Tri-(2-hydroxyethoxy)propane
†1,2,3-Tri-(2-hydroxy-*n*-propoxy)propane
Tri-α-propylene glycol *mono*methyl ether

29.09   Allyl glycidyl ether
1-Bromo-2,3-epoxypropane
†*n*-Butyl glycidyl ether
1-Chloro-2,3-epoxypropane
Dicyclopentadiene dioxide
Dieldrin
1,4-Di-(2,3-epoxypropoxy)butane
Endrin
†1,2-Epoxy-*n*-butane
Epoxybutane, mixed 1,2- and 2,3- isomers
αβ-Epoxyethylbenzene
Glycidol

29.10   α-Anhydroglucochloral
1-Bromo-2,2-diethoxyethane
8-*tert*Butyl-1,4-dioxaspiro[4,5]decane
1-Chloro-2,2-diethoxyethane
1,1-Diethoxy-3,7-dimethylocta-2,6-diene
†1,1-Diethoxy-*n*-hex-2-ene
1,1-Dimethoxy-3,7-dimethylocta-2,6-diene
†1,1-Dimethoxy-*n*-octane
1,3-Dioxan
1,3-Dioxolan containing not more than 0·02 per cent. by weight of water
1-Ethoxy-1,3,3-trimethoxypropane
2-Ethyl-2-methyl-1,3-dioxolan
Hexahydro-2,3,6,7-tetrahydroxy-1,4,5,8-tetraoxanaphthalene
Penthrichloral
4,4a,5,9b-Tetrahydroindeno[1,2-*d*]-1,3-dioxin
4,4a,9,9a-Tetrahydroindeno[2,1-*d*]-1,3-dioxin
1,1,3,3-Tetramethoxypropane

29.11   Acrylaldehyde
β-8′-Apocarotenal
4-*tert*Butylbenzaldehyde
3-(4-*tert*Butylphenyl)-2-methylpropionaldehyde
†*n*-Butyraldehyde
*iso*Butyraldehyde
*Crotonaldehyde containing not more than 4 per cent. by weight of water (until 6th March 1969)
*iso*Cyclocitral
2,4-Dihydroxybenzaldehyde
3,4-Dihydroxybenzaldehyde
2,3-Dimethoxybenzaldehyde
2,6-Dimethylhept-5-enal
3,7-Dimethylnona-2,6-dienal
2-Ethylhexanal
Glutaraldehyde
DL-Glyceraldehyde
Glycidaldehyde
Glyoxal

Tariff heading   *Description*

29.11
†*n*-Heptanal
†*n*-Hex-2-enal
4-(4-Hydroxy-4-methylpentyl)cyclohex-3-enaldehyde
Methacrylaldehyde
2-Naphthaldehyde
1,2,3,4,5,6,7,8-Octahydro-8,8-dimethyl-2-naphthaldehyde
Terephthalaldehyde
m-Tolualdehyde
3,5,5-Trimethylhexanal
2,6,10-Trimethylundec-10-enal
†*n*-Valeraldehyde
*iso*Valeraldehyde

29.12
4-Chlorobenzaldehyde (until 6th March 1969)
4-Chloro-3-nitrobenzaldehyde
3,4-Dichlorobenzaldehyde
2,4-Dinitrobenzaldehyde
2-Nitrobenzaldehyde
4-Nitrobenzaldehyde
5-Nitrosalicylaldehyde
Sodium 2-formylbenzenesulphonate

29.13
Acetoin
Acetoin dimer
Acetonylacetone
Acetovanillone
4-Acetyl-6-*tert*butyl-1,1-dimethylindane
7-Acetyl-6-ethyl-1,2,3,4-tetrahydro-1,1,4,4-tetramethylnaphthalene
7-Acetyl-2-methyl-5-*iso*propylbicyclo[2,2,2]oct-2-ene
4-Acetyl-3,7,7-trimethylbicyclo[4,1,0]hept-2-ene
Benzoin
†*p*-Bromo-*n*-valerophenone
Butanedione
†*n*-Butyrophenone
(+)-Camphor
Canthaxanthin
L-Carvone
Chloranil
†*p*-Chloro-*n*-butyrophenone
2-Chlorocyclohexanone
2-[α-(4-Chlorophenyl)phenylacetyl]indane-1,3-dione
Cycloheptadecanone
Cycloheptadec-9-enone
Cycloheptanone
Cyclohexane-1,3-dione
*Cyclo-octanone (until 3rd July 1969)
Cyclopentadecanone
†4-*n*-Decyloxy-2-hydroxybenzophenone
Dibenzo[*a,i*]pyrene-5,8-dione
1,3-Dichloroacetone
2,5-Dichloro-*p*-benzoquinone
3,3:20,20-Di(ethylenedioxy)-17α-hydroxypregn-5-en-11-one
1,3-Dihydroxyacetone
2,4-Dihydroxyacetophenone
2,6-Dihydroxyacetophenone
2,2′-Dihydroxy-4,4′-dimethoxybenzophenone
2,2′-Dihydroxy-4-methoxybenzophenone
5,11α-Dihydroxy-6β-methyl-5α-pregnane-3,20-dione
11β,17α-Dihydroxypregna-1,4-diene-3,20-dione
11β,21-Dihydroxypregna-4,17(20)-dien-3-one
3β,17α-Dihydroxy-5β-pregnane-11,20-dione
11β,21-Dihydroxypregna-1,4,17(20)-trien-3-one

Tariff heading   *Description*

29.13   11β,17α-Dihydroxypregn-4-ene-3,20-dione
           3β,17α-Dihydroxypregn-5-en-20-one
           4,4-Dimethoxybutan-2-one
           2,6-Dimethylheptan-4-one
           6,10-Dimethylundeca-5,9-dien-2-one
           3,17-Dioxoandrost-4-en-19-al
           1,1-Diphenylacetone
           Dydrogesterone
           2-Ethylanthraquinone
           17,17-Ethylenedioxyandrosta-1,4-dien-3-one
           13β-Ethyl-3-methoxygona-2,5(10)-diene-17-one
           Fenchone
           Flumethasone
           Fluorenone
           6α-Fluoro-17α,21-dihydroxy-16α-methylpregn-4-ene-3,20-dione
           6α-Fluoro-21-hydroxy-16α,17α-*iso*propylidenedioxypregn-4-ene-
               3,20-dione
           Fluorometholone
           Flurandrenolone
           †*n*-Heptan-2-one
           †*n*-Heptan-3-one
           3*H*,3*H*-Hexafluoroacetylacetone
           †2-*n*-Hexylcyclopent-2-enone
           †2-*n*-Hexylidenecyclopentanone
           2-Hydroxyacetophenone
           4-Hydroxyacetophenone
           4-Hydroxybenzophenone
           2-Hydroxy-3-methylcyclopent-2-enone
           †2-Hydroxy-4-*n*-octyloxybenzophenone
           17α-Hydroxypregna-1,4-diene-3,11,20-trione
           3β-Hydroxypregn-5-en-20-one
           4-Hydroxypropiophenone
           17β-Hydroxy-4,5-seco-19-norandrostane-3,5-dione
           (±)-*iso*Menthone
           Mesityl oxide
           Methandienone
           4-Methoxy-4-methylpentan-2-one
           4-(4-Methoxyphenyl)-3-methylbutan-2-one
           †*p*-Methyl-*n*-butyrophenone
           5-Methylheptan-3-one
           5-Methylhexan-2-one
           6-Methyl-α-ionone
           †3-Methyl-2-(*n*-pent-2-enyl)cyclopent-2-enone
           4-Methyl-4-phenylpentan-2-one
           4-Methyl-4-*p*-tolylpentan-2-one
           Musk ketone
           1,4-Naphthaquinone
           †*n*-Nonan-2-one
           Norethandrolone
           Norethisterone
           (±)-Norgestrel
           †*n*-Octan-3-one
           Oestr-5(10)-ene-3,17-dione
           Oestr-4-en-17-one
           3-Oxodinorchol-4-en-22-al
           Oxymetholone
           †*n*-Pentan-2-one
           Pentan-3-one
           4-*tert*Pentylcyclohexanone
           Phenacyl bromide

Tariff heading *Description*

29.13 Pinacolone
Pyruvaldehyde
Sodium 2,2′-dihydroxy-4,4′-dimethoxybenzophenone-5-sulphonate
2,4,2′,4′-Tetrahydroxybenzophenone
Tetramethylcyclobutane-1,3-dione
2,5-Toluquinone, having a melting point of not less than 67·0° centigrade
*1,1,1-Trifluoroacetylacetone, of a purity not less than 99 per cent. (until 6th March 1969)
14α,17α,21-Trihydroxypregn-4-ene-3,20-dione
†*n*-Undecan-2-one
†*n*-Valerophenone
Zerumbone

29.14 Acrylic acid
Allethrin
Allyl 3-cyclohexylpropionate
Allyl methacrylate
Allyl trifluoroacetate
Aluminium acetate, basic
†Ammonium pentadecafluoro-*n*-octanoate
Arachidic acid
Arachidonic acid
Biphenyl-4-carboxylic acid
(−)-Bornyl acetate
4β-Bromo-17α,21-dihydroxy-5β-pregnane-3,11,20-trione 21-acetate
†*n*-Butane-1,3-diol dimethacrylate
Butane-1,4-diol dimethacrylate
*iso*Butyl acrylate
4-*tert*Butylbenzoic acid
2-*sec*Butyl-4,6-dinitrophenyl 3-methylcrotonate
*tert*Butyl 2-ethylperbutyrate
†*n*-Butyric acid
*iso*Butyric acid
Calcium sorbate
Chloroacetic anhydride
Chloroacetyl chloride (until 1st May 1969)
2-Chlorocinnamic acid
3-(2-Chloroethoxy)-9α-fluoro-11β,21-dihydroxy-20-oxo-16α,17α-*iso*propylidenedioxypregna-3,5-diene-6-carbaldehyde 21-acetate
2-Chloro-4-nitrobenzoic acid
4-Chloro-3-nitrobenzoic acid
*Citronellyl 3-methylcrotonate (until 6th March 1969)
Crotonic acid
Cyclopent-2-enyl cyclohexylacetate
Cyclopropanecarboxyl chloride
Decahydro-2-naphthyl acetate
†*n*-Dec-2-enoic acid
Decyl acrylate, mixed isomers
Dichloroacetic acid
Dichloroacetyl chloride
Dihydrocarveyl acetate
Dihydrocarveyl propionate
17α,21-Dihydroxy-16α-methylpregna-1,4,9(11)-triene-3,20-dione 21-acetate
17α,21-Dihydroxypregn-4-ene-3,20-dione 21-acetate
3β,17α-Dihydroxypregn-5-en-20-one 3-acetate
3α,20-Dihydroxy-5β-pregn-17(20)-en-11-one diacetate
3β,11α-Dihydroxy-5α-pregn-16-en-20-one diacetate
1,1-Dimethyl-5-methylenehept-6-enyl acetate

Tariff heading   *Description*
29.14   (−)-3,7-Dimethyloct-6-enyl acetate
           †1,1-Dimethyl-2-phenylethyl *n*-butyrate
           1,1-Dimethyl-3-phenylpropyl acetate
           cis-3,3-(2,2-Dimethyltrimethylenedioxy)-6β-methyl-5α-pregn-
               17(20)-ene-5,11β,21-triol 21-acetate
           (±)-1,5-Dimethyl-1-vinylhept-4-enyl acetate
           2,5-Dinitrobenzoic acid
           Drostanolone propionate
           Ethanediol dimethacrylate
           Ethyl β-8′-apocarotenoate
           Ethyl fluoroacetate
           2-Ethyl-2-hydroxymethylpropanediol trimethacrylate
           Ethyl methacrylate
           Ethyl trichloroacetate
           Ethynodiol diacetate
           Fenchyl acetate
           Flumethasone 21-pivalate
           9α-Fluoro-11β,17α-dihydroxypregn-4-ene-3,20-dione 17-acetate
           Geranyl 5,9,13-trimethyltetradeca-4,8,12-trienoate
           Glycerol 1,3-dipropionate
           Glycerol tripropionate
           Glycidyl methacrylate (until 3rd July 1969)
           †Heptafluoro-*n*-butyric acid
           †*n*-Heptanoic acid
           †*n*-Hept-2-enoic acid
           †*n*-Heptyl acrylate
           †*n*-Hex-3-enoic acid
           †17α-Hydroxypregn-4-ene-3,20-dione *n*-heptanoate
           †17α-Hydroxypregn-4-ene-3,20-dione *n*-hexanoate
           Iodoacetic acid
           Lead tetra-acetate
           Linalyl cinnamate
           Medroxyprogesterone acetate
           †3-Methoxy-*n*-butyl acetate
           2-Methoxyethyl chloroformate
           Methyl acetate of a purity not less than 98 per cent.
           Methyl 2-chloro-3-(4-chlorophenyl)propionate
           Methyl chloroformate
           3-(4-Methylcyclohex-3-enyl)but-3-enyl acetate
           Methyl cyclopropanecarboxylate
           Methyl formate
           †Methyl *n*-hexanoate of a purity not greater than 98 per cent.
           Methyl 1-methyl-4-*iso*propylbicyclo[2,2,2]oct-2-ene-6-carboxylate
           *Methyl *p*-toluate (until 6th March 1969)
           †3-Methyl-*n*-valeric acid
           †4-Methyl-*n*-valeric acid
           1-Naphthoic acid
           (±)-Nerolidyl acetate
           (±)-Nerolidyl *iso*butyrate
           (±)-Nerolidyl formate
           (±)-Nerolidyl propionate
           2-Nitrobenzoic acid
           4-Nitrobenzoic acid
           2-Nitrocinnamic acid
           3-Nitrocinnamic acid
           4-Nitrocinnamic acid
           4-Nitrophenylacetic acid
           †*n*-Nonanoic acid

Tariff heading	Description

29.14 †*n*-Non-3-enoic acid
Nonyl acetate, mixed isomers, having a specific rotation at 20° centigrade to the D line of sodium of between $-9°$ and $-13°$
†*n*-Non-2-ynoic acid
Norethisterone acetate
†*n*-Octanoic acid (until 3rd July 1969)
†*n*-Oct-2-ynoic acid
†Pentadecafluoro-*n*-octanoic acid
Pentafluoropropionic acid
Pent-4-enoic acid
†2-Phenyl-*n*-butyric acid
Phenyl chloroformate
2-Phenylethyl cinnamate
Pivalic acid
Potassium sorbate
2-(4-*iso*Propenylcyclohex-1-enyl)ethyl formate
Propiolic acid
Propionic anhydride
†*n*-Propyl acrylate
*iso*Propyl acrylate
Sodium fluoroacetate
Sodium formate
†Sodium pentadecafluoro-*n*-octanoate
Sodium trichloroacetate
Sodium trifluoroacetate
Tetragol di-(2-ethylhexanoate)
Tetragol dimethacrylate
o-Toluic acid ($-$COOH at 1)
m-Toluic acid ($-$COOH at 1)
p-Toluic acid ($-$COOH at 1)
Tricyclo[5,2,1,0^{2,6}]dec-4-en-8-yl acetate
Tricyclo[5,2,1,0^{2,6}]dec-4-en-8-yl formate
Triethyl orthoacetate
Triethyl orthopropionate
Trifluoroacetic acid
Trigol di-(2-ethylbutyrate)
Trigol dimethacrylate
$3\beta,17\alpha,21$-Trihydroxypregn-5-en-20-one 21-acetate
4,7,7-Trimethylbicyclo[4,1,0]hept-4-en-3-ylmethyl acetate
Trimethyl orthoformate
2,2,4-Trimethylpentane-1,3-diol 1-*iso*butyrate
2,2,4-Trimethylpentane-1,3-diol di*iso*butyrate
2,4,6-Trinitrobenzoic acid which yields not more than $0\cdot1$ per cent. by weight of sulphated ash
Undec-10-enoic acid
Vaccenic acid
*iso*Valeric acid
†Vinyl *n*-butyrate
Vinyl chloroacetate
Vinyl 2-ethylhexanoate
Vinyl propionate
†Zinc *n*-heptanoate

29.15 *cis*Aconitic acid
Ammonium ferric oxalate
Azelaic acid
Benzenedicarboxylic acid, mixed isomers
Benzene-1,2,4-tricarboxylic anhydride
Bicyclo[2,2,1]hept-5-ene-2,3-dicarboxylic acid
Bicyclo[2,2,1]hept-5-ene-2,3-dicarboxylic anhydride
Biphenyl-2,2′-dicarboxylic acid

Tariff heading   *Description*

29.15   †*n*-Butyl hydrogen itaconate
         Calcium malonate
         Cyclohexane-1,2-diacetic acid
         Cyclohexane-1,2-dicarboxylic anhydride
         Cyclohex-4-ene-1,2-dicarboxylic anhydride
         †Di-*n*-butyl itaconate
         Dichloromaleic anhydride
         Dimethyl itaconate
         Dimethyl maleate
         Dioctyl 2*H*,3*H*-hexachlorobicyclo[2,2,1]hept-5-ene-2,3-dicarboxylate,
             mixed isomers
         †Di-*n*-octyl phthalate
         Di(tridecyl) sodium-sulphosuccinate, mixed isomers
         Dodecane-1,12-dioic acid
         Dodecenylsuccinic acid, mixed isomers
         Ethanediol cyclic brassylate
         Glutaric anhydride
         2*H*,3*H*-Hexachlorobicyclo[2,2,1]hept-5-ene-2,3-dicarboxylic acid
         2*H*,3*H*-Hexachlorobicyclo[2,2,1]hept-5-ene-2,3-dicarboxylic anhydride
         1,8,9,10,11,11-Hexachlorotricyclo[6,2,1,0^{2,7}]undec-9-ene-
             4,5-dicarboxylic anhydride
         Hexafluoroglutaric acid
         Hexafluoroglutaryl chloride
         Hydroxydione sodium succinate
         Isophthalic acid
         Itaconic anhydride
         Malonic acid
         Methylbicyclo[2,2,1]hept-5-ene-2,3-dicarboxylic anhydride
         Oxalic acid (until 6th March 1969)
         Pimelic acid
         Pyromellitic dianhydride
         Sodium oxalate which, in the form in which it is imported, contains
             not less than 5·0 per cent. by weight of moisture and which contains
             in the dried material not more than 98·0 per cent. by weight of
             oxalates expressed as sodium oxalate, $Na_2C_2O_4$
         Suberic acid
         4-Sulphophthalic acid
         4-Sulphophthalic acid, diammonium salt
         Terephthaloyl chloride
         Tetrabromophthalic anhydride
         Tetrachlorophthalic anhydride

29.16   Acetone-1,3-dicarboxylic acid
         Aluminium hydroxide di-(*O*-acetylsalicylate)
         Antimony potassium tartrate, which satisfies the requirements of the
             British Pharmacopoeia
         †*n*-Butoxycarbonylmethyl-*n*-butyl phthalate
         †*n*-Butyl 4,4-di*tert*butylperoxyvalerate
         †*n*-Butyl glycollate
         †4-*n*-Butyryl-2,3-dichlorophenoxyacetic acid
         Calcium glucoheptonate, pyrogen free
         Calcium D-saccharate
         Carbenoxolone
         Carbenoxolone, disodium salt
         Cyclandelate
         2,5-Dichloro-6-methoxybenzoic acid
         Diethyl ethoxymethylenemalonate
         2,5-Dihydroxybenzoic acid
         3,4-Dihydroxybenzoic acid
         3,5-Dihydroxybenzoic acid
         2,2-Di(hydroxymethyl)propionic acid

Tariff heading	Description

29.16   3,4-Dihydroxyphenylacetic acid
2,3-Dimethoxybenzoic acid
3,5-Dimethoxybenzoic acid
3,4-Dimethoxyphenylacetic acid
Dimethyl methoxymethylenemalonate
Enoxolone
3,4-Epoxy-6-methylcyclohexylmethyl 3,4-epoxy-6-methylcyclohexane-
    carboxylate
Ethacrynic acid
Ethyl diethoxyacetate
Ethyl 2-hydroxy*iso*butyrate
Ethyl 2-hydroxy-2-methylbutyrate
Ethyl pyruvate
Ethyl sodioacetoacetate (until 6th March 1969)
Galacturonic acid
Glucuronic acid
Glycollic acid
Glyoxylic acid
2-(4-Hydroxybenzoyl)benzoic acid
3-Hydroxycinnamic acid
4-Hydroxy-3,5-dimethoxycinnamic acid
1-Hydroxy-2-naphthoic acid
2-Hydroxy-*m*-toluic acid
Laevulic acid
L-Malic acid
L-Mandelic acid
Manganese α-D-glucoheptonate
Methallenoestril
Mucic acid
Mucochloric acid
2-Oxo-2,3:4,6-di*iso*propylidenegulonic acid
2-Oxoglutaric acid
Oxydiacetic acid
Pentaerythritol tetra-3-(3,5-di*tert*butyl-4-hydroxyphenyl)propionate
3-Phenylsalicylic acid
Potassium gluconate
*iso*Propyl 4,4′-dichlorobenzilate
Pyruvic acid which, in the dry state, contains not more than 97 per
    cent. by weight of free acid calculated as pyruvic acid
Quinic acid
Shikimic acid
*tri*Sodium ($\pm$)-*iso*citrate
Sodium deoxycholate
Sodium 2,5-dihydroxybenzoate
Sodium 2-hydroxy-4-methoxybenzoate
($-$)-Tartaric acid
*meso*Tartaric acid
2,4,5-Trichlorophenoxyacetic acid
Triethyl *O*-acetylcitrate
3,7,12-Trioxo-5β-cholanic acid
Vanillic acid

29.17   †*n*-Dodecyl sodium sulphate

29.18   Cyclohexyl nitrate

29.19   Barium hydrogen 2-phosphoglycerate
Barium hydrogen 3-phospho-D-glycerate
Calcium phytate
Chloro-1-(2,4-dichlorophenyl)vinyl diethyl phosphate
1,2-Dibromo-2,2-dichloroethyl dimethyl phosphate

Tariff heading   *Description*

29.19   †Di-*n*-butyl 2,2-dichlorovinyl phosphate
           †Di-*n*-butyl phenyl phosphate
           2,2-Dichlorovinyl dimethyl phosphate
           Di-(2-ethylhexyl) sodium phosphate
           2-Ethylhexyl diphenyl phosphate
           Sodium phytate
           Tri-(2,3-dibromopropyl) phosphate
           Triethyl phosphate

29.20   2-*sec*Butyl-4,6-dinitrophenyl *iso*propyl carbonate
           Diallyl digol dicarbonate
           *Di-(4-*tert*butylcyclohexyl) peroxydicarbonate (until 6th March 1969)
           Diethyl pyrocarbonate
           Diphenyl carbonate
           Ethylene carbonate
           Propylene carbonate

29.21   *O*-4-Bromo-2,5-dichlorophenyl *OO*-diethyl phosphorothioate
           O-4-Bromo-2,5-dichlorophenyl *OO*-dimethyl phosphorothioate
           O-2,4-Dichlorophenyl *OO*-diethyl phosphorothioate
           OO-Diethyl *O*-4-nitrophenyl phosphorothioate
           OO-Diethyl phosphorochloridothioate
           †1,3-Di-(4-methyl-1,3,2-dioxaborinan-2-yloxy)-*n*-butane
           OO-Dimethyl *O*-3-methyl-4-nitrophenyl phosphorothioate
           OO-Dimethyl *O*-4-nitrophenyl phosphorothioate
           OO-Dimethyl *O*-2,4,5-trichlorophenyl phosphorothioate
           Di-(4,4,6-trimethyl-1,3,2-dioxaborinan-2-yl) oxide
           1,9,10,11,12,12-Hexachloro-4,6-dioxa-5-thiatricyclo[7,2,1,0^{2,8}]dodec-
                10-ene 5-oxide
           Phenyl phosphorodichloridate
           4,4'-*iso*Propylidenedicyclohexyl di-(4-[1-(4-hydroxycyclohexyl)-
                1-methylethyl]cyclohexyl phenyl phosphite)
           Tri-(2-ethylhexyl) phosphite
           Triethyl phosphite
           Trimethyl phosphite

29.22   Allylamine
           2-Aminobiphenyl
           4-Aminobiphenyl
           6-Aminochrysene (I.U.P.A.C. numbering)
           N-2-Amino-3,5-dibromobenzyl-*N*-cyclohexylmethylammonium chloride
           †4-Amino-1-diethylamino-*n*-pentane
           2-Amino-4,4'-dinitrobiphenyl
           4-Aminodiphenylamine
           3-Aminomethyl-3,5,5-trimethylcyclohexylamine
           8-Aminonaphthalene-1-sulphonic acid
           8-Aminonaphthalene-2-sulphonic acid
           Amitriptyline embonate
           Amitriptyline hydrochloride
           Benzidine
           Benzidine hydrochloride
           Benzphetamine hydrochloride
           3-Bromoaniline
           2-Bromo-5-trifluoromethylaniline
           4-Bromo-2-trifluoromethylaniline
           4-Bromo-3-trifluoromethylaniline
           †*n*-Butylamine
           *iso*Butylamine
           *sec*Butylamine
           *tert*Butylamine
           2-Chloro-*NN*-diethyl-4-nitroanilinium chloride zinc chloride
           N-3-Chloropropyldimethylammonium chloride, solid
           2-Chloro-5-trifluoromethylaniline

Tariff heading   *Description*

29.22   4-Chloro-2-trifluoromethylaniline
         4-Chloro-3-trifluoromethylaniline
         3-Cyclohexylaminopropylamine
         N-Cyclohexyldimethylamine
         N-Cyclohexylmethylamine
         Cyclopentamine hydrochloride
         Cyclopentamine 2-(4-hydroxybenzoyl)benzoate
         (Cyclopropylmethyl)ammonium chloride
         †*N-n*-Decyldimethylamine
         Diallylamine
         1,2-Diaminoethane (until 6th March 1969)
         1,2-Diaminoethane hydrate
         1,7-Diaminoheptane
         Di-(4-amino-3-methylcyclohexyl)methane
         1,8-Diaminonaphthalene
         1,2-Diaminopropane
         1,3-Diaminopropane
         Di-(3-aminopropyl)amine
         2,4-Diaminotoluene
         1,6-Diaminotrimethylhexane, mixed 2,2,4- and 2,4,4- isomers
         Diamylamine, mixed isomers
         6,8-Dianilinonaphthalene-1-sulphonic acid
         2,6-Dibromoaniline
         †Di-*n*-butylamine
         2,4-Dichloroaniline
         3,4-Dichloroaniline
         2,4-Dichlorobenzylamine
         3,4-Dichlorobenzylamine
         4,5-Dichloro-*o*-phenylenediamine
         Dicyclohexylamine
         NN'-Dicyclohexyl-*p*-phenylenediamine
         †1,3-Di(dimethylamino)-*n*-butane
         1,4-Di(dimethylamino)butane
         2-Diethylaminoethylamine
         3-Diethylaminopropylamine
         NN-Diethylaniline
         Diethylenetriamine (until 6th March 1969)
         NN'-Di-(1-ethyl-3-methylpentyl)-*p*-phenylenediamine
         NN-Diethyl-*p*-phenylenediamine
         2-Dimethylaminoethylamine
         3-Dimethylaminopropylamine
         3-Dimethylaminopropyne
         NN'-Di-(1-methylheptyl)-*p*-phenylenediamine
         †*NN*-Dimethyl-*n*-octylamine
         NN-Dimethyl-*p*-phenylenediamine
         6,10-Dimethyl-2,6,10,14-tetra-azapentadecane
         †2,6-Dinitro-*NN*-di-*n*-propyl-4-trifluoromethylaniline
         †Di-*n*-octylamine
         †Di-*n*-propylamine
         Di*iso*propylamine
         †*N-n*-Dodecyldimethylamine
         Ethansylate
         2-Ethylaniline
         N-Ethylaniline
         N-Ethyldi-(3-phenylpropyl)ammonium dihydrogen citrate
         N-Ethyl-1-naphthylamine
         N-Ethyl-*m*-toluidine
         Fencamfamin hydrochloride
         Fenfluramine hydrochloride
         2-Fluoroaniline
         4-Fluoroaniline

Tariff heading   *Description*

29.22   2-Fluoro-5-trifluoromethylaniline
4-Fluoro-2-trifluoromethylaniline
†*n*-Heptylamine
†*n*-Hexylamine
Mephentermine
3-Methylaminopropylamine
N-Methylaniline
3-Methylbenzylamine
1-Methylheptylamine
N-1-Methylheptyl-*N*′-phenyl-*p*-phenylenediamine
N-Methyl-1-methylprop-2-ynylamine
N-(2-Methyl-2-nitropropyl)-4-nitrosoaniline
N-Methyltaurine
N-Methyltaurine, sodium salt
1-Naphthylamine
2-Naphthylamine
4-Nitroaniline
4-Nitro-*m*-phenylenediamine
†*n*-Octylamine
Pargyline hydrochloride
NNN′N″N‴-Pentamethyldiethylenetriamine
†*n*-Pentylamine
*iso*Pentylamine
Phentermine
m-Phenylenediamine
p-Phenylenediamine
p-Phenylenediamine dihydrochloride
(±)-1-Phenylethylamine
Prenylamine lactate
†*n*-Propylamine
*iso*Propylamine
(−)-Propylhexedrine hydrochloride
Protriptyline hydrochloride
Sodium 4-aminonaphthalene-1-sulphonate
Spermidine
Spermidine trihydrochloride
Taurine
3,4,3′,4′-Tetra-aminobiphenyl tetrahydrochloride
Tetraethylenepentamine (until 6th March 1969)
5,6,7,8-Tetrahydro-1-naphthylamine
1,2,3,4-Tetrahydro-2-naphthylamine
5,6,7,8-Tetrahydro-2-naphthylamine
o-Tolidine
o-Tolidine dihydrochloride
m-Tolidine dihydrochloride
m-Tolidine di(hydrogen sulphate)
Tolpropamine hydrochloride
3-*p*-Toluidinonaphthalene-1-sulphonic acid
Triallylamine
†Tri-*n*-butylamine
2,4,5-Trichloroaniline
†Tri-*n*-decylamine
Triethylammonium 3β,17β-dihydroxyandrost-5-en-17α-ylpropiolate
Triethylenetetramine (until 6th March 1969)
2-Trifluoromethylaniline
4-Trifluoromethylaniline
†Tri-*n*-hexylamine
†Tri-*n*-octylamine
†Tri-*n*-pentylamine
Tri*iso*pentylamine
†Tri-*n*-propylamine

Tariff heading   *Description*

29.22   2,3-Xylidine
          2,5-Xylidine
          3,4-Xylidine

29.23   Acetaldehyde ammonia
          D-Alanine
          L-Alanine
          DL-Alanine
          4-Aminoacetophenone
          7-(4-Aminoanilino)-4-hydroxynaphthalene-2-sulphonic acid
          3-Aminobenzoic acid
          4-Aminobenzoic acid
          †2-Amino-*n*-butan-1-ol
          4-Aminobutyric acid
          5-Amino-2-chlorobenzoic acid
          2-Amino-5,2′-dichlorobenzophenone
          2-Amino-4,6-dichlorophenol
          1-Amino-3-diethylaminopropan-2-ol
          L-2-Amino-3-(3,4-dihydroxyphenyl)-2-methylpropionic acid
          DL-2-Amino-3-(3,4-dihydroxyphenyl)-2-methylpropionic acid
          2-Amino-1-(3,4-dihydroxyphenyl)propan-1-ol hydrochloride
          2-(2-Aminoethoxy)ethanol
          2-Aminoethyl dihydrogen phosphate
          N-(2-Aminoethyl)ethanolamine
          2-Amino-2-ethylpropane-1,3-diol
          6-Aminohexanoic acid
          2-Amino-2-methylpropane-1,3-diol
          2-Amino-2-methylpropan-1-ol
          5-Amino-1-naphthol
          3-Amino-2-naphthol
          2-Amino-5-nitrophenol
          (−)-2-Amino-1-(4-nitrophenyl)propane-1,3-diol
          3-Aminophenol
          4-Aminophenylacetic acid
          (+)-2-Aminopropan-1-ol
          3-Aminopropan-1-ol
          3-Aminopropionic acid
          4-Aminosalicylic acid (−COOH at 1)
          5-Aminosalicylic acid (−COOH at 1)
          Amylocaine hydrochloride
          7-Anilino-4-hydroxynaphthalene-2-sulphonic acid
          m-Anisidine
          Anthranilic acid
          L-Aspartic acid
          DL-Aspartic acid
          Bamethan sulphate
          Benzocaine
          (−)-2-Benzylaminopropan-1-ol
          (±)-2-Benzylaminopropan-1-ol
          Butacaine sulphate
          2-*tert*Butylaminoethyl methacrylate
          Calcium 3-aminopropionate
          Calcium 4-aminosalicylate (−COOH at 1)
          7-(4-Carboxymethoxyanilino)-4-hydroxynaphthalene-2-sulphonic acid
          Chlophedianol
          Chlophedianol hydrochloride
          5-Chloro-*o*-anisidine (−NH$_2$ at 1)
          4-Chloro-2,5-dimethoxyaniline (until 3rd July 1969)
          4-(4-Chlorophenoxy)aniline
          3-Chloro-6-phenoxyaniline
          Chlorphenoxamine hydrochloride

Tariff heading	*Description*
29.23	Clorprenaline hydrochloride

2,4-Diaminoanisole
2,4-Diaminoanisole *mono*sulphate
1,2-Diaminocyclohexane-*NNN′N′*-tetra-acetic acid
1,3-Diaminopropan-2-ol
1,3-Diaminopropan-2-ol-*NNN′N′*-tetra-acetic acid
3,9-Di-(3-aminopropyl)-2,4,8,10-tetraoxaspiro[5,5]undecane
o-Dianisidine
o-Dianisidine dihydrochloride of a purity not greater than 98·5 per cent.
1,15-Diaza-5,8,11-trioxapentadecane
2,6-Di*tert*butyl-4-dimethylaminomethylphenol
3,3′-Di(carboxymethoxy)benzidine, dipotassium salt
6,6′-Dichloro-*o*-dianisidine
†1,2-Di[di-(2-hydroxy-*n*-propyl)amino]ethane
Di-(2-dimethylaminoethyl) ether
2,2-Diethoxyethylamine
†2-Diethylaminoethyl 4-amino-2-*n*-propoxybenzoate *mono*hydrochloride
2-Diethylaminoethyl diphenylacetate hydrochloride
3-Diethylaminopropan-1-ol
5,5′-Dihydroxy-2,2′-dinaphthylamine-7,7′-disulphonic acid
3-(3,4-Dihydroxyphenyl)-DL-alanine
2-(3,4-Dihydroxyphenyl)ethylammonium chloride
†Di-(2-hydroxy-*n*-propyl)amine
†*NN*-Di-(2-hydroxy-*n*-propyl)aniline (until 6th March 1969)
2,5-Dimethoxyaniline (until 3rd July 1969)
N-2,2-Dimethoxyethylmethylamine
1-(3,4-Dimethoxyphenyl)-1-dimethylamino-4-phenylbutane hydrochloride
2-(3,4-Dimethoxyphenyl)ethylamine
β-Dimethylamino*iso*butyrophenone hydrochloride
2-Dimethylaminoethyl methacrylate (until 3rd July 1969)
6-Dimethylaminomethyl-2,5-xylenol hydrochloride (−OH at 1)
1-Dimethylaminopropan-2-ol
3-(3-Dimethylaminopropyl)-1,2:4,5-dibenzocycloheptadien-3-ol
1,4-Di-(2,4,6-trimethylanilino)anthraquinone
Embramine hydrochloride
Ethomoxane hydrochloride
Ethyl aminoacetate hydrochloride
2-Ethylaminoethanol, of which not less than 90 per cent. by volume distils between 165° and 170° centigrade at normal pressure and which contains not more than 0·5 per cent. by weight of water
Ethylenediamine-*NN′*-diacetic acid
Ethylenediamine-*NN′*-diacetic acid, cobalt complex
Ethylenediamine-*NN′*-di-[α-(2-hydroxyphenyl)acetic acid]
Ethylenediamine-*NN′*-di-[α-(2-hydroxyphenyl)acetic acid], iron complex
N-Ethyl-*N*-2-hydroxyethyl-*m*-toluidine
D-Glucosamine hydrochloride
Glutamic acid
Glycine
DL-Homoserine
1-(4-Hydroxyphenyl)-2-methylaminoethanol hydrogen tartrate
1-(4-Hydroxyphenyl)-2-methylaminoethanol tartrate
Iopanoic acid
Isatoic anhydride
Isoetharine mesylate
Isoxsuprine hydrochloride
L-Leucine
DL-Leucine

Tariff heading	*Description*
29.23	L-*iso*Leucine
	DL-*iso*Leucine
	L-*nor*Leucine
	DL-*nor*Leucine
	Levopropoxyphene napsylate
	L-Lysine
	DL-Lysine dihydrochloride
	L-Lysine ethyl ester dihydrochloride
	L-Lysine *mono*hydrochloride
	DL-Lysine *mono*hydrochloride
	Lyxosamine
	Magnesium glutamate hydrobromide
	Mannomustine dihydrochloride
	Mebeverine hydrochloride
	Meclofenoxate hydrochloride
	Metaraminol hydrogen (+)-tartrate
	3-Methoxypropylamine
	6-Methoxy-*m*-toluidine ($-NH_2$ at 1)
	2-Methylaminoethanol
	3-(3-Methylaminoprop-1-ynyl)-1,2:4,5-dibenzocycloheptadien-3-ol
	N-Methyldiethanolamine
	Orciprenaline sulphate
	DL-Ornithine *mono*hydrochloride
	Orphenadrine
	Orphenadrine dihydrogen citrate
	Orphenadrine hydrochloride
	Pentyl 4-dimethylaminobenzoate, mixed isomers
	5-*tert*Pentyl-2-phenoxyaniline
	o-Phenetidine
	m-Phenetidine
	p-Phenetidine (until 1st May 1969)
	L-3-Phenylalanine
	DL-3-Phenylalanine
	Potassium 4-aminosalicylate ($-COOH$ at 1)
	Potassium dimethylaminoacetate
	Potassium 2-methylaminopropionate
	Procaine
	Procaine hydrochloride
	Protokylol hydrochloride
	Proxymetacaine *mono*hydrochloride
	Sarcosine
	L-Serine
	DL-Serine
	Sodium 4-aminosalicylate ($-COOH$ at 1)
	Sodium hydrogen glutamate
	L-Threonine
	DL-Threonine
	Thymoxamine hydrochloride
	†Tri-(2-hydroxy-*n*-propyl)amine
	Trolnitrate phosphate
	Trometamol
	Tyramine hydrochloride
	L-Tyrosine
	DL-Tyrosine
	L-Valine
	DL-*nor*Valine
29.24	Benzethonium chloride
	Betaine
	Betaine hydrochloride
	Carbenoxolone, dicholine salt

Tariff heading	*Description*
29.24	Cetalkonium chloride
	1,3-Di(dimethylamino)propan-2-ol dimethiodide
	Edrophonium chloride
	Methylbenzethonium chloride
	Oxyphenonium bromide
	Tridihexethyl chloride
29.25	8-Acetamido-2-naphthol
	O-Acetyl-4′-chloro-3,5-di-iodosalicylanilide
	N-Acetyl-D-galactosamine
	N-Acetyl-D-glucosamine
	N-Acetyl-L-glutamine
	N-Acetyl-L-tyrosine
	Acrylamide
	Ambenonium chloride
	Ambucetamide
	7-(4-Aminobenzamido)-4-hydroxynaphthalene-2-sulphonic acid
	4-Aminohippuric acid
	L-α-Asparagine
	DL-α-Asparagine
	L-β-Asparagine
	Barbitone
	Barbitone sodium
	N-Bromoacetamide
	Bucetin
	†*N*-(*n*-Butoxymethyl)acrylamide
	*sec*Butylurea
	Carbachol
	O-Carbamoyl-β-methylcholine chloride
	Chloroacetamide
	4-Chlorobut-2-ynyl 3-chlorophenylcarbamate
	N-5-Chloro-2-(4-chloro-2-sulphophenoxy)phenyl-*N*′-3,4-dichloro- phenylurea
	2-Chloro-2-diethylcarbamoyl-1-methylvinyl dimethyl phosphate
	11a-Chloro-5-hydroxytetracycline 6,12-hemiacetal
	N-4-(4-Chlorophenoxy)phenyl-*N*′*N*′-dimethylurea
	α-Chloro-*N*-*iso*propylacetanilide
	†*N*-(3-Chloro-*p*-tolyl)-2-methyl-*n*-valeramide
	Chlorphenesin carbamate
	*N-Cyclo-octyl-*N*′*N*′-dimethylurea (until 6th March 1969)
	Cyclopropanecarboxyamide
	Diacrylamidomethane
	3′,4′-Dichloromethacrylanilide
	3,3′-Dichloro-5-trifluoromethyl-*NN*′-diphenylurea
	NN′-Di-(4-chloro-3-trifluoromethylphenyl)urea
	1,2-Di(diacetylamino)ethane
	Diethylcarbamoyl chloride
	2-(2,5-Dihydroxybenzamido)ethanol
	NN-Dimethylacetamide (until 3rd July 1969)
	Dimethylcarbamoyl chloride
	NN′-Dimethyl-*NN*′-dinitrosoterephthalamide
	NN-Dimethyl-*N*′-3-trifluoromethylphenylurea
	NN′-Dimethylurea containing not more than 0·005 per cent. by weight of iron calculated as Fe
	Di-(4-phenoxycarbonylaminophenyl)methane
	Ethosalamide
	Ethotoin
	Ethyl *N*-3-(1,2:5,6-dibenzocycloheptatrien-7-yl)propylmethylcarbamate
	1-Ethyl-1-methylprop-2-ynyl carbamate
	Etymide hydrochloride
	Fluoroacetamide
	Formamide

Tariff heading	*Description*
29.25	L-Glutamine
	DL-Glutamine
	N-Glycyl-L-*β*-asparagine
	N-Glycyl-DL-*β*-asparagine
	N-(Hydroxymethyl)acrylamide
	1-Hydroxymethyl-5,5-dimethylhydantoin, solid
	Iodipamide, dimeglumine salt
	Iodoacetamide
	Iothalamic acid
	Isopropamide iodide
	Lactamide
	Mebutamate
	Methacrylamide
	Methohexitone
	Methyl 4-acetamido-2-ethoxybenzoate
	Methyl 4-acetamido-5-chloro-2-methoxybenzoate
	Methyl carbamate
	Methyl 3-(*m*-tolylcarbamoyloxy)phenylcarbamate
	Metoclopramide dihydrochloride
	Metoclopramide *mono*hydrochloride
	1-Naphthyl methylcarbamate
	Nealbarbitone
	Niclosamide
	Oxethazaine
	Phenytoin sodium
	Pivalamide
	2-*iso*Propoxyphenyl methylcarbamate
	Sodium diatrizoate
	Styramate
	Tetramethylurea
	5,3′,4′-Trichlorosalicylanilide
	†*N*-Vanillyl-*n*-nonanamide
	Vinbarbitone sodium
29.26	Acetamidinium chloride
	α-(4-Aminophenyl)-α-ethylglutarimide
	L-Arginine
	L-Arginine *mono*hydrochloride
	*N*ª-Benzoyl-DL-arginine 2-naphthylamide hydrochloride
	Creatine
	3,5-Dichloro-*p*-benzoquinonechlorimine
	1,2-Di-(1,3-dimethylbutylideneamino)ethane
	Di-[2-(1,3-dimethylbutylideneamino)ethyl]amine
	1-(Di-[2-(1,3-dimethylbutylideneamino)ethyl]amino)-3-phenoxypropan-2-ol
	Di-(2,6-di*iso*propylphenyl)carbodi-imine
	†*n*-Dodecylguanidinium acetate
	N-(2-Ethylhexyl)bicyclo[2,2,1]hept-5-ene-2,3-dicarboxyimide
	N-Ethylmaleimide
	Glutethimide
	4-Guanidinobutyric acid
	Hexahydro-1,3,5-tri-(2-hydroxyethyl) 1,3,5-triazine
	Hexamine 3-chloroallylochloride (until 6th March 1969)
	Phenformin *mono*hydrochloride
	N-Phosphonocreatine, sodium salt
	3,4,5,6-Tetrahydrophthalimidomethyl 2,2-dimethyl-3-(2-methylprop-1-enyl)cyclopropanecarboxylate
	NNN′N′-Tetramethylguanidine
29.27	(−)-2-Acetamido-2-vanillylpropionitrile
	Acrylonitrile
	Barium 2-cyanoethyl phosphate

Tariff heading　　　　　　　　　　　　*Description*

29.27　　Benzonitrile
　　　　3-Bromopropionitrile
　　　　†*n*-Butyronitrile
　　　　Chloroacetonitrile
　　　　3-Chlorophenylacetonitrile
　　　　4-Chlorophenylacetonitrile
　　　　Cyanocyclopropane
　　　　3-Cyano-5-dimethylamino-2-methyl-3-phenylhexane
　　　　3-Cyclohexylaminopropionitrile
　　　　2,6-Dichlorobenzonitrile
　　　　2,3-Dichloro-5,6-dicyanobenzoquinone
　　　　NN-Di-2-cyanoethylformamide
　　　　αα'-Dicyano-*o*-xylene
　　　　αα'-Dicyano-*m*-xylene
　　　　αα'-Dicyano-*p*-xylene
　　　　4-Diethylaminobutyronitrile
　　　　†2-Dimethylamino-2,2-diphenyl-*n*-valeronitrile
　　　　3-Dimethylaminopropionitrile
　　　　2,2-Dimethylpropionitrile
　　　　Diphenylacetonitrile
　　　　†4-Di-*n*-propylaminobutyronitrile
　　　　4-Di*iso*propylaminobutyronitrile
　　　　Ethyl 2-cyano-3,3-diphenylacrylate
　　　　Ethyl 2-cyano-3-ethoxyacrylate
　　　　2-Ethylhexyl 2-cyano-3,3-diphenylacrylate
　　　　†*n*-Hexanonitrile
　　　　3-Hydroxypropionitrile
　　　　Mandelonitrile
　　　　Methacrylonitrile
　　　　2-Phenylpropionitrile
　　　　Phthalonitrile
　　　　Propionitrile
　　　　Succinonitrile
　　　　Tetracyanoethylene
　　　　o-Tolunitrile
　　　　o-Tolylacetonitrile
　　　　p-Tolylacetonitrile
　　　　Verapamil hydrochloride

29.28　　4-Anilinophenyldiazonium hydrogen sulphate
　　　　Azobenzene
　　　　4-*N*-Benzylethylaminophenyldiazonium zinc chloride
　　　　3,4-Dimethyl-6-D-ribitylaminoazobenzene
　　　　Sodium 6-diazo-5-hydroxynaphthalene-1-sulphonate
　　　　*tri*Sodium hydrogen 4,5-dihydroxy-3,6-di-(2-sulphophenylazo)-
　　　　　　naphthalene-2,7-disulphonate
　　　　2,5,4'-Triethoxy-4-biphenylyldiazonium zinc chloride

29.29　　*p*-Benzoquinone dioxime
　　　　p-Benzoquinone dioxime dibenzoate
　　　　Benzylideneaminoguanidinium tartrate
　　　　N-(4-Bromophenyl)-*N'*-methoxy-*N'*-methylurea
　　　　1-(2-Carboxyphenyl)-5-(2-hydroxy-5-sulphophenyl)-3-phenylformazan
　　　　N-(4-Chlorobenzoyl)-*N*-(4-methoxyphenyl)hydrazine
　　　　N-4-Chlorophenyl-*N'*-methoxy-*N'*-methylurea
　　　　2-Chloro-4,6-xylylhydrazinium chloride
　　　　Cyclopropanecarbohydrazide
　　　　Desferrioxamine
　　　　Desferrioxamine hydrochloride
　　　　Desferrioxamine mesylate
　　　　Di(dimethylglyoximato)diamminecobaltic nitrate
　　　　N-3,4-Dichlorophenyl-*N'*-methoxy-*N'*-methylurea

Tariff heading	*Description*
29.29	*NN*-Diethylhydroxylamine
	Diethyl naphthalimido phosphate
	Di-(17β-hydroxy-2α,17α-dimethyl-5α-androstan-3-ylidene)hydrazine
	NN-Dimethylhydrazine
	N-Hydroxyphthalimide
	Hydroxyurea
	Phenelzine hydrogen sulphate
	Pheniprazine *mono*hydrochloride
	Phenylhydrazine
	1-Phenylsemicarbazide
	Procarbazine hydrochloride
29.30	4-*tert*Butyl-2-chlorophenyl methyl methylphosphoramidate
	1-Chloro-2-*iso*cyanatobenzene
	1-Chloro-3-*iso*cyanatobenzene
	1-Chloro-4-*iso*cyanatobenzene
	1-Chloro-2-*iso*cyanatoethane
	*iso*Cyanatobenzene
	*iso*Cyanatocyclohexane
	1-*iso*Cyanato-4-fluorobenzene
	*iso*Cyanatomethane
	1-*iso*Cyanatonaphthalene
	†1-*iso*Cyanato-*n*-octadecane
	1-*iso*Cyanatopropane
	3-Cyano-5-dimethylamino-2-methyl-3-phenylhexane cyclamate
	1,2-Dichloro-4-*iso*cyanatobenzene
	1,4-Dichloro-2-*iso*cyanatobenzene
	Di-(4-*iso*cyanatocyclohexyl)methane
	4,4′-Di*iso*cyanato-3,3′-dimethoxybiphenyl
	4,4′-Di*iso*cyanato-3,3′-dimethylbiphenyl
	4,4′-Di*iso*cyanatodiphenylmethane of a purity not less than 85 per cent.
	1,6-Di*iso*cyanatohexane
	1,5-Di*iso*cyanatonaphthalene
	2,4-Di*iso*cyanatotoluene
	Dimethylamine-borine
	Hexamethylphosphoramide
	Tetra(dimethylamino)diboron
	4,4′,4″-Tri*iso*cyanatotriphenylmethane
29.31	*N*-Acetyl-L-cysteine
	N-Acetyl-DL-methionine
	Ambazone
	2-Aminobenzenethiol
	Ammonium phenylhydrazinodithioformate
	Benzenethiol
	Bithionol
	*iso*Bornyl thiocyanatoacetate
	Butane-1,4-dithiol
	†*n*-Butane-1-thiol
	4-*tert*Butylbenzenethiol
	Calcium 2-hydroxy-4-(methylthio)butyrate
	Chlordantoin
	2-Chloroallyl diethyldithiocarbamate
	4-Chlorophenylthiomethyl *OO*-diethyl phosphorodithioate
	L-Cystathionine
	DL-Cystathionine
	L-Cysteine
	L-Cysteine hydrochloride
	Cysteine methyl ester hydrochloride
	D-Cystine
	L-Cystine

Tariff heading	*Description*
29.31	Dapsone, of a purity less than 99 per cent.

†*n*-Decane-1-thiol
Di-(3-*tert*butyl-4-hydroxy-6-methylphenyl) sulphide
Di-(2-carboxyphenyl) disulphide
S-2,3-Dichloroallyl di*iso*propylthiocarbamate
Di-(4-chlorophenyl) sulphone
2,5-Dichlorophenylthiomethyl *OO*-diethyl phosphorodithioate
2,6-Dichlorothiobenzamide
Di-(2-cyanoethyl) sulphide
2-Diethylaminoethanethiol hydrochloride
OO-Diethyl 2-ethylthioethyl phosphorodithioate
OO-Diethyl *O*-2-ethylthioethyl phosphorothioate
Diethyl *S*-2-ethylthioethyl phosphorothioate
OO-Diethyl ethylthiomethyl phosphorodithioate
Di-(2-ethylhexyl) 4,4′-thiodibutyrate
Di-(2-hydroxyethyl) sulphide
Di-(6-hydroxy-2-naphthyl) disulphide
Di-(4-hydroxyphenyl) sulphone having a melting point not less than 236° centigrade
Dimercaprol
Dimethyl disulphide
Dimethyl *S*-2-(1-methylcarbamoylethylthio)ethyl phosphorothioate
OO-Dimethyl methylcarbamoylmethyl phosphorodithioate
OO-Dimethyl phthalimidomethyl phosphorodithioate
Dimethyl sulphide
Dimethyl sulphoxide
Di-(4-nitrophenyl) disulphide
1,4-Dioxan-2,3-dithiol di-(*OO*-diethyl phosphorodithioate)
Diphenyl disulphide
Diphenyl sulphide
NN′-Diphenylthiourea
3,6-Dithiaoctane-1,8-diol
*n-Dodecane-1-thiol (until 6th March 1969)
Dodecanethiol, mixed isomers
Ethane-1,2-dithiol
Ethanethiol
D-Ethionine
L-Ethionine
DL-Ethionine
Ethylcarbamoylmethyl *OO*-dimethyl phosphorodithioate
†*S*-Ethyl di-*n*-propylthiocarbamate
Ethylene-1,2-di-(*N′N′*-dimethylthiuram disulphide)
Ethyl methyl sulphide
O-2-Ethylthioethyl *OO*-dimethyl phosphorothioate
S-2-Ethylthioethyl dimethyl phosphorothioate
Glutathione
Glutathione disulphide
Glutathione, *mono*sodium salt
N-Glycyl-DL-methionine
Hexane-1,6-dithiol
†*n*-Hexane-1-thiol
DL-Homocysteine
2-Mercapto*iso*butyric acid
2-Mercaptoethanol
2-Mercaptoethylammonium chloride
3-Mercaptopropane-1,2-diol (until 4th September 1969)
2-Mercaptopropionic acid
3-Mercaptopropionic acid (until 4th September 1969)
Mercaptosuccinic acid
Methanethiol

Tariff heading   *Description*

29.31 Methionine
    2-Methoxyethylcarbamoylmethyl *OO*-dimethyl phosphorodithioate
    Methyl phenyl sulphide
    2-Methylpropane-2-thiol
    Methylsulphonal
    1-Naphthylthiourea
    Noxythiolin
    †*n*-Octane-1-thiol
    Pentachlorobenzenethiol
    †*n*-Pentane-1-thiol
    Potassium ethylxanthate
    †Potassium *n*-pentylxanthate
    Propane-1,3-dithiol
    Propane-1-thiol
    Propane-2-thiol
    †*S-n*-Propyl *n*-butylethylthiocarbamate
    Sodium *sec*butylxanthate
    Sodium ethylxanthate
    Sodium *iso*propylxanthate
    Sodium toluene-4-sulphinate
    Sulphonal
    2,4,5,4'-Tetrachlorodiphenyl sulphide
    2,4,5,4'-Tetrachlorodiphenyl sulphone
    N-(1,1,2,2-Tetrachloroethanesulphenyl)cyclohex-4-ene-
     1,2-dicarboxyimide
    OOO'O'-Tetraethyl methylene di(phosphorodithioate)
    Thioacetamide
    Thioacetanilide
    Thioacetic acid
    Thiobarbituric acid
    Thiocarlide
    *iso*Thiocyanatobenzene
    *iso*Thiocyanatomethane
    Thiodiacetic acid
    Thiomesterone
    Thiourea
    Tolnaftate
    Toluene-2-thiol
    S-2,3,3-Trichloroallyl di*iso*propylthiocarbamate
    Trichloromethanesulphenyl chloride
    N-(Trichloromethanesulphenyl)cyclohex-4-ene-1,2-dicarboxyimide
    N-(Trichloromethanesulphenyl)phthalimide
    Zinc di-(2-benzamidophenyl sulphide)
    Zinc di(pentachlorophenyl sulphide)
    Zinc propylenebisdithiocarbamate

29.32 *o*-Arsanilic acid
    p-Arsanilic acid
    Bismuth *N*-glycollylarsanilate
    Cacodylic acid
    Phenylarsonic acid
    Sodium cacodylate
    Sodium hydrogen *p*-arsanilate
    *di*Sodium methylarsonate
    Triphenylarsine oxide

29.33 3,2-Mercurioxy-4-nitrotoluene
    Methylmercury hydroxide

29.34 Allyltrichlorosilane
    3-Aminopropyltriethoxysilane
    3-Aminopropyltrimethoxysilane
    †*n*-Butyl-lithium

Tariff heading   *Description*

29.34   *sec*Butyl-lithium
           3-Chloropropyltrimethoxysilane
           Di*iso*butylaluminium hydride
           Dicyclopentadienyliron
           Diethyl di-(2-hydroxyethyl)aminomethylphosphonate
           Dimethyl 2,2,2-trichloro-1-hydroxyethylphosphonate
           Diphenyldichlorosilane
           Diphenylsilanediol
           2-(3,4-Epoxycyclohexyl)ethyltrimethoxysilane
           O-Ethyl phenyl ethylphosphonodithioate
           3-Glycidyloxypropyltrimethoxysilane
           1-Hydroxyethylidenediphosphonic acid
           3-Methacryloyloxypropyltrimethoxysilane
           Methylcyclopentadienylmanganese tricarbonyl
           Methylvinyldichlorosilane
           Molybdenum hexacarbonyl
           Nitrilotri(methylphosphonic acid)
           Phenylphosphinic acid
           *penta*Sodium hydrogen nitrilotri(methylphosphonate)
           Sodium tetraphenylborate
           Tetramethylsilane
           †Tri-*n*-butylaluminium
           Triphenylphosphine
           Triphenyltin acetate
           Tungsten hexacarbonyl
           Vinyltrichlorosilane
           Vinyltriethoxysilane
           Vinyltri-(2-methoxyethoxy)silane

29.35   Acepromazine hydrogen maleate
           Acetoguanamine
           2-Acetothienone
           2-Acetylbenzofuran
           2-Acetyl-1,4-butyrolactone
           3-Acetyl-2,4-dimethylpyrrole
           N-Acetylhistamine
           3-Acetylindole
           5-Acetylindoline
           2-Acetylpyridine
           3-Acetylpyridine
           4-Acetylpyridine
           N^α-Acetyl-DL-tryptophan
           Acridine
           Acridone
           Adenine
           Adenine sulphate
           Adenosine
           Adenosine 3'-(dihydrogen phosphate)
           Adenosine 5'-(dihydrogen phosphate)
           Adenosine 5'-(dilithium hydrogen pyrophosphate)
           Adenosine 5'-(disodium dihydrogen triphosphate)
           Adenosine 5'-(tetrahydrogen triphosphate)
           Adenosine 5'-(tetrasodium triphosphate)
           Adenosine 5'-(trilithium pyrophosphate)
           Adenosine 5'-(trisodium pyrophosphate)
           S-Adenos-5'-yl-L-methionine iodide
           2-Allyloxypyridine
           Ambrettolide
           2-Aminobenzothiazole
           2-Aminobenzothiazole-6-carboxylic acid
           N^α-4-Aminobutyryl-L-histidine sulphate

Tariff heading   *Description*

29.35   5-Amino-4-chloro-2-phenylpyridazin-3-one
          5-Amino-1-di(dimethylamino)phosphinyl-3-phenyl-1,2,4-triazole
          5-Amino-3,4-dimethyl*iso*ooxazole
          4-Amino-2,6-dimethylpyrimidine
          2-(1-Aminoethyl)-3,4-di(hydroxymethyl)furan hydrochloride
          †4-Amino-5-methoxymethyl-2-*n*-propylpyrimidine
          5-Amino-3-methyl-1-phenylpyrazole
          2-Amino-4-methylpyrimidine
          3-Amino-5-morpholinomethyl-2-oxazolidone
          3-Amino-2-oxazolidone sulphate
          6-Aminopenicillanic acid
          4-Aminophenazone
          5-Amino-1-phenylpyrazole
          3-Amino-1-phenyl-5-pyrazolone
          6-Amino-2-picoline
          2-Amino-3-picoline
          2-Amino-4-picoline
          †1-(4-Amino-2-*n*-propyl-5-pyrimidylmethyl)-2-picolinium chloride
              *mono*hydrochloride
          Aminopterin
          4-Aminopyridine
          2-Aminopyrimidine
          3-Amino-1,2,4-triazole
          Ammonium hydrogen 7-oxabicyclo[2,2,1]heptane-2,3-dicarboxylate
          *di*Ammonium 7-oxabicyclo[2,2,1]heptane-2,3-dicarboxylate
          Angiotensin amide
          D-*iso*Ascorbic acid
          8-Aza-adenine
          Azapetine dihydrogen phosphate
          Aziridine
          Bamipine *mono*hydrochloride
          3,4-Benzacridine
          2-[2-(4-Benzhydrylpiperazin-1-yl)ethoxy]ethanol dihydrochloride
          2-Benzhydrylpyridine
          3-Benzhydrylpyridine
          4-Benzhydrylpyridine
          Benzimidazole
          Benziodarone
          Benzoguanamine
          5,6-Benzoquinoline
          N-Benzothiazol-2-yl-*NN*′-dimethylurea
          6-Benzylaminopurine
          †3-Benzyl-1-methyl-2-*n*-undecylimidazolium bromide
          Biperiden
          Biperiden hydrochloride
          4,4′-Biphenyldiyldi-(2,5-diphenyltetrazolium chloride)
          2,2′-Biquinolyl
          Bisacodyl
          5-Bromo-3-*sec*butyl-6-methyluracil
          5-Bromo-2′-deoxycytidine
          5-Bromo-2′-deoxyuridine
          5-Bromoindole
          5-Bromoindole-3-aldehyde
          5-Bromo-6-methyl-3-*iso*propyluracil
          2-Bromothiophen
          5-Bromouracil
          Brompheniramine hydrogen maleate
          Buclizine dihydrochloride
          Bupivacaine hydrochloride
          †2-*n*-Butoxyethyl nicotinate

Tariff heading	Description
29.35	†2-*n*-Butoxypyridine

*tert*Butyl 1-(4-chlorobenzoyl)-5-methoxy-2-methylindol-3-ylacetate
3-*tert*Butyl-5-chloro-6-methyluracil
2-(3-*tert*Butyl-2-hydroxy-5-methylphenyl)-5-chlorobenzotriazole
*tert*Butyl 5-methoxy-2-methylindol-3-ylacetate
2-*iso*Butylquinoline
6-*iso*Butylquinoline
6-*tert*Butylquinoline
1,4-Butyrolactone
2-Carbamoyloxymethyl-1-methyl-5-nitroimidazole
Carbinoxamine hydrogen maleate
1-(Carboxymethyl)pyridinium chloride, pyridinium salt
Chlordiazepoxide
Chlordiazepoxide *mono*hydrochloride
1-(4-Chlorobenzyl)-2-methylbenzimidazole hydrochloride
2-(4-Chlorobenzyl)pyridine
6-Chloro-2-chloromethyl-4-phenylquinazoline
　　3-oxide hydrochloride
5-Chloro-2-(3,5-di*tert*butyl-2-hydroxyphenyl)benzotriazole
7-Chloro-10-(2-dimethylaminoethyl)dibenzo[*b*,*e*]-1,4-diazepin-11-one
　　*mono*hydrochloride
O-3-Chloro-4-methylcoumarin-7-yl *OO*-diethyl phosphorothioate
(6-Chloro-2-oxobenzoxazolin-3-yl)methyl *OO*-diethyl
　　phosphorodithioate
6-Chloropurine
2-Chloropyridine
2-Chloroquinoline
2-Chlorothiophen
Chlorprothixene
Chlorthenoxazin
Chlorzoxazone
(±)-*iso*Citric acid lactone
Clorazepic acid, dipotassium salt
Cocarboxylase
Coenzyme A
2,4,6-Collidine
Creatinine
Creatinine hydrochloride
o-Cresolphthalein-6,6′-di(methylaminodiacetic acid)
Cumetharol
5-Cyanoindole
3-Cyano-4-methoxymethyl-6-methyl-5-nitro-2-pyridone
4-Cyano-1-methyl-4-phenylazacycloheptane
2-Cyanophenothiazine
Cyanuric acid
Cyanuric chloride
3-Cyclohexyl-1,2,3,4,6,7-hexahydro-2,4-dioxocyclopentapyrimidine
Cyclomethycaine hydrogen sulphate
2-Cyclopentyl-2-(2-thienyl)glycollic acid
Cyproheptadine hydrochloride
Cytidine
Cytidine dihydrogen phosphate, mixed 2′- and 3′- isomers
Cytosine
Debrisoquine sulphate
Decahydro-4a-hydroxy-2,8,8-trimethyl-2-naphthoic acid lactone
Dehydracetic acid of a purity not less than 96 per cent.
2′-Deoxyadenosine
2′-Deoxycytidine 5′-(disodium phosphate)
2′-Deoxycytidine hydrochloride
2′-Deoxyguanosine

Tariff heading	Description
29.35	2′-Deoxyguanosine 5′-(disodium phosphate)
	2′-Deoxyuridine
	Dextromethorphan
	Dextromethorphan hydrobromide
	Dextromoramide hydrogen (+)-tartrate
	2,5-Diamino-7-ethoxyacridinium lactate
	2,6-Diaminopyridine
	Diamthazole
	1,4-Diazabicyclo[2,2,2]octane
	Diazepam
	Diazoxide
	Dibenzofuran
	NN′-Di(benzothiazol-2-ylthiomethyl)urea
	*3,5-Dibenzyltetrahydro-1,3,5-thiadiazine-2-thione
	2-(3,5-Ditertbutyl-2-hydroxyphenyl)benzotriazole
	1-(2,3-Dichloroallyl)pyridinium chloride
	3,5-Dichloro-4-hydroxylutidine
	Dichloro-1,3,5-triazinetrione
	Dichloro-1,3,5-triazinetrione, potassium derivative
	Dichloro-1,3,5-triazinetrione, sodium derivative
	1,3-Di-(3-isocyanato-4-methylphenyl)-1,3-diazacyclobutane-2,4-dione
	2,3-Dicyano-1,4-dithia-anthraquinone
	NN-Dicyclohexylbenzothiazole-2-sulphenamide
	5-(2-Diethylaminoethyl)-3-phenyl-1,2,4-oxadiazole dihydrogen citrate
	5-(2-Diethylaminoethyl)-3-phenyl-1,2,4-oxadiazole dihydrogen phosphate
	Diethyl phenyl-2-pyridylmethylmalonate hydrochloride
	2,4-Diethyl-6-isopropoxy-1,3,5-triazine
	OO-Diethyl O-pyrazin-2-yl phosphorothioate
	α-(4-[4,4-Di-(4-fluorophenyl)butyl]piperazin-1-yl)acet-2′,6′-xylidide
	1-(1-[4,4-Di-(4-fluorophenyl)butyl]-4-piperidyl)benzimidazolin-2-one
	Dihydrallazine monosulphate
	4,5-Dihydro-2,3:6,7-dibenzazepine
	(±)-2,3-Dihydro-4-methyl-2-(2-methylprop-1-enyl)pyran
	Dihydronicotinamide-adenine dinucleotide, disodium salt
	Dihydronicotinamide-adenine dinucleotide phosphate, tetrasodium salt
	2,3-Dihydropyran
	3-(3β,17β-Dihydroxyandrost-5-en-17α-yl)propionic acid lactone
	2,4-Dihydroxyquinoline
	2,4-Dihydroxyquinoline, disodium derivative
	2,4-Dihydroxyquinoline, monosodium derivative
	Dimethindene hydrogen maleate
	Dimethisoquin monohydrochloride
	Dimethoxanate monohydrochloride
	11-(3-Dimethylaminopropylidene)-6,11-dihydrodibenz[b,e]oxepin hydrochloride
	11-(3-Dimethylaminopropylidene)-6,11-dihydrodibenzo[b,e]thiepin hydrochloride
	5,6-Dimethylbenzimidazole
	OO-Dimethyl morpholinocarbonylmethyl phosphorodithioate
	OO-Dimethyl 4-oxobenzotriazin-3-ylmethyl phosphorodithioate
	2,3-Dimethyl-1-phenyl-4-isopropyl-5-pyrazolone
	4,4-Dimethyl-1-phenyl-3-pyrazolidone
	2,5-Dimethylpyrazine
	2,6-Dimethylquinoline
	2,4-Dimethylthiophan 1,1-dioxide
	1,5-Di-(5-nitro-2-furyl)pentadien-3-one amidinohydrazone hydrochloride
	Diosgenin
	Diperodon

Tariff heading   *Description*

29.35   Diperodon hydrochloride
               Diphenoxylate hydrochloride
               Diphenylpyraline hydrochloride
               NN-Di*iso*propylbenzothiazole-2-sulphenamide
               †Di-*n*-propyl pyridine-2,5-dicarboxylate
               Dipyridamole
               1,3-Di-(2-pyridylimino)*iso*indoline
               Dipyrone
               Di(pyrrobutamine) napadisylate
               Distigmine bromide
               Dithiazanine iodide
               Ellagic acid
               Ethionamide
               2-Ethoxy-3,4-dihydropyran
               7-Ethoxy-4-methylcoumarin
               2-Ethylamino-4-methylthio-6-*iso*propylamino-1,3,5-triazine
               Ethyl 6,7-di*iso*butoxy-4-hydroxyquinoline-3-carboxylate
               2-Ethyl-3-hydroxy-4-pyrone
               Ethyl 7-methyl-4-oxo-1,8-naphthyridine-3-carboxylate
               N-Ethyl-*N*′-(5-nitrothiazol-2-yl)urea
               5-Ethyl-2-picoline
               2-Ethylpiperidine
               Fentanyl
               Fentanyl dihydrogen citrate
               Flavin-adenine dinucleotide
               Fluanisone
               Fluopromazine *mono*hydrochloride
               Fluorescein-2′,7′-di(methylaminodiacetic acid)
               1-[3-(4-Fluorobenzoyl)propyl]-4-hydroxy-4-
                    (3-trifluoromethylphenyl)piperidine
               1-[3-(4-Fluorobenzoyl)propyl]-4-hydroxy-4-
                    (3-trifluoromethylphenyl)piperidinium chloride
               1-(1-[3-(4-Fluorobenzoyl)propyl]-4-piperidyl)benzimidazolin-2-one
                    hydrochloride
               1-(1-[3-(4-Fluorobenzoyl)propyl]-1,2,3,6-tetrahydro-4-
                    pyridyl)benzimidazolin-2-one
               5-Fluorouracil
               †Fluphenazine *O*-*n*-decanoate
               Fluphenazine dihydrochloride
               Furan
               Furfuraldehyde
               3-(2-Furyl)acrylic acid
               D-Glucuronolactone
               Glycopyrronium bromide
               Guanethidine *mono*sulphate
               2-Guanidinobenzimidazole
               Guanine
               Guanine hydrochloride
               Guanosine 3′-(dihydrogen phosphate)
               Guanosine 5′-(disodium phosphate)
               Haematoporphyrin
               *Haematoporphyrin dihydrochloride (until 6th March 1969)
               Haloperidol
               Hecogenin
               Hecogenin acetate
               †10-(3-[4-(2-*n*-Heptanoyloxyethyl)piperazin-1-yl]propyl)-2-
                    trifluoromethylphenothiazine
               †*N*-*n*-Hexadecyl-*N*-[2-(*N*-4-methoxybenzyl-2-
                    pyrimidylamino)ethyl]dimethylammonium bromide
               1,3,4,6,7,8-Hexahydro-4,6,6,7,8,8-hexamethylindeno-[5,6-*c*]pyran
               Hexahydro*iso*nicotinamide

Tariff heading   *Description*

29.35   Hexa(methoxymethyl)melamine
           *1,6-Hexanolactam
           †1,4-*n*-Hexanolactone
           1,6-Hexanolactone
           Hexetidine
           Hexocyclium methylsulphate
           †2-*n*-Hexyl-1,4-butyrolactone
           Histamine acid phosphate
           Histamine di-(3,4-dichlorobenzenesulphonate)
           Histamine dihydrochloride
           L-Histidine
           L-Histidine *mono*hydrochloride
           DL-Histidine *mono*hydrochloride
           Hydrallazine hydrochloride
           2-Hydrazinobenzothiazole
           2-Hydroxycarbazole
           2-Hydroxycarbazole-3-carboxylic acid
           Hydroxychloroquine *mono*sulphate
           †1-(2-Hydroxyethyl)-2-*n*-nonylimidazoline
           3-Hydroxy-5-hydroxymethyl-4-methoxymethyl-2-picolinium chloride
           4-Hydroxy-1-methylpiperidine
           7-Hydroxy-7-(1-methyl-4-piperidyl)-1,2:5,6-dibenzocycloheptatriene
               hydrochloride
           8-Hydroxynaphth[1,2-*d*]imidazole
           2-(2-Hydroxyphenyl)benzotriazole
           4-Hydroxypiperidine
           L-Hydroxyproline
           3-Hydroxypyridine
           1-Hydroxypyridine-2-thione, sodium derivative
           5-(α-Hydroxy-α-2-pyridylbenzyl)-7-(α-2-
               pyridylbenzylidene)bicyclo[2,2,1]hept-5-ene-2,3-dicarboxyimide
           6-Hydroxyquinoline
           4-Hydroxy-DL-tryptophan
           5-Hydroxy-DL-tryptophan
           Hydroxyzine dihydrochloride
           Hydroxyzine embonate
           Idoxuridine
           Imidazole
           Imidazol-1-ylacetic acid
           3-(Imidazol-4-yl)propionic acid
           Imperatorin
           Indole
           Indole-3-carboxylic acid
           Indole-5-carboxylic acid
           Indomethacin
           Inosine
           Inosine 5'-(disodium phosphate)
           Inosine 5'-(trisodium pyrophosphate)
           6-Iodopurine
           Iproniazid *mono*phosphate
           Isatin
           Isocarboxazid
           Isoniazid
           Isothipendyl *mono*hydrochloride
           Lepidine
           Leptazol
           Levallorphan hydrogen tartrate
           Levorphanol hydrogen tartrate
           2,3-Lutidine
           2,5-Lutidine
           3,4-Lutidine

Tariff heading　　　　　　　　　　　*Description*

29.35　　Maltol
Mebhydrolin napadisylate
Meclozine dihydrochloride
Mepenzolate bromide
2-Mercaptobenzimidazole
6-Mercaptopurine
Methapyrilene 2-(4-hydroxybenzoyl)benzoate
Methdilazine *mono*hydrochloride
Methixene hydrochloride
Methotrexate
5-Methoxyindole
2-Methoxyphenothiazine
α-(4-Methoxyphenyl)piperidinoacetamide
α-(4-Methoxyphenyl)piperidinoacetonitrile
α-(4-Methoxyphenyl)pyrrolidinoacetamide
α-(4-Methoxyphenyl)pyrrolidinoacetonitrile
8-Methoxypsoralen
6-Methoxyquinoline
Methyl 3-amino-5,6-dichloropyrazine-2-carboxylate
6-Methylaminopurine
2-Methylbenzoselenazole
3-Methylbenzothiazolium toluene-4-sulphonate
3-Methylchromone
†Methyl 7-diethylamino-4-hydroxy-6-*n*-propylquinoline-3-carboxylate
6-Methyl-1,3-dithiolo[4,5-*b*]quinoxalin-2-one
Methylenedi-(1,6-hexanolactam), mixed isomers
2-Methylfuran
1-Methylimidazol-4-ylacetic acid
2-Methylindole
1-Methylindole-2-carboxylic acid
2-Methyl-4-nitroimidazole
3-Methyl-1-(4-nitrophenyl)-5-pyrazolone
Methyl phenidate *mono*hydrochloride
6-Methylpicolinic acid
1-Methylpiperazine
3-(2-Methylpiperidino)propan-1-ol
1-Methyl-4-piperidone
N-Methyl-3-piperidylmethanol
Methyl 2-pyridylacetate
Methyl 4-pyridylacetate
1-Methylpyrrole
1-Methyl-2-pyrrolidone
2-Methylthiophen
3-Methylthiophen
6-Methyl-2-thiouracil
4-Methylumbelliferone
Methyprylone
Metyrapone
DL-Mevalonic acid lactone
4-Morpholinobutyronitrile
2-(Morpholinodithio)benzothiazole
N-(Morpholinomethyl)pyrazinecarboxyamide
α-Morpholinophenylacetamide
α-Morpholinophenylacetonitrile
3-Morpholino-1-phenyl-1-(2-thienyl)propan-1-ol methiodide
3-Morpholinopropionitrile
Nalidixic acid
2-(1-Naphthyl)-5-phenyloxazole
Nialamide
Nicotinamide-adenine dinucleotide

Tariff heading	Description
29.35	Nicotinamide-adenine dinucleotide phosphate, *mono*sodium salt

Nicotinyl alcohol
*iso*Nicotinyl alcohol
Nifuratel
Nitrazepam
5-Nitroindole
Nitron
2-Nitrothiophen
1,3,4,5,6,7,8,8-Octachloro-1,3,3a,4,7,7a-hexahydro-
    4,7-methano*iso*benzofuran
1,4,4a,4b,5,8,8a,8b-Octahydrodibenzofuran-4b-aldehyde
1,8-Octanolactam
7-Oxabicyclo[2,2,1]heptane-2,3-dicarboxylic acid
12-Oxa-1,16-hexadecanolactone
Oxazepam
Oxymetazoline hydrochloride
Oxyphencyclimine hydrochloride
Pancuronium bromide
(−)-Pantolactone
(±)-Pantolactone, which yields on hydrolysis not more than 5 parts per
    million by weight of cyanides calculated as CN
Pemoline
1,15-Pentadecanolactone
†1,4-*n*-Pent-2-enolactone
Penthienate hydrochloride
Penthienate methobromide
Phenazone
Phenazopyridine *mono*hydrochloride
Phenbutrazate hydrochloride
Pheniramine hydrogen maleate
Phenmetrazine hydrochloride
Phenodioxin
Phenolphthalein, which satisfies the requirements of the British
    Pharmacopoeia
Phenoperidine
Phenoperidine hydrochloride
2-Phenoxypyridine
Phenprocoumon
Phentolamine *mono*mesylate
4-(*N*-Phenylamidino)thiazole hydrochloride
Phenylbutazone
2-Phenylcinchoninic acid
2-Phenylindole
α-Phenylpiperidinoacetamide
α-Phenylpiperidinoacetonitrile
α-Phenylpyrrolidinoacetamide
2-Picoline
3-Picoline
4-Picoline
Picoline, mixed isomers
Picolinic acid
Pipazethate *mono*hydrochloride
Pipenzolate bromide
4-Piperidinobutyronitrile
Piperidolate hydrochloride
Potassium 4-amino-3,5,6-trichloropicolinate
Potassium hydrogen 7-oxabicyclo[2,2,1]heptane-2,3-dicarboxylate
*di*Potassium 7-oxabicyclo[2,2,1]heptane-2,3-dicarboxylate
Pramoxine hydrochloride
L-Proline

Tariff heading   *Description*

29.35   DL-Proline
           Prolintane hydrochloride
           Propantheline bromide
           1,3-Propiolactone
           Propiomazine hydrogen maleate
           †2-*n*-Propylpyridine
           †6-*n*-Propylthiouracil
           Prothionamide
           Prothipendyl *mono*hydrochloride
           Pyrazinamide
           Pyrazole
           Pyridine
           Pyridine-2,3-dicarboxylic acid
           2-Pyridone
           3-Pyridylacetic acid
           2-Pyridylacetic acid hydrochloride
           4-Pyridylacetic acid hydrochloride
           3-Pyridylacetonitrile
           3-Pyridyl dimethylcarbamate
           1-(4-Pyridyl)pyridinium chloride
           Pyrimidine
           Pyritinol dihydrochloride
           Pyrrobutamine pentahydrogen diphosphate
           Pyrrolidine
           4-Pyrrolidinobutyronitrile
           2-Pyrrolidone
           3-Pyrroline
           Quinoline (until 3rd July 1969)
           *iso*Quinoline
           Skatole
           Sodium D-*iso*ascorbate
           Sodium dehydracetate
           Sodium deoxyribonucleate
           *di*Sodium 7-oxabicyclo[2,2,1]heptane-2,3-dicarboxylate
           Sodium 2-phenylcinchoninate
           Sodium ribonucleate
           Sodium 6,8-thioctamidoacetate
           Spironolactone
           Tetrabenazine
           Tetrachlorothiophen
           Tetracosactide hexa-acetate
           Tetra(dichloro-1,3,5-triazinetrione)-trichloro-1,3,5-triazinetrione
              complex, tetrapotassium derivative
           Tetrahydro-2,5-dimethoxyfuran
           Tetrahydro-3,5-dimethyl-1,3,5-thiadiazine-2-thione
           Tetrahydrofuran
           Tetrahydrofurfuryl alcohol
           Tetrahydro-2-methylfuran
           (+)-Tetrahydro-4-methyl-2-(2-methylprop-1-enyl)pyran
           (−)-Tetrahydro-4-methyl-2-(2-methylprop-1-enyl)pyran
           Tetrahydro-4-methyl-6-ureido-2-pyrimidone
           2-(Tetrahydro-5-methyl-5-vinyl-2-furyl)propan-2-ol
           †3-(Tetrahydro-2-*n*-pentyl-3-furyl)-1-[3-(tetrahydro-2-*n*-pentyl-3-furyl)-
              propoxy]propan-1-ol
           Tetrahydrozoline *mono*hydrochloride
           Thenyldiamine *mono*hydrochloride
           Thiabendazole
           Thiethylperazine di(hydrogen maleate)
           6,8-Thioctamide
           5,8-Thioctic acid

Tariff heading	Description

29.35   Thioguanine
Thionaphthen
Thiophen
Thioridazine
Thioridazine *mono*hydrochloride
Thioxolone
Thymidine
Thymine
Thymolphthalein-2,2'-di(methylaminodiacetic acid)
Tigogenin acetate
Triallyl cyanurate
Triaziridin-1-ylphosphine oxide
2-(3-Trifluoromethylanilino)nicotinic acid
4,4,4-Trifluoro-1-(2-thienyl)butane-1,3-dione
Tri-(2-hydroxyethyl)-1,3,5-triazinetrione
Trimetaphan *mono*-(+)-camphorsulphonate
Trimetazidine dihydrochloride
Tri-(2-methylaziridin-1-yl)phosphine oxide
NN'-Trimethyleneurea
Tripelennamine citrate
Tripelennamine *mono*hydrochloride
Tryptamine hydrochloride
L-Tryptophan
DL-Tryptophan
Uracil
Uric acid
Uridine
Uridine 3'-(dihydrogen phosphate)
Uridine 5'-(disodium dihydrogen triphosphate)
Usnic acid
5-Vinyl-2-picoline (until 3rd July 1969)
N-Vinyl-2-pyrrolidone
Viprynium embonate
Visnadine
Xanthen-9-carboxylic acid
Xanthine
Xanthurenic acid
Xylometazoline hydrochloride
Zinc di-(2-thiobenzimidazole)
Zoxazolamine

29.36   Acetohexamide
4-Acetylbenzenesulphonamide
*N*¹-Acetylsulphamethoxypyridazine
4-Amino-*N*-ethyl-*N*-(2-methanesulphonamidoethyl)-*m*-toluidine
     sesquisulphate (-NH₂ at 1)
Benzthiazide
3-*iso*Butyl-6-chloro-3,4-dihydrobenzo-1,2,4-thiadiazine-7-sulphonamide
     1,1-dioxide
Chloramine T
5-Chloroaniline-2,4-disulphonamide
3-Chloro-6-sulphanilamidopyridazine
Chlorpropamide
Clopamide
Cyclopenthiazide
Cyclothiazide
N-Dichlorofluoromethylthio-*N'N'*-dimethyl-*N*-phenylsulphamide
Dichlorphenamide
Dimethothiazine mesylate
2-Dimethylsulphamoylphenothiazine
Epithiazide

Tariff heading	Description
29.36	Ethiazide

29.36 Ethiazide
Ethyl 4-acetylbenzenesulphonylcarbamate
N'-Ethyl-p-toluidine-3-sulphonanilide (-NH$_2$ at 1)
2-Methoxy-3-sulphanilamidopyrazine
Methyclothiazide
3-Methyl-1-phenyl-5-sulphanilamidopyrazole
Polythiazide
Probenecid
Quinethazone
Sulphadimethoxine
Sulphadimidine esylate, sodium derivative
Sulphamerazine
Sulphamethoxazole
Sulphamethoxypyridazine
Sulphormethoxine
Teclothiazide potassium
Thioproperazine dimesylate
Thiothixene
Tolazamide

29.37 o-Cresolsulphonephthalein-6,6'di(methylaminodiacetic acid)
o-Cresolsulphonephthalein-6,6'di(methylaminodiacetic acid),
    tetrasodium salt
4,5,6,7,3',5',3'',5''-Octabromophenolsulphonephthalein
1,3-Propanesultone
Sulthiame
Thymolsulphonephthalein-2,2'-di(methylaminodiacetic acid)

29.38 L-Ascorbic acid
Ascorbyl palmitate
D-Biotin
Carotene
Dexpanthenol
Ergosterol
$(+)$-N-(3-Ethoxypropyl)-2,4-dihydroxy-3,3-dimethylbutyramide
Phytomenadione
Pteroylmonoglutamic acid
Pyridoxal 5-(dihydrogen phosphate)
Riboflavine
Sodium D-pantothenate
D-γ-Tocopherol

29.39 $(+)$-Aldosterone
Chlormadinone acetate
3-Cyclopentyloxy-17α-ethynyloestra-1,3,5(10)-trien-17β-ol
3-Cyclopentyloxy-17α-hydroxypregna-3,5-dien-20-one acetate
3-Cyclopentyloxypregna-3,5-dien-20-one
Deoxycorticosterone acetate
Deoxycorticosterone 21-D-glucoside
Deoxycorticosterone pivalate
Dexamethasone 21-(disodium phosphate)
Dexamethasone 21-isonicotinate
Dexamethasone 21-(3-sodium-sulphobenzoate)
Fludrocortisone 21-acetate
Fluocinolone acetonide
6α-Fluoro-11β,21-dihydroxy-16α,17α-isopropylidenedioxypregna-
    1,4-diene-3,20-diore
9α-Fluoro-11β,17α,21-trihydroxypregna-1,4-diene-3,20-dione 21-acetate
Fluoxymesterone
Follicle stimulating hormone (FSH) and luteinising hormone (LH),
    mixed
Nandrolone laurate

Tariff heading	Description

29.39
- (−)-Noradrenaline
- (−)-Noradrenaline hydrogen tartrate
- †17β-Oestradiol di-*n*-undecanoate
- †17β-Oestradiol 17-*n*-valerate
- Oxymesterone
- Oxytocin
- Oxytocin dihydrogen citrate
- Paramethasone 21-acetate
- Prednisolone 21-pivalate
- Prednisolone 21-(3-sodium-sulphobenzoate)
- Prednisolone 21-*O*-stearoylglycollate
- Prednylidene
- Quinestradol
- Testosterone 3-cyclohexylpropionate
- †Testosterone *n*-heptanoate
- DL-Thyroxine sodium
- Triamcinolone
- Triamcinolone acetonide
- Vasopressin
- Vasopressin tannate

29.40
- Urokinase

29.41
- Aesculin
- Digitalin
- Digitonin
- Digitoxin
- Ouabain
- Salicin

29.42
- 18β-Acetoxy-10β,17α-dimethoxy-16β-methoxycarbonyl-3-oxo-2,3-seco-20α-yohimbane
- Alcuronium chloride
- Arecoline
- Arecoline-acetarsol
- Arecoline hydrobromide
- Bamifylline hydrochloride
- Berberine hydrogen sulphate
- Bicuculline
- 2-Bromo-*NN*-diethyl-D-lysergamide hydrogen tartrate
- Bulbocapnine hydrochloride
- Cinchonidine
- Cinchonidine sulphate
- Cinchonine
- Cinchonine *mono*hydrochloride
- Cinchonine sulphate
- Cocaine, of a purity not greater than 97·5 per cent. by weight
- Colchicine
- Demecolcine
- Deptropine dihydrogen citrate
- Deserpidine
- Dihydroergocornine
- Dihydroergocristine
- Dihydroergocryptine
- Dihydroergotamine *mono*mesylate
- 7,8-Dihydro-14-hydroxy-6-methylene-6-deoxymorphine
- Dimenhydrinate
- *pseudo*Ephedrine
- *pseudo*Ephedrine hydrochloride
- Ergotamine tartrate
- Ethyl quinine carbonate
- Galanthamine hydrobromide

Tariff heading   *Description*

29.42   Galegine sulphate
            Harmalol
            Harmine
            †1-*n*-Hexyltheobromine
            Hydromorphone hydrochloride
            18β-Hydroxy-10,17α-dimethoxy-20α-yohimbane-16β-carboxylic acid
                lactone
            †Hyoscine *n*-butylobromide
            Lobeline hydrochloride
            Lobeline sulphate
            (+)-Lysergic acid
            Lysergide tartrate-methanol complex
            Meralluride
            Mescaline hydrochloride
            Mescaline sulphate
            Methoserpidine
            Methylergometrine maleate
            Methysergide hydrogen maleate
            Papaverine
            Papaverine hydrochloride
            Papaverine hydrogen sulphate
            Phenmetrazine theoclate
            Reserpine
            Sparteine *mono*sulphate
            Syrosingopine
            Tomatidine
            Vinblastine sulphate
            Vincristine sulphate
            Xanthinol nicotinate
            Yohimbine *mono*hydrochloride

29.43   D-Arabinose
            L-Arabinose
            Calcium bromide lactobionate
            Calcium gluconate lactobionate
            D-Erythrose
            Fructose 1-(barium phosphate)
            Fructose tetranicotinate, mixed isomers
            L-Fucose
            D-Galactose
            Galactose 6-(barium phosphate)
            Gentiobiose
            Lactobionic acid
            D-Lyxose
            Maltose
            D-Mannose
            Mannose 6-(barium phosphate)
            D-Melezitose dihydrate
            Methyl α-D-xyloside
            Methyl β-D-xyloside
            Phenyl β-D-glucoside
            Raffinose
            L-Rhamnose
            D-Ribose
            Ribose 5-(barium phosphate)
            Sorbose
            Sucrose benzoate having a benzoyl content of not less than 80 per cent.
                by weight calculated as benzoic acid
            Sucrose diacetate hexa*iso*butyrate
            Turanose

Tariff heading	*Description*
29.43	P^1-Uridine-5′ P^2-glucose-1 disodium pyrophosphate
	D-Xylose
29.44	Amphotericin B
	Bacitracin methylenedisalicylate
	Bacitracin zinc
	Calcium amphomycin
	Capreomycin disulphate
	Chloramphenicol 3-cinnamate
	Chloramphenicol sodium succinate
	Clomocycline, sodium salt
	Colistin sulphate
	Colistin sulphomethate sodium
	Cycloserine
	Diethanolammonium fusidate
	3-[2-(3,5-Dimethyl-2-oxocyclohexyl)-2-hydroxyethyl]glutarimide
	Erythromycin ethyl succinate
	Erythromycin glucoheptonate
	Erythromycin lactobionate
	Framycetin sulphate
	Fumagillin
	Fusafungin
	Gentamicin sulphate
	Gramicidin
	Hygromycin B
	Kanamycin sulphates
	Kojic acid
	Lincomycin hydrochloride
	Lymecycline
	Methacycline
	Methacycline hydrochloride
	3-(4-Methylpiperazin-1-yliminomethyl)rifamycin SV
	Novobiocin
	Novobiocin calcium
	Novobiocin sodium
	Nystatin
	Oleandomycin *mono*phosphate
	Paromomycin
	Paromomycin sulphates
	Rolitetracycline nitrate
	Rubidomycin hydrochloride
	Sodium fusidate
	Spectinomycin dihydrochloride
	Spectinomycin sulphate
	Spiramycin
	Thiostrepton
	Triacetyloleandomycin
	Tyrothricin
	Vancomycin hydrochloride
	Viomycin pantothenate sulphate
	Viomycin sulphate
	Virginiamycin
	Xanthocillin
29.45	Boron trifluoride-ethylamine complex
	Potassium *tert*butoxide
	Potassium methoxide
	Sodium ethoxide
	Sodium methoxide
30.01	Grafts of bone or cartilage, defatted, dried and packed in vacuum

Tariff heading   *Description*

30.03   Digitalin, being a mixture of digitalis glycosides standardised with the
           addition of lactose or other diluent

           Preparations consisting of not less than 3·4 per cent. by weight of
           3-cyclopentyloxy-17α-hydroxypregna-3,5-diene-20-one acetate dis-
           solved in fixed vegetable oil

           †Preparations consisting of not less than 10 per cent. by weight of
           methenolone *n*-heptanoate dissolved in fixed vegetable oil

           Preparations consisting of not less than 0·14 per cent. by weight of
           quinestradol dissolved in fixed vegetable oil

           Preparations containing either (*a*) not less than 0·8 per cent. by weight
           of thiotepa and not less than 95 per cent. by weight of polyethylene
           glycol ethers or (*b*) not less than 9·5 per cent. by weight of thiotepa

           Preparations containing leucovorin calcium equivalent to not less than
           2·7 grammes and not more than 3·6 grammes of leucovorin per litre

           Preparations containing not less than 18 per cent. by weight and not
           more than 58 per cent. by weight of frusemide

           Preparations containing not less than 18 per cent. by weight of
           2-(4-chloroanilino)-5-(4-chlorophenyl)-3,5-dihydro-3-*iso*propylimino-
           phenazine

           Preparations containing not less than 15 per cent. by weight of
           O-(3-chloro-4-methylcoumarin-7-yl) *OO*-diethyl phosphorothioate

           Preparations containing not less than 2·5 per cent. by weight of
           colistin sulphate

           Preparations containing not less than 50 per cent. by weight of
           fluanisone calculated on the dry material

           Preparations containing not less than 0·45 per cent. by weight of
           fusafungin and not less than 99 per cent. by weight of squalane

           Preparations containing not less than 0·18 per cent. by weight of
           fusafungin and not less than 80 per cent. by weight of volatile
           propellents

           Preparations containing not less than 95 per cent. by weight of lactose
           and not less than 0·3 per cent. by weight of uramustine

           Preparations containing not less than 1·2 per cent. by weight of
           methylprednisolone

           Preparations containing not less than 1 per cent. by weight of
           orciprenaline sulphate and not less than 96 per cent. by weight of
           propellent gases liquefied under pressure

           Preparations containing not less than 0·13 per cent. by weight of
           tramazoline hydrochloride, not less than 0·02 per cent. by weight of
           dexamethasone 21-*iso*nicotinate, and not less than 96 per cent. by
           weight of volatile propellents

           Preparations containing sodium salts of methotrexate equivalent to not
           less than 20 per cent. by weight and not more than 60 per cent. by
           weight of methotrexate

           Preparations, in the form of capsules, the contents of which include
           not less than 70 per cent. by weight of acetazolamide

           Preparations, in the form of cream, containing not less than 70 per
           cent. by weight of water and not less than 0·8 per cent. by weight of
           chlordantoin

           Preparations, in the form of suppositories, containing not less than
           0·25 per cent. by weight of bisacodyl

           Preparations, in the form of tablets, containing aminopterin sodium
           equivalent to not less than 0·35 per cent. by weight and not more
           than 0·45 per cent. by weight of aminopterin

           Preparations, in the form of tablets, containing not less than 1·8 per
           cent. by weight and not more than 2·3 per cent. by weight of
           methotrexate

           Preparations, in the form of tablets, containing not less than 4 per cent.
           by weight of orciprenaline sulphate

Tariff heading	*Description*
31.02	Mixtures consisting of ammonium nitrate and ammonium sulphate and containing not less than 25 per cent. by weight and not more than 27 per cent. by weight of nitrogen expressed as N (until 3rd July 1969)
32.07	Dispersions of carbon black in artificial plastics, containing not less than 6 per cent. by weight of carbon black, not less than 40 per cent. by weight of cellulose acetate butyrate and not less than 35 per cent. by weight of acrylic resin
	Preparations consisting of titanium dioxide dispersed in nylon 6, containing not less than 18 per cent. by weight and not more than 22 per cent. by weight of titanium dioxide
35.04	Protein substances of which, when 20 grammes are shaken for 2 hours at 20° centigrade with ethanol of a strength of 90 per cent. by volume, not more than 0·2 millilitre remains undissolved
37.01	Diazo film in sheets, being film which is capable, when developed by heating at between 105° and 135° centigrade, of producing a positive image consisting of light-scattering cavities in an otherwise transparent coating (until 6th March 1969)
37.02	Diazo film in rolls, being film which is capable, when developed by heating at between 105° and 135° centigrade, of producing a positive image consisting of light-scattering cavities in an otherwise transparent coating (until 6th March 1969)
37.03	Diazo paper, unexposed, being paper which is capable, when developed by heating at between 105° and 135° centigrade, of producing a positive image consisting of light-scattering cavities in an otherwise transparent coating (until 6th March 1969)
38.03	Activated carbon, not being of animal origin, which, in the form in which it is imported, on subjection to extraction with acetic acid of a strength of 30 per cent. by weight at 50° centigrade for 30 minutes, yields (*a*) a total of extractable solids which, when dried at 105° centigrade, does not exceed 0·2 per cent. by weight of the material and (*b*) extractable phosphate, which expressed in terms of phosphorus pentoxide, does not exceed 50 parts per million by weight of the material
38.05	Tall oil, crude
38.11	Preparations containing not less than 0·2 per cent. by weight of 2-[α-(4-chlorophenyl)phenylacetyl]indane-1,3-dione and not less than 95 per cent. by weight of hydrocarbon oil
	Preparations containing not less than 7 per cent. by weight of 2,6-dichlorothiobenzamide and not more than 15 per cent. by weight of materials soluble in diethyl ether
	Preparations, in powder form, containing not less than 17 per cent. by weight of triphenyltin hydroxide
	Preparations, liquid, containing not less than 35 per cent. by weight of 4-chlorophenylthiomethyl *OO*-diethyl phosphorodithioate
	Preparations, liquid, containing not less than 40 per cent. by weight of *OO*-diethyl *O*-pyrazin-2-yl phosphorothioate
	†Preparations, liquid, containing not less than 65 per cent. by weight of *S*-ethyl di-*n*-propylthiocarbamate
	†Preparations, liquid, containing not less than 65 per cent. by weight of *S*-*n*-propyl *n*-butylethylthiocarbamate
	Preparations, solid, containing not less than 45 per cent. by weight of *OO*-dimethyl phthalimidomethyl phosphorodithioate
	Preparations, solid, containing not less than 90 per cent. by weight of sodium ethylenebisdithiocarbamate
	Prepared cereal baits containing not less than 0·4 per cent. by weight and not more than 1 per cent. by weight of 5-(α-hydroxy-α-2-pyridylbenzyl)-7-(α-2-pyridylbenzylidene)bicyclo[2,2,1]hept-5-ene-2,3-dicarboxyimide

Tariff heading | *Description*

38.14   Prepared oil additives, consisting of hydrocarbon oil and organic compounds of antimony, and containing not less than 6 per cent. by weight and not more than 13 per cent. by weight of antimony calculated as Sb

Prepared oil additives containing not less than 5 per cent. by weight of calcium calculated as Ca when determined by titration with a solution of perchloric acid in acetic acid, and not more than 5·5 per cent. by weight of calcium calculated as Ca when determined by the Institute of Petroleum method No. 111/49T

Prepared oil additives, having a viscosity at 99° centigrade of not less than 20 centistokes, containing not less than 2·5 per cent. by weight and not more than 4·5 per cent. by weight of zinc calculated as Zn, and containing not less than 2 per cent. by weight of phosphorus calculated as P

38.15   Prepared rubber accelerators, being sulphides of alkylphenols, and containing not less than 20 per cent. by weight and not more than 30 per cent. by weight of sulphur in all

Prepared rubber accelerators containing not less than 80 per cent. by weight of *NNN'*-trimethylthiourea

38.19   Amines, mixed primary aromatic, containing not less than 4·5 per cent. by weight and not more than 5·5 per cent. by weight of nitrogen calculated as N

Chlordane

Cultured crystals, weighing not less than two and a half grammes of barium fluoride

Mixed alkenylsuccinic anhydrides having a saponification value not less than 505

Mixed alkyl selenides containing not less than 14 per cent. by weight and not more than 21 per cent. by weight of combined selenium

Mixed alkyl-substituted benzenesulphonic acids having an acid value not greater than 125

Poly-(3,4-diacetyl-5-thiothien-2-yl) which on ignition yields not more than 10 per cent. by weight of ash

Polyglyoxal

Preparations consisting of acrylamide with not less than 2 per cent. by weight and not more than 12 per cent. by weight of diacrylamido-methane

Preparations consisting of calcium tetrahydrogen diorthophosphate and aluminium compounds, and containing not less than 1·5 per cent. by weight and not more than 2·5 per cent. by weight of aluminium calculated as Al_2O_3

Preparations consisting of 1-chloro-1,1-difluoroethane and 1,1-difluoroethane, and containing not less than 40 per cent. by weight and not more than 50 per cent. by weight of 1,1-difluoroethane

Preparations consisting of clay and not less than 30 per cent. by weight and not more than 40 per cent. by weight of *N*-methyl-*N*,4-dinitrosoaniline

Preparations containing not less than 85 per cent. by weight of aluminium compounds calculated as Al_2O_3, and not less than 10 per cent. by weight of molybdenum compounds calculated as MoO_3, and of which not more than 10 per cent. by weight is retained by a sieve having a nominal width of aperture of 1·2 millimetres and conforming to British Standard 410:1962

Preparations containing not less than 55 per cent. by weight of melamine compounds calculated as melamine and not less than 12 per cent. by weight of peroxides calculated as hydrogen peroxide

Preparations, gaseous, containing not less than 0·002 per cent. by volume and not more than 1·5 per cent. by volume of antimony compounds calculated as stibine, and having a value not less than £15 per cubic metre at standard temperature and pressure

Tariff heading   *Description*

38.19   Preparations, gaseous, containing not less than 0·002 per cent. by volume and not more than 1·5 per cent. by volume of arsenic compounds calculated as arsine, and having a value not less than £15 per cubic metre at standard temperature and pressure

Preparations, gaseous, containing not less than 0·002 per cent. by volume and not more than 1·5 per cent. by volume of boron compounds calculated as diborane, and having a value not less than £15 per cubic metre at standard temperature and pressure

Preparations, gaseous, containing not less than 0·002 per cent. by volume and not more than 1·5 per cent. by volume of phosphorus compounds calculated as phosphine, and having a value not less than £15 per cubic metre at standard temperature and pressure

Preparations, gaseous, containing not less than 0·002 per cent. by volume and not more than 1·5 per cent. by volume of selenium compounds calculated as hydrogen selenide, and having a value not less than £15 per cubic metre at standard temperature and pressure

Preparations, gaseous, containing not less than 0·5 per cent. by volume and not more than 6 per cent. by volume of silicon compounds calculated as silane, and having a value not less than £40 per cubic metre at standard temperature and pressure

Prepared catalysts consisting of phosphoric acids and siliceous earth and containing not less than 55 per cent. by weight and not more than 70 per cent. by weight of phosphates calculated as P_2O_5

Prepared catalysts, in the form of spheres, containing silver or silver oxide dispersed with alumina or silica or compounds thereof, and which contain not less than 7 per cent. by weight and not more than 20 per cent. by weight of total silver calculated as Ag (until 3rd July 1969)

Prepared catalysts which in the dry state contain not less than 5 per cent. by weight of nickel compounds calculated as Ni and not less than 50 per cent. by weight of phosphate calculated as PO_4

39.01   Nylon 6 in the forms covered by Note 3(*b*) of Chapter 39, containing not more than 2 per cent. by weight of titanium dioxide and not more than 2·5 per cent. by weight of carbon black, but not otherwise compounded

Phenoxy resins, not plasticised or otherwise compounded, being thermoplastic polyaddition products of 2,2-di-(4-hydroxyphenyl)-propane and 1-chloro-2,3-epoxypropane and having an epoxide content of less than 0·8 per cent. by weight calculated as ethylene oxide

Poly-[2,2-di-(4-hydroxyphenyl)propane carbonate] moulding compounds, containing glass fibres which amount to not less than 25 per cent. by weight of the product and not more than 45 per cent. by weight of the product (until 6th March 1969)

Poly-[2,2-di-(4-hydroxyphenyl)propane carbonate], uncompounded, or compounded with other materials which do not exceed 3 per cent. by weight of the product

Polynoxylin

Resins, being products of the condensation of adipic acid with a mixture of propane-1,2-diol and ethanediol of which the ethanediol content is not less than 50 per cent. by weight, and having:—

    (*a*) an acetyl value not less than 34 and not more than 38,

    (*b*) an acid value not more than 1,

    (*c*) a colour not deeper than 50 Hazen units, and

    (*d*) a viscosity at 40° centigrade of not less than 70 seconds and not more than 125 seconds, for a free fall of 20 centimetres of a steel sphere ⅛ inch in diameter, in a tube of internal diameter 3·5 centimetres, when determined by the method of British Standard 188:1957, part 3

Tariff heading	*Description*
39.02	Polystyrene sheet, in rolls, colourless, of a thickness not less than 0·1 millimetre and not greater than 0·9 millimetre and having a light transmission not less than 85 per cent.
	Poly(vinyl butyral) sheet, of a thickness not greater than 0·8 millimetre and of a width not less than 35 centimetres
	Poly(vinyl chloride) having an apparent density of not more than 0·3 grammes per millilitre and a viscosity number of not less than 170 when tested by the methods described in British Standard 2782:1965 and of which not more than 5 per cent. by weight is retained by a sieve having a nominal width of aperture of 150 microns and conforming to British Standard 410:1962
39.03	Carboxymethylcellulose, aluminium salt
	Cellulose acetate, where the weight of the acetyl content, calculated as acetic acid, is not less than 60 per cent. of the weight of the cellulose acetate, not being cellulose acetate plasticised or otherwise compounded
	Cellulose acetate butyrate compounded with other materials which do not exceed 25 per cent. by weight of the product, in the forms covered by Note 3(b) of Chapter 39
	Cellulose acetate butyrate, not plasticised or otherwise compounded
	Cellulose acetate propionate, not plasticised or otherwise compounded
	Cellulose propionate, not plasticised or otherwise compounded
	2-Diethylaminoethylcellulose
	Ethylcellulose
	Ethylhydroxyethylcellulose
	Hydroxyethylcellulose
	Hydroxypropylcellulose
	Scrap exposed X-ray film (until 1st May 1969)
40.11	Non-pneumatic tyres not less than 37 inches in outside diameter, moulded in one piece and not mounted on a metal ring on the inside circumference (until 6th March 1969)
44.09	*Cleft pales, stub-pointed, not less than 3 feet nor more than 6 feet in length, split from stems or branches of sweet chestnut of not less than 4 inches girth (until 6th March 1969)
49.11	Identification kits, consisting essentially of a series of transparent slides or foils printed to depict individual characteristics of the human face or head; parts of such kits (until 3rd July 1969)
51.01	Yarn wholly of polytetrafluoroethylene (until 1st May 1969)
51.02	Monofil wholly of fluorocarbon polymer (until 1st May 1969)
69.09	Catalyst carriers in the form of spheres, consisting of aluminium oxide and silica whether or not combined together, and containing not more than 12·5 per cent. by weight of total silica, and of which (a) not less than 99 per cent. by weight passes a sieve having a nominal width of aperture of 2·40 millimetres and (b) not less than 99 per cent. by weight is retained by a sieve having a nominal width of aperture of 1·00 millimetre (both sieves conforming to British Standard 410:1962)
70.01	Glass in the mass (other than optical glass) containing not less than 5 per cent. and not more than 11 per cent. by weight of fluorine calculated as F
70.03	Amber-coloured tubing of soda glass, not being glass containing 0·25 per cent. or more of cadmium, free or combined, calculated as Cd (until 3rd July 1969)
	Tubing of neutral glass, in straight lengths and capable of passing a test corresponding with the test for limit of alkalinity of glass prescribed by British Pharmacopeia, 1953, not including (a) glass with a content of more than 85 per cent. of silica and boric oxide together, or (b) glass of fused silica or fused quartz (until 3rd July 1969)

Tariff heading   *Description*

70.10   Carboys having a capacity of not less than 5 gallons (until 3rd July 1969)

70.18   Optical glass in the mass containing not less than 5 per cent. by weight and not more than 11 per cent. by weight of fluorine calculated as F

Optical glass in the mass or in the form of slabs or moulded lens blanks, containing not more than $56 \cdot 9$ per cent. by weight nor less than $55 \cdot 9$ per cent. by weight of lead expressed as Pb, having a density of not more than $4 \cdot 65$ grammes nor less than $4 \cdot 25$ grammes per cubic centimetre and having a light transmission for a 1 inch path of not less than 40 per cent. at a wavelength of 4,500 ångströms (until 1st May 1969)

Optical glass in the mass or in the form of slabs or moulded lens blanks, containing not more than $60 \cdot 7$ per cent. by weight nor less than $59 \cdot 7$ per cent. by weight of lead expressed as Pb, having a density of not more than $4 \cdot 93$ grammes nor less than $4 \cdot 53$ grammes per cubic centimetre and having a light transmission for a 1 inch path of not less than 40 per cent. at a wavelength of 4,500 ångströms (until 1st May 1969)

Optical glass in the mass or in the form of slabs or moulded lens blanks, containing not more than $63 \cdot 1$ per cent. by weight nor less than $62 \cdot 1$ per cent. by weight of lead expressed as Pb, having a density of not more than $5 \cdot 11$ grammes nor less than $4 \cdot 71$ grammes per cubic centimetre and having a light transmission for a 1 inch path of not less than 40 per cent. at a wavelength of 4,500 ångströms (until 1st May 1969)

Optical glass in the form of sheets, slabs or moulded lens blanks, having, with reference to the D line of sodium, a refractive index (n_D) not less than $1 \cdot 5625$ and not greater than $1 \cdot 5650$ and a dispersive power (v_D) not less than $60 \cdot 0$ and not greater than $61 \cdot 5$ (until 1st May 1969)

Optical glass in the form of sheets, slabs or moulded lens blanks, having, with reference to the D line of sodium, a refractive index (n_D) not less than $1 \cdot 612$ and not greater than $1 \cdot 615$ and a dispersive power (v_D) not less than $43 \cdot 5$ and not greater than $45 \cdot 0$; having also at a wavelength of 400 nanometres a light transmission for a 25 millimetres path of not less than 83 per cent.; and which acquires no visible stain when kept for 15 minutes at a temperature of 25° centigrade in contact with a buffered sodium acetate solution having a pH value of $4 \cdot 6$ (until 1st May 1969)

70.20   Glass fibres, loose, unfelted, having a diameter not greater than 3 microns

73.06   *Iron or steel ingots of a tapered shape, of a weight of 10 tons or over per ingot, and with dimensions at the greater end of not less than 1,000 mm by 825 mm and at the lesser end of not less than 970 mm by 780 mm (until 6th March 1969)

73.07   *Iron or steel slabs not less than 29 inches wide, not less than $4\frac{1}{2}$ inches thick, and not less than 15 feet long (until 6th March 1969)

73.14   Iron or steel wire of a diameter not less than $0 \cdot 019$ inch nor more than $0 \cdot 200$ inch, and having a coating of nickel of not less than $0 \cdot 0001$ inch in thickness (until 3rd July 1969)

73.15   Cold-rolled steel strip, with dressed edges, in coils, the strip being not less than $0 \cdot 002$ inch nor more than $0 \cdot 007$ inch in thickness and not less than $\frac{1}{4}$ inch nor more than 4 inches in width, containing not less than 16 per cent. by weight nor more than 18 per cent. by weight of chromium and not less than 6 per cent. by weight nor more than 8 per cent. by weight of nickel and being of a tensile strength of not less than 115 tons per square inch (until 3rd July 1969)

Tariff heading   *Description*

73.15   Cold-rolled steel strip, with dressed edges, in coils, the strip being not less than 0·002 inch nor more than 0·040 inch in thickness and not less than $\frac{1}{16}$ inch nor more than 4 inches in width, containing not less than 16 per cent. by weight nor more than 18 per cent. by weight of chromium, and not less than 6 per cent. by weight nor more than 8 per cent. by weight of nickel, and being of a tensile strength of not less than 120 tons per square inch (until 3rd July 1969)

Single strand alloy steel wire coated with niobium alloy containing tin and with an outer coating of silver (until 3rd July 1969)

Steel wire, containing not less than 0·60 per cent. by weight and not more than 0·90 per cent. by weight of total carbon, being not less than 300 microns and not more than 540 microns in diameter, and having a coating of copper of not less than 15 microns and not more than 40 microns in thickness (until 3rd July 1969)

Steel wire containing not less than 23 per cent. by weight of chromium, not less than 18 per cent. by weight of nickel and not less than 0·35 per cent. by weight of total carbon, and weighing not less than 8·0 grammes and not more than 33·0 grammes per metre (until 3rd July 1969)

73.19   Hot rolled seamless circular steel tubes of an outside diameter of not less than 19½ inches and not more than 24½ inches, and of a wall thickness of not less than $\frac{7}{16}$ inch and not more than $\frac{5}{8}$ inch (until 1st May 1969)

74.05   Tape consisting of a layer of niobium alloy containing tin, laminated between two layers of copper foil whether or not coated with tin, and being (*a*) not less than 0·25 inch nor more than 0·75 inch in width and (*b*) not more than 0·005 inch in thickness (until 3rd July 1969)

76.03   Aluminium discs of a minimum value of 8s. per lb., not less than 6 inches nor more than 18 inches in diameter and not less than 0·033 inch nor more than 0·036 inch in thickness and which, when either face is placed on a flat surface, do not deviate from the flat by more than 0·010 inch at any point (until 1st May 1969)

76.16   Aluminium can ends, having a diameter of not less than 2·9 inches nor more than 3 inches, and incorporating a riveted tab for opening by means of scored lines (until 3rd July 1969)

81.02   Molybdenum, of a purity not less than 99·8 per cent., in the form of rods (whether or not threaded at the ends) not less than 55 inches nor more than 100 inches in length and not less than $1\frac{7}{32}$ inches nor more than $2\frac{1}{16}$ inches in diameter

Molybdenum, of a purity not less than 99·8 per cent., in the form of rods of not less than 18 inches and not more than 100 inches in length and of not less than 2¼ inches and not more than 4¼ inches in diameter and whether or not threaded at the ends

81.04   Chromium, electrolytic, in the form of cathode chips, which contains not more than 0·10 per cent. by weight of total oxygen, not more than 0·015 per cent. by weight of total aluminium, and not more than 0·001 per cent. by weight of aluminium compounds insoluble in boiling 5N hydrochloric acid and in boiling fuming perchloric acid, and estimated as Al

Hafnium crystal bars consisting of hafnium wire on which hafnium crystals have been deposited

Manganese metal of a purity not less than 96 per cent. and not more than 99·5 per cent. and containing not more than 1·0 per cent. by weight of carbon and not more than 3·0 per cent. by weight of iron (until 1st May 1969)

Tariff heading	*Description*

81.04   Vanadium, unwrought, of a purity not less than 99 per cent. and containing not more than 0·1 per cent. by weight of iron calculated as Fe

Zirconium sponge

83.13   Tinplate caps for sealing jars, of an internal diameter on the rim of not less than 2·001 inches and not more than 2·031 inches and a depth of not less than 0·430 inch and not more than 0·440 inch stamped from tinplate of nominal thickness of 0·0077 inch or of 0·0060 inch, with an internal curl, a vinyl coating applied to the internal surface and a plasticised lining compound deposited on the internal side wall and top sealing panel to form a sealing gasket (until 3rd July 1969)

Tinplate caps for sealing jars, of an internal diameter on the rim of not less than 1·580 inches and not more than 1·610 inches and a maximum depth of not less than 0·415 inch and not more than 0·425 inch stamped from tinplate of nominal thickness of 0·0055 inch or of 0·0066 inch, with an internal curl, a vinyl coating applied to the internal surface and a plasticised lining compound deposited on the internal side wall and top sealing panel to form a sealing gasket (until 3rd July 1969)

84.06   Combined crankcase and cylinder block castings of iron or steel, of a weight exceeding 291 lb. but not exceeding 308 lb., of a kind used in motor vehicle engines of 3 cylinder, direct injection, water-cooled, 2-stroke horizontally opposed piston type

85.14   Microphones, of a kind for incorporation in deaf aids, approximately rectangular in shape, with a maximum thickness not exceeding 0·165 inch and a total of the length and width not exceeding 0·675 inch, exclusive of sound tube (until 3rd July 1969)

85.15   Loran receivers incorporating direct reading indicators, designed to operate only on frequencies of 1,700 kilocycles per second or more (until 1st May 1969)

85.18   Tantalum capacitors greater than 10 microfarads in capacitance, of a kind for incorporation in deaf aids, with a maximum length not exceeding 7 millimetres exclusive of leads and with a transverse cross section having a circumference not exceeding 14 millimetres (until 3rd July 1969)

Tantalum capacitors, of a kind for incorporation in deaf aids, with a maximum length not exceeding 7 millimetres exclusive of leads and with a transverse cross section having a circumference not exceeding 10 millimetres (until 3rd July 1969)

85.19   Carbon track volume controls of a kind for incorporation in deaf aids, being of drum type with a cylindrical drum not exceeding 12 millimetres in diameter and 4 millimetres in thickness (until 3rd July 1969)

85.20   Glass neon discharge lamps, having a metal cap fitted to each end and not exceeding 1 inch in overall length and ½ inch in diameter over the caps

85.23   Insulated tape incorporating a layer of niobium alloy containing tin, laminated between two layers of copper foil, whether or not coated with tin and being (*a*) not less than 0·25 inch nor more than 0·75 inch in width and (*b*) not more than 0·005 inch in thickness (until 3rd July 1969)

90.01   Lenses, prisms, mirrors and other optical elements, not optically worked, of barium fluoride

Lenses, prisms, mirrors and other optical elements, not optically worked, of thallium bromide-iodide (until 3rd July 1969)

Tariff heading	Description
90.01	Material consisting of a polarising film supported on one or both sides by transparent material, and analysers and polarisers made therefrom
	Optical windows of zinc sulphide, unmounted
	Photographic process screens of the contact type, consisting of a base of cellulose acetate or of poly(ethylene terephthalate) on which is a regularly spaced pattern of grey-coloured or magenta-coloured dots (until 3rd July 1969)
90.17	Ampoule injectors consisting of a glass reservoir connected to a flexible plastic tube in which is inserted a hypodermic needle protected by a removable plastic sheath, of a total length not exceeding 10 centimetres (until 3rd July 1969)
	Endoradiosondes for the measurement of pH; and specialised receiving and recording apparatus therefor (until 6th March 1969)
90.19	Aortic heart valves (until 3rd July 1969)
	Earphones, of a kind for incorporation in deaf aids, approximately rectangular in shape, with a maximum thickness not exceeding 0·165 inch and a total of the length and width not exceeding 0·675 inch exclusive of sound tube (until 3rd July 1969)
	Mitral heart valves (until 3rd July 1969)
90.20	Beryllium metal windows of a thickness less than 0·004 inch for X-ray tubes
90.29	Scintillation phosphors of europium-activated lithium iodide

SCHEDULE 2

IMPORT DUTIES (TEMPORARY EXEMPTIONS) ORDERS REVOKED

Number and year of Order	Reference
No. 9 of 1967	S.I. 1967/1847 (1967 III, p. 4913).
No. 1 of 1968	S.I. 1968/252 (1968 I, p. 766).
No. 2 of 1968	S.I. 1968/641 (1968 I, p. 1473).
No. 3 of 1968	S.I. 1968/978 (1968 II, p. 2584).
No. 4 of 1968	S.I. 1968/1384 (1968 II, p. 3939).
No. 5 of 1968	S.I. 1968/1721 (1968 III, p. 4642).

EXPLANATORY NOTE

(*This Note is not part of the Order.*)

This Order provides that the goods listed in Schedule 1 shall be exempt, or shall continue to be exempt, from import duty until 1st January 1970, except for items for which an earlier day is specified. Descriptions of goods which were not exempt at the date of this Order are marked *.

Some goods, the exemption of which is continued by this Order, appear under a description which has been modified to make it specifically clear that the exemption relates only to the normal isomer of the substance concerned: descriptions so modified are marked †.

The Order also continues until 1st January 1970 the partial exemption for photographic film base of cellulose acetate.

STATUTORY INSTRUMENTS

1968 No. 1952

TRIBUNALS AND INQUIRIES

The Town and Country Planning Appeals (Determination by Appointed Persons) (Inquiries Procedure) Rules 1968

Made - - -	*9th December* 1968
Laid before Parliament	*16th December* 1968
Coming into Operation	*1st January* 1969

The Lord Chancellor, in exercise of the powers conferred upon him by section 7A of the Tribunals and Inquiries Act 1958(**a**) (inserted in that Act by section 33 of the Town and Country Planning Act 1959(**b**)) as applied by section 26 of the Town and Country Planning Act 1968(**c**) and after consultation with the Council on Tribunals, hereby makes the following Rules:—

Citation and Commencement

1.—(1) These Rules may be cited as the Town and Country Planning Appeals (Determination by Appointed Persons) (Inquiries Procedure) Rules 1968.

(2) These Rules shall come into operation on 1st January 1969 but shall not affect any appeal brought before that date.

Application of Rules

2.—(1) These Rules apply—

(*a*) to local inquiries held by a person appointed by the Minister of Housing and Local Government or by the Secretary of State for Wales for the purpose of appeals to the said Minister or Secretary of State under section 23 of the Town and Country Planning Act 1962(**d**), where such appeals fall to be determined by the said person instead of by the said Minister or Secretary of State by virtue of the powers contained in Part III of the Town and Country Planning Act 1968 and of regulations made thereunder and (to the extent provided in rule 17) to hearings before such a person for the purposes of any such appeal;

(*b*) to local inquiries held by a person appointed by the said Minister or the said Secretary of State for the purpose of appeals to the said Minister or Secretary of State under a tree preservation order, where such appeals fall to be determined as aforesaid, and (to the extent provided in rule 17) to hearings before such a person for the purpose of any such appeal, subject to the following modifications, that is to say—

(i) rule 4 shall not apply and the references in these Rules to section 17 parties shall be omitted;

(ii) references to development shall be construed as references to the cutting down, topping, or lopping of trees;

(**a**) 1958 c. 66.
(**c**) 1968 c. 72.
(**b**) 1959 c. 53.
(**d**) 1962 c. 38.

(iii) references to permission shall be construed as references to consent;

(c) to local inquiries held by a person appointed by the said Minister or the said Secretary of State for the purpose of appeals to the said Minister or Secretary of State under paragraph 7 of schedule 5 to the Town and Country Planning Act 1968, where such appeals fall to be determined as aforesaid, and (to the extent provided in rule 17) to hearings before such a person for the purpose of any such appeal, subject to the following modifications, that is to say—

    (i) references to development shall be construed as references to works for the demolition, alteration or extension of a listed building;

    (ii) references to permission shall be construed as references to a listed building consent;

(d) to local inquiries held by a person appointed by the said Minister or the said Secretary of State for the purpose of appeals to the said Minister or Secretary of State under the Town and Country Planning (Control of Advertisements) Regulations 1960(a), where such appeals fall to be determined as aforesaid, and (to the extent provided in rule 17) to hearings before such a person for the purpose of any such appeal, subject to the following modifications, that is to say—

    (i) rule 4 shall not apply and the references in these Rules to section 17 parties shall be omitted;

    (ii) references to development shall be construed as references to the display of advertisements;

    (iii) references to permission shall be construed as references to consent.

(2) These Rules apply in relation to Greater London, as defined in section 2(1) of the London Government Act 1963(b), subject to the modifications specified in rule 18.

Interpretation

3.—(1) In these Rules, unless the context otherwise requires—

" the Act " means the Town and Country Planning Act 1962;

" the Act of 1968 " means the Town and Country Planning Act 1968;

" the Minister " means either the Minister of Housing and Local Government or the Secretary of State for Wales, as the case may be;

" appointed person " means the person appointed by the Minister to determine the appeal;

" inquiry " means a local inquiry to which these Rules apply;

" the land " means the land (including trees and buildings) to which the inquiry relates;

" local authority " has the meaning assigned by section 221(1) of the Act (as amended by section 29(5) of the London Government Act 1963);

" local planning authority " means—

    (a) the local planning authority (within the meaning of section 2 of the Act) for the area in which the land is; or

    (b) an authority exercising delegated functions on behalf of that authority;

" section 17 parties " means persons from whom representations are received by the local planning authority in pursuance of section 17(3) of the Act, or by the Minister in pursuance of section 17(3) as applied by

---

(a) S.I. 1960/695 (1960 III, p. 3253).   (b) 1963 c. 33.

section 23(6) of the Act, within the time prescribed and, in relation to appeals brought under paragraph 7 of schedule 5 to the Act of 1968, persons from whom representations are received, in pursuance of regulations made under paragraph 2 of the said schedule, within the time prescribed;

" tree preservation order " means an order under section 29 of the Act;

" trees " includes groups of trees and woodlands.

(2) References in these Rules to section 17 of the Act shall be construed as including where appropriate references to the regulations made under paragraph 2 of schedule 5 to the Act of 1968.

(3) The Interpretation Act 1889(a) shall apply to the interpretation of these Rules as it applies to the interpretation of an Act of Parliament.

Preliminary information to be supplied by local planning authority

4. The local planning authority, on being notified by the Minister of the intention to proceed with the consideration of an appeal to which these Rules apply and of the name and address of any person who, pursuant to the provisions of section 17 of the Act, has made representations to the Minister, shall forthwith inform the appellant in writing of the name and address of every section 17 party and the Minister of all such persons who have made representations to the local planning authority.

Notification of Inquiry

5.—(1) A date, time and place for the holding of the inquiry shall be fixed and may be varied by the Minister, who shall give not less than 42 days' notice in writing of such date, time and place to the appellant and to the local planning authority and to all section 17 parties at the addresses furnished by them:

Provided that—

    (i) with the consent of the appellant and of the local planning authority, the Minister may give such lesser period of notice as shall be agreed with the appellant and the local planning authority and in that event he may specify a date for service of the statements referred to in rule 7(1) later than the date therein prescribed;

    (ii) where it becomes necessary or advisable to vary the time or place fixed for the inquiry, the Minister shall give such notice of the variation as may appear to him to be reasonable in the circumstances.

(2) Without prejudice to the foregoing provisions of this rule, the Minister may require the local planning authority to take one or more of the following steps, namely—

    (*a*) to publish in one or more newspapers circulating in the locality in which the land is such notices of the inquiry as he may direct;

    (*b*) to serve notice of the inquiry in such form, and on such persons or classes of persons as he may specify;

    (*c*) to post such notices of the inquiry as he may direct in a conspicuous place or places near to the land;

but the requirements as to the period of notice contained in paragraph (1) of this rule shall not apply to any such notices.

(3) Where the land is under the control of the appellant he shall, if so required

---

(a) 1889 c. 63.

by the Minister, affix firmly to some object on the land, in such a manner as to be readily visible to and legible by the public, such notice of the inquiry as the Minister may specify, and thereafter for such period before the inquiry as the Minister may specify the appellant shall not remove the notice, or cause or permit it to be removed.

Notification of identity of appointed person

6. The Minister shall give to the appellant, to the local planning authority and to all section 17 parties written notice informing them of the name of the appointed person:

Provided that, where, in exercise of his powers under section 23 of the Act of 1968, the Minister has appointed another person to determine the appeal in the place of a person previously appointed for that purpose and it is not practicable to give written notice of the new appointment before the inquiry is held, in lieu of the Minister's giving such notice the person holding the inquiry shall, at the commencement thereof, announce his own name and the fact of his appointment.

Statements to be served before Inquiry

7.—(1) Not later than 28 days before the date of the inquiry (or such later date as the Minister may specify under proviso (i) to paragraph (1) of rule 5), the local planning authority shall serve on the appellant and on the section 17 parties a written statement of any submission which the local planning authority propose to put forward at the inquiry and shall supply a copy of the statement to the Minister for transmission to the appointed person.

(2) Where a government department has expressed in writing the view that the application should not be granted, either wholly or in part, or should be granted only subject to conditions or, in the case of an appeal under a tree preservation order, should be granted together with a direction requiring the replanting of trees and the local planning authority propose to rely on such expression of view in their submissions at the inquiry, they shall include it in their statement and shall supply a copy of the statement to the government department concerned.

(3) Where the local planning authority intend to refer to, or put in evidence at the inquiry, documents (including maps and plans), the authority's statement shall be accompanied by a list of such documents, together with a notice stating the times and place at which the documents may be inspected by the appellant and the section 17 parties; and the local planning authority shall afford them a reasonable opportunity to inspect and, where practicable, to take copies of the documents.

(4) The local planning authority shall afford any other person interested a reasonable opportunity to inspect and, where practicable, to take copies of any document referred to in the preceding paragraph of this rule, as well as of any statement served on the authority by the appellant under paragraph (5) of this rule.

(5) The appellant shall, if so required by the Minister, serve on the local planning authority, on the section 17 parties and on the Minister for transmission to the appointed person, within such time before the inquiry as the Minister may specify, a written statement of the submissions which he proposes to put forward at the inquiry; and such statement shall be accompanied by a list of any documents (including maps and plans) which the appellant intends to refer to or put in evidence at the inquiry and he shall, if so required by the Minister, afford the local planning authority and the section 17 parties a reasonable opportunity to inspect and, where practicable, to take copies of such documents.

Appointed person may act in place of the Minister

8. The appointed person may himself in place of the Minister take such steps as the Minister is required or enabled to take under or by virtue of rule 5, rule 7(1) or (5), rule 9A(1) or (2) (as provided by rule 18 of these Rules) or rule 10(1) or (2).

Appearances at Inquiry

9.—(1) The persons who are entitled to appear at the inquiry shall be—

(a) the appellant;

(b) the local planning authority (within the meaning of section 2 of the Act) for the area in which the land is;

(c) where the land is in a united district for which a joint planning board has been constituted under section 2 of the Act, the council of the administrative county in which the land is;

(d) where the land is not in Greater London or a county borough, the council of the county district in which the land is, or the Council of the Isles of Scilly, as the case may be;

(e) section 17 parties;

(f) where the land is in an area designated as the site of a new town, the development corporation of the new town;

(g) any persons on whom the Minister or the appointed person has required notice to be served under rule 5(2)(b).

(2) Any other person may appear at the inquiry at the discretion of the appointed person.

(3) A local authority may appear by their clerk or by any other officer appointed for the purpose by the local authority, or by counsel or solicitor; and any other person may appear on his own behalf or be represented by counsel, solicitor or any other person.

(4) Where there are two or more persons having a similar interest in the matter under inquiry, the appointed person may allow one or more persons to appear for the benefit of some or all of the persons so interested.

Representatives of Government Departments at Inquiry

10.—(1) Where a government department has expressed in writing the view that the application should not be granted, either wholly or in part, or should be granted only subject to conditions or, in the case of an appeal under a tree preservation order, should be granted together with a direction requiring the replanting of trees and the local planning authority have included this view in their statement as required by rule 7(2), the appellant may, not later than 14 days before the date of the inquiry, apply in writing to the Minister for a representative of the government department concerned to be made available at the inquiry.

(2) The Minister shall transmit any application made to him under the last foregoing paragraph to the government department concerned, who shall make a representative of the department available to attend the inquiry.

(3) A representative of a government department who, in pursuance of this rule, attends an inquiry on an appeal, shall be called as a witness by the local planning authority and shall state the reasons for the view expressed by his department and included in the authority's statement under rule 7(2), and shall

give evidence and be subject to cross-examination to the same extent as any other witness.

(4) Nothing in the last foregoing paragraph shall require a representative of a government department to answer any question which in the opinion of the appointed person is directed to the merits of government policy and the appointed person shall disallow any such question.

Procedure at Inquiry

11.—(1) Except as otherwise provided in these Rules, the procedure at the inquiry shall be such as the appointed person shall in his discretion determine.

(2) Unless in any particular case the appointed person with the consent of the appellant otherwise determines, the appellant shall begin and shall have the right of final reply; and the other persons entitled or permitted to appear shall be heard in such order as the appointed person may determine.

(3) The appellant, the section 17 parties and the local planning authority shall be entitled to call evidence and cross-examine persons giving evidence, but any other person appearing at the inquiry may do so only to the extent permitted by the appointed person.

(4) The appointed person shall not require or permit the giving or production of any evidence, whether written or oral, which would be contrary to the public interest; but, save as aforesaid, any evidence may be admitted at the discretion of the appointed person, who may direct that documents tendered in evidence may be inspected by any person entitled or permitted to appear at the inquiry and that facilities be afforded him to take or obtain copies thereof.

(5) The appointed person may allow the local planning authority or the appellant, or both of them, to alter or add to the submissions contained in any statement served under paragraph (1) or (5) of rule 7, or to any list of documents which accompanied such statement, so far as may be necessary for the purpose of determining the questions in controversy between the parties, but shall (if necessary by adjourning the inquiry) give the appellant or the local planning authority, as the case may be, and the section 17 parties an adequate opportunity of considering any such fresh submission or document; and the appointed person may make to the Minister a recommendation as to the payment of any additional costs occasioned by any such adjournment.

(6) If any person entitled to appear at the inquiry fails to do so, the appointed person may proceed with the inquiry at his discretion.

(7) The appointed person shall be entitled (subject to disclosure thereof at the inquiry) to take into account any written representations or statements received by him before the inquiry from any person.

(8) The appointed person may from time to time adjourn the inquiry and, if the date, time and place of the adjourned inquiry are announced before the adjournment, no further notice shall be required.

Site Inspections

12.—(1) The appointed person may make an unaccompanied inspection of the land before or during the inquiry without giving notice of his intention to the persons entitled to appear at the inquiry.

(2) The appointed person may, and shall if so requested by the appellant or the local planning authority before or during the inquiry, inspect the land

after the close of the inquiry and shall, in all cases where he intends to make such an inspection, announce during the inquiry the date and time at which he proposes to do so.

(3) The appellant, the local planning authority and the section 17 parties shall be entitled to accompany the appointed person on any inspection after the close of the inquiry; but the appointed person shall not be bound to defer his inspection if any person entitled to accompany him is not present at the time appointed.

Procedure after Inquiry

13.—(1) If, after the close of the inquiry, the appointed person proposes to take into consideration any new evidence (including expert opinion on a matter of fact) or any new issue of fact (not being a matter of government policy) which was not raised at the inquiry and which he considers to be material to his decision, he shall not come to a decision without first notifying the appellant, the local planning authority and any section 17 party who appeared at the inquiry of the substance of the new evidence or of the new issue of fact and affording them an opportunity of making representations thereon in writing within 21 days or of asking within that time for the re-opening of the inquiry.

(2) The appointed person may in any case if he thinks fit cause the inquiry to be re-opened and shall cause it to be re-opened if asked to do so in accordance with the foregoing paragraph; and if the inquiry is re-opened, paragraphs (1) and (2) of rule 5 shall apply as they applied to the original inquiry, with the modifications that, for the figure " 42 " in paragraph (1), there shall be substituted the figure " 28 " and, for references to the Minister wherever they occur, there shall be substituted references to the appointed person.

Costs

14. Where any person makes application at any inquiry for an award of costs, the appointed person shall report in writing the proceedings on such application to the Minister and may in such report draw attention to any considerations which appear to him to be relevant to the Minister's decision on the matter.

Notification of decision

15. Unless the Minister has, under section 22 of the Act of 1968, directed that the appeal shall be determined by the Minister, the appointed person shall notify his decision and his reasons therefor in writing to the appellant, the section 17 parties and the local planning authority and to any person who, having appeared at the inquiry, has asked to be notified of the decision.

Service of notices by post

16. Notices or documents required or authorised to be served or sent under the provisions of any of these Rules may be sent by post.

Hearings

17. These Rules, except paragraphs (2) and (3) of rule 5 and rule 9(1)(g), shall apply to any such hearing as is mentioned in rule 2, and for that purpose references in these Rules to an inquiry shall be construed as references to such a hearing.

Application to Greater London

18. In their application to Greater London these Rules shall apply with the following modifications:—

(i) In rule 3, after the definition of " the Act ", there shall be added—

" ' the Act of 1963 ' means the London Government Act 1963; " and, for the definition of "local planning authority ", the following definition shall be substituted:—

" ' local planning authority ' means—

(a) in relation to the appeals referred to in rule 2(1)(a), the authority which, by virtue of section 24 of the Act of 1963 or of regulations made under that section, is the local planning authority in relation to the class of development concerned in the area of Greater London where the land is; or

(b) in relation to the appeals referred to in rule 2(1)(b), (c) or (d), either the Common Council of the City of London or the council of the London borough in which the land is, as the case may be."

(ii) Rule 4 shall be re-numbered rule 4(1) and, at the end of the same the following paragraph shall be added:—

"(2) Where either—

(a) in pursuance of regulations under section 24(6) of the Act of 1963, the application which is the subject of the appeal was required to be referred to the Greater London Council, or

(b) in pursuance of paragraph 5 of schedule 5 to the Act of 1968, notification of the application for listed building consent was required to be given to the Greater London Council,

and, in either case, that Council has either—

(i) issued a direction to the local planning authority in whose area the land is as to the manner in which the application is to be dealt with or determined, or

(ii) (whether before or after the appeal to the Minister) otherwise expressed an opinion to such local planning authority on any such application,

the Greater London Council shall, at the request of the local planning authority, forthwith furnish to them a statement in writing of their reasons for that direction or opinion."

(iii) At the end of rule 7, the following paragraph shall be added:—

" (6) In a case falling within rule 4(2) the local planning authority shall include in their statement particulars of the direction or opinion of the Greater London Council and of the reasons given for it."

(iv) For rule 9(1)(b) there shall be substituted the following:—

" (b) the local planning authority and—

(i) where the application was required to be referred under section 24(6) of the Act of 1963, or required to be notified under paragraph 5 of schedule 5 to the Act of 1968, the Greater London Council, or

(ii) where the Greater London Council is the local planning authority, the Common Council of the City of London or the council of the London borough in which the land is, as the case may be."

(v) After rule 9, the following rule shall be inserted:—

" *Representatives of the Greater London Council at Inquiry*

9A.—(1) In a case falling within rule 4(2), the appellant or the local planning authority may, not later than 14 days before the date of the inquiry, apply in writing to the Minister for a representative of the Greater London Council to be made available at the inquiry.

(2) The Minister shall transmit any application made to him under the last foregoing paragraph to the Greater London Council who shall make a representative of the Council available to attend the inquiry.

(3) A representative of the Greater London Council who, in pursuance of this rule, attends an inquiry shall be called as a witness by the local planning authority and shall give evidence and be subject to cross-examination to the same extent as any other witness."

Dated 9th December 1968.

Gardiner, C.

EXPLANATORY NOTE

(This Note is not part of the Rules.)

These Rules prescribe the procedure to be followed at local inquiries and hearings held in connection with appeals to the Minister of Housing and Local Government or the Secretary of State for Wales (*a*) under section 23 of the Town and Country Planning Act 1962, or (*b*) in respect of tree preservation orders, or (*c*) in respect of listed building consents, or (*d*) under the Town and Country Planning (Control of Advertisements) Regulations 1960, where such appeals fall to be determined by a person appointed for the purpose by the Minister or the Secretary of State in accordance with regulations made under section 21 of the Town and Country Planning Act 1968.

The principal provisions are as follows:

Rules 4 and 5 prescribe the procedure before an inquiry. Not less than 42 days' notice of the inquiry must be given, unless the parties agree to shorter notice.

Rule 6 provides that the Minister concerned shall notify the parties in writing of the name of the person appointed to determine the appeal and makes provision for notifying any change in the appointment.

Rule 7 requires the local planning authority to serve on the appellant and on any owner or agricultural tenant who has made representations under section 17 of the Town and Country Planning Act 1962, or under regulations made under paragraph 2 of schedule 5 to the Town and Country Planning Act 1968, a statement of the submissions which the authority propose to put forward at the inquiry. The statement must include any views expressed in writing by a government department in opposition to the application on which the authority propose to rely. Any persons interested must be given a reasonable opportunity of inspecting and taking copies of the statement. The appellant may also be required to serve a written statement of the submissions which he proposes to put forward at the inquiry.

Rule 8 makes provision for the appointed person, instead of the Minister, to carry out certain of the procedural steps.

Rule 9 describes the persons who may appear at the inquiry, while rule 10 provides for the representation at the request of the appellant of any government department which has expressed views in opposition to the application.

Rule 11 prescribes the procedure at the inquiry and rule 12 makes provision for the inspection of the site by the person appointed to determine the appeal.

Rule 13 provides that if the appointed person proposes to take into consideration any new evidence or new issue of fact which was not raised at the inquiry and which he considers to be material to his decision, he must not come to a decision without first giving the appellant, the local planning authority and any " section 17 party " who appeared at the inquiry an opportunity of making representations or of having the inquiry re-opened.

Rule 14 requires the appointed person to report to the Minister any proceedings on any application at the inquiry for an award of costs.

Rule 15 requires the appointed person to notify his decision and reasons to the appellant, " section 17 parties ", the local planning authority and to any other person who appeared at the inquiry and has asked to be notified.

Rule 18 contains adaptations of the rules in regard to Greater London.

STATUTORY INSTRUMENTS

1968 No. 1953

TRIBUNALS AND INQUIRIES

The Town and Country Planning (Inquiries Procedure) (Amendment) Rules 1968

Made - - - -	9*th December* 1968
Laid before Parliament	16*th December* 1968
Coming into Operation	1*st January* 1969

The Lord Chancellor, in exercise of the powers conferred upon him by section 7A of the Tribunals and Inquiries Act 1958(**a**) (inserted in that Act by section 33 of the Town and Country Planning Act 1959(**b**)) and after consultation with the Council on Tribunals, hereby makes the following Rules:—

1.—(1) These Rules may be cited as the Town and Country Planning (Inquiries Procedure) (Amendment) Rules 1968, and the Town and Country Planning (Inquiries Procedure) Rules 1965(**c**) and these Rules may be cited together as the Town and Country Planning (Inquiries Procedure) Rules 1965 and 1968.

(2) These Rules shall come into operation on 1st January 1969 but shall not affect any application referred to the Minister or appeal brought before that date.

(3) The Interpretation Act 1889(**d**) shall apply to the interpretation of these Rules as it applies to the interpretation of an Act of Parliament.

2. The Town and Country Planning (Inquiries Procedure) Rules 1965 are hereby amended as follows:—

(*a*) In rule 2(1):—

(i) for the words "These Rules apply—" there shall be substituted the words:—

"These Rules do not, except to the extent provided by paragraph (3) of this rule, apply to inquiries held under the provisions of Part III of the Town and Country Planning Act 1968(**e**), but save as aforesaid apply—";

(ii) for the reference in paragraph (*b*) to the Minister of Land and Natural Resources there shall be substituted a reference to the Minister of Housing and Local Government; and

(iii) for paragraph (*c*) there shall be substituted the following paragraph:—

"(*c*) to local inquiries caused by the Minister of Housing and Local Government or by the Secretary of State for Wales to be held for the purpose of applications referred to him and appeals to him under Part I of schedule 5 to the Town and Country Planning Act 1968 and (to the extent provided in rule 15) to hearings before a person appointed by the Minister or by the Secretary of State, as the case may be, for the purpose of any such application or appeal, subject to the following modifications:—

(a) 1958 c. 66.
(c) S.I. 1965/473 (1965 I p. 1204).
(e) 1968 c. 72.

(b) 1959 c. 53.
(d) 1889 c. 63.

> > (i) references to development shall be construed as references to works for the demolition, alteration or extension of a listed building;
> > (ii) references to permission shall be construed as references to a listed building consent."

(*b*) At the end of rule 2 there shall be inserted the following paragraph:—

"(3) Where the Minister of Housing and Local Government or the Secretary of State for Wales, in exercise of his powers under section 22 of the Town and Country Planning Act 1968, directs that an appeal, (which, by virtue of section 21 of that Act and the regulations made thereunder, falls to be determined by a person appointed by the Minister or by the Secretary of State, as the case may be), shall, instead of being determined by that person, be determined by the Minister or the Secretary of State, these Rules apply in relation to any step taken or thing done after the giving of the said direction, but do not affect any step taken or thing done before the giving of such direction."

(*c*) For rule 3 there shall be substituted the following rule:—

"3.—(1) In these Rules, unless the context otherwise requires—

'the Act' means the Town and Country Planning Act 1962;

'the Act of 1968' means the Town and Country Planning Act 1968;

'the Minister' means the Minister who causes the inquiry to be held;

'applicant' in the case of an appeal means the appellant;

'inquiry' means a local inquiry to which these Rules apply;

'appointed person' means the person appointed by the Minister to hold the inquiry;

'the land' means the land (including trees and buildings) to which the inquiry relates;

'listed building' and 'listed building consent' have the meanings assigned to them in section 40 of the Act of 1968;

'local authority' has the meaning assigned to it by section 221(1) of the Act;

'local planning authority' means (*a*) the local planning authority (within the meaning of section 2 of the Act) for the area in which the land is, or (*b*) an authority exercising delegated functions on behalf of that authority;

'referred application' means an application referred to the Minister under section 22 of the Act, or that section as applied by a tree preservation order, or under regulation 28 of the Town and Country Planning (Control of Advertisements) Regulations 1960(a), or under paragraph 3 of Schedule 5 to the Act of 1968;

'section 17 parties' means—

> (i) in relation to referred applications, persons from whom representations are received within the time prescribed, (*a*) in pursuance of section 17(2) or (3) of the Act, as applied by section 22(4), or (*b*) in the case of applications referred under paragraph 3 of schedule 5 to the Act of 1968, in pursuance of regulations made under paragraph 2 of the said schedule; and

---

(a) S.I. 1960/695 (1960 III, p. 3253).

(ii) in relation to appeals, persons from whom representations are received within the time prescribed (*a*) by the local planning authority in pursuance of section 17(3) of the Act, or by the Minister in pursuance of section 17(3) as applied by section 23(6), or (*b*) in the case of appeals brought under paragraph 7 of schedule 5 to the Act of 1968, in pursuance of regulations made under paragraph 2 of the said schedule;

'tree preservation order' means an order under section 29 of the Act;

'trees' includes groups of trees and woodlands.

(2) References in these Rules to section 17 of the Act shall be construed as including where appropriate references to regulations made under paragraph 2 of schedule 5 to the Act of 1968.

(3) The Interpretation Act 1889 shall apply to the interpretation of these Rules as it applies to the interpretation of an Act of Parliament."

(*d*) In rule 16, for paragraphs (*a*), (*b*) and (*d*) there shall be substituted the following paragraphs:—

"(*a*) In rule 3, after the definition of 'the Act' there shall be added—

" 'the Act of 1963' means the London Government Act 1963"(**a**); and, for the definition of 'local planning authority', the following definition shall be substituted:—

" 'local planning authority' means—

(i) in relation to the applications and appeals referred to in rule 2(1)(*a*), the authority which, by virtue of section 24 of the Act of 1963 or of regulations made under that section is the local planning authority in relation to the class of development concerned in the area of Greater London where the land is; or

(ii) in relation to the appeals referred to in rules 2(1)(*b*), (*c*) and (*d*), either the Common Council of the City of London or the Council of the London borough in which the land is, as the case may be."

'(*b*) At the end of rule 4 the following paragraph shall be added:—

"(3) Where either—

(*a*) in pursuance of regulations under section 24(6) of the Act of 1963, the application which is before the Minister or which is the subject of the appeal was required to be referred to the Greater London Council, or

(*b*) in pursuance of paragraph 5 of schedule 5 to the Act of 1968, notification of the application for listed building consent was required to be given to the Greater London Council,

and, in either case, that Council has either—

(i) issued a direction to the local planning authority in whose area the land is as to the manner in which the application is to be dealt with or determined, or

---

(**a**) 1963 c. 33.

(ii) (whether before or after the reference to the Minister or the appeal) otherwise expressed an opinion to such local planning authority on any such application,

the Greater London Council shall, at the request of the local planning authority, forthwith furnish to them a statement in writing of their reasons for that direction or opinion." "

"(d) For rule 7(1)(b) there shall be substituted the following:—

"(b) the local planning authority and—

(i) where the application was required to be referred under section 24(6) of the Act of 1963, or required to be notified under paragraph 5 of schedule 5 to the Act of 1968, the Greater London Council, or

(ii) where the Greater London Council is the local planning authority, the Common Council of the City of London or the council of the London borough in which the land is, as the case may be." "

Dated 9th December 1968. *Gardiner, C.*

EXPLANATORY NOTE
(This Note is not part of the Rules.)

These Rules amend the Town and Country Planning (Inquiries Procedure) Rules 1965 by substituting, for the previous references to applications for consent under a building preservation order and appeals under such an order, a provision including within the scope of the Rules local inquiries held into appeals brought, or applications referred, to the Minister of Housing and Local Government or the Secretary of State for Wales in respect of listed building consents under Part I of schedule 5 to the Town and Country Planning Act 1968. Consequential amendments are made, in particular to the definition of "section 17 parties" in the 1965 Rules so as to include persons who, by regulations made under the provisions of that schedule, have been given a status corresponding to that of persons making representations under section 17(3) of the Town and Country Planning Act 1962, and provision is made for references to "section 17" to include references to such regulations.

These Rules also provide that, where the Minister or the Secretary of State directs under section 22 of the Act of 1968 that an appeal, which has been proceeding as an appeal to be determined by an appointed person, shall instead be determined by the Minister or the Secretary of State, the Rules of 1965 shall apply to all subsequent steps taken or things done in the appeal.

Account has also been taken of the transfer, under the Ministry of Land and Natural Resources (Dissolution) Order 1967 (S.I. 1967/156), of functions formerly exercised in regard to tree preservation orders in England by the Minister of Land and Natural Resources to the Minister of Housing and Local Government.

STATUTORY INSTRUMENTS

1968 No. 1954

BUILDING SOCIETIES

The Building Societies (Accounts and Annual Return etc.) Regulations 1968

Made - - - -	*9th December* 1968
Laid before Parliament	*18th December* 1968
Coming into Operation	*19th December* 1968

The Chief Registrar of Friendly Societies, with the consent of the Treasury, in exercise of the powers conferred upon him by sections 78(2), 88(3) and 91(2) of the Building Societies Act 1962(a), and of all other powers enabling him in that behalf, hereby makes the following Regulations:—

1.—(1) These Regulations may be cited as the Building Societies (Accounts and Annual Return etc.) Regulations 1968, and shall come into operation on 19th December 1968.

(2) The Interpretation Act 1889(b) shall apply to the interpretation of these Regulations as it applies to the interpretation of an Act of Parliament.

2. The Revenue and Appropriation Account and Balance Sheet of a building society relating to a financial year ending on or after 31st December 1968 shall contain the particulars and be in the form set out in Part I of the Schedule hereto, except that any heading contained therein may be omitted if the entries in respect of such heading would be "Nil".

3. There shall be included against every heading in

(*a*) the Revenue and Appropriation Account, the corresponding amounts for the immediately preceding financial year; and

(*b*) the Balance Sheet, the corresponding amounts at the end of the immediately preceding financial year.

4. The annual return required to be made by a building society under section 88(1) of the Building Societies Act 1962 and relating to a financial year ending on or after 31st December 1968 shall contain the information and be in the form set out in Part II of the Schedule hereto, except that a return relating to a financial year ending on or before 30th December 1969 is not hereby required to contain in Section "A" of Schedule No. 3 thereof information as to advances secured on new properties.

5. The annual return and every statement or report annexed thereto shall be made on sheets of paper of the size 13 inches by 8 inches.

(a) 1962 c. 37.   (b) 1889 c. 63.

6. Where appropriate, the word "Nil" shall be inserted against any heading contained in any Schedule to the annual return, or against the whole of any such Schedule, as the case may require.

7. The auditors of a building society shall not be required to deal in their report on any annual return with the following matters contained therein:—

    (*a*) the information contained in the annual return up to and excluding the Revenue and Appropriation Account;

    (*b*) the information contained in—

        (i) Schedule No. 2;

        (ii) Schedule No. 3;

        (iii) Section "B" of Schedule No. 4.

8. If in the Revenue and Appropriation Account of a building society or in the Revenue and Appropriation Account contained in the annual return an amount is charged to revenue by way of provision for depreciation or diminution in value of assets, and an amount is also so charged by way of provision for renewal of those assets, the last-mentioned amount shall be shown separately.

9. If in the said Accounts the amount charged to revenue by way of depreciation or diminution in value of assets (other than investments) has been determined otherwise than by reference to the amount of those assets as determined for making up the Balance Sheet, that fact shall be stated.

10. The expression "Expenses", where it occurs in the heading "Directors' Fees and Expenses" contained in the said Accounts, includes, in relation to a director, any sum paid by way of expenses allowance and the estimated money value of any other benefits received by him otherwise than in cash in so far as those sums and benefits are charged to United Kingdom income tax, and any contribution paid in respect of him, as a director, under any pension scheme.

11. The expression "Remuneration", where it occurs in the heading "Remuneration of Auditors" contained in the said Accounts, includes any sums paid by a building society in respect of the auditors' expenses.

12. There shall, if it is not otherwise shown, be stated by way of note to the said Accounts every material respect in which items shown therein are affected

    (*a*) by transactions of an exceptional or non-recurrent nature; or

    (*b*) by any change in the basis of accounting.

13. The following matters shall be stated by way of note to the Balance Sheet of a building society, and to the Balance Sheet contained in the annual return, or in a statement or report annexed thereto respectively, if not otherwise shown—

    (*a*) particulars of any moneys owing by the society in respect of deposits, loans and overdrafts which are wholly or partially secured;

    (*b*) the general nature of any contingent liability not provided for, and, where practicable, the estimated amount of that contingent liability, if it is material;

2m

(c) where practicable, the aggregate amount or estimated amount, if it is material, of—

   (i) contracts for capital expenditure, so far as not provided for, and

   (ii) capital expenditure authorised by the directors which has not been contracted for;

(d) where the amounts of the separate reserves or provisions as compared with the amounts at the end of the immediately preceding financial year show any increases or decreases, the sources from which the increases have been derived and how the amounts of any decreases have been applied;

(e) the method of arriving at the amount at which any office premises, office equipment and other fixed assets are shown, and, where the amount is arrived at by a valuation made during the financial year ending with the date of the Balance Sheet, the names of the persons who valued such fixed assets or particulars of their qualifications for doing so and (whichever is stated) the bases of valuation used by them;

(f) if there are included amongst fixed assets under any heading assets that have been acquired during the financial year ending with the date of the Balance Sheet, the aggregate amount of the assets acquired as determined for the purpose of making up the Balance Sheet, and if during that year any fixed assets included under a heading in the Balance Sheet made up with respect to the immediately preceding financial year have been disposed of or destroyed, the aggregate amount thereof as determined for the purpose of making up that Balance Sheet;

(g) where interest accrued on investments is shown gross and the amount of corporation tax attributable thereto has not been fully provided for, the fact that no such provision has been made.

14. The Building Societies (Accounts and Annual Return etc.) Regulations 1964(a) and the Building Societies (Accounts and Annual Return etc.) (Amendment) Regulations 1966(b) are hereby revoked, but not so as to affect their operation in relation to the accounts and annual return of a building society relating to a financial year ending before 31st December 1968.

Dated 9th December 1968.

                                        S. D. Musson,

                                        Chief Registrar of Friendly Societies.
We consent to these Regulations.

Dated 9th December 1968.

                                        J. McCann,

                                        Walter Harrison,

                                        Two of the Lords Commissioners of
                                        Her Majesty's Treasury.

(a) S.I. 1964/1475 (1964 III, p. 3441).   (b) S.I. 1966/1023 (1966 II, p. 2467).

SCHEDULE

PART I

ANNUAL ACCOUNTS

....Building Society

Register No...............................B

Registered Chief Office...

Revenue and Appropriation Account for the year ended.................................

	£		£
Management Expenses:—		Interest charged to borrowers on Mortgages	
Directors' Fees and Expenses			
Remuneration and Expenses of Staff		Recoverable from H.M. Government under Option Mortgage Scheme	
Remuneration of Auditors ...			
Office Accommodation and Office Expenses			
Advertising		Interest and Dividends from Investments (gross)	
Commission and Agency Fees			
Other Expenses:—		Bank Interest	
....			
....		Rents and other Income from letting Office Premises ...	
....			
Total Management Expenses ...		Valuation Fees and Expenses...	
Depreciation:—			
	£	Entrance Fees and other amounts paid by borrowers as consideration for advances	
Office Premises ...			
Other Assets ...			
		Other Fees and Fines	
Valuation Fees and Expenses payable to Directors, Manager or Secretary		Commission (Insurance etc.) ...	
Other Valuation Fees and Expenses		Other Income:—	
Losses on Mortgages		....	
Other Expenditure:—		....	
....		....	
....		....	
Interest on Loans (including overdrafts) from Bank		....	
Interest on Deposits and Loans (not from Bank) ...	£	....	
Add Income Tax on deposit and loan interest			
Interest to Shareholders for period ended ...	£	Note:	
....		Income Tax on share, deposit and loan interest relates to	
Add Income Tax on Share Interest ...			
Proposed Interest to Shareholders for period ended ...	£	....	
....		....	
Add Income Tax on Share Interest ...			

continued on next page

ANNUAL ACCOUNTS—*continued*

Corporation Tax for period ended ....(at.........per cent.)			
Balance carried down			
Other Debits and Appropriations:-		Balance brought down... ... Balance brought forward from last year ... ... Other Credits and Appropriations:—	
....		....	
....		....	
....		....	
....		....	
....		....	
....		....	
Balance carried forward			

Balance Sheet as at....................................

	£		£
Due to Investing Shareholders ...		Balance due or outstanding on Mortgages:-	
		From persons other than bodies corporate where total indebtedness	
Advances from H.M. Government under the House Purchase and Housing Act 1959 ...		(a) does not exceed £10,000 (b) exceeds £10,000 ...	
Deposits and Loans (not from bank).		From Housing Societies where section 8 of the Housing Act 1964 applies to the advance...	
Loans (including overdrafts) from Bank		From other bodies corporate...	
		Total	
Deferred Liability:—		*Less* provision for anticipated losses on Mortgages... ...	
Corporation Tax for period ended.................................. payable		Mortgage Assets	
		Investments:—	
Other Liabilities:—	£	Quoted:—	£
Corporation Tax for period ended......... payable..............		Final redemption date in not more than 5 years ... Others ... ... (market value £.....................)	
Income Tax		Unquoted:— Repayable in not more than 6 months	
		Repayable in more than 6 months ...	
		Total Investments ...	
Proposed Interest for period ended................................ (including appropriate Income Tax)		Interest Accrued ...	
		Investments and Interest Accrued	
Provisions:—		Cash at Bank and in Hand ...	
....		Debtors ... ... Office Premises:— Freehold ... ... Leasehold (50 or more years unexpired) ... ... Leasehold (less than 50 years unexpired).	
Special Reserves:—			
...............................Reserve ....Reserve		Office Equipment ... ... Other Assets:—	
		....	

continued on next page

Balance Sheet as at........................—*continued*

General Reserve and Balance carried forward:—	£				
General Reserve ...			....		
			....		
Balance carried fwd.			....		
			....		
			....		
			Balance (loss) carried forward		

Signature of Director...

Signature of Director...

Signature of Manager or Secretary...

PART II

To be submitted in duplicate

BUILDING SOCIETIES ACT 1962

ANNUAL RETURN FOR FINANCIAL YEAR ENDED.....................................

Name of Society...Building Society Register Number ....

Registered Chief Office..

Date on which Annual General Meeting* was/will be held...
(*Delete as appropriate)
The following details on this page should be given as at the end of the financial year

Total Membership of Society ... ...

Number of Investing Shareholders ... ...

Number of Borrowers   ... ...

Number of Creditors for Deposits and Loans ... ...

NAMES AND ADDRESSES OF DIRECTORS, ETC.,

	Name	Address
Directors or Committee of Management		
Manager		
Secretary		

Number of Branch Offices staffed full time by employees of the Society............................

Number of Staff employed by the Society:

	Full Time	Part Time
Chief and Administrative Offices		
Branch Offices		
Total ...		

REVENUE AND APPROPRIATION ACCOUNT

	£		£
Management Expenses:—		Interest charged to borrowers on Mortgages	
Directors' Fees and Expenses			
Remuneration and Expenses of Staff		Recoverable from H.M. Government under Option Mortgage Scheme	
Remuneration of Auditors ...			
Office Accommodation and Office Expenses			
Advertising		Interest and Dividends from Investments (gross)	
Commission and Agency Fees			
Other Expenses:—		Bank Interest	
....			
....		Rents and other income from letting Office Premises ...	
....			
Total Management Expenses ...			
Depreciation:—	£	Valuation Fees and Expenses ...	
Office Premises ...		Entrance Fees and other amounts paid by borrowers as consideration for advances ...	
Other Assets ...			
		Other Fees and Fines	
Valuation Fees and Expenses payable to Directors, Manager or Secretary		Commission (Insurance, etc.) ...	
Other Valuation Fees and Expenses		Other Income:—	
Losses on Mortgages		....	
Other Expenditure:—			
....		....	
....		....	
....		....	
Interest on Loans (including overdrafts) from Bank		....	
Interest on Deposits and Loans (not from Bank) ...	£	....	
		....	
Add Income Tax on deposit and loan interest		....	
Interest to shareholders for period ended	£		
Add Income Tax on Share Interest ...		Note: Income Tax on share, deposit and loan interest relates to	
Proposed Interest to Shareholders for period ended ...	£	....	
		....	
....		....	
Add Income Tax on Share Interest ...			
Corporation Tax for period ended .... (at.........per cent.)			

continued on next page

REVENUE AND APPROPRIATION ACCOUNT—*continued*

Balance carried down			
Other Debits and Appropriations:- .... Balance carried forward		Balance brought down ... Balance brought forward from last year ... ... Other Credits and Appropriations:—	

Balance Sheet as at.................................

	£		£
Due to Investing Shareholders (classified in Schedule No. 2) (*as per Schedule No.* 1)		Balance due or outstanding on Mortgages (*as per Schedule No.* 1):—	
		From persons other than bodies corporate where total indebtedness	
Advances from H.M. Government under the House Purchase and Housing Act 1959 (*as per Schedule No.* 1.)		(a) does not exceed £10,000 (b) exceeds £10,000... ...	
		From Housing Societies where section 8 of the Housing Act 1964 applies to the advance	
Deposits and Loans (not from bank) (classified in Schedule No. 2) (*as per Schedule No.* 1)		From other bodies corporate	
		Total	
Loans (including overdrafts) from Bank		*Less* provision for anticipated losses on Mortgages ...	
Deferred Liability:— Corporation Tax for period ended................................. payable		Mortgage Assets	
		Investments (classified in Schedule No. 8):—	

	£		£
Other Liabilities:—		Quoted:— Final redemption date in not more than 5 years ... Others ... ... (market value £..................)	
Corporation Tax for period ended......... payable			
Income Tax ...		Unquoted:— Repayable in not more than 6 months ... ... Repayable in more than 6 months ...	
....		Total Investments (*as per Schedule No.* 1) ... ... Interest Accrued	
Proposed Interest for period ended................................ (including appropriate Income Tax)		Investments and Interest Accrued ... ... (*as per Schedule No.* 8)	
		Cash at Bank and in Hand ...	
		Debtors	
Provisions:—		Office Premises:— Freehold	
....		Leasehold (50 or more years unexpired)	
		Leasehold (less than 50 years unexpired)	

continued on next page

Balance Sheet as at.................................—*continued*

Special Reserves:—		Office Equipment	
................................Reserve		Other Assets:—	
................................Reserve		....	
		....	
General Reserve and Balance		....	
carried forward:—	£	....	
		....	
General Reserve ...		....	
Balance carried fwd.		....	
		Balance (loss) carried forward	

SCHEDULE No. 1

Summary of Share, Deposit and Loan, Mortgage and Investment transactions during the financial year.

Balances at beginning of Year	Additions during Year (state total amounts added and not excess of additions over deductions)	Deductions during Year (state total amounts deducted and not excess of deductions over additions)	Balances at end of Year
£	£	£	£
Due to Shareholders:— Shares ... ... Interest ... ... Total	Subscriptions received ... ... Interest ... ... Other credits:— .... Total...	Shares withdrawn ... ... Interest paid out ... ... Total... ... Other Debits:— .... Total... ...	Due to Shareholders:— Shares ... ... Interest ... ... Total... ...
Advances from H.M. Government (House Purchase and Housing Act 1959)	Interest	Repayments (including interest)	Advances from H.M. Government ... ...
Due to Depositors and Loanholders (other than Banks)	Deposits and Loans received ... Interest ... ... Other Credits:— .... Total...	Deposits and Loans withdrawn Interest paid out ... ... Total... ... Other Debits:— .... Total... ...	Due to Depositors and Loan-holders ... ...
Due on Mortgages	Advances made ... ... (for analysis see Schedule No. 3 "A"), Interest charged to Borrowers Insurance premiums ... ... Other Debits:— .... Total...	Repayments (including interest and insurance premiums) Losses on Mortgages ... ... Other Credits:— .... Total... ...	Due on Mortgages ... ...
Investments ... ... (excluding interest accrued)	Investments made ((for analysis see Schedule No. 7 "A"") Profits on realisation ... ... Other Debits:— .... Total...	Investments realised (for analysis see Schedule No. 7 "B") Losses on realisation ... ... Depreciation ... ... Other Credits:— .... Total...	Investments ... ... (excluding interest accrued)

Schedule No. 2

Details of Shares, Deposits and Loans (not from Bank) and Mortgages with particular reference to normal interest rates.

	Interest rate in force at end of financial year %	Amount due at end of financial year £
1. Shares (a) Classes of Shares		
....		
....		
....		
....		
....		
....		
(b) Interest not credited to share capital		
Total		
2. Deposits and Loans (not from Bank) (Classified according to notice required for repayment)	%	£
....		
....		
....		
....		
....		
....		
Total		

	Number of Holdings	Total Amount £
3. Particulars of holdings at end of financial year exceeding £10,000 (excluding any holdings where the aggregate holding of a husband and his wife does not exceed £20,000) Shares ... ... Deposits and Loans (excluding advances from H.M. Government) ...		

	Interest rate in force at end of financial year %	
4. Mortgages (classified according to normal interest rates)		
....		
....		
....		
....		
....		
....		

continued on next page

SCHEDULE NO. 2—*continued*

The highest interest rate charged on any mortgage during the financial year was:—

The lowest interest rate charged on any mortgage during the financial year (excluding special arrangements with staff) was:—

Particulars of any charges made to borrowers as consideration for advances in addition to the normal interest charges:—

5. Details of any changes in normal interest rates made during the financial year:—

....

....

....

....

SCHEDULE No. 3 SECTION "A"

Analysis of amounts advanced on mortgage during the financial year.

1	Advances other than to Housing Societies to which Section 8 of the Housing Act 1964 applies						Advances to Housing Societies to which Section 8 of the Housing Act 1964 applies	Total
	Type of property on which advance is secured and, to the best of the Society's knowledge and belief, its intended use							
	Dwellings (including sites for such dwellings and buildings under construction)				Business and Other Properties			
	Wholly to be occupied by borrower	Partly to be occupied by borrower	Wholly to be let by borrower	Under construction and to be put up for sale by borrower	Including some dwelling accommodation to be occupied by borrower	Other		
	2	3	4	5	6	7	8	9
	£	£	£	£	£	£	£	£
*New Mortgages:—								
On......... Mortgages where advance agreed to will not exceed £3,000								
(a) to bodies corporate								
(b) to persons								
On......... Mortgages where advance agreed to will exceed £3,000 but will not exceed £5,000								
(a) to bodies corporate								
(b) to persons								
On......... Mortgages where advance agreed to will exceed £5,000 but will not exceed £10,000								
(a) to bodies corporate								
(b) to persons								
On......... Mortgages where advance agreed to will exceed £10,000 but will not exceed £25,000								
(a) to bodies corporate								
(b) to persons								
On......... Mortgages where advance agreed to will exceed £25,000								
(a) to bodies corporate								
(b) to persons ... Total ...								
On......... New Mortgages								
Instalment Mortgages:—								
Second or subsequent advances								
On......... Mortgages where the first advance was made before commencement of the financial year								
†Existing Mortgages other than Instalment Mortgages:—								
On......... Mortgages								
On......... Mortgages ... ... Total ...								
On......... Mortgages secured on new properties								
Including advances on........Mortgages in respect of property already mortgaged to the society.								

*Excluding ⎱ further advances in respect of property already mortgaged to the society.
†Including ⎰

SCHEDULE NO. 3—*continued*

SECTION "B"

Amounts advanced on Mortgage during the financial year according to initial mortgage term.

Initial mortgage term of 26 years or more	Initial mortgage term 5 years or more but less than 26 years	Initial mortgage term less than 5 years	Total
£	£	£	£

SECTION "C"

The amount advanced on mortgage during the financial year included:—

£............advanced on......... Mortgages to which the Option Mortgage Scheme was applied, including

£............advanced on......... Mortgages guaranteed under Section 30 of the Housing Subsidies Act 1967.

SCHEDULE NO. 4

SECTION "A"

Analysis of Special Advances made during the financial year.

	Number of Advances	Total Amount
		£
1. Special Advances to persons other than bodies corporate (excluding special advances by virtue of Section 21(7) of the 1962 Act) who as a result were indebted:— by not more than £25,000 ... ... by more than £25,000		
Total		
2. Special Advances to bodies corporate (excluding special advances by virtue of Section 21(7) of the 1962 Act) (classified in Section "B" of this Schedule)		
Total		
3. Transfers of mortgages where no new advance is made but which rank as special advances by virtue of Section 21(7) of the 1962 Act		
Total		

SCHEDULE No. 4—*continued*

SECTION "B"

Particulars of every special advance made during the financial year to a body corporate (excluding special advances by virtue of Section 21(7) of the 1962 Act).

Register No. of Company	Type of Property	Valuation of Property	Amount of Advance	Observations
1	2	3	4	5
		£	£	
Total ...				

SCHEDULE No. 5

Mortgages at end of financial year.

1. At end of financial year a total of
   £....................................was due or outstanding on.................mortgages

2. The balance due or outstanding on mortgages included:

   £...............on......... Mortgages on Property of which the society has been more than 12 months in possession.

   £...............on......... Mortgages on Property of which the society is not in possession, or has been in possession for not more than 12 months, where the payments are more than 12 months in arrear.

   £...............on......... Mortgages on Property for which Receivers or Managers have acted for more than 12 months.

   £...............in respect of (*a*) advances to bodies corporate (excluding advances to which Section 8 of the Housing Act 1964 applies) and (*b*) advances to a person indebted in a total amount exceeding £10,000 representing ......per cent. of the total balance due or outstanding on Mortgages.

SCHEDULE No. 6

SECTION "A"

Names of Banks in which Society's funds were held on current and deposit accounts during financial year:—

....
....
....
....
....
....
....
....

SECTION "B"

Particulars of monies held during the financial year on deposit with or on loan to a Bank for a fixed period exceeding 2 months or at more than 2 months notice.

	Amount	Period of deposit or loan or notice required for repayment
1. Name of Bank	£	
....		
....		
....		
....		
....		
....		
....		
....		
....		
....		
....		
....		
2. Amount on deposit or loan with banks at end of year and repayable:		
(a) in more than 2 but not more than 6 months.		
(b) in more than 6 months. ...		

SECTION "C"

Particulars of Loans (including Overdrafts) from Banks

1. Maximum indebtedness in respect of loan(s) (including over-draft(s)) from bank(s) at any time during the financial year £...........................

2. Total number of days during the financial year when the society was indebted in respect of loan(s) (including over-draft(s)) from bank(s)   ...   .days

SCHEDULE NO. 7
SECTION "A"

Particulars of Investments made by the Society during the financial year.

QUOTED

	Latest date of redemption WITHIN 5 YEARS from date of purchase 1	Latest date of redemption AFTER 5 YEARS but WITHIN 15 YEARS from date of purchase 2	Latest date of redemption AFTER 15 YEARS but WITHIN 25 YEARS from date of purchase 3	Total 4
	Purchase Price £	Purchase Price £	Purchase Price £	Purchase Price £
British Government and British Government Guaranteed Securities				
Commonwealth Securities				
Local Authority Securities				
Other Quoted Securities				
Total				

UNQUOTED

	Repayable in NOT MORE THAN 6 MONTHS from date of purchase 1	Repayable AFTER 6 MONTHS but WITHIN 2 YEARS from date of purchase 2	Repayable AFTER 2 YEARS but WITHIN 5 YEARS from date of purchase 3	Total 4
	Purchase Price £	Purchase Price £	Purchase Price £	Purchase Price £
Tax Reserve Certificates				
Defence Bonds, National Development Bonds, Ulster Development Bonds and British Savings Bonds ...				
Treasury Bills and Northern Ireland Treasury Bills				
*Deposits at not more than 7 days notice:—				
Period from the making of the deposit after which notice is permissible:				
(a) Local Authorities (i) not exceeding 3 months				
(ii) exceeding 3 months but not one year ...				
(b) Other Authorities (i) not exceeding 3 months				
(ii) exceeding 3 months but not one year ...				
Loans secured by way of mortgage:—				
(a) Local Authorities				
(b) Other Authorities				
Total				

*Where there is a change in the interest rate of an investment within these categories and the other conditions remain the same the transaction need not be shown.

SCHEDULE No. 7—*continued*

SECTION "B"

Particulars of Investments realised by the Society during the financial year.

QUOTED

	Latest date of redemption WITHIN 5 YEARS from date of realisation	Latest date of redemption AFTER 5 YEARS but WITHIN 15 YEARS from date of realisation	Latest date of redemption AFTER 15 YEARS but WITHIN 25 YEARS from date of realisation	Latest date of redemption AFTER 25 YEARS from date of realisation, redeemable only at option of issuer or with no fixed date of redemption	Total
	1	2	3	4	5
	Proceeds of Realisation £	Proceeds of Realisation £	Proceeds of Realisation £	Proceeds of Realisation £	Proceeds of Realisation £
British Government and British Government Guaranteed Securities					
Commonwealth Securities					
Local Authority Securities					
Other Quoted Securities					
Total					

UNQUOTED

	Proceeds of Realisation £
Tax Reserve Certificates	
Defence Bonds, National Development Bonds, Ulster Development Bonds and British Savings Bonds	
Treasury Bills and Northern Ireland Treasury Bills	
*Deposits at not more than 7 days notice (a) Local Authorities	
(b) Other Authorities	
Loans secured by way of mortgage (a) Local Authorities	
(b) Other Authorities	
Other Unquoted Investments	
Total	

* The Society has not realised any loan to a local or other authority by exercise of a "stress clause" (i.e. on the society's demand for payment before maturity due to exceptional circumstances).

* The society has realised the following loan(s) to a local or other authority by exercise of a "stress clause" (i.e. on the society's demand for payment before maturity due to exceptional circumstances).

Description of Investment	Proceeds of Realisation £
Total ...	

*Delete as appropriate.

*Where there is a change in the interest rate of an investment within these categories and the other conditions remain the same the transaction need not be shown.

SCHEDULE No. 8

Particulars of Investments held by the Society as at end of financial year.

QUOTED	Final redemption date IN NOT MORE THAN 5 YEARS from date of Balance Sheet		Final redemption date AFTER 5 YEARS but WITHIN 15 YEARS from date of Balance Sheet		Final redemption date AFTER 15 YEARS but WITHIN 25 YEARS from date of Balance Sheet		Final redemption date MORE THAN 25 YEARS from date of Balance Sheet (including undated)		Amounts included in Balance Sheet	
	Nominal Value	Book Value	Nominal Value	Book Value	Nominal Value	Book Value	Nominal Value	Book Value	*Market Value	Book Value
	£	£	£	£	£	£	£	£	£	£
British Government and British Government Guaranteed Securities										
Commonwealth Securities										
Local Authority Securities										
Other Quoted Securities										
Total										
	*Market Value: £		*Market Value: £		*Market Value: £		*Market Value: £			

UNQUOTED	Repayable in NOT MORE THAN 6 MONTHS	Repayable AFTER 6 MONTHS but WITHIN 2 YEARS from date of Balance Sheet	Repayable AFTER 2 YEARS but WITHIN 5 YEARS from date of Balance Sheet	Repayable AFTER 5 YEARS from date of Balance Sheet but at some fixed date	Amounts included in Balance Sheet
	£	£	£	£	£
Tax Reserve Certificates					
Defence Bonds, National Development Bonds, Ulster Development Bonds and British Savings Bonds					
Treasury Bills and Northern Ireland Treasury Bills					
Deposits at not more than 7 days notice:— Period from the end of the financial year after which notice is permissible:—					
(a) Local Authorities (i) not exceeding 3 months					
(ii) exceeding 3 months but not one year					
(b) Other Authorities (i) not exceeding 3 months					
(ii) exceeding 3 months but not one year					
Loans secured by way of mortgage:—					
(a) Local Authorities					
(b) Other Authorities					
Other Unquoted Investments					
Total					

Total Quoted and Unquoted ... ...

Interest Accrued ... ...

Total ... ...

* At mid-market prices adjusted for net accrued interest where necessary.

SCHEDULE No. 9

SECTION "A"

Particulars of advances made during the financial year covered by the annual return to any director or the manager or secretary of the society or to any person who, after the making of the advance, became a director or manager or the secretary of the society in that year, distinguishing between (a) new advances and (b) transfers with the consent of the society of properties subject to mortgages in favour of the society.

Roll No. 1	Type of Property 2	Valuation of Property 3	Amount of Advance 4	Whether new advance or transfer and any further observations 5
		£	£	
	Total ...			

SECTION "B"

Particulars of advances made during the financial year covered by the annual return to (i) a company or other body corporate in which, when the advance was made, or at any later time in that financial year, a director or the manager or secretary of the society held, either directly or through a nominee, shares the nominal value of which exceeded two and a half per cent. of the total paid up share capital of the company or other body corporate, or (ii) a company or other body corporate of which, when the advance was made, or at any later time in that financial year, a director or the manager or secretary of the building society was a director, general manager, secretary or other similar officer, distinguishing between (a) new advances and (b) transfers with the consent of the society of properties subject to mortgages in favour of the society.

Register No. of Company 1	Type of Property 2	Valuation of Property 3	Amount of Advance 4	Particulars of each Officer's Shareholdings which exceed two and a half per cent. of Total Paid-up Share Capital		Whether new advance or transfer and any further observations 7
				Officer's Shareholdings in Company or other body corporate 5	Percentage of Officer's Shareholdings to Total Paid-up Share Capital 6	
		£	£			
	Total ...					

Signature of Director...

Signature of Director..

Signature of Manager or Secretary...

EXPLANATORY NOTE

(This Note is not part of the Regulations.)

These Regulations prescribe the form of, and the particulars to be contained in, the Revenue and Appropriation Account and Balance Sheet which are required to be laid before the annual general meeting of a building society. They also prescribe the form of, and the particulars to be contained in, the annual return which a building society is required to make to the Chief Registrar of Friendly Societies.

The Regulations supersede the Building Societies (Accounts and Annual Return etc.) Regulations 1964 (S.I. 1964/1475) and the Building Societies (Accounts and Annual Return etc.) (Amendment) Regulations 1966 (S.I. 1966/1023). The main changes in the prescribed forms, apart from changes in lay-out, are consequential upon the raising of the special advance limit to £10,000 and the introduction of the Option Mortgage Scheme.

STATUTORY INSTRUMENTS

1968 No. 1956

LOCAL GOVERNMENT, ENGLAND AND WALES

The Rate Support Grant Order 1968

Made - - - - -	*27th November* 1968
Laid before the House of Commons	*3rd December* 1968
Coming into Operation -	*10th December* 1968

The Minister of Housing and Local Government, with the consent of the Treasury and after consultation with the associations of local authorities appearing to him to be concerned and the local authority with whom consultation appeared to him to be desirable, in exercise of his powers under section 2 of the Local Government Act 1966(**a**) and of all other powers enabling him in that behalf, hereby makes the following order:—

Title and commencement

1. This order may be cited as the Rate Support Grant Order 1968 and shall come into operation on the day following the day on which it is approved by a resolution of the Commons House of Parliament.

Interpretation

2.—(1) The Interpretation Act 1889(**b**) shall apply for the interpretation of this order as it applies for the interpretation of an Act of Parliament.

(2) In this order—

"the Act" means the Local Government Act 1966;

"the Minister" means the Minister of Housing and Local Government;

"each year" means the year 1969–70 and the year 1970–71.

Rate support grants for 1969–70 *and* 1970–71

3. For the purposes of rate support grants for the year 1969–70 and the year 1970–71 this order hereby fixes and prescribes—

(1) As the aggregate amounts of the rate support grants and the amounts of the needs element, the resources element and the domestic element, the amounts set out in the following table:—

	1969–70	1970–71
Aggregate of rate support grants:	£1,528,000,000	£1,633,000,000
comprising—		
the needs element:	£1,230,000,000	£1,297,000,000
the resources element:	£225,000,000	£236,000,000
the domestic element:	£73,000,000	£100,000,000

(**a**) 1966 c. 42.   (**b**) 1889 c. 63.

(2) In pursuance of paragraph 1 of Part III of Schedule 1 to the Act—

As the amount in the pound which in the opinion of the Minister corresponds to the amount of the domestic element for that year—

For the year 1969–70:	15d;
For the year 1970–71:	20d;

(3) In respect of the matters which under Part I of Schedule 1 to the Act are to be or may be prescribed in relation to the under-mentioned payments comprised in the needs element—

(a) The basic payment under paragraph 2

    (i) As the sum to be multiplied by the population—

For the year 1969–70:	£14·70;
For the year 1970–71:	£15·03;

    (ii) As the sum to be multiplied by the estimated number of persons under 15 years of age in the population—

For the year 1969–70:	£1·15;
For the year 1970–71:	£1·17;

(b) The supplementary payment under paragraph 3

As the sum to be multiplied by the estimated number of persons under 5 years of age in the population—

For the year 1969–70:	£1·04;
For the year 1970–71:	£1·05;

(c) The supplementary payment under paragraph 4

As the sum to be multiplied by the estimated number of persons over 65 years of age in the population—

For the year 1969–70:	£1·04;
For the year 1970–71:	£1·05;

(d) The supplementary payment under paragraph 5

    (i) As the number of education units per 1,000 of the population to be exceeded as a condition of payment—

For each year:	200;

    (ii) As the sum to be multiplied by the excess and by the population to determine the amount of the payment—

For the year 1969–70:	£0·079;
For the year 1970–71:	£0·081;

(e) The supplementary payment under paragraph 6

    (i) As the number of persons per acre in the area of the authority to be exceeded as a condition of payment—

For each year:	18;

    (ii) As the percentage by which the excess is to be multiplied—

For each year:	$\frac{1}{2}$ per cent.;

(f) The supplementary payment under paragraph 7

    (i) As the number of road-miles per 1,000 of the population in the area of the authority to be exceeded as a condition of payment—

For each year:	2;

(ii) As the fraction of the basic payment—

For each year: $\frac{7}{10}$;

(iii) As the percentage of the basic payment to be multiplied by the road-mileage per 1,000 of the population in the area of the authority—

For each year: $2\frac{1}{4}$ per cent.;

(g) The supplementary payment under paragraph 8

(i) As the sum by which the road-mileage of the area of the authority (excluding trunk roads) is to be multiplied—

For the year 1969–70:   £262;
For the year 1970–71:   £268;

(ii) As the sum by which the road-mileage of the roads in the area of the authority classified as principal roads under section 27 of the Act (hereinafter called "the prescribed sum") is to be multiplied—

For the year 1969–70:   £1,281;
For the year 1970–71:   £1,311;

(iii) As the number per mile of the roads so classified of which the population is to fall short—

For each year: 4,000;

(iv) As the number per mile of the roads so classified which the population is to exceed—

For each year: 5,500;

(v) As the sum by which the prescribed sum is to be reduced for each 100 persons in the short-fall—

For the year 1969–70:   £24·75;
For the year 1970–71:   £25·35;

(vi) As the sum by which the prescribed sum is to be increased for each 100 persons in the excess—

For the year 1969–70:   £32·28;
For the year 1970–71:   £33·04;

(vii) As the sum below which the prescribed sum shall not be reduced—

For the year 1969–70:   £786;
For the year 1970–71:   £804;

(h) The supplementary payment under paragraph 9

(i) As the period over which the decline of population is to be estimated—

For each year: 10 years;

(ii) As the percentage of the decline to be exceeded as a condition of payment—

For each year: $\frac{1}{2}$ per cent.;

(iii) As the number by which the excess is to be multiplied to determine the amount of the payment—

For each year: 1;

(i) The supplementary payment under paragraph 10

As the percentage of the basic payment appearing to the Minister to be appropriate in relation to authorities whose areas lie wholly or partly within the metropolitan district—

For each year: 5 per cent.

Given under the official seal of the Minister of Housing and Local Government on 27th November 1968.

(L.S.)

Anthony Greenwood,
Minister of Housing and
Local Government.

We consent to this order.

W. Harrison,

J. McCann,

Two of the Lords Commissioners
of Her Majesty's Treasury.

27th November 1968.

EXPLANATORY NOTE
(This Note is not part of the Order.)

This Order, which came into operation on 10th December 1968, fixes and prescribes for the years 1969–70 and 1970–71—

(*a*) the aggregate amounts of the rate support grants payable under Part I of the Local Government Act 1966 to the councils of counties, county boroughs and county districts in England and Wales, the Greater London Council, the councils of London Boroughs, the Common Council of the the City of London and the Council of the Isles of Scilly;

(*b*) the division of these aggregate amounts between the needs element (which is not payable to councils of county districts or, subject to provision to the contrary by regulations under the Act, to the Greater London Council), the resources element and the domestic element (which is not payable to county councils or the Greater London Council);

(*c*) the amount by which rating authorities are to reduce the amount in the pound of the general rate which they would otherwise levy on dwelling-houses in their areas so as to take account of the amount of the domestic element for these years; and

(*d*) matters which are to be, or may be, prescribed under Part I of Schedule 1 to the Act, which determines the amount of the needs element payable to any authority.

STATUTORY INSTRUMENTS

1968 No. 1958 (C. 29) (S. 174)

EVIDENCE

The Law Reform (Miscellaneous Provisions) (Scotland) Act 1968 (Commencement No. 1) Order 1968

Made - - - *6th December* 1968

In exercise of the powers conferred on me by section 22(5) of the Law Reform (Miscellaneous Provisions) (Scotland) Act 1968**(a)**, I hereby make the following order:—

1. Sections 10, 11 and 12 of the Law Reform (Miscellaneous Provisions) (Scotland) Act 1968 shall come into operation on 1st January 1969.

2. This order may be cited as the Law Reform (Miscellaneous Provisions) (Scotland) Act 1968 (Commencement No. 1) Order 1968.

William Ross,
One of Her Majesty's
Principal Secretaries of State.

St. Andrew's House,
Edinburgh, 1.
6th December 1968.

EXPLANATORY NOTE

(This Note is not part of the Order.)

This Order brings into force on 1st January 1969 those provisions of the Law Reform (Miscellaneous Provisions) (Scotland) Act 1968 which make convictions and findings of adultery and of paternity admissible in evidence in subsequent civil proceedings, and which make convictions conclusive evidence of offences in subsequent defamation actions.

(a) 1968 c. 70.

STATUTORY INSTRUMENTS

1968 No. 1961 (S.177)

ARMS AND AMMUNITION

The Firearms (Variation of Fees) (Scotland) Order 1968

Made - - - -	*2nd December* 1968
Laid before Parliament	17th *December* 1968
Coming into Operation	1st *January* 1969

In exercise of the powers conferred on me by section 43 of the Firearms Act 1968(a) and of all other powers enabling me in that behalf, I hereby make the following order:—

1. Section 32 of the Firearms Act 1968 (which makes payable a fee of 5s. 0d. for the grant, and 2s. 6d. for the renewal, replacement or variation, of firearm and shotgun certificates, and grants certain exemptions) shall be amended by the substitution, for subsection (1) of that section, of the following subsection:—

"(1) Subject to this Act, there shall be payable—

(*a*) on the grant of a firearm certificate, a fee of £2 10s. 0d.;

(*b*) on the renewal of a firearm certificate or on the replacement of such a certificate which has been lost or destroyed, a fee of £1 5s. 0d.;

(*c*) on any variation of a firearm certificate (otherwise than when it is renewed or replaced at the same time) so as to increase the number of firearms to which the certificate relates, a fee of £1 5s. 0d.;

(*d*) on the grant or renewal of a shotgun certificate, a fee of 15s. 0d.; and

(*e*) on the replacement of a shotgun certificate which has been lost or destroyed, a fee of 7s. 6d.".

2. Section 32 of the Firearms Act 1968 shall be further amended by the insertion, after subsection (3) thereof, of the following subsection:—

"(3A) No fee shall be payable on the grant, variation or renewal of a firearm certificate which relates solely to and, in the case of a variation, will continue when varied to relate solely to a signalling device which, when assembled and ready to fire, is not more than six inches long and which is designed to discharge a flare, or to ammunition for such a device.".

3. Section 35 of the Firearms Act 1968 (which relates to the fees payable for the registration and renewal of registration of a firearms dealer) shall be amended by the substitution:—

(*a*) in subsection (1) thereof, of the words "a fee of £20" for the words "a fee of £5"; and

(*b*) in subsection (3) thereof, of the words "a fee of £4" for the words "a fee of £1".

(**a**) 1968 c. 27.

4. This order may be cited as the Firearms (Variation of Fees) (Scotland) Order 1968 and shall come into operation on 1st January 1969.

William Ross,
One of Her Majesty's Principal
Secretaries of State.

St. Andrew's House,
Edinburgh.
2nd December 1968.

EXPLANATORY NOTE

(This Note is not part of the Order.)

This Order increases in relation to Scotland the fees payable in respect of firearm and shotgun certificates, and also those payable on the registration or renewal of registration of a firearms dealer.

It also provides for no fee to be payable for a firearm certificate which relates only to a signalling device of the kind described in Article 2.

STATUTORY INSTRUMENTS

1968 No. 1963 (S.178)

POLICE

The Police (Scotland) Amendment (No. 2) Regulations 1968

Made - - -	*6th December* 1968
Laid before Parliament	*17th December* 1968
Coming into Operation	*20th December* 1968

In exercise of the powers conferred on me by section 26 of the Police (Scotland) Act 1967(**a**) and of all other powers enabling me in that behalf, and after consulting the Police Council for Great Britain, in accordance with section 26(8) of the said Act of 1967, I hereby make the following regulations :—

PART I

1. These regulations may be cited as the Police (Scotland) Amendment (No. 2) Regulations 1968.

2. The Police (Scotland) Regulations 1968(**b**) (hereinafter referred to as the principal regulations) shall have effect subject to the amendments specified in Part II of these regulations.

PART II

3. In Schedule 6 of the principal regulations (which relates to motor vehicle allowances)—

(*a*) for the table in sub-paragraph (1) of paragraph 1 there shall be substituted the following table :—

TABLE

Cylinder capacity	Annual rate of fixed element	Mileage element	
		Basic rate per mile	Reduced rate per mile
1,200 c.c. or more but less than 1,700 c.c.	£85	7½d.	4¾d.
1,000 c.c. or more but less than 1,200 c.c.	£75	6¾d.	4¼d.
Less than 1,000 c.c.	£68	6d.	3¾d.

(a) 1967 c. 77.   (b) S.I. 1968/716 (1968 II, p. 2024).

(b) for the table in paragraph 2 there shall be substituted the following table: —

TABLE

Cylinder capacity	Rate per mile
1,200 c.c. or more but less than 1,700 c.c.	1s. 1¾d.
1,000 c.c. or more but less than 1,200 c.c.	1s. 0¼d.
Less than 1,000 c.c.	11d.

4.—(1) In the year ending 30th April 1969 a motor vehicle allowance payable under regulation 50 of the principal regulations shall be calculated as hereinafter provided.

(2) So far as the motor vehicle allowance falls to be calculated by reference to completed months of authorised use ending, or mileage of authorised use performed, on or after 1st August 1968, it shall be calculated in accordance with the principal regulations as amended by regulation 3 of these regulations, which shall have effect accordingly.

(3) Nothing in regulation 3 of these regulations shall affect the calculation of the motor vehicle allowance so far as it falls to be calculated by reference to completed months of authorised use ending, or mileage of authorised use performed, before 1st August 1968.

5. These regulations shall come into operation on 20th December 1968 and, save as provided in regulation 4 hereof, shall have effect as from that date.

William Ross,
One of Her Majesty's Principal
Secretaries of State.

St. Andrew's House,
Edinburgh, 1.
6th December 1968.

EXPLANATORY NOTE

(This Note is not part of the Regulations.)

These Regulations amend the Police (Scotland) Regulations 1968 to provide for increases in the rates of motor vehicle allowances in respect of motor cars. These allowances are payable on an annual basis and are calculated by reference to completed months of authorised use and mileage performed in the year in question. Regulation 4 makes transitory provision for the calculation of these allowances in the year ending 30th April 1969 and provides (in exercise of the power conferred by section 26(3) of the Police (Scotland) Act 1967) that regulation 4 shall have effect as from 1st August 1968 as respects the calculation of motor vehicle allowances by reference to months of use completed, or mileage performed, on or after that date.

STATUTORY INSTRUMENTS

1968 No. 1965

OPTICIANS

The General Optical Council (Registration and Enrolment Rules) Order of Council 1968

Made - - - - 11th December 1968

At the Council Chamber, Whitehall, the 11th day of December 1968

By the Lords of Her Majesty's Most Honourable Privy Council

Whereas in pursuance of section 7 of the Opticians Act 1958(a) the General Optical Council have made rules entitled "The Registration and Enrolment Rules 1968 ":

And whereas by subsection (5) of the said section such rules shall not come into force until approved by Order of the Privy Council:

Now, therefore, Their Lordships, having taken the said rules into consideration, are hereby pleased to approve the same as set out in the Schedule to this Order.

This Order may be cited as the General Optical Council (Registration and Enrolment Rules) Order of Council 1968.

W. G. Agnew.

SCHEDULE

THE REGISTRATION AND ENROLMENT RULES 1968

The General Optical Council, in exercise of their powers under section 7 of the Opticians Act 1958, hereby make the following rules :—

Interpretation

1. These rules may be cited as the Registration and Enrolment Rules 1968.

2. In these rules, unless the context otherwise requires, the following expressions have the respective meanings hereby assigned to them :—

"the Act " means the Opticians Act 1958 ;

"appropriate form " means an application form issued by the Council for the type of application in question and a requirement that an application shall be made on the appropriate form shall imply that the Council are entitled to require the completion of the form ;

"the Council " means the General Optical Council established under the Act ;

"dispensing optician ", "enrolled ", "enrolment ", "list ", "optical appliance ", "ophthalmic optician ", "register " and "registered optician " have the meanings given them by section 30(1) of the Act ;

"financial year " means the financial year of the Council running from the first day of April to the thirty-first day of March ;

(a) 1958 c. 32.

" practice address " means an address at which the applicant provides ophthalmic services including testing sight as defined by section 30(2) of the Act, or the fitting and supply of optical appliances, or both, except an address at which he provides such services only in the following circumstances: —

    (*a*) when working as an employee of a registered medical practitioner or registered optician, or of an authority or person carrying on a hospital, clinic, nursing home or other institution providing medical or surgical treatment, or of a Minister of the Crown or Government department (including a department of the Government of Northern Ireland), or

    (*b*) when working as director, secretary or employee of an enrolled body corporate, or

    (*c*) in an emergency or in the place of a registered optician who is ill or on holiday ;

" the Registrar " means the registrar of the Council.

3. The Interpretation Act 1889(**a**) applies to the interpretation of these rules as it applies to the interpretation of an Act of Parliament.

The Registers and Lists

4. Each register shall contain the following particulars of each optician registered therein :—

(*a*) Full name.

(*b*) Permanent address with an indication whether or not he works there as an ophthalmic or dispensing optician.

(*c*) Practice addresses, if any, other than the permanent address.

(*d*) Qualifications held by the optician and recognised by the Council under section 3(2) or section 3(4), or approved by the Council under section 5, of the Act.

(*e*) Other optical, academic or professional qualifications approved by the Council for inclusion in the register.

5. Each list shall contain the following particulars of each body corporate enrolled therein : —

(*a*) Name.

(*b*) Principal place of business.

(*c*) The addresses of all places at which the body corporate carries on business as ophthalmic or dispensing opticians and the name under which such business is carried on at each such place.

6. The Registrar shall have authority to refuse to enter a name in a register or list, and to refuse to transfer or restore a name to a register or list, until the fees prescribed by these rules for the entry, transfer or restoration have been paid.

Applications for Registration or Enrolment

7. An application to the Council for the inclusion of a name in the register or the name of a body corporate in the list shall be made on the appropriate form. The Council may require in a particular case such evidence in verification of the information given on the appropriate form as in their view is necessary to establish whether the applicant is entitled to be registered or the body corporate to be enrolled.

Transfer from one Register or List to another

8. An application for the transfer of the name of a registered optician from one register to another or for the transfer of the name of an enrolled body corporate from one list to the other shall be accompanied by such information as the Council may reasonably require for establishing whether the applicant

---

(**a**) 1889 c. 63.

is entitled to be registered in the other register or the body corporate to be enrolled in the other list. Where the Council are satisfied that the applicant or body corporate is so entitled, they shall delete the name of the applicant from one register and insert it in the other, or, as the case may be, shall delete the name of the body corporate from one list and insert it in the other.

Retention of a name in the Register or List and removal for non-payment of fee

9. Not later than the fourteenth day of March in each year the Registrar shall send to the permanent address of every registered optician the appropriate form of application for the retention of a name in the register, and to the principal place of business of every body corporate the appropriate form of application for retention of a name in the list together, in each case, with a notice of the fees payable and a warning that non-payment entails erasure from the register or list respectively, but failure by a registered optician or enrolled body corporate to receive a form or notice shall not constitute a ground for retention or restoration of a name.

10. Where the Registrar shall not have received by the thirty-first day of March in any year a retention fee or fee for retention of enrolment due on that date he shall send a warning that failure to pay the fee will result in the removal from the register or the list of the name in relation to which the fee was due, and if the fee is not received within fourteen days of the issue of the warning he shall remove the name from the register or list.

Changes in particulars notified to the Council

11. A registered optician shall notify the Council within one month of any of the following changes bearing on the particulars entered in the register :—

(i) Change of name.

(ii) Change or abandonment of any address entered in the register or addition of any further practice address to those entered in the register.

(iii) Loss of any qualification entered in the register.

12. An enrolled body corporate shall notify the Council within one month of any of the following changes bearing on the particulars entered in the list :—

(i) Change of name.

(ii) Change or abandonment of any address entered in the list.

(iii) Inception by the body corporate of business as ophthalmic or dispensing opticians at an address additional to those entered in the list, the notification to include the name under which business is carried on at the additional address.

13. An enrolled body corporate shall notify the Council forthwith if at any time any particulars supplied by it in or in support of its application for enrolment no longer apply in any respect which may materially affect the application to the body corporate of any of the conditions of enrolment set out in section 4(2) of the Act.

Alteration or removal of an entry in the Register or List

14. When the Registrar receives information that an entry in the register or the list has become incorrect, or application is made by or on behalf of a registered optician or an enrolled body corporate for an entry in the register or list to be altered, if he has satisfied himself by means of a statutory declaration or otherwise that the information is true or the ground of the application is sufficient, he shall make the required correction or alteration. No charge shall be made for a correction or alteration under this rule unless it involves the inclusion in the register or list of additional particulars in respect of which increased fees are chargeable under Rule 22 or Rule 27 of these rules, in which case the amount added by those rules to the registration and enrolment fees in respect of the insertion of additional particulars shall be chargeable.

15. The Registrar may remove from the register or the list the name of any registered optician or enrolled body corporate upon receipt of a written application by or on behalf of the registered optician or enrolled body corporate stating the grounds on which the application is made and accompanied by a statutory declaration that the applicant is not aware of any reason for the institution of proceedings which might lead to the erasure of the name under section 11 or section 13 of the Act.

16. The Registrar shall erase from the register or the list the name of any registered optician or enrolled body corporate in respect of which he shall receive a direction to that effect from the Disciplinary Committee under section 11 or section 13 of the Act, on the date upon which such direction takes effect in accordance with section 14 of the Act.

Restoration of a name to the Register or List

17. Subject to the provisions of section 12 and section 13 of the Act, the Council may restore a name to the register on receipt of an application accompanied by: —

(i) the fee prescribed by Rule 25 and the fee due under Rules 19 and 24 of these rules for the period to which the application relates, and

(ii) where the name of the applicant has not been included in the register during any of the five financial years immediately preceding that in which the application is made, evidence establishing to the satisfaction of the Council his identity and good character.

18. Subject to the provisions of section 12 and section 13 of the Act, the Council may restore a name to the list on receipt of an application accompanied by :—

(i) the fee prescribed by Rule 31 and the fee due under Rules 26 and 30 of these Rules for the period to which the application relates, and

(ii) evidence establishing to the satisfaction of the Council the continuance of entitlement to enrolment.

Fees payable by Ophthalmic and Dispensing Opticians

19. The fee for the entry of a name in the register and the retention of the name for the period specified in Rule 21 of these rules shall be called the registration fee. A further fee shall be charged for the retention of a name in the register for each financial year beyond the period covered by the registration fee and shall be called the retention fee.

20. The registration fee shall be paid at the time of the application for registration. The fee shall be £8 except that it shall be £5 only for a person who first applies for registration either within six months of the date when he first became entitled to receive a qualification recognised by the Council for the purpose of section 3(2) or section 3(4), or approved by the Council under section 5, of the Act, or within three years of that date and within six months of the date when he has completed practical experience required by the Council under section 3 of the Act.

21. Subject to the provisions of sections 11, 13 and 14 of the Act, the registration fee shall entitle a registered optician to the retention of his name in the register until the end of the financial year in which his name was first included therein :

Provided that a registration fee paid in the financial year ending on the 31st day of March 1969 shall cover the retention of the name in the register until the 31st day of March 1970.

22. The registration fee shall cover the inclusion in the register of particulars inserted under paragraphs (a), (b), (d) and (e) of Rule 4 of these rules, but shall be increased by £1 for each address entered under paragraph (c) of that rule.

23. The fee for transfer of a name from one register to another shall be £2 and shall be paid at the time of the application for the transfer.

24. The retention fee shall be £3 per annum, and shall be paid before the beginning of the financial year to which it relates. It shall cover the retention in the register of particulars under paragraphs (a), (b), (d) and (e) of Rule 4 of these rules but shall be increased by £1 per annum for each address entered under paragraph (c) of that rule.

25. The fee for restoration of a name to the register shall be £2 and shall be additional to the retention fee for any year during which the name is included in the register.

Fees payable by bodies corporate

26. The fee for the entry of a name of a body corporate in the list and the retention of the name for the period specified in Rule 28 of these rules shall be called the enrolment fee. A further fee shall be charged for retention of such a name in the list for each financial year beyond the period covered by the enrolment fee and shall be called the fee for retention of enrolment.

27. The enrolment fee shall be paid at the time of the application for enrolment and shall be £2. The fee shall cover the entry in the list of particulars inserted under paragraphs (a) and (b) of Rule 5 of these rules but shall be increased by £1 for each address inserted under paragraph (c) of that rule other than the address of the principal place of business.

28. Subject to the provisions of sections 11, 13 and 14 of the Act, the enrolment fee shall entitle an enrolled body corporate to the retention of its name in the list until the end of the financial year in which the name was first included therein:

Provided that an enrolment fee paid in the financial year ending on the 31st day of March 1969 shall cover the retention of the name in the list until the 31st day of March 1970.

29. The fee for transfer of the name of a body corporate from one list to the other shall be £2 and shall be paid at the time of the application for the transfer.

30. The fee for retention of enrolment shall be £2 per annum, and shall be paid before the beginning of the financial year to which it relates. It shall cover the retention in the list of the principal place of business and shall be increased by £1 per annum for each further address retained in the list.

31. The fee for restoration of a name to the list shall be £2 and shall be additional to the fee for retention of enrolment for any year during which the name is included in the list.

Operation of these rules

32. These rules shall come into operation on the 1st day of April 1969, and the Registration and Enrolment Rules 1959, as amended by the Registration and Enrolment (Amendment) Rules 1963, 1965 and 1968, shall cease to have effect on that date.

Sealed on the 6th day of November 1968.

Attested by :

G. R. ROUGIER,
Member of Council.

L.S.

RONALD RUSSELL,
Member of Council.

A. T. GERARD,
Registrar.

EXPLANATORY NOTE

(This Note is not part of the Order.)

The rules approved by this Order consolidate, with amendments, the rules relating to the registration and enrolment of opticians.

The principal change effected by the rules is that after 31st March 1969 the payment of a registration or enrolment fee will cover only the year to which the fee relates and not, as hitherto, the following year also.

STATUTORY INSTRUMENTS

1968 No. 1966

HIGHWAYS, ENGLAND AND WALES

The Special Roads (Classes of Traffic) (England and Wales) Order 1968

Made	-	-	-	*7th November* 1968
Laid before Parliament			*20th November* 1968
Coming into Operation			*15th December* 1968

The Minister of Transport, in exercise of his powers under section 12(3) of the Highways Act 1959(**a**), and of all other powers him enabling in that behalf, hereby makes the following Order :—

1.—(1) This Order may be cited as the Special Roads (Classes of Traffic) (England and Wales) Order 1968, and shall come into operation on the fifth day following the day it is approved by Parliament.

(2) In this Order, "Schedule 4 to the Act of 1959" means Schedule 4 to the Highways Act 1959, as amended by the Special Roads (Classes of Traffic) Order 1961(**b**).

(3) The Interpretation Act 1889(**c**) shall apply for the interpretation of this Order as it applies for the interpretation of an Act of Parliament.

2. The composition of the class of traffic specified in Schedule 4 to the Act of 1959 as Class II shall be varied by adding at the end of the specification of the said Class II in that Schedule the following paragraph—

"Light locomotives, being motor vehicles on which is mounted apparatus designed to lift a disabled motor vehicle or trailer, and any such disabled vehicle or any towing implement drawn by such a locomotive, the said locomotives being vehicles in respect of which the following condition is satisfied, that is to say, that the maximum speed at which the vehicle, when not drawing a trailer, may be driven under section 78 of the Road Traffic Regulation Act 1967(**d**) on roads which are not special roads is not less than twenty miles per hour.".

3. In Schedule 4 to the Act of 1959, there shall be added at the end of the last paragraph (which relates to the interpretation of that Schedule) the words "and 'towing implement' has the same meaning as in the Motor Vehicles (Construction and Use) Regulations 1966(**e**).".

Given under the Official Seal of the Minister of Transport the 7th November 1968.

(L.S.)

Richard Marsh,
Minister of Transport.

(**a**) 7 & 8 Eliz. 2. c. 25.　　　　　(**b**) S.I. 1961/1210 (1961 II, p. 2408).
(**c**) 52 & 53 Vict. c. 63.　　　　　(**d**) 1967 c. 76.
(**e**) S.I. 1966/1288 (1966 III, p. 3493).

EXPLANATORY NOTE

(This Note is not part of the Order.)

Schedule 4 to the Highways Act 1959. as amended by the Special Roads (Classes of Traffic) Order 1961. specifies classes of traffic for the purposes of special roads.

This Order by adding to Class II of that Schedule breakdown vehicles of up to eleven and a half tons in weight and disabled vehicles drawn thereby. will enable them to use motorways.

STATUTORY INSTRUMENTS

1968 No. 1968

WAGES COUNCILS

The Wages Regulation (Milk Distributive) (Scotland) (Amendment) Order 1968

Made	-	-	-	11*th December* 1968
Coming into Operation				15*th January* 1969

Whereas the Secretary of State has received from the Milk Distributive Wages Council (Scotland) the wages regulation proposals set out in the Schedule hereto ;

Now, therefore, the Secretary of State in exercise of her powers under section 11 of the Wages Councils Act 1959(**a**), and of all other powers enabling her in that behalf, hereby makes the following Order :—

1. This Order may be cited as the Wages Regulation (Milk Distributive) (Scotland) (Amendment) Order 1968.

2.—(1) In this Order the expression "the specified date" means the 15th January 1969, provided that where, as respects any worker who is paid wages at intervals not exceeding seven days, that date does not correspond with the beginning of the period for which the wages are paid, the expression "the specified date" means, as respects that worker, the beginning of the next such period following that date.

(2) The Interpretation Act 1889(**b**) shall apply to the interpretation of this Order as it applies to the interpretation of an Act of Parliament.

3. The wages regulation proposals set out in the Schedule hereto shall have effect as from the specified date.

Signed by order of the Secretary of State.
11th December 1968.

A. A. Jarratt,
Deputy Under Secretary of State,
Department of Employment and Productivity.

Article 3   **SCHEDULE**

STATUTORY MINIMUM REMUNERATION

The Wages Regulation (Milk Distributive) (Scotland) Order 1967(**c**) (Order M.D.S. (91)) shall have effect as if in the Schedule thereto :—

1. for paragraph 2 there were substituted the following paragraph :—

(**a**) 1959 c. 69.   (**b**) 1889 c. 63.

(**c**) S.I. 1967/772 (1967 II, p. 2289).

"GENERAL MINIMUM TIME RATES
MALE OR FEMALE WORKERS

2. The general minimum time rates applicable to male or female workers are as follows:—

	Per week s. d.
(1) Foremen	*244 0*
(2) Forewomen	*244 0*
(3) Chargehands	*210 6*
(4) Male Clerks aged 22 years or over	*235 6*

(5) The following workers:—

    (*a*) All other male workers

    (*b*) *Roundswomen and female workers employed in garaging, pasteurising or milk sterilising*

the said workers being aged:—

	Per week s. d.
21 years or over	*230 6*
20 and under 21 years	*188 6*
19 ,, ,, 20 ,,	*178 6*
18 ,, ,, 19 ,,	*159 6*
17 ,, ,, 18 ,,	*127 6*
16 ,, ,, 17 ,,	*107 6*
under 16 years	*95 6*

(6) All other female workers (including *Assistant Roundswomen*, Clerks and Shop Assistants) being aged:—

	Per week s. d.
21 years or over	*179 6*
20 and under 21 years	*156 6*
19 ,, ,, 20 ,,	*149 6*
18 ,, ,, 19 ,,	*140 6*
17 ,, ,, 18 ,,	*112 6*
16 ,, ,, 17 ,,	*96 0*
under 16 years	*90 0*"

2. in paragraph 17, which relates to definitions, there were inserted the following:—

"' *ASSISTANT ROUNDSWOMAN*' means a worker wholly or mainly employed in assisting any person carrying out the duties normally performed by a roundswoman whether or not such person is a roundswoman as defined in this Schedule.

' *ROUNDSWOMAN*' means a worker wholly or mainly employed as a saleswoman on a definite or established route and responsible for keeping account of retail sales to customers and of any cash or tokens received in payment and who is not accompanied, save in exceptional circumstances, by any other person who exercises control or supervision."

EXPLANATORY NOTE

(*This Note is not part of the Order.*)

This Order, which has effect from 15th January 1969, amends the Wages Regulation (Milk Distributive) (Scotland) Order 1967 (Order M.D.S. (91)) by increasing the statutory minimum remuneration fixed by that Order.

New provisions are printed in italics.

STATUTORY INSTRUMENTS

1968 No. 1970

ROAD TRAFFIC

The Road Traffic Accidents (Payments for Treatment) (England and Wales) Order 1968

Made - - -	*10th December* 1968
Laid before Parliament	*19th December* 1968
Coming into Operation	*1st January* 1969

The Secretary of State for Social Services, in exercise of his powers under section 5 of and Schedule 3 to the Public Expenditure and Receipts Act 1968(**a**), and of all other powers enabling him in that behalf, hereby makes the following order :—

1.—(1) This order may be cited as the Road Traffic Accidents (Payments for Treatment) (England and Wales) Order 1968 and shall come into operation on 1st January 1969.

(2) The Interpretation Act 1889(**b**) applies to the interpretation of this order as it applies to the interpretation of an Act of Parliament.

2. Subject to article 4 of this order, in the proviso to section 212(1) of the Road Traffic Act 1960(**c**) (which provides that the maximum amount of payments by authorised insurers or owners of vehicles under the sub-section for hospital treatment of traffic casualties shall be £50 for each person treated as an in-patient and £5 for each person treated as an out-patient) for the sum of £50 there shall be substituted the sum of £200 and for the sum of £5 there shall be substituted the sum of £20.

3. Subject as aforesaid, in section 213(1) of the said Act (which provides a fee of 12s. 6d. for emergency treatment of traffic casualties) for the sum of 12s. 6d. there shall be substituted the sum of 25s.

4. This order shall apply only where an accident giving rise to the death or bodily injury in respect of which a payment is made under the said section 212, or claimed under the said section 213, occurred after the coming into operation of this order.

Signed by authority of the Secretary of State for Social Services.

David Ennals,
Minister of State,
Department of Health and Social Security.

10th December 1968.

(**a**) 1968 c. 14.   (**b**) 1889 c. 63.   (**c**) 1960 c. 16.

EXPLANATORY NOTE
(This Note is not part of the Order.)

This Order alters the maximum amounts payable under section 212(1) of the Road Traffic Act 1960 and the fee payable under section 213(1). The maximum payments for hospital treatment under section 212(1) are increased from £50 to £200 in respect of persons treated as in-patients and from £5 to £20 for persons treated as out-patients. The fee for emergency treatment under section 213(1) is increased from 12s. 6d. to 25s. The alterations apply only in respect of accidents occurring on or after 1st January 1969.

STATUTORY INSTRUMENTS

1968 No. 1972

TOWN AND COUNTRY PLANNING, ENGLAND AND WALES

The Town and Country Planning (Determination of appeals by appointed persons) (Prescribed Classes) Regulations 1968

Made - - - -	12th December 1968
Laid before Parliament	17th December 1968
Coming into Operation	1st January 1969

The Minister of Housing and Local Government, in exercise of the powers conferred on him by sections 21 and 104 of the Town and Country Planning Act 1968(a) and all of other powers enabling him in that behalf, hereby makes the following regulations:—

Citation and commencement

1.—(1) These regulations may be cited as the Town and Country Planning (Determination of appeals by appointed persons) (Prescribed Classes) Regulations 1968.

(2) These regulations shall come into operation on 1st January 1969 but shall not affect any appeals notice of which was given before that date.

Interpretation

2.—(1) In these regulations, unless the context otherwise requires—

"the Act" means the Town and Country Planning Act 1968;

"the principal Act" means the Town and Country Planning Act 1962(b);

"the Minister concerned" means, except as respects Wales, the Minister of Housing and Local Government and, as respects Wales, the Secretary of State; and "Wales" includes Monmouthshire;

"local planning authority", except in regulation 5, means—

(a) the local planning authority (within the meaning of section 2 of the principal Act) for the area in which the land is situate; or

(b) in relation to appeals affecting land within Greater London, the authority which, by virtue of section 24 of the London Government Act 1963(c), or of regulations made under that section, is the local planning authority in relation to the class of development concerned in the area of Greater London where the land is;

(c) an authority exercising delegated functions on behalf of any such authority as is mentioned in (a) or (b) above—

as the case may be;

"building" and "building operations" and "engineering operations" have

---

(a) 1968 c. 72.   (b) 1962 c. 38.
(c) 1963 c. 33.

the meanings assigned to them in the principal Act;

"dwellinghouse" means a building used for a residential purpose and includes a flat or other separate dwelling which is comprised in a larger building of which it forms part;

"the General Development Order" means the Town and Country Planning General Development Order 1963**(a)**;

"local authority" has the meaning assigned to it by section 221(1) of the principal Act (as amended by section 29(5) of the London Government Act 1963);

"operational land" has the meaning assigned to it by section 221(1) of the principal Act as affected by section 69 of the Act;

"statutory undertakers" means persons authorised by any enactment to carry on any railway, light railway, tramway, road transport, water transport, canal, inland navigation, dock, harbour, pier or lighthouse undertaking or any undertaking for the supply of electricity, gas, hydraulic power or water or the British Airports Authority and includes companies which are deemed to be statutory undertakers by virtue of section 141(2) of the Transport Act 1968**(b)**.

(2) References in these regulations to the use of land or buildings for residential purposes shall be construed as excluding a use falling within any of Classes XI, XII, XIV or XVI of the Schedule to the Town and Country Planning (Use Classes) Order 1963**(c)**, and references to development for residential purposes shall be construed accordingly.

(3) For the purposes of Class 1 of Schedule 1 to these regulations, 0.8 hectares shall be deemed to be the equivalent of 2 acres.

(4) For the purposes of Schedule 2 to these regulations, development of land is concurrently the subject of another appeal to the Minister concerned or of an application referred to him, where that appeal or application comes into the jurisdiction of the Minister concerned within the period of one month before or after the giving of notice of the appeal to which Schedule 1 of these regulations relates.

(5) The Interpretation Act 1889**(d)** applies to the interpretation of these regulations as it applies to the interpretation of an Act of Parliament.

Classes of appeals for determination by appointed persons

3. Subject to the next following regulation, the Minister of Housing and Local Government hereby prescribes the following classes of appeals as appeals to be determined in accordance with the provisions of Part III of the Act by a person appointed for the purpose by the Minister concerned instead of by such Minister, namely, appeals under section 23 of the principal Act (appeals against planning decisions), as originally enacted or as applied by section 24 of that Act (appeal in default of planning decision) where the development in question falls wholly within any one or more of the classes of case specified in Schedule 1 to these regulations.

Classes of appeals reserved for determination by the Minister concerned

4. The foregoing regulation shall not apply to any such appeal as is mentioned in that regulation if it relates to development falling within any one or more of the classes of case specified in Schedule 2 to these regulations.

(a) S.I. 1963/709 (1963 I, p. 862).   **(b)** 1968 c. 73.
(c) S.I. 1963/708 (1963 I, p. 857).   **(d)** 1889 c. 63.

Publicity for directions under section 21(1) of the Act.

5.—(1) For the purposes of this regulation "local planning authority" means either a London Borough Council or the Common Council of the City of London or a local planning authority within the meaning of section 2 of the principal Act, as the case may be.

(2) On the making by the Minister concerned of a direction under section 21(1) of the Act he may by notice in writing enclosing a copy of the direction require the local planning authority of any area for which the direction has effect to publish as soon as may be a notice in at least one newspaper circulating in the area; and this notice shall contain a concise statement of the effect of the direction and shall specify the place or places where a copy of the direction and (where the direction affects less than the whole of the area of the local planning authority) a map defining the area for which the direction has effect, may be seen at all reasonable hours.

SCHEDULE 1

CLASSES OF APPEALS FOR DETERMINATION BY APPOINTED PERSONS

Appeals in respect of development by operations

1. The development for residential purposes of land not exceeding 2 acres in extent where the application for planning permission is expressed to be an outline application within the terms of article 5(2) of the General Development Order and the appeal arises therefrom or on an application for approval required under the General Development Order.

2. The erection, or the enlargement or other alteration, of a building or buildings for use as not more than 10 dwellinghouses, where the application for planning permission is not expressed to be an outline application.

3. The carrying out of building, engineering or other operations on land for a purpose ancilliary to the existing use of land for residential purposes or ancillary or incidental to development of land for residential purposes.

Appeals in respect of changes in use

4. The change in the use of a building or buildings to use as not more than 10 dwellinghouses.

5. The change in the use of a building or buildings in use as not more than 10 dwellinghouses to another use for residential purposes.

SCHEDULE 2

CLASSES OF CASES EXCEPTED FROM SCHEDULE 1

Where the development the subject of the appeal is:—

1. Development in respect of which the Minister concerned has given a direction under the provisions of article 8 of the General Development Order.

2. Development in respect of which the Minister of Transport or, in Wales, the Secretary of State has given a direction under article 9(2) of the General Development Order.

3. Development by a local authority.

4. Development by statutory undertakers on operational land or on land in the case of which the circumstances mentioned in section 70(2) of the Act apply.

5. Development by the National Coal Board on land of a class specified in regulations made pursuant to section 204 of the principal Act.

6. Development for which planning permission has been refused by a local planning authority, or granted by them subject to conditions, where the local planning authority have included in their reasons for such decision the statement that such decision has been made following an expression of views, by a government department or new town development corporation, that the application should not be granted wholly or in part, or should be granted only subject to conditions.

7. Development where the same development is concurrently the subject or part of the subject of another appeal to the Minister concerned or of an application referred to him, under any provisions of the Act or the principal Act.

8. Development where the same land is concurrently the subject or part of the subject of another appeal to the Minister concerned or of an application referred to him, in respect of development wholly or partly outside the classes specified in Schedule 1 to these regulations.

Given under the official seal of the Minister of Housing and Local Government on 12th December 1968.

(L.S.)
                                  Anthony Greenwood,
Minister of Housing and
Local Government.

EXPLANATORY NOTE

(This Note is not part of the Regulations.)

These regulations prescribe classes of planning appeals (set out in Schedule 1) which are to be determined by persons appointed for the purpose by the Minister of Housing and Local Government (in Wales and Monmouthshire, the Secretary of State) instead of being determined by the Minister or the Secretary of State.

Regulation 4 provides that certain excepted classes of appeals (set out in Schedule 2) which would otherwise fall within the prescribed classes are to continue to be determined by the Minister or the Secretary of State.

Regulation 5 provides for the advertisement by local planning authorities of any direction made by the Minister or the Secretary of State under section 21(1) of the Town and Country Planning Act 1968 whereby specified classes of appeals are to be determined by him instead of by an appointed person.

STATUTORY INSTRUMENTS

1968 No. 1973

PROFESSIONS SUPPLEMENTARY TO MEDICINE

The Professions Supplementary to Medicine (Registration Rules) (Amendment) Order of Council 1968

Made - - - *13th December* 1968

At the Council Chamber, Whitehall, the 13th day of December 1968

By the Lords of Her Majesty's Most Honourable Privy Council

Whereas in pursuance of section 2 of the Professions Supplementary to Medicine Act 1960(**a**) the Council for Professions Supplementary to Medicine has made rules entitled "The Registration (Amendment) Rules 1968":

And whereas by subsection (3) of the said section such rules shall not come into force until confirmed by Order of the Privy Council:

Now, therefore, Their Lordships, having taken the said rules into consideration, are hereby pleased to confirm the same as set out in the Schedule to this Order.

This Order may be cited as the Professions Supplementary to Medicine (Registration Rules) (Amendment) Order of Council 1968.

W. G. Agnew.

SCHEDULE

THE REGISTRATION (AMENDMENT) RULES 1968

The Council for Professions Supplementary to Medicine, in exercise of its powers under section 2 of the Professions Supplementary to Medicine Act 1960, hereby makes the following rules:—

1. These rules may be cited as the Registration (Amendment) Rules 1968.

2. The Registration Rules 1962, as scheduled to the Professions Supplementary to Medicine (Registration Rules) Order of Council 1962(**b**) and as subsequently amended (**c**), shall be further amended as follows:—

   (*a*) Rule 18 shall be deleted.

   (*b*) Rule 19 shall be deleted and the following rule shall be substituted therefor:—

   "19. (i) Registered members of each profession shall, before the dates set out opposite that profession in column 3 of the Schedule, pay a retention fee in respect of the year following that date.

   (ii) A member of a profession whose name is restored to the Register under Rule 13 shall pay a retention fee in respect of any unexpired portion of the year next ending upon the date set out opposite that profession in column 3 of the Schedule.

(a) 1960 c. 66.   (b) S.I. 1962/1765 (1962 II, p. 2130).
(c) There is no amendment which relates expressly to the subject matter of these rules.

(iii) Payment of any retention fee shall cover retention in a Register for the relevant period of particulars under paragraphs (*a*), (*b*), (*d*) and (*e*) of Rule 4 of these Rules but shall be increased by £1 per annum for each address registered under paragraph (*c*) of that Rule.

(iv) As from the 1st March 1969 the retention fee in respect of a year or any part of a year shall be £2."

EXPLANATORY NOTE

(This Note is not part of the Order.)

The rules approved by this Order alter the provisions as to the registration fees and retention fees payable to the Boards established under the Professions Supplementary to Medicine Act 1960.

STATUTORY INSTRUMENTS

1968 No. 1974

SEA FISHERIES

The Salmon and Migratory Trout (Drift-net Fishing) Licensing (Extension) Order 1968

Made - - -		*12th December* 1968
Laid before Parliament		*18th December* 1968
Coming into Operation		*15th February* 1969

The Minister of Agriculture, Fisheries and Food, and the Secretaries of State for Scotland and the Home Department (being the Secretaries of State concerned with the sea-fishing industry in Scotland and Northern Ireland respectively) in exercise of the powers conferred on them by section 4 of the Sea Fish (Conservation) Act 1967(**a**) and of all other powers enabling them in that behalf, with the approval of the Treasury, hereby make the following order:—

Citation and Commencement

1. This order may be cited as the Salmon and Migratory Trout (Drift-net Fishing) Licensing (Extension) Order 1968 and shall come into operation on 15th February 1969.

Interpretation

2.—(1) In this order—

"the principal order" means the Salmon and Migratory Trout (Drift-net Fishing) Licensing Order 1962(**b**) as amended (**c**).

(2) The Interpretation Act 1889(**d**) shall apply to the interpretation of this order as it applies to the interpretation of an Act of Parliament.

Extension of Period

3. Article 4 of the principal order shall be read and construed as if for the date 15th February 1969 there were substituted the date 15th February 1971.

(**a**) 1967 c. 84.　　　　　　　　(**b**) S.I. 1962/1393 (1962 II, p. 1520).
(**c**) The relevant amending instruments are S.I. 1964/1963, 1965/2023, 1966/1546 (1964 III, p. 4290; 1965 III, p. 5989; 1966 III, p. 4380).
(**d**) 1889 c. 63.

In witness whereof the Official Seal of the Minister of Agriculture, Fisheries and Food is hereunto affixed on 4th December 1968.

(L.S.)   *Cledwyn Hughes,*
                              Minister of Agriculture, Fisheries and Food.

Given under the Seal of the Secretary of State for Scotland on 6th December 1968.

(L.S.)   *William Ross,*
                                  Secretary of State for Scotland.

Given under the hand of the Secretary of State for the Home Department on 10th December 1968.

James Callaghan,
                              Secretary of State for the Home Department.

Approved
12th December 1968.

Walter Harrison,
                                      B. K. O'Malley,
                              Two of the Lords Commissioners of
                                      Her Majesty's Treasury.

EXPLANATORY NOTE

(This Note is not part of the Order.)

The operation of the Salmon and Migratory Trout (Drift-net Fishing) Licensing Order 1962 (which prohibits drift-net fishing for salmon in specified waters around England and Wales except under the authority of a licence) is extended for a period of two years from 15th February 1969.

STATUTORY INSTRUMENTS

1968 No. 1975

SEA FISHERIES

The Salmon and Migratory Trout (Drift-net Fishing) Restrictions on Landing (Extension) Order 1968

Made - - -	*10th December* 1968
Laid before Parliament	*18th December* 1968
Coming into Operation	*15th February* 1969

The Minister of Agriculture, Fisheries and Food, and the Secretaries of State for Scotland and the Home Department (being the Secretaries of State concerned with the sea-fishing industry in Scotland and Northern Ireland respectively) in exercise of the powers conferred on them by section 6 of the Sea Fish (Conservation) Act 1967(a) and of all other powers enabling them in that behalf, after consultation with the Board of Trade hereby make the following order :—

Citation and Commencement

1. This order may be cited as the Salmon and Migratory Trout (Drift-net Fishing) Restrictions on Landing (Extension) Order 1968 and shall come into operation on 15th February 1969.

Interpretation

2.—(1) In this order—
"the principal order" means the Salmon and Migratory Trout (Drift-net Fishing) Restrictions on Landing Order 1962(b) as amended (c).

(2) The Interpretation Act 1889(d) shall apply to the interpretation of this order as it applies to the interpretation of an Act of Parliament.

Extension of Period

3. Article 3 of the principal order shall be read and construed as if for the date 15th February 1969 there were substituted the date 15th February 1971.

(a) 1967 c. 84.   (b) S.I. 1962/1394 (1962 II, p. 1522).
(c) The relevant amending instruments are S.I. 1964/1962, 1965/2024, 1966/1545 (1964 III, p. 4288; 1965 III, p. 5991; 1966 III, p. 4378).   (d) 1889 c. 63.

In witness whereof the Official Seal of the Minister of Agriculture, Fisheries and Food is hereunto affixed on 4th December 1968.

(L.S.) *Cledwyn Hughes,*
Minister of Agriculture, Fisheries and Food.

Given under the Seal of the Secretary of State for Scotland on 6th December 1968.

(L.S.) *William Ross,*
Secretary of State for Scotland.

Given under the hand of the Secretary of State for the Home Department on 10th December 1968.

James Callaghan,
Secretary of State for the Home Department.

EXPLANATORY NOTE

(This Note is not part of the Order.)

The operation of the Salmon and Migratory Trout (Drift-net Fishing) Restrictions on Landing Order 1962 (which prohibits the landing anywhere in Great Britain of salmon or migratory trout caught by drift-net in specified waters around Great Britain except that such landings may be legally effected if the catching of the fish off the coasts of England and Wales has been authorised by a River Authority licence or in waters outside territorial waters adjacent to England and Wales by a licence issued by the Minister of Agriculture, Fisheries and Food) is extended for two years from 15th February 1969.

STATUTORY INSTRUMENTS

1968 No. 1978 (L.23)

COUNTY COURTS

The County Courts (Race Relations Jurisdiction) Order 1968

Made - - - -	11*th December* 1968
Coming into Operation	15*th January* 1969

I, Gerald, Baron Gardiner, Lord High Chancellor of Great Britain, in exercise of the powers conferred on me by section 19(2) and (3) of the Race Relations Act 1968**(a)**, hereby make the following Order:—

1. The courts mentioned in column 1 of the schedule to this Order are hereby appointed to have jurisdiction to entertain proceedings under section 19 of the Race Relations Act 1968 and the districts of those courts for the purpose of such proceedings shall, in addition to their existing districts, include the districts of the courts mentioned opposite thereto in column 2 of the schedule.

2.—(1) This Order may be cited as the County Courts (Race Relations Jurisdiction) Order 1968 and shall come into operation on 15th January 1969.

(2) The Interpretation Act 1889**(b)** shall apply to the interpretation of this Order as it applies to the interpretation of an Act of Parliament.

Dated 11th December 1968.

Gardiner, C.

(a) 1968 c. 71.   (b) 1889 c. 63.

SCHEDULE

Column 1	Column 2	
Courts having jurisdiction	Court districts constituting enlarged districts	
Birmingham	Bridgnorth	Redditch
	Bromsgrove	Rugby
	Burton on Trent	Shrewsbury
	Coventry	Stafford
	Dudley	Stoke on Trent
	Evesham	Stourbridge
	Great Malvern	Stratford on Avon
	Hereford	Tamworth
	Kettering	Uttoxeter
	Kidderminster	Walsall
	Kington	Warwick
	Leek	Wellingborough
	Leominster	Wellington
	Lichfield	Welshpool
	Ludlow	West Bromwich
	Market Drayton	Whitchurch
	Newcastle under Lyme	Wolverhampton
	Nuneaton	Worcester
Bristol	Bath	Melksham
	Bridgwater	Minehead
	Bridport	Ross
	Cheltenham	Stroud
	Chippenham	Swindon
	Cirencester	Taunton
	Devizes	Thornbury
	Dursley	Trowbridge
	Frome	Warminster
	Gloucester	Wells
	Malmesbury	Weston super Mare
	Marlborough	Wincanton
		Yeovil
Cambridge	Bishops Stortford	Kings Lynn
	Bury St. Edmunds	Lowestoft
	Cromer	March
	Downham Market	Newmarket
	East Dereham	Norwich
	Ely	Peterborough
	Fakenham	Stowmarket
	Great Yarmouth	Sudbury
	Halesworth	Swaffham
	Hitchin	Thetford
	Huntingdon	Wisbech
	Ipswich	Woodbridge
Canterbury	Ashford	Margate
	Deal	Ramsgate
	Dover	Sheerness
	Folkestone	Sittingbourne
Cardiff	Aberdare	Chepstow
	Aberystwyth	Haverfordwest

Column 1	Column 2	
Courts having jurisdiction	Court districts constituting enlarged districts	
Cardiff (*cont.*)	Ammanford	Lampeter
	Bargoed	Llandovery
	Barry	Llanelli
	Blackwood, Tredegar	Merthyr Tydfil
	& Abertillery	Monmouth
	Brecknock	Neath & Port Talbot
	Bridgend	Newport (Mon.)
	Builth	Pontypool &
	Caerphilly	Abergavenny
	Cardigan	Pontypridd &
	Carmarthen	Ystradyfodwg
		Swansea
Carlisle	Barrow in Furness &	Whitehaven & Millom
	Ulverston	Windermere
	Kendal	Workington &
	Penrith & Appleby	Cockermouth
Exeter	Axminster & Chard	Newton Abbot
	Barnstaple	Okehampton
	Bideford	South Molton
	Holsworthy	Tiverton
	Honiton	Torquay
Leeds	Barnsley	Malton
	Beverley	Otley
	Bradford	Pontefract
	Bridlington	Ripon
	Dewsbury	Rotherham
	Doncaster	Scarborough
	Goole	Sheffield
	Great Driffield	Skipton
	Halifax	Thorne
	Harrogate	Wakefield
	Huddersfield	Whitby
	Keighley	York
	Kingston on Hull	
Manchester	Accrington	Leigh
	Altrincham	Liverpool
	Ashton under Lyne &	Macclesfield
	Stalybridge	Nelson
	Birkenhead	Northwich
	Blackburn	Oldham
	Blackpool	Preston
	Bolton	Rawtenstall
	Burnley	Rochdale
	Bury	Runcorn
	Congleton	St. Helens & Widnes
	Chester	Salford
	Chorley	Southport
	Crewe	Stockport
	Ellesmere Port	Todmorden
	Hyde	Warrington
	Lancaster	Wigan

Column 1	Column 2
Courts having jurisdiction	Court districts constituting enlarged districts
Newcastle upon Tyne	Alnwick — Hexham Barnard Castle — Middlesbrough Berwick upon Tweed — Morpeth Bishop Auckland — Northallerton Blyth — North Shields Consett — Richmond Darlington — South Shields Durham — Stockton on Tees Gateshead — Sunderland Hartlepool
Nottingham	Alfreton — Loughborough Ashby de la Zouch — Louth Boston — Mansfield Buxton — Market Harborough Chesterfield — Matlock Derby — Melton Mowbray East Retford — Newark Gainsborough — Oakham Grantham — Scunthorpe Great Grimsby — Skegness & Spilsby Hinckley — Sleaford Ilkeston — Spalding Leicester — Stamford Lincoln — Worksop
Oxford	Aylesbury — Northampton Banbury — Reading Bletchley & Leighton Buzzard — Thame Chipping Norton — Wallingford Newbury — Wantage Witney
Plymouth	Bodmin — Penzance Camelford — Redruth Helston — St. Austell Kingsbridge — Tavistock Launceston — Truro & Falmouth Liskeard Newquay
Southampton	Andover — Poole Arundel — Portsmouth Basingstoke — Ringwood Bournemouth — Salisbury Chichester — Shaftesbury Dorchester — Swanage Lymington — Weymouth Newport, Isle of Wight — Wimborne Minster Petersfield — Winchester
Westminster	Aldershot — Haywards Heath Amersham — Hemel Hempstead Barnet — Hertford Bedford — High Wycombe

Column 1	Column 2	
Courts having jurisdiction	Court districts constituting enlarged districts	
Westminster (*cont.*)	Biggleswade	Horsham
	Bloomsbury &	Ilford
	Marylebone	Kingston upon Thames
	Bow	Lambeth
	Braintree	Lewes
	Brentford	Luton
	Brentwood	Maidstone
	Brighton	Maldon
	Bromley	Mayor's &
	Chelmsford	City of London
	Clerkenwell	Reigate
	Colchester & Clacton	Rochester
	Cranbrook	Saint Albans
	Croydon	Sevenoaks
	Dartford	Shoreditch
	Dorking	Slough
	Eastbourne	Southend
	East Grinstead	Southwark
	Edmonton	Tonbridge
	Epsom	Tunbridge Wells
	Gravesend	Uxbridge
	Grays Thurrock	Wandsworth
	Guildford	Watford
	Harlow	West London
	Harwich	Willesden
	Hastings	Woolwich
		Worthing
Wrexham	Bala & Corwen	
	Bangor	
	Caernarvon	Llanidloes
	Conway, Llandudno &	Llanrwst
	Colwyn Bay	Machynlleth
	Denbigh & Ruthin	Mold
	Dolgellau	Newtown
	Holywell	Oswestry
	Knighton	Portmadoc & Blaenau
	Llandrindod Wells	Festiniog
	Llangefni, Holyhead &	Pwllheli
	Menai Bridge	Rhyl

EXPLANATORY NOTE

(*This Note is not part of the Order.*)

This Order appoints 16 county courts in England and Wales as courts to exercise jurisdiction in proceedings brought under the Race Relations Act 1968, and defines the districts of those courts as enlarged for the purpose of this jurisdiction. The courts are the Birmingham, Bristol, Cambridge, Canterbury, Cardiff, Carlisle, Exeter, Leeds, Manchester, Newcastle upon Tyne, Nottingham, Oxford, Plymouth, Southampton, Westminster and Wrexham County Courts.

STATUTORY INSTRUMENTS

1968 No. 1979

COMMONWEALTH TELEGRAPHS

The Commonwealth Telegraphs
(Cable and Wireless Ltd. Pension) Regulations 1968

Made - - - -	12*th December* 1968
Laid before Parliament	19*th December* 1968
Coming into Operation	1*st January* 1969

I, The Right Honourable John Thomson Stonehouse, M.P., Her Majesty's Postmaster General, with the consent of the Minister for the Civil Service(a), by virtue of the powers vested in me by section 6 of the Commonwealth Telegraphs Act 1949(b) as amended by section 28 of the Post Office Act 1961(c) and of all other powers enabling me in this behalf, do hereby make the following regulations:

1.—(1) These regulations shall be read as one with the Commonwealth Telegraphs (Cable and Wireless Ltd. Pension) Regulations 1955(d) and the Commonwealth Telegraphs (Cable and Wireless Ltd. Pension) Regulations 1962(e).

(2) The Interpretation Act 1889(f) shall apply for the interpretation of these regulations as it applies for the interpretation of an Act of Parliament.

2. The following shall be substituted for regulation 2(1)(*c*) of the Commonwealth Telegraphs (Cable and Wireless Ltd. Pension) Regulations 1962 (which regulation provides for Cable and Wireless Ltd. to establish a widows' pension scheme):

"(*c*) dies, whether prior to or after his being retired from pensionable service in the Post Office."

3. These regulations may be cited as the Commonwealth Telegraphs (Cable and Wireless Ltd. Pension) Regulations 1968 and shall come into operation on the 1st day of January 1969.

Dated 11th December 1968.

John Stonehouse,
Her Majesty's Postmaster General.

Consent of the Minister for the Civil Service given under his Official Seal 12th December 1968.

(L.S.)   *J. E. Herbecq,*
Authorised by the Minister for the Civil Service.

(a) See S.I. 1968/1656 (1968 III, p. 4485).   (b) 1949 c. 39.
(c) 1961 c. 15.   (d) S.I. 1955/1893 (1955 I, p. 500).
(e) S.I. 1962/196 (1962 I, p. 193).   (f) 1889 c. 63.

EXPLANATORY NOTE

(This Note is not part of the Regulations.)

The Commonwealth Telegraph (Cable and Wireless Ltd. Pension) Regulations 1962 made provision for Cable and Wireless Ltd. to establish an approved pension scheme for widows or children of certain former male employees of the Company who became employed in the Post Office as a result of the transfer of the United Kingdom assets of the Company into public ownership on the 1st September 1950 and who die prior to retirement from pensionable service in the Post Office. These regulations amend the 1962 regulations so as to enable a pension to be paid to the widow or children whether the employee dies prior to or after his retirement.

STATUTORY INSTRUMENTS

1968 No. 1980

TRANSPORT

The National Bus Company (Transfer of Additional Securities) Order 1968

Made - - -	12th December 1968
Coming into Operation	13th December 1968

The Minister of Transport makes this Order in exercise of his powers under section 28(4) of the Transport Act 1968(**a**) and of all other enabling powers :—

1. This Order may be cited as the National Bus Company (Transfer of Additional Securities) Order 1968, and shall come into operation on the 13th December 1968.

2. There shall be added to Schedule 7 to the Transport Act 1968 the following body, namely—

London Country Bus Services Limited

(being a body whose activities are similar to those of the bodies already listed in the said Schedule and whose securities are beneficially owned by the Transport Holding Company).

Sealed with the Official Seal of the Minister of Transport the 12th December 1968.

(L.S.)

T. L. Beagley,
An Under Secretary of
the Ministry of Transport.

EXPLANATORY NOTE

(This Note is not part of the Order.)

This Order adds London Country Bus Services Ltd., to the list of bodies in Schedule 7 to the Transport Act 1968 whose securities are to be transferred to the National Bus Company on 1st January 1969 by virtue of section 28(1) of the Transport Act 1968 and of the Transport Act 1968 (Commencement No. 1) Order 1968 (S.I. 1968/1822).

(**a**) 1968 c.73.

STATUTORY INSTRUMENTS

1968 No. 1982 (S.179)

ROADS AND BRIDGES, SCOTLAND

The Special Roads (Classes of Traffic) (Scotland) Order 1968

Made - - - -	13*th November* 1968
Laid before Parliament	20*th November* 1968
Coming into Operation	15*th December* 1968

In exercise of the powers conferred on me by section 2(3) of the Special Roads Act 1949(a), as read with the Transfer of Functions (Roads, Bridges and Ferries) Order 1955(b), and of all other powers enabling me in that behalf, I hereby make the following order:—

1.—(1) This order may be cited as the Special Roads (Classes of Traffic) (Scotland) Order 1968 and shall come into operation on the fifth day following the day it is approved by Parliament.

(2) In this order, "Schedule 2 to the Act of 1949" means Schedule 2 to the Special Roads Act 1949, as amended by the Special Roads (Classes of Traffic) (Scotland) Order 1964(c).

(3) The Interpretation Act 1889(d) shall apply for the interpretation of this order as it applies for the interpretation of an Act of Parliament.

2. The composition of the class of traffic specified in Schedule 2 to the Act of 1949 as Class II shall be varied by adding at the end of the specification of the said Class II in that Schedule the following paragraph—

"Light locomotives, being motor vehicles on which is mounted apparatus designed to lift a disabled motor vehicle or trailer, and any such disabled vehicle or any towing implement drawn by such a locomotive, the said locomotives being vehicles in respect of which the following condition is satisfied, that is to say, that the maximum speed at which the vehicle, when not drawing a trailer, may be driven under section 78 of the Road Traffic Regulation Act 1967(e) on roads which are not special roads is not less than twenty miles per hour."

3. In Schedule 2 to the Act of 1949, there shall be added at the end of the last paragraph (which relates to the interpretation of that Schedule) the words

(a) 1949 c. 32.
(b) S.I. 1955/1955 (1955 I, p.1205).
(c) S.I. 1964/1084 (1964 II, p. 2398).
(d) 1889 c. 63.
(e) 1967 c.76.

"and 'towing implement' has the same meaning as in the Motor Vehicles (Construction and Use) Regulations 1966(a).".

William Ross,
One of Her Majesty's Principal
Secretaries of State.

St. Andrew's House,
   Edinburgh, 1.

13th November 1968.

EXPLANATORY NOTE

(This Note is not part of the Order.)

Schedule 2 to the Special Roads Act 1949, as amended by the Special Roads (Classes of Traffic) (Scotland) Order 1964, specifies classes of traffic for the purposes of special roads.

This Order, by adding to Class II of that Schedule breakdown vehicles of up to 11½ tons in weight and disabled vehicles drawn thereby, will enable them to use motorways.

(a) S.I. 1966/1288 (1966 III, p. 3493).

STATUTORY INSTRUMENTS

1968 No. 1986

AGRICULTURE

GUARANTEED PRICES AND ASSURED MARKETS

The Eggs (Protection of Guarantees) Order 1968

Made - - -	16*th December* 1968
Laid before Parliament	19*th December* 1968
Coming into Operation	23*rd December* 1968

The Minister of Agriculture, Fisheries and Food and the Secretaries of State respectively concerned with agriculture in Scotland and Northern Ireland acting jointly in exercise of the powers conferred upon them by sections 5, 9(4) and 35(3) of the Agriculture Act 1957(**a**) and section 70 of the Agriculture Act 1967(**b**), and of all other powers enabling them in that behalf, hereby make the following order :—

Citation and commencement

1. This order may be cited as the Eggs (Protection of Guarantees) Order 1968 ; and shall come into operation on 23rd December 1968.

Interpretation

2.—(1) In this order, unless the context otherwise requires—

"approved mark" means, in relation to each of the descriptions of hen eggs and the description of duck eggs specified in column 2 of the Schedule to this order, the word relative to such description specified in column 3 of that Schedule, together with, in each case and in close proximity to that word, the registration number allotted by the Board to the packing station where the eggs are packed ;

"the Board" means the British Egg Marketing Board constituted by the British Egg Marketing Scheme 1956(**c**) which has effect as if made under the Agricultural Marketing Act 1958(**d**) ;

"container" means a container which is capable of holding not less than 15 dozen eggs ;

"duck eggs" means eggs in shell laid by domestic ducks in the United Kingdom ;

"first quality", in relation to duck eggs, means fresh and free from taint, the shells being clean and unstained, sound and of good texture and shape, the contents being free from visible blemish and discolouration, the yolk

---

(**a**) 1957 c. 57. (**b**) 1967 c. 22.
(**c**) S.I. 1956/2082 (1956 I, p. 66). (**d**) 1958 c. 47.

being central and translucent and the white being translucent with the air space not exceeding one-quarter of an inch in depth ;

"first quality", in relation to hen eggs, means fresh and free from taint, the shells being clean and unstained, sound and of good texture and shape, the contents being free from visible blemish and discolouration, the yolk being central, translucent and faintly but not clearly defined and the white being translucent with the air space not exceeding one-quarter of an inch in depth ;

"fresh eggs" means hen eggs and duck eggs which have not been preserved by cold or chemical storage or any other means ;

"hen eggs" means eggs in shell laid by domestic fowls in the United Kingdom ;

"the Ministers" means the Minister of Agriculture, Fisheries and Food and the Secretaries of State respectively concerned with agriculture in Scotland and Northern Ireland ;

"the Minister", in relation to any part of the United Kingdom, means either that one of the Ministers who is concerned with agriculture in that part, or that Minister and either or both of the others acting jointly ;

"packer" means any person appointed by the Board to purchase, grade and pack hen eggs on their behalf and includes the Board insofar as they exercise those functions ;

"sale by retail" means any sale to a person buying otherwise than for the purpose of resale but does not include a sale to a caterer for the purposes of his catering business, or a sale to a manufacturer for the purposes of his manufacturing business ; and "manufacturing" means using eggs, for the purposes of a trade or business (other than a catering business), in the composition, manufacture or preparation of any other product, and corresponding expressions have corresponding meanings.

(2) The Interpretation Act 1889(a) shall apply to the interpretation of this order as it applies to the interpretation of an Act of Parliament and as if this order and the orders hereby revoked were Acts of Parliament.

Marking of containers

3.—(1) Every packer shall, as soon as practicable, pack all eggs to which this article applies in containers, being the containers in which the eggs are to be removed from the packing premises, and each such container shall bear the approved mark relating to the eggs packed therein and shall contain eggs of not more than one weight grade. The approved mark shall appear distinctly and legibly in letters and figures not less than half an inch high and shall be applied by means of stamping with indelible ink or printing or by means of a label affixed to the container, or by more than one of those methods.

(2) The eggs to which this article applies are—

(*a*) all hen eggs purchased by a packer on behalf of the Board which weigh not less than one and a half ounces each and which are either of first quality or dirty but otherwise of first quality ;

(*b*) all duck eggs sold to the Board by a packer which are either of first quality or dirty but otherwise of first quality.

Restriction on sale, etc. and use for hatching of certain eggs

4. No person shall sell, offer or expose for sale or have in possession for sale for hatching or shall use for hatching, or cause or permit to be so used—

(**a**) 1889 c. 63.

(*a*) any hen eggs which weigh not less than one and a half ounces each and which are either of first quality or dirty but otherwise of first quality and as respects which he knows or has reason to believe that they have previously been purchased by a packer on behalf of the Board ;

(*b*) any duck eggs which are either of first quality or dirty but otherwise of first quality and as respects which he knows or has reason to believe that they have previously been sold by a packer to the Board.

Keeping and production of records

5.—(1) Every packer shall keep or cause to be kept and shall produce on demand by an authorised officer of the Minister or, in Northern Ireland, of the Ministry of Agriculture in Northern Ireland an accurate record of every purchase, sale and use of fresh eggs by him (whether or not on behalf of the Board), such record to distinguish between hen eggs and duck eggs and to include the following particulars :—

(*a*) the date of each purchase, sale and use ;

(*b*) the name and address of each person from whom he buys and to whom he sells any such eggs ;

(*c*) in each case the description or descriptions and number of such eggs bought, sold and used respectively, showing separately (except where this is not reasonably practicable) the number of eggs of each quality and weight grade ;

(*d*) the price or prices paid on each purchase and sale ;

and if so required by notice in writing served on him by or on behalf of the Minister any such record shall be kept in such form as the Minister shall prescribe in the said notice.

(2) Every packer shall retain the record of any transaction and use of eggs required to be kept pursuant to this article for two years from the date of such transaction or use.

Right of entry

6. Any authorised officer of the Minister or, in Northern Ireland, of the Ministry of Agriculture for Northern Ireland may at all reasonable times enter upon the land used for the storage, grading, packing, or sale other than by retail of hen eggs or duck eggs and may inspect and take samples of any such eggs found upon land so used.

Right to demand production of books, accounts and records

7. Any authorised officer of the Minister or, in Northern Ireland, of the Ministry of Agriculture for Northern Ireland may require any person concerned by way of trade or business in the storage, grading, packing, hatching or sale other than by retail of hen eggs or duck eggs to produce on demand books, accounts and records relating to the purchase and sale of any such eggs.

Service of notices

8.—(1) Any notice required or authorised by this order to be given to or served on any person shall be sufficiently given or served if it is delivered to him personally or left at his last known place of abode or business or sent to him by post in a letter addressed to him at the aforesaid place of abode or business.

(2) Any notice required or authorised by this order to be given to or served on an incorporated company or body shall be sufficiently given or served if

given to or served on the secretary or clerk of the company or body. For the purposes of this order and of section 26 of the Interpretation Act 1889, the proper address of such secretary or clerk shall be that of the registered or principal office of the company or body.

Delegation of functions as respects Northern Ireland

9. The functions conferred or imposed on the Minister by this order may be exercised in relation to Northern Ireland by the Minister of Agriculture for Northern Ireland.

Revocation

10. The Eggs (Protection of Guarantees) Order 1958(**a**) and the Eggs (Protection of Guarantees) (Amendment) Order 1961(**b**) are hereby revoked.

In Witness whereof the Official Seal of the Minister of Agriculture, Fisheries and Food is hereunto affixed on 16th December 1968.

(L.S.)   *Cledwyn Hughes,*
                          Minister of Agriculture, Fisheries and Food.

Given under the Seal of the Secretary of State for Scotland on 12th December 1968.

(L.S.)   *William Ross,*
                               Secretary of State for Scotland.

Given under the hand of the Secretary of State for the Home Department on 13th December 1968.

James Callaghan,
Secretary of State for the Home Department.

(**a**) S.I. 1958/957 (1958 I, p.80).   (**b**) S.I. 1961/90 (1961 I, p.151).

Article 2(1)

SCHEDULE

APPROVED MARKS

Column 1	Column 2		Column 3
Kind of Eggs	Description		Approved Mark
	State or Condition	Weight grade	
Hen eggs	First quality or dirty but otherwise of first quality	Not less than $2\frac{3}{16}$ ounces	LARGE
		Less than $2\frac{3}{16}$ ounces but not less than $1\frac{7}{8}$ ounces	STANDARD
		Less than $1\frac{7}{8}$ ounces but not less than $1\frac{5}{8}$ ounces	MEDIUM
		Less than $1\frac{5}{8}$ ounces but not less than $1\frac{1}{2}$ ounces	SMALL
Duck eggs	First quality or dirty but otherwise of first quality	All weights	DUCK

together with, in each case and in close proximity to the word, the registration number allotted by the Board to the packing station where the eggs are packed

EXPLANATORY NOTE

(This Note is not part of the Order.)

This order supersedes the Eggs (Protection of Guarantees) Order 1958, as amended.

The principal change is that packers are required to pack into containers bearing approved marks all hen and duck eggs which are eligible for subsidy and are sold to the British Egg Marketing Board through packing stations instead of being required to mark the eggs.

STATUTORY INSTRUMENTS

1968 No. 1987

WAGES COUNCILS

The Wages Regulation (Cutlery) Order 1968

Made - - -	16*th December* 1968
Coming into Operation	17*th January* 1969

Whereas the Secretary of State has received from the Cutlery Wages Council (Great Britain) the wages regulation proposals set out in the Schedules 1 and 2 hereof;

Now, therefore, having by virtue of her powers under Schedule 2 to the Prices and Incomes Act 1968(a) postponed the making of this Order, the Secretary of State in exercise of her powers under section 11 of the Wages Councils Act 1959(b), and of all other powers enabling her in that behalf, hereby makes the following Order:—

1. This Order may be cited as the Wages Regulation (Cutlery) Order 1968.

2.—(1) In this Order the expression "the specified date" means the 17th January 1969, provided that where, as respects any worker who is paid wages at intervals not exceeding seven days, that date does not correspond with the beginning of the period for which the wages are paid, the expression "the specified date" means, as respects that worker, the beginning of the next such period following that date.

(2) The Interpretation Act 1889(c) shall apply to the interpretation of this Order as it applies to the interpretation of an Act of Parliament and as if this Order and the Order hereby revoked were Acts of Parliament.

3. The wages regulation proposals set out in the Schedules 1 and 2 hereof shall have effect as from the specified date and as from that date the Wages Regulation (Cutlery) Order 1967(d) shall cease to have effect.

Signed by order of the Secretary of State.

16th December 1968.

A. A. Jarratt,
Deputy Under Secretary of State,
Department of Employment and
Productivity.

Article 3   SCHEDULE 1

The following minimum remuneration shall be substituted for the statutory minimum remuneration fixed by the Wages Regulation (Cutlery) Order 1967 (Order C.**T.** (84)).

(a) 1968 c. 42.	(b) 1959 c. 69.
(c) 1889 c. 63.	(d) S.I. 1967/1215 (1967 II, p. 3540).

STATUTORY MINIMUM REMUNERATION

PART I

GENERAL MINIMUM TIME RATES AND PIECE WORK BASIS TIME RATES

	Column 1 General minimum time rate per hour	Column 2 Piece work basis time rate per hour
	s. d.	s. d.
I.—MALE WORKERS OF 21 YEARS OF AGE OR OVER		
A.—WORKERS IN THE TABLE, BUTCHER, PALETTE, SHOE AND TOOL KNIFE, AND FORK AND STEEL AND KNIFE SHARPENER SECTION OF THE TRADE		
1. HAND FORGERS OF BLADES OR FORKS: (i.e. workers who, without supervision, forge entirely by hand from the bar or rod any kind of blade or fork used in this section of the trade and also mark and harden and temper the blade or fork where necessary)	5 8	6 6¼
2. FORGERS OF TABLE OR BUTCHER STEELS	5 7	6 5¼
3. ANNEALERS OF TABLE OR BUTCHER STEELS	5 5	6 2¾
4. STRIPPERS OF TABLE OR BUTCHER STEELS...	5 5	6 2¾
5. SCOURERS OF TABLE OR BUTCHER STEELS...	5 5	6 2¾
6. GOFFERS (MACHINE FORGERS, ROLLERS, STAMPERS) OF BLADES OR FORKS employed in:		
(a) Mooding from the bar	5 8	6 6¼
(b) Plating	5 8	6 6¼
(c) Bolstering moods or blanks or off the bar ...	5 8	6 6¼
(d) Drawing	5 8	6 6¼
(e) Cutting out or blanking	5 7	6 5¼
(f) Rolling	5 7	6 5¼
(g) Sateing	5 8	6 6¼
(h) Pronging forks	5 7	6 5¼
(i) Punching guard hole in forks	5 7	6 5¼
(j) Trapping forks	5 5	6 2¾
(k) Tanging	5 5	6 2¾
(l) Stamping	5 5	6 2¾

	Column 1 General minimum time rate per hour	Column 2 Piece work basis time rate per hour
	s. d.	s. d.
7. SMITHERS, HARDENERS AND TEMPERERS OF BLADES:		
(a) who smith and/or shape by hand, and who also mark and harden and temper the blades where necessary	5 7	6 5¼
(b) who by hand harden and temper throughout ...	5 7	6 5¼
(c) who by hand harden only or temper only, and who use a hand hammer in connection therewith ...	5 5	6 2¾
(d) who by hand harden only or temper only, and who do not use a hand hammer in connection therewith	5 5	6 2¾
(e) who harden by machine and who in connection therewith straighten the blades by hand	5 5	6 2¾
(f) who harden by machine and who do not straighten the blades by hand in connection therewith ...	5 4	6 1¾
(g) who flatten or straighten blades by drop stamp or power hammer	5 5	6 2¾
8. HAND GRINDERS OF BLADES:		
Grade I (i.e. hand grinders (other than hand grinders of grade II) employed on grinding from the rough blank, or whittening, or glazing, or finishing any kind of blade used in this section of the trade) ...	5 7	6 5¼
Grade II (i.e. hand grinders employed only in tumbling, or in neck grinding and glazing, or in blade buffing, or employed only in glazing palette blades, or putty blades, or scrapers)	5 5	6 2¾
9. HAND GRINDERS AND/OR HAND GLAZIERS OF FORKS ...	5 7	6 5¼
10. FORK GUARDERS:		
Grade I (i.e. workers who perform any of the following operations, viz.: forging guards or springs from bar steel, hardening or tempering springs, or boring holes in forks or guards)	5 7	6 5¼
Grade II (i.e. workers who perform any of the following operations, viz.: grinding or glazing guards, fitting springs or guards into guard holes, riveting guards to forks, filing or grinding rivet heads flush with shank, or fine glazing shanks)	5 5	6 2¾
11. HAND OR MACHINE GRINDERS OF TABLE OR BUTCHER STEELS	5 7	6 5¼
12. MACHINE GRINDERS OF BLADES:		
Grade I (i.e. foremen or charge-hands in the machine grinding branch)	5 7	6 5¼
Grade II (i.e. workers (other than foremen or charge-hands) who set up and work a grinding machine) ...	5 5	6 2¾
Grade III (i.e. workers who work a grinding machine but do not set it up)	5 4	6 1¾

	Column 1 General minimum time rate per hour	Column 2 Piece work basis time rate per hour
	s. d.	s. d.
13. SWAGERS OF BLADES:		
(a) working without supervision	5 7	6 5¼
(b) working under supervision	5 5	6 2¾
14. MACHINE FINISHERS OF BLADES:		
Grade I (i.e. foremen or charge-hands in the machine finishing branch)	5 7	6 5¼
Grade II (i.e. workers (other than foremen or charge-hands) who set up and work a finishing machine) ...	5 5	6 2¾
Grade III (i.e. workers who work a finishing machine but do not set it up)	5 4	6 1¾
15. MIRROR POLISHERS, ETCHERS, SERRATORS:		
(a) Foremen or charge-hands in the mirror polishing, etching (including electrical etching) or serrating branch...	5 7	6 5¼
(b) Mirror polishers	5 5	6 2¾
(c) Etchers (including clectrical etchers)	5 5	6 2¾
(d) Serrators	5 5	6 2¾
16. CUTLERS:		
Grade I (i.e. workers without supervision employed in preparing and assembling to the finished article any knife, fork, steel or knife sharpener hafted with any material, including those with caps and ferrules; or a charge-hand or teamster in charge of a team engaged in such work)	5 7	6 5¼
Grade II (i.e. workers under supervision employed in preparing or assembling parts for the work described in grade I)	5 5	6 2¾

B.—WORKERS IN THE SPRING KNIFE SECTION OF THE TRADE

17. SCALE TANG PRUNER BLADE HAND FORGERS (i.e. workers who, without supervision, forge entirely by hand from bar or rod steel, scale tang pruner blades and also mark and harden and temper the forged blades where necessary)	5 8	6 6¼
18. PEN AND POCKET BLADE HAND FORGERS (other than forgers of scale tang pruner blades) (i.e. workers who, without supervision, forge entirely by hand from bar or rod steel, any kind of blade (other than scale tang pruner blades) used in this section of the trade and also mark and harden and temper the forged blades where necessary)	5 7	6 5¼

	Column 1 General minimum time rate per hour	Column 2 Piece work basis time rate per hour
	s. d.	s. d.
19. MACHINE FORGERS:		
Grade I (i.e. machine forgers who set up their own tools)	5 5	6 2¾
Grade II (i.e. machine forgers who do not set up their own tools)	5 5	6 2¾
20. PEN AND POCKET BLADE SMITHERS (i.e. workers who, without supervision, smith and/or shape by hand from cut-out moods any kind of blade used in this section of the trade but who do not forge by hand from bar or rod steel)	5 5	6 2¾
21. MARKERS AND HARDENERS:		
Grade I (i.e. workers who both mark sides or tangs by hand and harden and temper)	5 7	6 5¼
Grade II (i.e. workers who either harden and temper or mark sides or tangs by hand or press either by controlled furnace or open hearth but who do not both harden and temper and mark)...	5 5	6 2¾
22. HAND GRINDERS AND FINISHERS	5 7	6 5¼
23. SWAGERS working without supervision	5 7	6 5¼
24. SCALE AND SPRING MAKERS:		
Grade I (i.e. scale and spring makers who set up their own tools)	5 7	6 5¼
Grade II (i.e. scale and spring makers who do not set up their own tools)	5 5	6 2¾
Scale and spring makers are workers who forge iron bolsters, stamp scales of nickel silver or iron and/or cut out webs, springs, moods or any other articles used in this section of the trade.		
25. MATERIAL PREPARERS (other than workers to whom the minimum rates for cutlers in paragraph 26 and for covering cutters in paragraphs 27 to 32 inclusive apply)	5 5	6 2¾
26. CUTLERS:		
Grade I (i.e. workers who are employed in preparing and assembling to the finished article or in assembling to the finished article the following types of knives), viz.:—		
Two-ended fitted work; sunk-joint two, three and four blades; all lobster work; ivory and bone budders; lock knives; sporting work (except common nutcracks, common screw knives and common black clocks); tyne knives; pruner knives (other than scale tang pruners)	5 7	6 5¼

	Column 1 General minimum time rate per hour	Column 2 Piece work basis time rate per hour
	s. d.	s. d.
26. CUTLERS—contd.		
Grade II (i.e. workers who are employed in preparing and assembling to the finished article or in assembling to the finished article (including hafting and setting-in) any types of knives (including scale tang pruner knives and cattle knives) other than those to which the minimum rate for grade I workers applies)	5 5	6 2¾
C.—WORKERS IN THE COVERING CUTTING SECTION OF THE TRADE		
27. IVORY CUTTERS:		
Grade I (i.e. workers who, without supervision, produce from the natural material, handles or scales for cutlery)	5 8	6 6¼
Grade II (i.e. workers who, under supervision, produce from the natural material, handles or scales for cutlery)	5 5	6 2¾
28. CELLULOID CUTTERS AND OTHER SYNTHETIC MATERIAL AND BONE CUTTERS:		
Grade I (i.e. workers who, without supervision, cut or shape from sheets, handles or scales for cutlery) ...	5 7	6 5¼
Grade II (i.e. workers who, under supervision, cut or shape from sheets, handles or scales for cutlery) ...	5 5	6 2¾
29. WOOD SCALE CUTTERS:		
Grade I (i.e. workers who, without supervision, cut to length, shape and run off, and who sharpen and set their saws)	5 7	6 5¼
Grade II (i.e. workers who saw or cut up under supervision)	5 5	6 2¾
30. PEARL CUTTERS (i.e. workers who, without supervision, cut pearl scales or handles for cutlery)	5 7	6 5¼
31. HORN SCALE CUTTERS:		
Grade I (i.e. workers who, without supervision, cut to length, shape and run off, and who sharpen and set their saws)	5 7	6 5¼
Grade II (i.e. workers who saw or cut up under supervision)	5 5	6 2¾
32. HORN SCALE PRESSERS	5 5	6 2¾

	Column 1 General minimum time rate per hour	Column 2 Piece work basis time rate per hour
	s. d.	s. d.
D.—WORKERS IN THE SCISSORS SECTION OF THE TRADE		
33. HAND FORGERS	5 7	6 5¼
34. DROP STAMPERS AND PRESSERS:		
Grade I (i.e. drop stampers and/or pressers, who set up their own tools)	5 7	6 5¼
Grade II (i.e. drop stampers and/or pressers, who do not set up their own tools)	5 5	6 2¾
35. CUTTERS-OUT OR TRIMMERS:		
Grade I (i.e. cutters-out or trimmers, who set up their own tools)	5 5	6 2¾
Grade II (i.e. cutters-out or trimmers, who do not set up their own tools)	5 4	6 1¾
36. FILERS:		
Grade I (i.e. filers of any scissors known in the trade as " filed-out " scissors)	5 7	6 5¼
Grade II (i.e. filers of any scissors except those specified in grade I)	5 5	6 2¾
37. BORERS AND HARDENERS:		
Grade I (i.e. borers and hardeners of any hand forged scissors or of any of the following classes of machine forged scissors, viz.: paper scissors, tailors' shears and trimmers, bent work, surgeons' scissors, polished work)	5 5	6 2¾
Grade II (i.e. borers and hardeners of any scissors except those specified in grade I)	5 5	6 2¾
38. HAND GRINDERS AND HAND FINISHERS:		
Grade I (i.e. hand grinders and/or hand finishers of any hand forged scissors or of any of the following classes of machine forged scissors, viz.: paper scissors, tailors' shears and trimmers, bent work, surgeons' scissors, polished work and all scissors " done twice ")	5 7	6 5¼
Grade II (i.e. hand grinders and/or hand finishers of any scissors " done once ", except scissors of cast metal or pressed wire)	5 5	6 2¦
Grade III (i.e. hand grinders and/or hand finishers of any scissors of cast metal or pressed wire)... ...	5 5	6 2¾

	Column 1 General minimum time rate per hour	Column 2 Piece work basis time rate per hour
	s. d.	s. d.
39. MACHINE GRINDERS:		
Grade I (i.e. foremen or charge-hands in the machine grinding branch)	5 7	6 5¼
Grade II (i.e. workers (other than foremen or charge-hands) who set up and work a grinding machine) ...	5 5	6 2¾
Grade III (i.e. workers who work a grinding machine but do not set it up)	5 4	6 1¾
40. PUTTERS-TOGETHER:		
Grade I (i.e. putters-together of any hand forged scissors or any of the following classes of machine forged scissors, viz.: paper scissors, tailors' shears and trimmers, bent work, surgeons' scissors, polished work and all scissors " done twice ") ...	5 7	6 5¼
Grade II (i.e. putters-together of any scissors " done once ", except scissors of cast metal or pressed wire)	5 5	6 2¾
Grade III (i.e. putters-together of any scissors of cast metal or pressed wire)	5 5	6 2¾
41. PLATERS:		
Grade I (i.e. platers who make up the solutions for plating and maintain and supervise the plating shop)	5 7	6 5¼
Grade II (i.e. all other platers not included under grade I)	5 4	6 1¾

E.—WORKERS IN THE RAZOR SECTION OF THE TRADE

WORKERS EMPLOYED IN CONNECTION WITH THE MAKING OF RAZORS OTHER THAN SAFETY RAZORS

For the purpose of the minimum rates set out in this section, hollow ground blades are blades ground on a stone not exceeding 8-in. in diameter. Flat side blades are blades ground on a stone exceeding 8-in. in diameter.

	Column 1	Column 2
42. HAND FORGERS AND HARDENERS who hand forge razor blades or harden hand forged or machine forged razor blades	5 7	6 5¼
43. DROP STAMPERS (machine forgers) of razor blades:		
Grade I (i.e. workers who set up their own tools) ...	5 7	6 5¼
Grade II (i.e. workers who do not set up their own tools)	5 5	6 2¾

	Column 1 General minimum time rate per hour	Column 2 Piece work basis time rate per hour
	s. d.	s. d.
44. CUTTERS-OUT OR TRIMMERS:		
Grade I (i.e. workers who set up their own tools) ...	5 5	6 2¾
Grade II (i.e. workers who do not set up their own tools)	5 4	6 1¾
45. HAND GRINDERS, HAND FINISHERS AND MACHINE GRINDERS of hand forged or machine forged blades:		
Grade I (i.e. workers employed on hollow ground blades)	5 7	6 5¼
Grade II (i.e. workers employed on "flat side" blades)	5 5	6 2¾
46. SETTERS-IN AND WHETTERS:		
Grade I (i.e. workers employed in setting-in or whetting hollow ground blades)	5 7	6 5¼
Grade II (i.e. workers employed in setting-in or whetting "flat side" blades)...	5 5	6 2¾
F.—WORKERS IN ALL SECTIONS OF THE TRADE		
47. WAREHOUSE BUFFERS AND WAREHOUSE WHETTERS:		
Employed on the operations of warehouse buffing or warehouse whetting	5 4	6 1¾
48. MALE WORKERS other than those to whom the minimum rates set out in paragraphs 1 to 47 apply	5 4	6 1¾

MALE LATE ENTRANTS

49. Notwithstanding the provisions of paragraphs 1 to 48 (inclusive), the general minimum time rate and piece work basis time rate applicable to a male worker who has entered or who shall hereafter enter the trade for the first time at or over the age of 21 years shall be as follows:—

During the first six months of employment in the trade ... ... 80 per cent.

During the second six months of employment in the trade ... 90 per cent.

of the general minimum time rate or piece work basis time rate otherwise appropriate under paragraphs 1 to 48 (inclusive).

After 12 months' employment in the trade the worker shall be entitled to the appropriate general minimum time rate or piece work basis time rate specified in paragraphs 1 to 48 (inclusive).

	Column 1 General minimum time rate per hour	Column 2 Piece work basis time rate per hour
	s. d.	s. d.
II.—MALE WORKERS UNDER 21 YEARS OF AGE		
50. Aged 20 years and under 21 years	3 10	4 5
„ 19 „ „ „ 20 „	3 6	4 0½
„ 18 „ „ „ 19 „	3 3	3 9
„ 17 „ „ „ 18 „	2 9½	3 2¾
„ 16 „ „ „ 17 „	2 6	2 10½
„ under 16 years	2 2½	2 6½

III.—FEMALE WORKERS

51. Workers employed on production (i.e. workers employed on any productive operations (including the operations of buffing and whetting wherever performed) up to and including the production of the finished article):—		
Aged 21 years or over	4 1	4 8½
„ 20 „ and under 21 years	3 8	4 2¾
„ 19 „ „ „ 20 „	3 6	4 0½
„ 18 „ „ „ 19 „	3 3½	3 9½
„ 17 „ „ „ 18 „	2 7½	3 0¼
„ 16 „ „ „ 17 „	2 5	2 9½
„ under 16 years	2 2	2 6
52. Warehouse workers (i.e. workers employed on warehousing operations such as receiving, storing, stockkeeping, distributing, inspecting, wiping, counting, wrapping, labelling, packing, boxing, dispatching; and similar operations) and any other workers (including workers employed in carrying) to whom the minimum rates in paragraph 51 do not apply:—		
Aged 21 years or over	3 11	4 6¼
„ 20 „ and under 21 years	3 5½	3 11¾
„ 19 „ „ „ 20 „	3 3½	3 9½
„ 18 „ „ „ 19 „	3 1	3 6¾
„ 17 „ „ „ 18 „	2 6	2 10½
„ 16 „ „ „ 17 „	2 3½	2 7¾
„ under 16 years	2 1½	2 5½

PART II

MINIMUM OVERTIME AND NIGHT WORK RATES
ALL WORKERS

53.—(1) Minimum overtime rates are payable as follows:—

(a) on a Sunday or customary holiday—
for all time worked ... ... double time

(b) in any week exclusive of Sunday or a customary holiday, for all time worked in excess of 40 hours—
  (i) for the first 5 hours ... ... time-and-a-quarter
  (ii) thereafter ... ... time-and-a-half

(2) In this paragraph the expressions "time-and-a-quarter", "time-and-a-half" and "double time" mean respectively:—

(a) in the case of a time worker, one and a quarter times, one and a half times and twice the general minimum time rate otherwise payable to the worker, and

(b) in the case of a piece worker—

(i) a time rate equal respectively to one quarter, one half and the whole of the piece work basis time rate otherwise applicable to the worker, and

(ii) in addition thereto, piece rates each of which would yield, in the circumstances of the case, to an ordinary worker at least the same amount of money as the said piece work basis time rate.

(3) In this paragraph the expression "customary holiday" means:—

(a) (i) in England and Wales—
Christmas Day (or, if Christmas Day falls on a Sunday, such weekday as may be appointed by national proclamation, or, if none is so appointed, the next following Tuesday), Boxing Day, Good Friday, Easter Monday, Whit Monday (or where another day is substituted therefor by national proclamation, that day) and August Bank Holiday;

(ii) in Scotland—
New Year's Day (or, if New Year's Day falls on a Sunday, the following Monday);

the local Spring holiday;

the local Autumn holiday; and

three other days (being days on which the worker normally works) in the course of a calendar year, to be fixed by the employer and notified to the worker not less than three weeks before the holiday;

or (b) in the case of each of the said days (other than a day fixed by the employer in Scotland and notified to the worker as aforesaid) a day substituted by the employer therefor, being either a day recognised by local custom as a day of holiday in substitution for the said day or a weekday agreed between the employer and the worker or his representative.

NIGHT WORK

54. For all time worked between 10 p.m. and 6 a.m. the minimum rate shall be the amount to which the worker is entitled under the other provisions of this Schedule with the addition of the following amount:—

(1) in the case of a time worker one third of the appropriate general minimum time rate;

(2) in the case of a piece worker one third of the appropriate piece work basis time rate.

PART III

GENERAL PROVISIONS
WORKERS EMPLOYED ON PIECE WORK

55. Subject to the provisions of Part II of this Schedule, a worker employed on piece work shall be paid piece rates each of which would yield, in the circumstances of the case, to an ordinary worker at least the same amount of money as the piece work basis time rate applicable to the worker.

WAITING TIME

56.—(1) A worker shall be entitled to payment of statutory minimum remuneration as aforesaid for all the time during which he is present on the premises of his employer unless he is so present either without his employer's consent, express or implied, or for some purpose unconnected with his work and other than that of waiting for work to be given to him to perform.

(2) A piece worker shall, during any time during which he is present as aforesaid and is not doing piece work, be entitled to payment of the general minimum time rate applicable to the workers of the class to which he belongs.

(3) Provisions (1) and (2) above do not apply when:—

(a) a worker is present on his employer's premises by reason only of the fact that he is resident thereon, or

(b) a worker is present on his employer's premises during normal meal times in a room or place in which no work is being done and is not waiting for work to be given to him to perform.

REMUNERATION IN RESPECT OF PERIODS OF SICKNESS OR INJURY

57. *Notwithstanding the preceding provisions of this Schedule but subject to this paragraph and to paragraphs 58 and 59, where a worker aged 18 or over is, throughout any day on which he normally works for the employer, absent from work by reason of incapacity for work due to proved sickness or injury, the minimum remuneration payable in respect of that day shall be one-fifth of the sick pay applicable to that worker under the provisions of paragraph 58:*

Provided that—

(1) *No remuneration shall be payable to a worker under this paragraph unless—*

(a) *the worker has been in the employer's continuous employment (within the meaning of the Contracts of Employment Act 1963) for not less than 104 weeks prior to the relevant date except that absence due to pregnancy or childbirth of not more than 12 weeks in any one instance shall be deemed not to break continuity of employment; or*

(b) *the worker has been employed as a worker to whom this Schedule applies for the aggregate of not less than 240 weeks (which need not be consecutive) falling within 260 weeks preceding the relevant date.*

(2) *Where the worker first became employed as a worker to whom this Schedule applies after 26th July 1967 no remuneration shall be payable to the worker under this paragraph unless he had not attained the age of 55 years at the relevant date.*

(3) *Once a worker becomes eligible for remuneration under the provisions of this paragraph he remains eligible for the whole time of active employment as a worker to whom this Schedule applies.*

(4) *For the purposes of this paragraph the expression "relevant date" shall be taken to be:—*

(a) *as respects a worker who was in employment on 26th July 1967 and who on that date would have been eligible for payments under this paragraph, that date; and*

(b) *in any other case the date, if any, on which the worker concerned first completed 104 weeks continuous employment under sub-paragraph (1)(a) or as the case may be 240 weeks employment under sub-paragraph (1)(b) prior to attaining the age of 55 years.*

(5) *No remuneration shall be payable to a worker under this paragraph for the first five consecutive working days of any period of absence and for these purposes days shall be treated as consecutive notwithstanding that a Saturday or Sunday or a holiday or a day upon which the worker does not normally work intervenes.*

(6) *No remuneration shall be payable to a worker under this paragraph in respect of any day of absence falling within the year commencing on 6th April 1968 or in any succeeding year commencing on 6th April where the number of days absence due to sickness or injury in any such year for which remuneration not less than that payable under this paragraph has been paid or is payable by the employer exceeds 30 days.*

(7) *Where a period of incapacity overlaps from one year ending 5th April to the next, the whole of the remuneration payable under this paragraph in respect thereof shall be regarded as having accrued in respect of the earlier year ending 5th April.*

(8) *Without prejudice to any other provision of this Schedule payment of remuneration under this paragraph shall be conditional upon the production (if required by the employer at any time) of a medical certificate.*

58. *The amount of remuneration payable to a worker by way of sick pay under paragraph 57 shall be—*

In respect of workers who during the four weeks immediately preceding the week which includes the first day of any period of absence have been employed—

(1) *for an average weekly number of hours which equals or exceeds 26—*

    (a) *in the case of an adult male worker, £5 per week;*

    (b) *in the case of an adult female worker, £2 10s. 0d. per week;*

    (c) *in the case of a male worker who has attained 18 years of age but is under 21 years of age £2 10s. 0d. per week;*

    (d) *In the case of a female worker who has attained 18 years of age but is under 21 years of age £1 5s. 0d. per week.*

(2) *for an average weekly number of hours which is less than 26—*

    (i) *in the case of an adult male worker, £2 10s. 0d. per week;*

    (ii) *in the case of an adult female worker, £1 5s. 0d. per week.*

59. *No remuneration shall be payable under paras. 57 and 58 where absence from work has been caused by—*

    (i) *War, invasion, act of foreign enemy, hostilities, civil war, rebellion, revolution, insurrection, or military or usurped power.*

    (ii) *Suicide or attempted suicide.*

    (iii) *Flying except as a passenger in a fully licensed aircraft.*

    (iv) *Engaging in winter sports abroad, ice-hockey, polo, hunting, mountaineering, racing (except on foot) or professional sport of any type.*

    (v) *Pregnancy or childbirth.*

    (vi) *Illness commencing or accident occurring before the relevant date (as defined in paragraph 57 (4)).*

APPLICATION OF RATES TO INCIDENTAL OPERATIONS

60. For the purposes of this Schedule the work of any class of worker to which a minimum rate is applicable includes any fixing of dies or tools, setting up of machines or tools, grinding of dies or tools, or any other similar work performed by that class of worker.

APPLICABILITY OF STATUTORY MINIMUM REMUNERATION

61. This Schedule applies to workers in relation to whom the Cutlery Wages Council (Great Britain) operates, that is to say, workers employed in Great Britain in the trade specified in the Schedule to the Trade Boards (Cutlery Trade, Great Britain) (Constitution and Proceedings) Regulations 1933(a), which reads as follows:—

"The Cutlery Trade, that is to say—

(1) the manufacture of

    (a) Knives of any kind with one or more than one blade, or one or more than one blade and any other components, including fish and dessert knives;

    (b) Carving Forks and all other Hafted Forks, including fish and dessert forks;

    (c) Steels and Hafted Knife Sharpeners;

    (d) Scissors, including tailors' and similar shears;

    (e) Razors;

    (f) Parts of any of the above articles including blades and components;

    (g) Blanks for any of the above parts or articles;

but excluding

(a) S.R. & O. 1933/1056 (Rev. XXIII, p. 471; 1933, p. 2035).

(2) the manufacture of—

(a) Parts when made by workers mainly engaged on work other than work specified in paragraph (1) hereof;

(b) Knives for use in machines;

(c) Garden Shears, Sheep Shears, Metal Cutting Shears or Secateurs;

(d) Safety Razors and component parts thereof;

(e) Surgical Instruments;

(f) Fish, Dessert or Butter Knives of the Spoon-handled type.

(3) The expression 'manufacture' includes hafting and finishing and all other operations and processes incidental or appertaining to manufacture."

SCHEDULE 2

HOLIDAYS AND HOLIDAY REMUNERATION

The Wages Regulation (Cutlery) (Holidays) Order 1967(a) (Order C.T. (83)), shall have effect as if in the Schedule thereto:—

1. for sub-paragraph (1) of paragraph 7 (which relates to holiday remuneration for annual holiday), there were substituted the following sub-paragraph:—

"7.—(1) Subject to the provisions of sub-paragraph (3)(b) of this paragraph and to the provisions of paragraph 8, a worker qualified to be allowed an annual holiday under this Schedule shall be paid by his employer in respect thereof, on the last pay day preceding such annual holiday, holiday remuneration as follows, that is to say:—

(a) in the case of an adult male worker other than an outworker, three-fiftieths of the amount specified in sub-paragraph (2) of this paragraph, but not exceeding £42 5s. 0d.;

(b) in the case of an adult female worker other than an outworker, three-fiftieths of the amount specified in sub-paragraph (2) of this paragraph, but not exceeding £35 17s. 6d.;

(c) in the case of a male or female worker under 21 years of age other than an outworker, three-fiftieths of the amount specified in sub-paragraph (2) of this paragraph, but not exceeding the amount obtained by multiplying by 120 the minimum hourly rate of remuneration applicable to the worker at the commencement of the holiday season;

(d) in the case of an outworker who is a grinder, three-fiftieths of 85 per cent. of the amount specified in sub-paragraph (2) of this paragraph;

(e) in the case of any other outworker, three-fiftieths of 90 per cent. of the amount specified in sub-paragraph (2) of this paragraph."

2. for sub-paragraph (2) of paragraph 9 (which relates to accrued holiday remuneration payable on termination of employment), there were substituted the following sub-paragraph:—

"(2) in respect of any employment since the preceding 5th April, a sum equal to the holiday remuneration which would have been payable to him if he could have been allowed an annual holiday in respect of that employment at the time of leaving it or,

(a) in the case of a male worker other than an outworker, a sum calculated at the rate of 17s. 3d. in respect of each week of employment since the said 5th April, whichever is the less;

(b) in the case of a female worker other than an outworker, a sum calculated at the rate of 14s. 8d. in respect of each week of employment since the said 5th April, whichever is the less."

(a) S.I. 1967/1360 (1967 III, p. 3994).

EXPLANATORY NOTE

(*This Note is not part of the Order.*)

This Order has effect from 17th January 1969. Schedule 1 sets out the minimum remuneration payable in substitution for that fixed by the Wages Regulation (Cutlery) Order 1967 (Order C.T.(84)), which is revoked and introduces for the first time new provisions for the payment of statutory minimum remuneration by way of sick pay.

Schedule 2 amends the Wages Regulation (Cutlery) (Holidays) Order 1967 (Order C.T. (83)), by increasing the maximum amount of holiday remuneration payable to a worker other than an outworker.

New provisions are printed in italics.

STATUTORY INSTRUMENTS

1968 No. 1988 (C.30)

FUGITIVE CRIMINAL

The Fugitive Offenders Act 1967 (Commencement No. 2) Order 1968

Made - - - *16th December* 1968

In exercise of the powers conferred on me by section 22 of the Fugitive Offenders Act 1967(**a**), I hereby make the following Order :—

1. In relation to any country to which Her Majesty is empowered by paragraph (*c*) of section 2(2) of the Fugitive Offenders Act 1967 (definition of "United Kingdom dependency") to apply the said section 2(2), the said Act shall come into force on 1st January 1969 for the purposes of all the provisions of the Act other than—

    (*a*) the purposes of any provision thereof conferring power on Her Majesty to make an Order in Council, and

    (*b*) the purposes of section 18(2) thereof,

for which purposes the said Act came into force on 25th August 1967 and 1st September 1967, respectively.

2. This Order may be cited as the Fugitive Offenders Act 1967 (Commencement No. 2) Order 1968.

James Callaghan,
One of Her Majesty's Principal
Secretaries of State.

Home Office,
Whitehall.
16th December 1968.

EXPLANATORY NOTE

(This Note is not part of the Order.)

This Order provides that the Fugitive Offenders Act 1967 shall come into force on 1st January 1969 for the purposes of all the provisions thereof which have not sooner come into force, so far as they relate to countries and territories outside Her Majesty's dominions in which She has jurisdiction, or over which She extends protection, in right of Her Government in the United Kingdom.

(**a**) 1967 c.68.

STATUTORY INSTRUMENTS

1968 No. 1989

POLICE

ENGLAND AND WALES

The Special Constables (Pensions) (Amendment) Regulations 1968

Made - - -	*16th December* 1968
Laid before Parliament	*30th December* 1968
Coming into Operation	*1st January* 1969

In exercise of the powers conferred on me by section 34 of the Police Act 1964(a) (as read with section 1(2) of the Police Pensions Act 1961(b)), I hereby make the following Regulations:—

1.—(1) In the application of the Police Pensions Regulations 1966(c) to the calculation of the pension of the widow, or the allowance of a child, of a special constable under the Instrument of 1966, those Regulations shall apply as amended by the Police Pensions (Amendment) Regulations 1968(d) (which amendments relate to increases in widows' and children's awards).

(2) In accordance with paragraph (1) of this Regulation, for Regulation 15(1) of the Instrument of 1966 (which, as set out in the Special Constables (Pensions) (Amendment) Regulations 1967(e), defines the expression "the principal Regulations") there shall be substituted the following paragraph:—

'(1) In these Regulations the expression "the principal Regulations" means the Police Pensions Regulations 1966 as amended by the Police Pensions (Amendment) (No. 2) Regulations 1967(f) and the Police Pensions (Amendment) Regulations 1968.'

2.—(1) For paragraph 1 of Schedule 1 to the Instrument of 1966 (which provides for the average pensionable pay of a special constable to be calculated in accordance with the Tables set out in that Schedule) there shall be substituted the following paragraph:—

"1.—(1) Subject to the provisions of this Schedule, for the purpose of calculating an award under these Regulations to or in respect of a special constable his average pensionable pay or average pensionable pay for a period of a week—

(a) in the case of a special constable last appointed such on or after 1st March 1967, shall be of an amount determined in accordance with sub-paragraph (2) of this paragraph;

(b) in the case of a special constable last appointed such before 1st March 1967 who ceased to hold that office on or after that date, shall be of an amount determined in accordance with sub-paragraph (2) of this paragraph or with sub-paragraph (3) thereof if the amount so calculated is higher;

(a) 1964 c. 48.
(b) 1961 c. 35.
(c) S.I. 1966/1582 (1966 III, p. 4894).
(d) S.I. 1968/530 (1968 I, p. 1269).
(e) S.I. 1967/1546 (1967 III, p. 4311).
(f) S.I. 1967/1500 (1967 III, p. 4204).

(c) in the case of a special constable who ceased to hold that office before 1st March 1967, shall be determined in accordance with sub-paragraph (3) of this paragraph.

(2) In a case in which this sub-paragraph applies, the average pensionable pay or average pensionable pay for a period of a week of a special constable shall be deemed to be of the like amount as his average pensionable pay or, as the case may be, his average pensionable pay for a week (within the meaning of the principal Regulations) would have been, at the date at which he ceased to hold that office, had his appointment and service at any time as a special constable for any police area been appointment and service in the rank of constable as a regular policeman in the police force for that area.

(3) In a case in which this sub-paragraph applies, the average pensionable pay or average pensionable pay for a period of a week of a special constable shall be deemed to be the sum set out, opposite to the period during which he ceased to hold that office, in the second column of the appropriate Table in this Schedule with the addition of the sum so set out in the third column of that Table for each completed year of service as a special constable from the date of his appointment as such, subject to the maximum, if any, so set out in the fourth column of that Table."

(2) In paragraph 2 of the said Schedule 1 (which relates to the reckoning of service for the purposes of paragraph 1) for the words "the preceding paragraph" there shall be substituted the words "paragraph 1(3) of this Schedule".

(3) In paragraph 3 of the said Schedule (which relates to additions to average pensionable pay in the case of special constables for the City of London or the Metropolitan Police District) for the words "paragraph 1" there shall be substituted the words "paragraph 1(3)".

(4) In paragraph 7 of the said Schedule 1 (which relates to the interpretation of the Schedule) after the words "a reference to a person's appointment as a special constable" there shall be inserted the words "otherwise than in paragraph 1(2) thereof".

3. In these Regulations any reference to the Instrument of 1966 is a reference to the Special Constables (Pensions) Regulations 1966(**a**), as amended(**b**).

4.—(1) These Regulations shall come into operation on 1st January 1969 and shall have effect—

(a) for the purposes of Regulation 1 thereof, as from that date;

(b) for the purposes of Regulation 2 thereof, as from 1st March 1967.

(2) These Regulations may be cited as the Special Constables (Pensions) (Amendment) Regulations 1968.

James Callaghan,
One of Her Majesty's Principal
Secretaries of State.

Home Office,
  Whitehall.
16th December, 1968.

(**a**) S.I. 1966/1590 (1966 III, p. 5008).
(**b**) The amending Regulations are S.I. 1967 1546 (1967 III. p. 4311).

EXPLANATORY NOTE

(This Note is not part of the Regulations.)

These Regulations amend the Special Constables (Pensions) Regulations 1966 which give to special constables and their dependants certain pension benefits for which members of police forces and their dependants are eligible.

The Police Pensions (Amendment) Regulations 1968 provide that certain benefits payable to dependants of members of police forces shall be increased. Regulation 1 of these Regulations provides for similar increases in the benefits payable to the dependants of special constables.

Awards under the Special Constables (Pensions) Regulations 1966 are calculated by reference to a scale of notional remuneration, referred to as average pensionable pay. Regulation 2 of these Regulations provides (subject to a saving in certain cases for the existing scale where more favourable) that in the case of a special constable who ceased to hold that office on or after 1st March 1967 this notional average pensionable pay should be of the like amount as the actual average pensionable pay of a member of a police force of the rank of constable with the same service as the special constable. Regulation 2 has retrospective effect to 1st March 1967 by virtue of Regulation 4(1)(b) (which is made in exercise of the power conferred by section 34(3) of the Police Act 1964).

STATUTORY INSTRUMENTS

1968 No. 1994 (S. 180)

ROAD TRAFFIC

The Road Traffic Accidents (Payments for Treatment) (Scotland) Order 1968

Made - - - -	*13th December* 1968
Laid before Parliament	*30th December* 1968
Coming into Operation	*1st January* 1969

In exercise of the powers conferred on me by section 5 of and Schedule 3 to the Public Expenditure and Receipts Act 1968(a), and of all other powers enabling me in that behalf, I hereby make the following order:—

1.—(1) This order may be cited as the Road Traffic Accidents (Payments for Treatment) (Scotland) Order 1968 and shall come into operation on 1st January 1969.

(2) The Interpretation Act 1889(b) applies for the interpretation of this order as it applies for the interpretation of an Act of Parliament.

2. Subject to article 4 of this order, in the proviso to section 212(1) of the Road Traffic Act 1960(c) (which provides that the maximum amount of payments by authorised insurers or owners of vehicles under the sub-section for hospital treatment of traffic casualties shall be £50 for each person treated as an in-patient and £5 for each person treated as an out-patient) for the sum of £50 there shall be substituted the sum of £200 and for the sum of £5 there shall be substituted the sum of £20.

3. Subject as aforesaid, in section 213(1) of the said Act (which provides a fee of 12s. 6d. for the emergency treatment of traffic casualties) for the sum of 12s. 6d. there shall be substituted the sum of 25s.

4. This order shall apply only where an accident giving rise to the death or bodily injury in respect of which a payment is made under the said section 212, or claimed under the said section 213, occurred after the coming into operation of this order.

William Ross,
One of Her Majesty's
Principal Secretaries of State.

St. Andrew's House,
Edinburgh, 1.
13th December 1968.

(a) 1968 c. 14.   (b) 1889 c. 63.   (c) 1960 c. 16.

EXPLANATORY NOTE

(This Note is not part of the Order.)

This order increases the maximum amounts payable for hospital treatment under section 212(1) of the Road Traffic Act 1960 from £50 to £200 in respect of persons treated as in-patients and from £5 to £20 for persons treated as out-patients. The fee for emergency treatment under section 213(1) is increased from 12s. 6d. to 25s. The alterations apply only in respect of accidents occurring on or after 1st January 1969.

STATUTORY INSTRUMENTS

1968 No. 1995 (S.181)

POLICE

The Special Constables (Pensions) (Scotland) Amendment Regulations 1968

Made - - -	16*th December* 1968
Laid before Parliament	30*th December* 1968
Coming into Operation	1*st January* 1969

In exercise of the powers conferred on me by section 26 of the Police (Scotland) Act 1967(**a**) (as read with section 1(2) of the Police Pensions Act 1961(**b**)) and of all other powers enabling me in that behalf, and after consultation with the Committee and such bodies and associations as are mentioned in section 26(9)(*b*) of the said Act of 1967, I hereby make the following regulations: —

Citation and commencement

1. These regulations may be cited as the Special Constables (Pensions) (Scotland) Amendment Regulations 1968 and shall come into operation on 1st January 1969 and shall have effect: —

(*a*) for the purposes of regulation 3 thereof, as from that date ;

(*b*) for the purposes of regulation 4 thereof, as from 1st March 1967.

Interpretation

2. In these regulations any reference to the Instrument of 1966 is a reference to the Special Constables (Pensions) (Scotland) Regulations 1966(**c**), as amended (**d**).

3.—(1) In the application of the Police Pensions Regulations 1966(**e**) to the calculation of the pension of the widow, or the allowance of a child, of a special constable under the Instrument of 1966, those regulations shall apply as amended by the Police Pensions (Amendment) Regulations 1968(**f**) (which amendments relate to increases in widows' and children's awards).

(2) In accordance with paragraph (1) of this regulation, for regulation 2(1) of the Instrument of 1966 (which, as set out in the Special Constables (Pensions) (Scotland) Amendment Regulations 1967, defines the expression "the principal regulations") there shall be substituted the following paragraph :—

'(1) In these regulations the expression "the principal regulations" means the Police Pensions Regulations 1966 as amended by the Police Pensions (Amendment) (No. 2) Regulations 1967(**g**) and the Police Pensions (Amendment) Regulations 1968.'.

(**a**) 1967 c. 77.
(**c**) S.I. 1966/1625 (1966 III, p. 5066).
(**e**) S.I. 1966/1582 (1966 III, p. 4894).
(**g**) S.I. 1967/1500 (1967 III, p. 4204).

(**b**) 1961 c. 35.
(**d**) S.I. 1967/1553 (1967 III, p. 4315).
(**f**) S.I. 1968/530 (1968 I, p. 1269).

4. For paragraph 1 of Schedule 1 to the Instrument of 1966 (which provides for the average pensionable pay of a special constable to be calculated in accordance with the Tables set out in that Schedule) there shall be substituted the following paragraph :—

"1.—(1) Subject to the provisions of this Schedule, for the purpose of calculating an award under these regulations to or in respect of a special constable his average pensionable pay or average pensionable pay for a period of a week—

(*a*) in the case of a special constable last appointed such on or after 1st March 1967, shall be of an amount determined in accordance with sub-paragraph (2) of this paragraph ;

(*b*) in the case of a special constable last appointed such before 1st March 1967 who ceased to hold that office on or after that date, shall be of an amount determined in accordance with sub-paragraph (2) of this paragraph or with sub-paragraph (3) thereof if the amount so calculated is higher ;

(*c*) in the case of a special constable who ceased to hold that office before 1st March 1967, shall be of an amount determined in accordance with sub-paragraph (3) of this paragraph.

(2) In a case in which this sub-paragraph applies, the average pensionable pay or average pensionable pay for a period of a week of a special constable shall be deemed to be of the like amount as his average pensionable pay or, as the case may be, his average pensionable pay for a week (within the meaning of the principal regulations) would have been, at the date at which he ceased to hold that office, had his appointment and service at any time as a special constable for any police area been appointment and service in the rank of constable as a regular policeman in the police force for that area.

(3) In a case in which this sub-paragraph applies, the average pensionable pay or average pensionable pay for a period of a week of a special constable shall be deemed to be the sum set out, opposite to the period during which he ceased to hold that office, in the second column of the appropriate Table in this Schedule with the addition of the sum so set out in the third column of that Table for each completed year of service as a special constable from the date of his appointment as such, subject to the maximum, if any, so set out in the fourth column of that Table.".

5. In paragraph 2 of the said Schedule 1 (which relates to the reckoning of service for the purposes of paragraph 1) for the words "the preceding paragraph" there shall be substituted the words "paragraph 1(3) of this Schedule".

6. In paragraph 6 of the said Schedule 1 (which relates to the interpretation of the Schedule) after the words "a reference to a person's appointment as a special constable" there shall be inserted the words "otherwise than in paragraph 1(2) thereof".

William Ross,
One of Her Majesty's Principal
Secretaries of State.

St. Andrew's House,
Edinburgh, 1.
16th December 1968.

EXPLANATORY NOTE
(This Note is not part of the Regulations.)

These Regulations amend the Special Constables (Pensions) (Scotland) Regulations 1966 which give to special constables and their dependants certain pension benefits for which members of police forces and their dependants are eligible.

The Police Pensions (Amendment) Regulations 1968 provide that certain benefits payable to dependants of members of police forces shall be increased. Regulation 3 of these Regulations provides for similar increases in the benefits payable to the dependants of special constables.

Awards under the Special Constables (Pensions) (Scotland) Regulations 1966 are calculated by reference to a scale of notional remuneration, referred to as average pensionable pay. Regulation 4 of these Regulations provides (subject to a saving in certain cases for the existing scale where more favourable) that in the case of a special constable who ceased to hold that office on or after 1st March 1967 this notional average pensionable pay should be of the like amount as the actual average pensionable pay of a member of a police force of the rank of constable with the same service as the special constable. Regulation 4 has retrospective effect to 1st March 1967 by virtue of Regulation 1(*b*) (which is made in exercise of the power conferred by section 26(4) of the Police (Scotland) Act 1967).

STATUTORY INSTRUMENTS

1968 No. 1996 (S. 182)

SHERIFF COURT, SCOTLAND

The Sheriff Courts (Race Relations Jurisdiction) (Scotland) Order 1968

Made - - - -	16th December 1968
Coming into Operation	31st December 1968

In exercise of the powers conferred on me by section 20(2) and (4) of the Race Relations Act 1968(a) and of all other powers enabling me in that behalf, I hereby make the following Order:—

1.—(1) This order may be cited as the Sheriff Courts (Race Relations Jurisdiction) (Scotland) Order 1968 and shall come into operation on 31st December 1968.

(2) The Interpretation Act 1889(b) shall apply for the interpretation of this order as it applies for the interpretation of an Act of Parliament.

2. The courts mentioned in Column 1 of the schedule to this Order are hereby appointed to have jurisdiction to entertain proceedings under section 20 of the Race Relations Act 1968, and there is hereby assigned to these courts as their districts for the purposes of such proceedings the sheriffdoms mentioned opposite thereto in Column 2 of the said schedule.

William Ross,
One of Her Majesty's
Principal Secretaries of State.

St. Andrew's House,
  Edinburgh, 1.
16th December 1968.

Article 2   SCHEDULE

Column 1	Column 2
The Sheriff Court at Edinburgh.	The Sheriffdoms of The Lothians and Peebles; and Roxburgh, Berwick and Selkirk.
The Sheriff Court at Glasgow.	The Sheriffdoms of Lanark, Stirling, Dunbarton and Clackmannan; Renfrew and Argyll; Ayr and Bute; and Dumfries and Galloway.
The Sheriff Court at Dundee.	The Sheriffdoms of Perth and Angus; Fife and Kinross; and Aberdeen, Kincardine and Banff.
The Sheriff Court at Inverness.	The Sheriffdoms of Inverness, Moray, Nairn and Ross and Cromarty; and Caithness, Sutherland, Orkney and Zetland.

(a) 1968 c. 71.   (b) 1889 c. 63.

EXPLANATORY NOTE

(This Note is not part of the Order.)

This Order appoints four Sheriff Courts in Scotland as courts to exercise jurisdiction in proceedings brought under the Race Relations Act 1968, and defines the districts of these courts as enlarged for the purpose of this jurisdiction. The courts are the Sheriff Courts at Edinburgh, Glasgow, Dundee and Inverness.

STATUTORY INSTRUMENTS

1968 No. 1997 (S.183)

JUSTICES OF THE PEACE
The Justices (Supplemental List) (Scotland) Rules 1968

Made - - -	*16th December* 1968
Coming into Operation	*1st January* 1969

In exercise of the powers conferred on me by section 4 of the Justices of the Peace Act 1949(**a**) (hereinafter referred to as "the Act") as read with the Transfer of Functions (Justices of the Peace) (Scotland) Order 1955(**b**) and section 6(2) of the Justices of the Peace Act 1968(**c**) and of all other powers enabling me in that behalf, I hereby make the following rules :—

1. These rules may be cited as the Justices (Supplemental List) (Scotland) Rules 1968 and shall come into operation on 1st January 1969.

2. The Interpretation Act 1889(**d**) applies for the interpretation of these rules as it applies for the interpretation of an Act of Parliament.

3. Subject to the provisions of these rules, there shall be kept in connection with every Commission of the Peace issued by Her Majesty a list to be called the "Supplemental List".

4.—(1) Subject to the provisions of these rules, the Clerk of the Peace for every county, and county of a city, shall enter in the Supplemental List kept for that county, or county of a city, the name of any person appointed a Justice by the Commission—

   (*a*) who is of the age of seventy years or over and neither holds nor has held high judicial office within the meaning of the Appellate Jurisdiction Act 1876(**e**) or

   (*b*) who applies to have his name entered therein and obtains the approval of the Secretary of State for such entry to be made ; or

   (*c*) whose name is directed by the Secretary of State to be so entered in pursuance of section 4(4) of the Act.

(2) As regards the year 1969 and the three following years, this rule shall apply as if the references in sub-paragraph (*a*) of paragraph (1) of this rule to the age of seventy years were a reference for 1969 to an age of seventy-four years, for 1970 to an age of seventy-three years, for 1971 to an age of seventy-two years and for 1972 to an age of seventy-one years.

5. These rules shall apply to a person who under the Local Government (Scotland) Act 1947(**f**) is a Justice of the Peace for any area by virtue of his office as Lord Provost, or Provost, or Chairman of a local authority as they apply to a Justice appointed by the Commission.

(**a**) 1949 c. 101.	(**b**) S.I. 1955/240 (1955 I, p. 1199).
(**c**) 1968 c. 69.	(**d**) 1889 c. 63.
(**e**) 1876 c. 59.	(**f**) 1947 c. 43.

6. The Clerk of the Peace shall remove from the Supplemental List—

(*a*) any name which the Secretary of State may direct him to remove from that list ; or

(*b*) the name of any person who has ceased to be a Justice.

7. These rules shall apply to a Justice of the Peace whether appointed before or after the coming into force of the rules.

8. The Justices (Supplemental List) Rules 1950(**a**), in so far as applying to Scotland, are hereby revoked.

William Ross,
One of Her Majesty's
Principal Secretaries of State.

St. Andrew's House,
Edinburgh, 1.
16th December 1968.

EXPLANATORY NOTE

(*This Note is not part of the Rules.*)

These Rules replace the Justices (Supplemental List) Rules 1950 in so far as they relate to Scotland, and they implement the changes made in the law by section 6(2) of the Justices of the Peace Act 1968.

(a) S.I. 1950/594 (1950 I, p. 1149).

STATUTORY   INSTRUMENTS

1968 No. 2001

CUSTOMS AND EXCISE

The European Free Trade Association (Drawback) (Amendment No. 2) Regulations 1968

Made - - - -	18*th December* 1968
Laid before the House of Commons	30*th December* 1968
Coming into Operation	1*st January* 1969

The Board of Trade, in pursuance of the powers conferred upon them by section 2 of the European Free Trade Association Act 1960(a), hereby make the following Regulations : —

1. The European Free Trade Association (Drawback) Regulations 1966(b), as amended(c), shall have effect as if for paragraph (*d*) of regulation 3 there were substituted the following : —

" (*d*) where drawback was claimed in connection with an exportation before 31st December 1966 of goods from one country in the Convention area to another such country (not being the United Kingdom) and the goods were re-exported to the United Kingdom from the latter country after that date without having undergone any operation or process of production or manufacture in that latter country ; ".

2. The Interpretation Act 1889(d) shall apply to the interpretation of these Regulations as it applies to the interpretation of an Act of Parliament.

3. These Regulations may be cited as the European Free Trade Association (Drawback) (Amendment No. 2) Regulations 1968 and shall come into operation on 1st January 1969.

Edmund Dell,
Minister of State,
Board of Trade.

18th December 1968.

EXPLANATORY NOTE

(This note is not part of the Regulations.)

These Regulations further amend the European Free Trade Association (Drawback) Regulations 1966.

The 1966 Regulations generally debar goods of Convention area origin from preferential treatment in connection with customs duties if they have been the subject of a claim for drawback on exportation from a Convention country. Regulation 3(*d*) of the 1966 Regulations provides an exception which is available only if the goods are cleared for home use in this country or for temporary duty-free admission before the end of 1968. These Regulations remove this limitation.

(a) 1960 c. 19.   (b) S.I. 1966/1481 (1966 III, p. 4088).
(c) The amendment is not relevant to these Regulations.   (d) 1889 c. 63.

STATUTORY   INSTRUMENTS

1968 No. 2002

FACTORIES

The Reports of Appointed Factory Doctors Order 1968

Made - - -	*17th December* 1968
Coming into Operation	*1st January* 1969

The Secretary of State by virtue of her powers under section 151(7) of the Factories Act 1961(a) and of all other powers enabling her in that behalf, hereby makes the following Order:—

1.—(1) This Order may be cited as the Reports of Appointed Factory Doctors Order 1968 and shall come into operation on 1st January 1969.

(2) The Reports of Appointed Factory Doctors Order 1967(b) is hereby revoked.

2. The Interpretation Act 1889(c) shall apply to the interpretation of this Order as it applies to the interpretation of an Act of Parliament, and as if this Order and the Order hereby revoked were Acts of Parliament.

3. The report to the Secretary of State required under section 151(7) of the Factories Act 1961 to be made each year by every appointed factory doctor as to examinations made and other duties performed by him in pursuance of that Act shall be made during the month of January in each year in respect of the year ended on the immediately preceding 31st December and shall be in the form set out in the Schedule to this Order.

Signed by order of the Secretary of State.
17th December 1968.

K. Barnes,.

Deputy Under Secretary of State,
Department of Employment and
Productivity.

(a) 1961 c. 34.   (b) S.I. 1967/1729 (1967 III, p. 4651).
(c) 1889 c. 63.

Article 3
F 520

SCHEDULE

FORM OF REPORT BY APPOINTED FACTORY DOCTOR
for the year ended 31st December

This report is to be forwarded to:
H.M. CHIEF INSPECTOR OF FACTORIES,
Department of Employment and Productivity,
Baynards House,
1 Chepstow Place,
Westbourne Grove,
LONDON, W.2.

NOT LATER THAN 31st January.

Tables I and II to be completed by an Appointed Factory Doctor for a District and by an Appointed Factory Doctor appointed to carry out medical examinations of young persons for particular works.

Table I—Examinations for Certificates of Fitness for Employment under the Factories Act
(Sections 99, 118 and 119 of Factories Act 1961)

M/c. Line Number	Young Persons presented as being between 15 and 18 years of age (Each examination of each young person to be counted)	Number of Certificates						Number of Rejections		M/c. Line Number
		Without Conditions		Conditional		Provisional				
		Male	Female	Male	Female	Male	Female	Male	Female	
	(1)	(2)	(3)	(4)	(5)	(6)	(7)	(8)	(9)	
1	FIRST EXAMINATION AFTER LEAVING SCHOOL for employment under the Factories Act									1
2	SUBSEQUENT examinations including annual and those due to change of employment and those following conditional or provisional certificates				—					2
3	Boys over 16 years of age for employment AT NIGHT		—		—				—	3
	TOTAL									

Table II—Causes of Rejection. (Columns (8) and (9) of Table I only)

Part 1

Defect or Disease	M/c Line Number	Number – Male	Number – Female
Malnutrition	4		
Undersize...	5		
Deformity	6		
Skin	7		
Pediculosis	8		
Eyes: Refractive errors ...	9		
Eyes: Other, or eyelids ...	10		
Mouth and teeth	11		
Nose	12		
Throat	13		
Ears: Defective hearing ...	14		
„ Other	15		
Glands	16		
Respiratory System: Tuberculosis ...	17		
„ Other	18		
Total Part 1			

Part 2

Defect or Disease	M/c Line Number	Number – Male	Number – Female
Circulatory System: Heart ...	4		
„ Anaemia	5		
Nervous System: Chorea ...	6		
„ Epilepsy ...	7		
„ Mental defect	8		
„ Other ...	9		
Bones and joints	10		
Specific fevers	11		
Rheumatism	12		
Hernia	13		
Other causes—specify ...	14		
	15		
	16		
	17		
	18		
Total Part 2			
Grand Total Parts 1 and 2			

[Please insert Signature overleaf]

Table III is to be completed by an Appointed Factory Doctor for a District or by a doctor appointed or approved under Regulations

Table III—Particulars of examinations undertaken in accordance with Special Regulations, and sections 75 and 128 of the Factories Act 1961

M/c. Line Number	(1)	Examinations (Each examination of each worker to be counted)		Suspensions*		Rejections on first examination as unfit	Certificates permitting return to work after suspension	M/c. Line Number
		Males (2)	Females (3)	Males (4)	Females (5)	(6)	(7)	
	DETAILS OF STATUTORY PERIODIC MEDICAL EXAMINATIONS							
	(Voluntary examinations should not be included)							
	(1) Under Special Regulations:							
	Chemicals:							
19	(a) Nitro and amido processes							19
20	(b) Chrome processes							20
21	Carcinogenic Substances							21
22	Chromium Plating and Anodic Oxidation							22
23	Diving Operations							23
24	Electric Accumulators							24
25	Heading of Yarn							25
	India Rubber:							
26	(a) Lead processes							26
27	(b) Fume processes							27
	Ionising Radiations:							
28	(a) Sealed Sources							28
29	(b) Unsealed Radioactive Substances							29
30	Lead Compounds (Carbonate, etc.)							30
	Lead Smelting, etc.:							
31	(a) Smelting of lead							31
32	(b) Making of flaked litharge							32
33	(c) Making of red and orange lead							33

34	Luminising... ... ...
35	Mule Spinning (Health) ... ...
36	Paint and Colour Works ... ...
37	Patent Fuel ... ...
	Pottery (Health and Welfare):
	(a) Lead processes (see Part I of the First Schedule to Regulations)—
38	(i) Frit, glaze and colour mixing, etc. ...
39	(ii) Flow material preparation, etc. ...
40	(iii) Colour blowing, etc. ... ...
41	(iv) Ground laying, colour dusting ...
42	(v) Colour grinding ... ...
43	(vi) Litho-transfer making ... ...
44	(vii) Other lead processes ... ...
	(b) Regulation 6(7)—
45	Lifting or carrying by young persons ...
	(c) Regulation 25(2)—
46	Colour blowing (Eyesight) ... ...
47	Tinning of Hollow-ware, etc. ... ...
48	Vitreous Enamelling of Metal or Glass ...
49	Work in Compressed Air... ... ...
	(2) Under s.75 or s.128 of the Factories Act 1961, and not included above (women and young persons only)
50	Processes involving use of Lead Compounds ...
51	**Total**

*Suspensions means suspensions of all descriptions (excluding initial rejections—see col. (6)) under Regulations, made at the periodic examination or otherwise. They include therefore those occasioned by notice of poisoning received by the Appointed Factory Doctor unless the worker has been suspended already by a medical practitioner appointed under the Regulations for the factory concerned.

—Indicates an entry is not applicable.

Signature of Doctor ....   Date ....

Address (Private Residence) ....

EXPLANATORY NOTE

(This Note is not part of the Order.)

This Order prescribes the form of report required to be made each year by appointed factory doctors under the Factories Act 1961 and the time at which the report is to be made.

The form of report prescribed by this Order is in substitution for that prescribed by the Reports of Appointed Factory Doctors Order 1967, which is revoked.

STATUTORY INSTRUMENTS

1968 No. 2003

PROBATION AND AFTER-CARE

The Probation (Conditions of Service) (Amendment No. 2) Rules 1968

Made	-	-	-	16*th December* 1968

Coming into Operation   16*th December* 1968

In pursuance of the powers conferred on me by Schedule 5 to the Criminal Justice Act 1948(**a**) and section 1 of the Police, Fire and Probation Officers Remuneration Act 1956(**b**), I hereby make the following Rules :—

1. In Rule 4(1) of the Probation (Conditions of Service) Rules 1965(**c**) for the figure "£75" (which was substituted by the Probation (Conditions of Service) (No. 3) Rules 1965(**d**)), there shall be substituted the figure "£90".

2.—(1) These Rules may be cited as the Probation (Conditions of Service) (Amendment No. 2) Rules 1968.

(2) These Rules shall come into operation forthwith and shall take effect from 1st May 1968.

James Callaghan,
One of Her Majesty's Principal
Secretaries of State.

Home Office,
Whitehall.

16th December 1968.

EXPLANATORY NOTE

(This Note is not part of the Rules.)

These Rules amend the Probation (Conditions of Service) Rules 1965, as amended, by increasing the London addition payable to certain probation officers from £75 to £90. By virtue of section 1 of the Police, Fire and Probation Officers Remuneration Act 1956 the Rules take effect from 1st May 1968.

(**a**) 1948 c. 58.   (**b**) 5 & 6 Eliz. 2. c.1.
(**c**) S.I. 1965/722 (1965 I, p. 2230).
(**d**) S.I. 1965/1520 (1965 II, p. 4405).

STATUTORY INSTRUMENTS

1968 No. 2005

FACTORIES

The Anthrax (Cautionary Notice) Order 1968

Made - - -		*17th December* 1968
Coming into Operation		*13th January* 1969

The Secretary of State in pursuance of Regulation 14 of the Regulations dated 20th December 1907 relating to processes involving the use of certain horse-hair(**a**), Regulation 2 of the Hides and Skins Regulations 1921(**b**) and Regulation 6 of the Tanning Welfare Order 1930(**c**) hereby prescribes for the purposes of the said Regulations the cautionary notice as to anthrax.

1.—(1) This Order may be cited as the Anthrax (Cautionary Notice) Order 1968 and shall come into operation on 13th January 1969.

(2) The Order prescribing the cautionary notice as to anthrax made by the Minister of Labour and National Service on 21st January 1958 is hereby revoked.

2. The Interpretation Act 1889(**d**) shall apply to the interpretation of this Order as it applies to the interpretation of an Act of Parliament, and as if this Order and the Order hereby revoked were Acts of Parliament.

3. The cautionary notice as to anthrax for the purposes of the said Regulations shall be in the form set out in the Schedule to this Order.

Signed by order of the Secretary of State.
17th December 1968.

K. Barnes,
Deputy Under Secretary of State,
Department of Employment and Productivity.

(**a**) S.R. & O. 1907/984 (Rev. VII, p. 354: 1907 p. 152).
(**b**) S.R. & O. 1921/2076 (Rev. VII, p. 349: 1921 p. 243).
(**c**) S.R. & O. 1930/312 (Rev. VII, p. 174: 1930 p. 512).
(**d**) 1889 c. 63.

EXPLANATORY NOTE
(This Note is not part of the Order.)

This Order prescribes the cautionary notice as to anthrax to be kept posted up in factories and other premises to which the Factories Act 1961 applies in which processes involving certain materials liable to be infected with anthrax are carried on. The notice prescribed by this Order supersedes that prescribed by the Order made by the Minister of Labour and National Service on 21st January 1958, which is revoked.

STATUTORY INSTRUMENTS

1968 No. 2006

ANIMALS

DESTRUCTIVE ANIMALS

The Coypus (Keeping) (Amendment) Regulations 1968

Made	- - -		17*th December* 1968
Coming into Operation			1*st January* 1969

The Minister of Agriculture, Fisheries and Food and the Secretary of State for Scotland in exercise of the power vested in them by section 2 of the Destructive Imported Animals Act 1932(a) and of all other powers enabling them in that behalf, acting jointly, with the approval of the Treasury, hereby make the following Regulations :—

Citation and commencement

1. These Regulations which may be cited as the Coypus (Keeping) (Amendment) Regulations 1968 shall come into operation on the 1st January 1969.

Amendment of the Coypus (Keeping) Regulations 1967

2. Regulation 4(2) of the Coypus (Keeping) Regulations 1967(b) is hereby amended by substituting the figure "£4" for the figure "£2".

In Witness whereof the official seal of the Minister of Agriculture, Fisheries and Food is hereunto affixed on 10th December 1968.

(L.S.)

Cledwyn Hughes,
Minister of Agriculture, Fisheries and Food.

Given under the seal of the Secretary of State for Scotland on 12th December 1968.

(L.S.)

William Ross,
Secretary of State for Scotland.

Approved on 17th December 1968.

Walter Harrison,
Joseph Harper,
Two of the Lords Commissioners
of Her Majesty's Treasury.

(a) 1932 c. 12.   (b) S.I. 1967/1873 (1967 III, p. 5088).

EXPLANATORY NOTE

(This Note is not part of the Regulations.)

These regulations increase the fee to be paid for a licence to keep coypus from £2 to £4, with effect from the 1st January 1969.

STATUTORY INSTRUMENTS

1968 No. 2007

ANIMALS

DESTRUCTIVE ANIMALS

The Mink (Keeping) (Amendment) Regulations 1968

Made - - -	*17th December* 1968
Coming into Operation—	
Paragraph (b) of Regulation 2	*1st January* 1970
Remainder	*1st January* 1969

The Minister of Agriculture, Fisheries and Food and the Secretary of State for Scotland in exercise of the power vested in them by section 2 of the Destructive Imported Animals Act 1932(a) and of all other powers enabling them in that behalf, acting jointly, with the approval of the Treasury, hereby make the following Regulations :—

Citation and commencement

1.—(1) These Regulations may be cited as the Mink (Keeping) (Amendment) Regulations 1968.

(2) These Regulations, with the exception of paragraph (*b*) of Regulation 2, shall come into operation on the 1st January 1969.

(3) Paragraph (*b*) of Regulation 2 shall come into operation on the 1st January 1970.

Amendment of the Mink (Keeping) Regulations 1967

2. The Mink (Keeping) Regulations 1967(**b**) are hereby amended as follows:—

(*a*) In subparagraph (*e*) of Regulation 3(1) for the word "near" there shall be substituted the words "within 4 feet of".

(*b*) In each of subparagraphs (i) and (ii) of Regulation 3(1)(*e*) for the figure "18" there shall be substituted the figure "12".

(*c*) In Regulation 4(2) for the figure "£3" there shall be substituted the figure "£6".

In Witness whereof the official seal of the Minister of Agriculture, Fisheries and Food is hereunto affixed on 10th December 1968.

(L.S.)

Cledwyn Hughes,
Minister of Agriculture, Fisheries and Food.

(**a**) 1932 c. 12.　　　　　　　　　　(**b**) S.I. 1967/1872 (1967 III, p.5082).

Given under the seal of the Secretary of State for Scotland on 12th December 1968.

(L.S.)   *William Ross.*
                                           Secretary of State for Scotland.

Approved on 17th December 1968.

                                                    Walter Harrison,
                                                    Joseph Harper,
                                           Two of the Lords Commissioners
                                              of Her Majesty's Treasury.

EXPLANATORY NOTE

(This Note is not part of the Regulations.)

These Regulations increase the fee for a licence to keep mink from £3 to £6, with effect from the 1st January 1969.

In addition these Regulations amend Regulation 3(1)(*e*) of the 1967 Regulations (which Regulation provides that no objects other than nest boxes, cages and cage-traps not more than 18 inches high shall be placed near the guard fences of mink enclosures) by reducing the permitted height of nest boxes, cages and cage-traps (when near guard fences) from 18 to 12 inches, and by substituting "within 4 feet of" for "near". The former amendment is to come into effect on the 1st January 1970, and the latter on the 1st January 1969.

STATUTORY INSTRUMENTS

1968 No. 2009

SUGAR

The Sugar (Surcharge Remission) Order 1968

Made - - - 18th December 1968

Laid before Parliament 30th December 1968

Coming into Operation 31st December 1968

The Minister of Agriculture, Fisheries and Food (hereinafter referred to as "the Minister") in exercise of the powers conferred upon him by section 58 of the Finance Act 1968(**a**) construed as one with the Sugar Act 1956(**b**), and of all other powers enabling him in that behalf, for the purpose of prescribing such goods as it appears to him to be expedient to prescribe for the purposes of subsection (1)(*b*) of that section in the interests of the national economy, hereby makes the following order :—

1.—(1) This order may be cited as the Sugar (Surcharge Remission) Order 1968 ; and shall come into operation on 31st December 1968.

(2) The Interpretation Act 1889(**c**) shall apply to the interpretation of this order as it applies to the interpretation of an Act of Parliament.

2. Goods of the descriptions specified in the Schedule to this order are hereby prescribed for the purposes of subsection (1)(*b*) of section 58 of the Finance Act 1968 (which authorises the Commissioners of Customs and Excise to remit or repay surcharge under section 7 of the Sugar Act 1956 if they are satisfied that the sugar in respect of which it is payable or has been paid will be, or has been, used in the manufacture of goods of any description prescribed for the above mentioned purposes, at the time when the sugar was or is so used, by an order made by the Minister).

In Witness whereof the Official Seal of the Minister of Agriculture, Fisheries and Food is hereunto affixed on 18th December 1968.

(L.S.)

Cledwyn Hughes,
Minister of Agriculture, Fisheries and Food.

(**a**) 1968 c. 44.   (**b**) 1956 c. 48.
(**c**) 1889 c. 63.

SCHEDULE

Anti-microbial substances produced by the culturing of living micro-organisms
Dextrans
Dyestuffs
Fructose
Gibberellic acid and its salts
Griseofulvin
Itaconic acid and its salts
Lactic acid and its salts
Mannitol
Polyols
Sodium glucoheptonate
Sorbitol
Water-soluble textile size

EXPLANATORY NOTE

(This Note is not part of the order.)

This order prescribes the descriptions of goods in respect of whose manufacture sugar surcharge may be remitted or repaid in accordance with the provisions of section 58(1)(*b*) of the Finance Act 1968.

STATUTORY INSTRUMENTS

1968 No. 2010 (L.24)

COUNTY COURTS

PROCEDURE

The County Court (Amendment) Rules 1968

Made - - - *17th December* 1968

Coming into Operation *15th January* 1969

1.—(1) These Rules may be cited as the County Court (Amendment) Rules 1968.

(2) In these Rules an Order and Rule referred to by number means the Order and Rule so numbered in the County Court Rules 1936(a), as amended (**b**).

(3) The Interpretation Act 1889(**c**) shall apply for the interpretation of these Rules as it applies for the interpretation of an Act of Parliament.

2. The following Rule shall be substituted for Order 2, Rule 11 :—

"Race Relations Act 1968

1968 c. 71. **11.**—(1) Proceedings under section 19 of the Race Relations Act 1968 may be commenced—

(*a*) in the court for the district in which the defendant or one of the defendants resides or carries on business ; or

(*b*) in the court for the district in which the act or any of the acts in respect of which the proceedings are brought took place.

(2) In this Rule "court" means a court appointed to have jurisdiction to entertain proceedings under the said section 19 and "district" means the district assigned to such a court for the purposes of that section."

3. The following Rule shall be substituted for Order 31, Rule 12 :—

Proceedings excluded 1913 c.31. 1968 c.71. **"12.** This Order shall not apply to an appeal under section 28 of the Pilotage Act 1913 or to proceedings under section 19 of the Race Relations Act 1968."

(**a**) S.R. & O. 1936/626 (1936 I, p. 282).
(**b**) There are no amendments which relate to the subject matter of these Rules
(**c**) 1889 c. 63.

We, the undersigned members of the Rule Committee appointed by the Lord Chancellor under section 102 of the County Courts Act 1959(a), having by virtue of the powers vested in us in this behalf made the foregoing Rules, do hereby certify the same under our hands and submit them to the Lord Chancellor accordingly.

Owen Temple-Morris.
D. O. McKee.
S. Granville Smith.
Connolly H. Gage.
Hugh Mais.
W. Ralph Davies.
E. A. Everett.
Brian D. Bush.
Arthur Figgis.
A. F. Stapleton Cotton.
D. A. Marshall.

I allow these Rules, which shall come into force on 15th January 1969. Dated 17th December 1968.

Gardiner, C.

EXPLANATORY NOTE

(This Note is not part of the Rules.)

These Rules amend the County Court Rules so as to make provision for proceedings under the Race Relations Act 1968.

(a) 1959 c. 22.

STATUTORY INSTRUMENTS

1968 No. 2011

TRANSPORT

PENSIONS AND COMPENSATION

The British Transport (Pensions of Employees) (No. 1) Order 1968

Made - - - -	*17th December* 1968
Laid before Parliament	*30th December* 1968
Coming into Operation	*31st December* 1968

The Minister of Transport and the Secretary of State, acting jointly, make this Order in exercise of their powers under section 74 of the Transport Act 1962(**a**), as read with section 136 of the Transport Act 1968(**b**), and of all other enabling powers :—

PART I

PRELIMINARY

Commencement, citation and interpretation

1.—(1) This Order shall come into operation on the 31st December 1968 and, except as mentioned in paragraph (2) of this Article, shall have effect from the 18th November 1968.

(2) Article 6 and Articles 8 to 12 of this Order shall have effect from the 31st December 1968.

(3) This Order may be cited as the British Transport (Pensions of Employees) (No. 1) Order 1968.

(4) In this Order, unless the context otherwise requires—

" the Act " means the Transport Act 1968 ;

" appropriate body ", in relation to an established scheme, means—

(i) where the scheme is one in relation to which the property, rights and liabilities of the Holding Company are transferred by Part IV of this Order, the nationalised transport body to which they are so transferred,

(ii) where a scheme does not fall within (i) above but is a scheme in relation to which the responsibility for making payments was placed, or the rights, liabilities and functions of the British Transport Commission were transferred, by the British Transport Reorganisation (Pensions of Employees) (No. 2) Order 1962(**c**) or the British Transport Reorganisation (Pensions of Employees) (No. 3) Order 1962(**d**) (as the case may be), the nationalised transport body (or if more than one, any one of those bodies) on which that responsibility rests, or in which those rights, liabilities and functions are vested, immediately after the 1st January 1969,

(iii) where the scheme does not fall within (i) or (ii) above but is a scheme in which employees of a nationalised transport body

---

(**a**) 10 & 11 Eliz. 2. c. 46.   (**b**) 1968 c. 73.
(**c**) S.I. 1962/2715 (1962 III, p. 3692).   (**d**) S.I. 1962/2758 (1962 III, p. 3866).

which is a subsidiary of a Board or the Holding Company are participating immediately before the 1st January 1969, whichever of the following bodies, namely, a Board, a new authority and the Holding Company, is the body of which the said nationalised transport body is a subsidiary immediately after the 1st January 1969,

(iv) in all other cases, the nationalised transport body which has established the scheme ;

" Board " means any of the following bodies, namely—

the British Railways Board,

the London Transport Board,

the British Transport Docks Board, and

the British Waterways Board ;

" the Bus Company " means the National Bus Company established under section 24 of the Act ;

" established scheme " has the meaning given to that expression in Article 2(1) of this Order ;

" the freightliner company " and " the freight sundries company " mean the companies so referred to in section 5(2) of the Act ;

" the Freight Corporation " means the National Freight Corporation established under section 1 of the Act ;

" the Holding Company " means the Transport Holding Company ;

" the Minister " means—

(a) for the purposes of matters relating only to the Scottish Group (including any subsidiary of that Group), the Secretary of State,

(b) for the purposes of matters relating both to the Scottish Group (including any subsidiary as aforesaid) and to other nationalised transport bodies, the Minister of Transport and the Secretary of State acting jointly, and

(c) for all other purposes, the Minister of Transport ;

" member ", in relation to a pension scheme, means a person who has pension rights thereunder whether or not he is a participant therein, and " membership " shall be construed accordingly ;

" nationalised transport body " means any of the following—

(a) a Board,

(b) the Holding Company,

(c) a new authority,

(d) a subsidiary of a Board, the Holding Company or a new authority ;

" new authority " means any of the following bodies, namely—

the Freight Corporation,

the Bus Company, and

the Scottish Group ;

" past member ", in relation to a pension scheme, means a member whose pensionable service has ceased ;

" the Railways Board " means the British Railways Board ;

" the Scottish Group " means the Scottish Transport Group established under section 24 of the Act ;

" subsidiary ", in relation to a nationalised transport body, has the same meaning as in the Transport Act 1962, and in this connection no account shall be taken of the provisions of section 51(5) of the Act ;

" term ", in relation to a pension scheme, includes any rule or provision of the scheme, or of any statutory provision relating to the scheme, or of any trust deed or other instrument made for the purposes of the scheme ; and

" transport pension scheme " means a pension scheme which relates in whole or in part to the provision of pensions in respect of service rendered in the employment of a nationalised transport body.

(5) Unless the context otherwise requires, references in this Order to the provisions of any enactment or instrument shall be construed as references to those provisions as amended, re-enacted or modified by or under any subsequent enactment or instrument.

(6) The Interpretation Act 1889(a) shall apply for the interpretation of this Order as it applies for the interpretation of an Act of Parliament.

Application of the Order

2.—(1) This Order applies to every established scheme, that is to say, to every transport pension scheme which is in existence on the 1st January 1969 and which is either—

(a) an existing scheme within the meaning of the British Transport Reorganisation (Pensions of Employees) (No. 1) Order 1964(b), or

(b) a pension scheme established under section 74 of the Transport Act 1962, or

(c) any other pension scheme in which employees of, or of a subsidiary of, the Railways Board or the Holding Company are participating immediately before the 1st January 1969.

(2) Every established scheme shall, subject to the provisions of paragraph (3) of this Article, be construed and have effect as if the provisions of this Order were terms of the scheme, any other term thereof, whether express or implied, to the contrary notwithstanding, and each nationalised transport body shall, for the purposes of giving effect to this Order, be bound by the terms of every such scheme.

(3) The rights to continue to participate in or to enter or re-enter an established scheme given by this Order shall be additional to any similar rights existing under the terms of that scheme apart from the provisions of this Order and nothing in this Order shall derogate from such rights where they subsist.

PART II

ADAPTATION AND EXTENSION OF CERTAIN ORDERS

Extension of inter-availability of pension schemes

3. The British Transport Reorganisation (Pensions of Employees) (No. 1) Order 1964 (which enables employees of one nationalised transport body to continue to participate in, or to re-enter, pension schemes of another nationalised transport body) (except Article 5 thereof) shall have effect as if—

(a) the expression " Board " therein included each of the new authorities,

<hr/>

(a) 52 & 53 Vict. c. 63. (b) S.I. 1964/1329 (1964 II, p. 3034).

(b) the expression "existing scheme" therein included any established scheme,

(c) the expression "the Minister" therein had the same meaning as in this Order,

(d) in relation to any established scheme, the expression "successor body" therein had the same meaning as the expression "appropriate body" has in this Order, and

(e) in relation to a scheme where the property, rights and liabilities of the Holding Company are transferred by Part IV of this Order, the expression "the appropriate Transfer Order" therein included this Order.

Contribution obligations of nationalised transport bodies and pension rights of persons who become members or directors of such bodies

4. Articles 13, 14 and 16 of the British Transport Reorganisation (Pensions of Employees)(No.3) Order 1962(a)(which make provision for one nationalised transport body to make contributions to another such body and for preserving the pension rights of certain persons who become members or directors of a nationalised transport body), and Article 1 of that Order (which contains definitions) in its application to the said Articles 13, 14 and 16, shall have effect as if—

(a) the expression "Board" therein included each of the new authorities,

(b) the expression "existing scheme" therein included any established scheme,

(c) the expression "the Minister" therein had the same meaning as in this Order,

(d) in relation to any established scheme, the expression "successor body" therein had the same meaning as the expression "appropriate body" has in this Order, and there were substituted for so much of the definition of the expression "responsible employing body" therein as relates to a past member of an existing scheme, the following—

"(b) for a past member of an existing scheme, the nationalised transport body in which is vested under such one or more of the following Acts as may be relevant, that is to say, the Transport Act 1947(b), the Transport Act 1962 and the Transport Act 1968, the particular undertaking, or the particular part of an undertaking (as the case may be), in connection with which he was employed immediately before his pensionable service ended," and

(e) in the said Article 14—

(i) the expressions "the provisions of this Order" and "the foregoing provisions of this Order" included the provisions of the present Order,

(ii) the references to liabilities or functions transferred to a body under that Order included a reference to liabilities or functions transferred to a body by this Order or otherwise falling to be borne or exercised by a body in consequence of this Order, and

(iii) in relation to a scheme where the property, rights and liabilities of the Holding Company are transferred by Part IV of this Order, the references to a power which immediately before the vesting date was exercisable by the Commission included a reference to a power which immediately before the 1st January 1969 was exercisable by the Holding Company.

(a) S.I. 1962/2758 (1962 III, p. 3866).   (b)10 & 11 Geo. 6. c. 49.

PART III

ADDITIONAL ELIGIBILITY

Persons having no pension rights under an established scheme and becoming employees of a new authority or of certain subsidiaries before 1st January 1969

5. Where a person who has no pension rights under an established scheme enters before the 1st January 1969 the employment of a new authority or of the freightliner company or the freight-sundries company after leaving the employment of the Railways Board, the Holding Company or a subsidiary of that Board or Company, he shall be eligible to become a member of that established scheme to the same extent and on the same basis as he would have been so eligible if, instead of entering the employment of that new authority or company, he had been continuing in comparable employment of the Railways Board, the Holding Company or the subsidiary of that Board or Company (as the case may be).

Certain transfers not to affect eligibility to join pension schemes

6. Where, by reason of a transfer under any of the following provisions of the Act, namely, sections 4(1), 4(4), 5(3)(*a*) or (*b*), 7(5) or (6), 8(4), 28(1), (2) or (5), 29(2) or 53(2), a person ceases to be employed by one nationalised transport body and becomes employed by another such body, or the employer of a person ceases to be a subsidiary of one nationalised transport body and becomes a subsidiary of another such body, and that person is not, immediately before the transfer, a member of an established scheme, then he shall, notwithstanding the transfer, be eligible to become a member of that established scheme to the same extent and on the same basis as he would have been so eligible if the transfer had not occurred.

Designation of pension schemes for employees or new authorities or their subsidiaries, if no other pension schemes are available

7. Where on or after the 18th November 1968 a person enters any employment specified in the Table below (whether by reason of becoming an employee of a particular nationalised transport body or by reason of a change in the terms and conditions of his existing employment by such a body) and apart from the provisions of this Article that person would not be eligible to become a member of a transport pension scheme appropriate to the employment which he is entering, then he shall be eligible to become a member of the established scheme specified in that Table in relation to that employment :—

TABLE

Employment	*Established Scheme*
1. Employment by the Freight Corporation or by a subsidiary of that Corporation (not being a body mentioned at 5 below) on terms and conditions which would have created eligibility for membership of the scheme opposite if the employment entered had been that of British Road Services Limited.	British Road Services (Salaried Staff) Group Superannuation Fund.

Employment : continued	*Established Scheme : continued*
2. Employment by any of the bodies at 1 above on terms and conditions which would have created eligibility for membership of the scheme opposite if the employment entered had been that of British Road Services Limited.	British Road Services (Male Wages Grades) Group Pension Fund.
3. Employment by the Bus Company or by a subsidiary of that Company on terms and conditions which would have created eligibility for membership of the scheme opposite if the employment entered had been that of Tilling Association Limited.	Tilling Group Pension Fund.
4. Employment by the Scottish Group or by a subsidiary of that Group on terms and conditions which would have created eligibility for membership of the scheme opposite if the employment entered had been that of Scottish Bus Group Limited.	Scottish Bus Group Pension Fund.
5. Employment by the freightliner company or the freight-sundries company or by a subsidiary of either of those companies on terms and conditions which would have created eligibility for membership of the scheme opposite if the employment entered had been that of the Railways Board.	London and North Eastern Railway Superannuation Fund.
6. Employment by any of the bodies mentioned at 5 above on terms and conditions which would have created eligibility for membership of the scheme opposite if the employment entered had been that of the Railways Board.	British Railways (Wages Grades) Pension Fund.

Part IV

Transfer of Rights and Liabilities of Holding Company

Application of Part IV

8.—(1) This Part of this Order makes provision, in the case of the transfers mentioned in paragraph (2) of this Article, for the transfer of property, rights and liabilities of the Holding Company relating to pensions and pension schemes.

(2) The transfers referred to in paragraph (1) of this Article are the transfers of securities, rights and liabilities of the Holding Company—

(a) to the Freight Corporation under section 4(1) or (4) of the Act,

(b) to the Bus Company under section 28(1) or (5) of the Act, and

(c) to the Scottish Group under section 28(2) or (5) of the Act.

Transfer of property, rights and liabilities

9.—(1) The property, rights and liabilities of the Holding Company relating to the established schemes which are specified in Parts 1, 2 and 3 of the Schedule to this Order (including any functions of that Company in relation to those schemes and any securities or other property held by that Company in trust for those schemes) shall be respectively transferred to the Freight Corporation, the Bus Company and the Scottish Group.

(2) All such property, rights and liabilities of the Holding Company (including as aforesaid) relating to the Railway Clearing System Superannuation Fund Scheme as were transferred to that Company by the British Transport Reorganisation (Pensions of Employees) (No. 3) Order 1962 shall be transferred to the Freight Corporation.

Transfer of certain liabilities

10.—(1) The liability of the Holding Company to make, in relation to any such person as is mentioned in this paragraph, payments or contributions to some other nationalised transport body under any of the provisions mentioned in paragraph (2) of this Article shall be transferred to the Freight Corporation, the Bus Company or the Scottish Group according as the person in relation to whom the payments or contributions fall to be made becomes, on the date of the relevant transfer mentioned in Article 8(2) above, an employee of such body or of a subsidiary of such body, or would then have become such an employee had he been in the employment of a nationalised transport body immediately before that date.

(2) The provisions referred to in paragraph (1) of this Article are the provisions of—

(a) Article 5 of the British Transport Reorganisation (Pensions of Employees) (No. 1) Order 1962(a),

(b) Articles 13 and 14 of the British Transport Reorganisation (Pensions of Employees) (No. 3) Order 1962(b),

(c) Article 10 of the British Transport Reorganisation (Pensions of Employees) (No. 4) Order 1962(c),

(d) Articles 7 and 8 of the British Transport Reorganisation (Pensions of Employees) (No. 1) Order 1964.

General provisions as to transfers

11.—(1) All the transfers of property, rights and liabilities of the Holding Company provided for in this Part of this Order shall take place on the 1st January 1969 and shall be transfers subject to the provisions of this Order, and the property, rights and liabilities hereby transferred shall by virtue of this Order vest on that date in the bodies to which they are respectively transferred.

(2) The provisions of paragraphs 7 to 13 of Schedule 4 to the Act (so far as relevant) shall apply in relation to the transfers provided for in this Part of this Order but subject to the following modifications, that is to say,

the word "agreement" in those paragraphs shall include any trust deed, rules or other instrument relating to an established scheme, and the references to rights or liabilities in those paragraphs shall include references to functions.

(a) S.I. 1962/2714 (1962 III, p. 3688).   (b) S.I. 1962/2758 (1962 III, p. 3866).
(c) S.I. 1962/2793 (1962 III, p. 4020).

(3) Nothing in this Part of this Order shall affect the tenure of office of any person appointed or nominated by the Holding Company before the 1st January 1969 in the exercise of any power conferred on that Company by any term of an established scheme or otherwise exercisable by that Company in relation to an established scheme.

PART V

PAYMENT OF PENSIONS BY NEW AUTHORITIES AND THEIR SUBSIDIARIES

Consent of Minister to payment of pensions

12.—(1) Except as provided by this Article, a new authority and any subsidiary of a new authority shall not without the consent of the Minister pay any pension or enter into any obligation under a pension scheme.

(2) Paragraph (1) shall not apply to—

(*a*) the payment of any pension in accordance with the terms of an established scheme as those terms stand immediately after the 1st January 1969 or are subsequently modified with the consent of the Minister, or

(*b*) the payment of any pension in pursuance of an obligation under a pension scheme entered into with the consent of the Minister after the said date, being a payment in accordance with that obligation as it subsists when first entered into or as it is subsequently modified with the said consent.

(3) Any consent given by the Minister for the purposes of this Article may be given for any case or description of case specified in the consent and may be given subject to conditions.

Given under the Official Seal of the Minister of Transport the 13th December 1968.

(L.S.)
            Richard Marsh,
            Minister of Transport.

            William Ross,
         One of Her Majesty's Principal
           Secretaries of State.

Dated the 17th December 1968.

SCHEDULE

Article 9(1)

PART 1

ESTABLISHED SCHEMES—THE FREIGHT CORPORATION

British Road Services (Salaried Staff) Group Superannuation Fund.
British Road Services (Male Wages Grades) Group Pension Fund.
Burnley Equitable Co-operative & Industrial Society Ltd.
    Superannuation Scheme—Divided.
Chas. A. Wells Endowment Fund—Divided.
Coast Lines Superannuation Fund Association—Divided.
Foremen & Staff Mutual Benefit Society—Divided.
Furness Withy Superannuation Scheme—Divided.
Hay's Wharf Companies Superannuation Fund—Section B.
Rudd Endowment Fund.
Superannuation Fund Association of Chaplins Ltd.

Insurance Funds:—

  Eagle Star Insurance Co. Ltd.:—

    Fairclough Staff Pension Scheme.

    Scribbans Kemp Pension Scheme:—
      Hirst and Payne.
      Red Arrow Deliveries.

  Equity and Law Life Assurance Society Ltd.:—
    E. & E. J. Shaw Ltd. Pension & Life Assurance Scheme.
    Morton's (Coventry) Ltd. Pension & Life Assurance Scheme.

  Prudential Assurance Co. Ltd.:—
    J. Gerrard Transport Ltd. Scheme.

  Scottish Provident Institution:—
    H. & G. Dutfield Ltd. Staff Endowment Scheme.
    Lawther & Harvey Ltd. Pension & Life Assurance Scheme.

  Sun Life Assurance Society Ltd.:—
    George Read (Transport) Ltd.
    R. J. Weeks & Co. Ltd. Staff Superannuation Scheme.
    Springfield Carriers Ltd. Staff Superannuation Scheme.
    The Tayforth Group Staff Pension Fund.
    The Tayforth Group Operatives Pension Fund.
    W. A. & A. G. Spiers Ltd. Staff Assurance Scheme.

Insurance Schemes:—

  Colonial Mutual Life Assurance Society Ltd.:—

A.C.S. Motors Ltd.	H. & G. Dutfield Ltd.
Adamsons Limited.	Harold Wood & Sons Ltd.
Barrack & Fenton Ltd.	H. H. Hawker Ltd.
Bennets Haulage.	J. & G. Barrack Ltd.
Blackford Bros. Ltd.	J. Arnott (Contractors) Ltd.
Cowan & Co.	J. Gupwell Transport Ltd.
Crouchers Ltd.	J. Harvey (Hauliers) Ltd.
D. West & Sons Ltd.	J. Keetch & Son.
Direct Transport (Wellingbro.) Ltd.	Jennens Bros. Transport Ltd.
Donaldson Wright.	Macks Hauliers.
F. Crowther & Son (Wakefield) Ltd.	Marshalls—St. Helens.
F. D. Hulse Ltd.	Munro's Motor Transport Co.
Fisher Renwick Ltd.	P. X. Ltd.
G. H. Atkins & Sons.	R. Keetch & Son Ltd.
Guest Transport Ltd.	Robin Hood Transport Ltd.
Harding Bros. Transport Ltd.	Robinson Transport (Beccles) Ltd.

S. Oatley & Sons Ltd.
Swindon Transport Ltd.
T. Goy & Sons Ltd.
Tees-side Motor Transport Ltd.
Topham Bros.
Union Road Transport.

Wm. Clarke (Nottingham) Ltd.
W. Hesford Ltd.
W. Hill.
W. Wisely & Sons Ltd.
Youngs Express Deliveries.

Eagle Star Insurance Co. Ltd.: —
T. M. Fairclough & Son Ltd. Group Life Assurance Scheme.

Equity & Law Life Assurance Society Ltd.: —
Furness & Parker Ltd.

Friends' Provident & Century Life Office: —
Southern Roadways Ltd. Endowment.

Legal & General Assurance Society Ltd.: —
Ardwick Haulage.
Castle Bros. (Hauliers) Limited Staff Assurance Scheme.
C. Scott's Road Services Ltd. Life Assurance Scheme.
S. J. Jeffrey Ltd. Staff Assurance Scheme.

National Employers' Life Assurance Co. Ltd.: —
F. Crowther & Son (Wakefield) Ltd.

National Mutual Life Association of Australasia: —
Castleford Transport Ltd. Pension Scheme.

National Provident Institution:—
N. Francis & Co. Ltd.

Northern Assurance Company: —
James Express Carriers Ltd.

Norwich Union Life Insurance Society: —
Corringdon Ltd.

Phoenix Assurance Co. Ltd.: —
Davies & Brownlow Ltd. Staff Pension Scheme.

Provident Mutual Life Assurance Association: —
Carter Paterson Ltd.
Hay's Wharf Cartage Co., Pickfords Ltd., & Carter Paterson & Co. Ltd.
Joseph Nall & Co. Ltd.

Royal Exchange Assurance Co. Ltd.: —
Carter Paterson Ltd.

Scottish Widows' Fund and Life Assurance Society: —
Atlantic Steam Navigation Co. Ltd. Pension and Life Insurance Schemes.
H. Viney & Co. Pension & Life Assurance Plan.

Sun Life of Canada: —
D. M. Smith Road Transport Staff Scheme.
G. & B. Watson—B. E. Palmer Ltd.
H. & R. Duncan Ltd.
J. Robertson Group Superannuation.
Northern Motor Utilities Pension Scheme.
T. Brown Transport Pension Scheme.
W. A. Mitchell Road Transport.

Pension schemes for former Road Haulage Undertakings to which the Transferred Undertakings (Pensions of Employees) (No. 2) Regulations 1952(a) and the British Transport Commission (Pensions of Employees) Regulations 1953(b) apply, not being schemes otherwise specified in this Part of this Schedule.

(a) S.I. 1952/1612 (1952 II, p. 2248).   (b) S.I. 1953/1445 (1953 II, p. 1472).

PART 2

ESTABLISHED SCHEMES—THE BUS COMPANY

Bristol Tramways and Carriage Co. Ltd. Superannuation Scheme.
City Widows' Pension Fund.
Foremen and Staff Mutual Benefit Society.
The British Electrical Endowment Fund.
Tillings Endowment Funds.
Tilling Group Pension Fund.

Insurance Funds:—

General & Life Assurance Co.:—
West Riding Automobile Co. Ltd. E.P.T. Master Pension Plan.
West Riding Automobile Co. Ltd. Pension Assurance Plan.

Legal and General Assurance Society Ltd.:—
B.E.T. Group Pension Fund and B.E.T. Group Endowment Scheme.
The B.E.T. Retirement Benefits Scheme.
The Superannuation Fund of Shamrock and Rambler Motor Coaches Ltd.

Insurance Schemes:—

Equity and Law Life Assurance Society Ltd.:—
West Yorkshire Road Car Co. Ltd. (S. Ledgard Ltd.).

Friends Provident and Century Life:—
Scout Motor Services Ltd. Works Provident Fund.

Legal and General Assurance Society Ltd.:—
Red & White Services Limited.
United Welsh Services Ltd.
East Kent Group Pension Scheme.

Provident Mutual Life Assurance Association:—
Brighton, Hove & District Omnibus Co. Ltd.
Durham District Services Ltd.
Eastern Coach Works Ltd.
Eastern Counties Omnibus Co. Ltd.
Maidstone & District Motor Services Ltd. Staff Pension Scheme.
Ribble Pension and Assurance Scheme.
Southdown Motor Services Pension Scheme.
The Aldershot & District Traction Co. Staff Pension Scheme.
Tilling Staff Welfare Society—Section 1.
United Automobile Services Ltd.
United Counties Omnibus Co. Ltd.
West Yorkshire Road Car Co. Ltd.
Wilts and Dorset Motor Services Ltd.

Prudential Assurance Co. Ltd.:—
B.M.M.O. Pension Scheme.

Sun Life Assurance Society:—
Greenslades Tours Superannuation Scheme.

" Bristol " Supplementary Pension Scheme.

Customary and ex gratia pension practices of the Tilling Group of Companies (which for this purpose includes Eastern Coachworks Ltd. and Bristol Commercial Vehicles Ltd.).

Property, rights and liabilities of the Holding Company relating to any established scheme not otherwise specified in this Part of this Schedule for the provision of pensions for staff employed by companies formerly owned by the British Electrical Traction Company Limited or any of its subsidiaries.

PART 3

ESTABLISHED SCHEMES—THE SCOTTISH GROUP

Scottish Bus Group Pension Fund.

Customary and ex gratia pension practices of the Scottish Bus Group Ltd. and Associated Companies.

EXPLANATORY NOTE

(This Note is not part of the Order.)

This Order makes provision for certain changes in connection with established pension schemes in the nationalised transport industry consequent on the setting up of the new authorities (the National Freight Corporation, the National Bus Company and the Scottish Transport Group) by the Transport Act 1968.

By Article 3, the Order extends to staff of the new authorities (and their subsidiaries) the same facility to join and re-enter pension schemes as is conferred on the staff of the existing Boards and the Transport Holding Company (and their subsidiaries) by the British Transport Reorganisation (Pensions of Employees) (No. 1) Order 1964.

By Article 4, the Order provides that Articles 13, 14 and 16 of the British Transport Reorganisation (Pensions of Employees) (No. 3) Order 1962 (which make provision for one nationalised transport body to make contributions to another such body and for preserving the pension rights of certain persons who become members or directors of a nationalised transport body) and so much of Article 1 of that Order as contains definitions of expressions used in the said Articles 13, 14 and 16 are to have effect with modifications to meet the new circumstances arising from the provisions of the Act of 1968 and of the present Order.

Provision is made in Articles 5 to 7 to confer on staff of the new authorities (and their subsidiaries) additional eligibility to join pension schemes.

In Articles 8 to 11 the Order provides for the transfer to the new authorities of the property, rights and liabilities of the Transport Holding Company in relation to certain established pension schemes for which that Company is at present responsible.

The Order places an obligation on the new authorities and their subsidiaries to obtain the consent of the Minister of Transport, or the Secretary of State, before entering into any new pension obligations or amending any established pension scheme (Article 12).

The Order, except for Articles 6 and 8 to 12, has effect from 18th November 1968 by virtue of S. 74(7) of the Transport Act 1962.

STATUTORY INSTRUMENTS

1968 No. 2012

TRANSPORT

PENSIONS AND COMPENSATION

The British Transport (Pensions of Employees) (No. 2) Order 1968

Made - - - -	17th December 1968
Laid before Parliament	30th December 1968
Coming into Operation	31st December 1968

The Minister of Transport and the Secretary of State, acting jointly, make this Order in exercise of their powers under section 74 of the Transport Act 1962(a), as read with section 136 of the Transport Act 1968(b), and of all other enabling powers: —

Commencement, citation and interpretation

1.—(1) This Order shall come into operation on the 31st December 1968 and shall have effect from the 18th November 1968.

(2) This Order may be cited as the British Transport (Pensions of Employees) (No. 2) Order 1968.

(3) In this Order, unless the context otherwise requires—

" the Act " means the Transport Act 1968 ;

" accrued pension rights " has the meaning assigned to that expression in paragraph (4) of this Article ;

" an actuary " means a Fellow of the Institute of Actuaries or of the Faculty of Actuaries in Scotland ;

" the appropriate body ", in relation to a pension scheme under which pensions are provided in respect of service rendered in the employment of a nationalised transport body, means—

(i) where the scheme is one in relation to which the property, rights and liabilities of the Holding Company are transferred by the British Transport (Pensions of Employees) (No. 1) Order 1968(c), the nationalised transport body to which they are so transferred,

(ii) where the scheme does not fall within (i) above but is a scheme in relation to which the responsibility for making payments was placed, or the rights, liabilities and functions of the Commission were transferred, by the British Transport Reorganisation (Pensions of Employees) (No. 2) Order 1962(d), or the British Transport Reorganisation (Pensions of Employees) (No. 3) Order 1962(e), (as the case may be), the nationalised transport body (or if more than one, any one of those bodies) on which that responsibility for the time being rests or in which those rights, liabilities and functions are for the time being vested,

(iii) where the scheme does not fall within (i) or (ii) above but is a scheme in which employees of a nationalised transport body which

---

(a) 10 & 11 Eliz. 2. c. 46. (b) 1968 c. 73. (c) S.I. 1968/2011 (1968 III, p. 5450).
(d) S.I. 1962/2715 (1962 III, p. 3692). (e) S.I. 1962/2758 (1962 III, p. 3866).

is a subsidiary of a Board or the Holding Company are participating immediately before the 1st January 1969, whichever of the
following bodies, namely, a Board, the Freight Corporation, the
Bus Company, the Scottish Group and the Holding Company, is
the body of which the said nationalised transport body is a subsidiary immediately after the 1st January 1969, and

(iv) in all other cases, the nationalised transport body which has
established the scheme ;

" a Board " means any of the following bodies, namely—

the British Railways Board,

the London Transport Board,

the British Transport Docks Board,

the British Waterways Board ;

" the Bus Company " means the National Bus Company established
under section 24 of the Act ;

" the Commission " means the British Transport Commission ;

" discharged officer " means an officer who loses his employment as
an officer by reason of a relevant event (the cause of the loss having arisen
not later than the end of 10 years after the date of the event in question)
and who does not thereupon enter the employment of another nationalised
transport body, and " discharge " in relation to a discharged officer means
such loss of employment ;

" the Freight Corporation " means the National Freight Corporation
established under section 1 of the Act ;

" funded scheme " means a scheme, not being an insurance scheme,
which relates in whole or in part to providing pensions in respect of
service rendered in the employment of a nationalised transport body, such
pensions being payable out of a fund held by any person for the purposes
of the scheme ;

" general scheme " means a scheme, not being a funded scheme or an
insurance scheme, which relates in whole or in part to providing pensions
in respect of service rendered in the employment of a nationalised transport
body ;

" the Holding Company " means the Transport Holding Company established under section 29 of the Transport Act 1962 ;

" insurance scheme " means a scheme for providing pensions in respect
of service rendered in the employment of a nationalised transport body by
way of contracts or policies made or effected with an assurance company
carrying on life assurance business within the meaning of the Insurance
Companies Act 1958(a) (including contracts or policies made with such a
company for the purpose of implementing any form of private superannuation fund) ;

" member ", in relation to a pension scheme, means a person who has
pension rights thereunder whether or not he is a participant therein, and
" membership " shall be construed accordingly ;

" the Minister " means the Minister of Transport ;

" nationalised transport body " means any of the following : —

a Board,

the Holding Company,

(a) 6 & 7 Eliz. 2. c. 72.

the Freight Corporation,

the Bus Company,

the Scottish Group,

a subsidiary of any of the foregoing bodies ;

" non-participating employment " has the meaning assigned to it by section 56(1) of the National Insurance Act 1965(a) ;

" normal retiring age " means—

(i) in relation to a discharged officer who immediately before his discharge was, by virtue of the terms of his employment or the terms of the pension scheme associated with that employment, subject to a requirement to retire from that employment before attaining the age of 65 years (if a man) or 60 years (if a woman), the age at which he would have been required by those terms to retire if he had not been discharged,

(ii) in relation to a discharged officer who immediately before his discharge had the right of continuing in his employment as an officer beyond the age of 65 years (if a man) or 60 years (if a woman), the minimum age at which he could, by the terms of his employment or the terms of his pension scheme, be required to retire or, if there is no such age, his actual age at the time when he could have been required by those terms to retire if he had not been discharged, and

(iii) in all other cases, 65 years for men and 60 years for women ;

" officer " means a person employed (whether as member, director or holder of some other office or appointment, or as a servant) by any of the following bodies, that is to say—

the Railways Board,

the Freight Corporation,

the Bus Company,

the Scottish Group,

the Holding Company,

a subsidiary of any of the foregoing bodies,

and " employment as an officer " means such employment by any of those bodies ;

" pensionable service " means service ranking for benefit under a pension scheme ;

" relevant event " means any one of the events specified in paragraph (a), (b), (c) or (but only where the existing operator as defined in Schedule 6 to the Act whose consent is revoked is a nationalised transport body) (d) of section 135(1) of the Act :

" the Railways Board " means the British Railways Board ;

" the Scottish Group " means the Scottish Transport Group established under section 24 of the Act ;

" subsidiary ", in relation to a nationalised transport body, has the same meaning as in the Transport Act 1962 (the provisions of section 51(5) of the Act being disregarded) ; and

(a) 1965 c. 51.

" tribunal " means a referee or board of referees appointed by the Secretary of State for Employment and Productivity after consultation with the Lord Chancellor or, where the proceedings are to be held in Scotland, after consultation with the Secretary of State.

(4) In this Order the expression " accrued pension rights ", in relation to a discharged officer, means any right to the payment on or after his reaching normal retiring age or on or after the happening of any other contingency (which expression includes the exercise of any right to receive a pension on retirement before reaching normal retiring age) carrying entitlement to pension under his scheme—

(a) if his scheme is an insurance scheme, of the pension which would have been payable to or in respect of him by virtue of any premiums paid by or in respect of him under the scheme up to the date of his discharge ; or

(b) if his scheme is a funded scheme or a general scheme and the scheme is a scheme under which the pension rights are related by some specific proportion to pensionable service and pensionable emoluments, of a pension payable to or in respect of him calculated at such fraction or fractions of his pensionable emoluments in respect of each year or part of a year of his pensionable service as would have been applicable under that scheme in the calculation of the pension, if he had at the date of his discharge reached normal retiring age, or, as the case may be, if the other contingency had then happened and there had been no requirement of the scheme as to a minimum qualifying period of service ; or

(c) if his scheme is a funded scheme or a general scheme and the scheme is a scheme under which the pension rights are not related by some specific proportion to pensionable service and pensionable emoluments, of a pension payable to or in respect of him calculated on reaching normal retiring age or, as the case may be, on the happening of the other contingency, as follows : —

(i) on reaching normal retiring age, the pension which would have been payable under the scheme had he continued to be a member of the scheme until that age without increase of emoluments, but reduced in the proportion which the number of years of pensionable service under the scheme before the date of his discharge bears to the number of years of pensionable service which he would have rendered had he continued to be a member of the scheme until normal retiring age ; or

(ii) on the happening of the other contingency, the pension which would have been payable under the scheme if the contingency had happened on the date of his discharge with the corresponding emoluments and length of service and there had been no requirement of the scheme as to a minimum qualifying period of service :

Provided that for the purpose of ascertaining the amount of any pension under sub-paragraphs (b) and (c) of this paragraph no account shall be taken of any right to payments of pension on account of temporary periods of incapacity which exceed in total amount or total period of payment the maximum amount or period laid down in the relevant scheme.

(5) Unless the context otherwise requires, references in this Order to the provisions of any Act of Parliament or instrument made thereunder shall be construed as references to those provisions as amended, re-enacted or modified by or under any subsequent Act or instrument.

(6) The Interpretation Act 1889(**a**) shall apply for the interpretation of this Order as it applies for the interpretation of an Act of Parliament.

Return of contributions

2. Where a discharged officer is entitled under his pension scheme, on his discharge, to receive any payment by way of a return of contributions paid by or in respect of him, with or without interest thereon, he may, at any time within three months of the date of his discharge exercise his right to receive such a payment ; and where such a right is exercised by any person the subsequent provisions of this Order shall not apply to him, and the persons administering the scheme, the persons in whom any fund held for the purposes of the scheme is vested, and the appropriate body shall be discharged from all other liability under the scheme to or in respect of that officer or to any other person by reason of that right having been exercised.

Funded schemes

3.—(1) Subject to the provisions of this Order, this and the next two succeeding Articles shall apply to every discharged officer who at the date of his discharge has accrued pension rights under a funded scheme.

(2) In respect of a discharged officer to whom this Article applies, the appropriate body may, not later than 3 months after the date of his discharge, make such arrangements with the persons administering the scheme as shall secure to him his accrued pension rights.

(3) Any arrangements made under the last foregoing paragraph may be terminated by the appropriate body at any time upon giving to the persons administering the scheme 3 months' previous notice in writing.

(4) Notwithstanding anything to the contrary in any such scheme as aforesaid or any statutory provisions relating thereto or trust deeds, rules or other instruments made for the purposes thereof, the persons administering the scheme shall be authorised to make such arrangements (including the disposal of funds held for the purposes of the scheme) as are referred to in paragraph (2) of this Article and the said scheme, statutory provisions, trust deeds, rules and other instruments shall be construed accordingly and as though provision was duly made in the scheme for any arrangements so made.

4.—(1) Where no such arrangements as are mentioned in Article 3 of this Order are made in relation to a discharged officer to whom this Article applies, or where such arrangements, if made, have been duly terminated, the persons in whom any funds held for the purposes of the scheme are vested shall transfer to the appropriate body a sum which equals in amount either—

(*a*) the transfer value at the date of his discharge or the date on which the arrangements are terminated, as the case may be, of his pension rights as defined for the purposes of the scheme, or

(*b*) in the absence of such a definition, the estimated capital value at that date of his accrued pension rights,

with compound interest from the date of his discharge or the date on which the arrangements are terminated, as the case may be, until such sum is transferred to the appropriate body ; and upon such sum being transferred, the appropriate body shall indemnify the persons in whom the said sum is vested against any liability for the payment of income tax in respect of the sum transferred to that body, and, without prejudice to their liability

---

(**a**) 52 & 53 Vict. c. 63.

under arrangements made in accordance with Article 3 of this Order or under the preceding provisions of this Article, as from the date of the discharge of such discharged officer, the persons administering the scheme, and the persons in whom the said fund is vested, shall be discharged from all liability under the scheme to or in respect of that discharged officer or to any other person by reason of the transfer.

(2) The reference in paragraph (1) of this Article to compound interest shall be construed as a reference to compound interest at the same rate and with the same rests as were applied—

(a) in a case where the sum to be transferred is that referred to in sub-paragraph (a) of the said paragraph, for the purposes of the last periodical actuarial valuation of the fund held for the purposes of the scheme ; and

(b) in any other case, for the purposes of calculating the estimated capital value of the accrued pension rights referred to in that paragraph.

(3) The sum to be transferred to the appropriate body under the provisions of paragraph (1) of this Article shall be transferred within 6 months after the date of the discharge of the officer concerned or, where any such arrangements as are referred to in paragraph (2) of the last preceding Article have been made, the date on which the arrangements are duly terminated, as the case may be.

(4) The sum referred to in paragraph (1)(b) of this Article shall be determined by an actuary appointed by the appropriate body and the fees of any actuary so appointed shall be defrayed by the appropriate body.

5.—(1) Subject to the provisions of this Article, where in relation to a discharged officer to whom this Article applies a sum has been transferred to the appropriate body under the provisions of the last preceding Article, the appropriate body shall pay to or in respect of that officer : —

(a) as from his reaching normal retiring age, or as from the happening of any other contingency carrying entitlement to pension under the scheme, the payment or payments comprised in his accrued pension rights ; or

(b) at the option of the appropriate body in any case where the sum does not exceed £250 and where the officer concerned has not at any time before his discharge been in non-participating employment or, if he has so been, a payment in lieu of graduated contributions has been made in respect of his non-participating employment in accordance with section 58 of the National Insurance Act 1965, (such option to be exercised not later than 6 months after the date of his discharge), a lump sum equal in amount to the estimated capital value of his accrued pension rights at the date when the option is exercised, as determined by an actuary appointed by the appropriate body, reduced by the aggregate of—

(i) any sum which the persons in whom the fund held for the purposes of that scheme is vested may become liable to pay by way of income tax in respect of the amount transferred by way of transfer value or estimated capital value, and

(ii) in a case where a payment in lieu of graduated contributions has been made under section 58 of the National Insurance Act 1965 on the discharge of the officer concerned and the period taken into account in fixing the amount of that payment includes any period of his pensionable service under that scheme, the smaller of the following two sums—

(A) one-half of so much of that payment in lieu of graduated contributions as is referable to that period of pensionable service, and

(B) the estimated capital value (determined as aforesaid) of the pension rights which have accrued to him under that scheme in respect of that period of pensionable service :

Provided that for the purposes of this paragraph, the expression " accrued pension rights " excludes any pension payable during the period for which any such arrangements as are referred to in Article 3(2) of this Order are in force.

(2) Except as provided in paragraph (1)(*b*) of this Article, the payment or payments comprised in the accrued pension rights of a discharged officer to whom this Article applies shall not be capable of surrender, commutation or assignment otherwise than in accordance with the rules of his pension scheme.

(3) The appropriate body may discharge its liability under paragraph (1)(*a*) of this Article by making such arrangements with a life assurance company as will secure to or in respect of the discharged officer concerned, as from his reaching normal retiring age or as from the happening of any other contingency carrying entitlement to pension under his pension scheme, the payment or payments comprised in his accrued pension rights.

(4) Except as aforesaid, the appropriate body shall be under no liability to or in respect of the discharged officer concerned by reason of any rights under or arising out of his membership of the scheme.

Insurance Schemes

6.—(1) Subject to the provisions of this Order, this Article shall apply to every discharged officer who at the date of his discharge has accrued pension rights under an insurance scheme.

(2) In respect of a discharged officer to whom this Article applies, the appropriate body shall, not later than 3 months after the date of his discharge, make such arrangements with the persons administering the scheme and the life assurance company concerned as shall secure to or in respect of that discharged officer on his reaching normal retiring age, or on the happening of any other contingency carrying entitlement to pension under the scheme, the payment or payments comprised in his accrued pension rights.

(3) Any arrangements made under paragraph (2) of this Article shall, in any case where the payments to be secured thereunder to or in respect of a discharged officer on his reaching normal retiring age do not exceed £13 per annum and where the officer concerned has not at any time before his discharge been in non-participating employment or, if he has so been, a payment in lieu of graduated contributions has been made in respect of his non-participating employment in accordance with section 58 of the National Insurance Act 1965, provide that the life assurance company may, at any time within 3 months of the making of the arrangements, discharge its liability thereunder by paying to or in respect of the discharged officer concerned a lump sum equal in amount to the estimated capital value of his accrued pension rights as at the date on which the arrangements are

made, determined in such manner as may be provided by the arrangements so made, and adjusted, in such manner as may be provided by the arrangements, in respect of the aggregate of:—

(a) any sum which the persons administering the scheme may become liable to pay by way of income tax in consequence of the payment of the said lump sum, and

(b) in a case where a payment in lieu of graduated contributions has been made under section 58 of the National Insurance Act 1965 on the discharge of the officer concerned and the period taken into account in fixing the amount of that payment includes any period of his pensionable service under that scheme, the smaller of the following two sums—

(i) one-half of so much of that payment in lieu of graduated contributions as is referable to that period of pensionable service, and

(ii) the estimated capital value (determined as aforesaid) of the pension rights which have accrued to him under that scheme in respect of that period of pensionable service.

(4) Notwithstanding anything to the contrary in such scheme as aforesaid or any statutory provisions relating thereto or trust deeds, rules or other instruments made for the purposes thereof, the persons administering the scheme and the life assurance company concerned shall be authorised to make such arrangements (including the disposal of any funds held for the purposes of the scheme) as are referred to in paragraph (2) of this Article and the said scheme, statutory provisions, trust deeds, rules and other instruments shall be construed accordingly and as though provision was duly made in the scheme for any arrangements so made.

(5) Except as provided in paragraph (3) of this Article, the arrangements aforesaid shall ensure that the payment or payments comprised in the accrued pension rights of the officer concerned shall not be capable of surrender, commutation or assignment otherwise than in accordance with the rules of his pension scheme.

General Schemes

7.—(1) Subject to the provisions of this Order, this Article shall apply to every discharged officer who at the date of his discharge has accrued pension rights under a general scheme.

(2) The appropriate body shall pay to or in respect of a discharged officer to whom this Article applies—

(a) as from his reaching normal retiring age, or as from the happening of any other contingency carrying entitlement to pension under the scheme, the payment or payments comprised in his accrued pension rights ; or

(b) at the option of the appropriate body in any case where the sum does not exceed £250 and where the officer concerned has not at any time before his discharge been in non-participating employment or, if he has so been, a payment in lieu of graduated contributions has been made in respect of his non-participating employment in accordance with section 58 of the National Insurance Act 1965, (such option to be exercised not later than 6 months after the date of his discharge), a lump sum equal in amount to the estimated capital value of his accrued pension rights at the date when the option is exercised, as determined by an actuary appointed by the appropriate body, reduced by the aggregate of—

(i) any sum payable by way of income tax in consequence of the payment of the said lump sum, and

(ii) in a case where a payment in lieu of graduated contributions has been made under section 58 of the National Insurance Act 1965 on the discharge of the officer concerned and the period taken into account in fixing the amount of that payment includes any period of his pensionable service under that scheme, the smaller of the following two sums:—

(A) one-half of so much of that payment in lieu of graduated contributions as is referable to that period of pensionable service, and

(B) the estimated capital value (determined as aforesaid) of the pension rights which have accrued to him under that scheme in respect of that period of pensionable service.

(3) Except as provided in paragraph (2)(*b*) of this Article, the payment or payments comprised in the accrued pension rights of the officer concerned shall not be capable of surrender, commutation or assignment otherwise than in accordance with the rules of his pension scheme.

(4) The appropriate body may discharge its liability under paragraph (2)(*a*) of this Article by making such arrangements with a life assurance company as will secure to or in respect of the discharged officer concerned as from his reaching normal retiring age or as from the happening of any other contingency carrying entitlement to pension under the scheme, the payment or payments comprised in his accrued pension rights.

(5) Except as aforesaid, the appropriate body shall be under no liability to or in respect of the discharged officer concerned by reason of any rights under or arising out of his membership of the scheme.

Transfer of pension rights

8.—(1) Subject to the provisions of this Order, this Article shall apply to (and only to) every discharged officer who at the date of his discharge is a participant in a funded scheme, or who, having immediately before entering the employment of the Commission been a participant in a funded scheme, is at the date of his discharge a member of a general scheme by virtue of Regulations made by the Minister under section 98 of the Transport Act 1947(**a**).

(2) In respect of any discharged officer to whom this Article applies, and who, within a period of 12 months from the date of his discharge, obtains other employment in connection with which he has pension rights under another pension scheme (being a scheme approved in whole or in part by the Commissioners of Inland Revenue under section 379 of the Income Tax Act 1952(**b**) or otherwise approved by them for the purposes of this Article), the appropriate body may, subject to the provisions of this Article, make arrangements with the persons administering that other scheme and, in the case of a participant in a funded scheme, with the persons administering that scheme, for the transfer to the persons administering that other scheme of a sum which equals in amount either—

(*a*) the transfer value at the date on which the arrangements are made of his pension rights as defined for the purposes of his existing scheme, or

---

(a) 10 & 11 Geo. 6. c. 49.   (b) 15 & 16 Geo. 6 & 1 Eliz. 2. c. 10.

(*b*) in the absence of such a definition, the estimated capital value at that date of his accrued pension rights,

with compound interest from the date on which the arrangements are made until such transfer is made :

Provided that no such arrangements shall be concluded unless and until the appropriate body has communicated the terms thereof to the discharged officer concerned, has furnished him with a copy of a certificate given by the actuary of that other pension scheme certifying that the pension rights to be conferred on him under the arrangements, if made, will be actuarially equivalent to his accrued pension rights under his former scheme, and has obtained his consent to the making of the arrangements.

(3) The reference in paragraph (2) of this Article to compound interest shall be construed as a reference to compound interest at the same rate and with the same rests as were applied—

(*a*) in a case where the sum to be transferred is that referred to in sub-paragraph (*a*) of the said paragraph, for the purposes of the last periodical actuarial valuation of the fund held for the purposes of the scheme ; and

(*b*) in any other case, for the purposes of calculating the estimated capital value of the accrued pension rights referred to in that paragraph.

(4) The sum to be transferred under any such arrangements as are referred to in paragraph (2) of this Article shall be determined by an actuary appointed by the appropriate body and the fees of any actuary so appointed shall be defrayed by the appropriate body.

(5) The persons administering any pension scheme to whom any sum is transferred under any such arrangements as are referred to in paragraph (2) of this Article shall indemnify the appropriate body or, where the sum is transferred in respect of a participant in a funded scheme, the persons in whom any fund held for the purposes of the funded scheme is vested, against any liability for the payment of income tax in respect of the sum so transferred.

(6) Notwithstanding anything to the contrary in any such scheme as is referred to in the foregoing provisions of this Article or any statutory provisions relating thereto or trust deeds, rules or other instruments made for the purposes thereof, the appropriate body and the persons administering the scheme shall be authorised to make such arrangements (including the disposal of funds held for the purposes of any funded scheme) as are referred to in paragraph (2) of this Article and the said scheme, statutory provisions, trust deeds, rules and other instruments shall be construed accordingly and as though provision was duly made in the scheme for any arrangements so made.

Avoidance of diminution in or loss of pension rights of officers who are not discharged

9.—(1) Subject to the provisions of this Order, this Article shall apply to every officer who is a member of a pension scheme under which he has pension rights in connection with his service in the employment of a nationalised transport body, and who (though not discharged) suffers a diminution of his emoluments, or a change in the nature or terms of his employment, by reason of a relevant event, the cause of such diminution or change having arisen not later than the end of 10 years after the date of the event in question.

(2) An officer to whom this Article applies as a result of a diminution of his emoluments may (without prejudice to any other power he may

have in that behalf) with the consent of the appropriate body and the persons administering the pension scheme continue his premiums or contributions under the scheme and continue to have premiums or contributions paid in respect of him thereunder and to be entitled to the benefits thereof by reference to the amount of his emoluments before they were first so diminished ; and notwithstanding anything to the contrary contained therein, every such scheme and any statutory provisions relating thereto and all trust deeds, rules and other instruments made for the purposes thereof, shall be construed accordingly and as though the provisions of this paragraph were a term of the scheme.

(3) An officer to whom this Article applies as a result of a change in the nature or terms of his employment, the change being such as would terminate his membership of the pension scheme, shall have the right, if he gives notice in writing to that effect to the persons administering the scheme within 3 months of the date of such change, to continue to be a member of the scheme so long as he remains in the employment of a nationalised transport body and to be treated as having been such from the date of such change and as subject to the like conditions as to payment of premiums or contributions and otherwise in all respects as if that change had not taken place ; and notwithstanding anything to the contrary contained therein, every such scheme and any statutory provisions relating thereto and all trust deeds, rules and other instruments made for the purposes thereof, shall be construed accordingly and as though the provisions of this paragraph were a term of the scheme.

(4) Where an officer who is entitled to give notice under paragraph (3) of this Article to the persons administering a pension scheme does not give that notice within the time prescribed thereby, the provisions of this Order (other than Article 2) shall apply in respect of him as if he were a discharged officer and as if the date of the change in the nature or terms of his employment which entitles him to give the said notice were the date of his discharge.

Payment of contributions towards liability of appropriate body

10. Where by reason of any provision of this Order any liability falls upon the appropriate body for a pension scheme in respect of a discharged officer or an officer to whom Article 9 of this Order applies and—

(*a*) in the case of a discharged officer, he was not an officer of, or of any subsidiary of, that body immediately before his discharge, and

(*b*) in the case of an officer to whom Article 9 of this Order applies, he was not an officer of, or of any subsidiary of, that body immediately before the occurrence of the diminution of his emoluments or the change in the nature or terms of his employment,

then whichever of the following bodies, that is to say, the Railways Board, the Freight Corporation, the Bus Company, the Scottish Group and the Holding Company, was the body by which, or by the subsidiary of which, he was employed immediately before the discharge or occurrence aforesaid, shall make such payment by way of contribution to the liability of the appropriate body as may be just in all the circumstances ; and if there is any disagreement between the bodies concerned as to the obligations of any such body as aforesaid under this Article, the matter shall, on the application of either body, be referred for decision to the Minister and the Secretary of State jointly, in a case involving the Scottish Group, or to the Minister in all other cases, and the decision of the Minister and the Secretary of State or the decision of the Minister (as the case may be) shall be final.

Determination of Disputes

11. Without prejudice to the provisions of Article 10 of this Order any question arising between the appropriate body and any person as to whether that person is a member of a pension scheme, and any question arising between the appropriate body and a member of a pension scheme as to the application or effect of any of the provisions of Articles 3(2), 5(1)(*a*), 5(3), 6(2), 7(2)(*a*) or 7(4) of this Order shall in default of agreement between the parties concerned be referred to a tribunal.

Given under the Official Seal of the Minister of Transport the 13th December 1968.

(L.S.)

Richard Marsh,
Minister of Transport.

William Ross,
One of Her Majesty's Principal
Secretaries of State.

Dated the 17th December 1968.

EXPLANATORY NOTE

(This Note is not part of the Order.)

This Order deals with the preservation of the pension rights of persons who because of any of the various reorganisations in the nationalised transport industry provided for in the Transport Act 1968 either lose their employment or suffer diminution of emoluments or a change in the nature or terms of their employment.

In the case of a person who loses his employment, the pension accrued up to the date on which he was discharged is normally to be paid to him at age 65 (age 60 for a woman) or at such time as, by the terms of his employment or of his pension scheme, he would have been entitled to receive a pension (Articles 3(2), 5(1)(*a*), 6(2) and 7(2)(*a*)). A discharged person may, however, elect within 3 months of his discharge to have a return of contributions if the rules of his pension scheme permit this ; but, if he does so, he will have no other rights under the Order (Article 2). Where the value of the accrued pension rights is small, the appropriate body as defined in Article 1(3) (or in the case of an insurance scheme, the life assurance company) may, in certain circumstances and at their option, commute their liability by an immediate lump sum payment (Articles 5(1)(*b*), 6(3) and 7(2)(*b*)).

The appropriate body may discharge its liability to preserve a discharged person's accrued pension rights by arranging for a life assurance company to make the payments at the appropriate time (Articles 5(3) and 7(4)).

In certain cases, where the new employment obtained by a discharged person is pensionable, the appropriate body may, with the prior agreement of the discharged person, pay or arrange for the payment to that person's new pension scheme of the sum representing the value of that person's rights in his former scheme (Article 8).

A person who does not lose his employment but who suffers a reduction in pay may be allowed to continue to contribute to, and benefit from, his pension scheme on the basis of his former pay. Similarly, if such a person is transferred from a pensionable to a non-pensionable grade he can, within 3 months, choose to remain in his pension scheme, though if he does not choose to do this his pension rights will be preserved in the same way as if he had been discharged (Article 9).

Provision is made for contributions between the nationalised transport bodies (Article 10) and for the settlement of disputes (Article 11).

The Order has effect from 18th November 1968, by virtue of S. 74(7) of the Transport Act 1962.

STATUTORY INSTRUMENTS

1968 No. 2015

SUGAR

The Sugar (Rates of Surcharge and Surcharge Repayments) (No. 8) Order 1968

Made - - - -	*19th December* 1968
Laid before Parliament	*23rd December* 1968
Coming into Operation	*24th December* 1968

The Minister of Agriculture, Fisheries and Food, in exercise of the powers conferred on him by sections 7(4), 8(6) and 33(4) of the Sugar Act 1956(a) having effect subject to the provisions of section 3 of, and Part II of Schedule 5 to, the Finance Act 1962(b), and section 58 of the Finance Act 1968 (c) and of all other powers enabling him in that behalf, with the concurrence of the Treasury, on the advice of the Sugar Board, hereby makes the following order:—

1.—(1) This order may be cited as the Sugar (Rates of Surcharge and Surcharge Repayments) (No. 8) Order 1968; and shall come into operation on 24th December 1968.

(2) The Interpretation Act 1889(d) shall apply for the interpretation of this order as it applies for the interpretation of an Act of Parliament.

2. Notwithstanding the provisions of Article 2 of the Sugar (Rates of Surcharge and Surcharge Repayments) (No. 7) Order 1968(e), the rates of surcharge payable under and in accordance with the provisions of section 7 of the Sugar Act 1956, having effect as aforesaid, in respect of sugar and invert sugar imported or home produced or used in the manufacture of imported composite sugar products shall on and after 24th December 1968 be those rates specified in Schedule 1 to this order.

3. For the purpose of section 8(3)(b) of the Sugar Act 1956, having effect as aforesaid, the rates of surcharge repayments in respect of invert sugar produced in the United Kingdom from materials on which on or after 24th December 1968 sugar duty has been paid or, by virtue of paragraph 1 of Part II of Schedule 5 to the Finance Act 1962, is treated as having been paid shall, notwithstanding the provisions of Article 3 of the Sugar (Rates of Surcharge and Surcharge Repayments) (No. 7) Order 1968 be those specified in Schedule 2 to this order.

(a) 1956 c. 48.   (b) 1962 c. 44.
(c) 1968 c. 44.   (d) 1889 c. 63.
(e) S.I. 1968/1883 (1968 III, p. 5024).

In Witness whereof the Official Seal of the Minister of Agriculture Fisheries and Food is hereunto affixed on 18th December 1968.

(L.S.)   *R. P. Fraser*,

Authorised by the Minister.

We concur.

19th December 1968.

E. Alan Fitch,
Walter Harrison,

Two of the Lords Commissioners of
Her Majesty's Treasury.

SCHEDULE 1

PART I

SURCHARGE RATES FOR SUGAR

Polarisation	Rate of Surcharge per cwt.	
	s.	d.
Exceeding—		
99°	25	8·0
98° but not exceeding 99°	24	2·4
97° „ „ „ 98°	23	7·3
96° „ „ „ 97°	22	11·9
95° „ „ „ 96°	22	4·5
94° „ „ „ 95°	21	9·1
93° „ „ „ 94°	21	1·7
92° „ „ „ 93°	20	6·4
91° „ „ „ 92°	19	11·0
90° „ „ „ 91°	19	3·6
89° „ „ „ 90°	18	8·2
88° „ „ „ 89°	18	0·8
87° „ „ „ 88°	17	6·6
86° „ „ „ 87°	17	0·5
85° „ , „ 86°	16	6·9
84° „ „ „ 85°	16	1·4
83° „ „ „ 84°	15	7·8
82° „ „ „ 83°	15	2·3
81° „ „ „ 82°	14	9·4
80° „ „ „ 81°	14	4·4
79° „ „ „ 80°	13	11·5
78° „ „ „ 79°	13	6·6
77° „ „ „ 78°	13	1·6
76° „ „ „ 77°	12	8·7
Not exceeding 76°	12	3·8

Part II

Surcharge Rates for Invert Sugar

Sweetening matter content by weight	Rate of Surcharge per cwt.
	s. d.
70 per cent. or more	16 3
Less than 70 per cent. and more than 50 per cent.	11 8
Not more than 50 per cent.	5 9

SCHEDULE 2

Surcharge Repayment Rates for Invert Sugar

Sweetening matter content by weight	Rate of Surcharge Repayment per cwt.
	s. d.
More than 80 per cent.	19 3
More than 70 per cent. but not more than 80 per cent.	16 3
More than 60 per cent. but not more than 70 per cent.	11 8
More than 50 per cent. but not more than 60 per cent.	9 3
Not more than 50 per cent. and the invert sugar not being less in weight than 14 lb. per gallon	5 9

EXPLANATORY NOTE

(This Note is not part of the Order.)

This order prescribes—

(*a*) reductions equivalent to 2s. 4d. per cwt. of refined sugar in the rates of surcharge payable on sugar and invert sugar which become chargeable with surcharge on or after 24th December 1968;

(*b*) correspondingly reduced rates of surcharge repayment in respect of invert sugar produced in the United Kingdom from materials on which surcharge has been paid.

STATUTORY INSTRUMENTS

1968 No. 2016

SUGAR

The Composite Sugar Products (Surcharge and Surcharge Repayments—Average Rates) (No. 8) Order 1968

Made - - - -	*19th December* 1968
Laid before Parliament	*23rd December* 1968
Coming into Operation	*24th December* 1968

Whereas the Minister of Agriculture, Fisheries and Food (hereinafter called " the Minister ") has on the recommendation of the Commissioners of Customs and Excise (hereinafter called " the Commissioners ") made an order(a) pursuant to the powers conferred upon him by sections 9(1) and 9(4) of the Sugar Act 1956(b), having effect subject to the provisions of section 3 of, and Part II of Schedule 5 to, the Finance Act 1962(c), to the provisions of section 52(2) of the Finance Act 1966(d), and to the provisions of Section 58 of the Finance Act 1968(e), providing that in the case of certain descriptions of composite sugar products surcharge shall be calculated on the basis of an average quantity of sugar or invert sugar taken to have been used in the manufacture of the products, and that certain other descriptions of composite sugar products shall be treated as not containing any sugar or invert sugar, and that in the case of certain descriptions of goods in the manufacture of which sugar or invert sugar is used, surcharge repayments shall be calculated on the basis of an average quantity of sugar or invert sugar taken to have been so used:

Now, therefore, the Minister, on the recommendation of the Commissioners and in exercise of the powers conferred upon him by sections 9(1), 9(4) and 33(4) of the Sugar Act 1956, having effect as aforesaid, and of all other powers enabling him in that behalf, hereby makes the following order:—

1.—(1) This order may be cited as the Composite Sugar Products (Surcharge and Surcharge Repayments—Average Rates) (No. 8) Order 1968; and shall come into operation on 24th December 1968.

(2) The Interpretation Act 1889(f) shall apply for the interpretation of this order as it applies for the interpretation of an Act of Parliament.

2. Surcharge payable on or after 24th December 1968 under and in accordance with the Sugar Act 1956, having effect as aforesaid, in respect of sugar and invert sugar used in the manufacture of the descriptions of imported composite sugar products specified in column 2 of Schedule 1 to this order shall, notwithstanding the provisions of the Sugar (Rates of Surcharge and Surcharge Repayments) (No. 8) Order 1968(g) and the Composite Sugar Products (Surcharge and Surcharge Repayments—Average Rates) (No. 7) Order 1968(a), be calculated by reference to the weight or value, as the case may be, of the products at the rates specified in relation thereto in column 3 of the said Schedule.

(a) S.I. 1968/1884 (1968 III, p. 5027).   (b) 1956 c. 48.   (c) 1962 c. 44.
(d) 1966 c. 18.   (e) 1968 c. 44.   (f) 1889 c. 63.
(g) S.I. 1968/2015 (1968 III, p. 5475).

3. Imported composite sugar products other than those of a description specified in Schedules 1 and 2 to this order shall be treated as not containing any sugar or invert sugar for the purposes of surcharge payable on or after 24th December 1968.

4. Surcharge repayments payable on and after 24th December 1968 under and in accordance with the provisions of section 8 of the Sugar Act 1956, having effect as aforesaid, in respect of sugar and invert sugar used in the manufacture of the descriptions of goods specified in column 1 of Schedule 3 to this order shall, notwithstanding the provisions of the Sugar (Rates of Surcharge and Surcharge Repayments) (No. 8) Order 1968(a) and the Composite Sugar Products (Surcharge and Surcharge Repayments—Average Rates) (No. 7) Order 1968(b), be calculated by reference to the quantity of the goods at the rates specified in relation thereto in column 2 of the said Schedule.

In Witness whereof the Official Seal of the Minister of Agriculture, Fisheries and Food is hereunto affixed on 19th December 1968.

(L.S.)

R. P. Fraser,
Authorised by the Minister.

SCHEDULE 1

In this Schedule:—

" Tariff heading " means a heading or, where the context so requires, a subheading of the Customs Tariff 1959 (see paragraph (1) of Article 1 of the Import Duties (General) (No. 4) Order 1968(c)).

" Per cent." means, where it occurs in relation to any rate of surcharge, per cent. of the value for customs duty purposes of the product to which it relates.

Tariff heading	Description of Imported Composite Sugar Products	Rate of Surcharge
		per cwt. s. d.
04.02	Milk and cream, preserved, concentrated or sweetened, containing more than 10 per cent. by weight of added sweetening matter	11 5
17.02 (B) (2) and 17.05 (B)	Syrups containing sucrose sugar, whether or not flavoured or coloured, but not including fruit juices containing added sugar in any proportion:—	
	containing 70 per cent. or more by weight of sweetening matter	16 4
	containing less than 70 per cent., and more than 50 per cent., by weight of sweetening matter...	11 9
	containing not more than 50 per cent. by weight of sweetening matter	5 8

(a) S.I. 1968/2015 (1968 III, p. 5475).   (b) S.I. 1968/1884 (1968 III, p. 5027).
(c) S.I. 1968/679 (1968 I, p. 1519).

Tariff heading	Description of Imported Composite Sugar Products	Rate of Surcharge
		per cwt. s. d.
17.02 (F) ...	Caramel:—	
	Solid	25 8
	Liquid	18 0
17.04	Sugar confectionery, not containing cocoa	20 11
18.06	Chocolate and other food preparations containing cocoa:—	
	Chocolate couverture not prepared for retail sale; chocolate milk crumb, liquid	11 5
	Chocolate milk crumb, solid	14 1
	Solid chocolate bars or blocks, milk or plain, with or without fruit or nuts; other chocolate confectionery consisting wholly of chocolate or of chocolate and other ingredients not containing added sugar, but not including such goods when packed together in retail packages with goods liable to surcharge at a higher rate	11 7
	Other	14 10
		per cent.
19.08	Pastry, biscuits, cakes and other fine bakers' wares containing added sweetening matter:—	
	Biscuits	$5\frac{1}{2}$
	Other	$3\frac{3}{10}$
20.01	Vegetables and fruit, prepared or preserved by vinegar or acetic acid, containing added sweetening matter	$7\frac{7}{10}$
20.03	Fruit preserved by freezing, containing added sugar	$2\frac{3}{4}$
		per cwt. s. d.
20.04	Fruit, fruit-peel and parts of plants, preserved by sugar (drained, glacé or crystallised)	16 10
20.05	Jams, fruit jellies, marmalades, fruit purée and fruit pastes, being cooked preparations, containing added sweetening matter	16 2
		per cent.
20.06	Fruit otherwise prepared or preserved, containing added sweetening matter:—	
	Ginger	11
	Other	$2\frac{3}{4}$

SCHEDULE 2

Tariff heading	Description of Imported Composite Sugar Products
17.05 (A) and (B)	Sugar and invert sugar, flavoured or coloured.

SCHEDULE 3

Description of goods	Rate of surcharge repayment per bulk barrel of 36 gallons
Lager	1s. 0·8d.
All beer other than lager	11·4d.

EXPLANATORY NOTE

(This Note is not part of the Order.)

This order provides for reductions on and after 24th December 1968 in the average rates of surcharge payable on imported composite sugar products of the descriptions specified in Schedule 1 and in the average rates of surcharge repayment in respect of exported goods of the descriptions specified in Schedule 3. These correspond to the reductions in surcharge rates effected by the Sugar (Rates of Surcharge and Surcharge Repayments) (No. 8) Order 1968 (S.I. 1968/2015). Provision is also made for certain imported composite sugar products to be treated as not containing any sugar or invert sugar.

STATUTORY INSTRUMENTS

1968 No. 2019

EXCHANGE CONTROL

The Exchange Control (Authorised Dealers and Depositaries) (Amendment) (No. 4) Order 1968

Made - - -	*19th December* 1968
Coming into Operation	*31st December* 1968

The Treasury, in exercise of the powers conferred upon them by sections 36(5) and 42(1) of the Exchange Control Act 1947(**a**), hereby make the following Order :—

1. Schedule 2 to the Exchange Control (Authorised Dealers and Depositaries) Order 1968(**b**) shall be amended as follows :—

(*a*) by inserting the words "Baer International Ltd., Julius." after the words "Australia and New Zealand Bank Ltd." ;

(*b*) by deleting the words "Barclays Bank (France) Ltd." ;

(*c*) by inserting the words "Barclays Bank (London and International) Ltd." after the words "Barclays Bank Ltd.".

2. This Order shall extend to the Channel Islands, and any reference in this Order to the Exchange Control Act 1947 includes a reference to that Act as extended by the Exchange Control (Channel Islands) Order 1947(**c**).

3. The Interpretation Act 1889(**d**) shall apply for the interpretation of this Order as it applies for the interpretation of an Act of Parliament.

4. This Order may be cited as the Exchange Control (Authorised Dealers and Depositaries) (Amendment) (No. 4) Order 1968, and shall come into operation on 31st December 1968.

Walter Harrison,
B. K. O'Malley,
Two of the Lords Commissioners
of Her Majesty's Treasury.

19th December 1968.

EXPLANATORY NOTE

(*This Note is not part of the Order.*)

This Order amends the list of persons authorised by the Treasury under the Exchange Control Act 1947 to act as dealers in gold and foreign currencies and as depositaries for the purpose of the deposit of securities.

(**a**) 1947 c.14.   (**b**) S.I. 1968/1634 (1968 III, p. 4457).
(**c**) S.R. & O. 1947/2034 (Rev. VI, p. 1001: 1947 I, p.660).
(**d**) 1889 c.63.

STATUTORY   INSTRUMENTS

1968 No. 2021

JUSTICES OF THE PEACE

The Justices (Lancashire Supplemental List) Rules 1968

Made -   -   -   -   *19th December* 1968
Coming into Operation   *1st January* 1969

The Chancellor of the Duchy and County Palatine of Lancaster, in exercise of the powers conferred on him by section 4 of the Justices of the Peace Act 1949(**a**) and by virtue of section 2 of the Justices of the Peace Act 1968(**b**), hereby makes the following Rules:—

1.—(1) These Rules may be cited as The Justices (Lancashire Supplemental List) Rules 1968 and shall come into force on 1st January 1969 :

Provided that, as regards the year 1969 and the three following years, the references in paragraphs (*a*) and (*b*) in Rule 2 to the age of seventy years shall be deemed to be references for 1969 to an age of seventy-four years, for 1970 to an age of seventy-three years, for 1971 to an age of seventy-two years and for 1972 to an age of seventy-one years ; and if, at the beginning of any of these years or of the year 1973, a person is of or over the age relevant for that year to those paragraphs he shall be treated, for the purposes of those paragraphs, as having held since attaining that age any office mentioned in the said paragraph (*a*) (i) which he holds at the beginning of that year.

(2) The Interpretation Act, 1889(**c**), applies for the interpretation of these Rules as it applies for the interpretation of an Act of Parliament.

2. There shall be kept in connection with the Commission of the Peace for the County Palatine of Lancaster and the Commission of the Peace for every borough within the said County Palatine having a separate Commission of the Peace a list to be called the " Supplemental List ".

3. Subject to the provisions of these Rules there shall be entered in the appropriate Supplemental List the name of any person appointed a Justice by any Commission aforementioned,

(*a*) who is of the age of seventy years or over and neither

    (i) on attaining the age of seventy years holds or has held office as chairman or deputy chairman of a Court of Quarter Sessions or as a recorder of a borough (including recorder of the cities of Liverpool or Manchester) nor

    (ii) holds or has held high judicial office within the meaning of the Appellate Jurisdiction Act 1876(**d**) ; or

(*b*) who, after attaining the age of seventy years while holding an office mentioned in paragraph (*a*) (i) above, no longer holds any such office and who neither holds nor has held high judicial office ; or

(*c*) who is of the age of seventy-five years or over ; or

(*d*) who applies to have his name entered therein and obtains the approval of the Chancellor of the Duchy for such entry to be made ; or

---

(**a**) 1949 c. 101.   (**b**) 1968 c. 69.   (**c**) 1889 c. 63.   (**d**) 1876 c. 59.

(*e*) whose name is directed by the Chancellor of the Duchy to be so entered in pursuance of Subsection (4) of Section 4 of the Justices of the Peace Act 1949(**a**).

4. There shall be removed from the Supplemental List—

(*a*) any name which the Chancellor of the Duchy may so direct ; or

(*b*) the name of any person who has ceased to be a Justice.

5. These Rules shall apply to a Justice of the Peace whether appointed before or after the coming into force of the Rules and the lists kept in accordance with the Justices (Lancashire Retired List) Rules 1950(**b**) shall be deemed to be Supplemental Lists for the purposes of this Order.

6. The Justices (Lancashire Retired List) Rules 1950 are hereby revoked.

Dated the 19th day of December 1968.

Fred Lee.

EXPLANATORY NOTE

(This Note is not part of the Rules.)

The purpose of this Order, which revokes the 1950 Rules, is to provide for the removal of the names of Justices from Active Lists of Commissions of the Peace in Lancashire. It particularly provides, in accordance with the Justices of the Peace Act 1968, for the phased reduction of the maximum age for service on the Bench from 75 as at present to the age of 70 which will be reached in 1973.

(**a**) 1949 c. 101.   (**b**) S.I. 1950/567 (1950 I, p. 1148).

STATUTORY INSTRUMENTS

1968 No. 2028

DEFENCE

The Air Force Act 1955 (Continuation) Order 1968

Laid before Parliament in draft

Made - - - *20th December* 1968

At the Court at Buckingham Palace, the 20th day of December 1968

Present,

The Queen's Most Excellent Majesty in Council

Whereas a draft of the following Order in Council has been laid before Parliament and approved by resolution of each House of Parliament:

Now, therefore, Her Majesty, in pursuance of section 1(2) of the Armed Forces Act 1966(a), is pleased, by and with the advice of Her Privy Council, to order, and it is hereby ordered, as follows:—

1. The Air Force Act 1955(b) shall continue in force for a period of twelve months beyond the 31st December 1968, that date being the date on which it would otherwise expire.

2. This Order may be cited as the Air Force Act 1955 (Continuation) Order 1968.

W. G. Agnew.

(a) 1966 c.45. **(b)** 1955 c.19.

STATUTORY INSTRUMENTS

1968 No. 2029

DEFENCE

The Army Act 1955 (Continuation) Order 1968

Laid before Parliament in draft
Made - - - - *20th December* 1968

At the Court at Buckingham Palace, the 20th day of December 1968

Present,

The Queen's Most Excellent Majesty in Council

Whereas a draft of the following Order in Council has been laid before Parliament and approved by resolution of each House of Parliament :

Now, therefore, Her Majesty, in pursuance of section 1(2) of the Armed Forces Act 1966(a), is pleased, by and with the advice of Her Privy Council, to order, and it is hereby ordered, as follows :—

1. The Army Act 1955(b) shall continue in force for a period of twelve months beyond the 31st December 1968, that date being the date on which it would otherwise expire.

2. This Order may be cited as the Army Act 1955 (Continuation) Order 1968.

W. G. Agnew.

(a) 1966 c. 45.   (b) 1955 c. 18.

STATUTORY   INSTRUMENTS

1968 No. 2030

CARIBBEAN AND NORTH ATLANTIC TERRITORIES

The Cayman Islands (George Town Election) Order 1968

Made - - - -	*20th December* 1968
Laid before Parliament	*20th December* 1968
Coming into Operation	*On publication in accordance with section* 1(1)

At the Court at Buckingham Palace, the 20th day of December 1968

Present,

The Queen's Most Excellent Majesty in Council

Whereas writs were issued on 2nd July 1968 in pursuance of the Elections Law(a) of the Cayman Islands for the purpose of a general election of members of the Legislative Assembly specifying that, if necessary, the poll should be taken in the respective electoral districts established by that Law on 7th November 1968 between the hours of seven o'clock in the forenoon and six o'clock in the afternoon:

And whereas the proceedings at the poll at the polling station for the second electoral district (hereinafter referred to as "the district of George Town") were stopped at approximately four o'clock in the afternoon on that day in order to preserve peace and order:

Now, therefore, Her Majesty, by virtue of the powers conferred upon Her by section 5 of the West Indies Act 1962(b) and the powers reserved to Her by section 57 of the Constitution of the Cayman Islands contained in the Schedule to the Cayman Islands (Constitution) Order 1965(c), is pleased, by and with the advice of Her Privy Council, to order, and it is hereby ordered, as follows:—

1.—(1) This Order may be cited as the Cayman Islands (George Town Election) Order 1968 and shall be published in the Cayman Islands by Government Notice and come into operation on the day on which it is so published. Citation, commencement and construction.

(2) This Order shall be construed as one with the Elections Law of the Cayman Islands as in force immediately before the coming into operation of this Order, and accordingly the Interpretation Law(d) of the Cayman Islands as so in force shall apply for the purpose of interpreting and otherwise in relation to this Order as it applies for the purpose of interpreting and in relation to the Elections Law.

(a) Laws of the Cayman Islands, Rev. Edn., c. 45.   (b) 1962 c. 19.
(c) S.I. 1965/1860 (1965 III, p. 5588).
(d) Laws of the Cayman Islands, Rev. Edn. c. 70.

Poll on 7th November 1968 to be of no effect. **2.**—(1) The proceedings at the poll for the district of George Town on 7th November 1968 shall be of no effect:

Provided that—

(*a*) the used ballot papers (including ballot papers returned by post by absent voters· and the envelopes and declarations of identity relating thereto), the counterfoils of such ballot papers and the poll book used in connection therewith shall be dealt with in accordance with section 48 of the Elections Law as if they were election documents relating to an election held on that day ; and

(*b*) nothing in this subsection shall be construed as affecting the application of Part V of the Elections Law in relation to the proceedings at the aforementioned poll.

(2) No proceedings shall lie against the Administrator, any election officer or any other public officer in respect of any act done or omitted to be done by him for the purposes of, or in consequence of, the stopping of the proceedings at the poll for the district of George Town on 7th November 1968.

New poll to be held. **3.**—(1) Subject to the following provisions of this Order, a poll for the purpose of electing the members of the Legislative Assembly for the district of George Town from among the persons duly nominated as candidates in pursuance of the writ issued to the returning officer of that district on 2nd July 1968 shall be held in that district in accordance with the provisions of the Elections Law on such day and between such hours as the Administrator may by Government Notice appoint and the said writ shall accordingly have effect as if it had specified that day and those hours for the taking of a poll :

Provided that the day appointed under this subsection shall not be earlier than fourteen days after the day or, as the case may be, the last of the days appointed by the Administrator under section 4(3) of this Order.

(2) Where proceedings at the poll held in pursuance of subsection (1) of this section are interrupted or obstructed by riot or open violence or by the occurrence of any earthquake, hurricane, flood, fire, epidemic disease or other calamity, whether similar to the foregoing or not, the Administrator may adjourn the proceedings until such day as the Administrator shall then or subsequently appoint.

(3) Where the proceedings at the poll are adjourned—

(*a*) the hours of polling on the day to which they are adjourned shall be the same as for the original day ; and

(*b*) the provisions of subsection (2) of this section shall apply in relation to the proceedings on the day to which the proceedings are adjourned as they apply in relation to the proceedings on the original day.

Amendment of Register of Voters. **4.**—(1) Any person whose name does not appear in the Register of Voters in force under the Elections Law for the district of George Town (in this section referred to as " the Register ") and who claims that he was entitled on 29th April 1968 to have his name included on the preliminary list for that Register which was prepared with effect from that day may within five days after the day on which this Order comes into operation give notice in writing to the registering officer of that district stating his name, address and occupation and his place of residence on 29th April 1968 if different from that stated as his present address and claiming that he was so entitled and that his name should be included in the Register.

(2) The registering officer of the district of George Town shall, within three days after the expiration of the period of five days mentioned in subsection (1) of this section, publish in such manner as he thinks fit a list containing the names and addresses of the persons who have made claims under that subsection.

(3) The said claims shall be considered by the Magistrate at the Court House, George Town, on such day or days and commencing at such time thereon as the Administrator may by Government Notice appoint, and the registering officer shall accordingly produce to the Magistrate a copy of the list published under subsection (2) of this section and the claims received by him under subsection (1) of this section.

(4) If on considering any claim under this section the Magistrate is satisfied that the claimant was entitled as mentioned in subsection (1) of this section and, on the date of consideration of the claim, is not disqualified for registration under section 27 of the Constitution of the Cayman Islands he shall insert the claimant's name, together with his address and occupation, in the Register in the appropriate place according to the alphabetical order of surnames, and he shall not make any such insertion unless he is so satisfied.

(5) The decision of the Magistrate on any claim under this section shall be final and no appeal shall be allowed therefrom.

(6) On inserting any name in the Register under this section the Magistrate shall write his initials against that name, and he shall sign his name to every page of the Register when the same is finally settled.

(7) The Magistrate shall have power to adjourn the consideration of any claim under this section, and he shall have the same powers of keeping order within the Court House when sitting for the purposes of this section as the Judge of the Grand Court has when sitting as such.

(8) On completion of the revision of the Register in accordance with the provisions of this section the Magistrate shall cause the revised Register to be printed and bound and shall certify the printed and bound Register and date his certificate and shall transmit the revised Register to the Supervisor of Elections, and the revised Register shall be the Register of Voters for the purposes of the poll provided for by section 3 of this Order and shall remain in force as the Register of Voters for the district of George Town until the next such Register is compiled and comes into force.

5.—(1) For the purposes of sub-paragraphs (iv), (v) and (vi) of paragraph (a) of section 39(1) of the Elections Law the poll to be held in pursuance of this Order shall not be regarded as a poll at a general election, and accordingly a person who was entitled to be treated as an absent voter for the purposes of the poll commenced on 7th November 1968 by reason of an application based on a ground mentioned in any of those sub-paragraphs shall not by reason only of that application be so treated for the purposes of the poll to be held in pursuance of this Order. *Absent voters.*

(2) A person who gives notice under section 4(1) of this Order of his claim to be included in the Register may also apply in accordance

with the provisions of the Elections Law to be treated as an absent voter notwithstanding that at the time he so applies his name is not included in the Register, but the registering officer shall not allow any such application unless the Magistrate inserts the name of the applicant in the Register under section 4 of this Order.

W. G. Agnew.

EXPLANATORY NOTE

(This Note is not part of the Order.)

In the course of the general election of members of the Legislative Assembly of the Cayman Islands held on 7th November 1968 polling in the electoral district of George Town was stopped prematurely in order to preserve peace and order. This Order provides for a new poll to be held in that district and for persons who are not on the Register of Voters for that district but who claim that they were entitled to be included when the Register was being prepared to have an opportunity to claim inclusion on the Register before the new poll is held.

STATUTORY INSTRUMENTS

1968 No. 2031

FRIENDLY SOCIETIES

INDUSTRIAL AND PROVIDENT SOCIETIES

The Friendly and Industrial and Provident Societies (Channel Islands) Order 1968

Made - - - - 20th December 1968
Coming into Operation 1st January 1969

At the Court at Buckingham Palace, the 20th day of December 1968

Present,

The Queen's Most Excellent Majesty in Council

Her Majesty, in pursuance of the power conferred upon Her by section 22(1) of the Friendly and Industrial and Provident Societies Act 1968(a), is pleased, by and with the advice of Her Privy Council, to order, and it is hereby ordered, as follows :—

1. The Friendly and Industrial and Provident Societies Act 1968 shall extend to the Bailiwick of Jersey and to the Bailiwick of Guernsey, subject to the following modifications :—

(a) in section 6(8) the reference to the High Court shall be construed as a reference—

    (i) in Jersey, to the inferior number of the Royal Court of Jersey ;

    (ii) in Guernsey, Herm and Jethou, to the Royal Court of Guernsey sitting as an Ordinary Court ;

    (iii) in Alderney, to the Court of Alderney ;

    (iv) in Sark, to the Court of the Seneschal of Sark ;

(b) for section 8(2)(b) there shall be substituted the following paragraph :—

    " (b) he is—

        (i) an officer or servant (otherwise than as auditor) of a company which is a subsidiary of that society ; or

        (ii) a person who is a partner of or in the employment of a person who is an officer or servant (otherwise than as auditor) of such a company." ;

(c) in section 14(1) the reference to Great Britain shall be construed as including any of the Channel Islands.

2. This Order may be cited as the Friendly and Industrial and Provident Societies (Channel Islands) Order 1968 and shall come into operation on 1st January 1969.

W. G. Agnew.

(a) 1968 c. 55.

EXPLANATORY NOTE

(This Note is not part of the Order.)

This Order extends the Friendly and Industrial and Provident Societies Act 1968 to the Channel Islands with modifications.

STATUTORY   INSTRUMENTS

1968 No. 2032

FRIENDLY SOCIETIES

The Friendly Societies (Isle of Man) Order 1968

Made - - - -	*20th December* 1968
Coming into Operation	*1st January* 1969

At the Court at Buckingham Palace, the 20th day of December 1968

Present,

The Queen's Most Excellent Majesty in Council

Her Majesty, in pursuance of the power conferred upon Her by section 22(1) of the Friendly and Industrial and Provident Societies Act 1968(**a**), is pleased, by and with the advice of Her Privy Council, to order, and it is hereby ordered, as follows :—

1. The Friendly and Industrial and Provident Societies Act 1968, in so far as it relates to societies registered under the Friendly Societies Act 1896(**b**), shall extend to the Isle of Man, subject to the modification that in section 6(8) the reference to the High Court shall be construed as a reference to the Chancery Division of the High Court of the Isle of Man.

2. This Order may be cited as the Friendly Societies (Isle of Man) Order 1968 and shall come into operation on 1st January 1969.

W. G. Agnew.

EXPLANATORY NOTE

(This Note is not part of the Order.)

This Order extends the Friendly and Industrial and Provident Societies Act 1968 so far as it relates to friendly societies to the Isle of Man, with a modification.

(**a**) 1968 c. 55.   (**b**) 1896 c. 25.

STATUTORY INSTRUMENTS

1968 No. 2033

FUGITIVE CRIMINAL

The Fugitive Offenders (United Kingdom Dependencies) Order 1968

Laid before Parliament in draft

Made	-	-	-	*20th December* 1968
Coming into Operation				*1st January* 1969

At the Court at Buckingham Palace, the 20th day of December 1968

Present,

The Queen's Most Excellent Majesty in Council

Her Majesty, in exercise of the powers conferred upon Her by section 2(2)(*c*) and (3) of the Fugitive Offenders Act 1967(**a**), is pleased, by and with the advice of Her Privy Council, to make the following Order, a draft of which has been laid before Parliament and has been approved by resolution of each House of Parliament :—

1. Section 2(2) of the Fugitive Offenders Act 1967 (which defines the expression "United Kingdom dependency") shall apply to the countries specified in column 1 of the Schedule hereto (being countries outside Her Majesty's dominions in which Her Majesty has jurisdiction, or over which She extends protection, in right of Her Government in the United Kingdom).

2. In relation to the return of persons to, and in relation to persons returned from, a country specified in column 1 of the Schedule hereto, other than the British Solomon Islands Protectorate, the Fugitive Offenders Act 1967 shall have effect as if for any reference therein to the Governor there were substituted a reference to the person or government specified opposite to the country in question in column 2 of the said Schedule.

3. In relation to the return of persons to the New Hebrides, the Fugitive Offenders Act 1967 shall have effect as if at the end of section 3(1) thereof (which defines a relevant offence for the purposes of the Act) there were added the following proviso :—

"Provided that an offence of which a person is accused or has been convicted in the New Hebrides shall not be a relevant offence unless he is liable to be tried therefor or, as the case may be, has been convicted thereof, by the High Court of the Western Pacific or by the Joint Court established for the New Hebrides.".

(**a**) 1967 c.68.

4. This Order may be cited as the Fugitive Offenders (United Kingdom Dependencies) Order 1968 and shall come into operation on 1st January 1969.

W. G. Agnew.

SCHEDULE

Country	Government or person
British Solomon Islands Protectorate	—
Brunei	The Government of Brunei.
The New Hebrides	Her Majesty's High Commissioner for the Western Pacific or the Resident Commissioner for the New Hebrides acting with his authority.
Tonga	The Premier of Tonga.

EXPLANATORY NOTE

(This Note is not part of the Order.)

Section 2(2)(*c*) of the Fugitive Offenders Act 1967 relates to countries outside Her Majesty's dominions in which She has jurisdiction, or over which She extends protection, in right of Her Government in the United Kingdom. It provides that such countries to which section 2(2) is applied by Order in Council shall fall within the definition of "United Kingdom dependency" for the purposes of that Act. Article 1 of this Order applies section 2(2) to the countries specified in the Schedule.

As authorised by section 2(3), Article 2 provides for the modification of references in the 1967 Act to the Governor in relation to the return of persons to, and in relation to persons returned from, these countries, and Article 3 provides that a person shall be returned to the New Hebrides only if he is liable to be tried or, as the case may be, has been convicted, by the High Court of the Western Pacific or by the Joint Court established for the New Hebrides.

STATUTORY INSTRUMENTS

1968 No. 2034

INCOME TAX

The Double Taxation Relief (Taxes on Income) (Sweden) (No. 2) Order 1968

Laid before the House of Commons in draft

Made - - - *20th December* 1968

At the Court at Buckingham Palace, the 20th day of December 1968

Present,

The Queen's Most Excellent Majesty in Council

Whereas a draft of this Order was laid before the Commons House of Parliament in accordance with the provisions of section 347(6) of the Income Tax Act 1952(a), and an Address has been presented to Her Majesty by that House praying that an Order may be made in the terms of this Order :

Now, therefore, Her Majesty, in exercise of the powers conferred upon Her by section 347(1) of the said Income Tax Act 1952, as amended by section 39 and section 64 of the Finance Act 1965(b), and of all other powers enabling Her in that behalf, is pleased, by and with the advice of Her Privy Council, to order, and it is hereby ordered, as follows :—

1. This Order may be cited as the Double Taxation Relief (Taxes on Income) (Sweden) (No. 2) Order 1968.

2. It is hereby declared—

(*a*) that the arrangements specified in the Supplementary Protocol set out in the Schedule to this Order have been made with the Government of the Kingdom of Sweden with a view to affording relief from double taxation in relation to income tax, corporation tax, or capital gains tax and taxes of a similar character imposed by the laws of Sweden varying the arrangements set out in the Schedule to the Double Taxation Relief (Taxes on Income) (Sweden) Order 1961(c), as amended by the arrangements set out in the Schedule to the Double Taxation Relief (Taxes on Income) (Sweden) Order 1968(d) ; and

(*b*) that it is expedient that those arrangements should have effect.

W. G. Agnew.

(a) 15 & 16 Geo. 6 & 1 Eliz. 2. c. 10.　(b) 1965 c. 25.
(c) S.I. 1961/577 (1961 I, p. 1265).　(d) S.I. 1968/1105 (1968 II, p. 3057).

SCHEDULE

SUPPLEMENTARY PROTOCOL BETWEEN THE GOVERNMENT OF THE UNITED KINGDOM
OF GREAT BRITAIN AND NORTHERN IRELAND AND THE GOVERNMENT OF THE
KINGDOM OF SWEDEN, AMENDING THE CONVENTION FOR THE AVOIDANCE OF
DOUBLE TAXATION AND THE PREVENTION OF FISCAL EVASION WITH RESPECT TO
TAXES ON INCOME, SIGNED AT LONDON ON 28th JULY, 1960, AS MODIFIED BY THE
PROTOCOL SIGNED AT LONDON ON 25th MARCH, 1966

The Government of the United Kingdom of Great Britain and Northern Ireland
and the Government of the Kingdom of Sweden ;

Desiring to conclude a Supplementary Protocol to amend the Convention between
the Contracting Parties for the Avoidance of Double Taxation and the Prevention
of Fiscal Evasion with respect to Taxes on Income, signed at London on 28th July,
1960, as modified by the Protocol signed at London on 25th March, 1966, (hereinafter referred to as "the Convention") ;

Have agreed as follows:

ARTICLE 1

Paragraph (1) of Article I of the Convention shall be deleted and replaced by the
following:

"(1) The taxes which are the subject of this Convention are:

(*a*) in Sweden (and hereinafter referred to as "Swedish tax"):

    (i) the State income tax, including sailors tax and coupon tax ;

    (ii) the tax on undistributed profits of companies (*ersättningsskatt*) ;

    (iii) the tax on distributed income (*utskiftningsskatt*) ;

    (iv) the tax on public entertainers (*bevillningsavgift för vissa offentliga föreställningar*) ;

    (v) the communal income tax (*kommunal inkomstskatt*) ; and

    (vi) the State capital tax ;

(*b*) in the United Kingdom of Great Britain and Northern Ireland (and hereinafter referred to as "United Kingdom tax"):

    (i) the income tax (including surtax) ;

    (ii) the corporation tax ; and

    (iii) the capital gains tax."

ARTICLE 2

(1) Sub-paragraph (*g*) (i) of paragraph (1) of Article II of the Convention shall be
deleted and replaced by the following:

"(*g*) (i) the term "resident of the United Kingdom" means any person who is
resident in the United Kingdom for the purposes of United Kingdom tax but
does not include any individual who is liable to tax in the United Kingdom only
if he derives income from sources therein, and the term "resident of Sweden"
means any person who is resident in Sweden for the purposes of Swedish tax but
does not include any individual who is liable to tax in Sweden only if he derives
income from sources therein ; provided that".

(2) Paragraph (2) of Article II of the Convention shall be deleted and replaced by
the following:

"(2) Where under this Convention income from a source in one of the territories
is relieved from tax in that territory and, under the law in force in the other
territory, an individual, in respect of the said income, is subject to tax by reference
to the amount thereof which is remitted to or received in that other territory

and not by reference to the full amount thereof, then the relief to be allowed under this Convention in the first-mentioned territory shall apply only to so much of the income as is remitted to or received in the other territory."

ARTICLE 3

Article VII of the Convention shall be deleted and replaced by the following:

"*Article VII*

(1) Dividends paid by a company which is a resident of one of the territories to a resident of the other territory may be taxed in that other territory.

(2) Subject to paragraph (3) of this Article, dividends paid by a company which is a resident of one of the territories to a resident of the other territory may be taxed in the first-mentioned territory, and according to the law of that territory, but where such dividends are beneficially owned by a resident of the other territory the tax so charged shall not exceed:

(*a*) 5 per cent of the gross amount of the dividends if the recipient is a company (excluding a partnership) which:

(i) being a resident of Sweden controls directly or indirectly at least 25 per cent of the voting power of the company paying the dividends, or

(ii) being a resident of the United Kingdom controls directly or indirectly at least 25 per cent of the capital of the company paying the dividends;

(*b*) in all other cases 15 per cent of the gross amount of the dividends.

This paragraph shall not affect the taxation of the company in respect of the profits out of which the dividends are paid.

(3) Dividends paid before the date of entry into force of the Supplementary Protocol signed at London on 27th June, 1968, by a company which is a resident of one of the territories to a resident of the other territory who is subject to tax there in respect thereof (or would be so subject to tax there but for a provision in the Convention) shall be exempt from any tax which is chargeable in the first-mentioned territory on dividends in addition to the tax chargeable in respect of the profits or income of the company.

(4) The term "dividends" as used in this Article means income from shares, mining shares, founders' shares or other rights, not being debt-claims, participating in profits, as well as income from other corporate rights assimilated to income from shares by the taxation law of the territory of which the company making the distribution is a resident and, in the case of the United Kingdom, includes any item (other than interest or royalties exempt from United Kingdom tax under Article VIII or Article IX of this Convention) which under the law of the United Kingdom is treated as a distribution of a company.

(5) Where the company paying a dividend is a resident of the United Kingdom and the beneficial owner of the dividend, being a resident of Sweden, owns 10 per cent or more of the class of shares in respect of which the dividend is paid, then the exemption from tax and the limitation in the rate of tax provided for in paragraphs (2) and (3) of this Article shall not apply to the dividend to the extent that it can have been paid only out of profits which the company paying the dividend earned or other income which it received in a period ending twelve months or more before the relevant date. For the purposes of this paragraph the term "relevant date" means the date on which the beneficial owner of the dividend became the owner of 10 per cent or more of the class of shares in question. Provided that this paragraph shall not apply if the shares were acquired for bona fide commercial reasons and not primarily for the purpose of securing the benefit of this Article.

(6) The provisions of paragraphs (1), (2) and (3) shall not apply if the recipient of the dividends, being a resident of one of the territories, has in the other territory, of which the company paying the dividends is a resident a permanent establishment and the holding by virtue of which the dividends are paid is effectively connected with a trade or business carried on through such permanent establishment. In such a case the provisions of Article III shall apply.

(7) Where a company which is a resident of one of the territories derives profits or income from the other territory, that other territory may not impose any tax on the dividends paid by the company to persons who are not residents of that other territory, or subject the company's undistributed profits to a tax on undistributed profits, even if the dividends paid or the undistributed profits consist wholly or partly of profits or income arising in such other territory."

ARTICLE 4

Article VIII of the Convention shall be deleted and replaced by the following:

"*Article VIII*

(1) Interest derived and beneficially owned by a resident of one of the territories shall be exempt from tax in the other territory.

(2) The term "interest" as used in this Article means income from Government securities, bonds or debentures, whether or not secured by mortgage and whether or not carrying a right to participate in profits, and other debt-claims of every kind as well as all other income assimilated to income from money lent by the taxation law of the territory in which the income arises.

(3) The provisions of paragraph (1) of this Article shall not apply if the recipient of the interest, being a resident of one of the territories, has in the other territory a permanent establishment and the debt-claim from which the interest arises is effectively connected with a trade or business carried on through such permanent establishment. In such a case the provisions of Article III shall apply.

(4) Any provision in the law of one of the territories which relates only to interest paid to a non-resident company with or without any further requirement, or which relates only to interest payments between interconnected companies, with or without any further requirement, shall not operate so as to require such interest paid to a company which is a resident of the other territory to be left out of account as a deduction in computing the taxable profits of the company paying the interest as being a distribution.

(5) The exemption from tax provided for in paragraph (1) of this Article shall not apply to interest on any form of debt-claim dealt in on a stock exchange where the beneficial owner of the interest:

(*a*) does not bear tax in respect thereof in the territory of which it is a resident ; and

(*b*) sells (or makes a contract to sell) the debt-claim from which such interest is derived within three months of the date on which such beneficial owner acquired such debt-claim.

(6) Where, owing to a special relationship between the payer and the recipient or between both of them and some other person, the amount of the interest paid, having regard to the debt-claim for which it is paid, exceeds the amount which would have been agreed upon by the payer and the recipient in the absence of such relationship, the provisions of this Article shall apply only to the last-mentioned amount. In that case, the excess part of the payment shall remain taxable according to the law of each territory except that if the excess part of the interest is included in the taxable income of the payer, being a company, the tax levied on the excess part of the interest in the territory of which the payer is a resident shall not exceed the tax which would be charged if the interest was a dividend to which Article VII applies.

(7) The provisions of this Article shall not apply if the debt-claim in respect of which the interest is paid was created or assigned mainly for the purpose of taking advantage of this Article and not for bona fide commercial reasons."

ARTICLE 5

Article IX of the Convention shall be deleted and replaced by the following:

"*Article IX*

(1) Royalties derived and beneficially owned by a resident of one of the territories shall be exempt from tax in the other territory.

(2) The term "royalties" as used in this Article:

(*a*) means payments of any kind received as consideration for the use of, or the right to use, any copyright of literary, artistic or scientific work, any patent, trade mark, design or model, plan, secret formula or process, or for the use of, or the right to use, industrial, commercial or scientific equipment, or for information concerning industrial, commercial or scientific experience, but

(*b*) does not include any royalty or other amount paid in respect of the operation of a mine or quarry or of any other extraction of natural resources or in respect of cinematograph, including television, films.

(3) The provisions of paragraph (1) of this Article shall not apply if the recipient of the royalties, being a resident of one of the territories, has in the other territory a permanent establishment and the right or property giving rise to the royalties is effectively connected with a trade or business carried on through such permanent establishment. In such a case, the provisions of Article III shall apply.

(4) Any provision of the law of one of the territories which requires royalties paid by a company to be left out of account as a deduction in computing the company's taxable profits as being a distribution shall not operate in relation to royalties paid to a resident of the other territory. The provisions of this paragraph shall not apply to royalties paid to a company which is a resident of that other territory where:

(*a*) the same persons participate directly or indirectly in the management or control of the company paying the royalties and the company deriving the royalties, and

(*b*) more than 50 per cent of the voting power in the company deriving the royalties is controlled, directly or indirectly, by a person or persons resident in the territory in which the company paying the royalties is resident.

(5) Where, owing to a special relationship between the payer and the recipient, or between both of them and some other person, the amount of the royalties paid exceeds the amount which would have been agreed upon by the payer and the recipient in the absence of such relationship, the provisions of this Article shall apply only to the last-mentioned amount. In that case, the excess part of the payments shall remain taxable according to the law of each territory, except that if the excess part of the royalties is included in the taxable income of the payer, being a company, the tax levied on the excess part of the royalties in the territory of which the payer is a resident shall not exceed the tax which would be charged if the royalties were a dividend to which Article VII applies."

ARTICLE 6

Paragraph (3) of Article X of the Convention shall be deleted and replaced by the following:

"(3) The provisions of paragraphs (1) and (2) of this Article shall apply to income derived from the direct use or from the letting of immovable property or the use in any other form of such property, including income from agricultural or forestry enterprises."

ARTICLE 7

Article XII of the Convention shall be deleted and replaced by the following:

"Article XII

(1) Gains from the alienation of immovable property. as defined in paragraph (2) of Article X, may be taxed in the territory in which such property is situated.

(2) Gains from the alienation of movable property forming part of the business property of a permanent establishment which an enterprise of one of the territories has in the other territory or of movable property pertaining to a fixed base available to a resident of one of the territories in the other territory for the purpose of performing professional services, including such gains from the alienation of such a permanent establishment (alone or together with the whole enterprise) or of such a fixed base, may be taxed in the other territory. However, gains from the alienation of movable property of the kind referred to in paragraph (c) of Article XXI shall be taxable only in the territory in which such movable property is taxable according to the said Article.

(3) Gains from the alienation of any property other than those mentioned in paragraphs (1) and (2) shall be taxable only in the territory of which the alienator is a resident."

ARTICLE 8

Article XXII of the Convention shall be deleted and replaced by the following:

"Article XXII

(1) Subject to the provisions of paragraph (3) of this Article, individuals who are residents of Sweden shall be entitled to the same personal allowances, reliefs and reductions for the purposes of United Kingdom taxation as British subjects not resident in the United Kingdom.

(2) Subject to the provisions of paragraph (3) of this Article, individuals who are residents of the United Kingdom shall be entitled to the same personal allowances, reliefs and reductions for the purposes of Swedish tax as Swedish nationals not resident in Sweden.

(3) Nothing in this Convention shall entitle an individual who is a resident of one of the territories and whose income from the other territory consists solely of dividends, interest or royalties (or solely of any combination thereof) to the personal allowances, reliefs and reductions of the kind referred to in this Article for the purposes of taxation in that other territory."

ARTICLE 9

Article XXIII of the Convention shall be deleted and replaced by the following:

"Article XXIII

(1) (a) Subject to the provisions of the law of the United Kingdom regarding the allowance as a credit against United Kingdom tax of tax payable in a territory outside the United Kingdom (which shall not affect the general principle hereof) Swedish tax payable under the laws of Sweden and in accordance with this Convention, whether directly or by deduction. on profits, income or chargeable gains from sources within Sweden (excluding in the case of a dividend, tax payable in respect of the profits out of which the dividend is paid) shall be allowed as a credit against any United Kingdom tax computed by reference to the same profits. income or chargeable gains by reference to which Swedish tax is computed.

(*b*) Where such income is a dividend paid by a company which is a resident of Sweden to a company which is a resident of the United Kingdom and which controls directly or indirectly not less than one-tenth of the voting power in the former company, the credit shall take into account (in addition to any Swedish tax payable in respect of the dividend) the Swedish tax payable by that former company in respect of its profits.

For the purposes of this paragraph the term Swedish tax shall not include any capital tax.

(2) (*a*) Where a resident of Sweden derives income or owns capital which under the laws of the United Kingdom and in accordance with the provisions of this Convention may be taxed in the United Kingdom, Sweden shall allow:

(i) as a deduction from the tax on the income, an amount equal to the United Kingdom tax paid in respect of such income ;

(ii) as a deduction from the tax on the capital, an amount equal to any United Kingdom tax paid in respect of such capital.

The deduction in either case shall not, however, exceed that part of the income or capital tax, respectively, as computed before the deduction is given, which is appropriate, as the case may be, to the income or the capital which may be taxed in the United Kingdom.

(*b*) Where a resident of Sweden derives income or owns capital which in accordance with Article VI, the last sentence of paragraph (2) of Article XII, paragraph (1) of Article XIII and paragraph (*c*) of Article XXI shall be taxable only in the United Kingdom, such income or capital shall be exempt from Swedish tax ; however, the graduated rates of Swedish tax may be calculated as though income or capital thus exempted were included in the amount of the total income or capital.

(3) Notwithstanding the provisions of paragraph (2), dividends paid by a company which is a resident of the United Kingdom to a company which is a resident of Sweden shall be exempt from Swedish tax, provided that in accordance with the laws of Sweden the dividends would be exempt from tax if both companies had been residents of Sweden.

(4) For the purposes of this Article, profits or remuneration for personal (including professional) services performed in one of the territories shall, unless paragraph (2) of Article XIII applies, be deemed to be income from sources within that territory, and the services of an individual whose services are wholly or mainly performed in ships or aircraft operated by a resident of one of the territories shall be deemed to be performed in that territory.

(5) Where profits of an enterprise of one of the territories are also included in the profits of an enterprise of the other territory in accordance with Article IV, the amount of such profits included in the profits of both enterprises shall be treated for the purpose of this Article as income from a source in the other territory of the enterprise of the first-mentioned territory and credit shall be given accordingly under paragraph (1) or paragraph (2) of this Article."

ARTICLE 10

Article XXV of the Convention shall be deleted and replaced by the following:

"*Article XXV*

(1) Where a resident of a Contracting Party considers that the action of one or both of the Contracting Parties result or will result for him in taxation not in accordance with this Convention, he may, notwithstanding the remedies provided by the national laws of those parties, present his case to the taxation authority of the Contracting Party of which he is a resident.

(2) The taxation authority shall endeavour, if the objection appears to it to be justified and if it is not itself able to arrive at an appropriate solution, to resolve the case by mutual agreement with the taxation authority of the other Contracting Party, with a view to the avoidance of taxation not in accordance with this Convention.

(3) The taxation authorities of the Contracting Parties shall endeavour to resolve by mutual agreement any difficulties or doubts arising as to the interpretation or application of this Convention.

(4) The taxation authorities of the Contracting Parties may communicate with each other directly for the purpose of reaching an agreement in the sense of the preceding paragraphs."

ARTICLE 11

Paragraph (3) of Article XXVI of the Convention shall be deleted and replaced by the following:

"(3) The taxation on a permanent establishment which an enterprise of one of the territories has in the other territory shall not be less favourably levied in that other territory than the taxation levied on enterprises of that other territory carrying on the same activities. Nothing in this Article shall be construed as obliging either Contracting Party to grant to residents of the other Contracting Party any personal allowances, reliefs and reductions for taxation purposes on account of civil status or family responsibilities which it grants to its own residents, nor as conferring any exemption from tax in a territory in respect of dividends paid to a company which is a resident of the other territory."

ARTICLE 12

Article XXX of the Convention shall be deleted and replaced by the following:

"Article XXX

This Convention shall continue in effect indefinitely but either of the Contracting Parties may, on or before the thirtieth day of June in any calendar year after the year 1970 give, through diplomatic channels, notice of termination to the other Contracting Party and, in such event, this Convention shall cease to be effective:

(a) in Sweden:
  (i) in respect of taxes on income derived on or after 1st January in the calendar year next following that in which the notice is given ;
  (ii) in respect of capital tax assessed in or after the second calendar year following that in which the notice is given ;

(b) in the United Kingdom:
  (i) as respect income tax (including surtax) and capital gains tax for any year of assessment beginning on or after 6th April in the calendar year next following that in which the notice is given ;
  (ii) as respects corporation tax, for any financial year beginning on or after 1st April in the calendar year next following that in which the notice is given."

ARTICLE 13

(1) This Supplementary Protocol shall be ratified by the Contracting Parties in accordance with their respective constitutional and legal requirements. The instruments of ratification shall be exchanged at Stockholm as soon as possible.

(2) This Supplementary Protocol shall enter into force after the expiration of thirty days following the date on which the instruments of ratification are exchanged(**a**) and shall thereupon have effect:

(*a*) in Sweden:

    (i) in respect of taxes on income derived on or after 1st January in the calendar year beginning after the entry into force of this Supplementary Protocol; provided, however, that the provisions of paragraph (2) of Article XXIII of the Convention as amended by Article 9 of this Supplementary Protocol shall have effect from the date of entry into force of this Supplementary Protocol in so far as these provisions allow a credit against Swedish tax for United Kingdom tax on dividends paid on or after the date of entry into force of this Supplementary Protocol ;

    (ii) in respect of capital tax assessed in or after the calendar year beginning after the entry into force of this Supplementary Protocol ;

(*b*) in the United Kingdom:

    (i) as repects income tax and surtax for any year of assessment beginning on or after 6th April, 1967 ;

    (ii) as respects corporation tax for any financial year beginning on or after 1st April, 1964 ; and

    (iii) as respects capital gains tax for any year of assessment beginning on or after 6th April, 1965.

(3) Where any greater relief from tax in the United Kingdom would have been afforded by any provision of the Convention than is due under the Convention as amended by this Supplementary Protocol, any such provision as aforesaid shall continue to have effect in the United Kingdom for any year of assessment or financial year beginning before the entry into force of this Supplementary Protocol.

In witness whereof the undersigned, duly authorised thereto by their respective Governments, have signed this Supplementary Protocol.

Done in duplicate at London this 27th day of June, 1968, in the English and Swedish languages, both texts being equally authoritative.

For the Government of the United Kingdom
of Great Britain and Northern Ireland:

WILLIAM RODGERS

For the Government of the Kingdom of
Sweden:

LEIF BELFRAGE

(**a**) Instruments of ratification were exchanged on 29th November 1968.

EXPLANATORY NOTE

(This Note is not part of the Order.)

The Double Taxation Convention with Sweden signed on 28th July 1960 was amended by a Protocol signed on 25th March 1966.   The Supplementary Protocol scheduled to this Order makes certain further alterations to this Convention, the more important of which are as follows.

The rate of tax in the source country on dividends flowing from one country to the other is normally not to exceed 15 per cent in the case of portfolio investment and 5 per cent in the case of direct investment.   Interest and royalties flowing from one country to the other will (as hitherto) normally be exempt from tax in the source country.   Relief from tax on dividends, interest and royalties in the country of origin will however no longer depend on whether the recipient is subject to tax in the other country, but will instead depend on whether the income is beneficially owned by a resident of the other country. Capital gains arising from the disposal of immovable property may be taxed in the country where the property is situated, but gains arising from the disposal of other property are to be taxed only in the country of the taxpayer's residence unless they arise from the disposal of the assets of a permanent establishment or a fixed base which the taxpayer has in the other country.   There are also further provisions for consultation between the taxation authorities of the two countries.

The Supplementary Protocol is, in general, to take effect in the United Kingdom for corporation tax and capital gains tax for all years and for income tax and surtax for the fiscal year 1967/68 and subsequent years.

STATUTORY INSTRUMENTS

1968 No. 2035 (C. 31)

JUSTICES OF THE PEACE

The Justices of the Peace Act 1968 (Commencement No. 1) Order 1968

Made - - - -	*20th December* 1968
Laid before Parliament	*31st December* 1968
Coming into Operation	*1st February* 1969

At the Court at Buckingham Palace, the 20th day of December 1968

Present,

The Queen's Most Excellent Majesty in Council

Her Majesty, in exercise of the powers conferred on Her by section 7 of the Justices of the Peace Act 1968(**a**) and of all other powers enabling Her in that behalf, is pleased, by and with the advice of Her Privy Council, to order, and it is hereby ordered, as follows: —

1.—(1) Subject to paragraph 2, the provisions of section 1, other than the words from " but " to the end of subsection (5) and subsection (8), of, and of Schedule 1 to, the Act shall come into operation on 1st February 1969 :

Provided that any person who is on that date mayor of any borough (including a borough included in a rural district), chairman of the Greater London Council or chairman of a county council or district council (within the meaning of the Local Government Act 1933(**b**), shall continue to be a Justice of the Peace by virtue of that office until the expiration of his current term of office.

(2) So much of Part II of Schedule 5 to the Act as is set out in the Schedule to this Order shall come into operation on 1st February 1969.

2. Paragraph 9 of Schedule 3 to the Act, and so much of section 1(2) of the Act as relates to that paragraph, shall come into operation on 1st February 1969, but otherwise this Order shall not apply in relation to the City of London.

3. This Order may be cited as the Justices of the Peace Act 1968 (Commencement No. 1) Order 1968, and shall come into operation on 1st February 1969.

W. G. Agnew.

(**a**) 1968 c. 69.   (**b**) 1933 c. 51.

SCHEDULE

Chapter	Title or Short Title	Extent of Repeal
11 Hen. 6. c. 6.	—	The whole chapter
27 Hen. 8. c. 24.	The Jurisdiction in Liberties Act 1535.	Section 19, so far as un-repealed.
37 Hen. 8. c. 1.	The Custos Rotulorum Act 1545.	The whole Act, so far as unrepealed.
1 Edw. 6. c. 7.	The Justices of the Peace Act 1547.	The whole Act, so far as unrepealed.
3 Chas. 1. c. 1.	The Petition of Right.	Sections 3 to 5 and in section 8 the words from " And that no" to " de-tained ".
16 Chas. 1. c. 10.	The Habeas Corpus Act 1640.	Section 6.
1 Will. & Mary c. 21.	The Great Seal Act 1688.	Section 3.
6 & 7 Will. 4. c. 19.	The Durham (County Pala-tine) Act 1836.	Section 3.
24 & 25 Vict. c. 96.	The Larceny Act 1861.	Section 117.
24 & 25 Vict. c. 97.	The Malicious Damage Act 1861.	Section 73.
24 & 25 Vict. c. 98.	The Forgery Act 1861.	Section 51.
24 & 25 Vict. c. 100.	The Offences against the Person Act 1861.	Section 71.
28 & 29 Vict. c. 124.	The Admiralty Powers, &c. Act 1865,	Section 5.
37 & 38 Vict. c. 45.	The County of Hertford and Liberty of St. Alban Act 1874.	In section 5 the words " and custos rotulorum ", and the words " or the office of custos rotulorum ".
45 & 46 Vict. c. 50.	The Municipal Corporations Act 1882.	Section 157(2) from " and made " onwards. Section 163(4) from " and made " onwards. In section 168(2) the words " the making of a declara-tion as in the Eighth Schedule ". Sections 239, 240 and 249. Schedule 8, so far as un-repealed.
49 & 50 Vict. c. 31.	The Oxford University (Justices) Act 1886.	The whole Act.
51 & 52 Vict. c. 41.	The Local Government Act 1888.	Section 78(2) from " but " onwards.
3 & 4 Geo. 5. c. 27.	The Forgery Act 1913.	Section 12, so far as un-repealed.
6 & 7 Geo. 5. c. 50.	The Larceny Act 1916.	Section 37(5), so far as un-repealed.
23 & 24 Geo. 5. c. 51.	The Local Government Act 1933.	Section 3(5). Section 5(3) from " except " onwards. Section 18(7), (8) and (10). Section 20(3) from " and " onwards. Section 33(5). Section 34(2) from " except " onwards.
26 Geo. 5 & 1 Edw. 8. c. 16.	The Coinage Offences Act 1936.	Section 12(2) and (3).

Chapter	Title or Short Title	Extent of Repeal
12, 13 & 14 Geo. 6. c. 101.	The Justices of the Peace Act 1949.	In section 1(3) the words "Subject to the next following subsection", and section 1(4). Section 2. In section 4, subsection (4)(*a*) (from the beginning of the year 1969). Section 13(3) from "and" onwards. In section 20(4), in paragraph (*a*) the words from "clerk to a stipendiary magistrate" to "aforesaid and" and the last "or", and paragraph (*b*), but not as respects qualification by service before the coming into force of this repeal. Section 25(6). Section 33(2), from the passing of this Act (but not as respects a magistrate appointed before that time). Schedule 1. In Schedule 2, paragraph 19.
15 & 16 Geo. 6. & 1 Eliz. 2. c. 55.	The Magistrates' Courts Act 1952.	In section 118(3) the words from "appointed" to "1949".
4 & 5 Eliz. 2. c. 34.	The Criminal Justice Administration Act 1956.	Section 13(4) from the passing of this Act (but not as respects a magistrate appointed before that time).
5 & 6 Eliz. 2. c. 27.	The Solicitors Act 1957.	Section 33(3).
7 & 8 Eliz. 2. c. 22.	The County Courts Act 1959.	Section 11.
1963 c. 33.	The London Government Act 1963.	In Schedule 4, paragraph 5.
1964 c. 26.	The Licensing Act 1964.	In section 57(1) the words "Subject to the following provisions of this section", and section 57(3).
1964 c. 42.	The Administration of Justice Act 1964.	Section 5(3) from "and section 11" onwards. In section 13(2) the words "The custos rotulorum for the inner London area" and the words "for that area". Section 30(3) and (4). Section 33. In Schedule 3, in paragraph 11 the word "and"; paragraph 12(2); in paragraph 14(1) the words "3(1), 4 and"; paragraph 15; paragraph 19(1); paragraph 22(4)"; paragraph 24; and paragraph 28(3).

Chapter	Title or Short Title	Extent of Repeal
1965 c. 28.	The Justices of the Peace Act 1965.	Section 1(2), but not as respects qualification by service before the coming into force of this repeal.
1967 c. 58.	The Criminal Law Act 1967.	Section 7(4).

EXPLANATORY NOTE

(This Note is not part of the Order.)

The effect of section 1 of the Justices of the Peace Act 1968 is that a person shall no longer be a Justice of the Peace by virtue of his holding some other office. This Order brings that provision into force, but existing heads of local authorities will continue to be Justices by virtue of those offices until the end of their current terms of office.

The Order does not apply to the City of London, in respect of which a number of arrangements have to be made before the provisions of the Act can be brought into effect there, except to enable a Commission of the Peace for the City to be issued.

STATUTORY INSTRUMENTS

1968 No. 2038

MINISTERS OF THE CROWN

The Transfer of Functions (Sea Transport, etc.) Order 1968

Made - - - -	20th December 1968
Laid before Parliament	31st December 1968
Coming into Operation	1st January 1969

At the Court at Buckingham Palace, the 20th day of December 1968

Present,

The Queen's Most Excellent Majesty in Council

Her Majesty, in pursuance of section 1 of the Ministers of the Crown (Transfer of Functions) Act 1946(a), is pleased, by and with the advice of Her Privy Council, to order, and it is hereby ordered, as follows:—

Citation, interpretation and commencement

1.—(1) This Order may be cited as the Transfer of Functions (Sea Transport, etc.) Order 1968.

(2) The Interpretation Act 1889(b) applies for the interpretation of this Order as it applies for the interpretation of an Act of Parliament.

(3) This Order shall come into operation on 1st January 1969.

Transfer of functions, and consequential transfer of rights and liabilities

2.—(1) In relation to the functions exercised at the date of this Order by the Minister of Transport in connection with the provision, acquisition, management and disposal of ships and shipping accommodation and of machinery, plant and equipment for use in shipping or for the purposes of shipping (except any such functions not exercised by him through the sea transport division of his Ministry), and in relation to the functions exercised or exercisable by the Minister of Transport under the Marine and Aviation Insurance (War Risks) Act 1952(c), the Board of Trade shall replace the Minister of Transport.

(2) Any rights or liabilities of the Minister of Transport arising from an agreement or contract entered into in connection with any of the functions transferred by paragraph (1) above, or from any thing done under or in pursuance of any such agreement or contract, shall be rights and liabilities of the Board of Trade; and any outstanding rights and obligations of that Minister by reason of Part I of the War Risks Insurance Act 1939(d), shall be rights and obligations of the Board.

(a) 1946 c. 31.   (b) 1889 c. 63.   (c) 1952 c. 57.   (d) 1939 c. 57.

3.—(1) Without prejudice to the continued validity of anything done before the coming into operation of this Order, the Board of Trade shall also replace the Minister of Transport in relation to the functions exercised or exercisable by that Minister under or by virtue of any of the following:—

(a) section 143 of the Public Health Act 1936(**a**) (treatment and prevention of infectious diseases);

(b) section 64(1) of the Finance Act 1940(**b**) (remission of death duties in cases of members of crews killed in war);

(c) except as provided by paragraph (2) below, so much of any enactment in a local Act or of any provisional order as relates to the foreshore or tidal lands (with or without other land) and restricts the making or operation of byelaws affecting the foreshore or tidal lands.

(2) Paragraph (1)(c) above shall not apply where the power to make the byelaws is exercisable by a harbour authority for the purposes of their functions as harbour authority; and in this paragraph " harbour authority " means, in relation to Great Britain, a harbour authority within the meaning of the Harbours Act 1964(**c**) and, in relation to Northern Ireland a person in whom are vested by or under any enactment functions of improving, maintaining or managing a harbour, whether natural or artificial, or any port, haven or estuary.

Provisions supplementary to Article 2

4.—(1) For the purpose of giving effect to Article 2(1) and (2) above—

(a) in section 1(2)(b) of the Restriction of Advertisement (War Risks Insurance) Act 1939(**d**), as amended by section 8 of the Marine and Aviation Insurance (War Risks) Act 1952(**e**), for the words " Minister of Transport " there shall be substituted the words " Board of Trade "; and

(b) in the provisions other than section 8 of the Marine and Aviation Insurance (War Risks) Act 1952(**e**) any reference to the Minister of Transport shall have effect as a reference to the Board of Trade, except in so far as paragraph (2) below provides to the contrary; and

(c) so far as may be necessary for or in consequence of any transfer effected by Article 2(1) or (2), any agreement or contract shall have effect as if references to the Minister of Transport or to his officers or department (including references which are to be construed as such a reference) were references to the Board of Trade or to officers or the department of the Board.

(2) Paragraph (1)(b) above, in its application to section 7(1)(a) to (c) of the Marine and Aviation Insurance (War Risks) Act 1952(**e**) (which describe the instruments exempt under the section from certain provisions about stamp duty and from requirements of the Marine Insurance Act 1906(**f**)), shall not restrict the operation of section 7(1)(a) to (c) in relation to any agreement or contract entered into before the date when this Order comes into operation or to any policy or certificate issued in pursuance of or in connection with any such agreement or contract; and from that date approvals previously given under section 7(4) of the Act by the Minister of Transport shall have effect as approvals given by the Board of Trade under section 7(4) as modified by this Order.

(a) 1936 c. 49.	(b) 1940 c. 29.	(c) 1964 c. 40.
(d) 1939 c. 120.	(e) 1952 c. 57.	(f) 1906 c. 41.

(3) Article 2 above shall not affect the operation in relation to Government ships in the service of the Minister of Transport of the Order in Council(a) made on the 14th July 1921 under section 80 of the Merchant Shipping Act 1906(b) with reference to Government ships in the service of the Board of Trade, and that Order shall have effect both in relation to Government ships in the service of the Minister (with references to the Minister replacing the original references to the Board by virtue of the Ministry of War Transport (Dissolution) Order 1946(c)) and in relation to Government ships in the service of the Board; and accordingly as regards Government ships which at the coming into operation of this Order are in the service of the Minister in connection with functions transferred by Article 2 above, that Order shall thereupon apply to those ships as ships in the service of the Board of Trade, and the necessary alterations shall be made in the entries relating to the ships in the register book.

(4) Article 2 above shall not be taken to affect the exercise of any functions by a Minister of the Crown or government department other than the Minister of Transport and the Board of Trade, or to prejudice any powers exercisable in relation to the functions of Ministers of the Crown and government departments by virtue of Her Majesty's prerogative.

W. G. Agnew.

EXPLANATORY NOTE

(This Note is not part of the Order.)

This Order provides for the transfer from the Minister of Transport to the Board of Trade on the 1st January 1969 of—

(a) the functions in connection with the provision, acquisition, management and disposal of ships and shipping accommodation and with related matters exercised by the Sea Transport Division of the Ministry of Transport;

(b) the functions of the Minister under the Marine and Aviation Insurance (War Risks) Act 1952 (which empowers the Minister to undertake the insurance of ships, aircraft and cargoes against war risks); and

(c) certain miscellaneous functions of a minor nature relating to shipping and to the sea which are similar to those previously transferred to the Board of Trade by the Transfer of Functions (Shipping and Construction of Ships) Order 1965 (S.I. 1965/145).

(a) S.R. & O. 1921/1211 (Rev. XIV, p. 64; 1921, p. 544). (b) 1906 c. 48.
(c) S.R. & O. 1946/375 (Rev. XV, p. 229; 1946 I, p. 1009).

STATUTORY INSTRUMENTS

1968 No. 2044

POLICE

ENGLAND AND WALES

The Police Federation (Amendment) (No. 2) Regulations 1968

Made - - -	*19th December* 1968
Laid before Parliament	*3rd January* 1969
Coming into Operation	*6th January* 1969

In exercise of the powers conferred on me by section 44 of the Police Act 1964(**a**), and after consultation with the three Central Committees of the Police Federation for England and Wales sitting together as a Joint Committee, I hereby make the following Regulations :—

1. At the end of Regulation 10 of the principal Regulations (which relates to the emoluments of the secretary of the Police Federation) there shall be added the following paragraph :—

"(2) The Regulations for the time being in force under—

(*a*) section 33 of the Police Act 1964, in so far as they relate to leave, pay and allowances, and

(*b*) the Police Pensions Act 1948(**b**), except in so far as they relate to compulsory retirement on account of age,

shall have effect in relation to the secretary of the joint central committee as if he held the rank of chief inspector in the City of London police force so, however, that nothing in this paragraph shall be construed as transferring any rights or liabilities to the police authority maintaining that force.".

2. For paragraph 1(1) of Part II of Schedule 3 to the principal Regulations (which constitutes districts for the purposes of the election of women delegates to central conferences) there shall be substituted the following provision :—

"1.—(1) For the purposes of the election of women delegates to central conferences there shall be the following districts :—

(*a*) No. 1 District, comprising the county of Lancaster, the county boroughs of Barrow-in-Furness, Blackburn, Blackpool, Bolton, Burnley, Oldham, Preston, Rochdale, St. Helens, Southport, Warrington and Wigan, and the combined police areas known as the Cheshire police area, the Cumbria police area, the Liverpool and Bootle police area and the Manchester and Salford police area ;

(*b*) No. 2 District, comprising the county of Northumberland, the county boroughs of Kingston-upon-Hull, Newcastle-upon-Tyne, Teesside and Tynemouth and the combined police areas known as the Durham police area and the York and North-East Yorkshire police area ;

(**a**) 1964 c. 48.   (**b**) 1948 c. 24.

(c) No. 3 District, comprising the county boroughs of Bradford and Leeds, and the combined police areas known as the Derby county and borough police area, the Lincolnshire police area, the Nottinghamshire combined police area, the Sheffield and Rotherham police area and the West Yorkshire police area ;

(d) No. 4 District, comprising the county boroughs of Birmingham and Coventry, and the combined police areas known as the Leicester and Rutland police area, the Northampton and county police area, the Staffordshire county and Stoke-on-Trent police area, the Warwickshire police area, the West Mercia police area and the West Midlands police area ;

(e) No. 5 District, comprising the counties of Essex and Hertfordshire, the City of London, the county borough of Southend-on-Sea and the combined police areas known as the Bedfordshire and Luton police area, the Mid-Anglia police area, the Norfolk joint police area, the Suffolk police area and the Thames Valley police area ;

(f) No. 6 District, comprising the county of Surrey and the combined police areas known as the Hampshire police area, the Kent police area and the Sussex police area ;

(g) No. 7 District, comprising the counties of Gloucestershire and Wiltshire, the county borough of Bristol and the combined police areas known as the Devon and Cornwall police area, the Dorset and Bournemouth police area and the Somerset and Bath police area ;

(h) No. 8 District, comprising the county of Glamorgan, the county boroughs of Cardiff, Merthyr Tydfil and Swansea, and the combined police areas known as the Dyfed-Powys police area, the Gwent police area and the Gwynedd police area.".

3. In these Regulations any reference to the principal Regulations is a reference to the Police Federation Regulations 1965**(a)**, as amended **(b)**.

4. These Regulations may be cited as the Police Federation (Amendment) (No. 2) Regulations 1968 and shall come into operation on 6th January 1969.

James Callaghan,
One of Her Majesty's Principal
Secretaries of State.

Home Office,
  Whitehall.
19th December 1968.

(a) S.I. 1965/619 (1965 I, p. 1928).
(b) The relevant amending Regulations are S.I. 1968/24 (1968 I, p. 29).

EXPLANATORY NOTE

(This Note is not part of the Regulations.)

These Regulations amend the Police Federation Regulations 1965.

Regulation 1 provides that the regulations governing police leave, pay and allowances and pensions shall have effect in relation to the secretary of the Police Federation as if he were a chief inspector in the City of London police force.

Regulation 2 redefines the districts constituted for the purposes of the election of women delegates to central conferences of the Police Federation and takes account of the constitution, or reconstitution, of a number of combined police areas since the relevant provision of the 1965 Regulations was last amended.

STATUTORY INSTRUMENTS

1968 No. 2046

FOOD AND DRUGS

COMPOSITION AND LABELLING

The Canned Meat Product (Amendment) Regulations 1968

Made - - -	*19th December* 1968
Laid before Parliament	*3rd January* 1969
Coming into Operation	*4th January* 1969

The Minister of Agriculture, Fisheries and Food and the Secretary of State for Social Services, acting jointly, in exercise of the powers conferred on them by sections 4, 7 and 123 of the Food and Drugs Act 1955(**a**) and of all other powers enabling them in that behalf, hereby make the following regulations after consultation with such organisations as appear to them to be representative of interests substantially affected by the regulations and reference to the Food Hygiene Advisory Council under section 82 of the said Act (insofar as the regulations are made in exercise of the powers conferred by the said section 7) :—

Citation, commencement and interpretation

1.—(1) These regulations may be cited as the Canned Meat Product (Amendment) Regulations 1968 ; and shall come into operation on 4th January 1969.

(2) The Interpretation Act 1889(**b**) shall apply to the interpretation of these regulations as it applies to the interpretation of an Act of Parliament.

Amendment of the principal regulations

2. The Canned Meat Product Regulations 1967(**c**) shall be amended as follows :—

(*a*) by substituting for regulation 5(2) thereof the following paragraph :—

"(2) The minimum meat content required by regulation 6 of these regulations for any canned meat product (other than any canned sliced bacon, canned sausage, canned meat pie or canned sausage roll) shall include a lean meat content of not less than 60 per cent. of such minimum meat content." ;

(*b*) by substituting for sub-paragraph (*a*) of the proviso to paragraph (2) of regulation 6 thereof the following sub-paragraph :—

"(*a*) have a meat content of not less than 90 per cent. if—

(i) the meat in the product has been cured and the product has been cooked after canning and bears on a label on the container as a description, as or as part of or in immediate proximity to its name, the expression "cured meat" or the name of any variety of meat which is commonly or usually recognised as the name of a cured meat ; or

---

(**a**) 4 & 5 Eliz. 2.c.16. For the transfer of functions from the Minister of Health to the Secretary of State, see S.I. 1968/1699 (1968 III, p. 4585).

(**b**) 1889 c.63.　　　　　　　　　　　　(**c**) S.I. 1967/861 (1967 II, p. 2569).

    (ii) the meat in the product has been chopped or minced and the product has been cooked after canning and is such that it can be removed from the container as a single piece and can be sliced, and bears on a label on the container as a description, as or as part of or in immediate proximity to its name, such one of the following expressions as may be appropriate, namely, "chopped meat" or "minced meat" or "chopped X" or "minced X", and the description has been completed, where appropriate, by inserting at "X" the common or usual name of the meat present ;" ;

  (c) by deleting from regulation 6(8)(c)(i) thereof the words "as or" which follow immediately after the words "if there appears upon such label," ;

  (d) by inserting in regulation 8 thereof immediately after the word "deliver" the words "in a container" and by inserting in the said regulation immediately before the words "such canned meat product" the words "the container of".

In Witness whereof the Official Seal of the Minister of Agriculture, Fisheries and Food is hereunto affixed on 17th December 1968.

(L.S.)   *Cledwyn Hughes,*
                      Minister of Agriculture, Fisheries and Food.

Signed by authority of the Secretary of State for Social Services.

                            David Ennals,
                            Minister of State,
                  Department of Health and Social Security.
19th December 1968.

EXPLANATORY NOTE

(This Note is not part of the Regulations.)

These regulations amend the Canned Meat Product Regulations 1967 (which come into operation on 31st May 1969) by—

  (a) exempting canned sliced bacon from any requirement as to lean meat content ;

  (b) setting a separate standard for the meat content of chopped or minced meat which is suitable for slicing ;

  (c) restricting the use of the expression "ready meal" on the label of a canned meat product ;

  (d) applying labelling requirements to canned meat products only when such products are in containers.

STATUTORY INSTRUMENTS

1968 No. 2047

FOOD AND DRUGS

COMPOSITION AND LABELLING

The Sausage and Other Meat Product (Amendment) Regulations 1968

Made - - -	*19th December* 1968
Laid before Parliament	*3rd January* 1969
Coming into Operation	*4th January* 1969

The Minister of Agriculture, Fisheries and Food and the Secretary of State for Social Services, acting jointly, in exercise of the powers conferred on them by sections 4, 7 and 123 of the Food and Drugs Act 1955(a) and of all other powers enabling them in that behalf, hereby make the following regulations after consultation with such organisations as appear to them to be representative of interests substantially affected by the regulations and reference to the Food Hygiene Advisory Council under section 82 of the said Act (insofar as the regulations are made in exercise of the powers conferred by the said section 7) :—

Citation, commencement and interpretation

1.—(1) These regulations may be cited as the Sausage and Other Meat Product (Amendment) Regulations 1968 ; and shall come into operation on 4th January 1969.

(2) The Interpretation Act 1889(b) shall apply to the interpretation of these regulations as it applies to the interpretation of an Act of Parliament.

Amendment of the principal regulations

2. The Sausage and Other Meat Product Regulations 1967(c) shall be amended as follows :—

  (*a*) by inserting in regulation 3(*b*) thereof immediately after the words "any canned meat product" the words "(including any such product after removal from its container)" ;

  (*b*) by deleting from regulation 5(2)(*c*)(i) thereof the words "as or" which follow immediately after the words "if it bears,".

(**a**) 4 & 5 Eliz. 2. c.16.   For the transfer of functions from the Minister of Health to the Secretary of State, see S.I. 1968/1699 (1968 III, p. 4585).
(**b**) 1889 c.63.   (**c**) S.I. 1967/862 (1967 II, p.2583).

In Witness whereof the Official Seal of the Minister of Agriculture, Fisheries and Food is hereunto affixed on 17th December 1968.

(L.S.)   *Cledwyn Hughes,*
Minister of Agriculture, Fisheries and Food.

Signed by authority of the Secretary of State for Social Services.

David Ennals,
Minister of State,
Department of Health and Social Security.

19th December 1968.

EXPLANATORY NOTE

(This Note is not part of the Regulations.)

These regulations amend the Sausage and Other Meat Product Regulations 1967 (which come into operation on 31st May 1969) so as to—

(*a*) provide that the principal regulations do not apply to a canned meat product after removal from its container ;

(*b*) restrict the use of the expression "ready meal" in relation to a meat product.

STATUTORY INSTRUMENTS

1968 No. 2048

AGRICULTURE

MEAT AND LIVESTOCK COMMISSION

The Livestock and Livestock Products Industries (Payments for Scientific Research) Order 1968

Laid before Parliament in draft

Made - - -	19*th December* 1968
Coming into Operation	20*th December* 1968

The Minister of Agriculture, Fisheries and Food and the Secretary of State concerned with agriculture in Scotland, acting jointly in exercise of the powers conferred on them by section 16 of the Agriculture Act 1967(**a**) and of all other powers enabling them in that behalf, hereby make the following order a draft whereof has been laid before Parliament and approved by resolution of each House of Parliament:—

1.—(1) This order may be cited as the Livestock and Livestock Products Industries (Payments for Scientific Research) Order 1968, and shall come into operation on the day immediately following the day on which it is made.

(2) The Interpretation Act 1889(**b**) shall apply to the interpretation of this order as it applies to the interpretation of an Act of Parliament.

2. For the purpose of providing funds to be applied for the purpose of scientific research which is connected with the livestock industry and the livestock products industry and which is to be carried out by the Agricultural Research Council, the Meat and Livestock Commission (established under Part I of the Agriculture Act 1967) shall make payments as follows:—

   (*a*) a sum of £98,000 on or before the 31st March 1969;

   (*b*) a sum of £197,000 during the twelve months ending with the 31st March 1970;

   (*c*) a sum of £197,000 during the twelve months ending with the 31st March 1971; and

   (*d*) a sum of £197,000 during the twelve months ending with the 31st March 1972.

3. All sums to be paid by the Meat and Livestock Commission in accordance with the foregoing provisions of this order shall be paid by them into the Agricultural Research Council Deposit Account, being an account opened by Her Majesty's Paymaster General, such sums to be applied and dealt with by

---

(**a**) 1967 c. 22.   (**b**) 1889 c. 63.

the Agricultural Research Council for the purpose of scientific research to be carried out by them in connection with the livestock industry and the livestock products industry.

In Witness whereof the Official Seal of the Minister of Agriculture, Fisheries and Food is hereunto affixed on the 18th December 1968.

(L.S.)   *Cledwyn Hughes,*
Minister of Agriculture, Fisheries and Food.

Given under the Seal of the Secretary of State for Scotland on the 19th December 1968.

(L.S.)   *William Ross,*
Secretary of State for Scotland.

EXPLANATORY NOTE
(This Note is not part of the Order.)

This order requires the making of payments by the Meat and Livestock Commission for the purpose of providing funds for the purpose of scientific research, to be carried on by the Agricultural Research Council, in connection with the livestock industry and the livestock products industry.

STATUTORY INSTRUMENTS

1968 No. 2049

REGISTRATION OF BIRTHS, DEATHS, MARRIAGES, ETC.

ENGLAND AND WALES

The Registration of Births, Deaths and Marriages Regulations 1968

Made - - -		*18th December* 1968
Coming into Operation		*1st April* 1969

ARRANGEMENT OF REGULATIONS

PART I

PRELIMINARY

PART II

REGISTRATION OFFICERS

PART III

GENERAL PROVISIONS AS TO ENTRIES IN REGISTERS

Part IV

Birth Registration

Part V

Re-Registration of Births of Legitimated Persons

Part VI

Birth Entries of Adopted Children

Part VII

Registration of Still-Births

The Registrar General, in exercise of the powers conferred on him by sections 1, 3 and 12 of the Births and Deaths Registration Act 1926(a), paragraph 5 of Schedule 1 to the Industrial Assurance and Friendly Societies Act 1948(b), sections 35, 55 and 74 of the Marriage Act 1949(c), sections 1, 5, 7, 9, 11 (as amended by section 2 of the Population (Statistics) Act 1960(d)), 12 to 15, 20 to 24, 26, 29, 33, 39 and 41 of the Births and Deaths Registration Act 1953(e) and sections 6 to 8, 16, 19 and 20 of the Registration Service Act 1953(f) and

---

(a) 1926 c. 48.   (b) 1948 c. 39.
(c) 1949 c. 76.   (d) 1960 c. 32.
(e) 1953 c. 20.   (f) 1953 c. 37.

of all other powers enabling him in that behalf, with the approval of the Secretary of State for Social Services, hereby makes the following regulations :—

PART I

PRELIMINARY

Title and commencement

1. These regulations may be cited as the Registration of Births, Deaths and Marriages Regulations 1968 and shall come into operation on 1st April 1969.

Interpretation

2.—(1) In these regulations, unless the context otherwise requires—

"the Act" means the Births and Deaths Registration Act 1953 ;

"authorised person" has the same meaning as in the Marriage Act 1949 ;

"birth" does not include a still-birth ;

"borough" means a county borough or a London borough, and includes the City of London ;

"certificate of cause of death" means a certificate required to be signed by a medical practitioner pursuant to section 22 of the Act ;

"clerk" means the clerk of a council ;

"coroner" includes a deputy coroner and an assistant deputy coroner ;

"council", in relation to a district or sub-district, means the council of the county or borough in which the district or sub-district is situated and, in relation to an officer, means the council of the county or borough which contains the district or sub-district, as the case may be, within which he is authorised to act ;

"deputy officer" means a deputy superintendent registrar, a deputy registrar of births and deaths or a deputy registrar of marriages ;

"description", in relation to a coroner, means his official designation and the area of his jurisdiction ;

"enactment" includes any instrument made under an Act ;

"entry" means a record of the particulars relating to a birth, still-birth, death or marriage completed by the registrar in the appropriate spaces in form 1, 4, 5, 9 or 23 ;

"interim officer" means an interim superintendent registrar or an interim registrar of births and deaths ;

"local scheme", in relation to an officer, means the scheme in force under section 13 of the Registration Service Act 1953 (which provides for local schemes of registration) in the county or borough which contains the district or the sub-district, as the case may be, within which he is authorised to act ;

"maiden surname", in relation to a woman, means the surname under which she contracted her marriage (or, where she has married more than once, her first marriage ;)

"medical practitioner" means a registered medical practitioner ; and in relation to a medical practitioner who has signed a certificate, "name and qualification" means his name as stated on the certificate and his registered professional qualification ;

"midwife" means a certified midwife within the meaning of the Midwives Act 1951(**a**) ;

(**a**) 1951 c. 53.

"name", in relation to a person, includes a surname except in regulations 18, 25, 73 and 82, and in forms 1, 2 and 3 ;

"non-salaried officer" means an officer to whom section 18 of the Registration Service Act 1953 (which relates to non-salaried officers) applies, an interim officer who, on the vacation by such an officer of his office, takes on his duties or an officer appointed under section 7 of the said Act (which provides for the appointment of additional registrars of marriage) ;

"occupation" includes rank or profession ;

"officer" means a superintendent registrar, a registrar, a deputy officer or an interim officer ;

"principal officer" means an officer other than a deputy officer ;

"registrar" means a registrar of births and deaths or a registrar of marriages ;

"registration office" means the office of superintendent registrar, registrar of births and deaths or registrar of marriages ;

"short certificate of birth" means a certificate of birth under section 33 of the Act (which provides for the issue of short certificates of birth) ;

(2) All institutions maintained wholly or mainly from public funds or charitable endowments or subscriptions or any combination thereof shall be public institutions for the purposes of section 41 of the Act (which relates to interpretation).

(3) In these regulations, unless the context otherwise requires, any reference to any enactment shall be construed as a reference to that enactment as amended by or under any subsequent enactment.

(4) Any reference in these regulations to a numbered regulation or schedule shall, unless the reference is to a regulation of or a schedule to a specified enactment, be construed as a reference to the regulation or schedule bearing that number in these regulations.

(5) Any reference in any regulation in these regulations to a numbered paragraph shall, unless the reference is to a paragraph of a specified regulation, be construed as a reference to the paragraph bearing that number in the first mentioned regulation.

(6) Any reference to a numbered form shall be construed as a reference to the form bearing that number in Schedule 1 ; and any reference to a numbered space or column on a form shall be construed as a reference to the space or column bearing that number on that form.

(7) The Interpretation Act 1889(a) shall apply to the interpretation of these regulations as it applies to the interpretation of an Act of Parliament and as if these regulations and the regulations hereby revoked were Acts of Parliament.

Provision where date or place of birth or death is unknown

3. Where a new-born living or still-born child is found exposed or a dead body is found—

(*a*) if the date of the birth of the child or of the death of the deceased person is unknown, references in these regulations to the doing of anything within a specified period after the birth or death shall be construed

---

(a) 1889 c. 63.

as references to the doing thereof within the same period after the child or the dead body was found ;

(b) if the place of birth of the child or the place of death of the deceased person is unknown, references in these regulations to the place where a birth or death occurred shall be construed as references to the place where the child or the dead body was found.

PART II

REGISTRATION OFFICERS

Qualifications for appointment

4. A candidate for appointment to a registration office must be qualified in accordance with the following conditions :—

(a) he must produce satisfactory evidence as to character ;

(b) he must have attained the age of 21 ;

(c) he must not have attained the age of 65 ;

(d) if he has attained the age of 55 he must—

(i) in the case of a candidate for appointment as superintendent registrar, previously have held a registration office or deputy registration office for at least 5 years in the aggregate ;

(ii) in the case of a candidate for appointment to any other registration office, previously have held a registration office or a deputy registration office for a period in the aggregate at least equal to that which has elapsed since he attained the age of 55:

Provided that the council may appoint a candidate who is not qualified under paragraph (c), or a candidate who is not qualified under paragraph (d), if the Registrar General is satisfied that there is no other suitable candidate for appointment.

Disqualifications for appointment

5. Notwithstanding the provisions of regulation 4, no person shall be qualified for appointment—

(a) to any registration office—

(i) if he has been declared bankrupt and has not subsequently obtained his discharge, or if he has made any composition or arrangement with his creditors and has not subsequently paid his debts in full or obtained a certificate of discharge ;

(ii) if he has been dismissed from any office by the Registrar General and the Registrar General does not consent to the appointment ;

(iii) if he is, or has been during the 12 months preceding the date on which the appointment is to take effect, a member of the council or of a committee of the council having duties in relation to the appointment of registration officers ;

(iv) if he is an officer or servant, other than the clerk or deputy clerk, of a local authority employed by them in the performance of duties relating to their functions as a burial authority ;

(v) if he holds any office as authorised person, secretary (for marriages) of a synagogue or registering officer of the Society of Friends ;

(vi) if he is a minister of religion, a medical practitioner, a midwife, an undertaker or other person concerned in a burial or cremation business, a person engaged in any business concerned with life insurance, or a person engaged in any other calling which would conflict with or prevent the proper performance in person of the duties of the office for which he is a candidate ;

(b) as superintendent registrar, if he holds office as a registrar or any deputy registration office ;

(c) as registrar, if he holds office as a superintendent registrar or is a coroner.

Powers and duties of deputy

6.—(1) Subject to the provisions of regulation 9, a deputy may in the absence of his principal perform any of the duties of his principal, notwithstanding that his absence may not be unavoidable or occasioned by illness ; and a deputy registrar may register—

(a) a birth, still-birth or death in respect of which his principal acts as informant, or

(b) a marriage to which his principal is a party or witness.

(2) Subject as aforesaid, a deputy may, while his principal is performing any duties of his office, perform any of the duties of his principal which are not reserved to the principal under the local scheme.

(3) As soon as a deputy has acted continuously as such for one month in the absence of the principal he shall make a report of the fact to the Registrar General, stating to the best of his ability the circumstances to which the principal's absence from duty is due and the date when the principal expects to resume his duties.

Vacation of office

7.—(1) A superintendent registrar or a registrar may resign his office by giving to the clerk such notice in writing as may have been determined at the time of his appointment ; and at the same time he shall inform the Registrar General accordingly.

(2) When a deputy to a superintendent registrar or to a registrar ceases to hold office, the superintendent registrar or the registrar, as the case may be, shall inform the clerk and the Registrar General.

Lists of officers, offices and hours of attendance

8.—(1) A superintendent registrar shall from time to time, at such intervals as he may with the approval of the clerk think fit, cause to be printed a list of the principal officers holding office within his district, stating their names, head offices and stations and their days and hours of attendance, and shall furnish two copies of the list to the Registrar General and one copy each to—

(i) the superintendent registrar of each district adjoining his district ;

(ii) the chief officer of every hospital in the district ;

(iii) the chief officer of every police station in the district ;

(iv) every coroner having jurisdiction in the district ;

(v) the clerk of the council of every urban or rural district and parish wholly or partly situated in the district;

(vi) every medical practitioner and midwife practising in the district; and

(vii) such other persons as he may consider expedient for the convenience of the public;

and in the event of any changes in the list he shall notify the change to the persons to whom the list has been supplied.

(2) A superintendent registrar and a registrar of births and deaths shall cause to be exhibited and maintained outside his office and out-stations (if any) a notice stating his name, his official description, the name of his district or sub-district and the hours when his office and out-stations (if any) are open to the public.

Duality of function

9.—(1) A registrar shall not register—

(a) a birth, still-birth or death of which he is an informant, or

(b) a marriage to which he is a party or a witness.

(2) A person who holds jointly the offices of registrar and deputy superintendent registrar shall not perform any of the duties of the superintendent registrar in relation to any duties which he performs as registrar.

General conduct, etc. of officers

10.—(1) An officer shall not, while discharging his official duties with any person attending upon him at his office or otherwise coming into communication with him in his official capacity, transact or attempt to transact or to further the transaction of any business of a private nature, either on his own behalf or on behalf of any other person or body.

(2) An officer shall not, without the express authority of the Registrar General, publish or communicate to any person, otherwise than in the ordinary course of the performance of his official duties, any information acquired by him while performing those duties.

(3) An officer shall comply with any instruction or direction, whether particular or general, given to him by the Registrar General in any matter relating to the due performance by the officer of his duties in the execution of any enactment relating to his functions (not being a matter for which specific provision is made).

Statistical returns

11. A superintendent registrar or a registrar shall at such times and in such manner as the Registrar General may direct send to the Registrar General such information concerning births, still-births, deaths and marriages as he may require to be extracted from the records kept by the officer.

Inspection, etc., of books

12. Every officer shall submit all books and forms in his possession to inspection by any person authorised in that behalf by the Registrar General, and shall if so required by the Registrar General give him a statement as to the books and forms in his possession.

PART III

GENERAL PROVISIONS AS TO ENTRIES IN REGISTERS

Registration in more than one place

13.—(1) A registrar shall not register a birth, still-birth or death which has already been registered unless—

(*a*) the provisions of regulation 45 or 55 apply or

(*b*) the Registrar General gives his authority.

(2) If it appears to a registrar that a birth, still-birth or death has nevertheless been registered more than once, he shall—

(*a*) if there is no material difference in the particulars recorded, write in the margin of every entry but the original the words "Inadvertently re-registered. For correct entry see No............ Register No.............", inserting the number of the original entry and the number of the register in which it is recorded ;

(*b*) if there is any material difference, report the matter to the Registrar General and make such note in the margin of the entry as the Registrar General may authorise.

(3) Where a birth, still-birth or death is re-registered on the authority of the Registrar General, the registrar making the new entry and the registrar or superintendent registrar having custody of the register in which the original entry was made shall make such notes (if any) in the margin of the respective entries as the Registrar General may direct.

Cancellation of entry space

14. Where during the registration of a birth, still-birth, death or marriage it appears to the registrar that he cannot enter the particulars required in any space or column on the appropriate form (other than space 17 on form 1), then, subject to any other provision of these regulations, he shall draw a line in ink through that space or column before the informant is called upon to certify the entry.

Signature by mark or in foreign characters

15. Where a person who is required under any provision of these regulations to sign his name in a register makes a mark or signs in characters other than those used in the English or Welsh languages, the registrar shall write against the mark or signature the words "The mark (or signature) of ....", inserting the name of the person.

PART IV

BIRTH REGISTRATION

Particulars to be registered

16. The particulars concerning a birth required to be registered pursuant to section 1 of the Act (which requires prescribed particulars of births to be registered) shall, subject to the provisions of this Part of these regulations, be the particulars required in spaces 1 to 13 in form 1 ; and form 1 shall be the prescribed form for birth registration for the purposes of section 5 of the Act (which provides for registration of births free of charge).

Particulars as at date of birth

17. Subject to the provisions of regulation 18(4) and (5), under this part of these regulations the particulars to be recorded in respect of the parents of a child shall be the particulars appropriate as at the date of birth of the child.

Manner of registration

18.—(1) On receiving from an informant, at any time within 3 months after the date of a birth which occurred in his sub-district, information of the particulars required by regulation 16, the registrar shall register the birth in the presence of the informant by inserting in form 1 the particulars required in spaces 1 to 13 subject to the provisions of this regulation.

(2) With respect to space 1 (Date and place of birth)—

    (*a*) if more than one living child is born at a confinement the registrar shall enter the time of birth after the date of birth in each entry respectively ;

    (*b*) if the birth is that of a new-born child found exposed and the date and place of birth are unknown, the registrar shall enter the words "On or about........." and the approximate date of birth followed by the words "Found at .... on ....", with the relevant place and date.

(3) With respect to space 2 (Name and surname) the surname to be entered shall be the surname by which at the date of the registration of the birth it is intended that the child shall be known and, if a name is not given, the registrar shall enter the surname preceded by a horizontal line.

(4) With respect to spaces 4 and 6 (Father's name, surname and occupation)—

    (*a*) if after the child's birth the father acquired a surname different from that borne by him at the date of the birth, the registrar shall enter the name and surname as at the date of the birth, followed by the acquired surname preceded by the word "now" or, if the father is deceased, by the word "afterwards" ;

    (*b*) if the child was illegitimate, the registrar shall not complete space 6 unless the name and surname of a person acknowledging himself to be the father of the child have been entered in space 4 pursuant to section 10 of the Act (which makes provision as to the father of an illegitimate child) ;

    (*c*) if the father is deceased, the registrar shall enter below the particulars in space 6 the word "deceased" ;

    (*d*) if the father has changed his occupation since the birth of the child, the registrar shall enter in space 6 after the occupation as at the date of the birth, the occupation as at the date of registration preceded by the word "now".

(5) With respect to space 7 (Mother's name and surname)—

    (*a*) if after the birth of the child the mother acquired by marriage or otherwise a surname different from that borne by her at the date of the birth, the registrar shall enter the name and surname as at the date of the birth, followed by the acquired surname preceded by the word "now" or, if the mother is deceased, by the word "afterwards" ;

    (*b*) if the child was illegitimate and the mother was engaged before the birth in gainful employment, the registrar shall enter particulars of the occupation unless pursuant to paragraph (4) an entry is made of the father's occupation.

(6) With respect to space 13 (Informant's address)—

(a) the address required shall be the address as at the date of registration of the birth ;

(b) if in pursuance of section 10 of the Act an entry has been made of the name of the person acknowledging himself to be the father of the child, the registrar shall enter that person's address, followed by the mother's address if different ;

(c) except as provided by sub-paragraph (b) of this paragraph, the registrar shall not enter the address of the informant if that address is the same as the mother's usual address.

Verification of particulars

19. After completing spaces 1 to 13 in form 1 the registrar shall call upon the informant to verify the particulars entered ; and if it appears that any error has been made in those particulars, the registrar shall thereupon in the presence of the informant make the necessary correction in the manner provided in regulation 72.

Signatures

20.—(1) The registrar shall call upon the informant to sign the entry in space 14.

(2) If, in pursuance of section 10 of the Act, an entry has been made of the name of the person acknowledging himself to be the father, the registrar shall call first upon that person and then upon the mother to sign the entry.

Signature, etc. of registrar

21. When the registrar has signed the entry in space 16 he shall add his official description.

Registration after 3 months but within 12 months

22. Where an informant attends before a superintendent registrar to make a declaration under section 6(1)(b) of the Act (which relates to registration after 3 but within 12 months of birth) the superintendent registrar shall supply a form of declaration provided by the Registrar General.

Registration after 12 months

23.—(1) Where a registrar or a superintendent registrar is informed that a birth which occurred more than 12 months previously has not been registered, he shall make a report to the Registrar General stating to the best of his knowledge and belief the particulars required to be registered concerning the birth, the source of his information and the name and address of any qualified informant available to give information for the registration.

(2) Where an informant attends, pursuant to the written authority of the Registrar General, to give information for the registration of a birth which occurred more than 12 months previously, the superintendent registrar shall—

(a) ascertain from the informant the particulars required to be registered concerning the birth, enter them in a form of declaration provided by the Registrar General, read or show the form to the informant and, after correcting any error, require the informant to sign the declaration ; and

(*b*) attest the declaration.

(3) On registering the birth pursuant to this regulation the registrar shall enter immediately after the date of registration the words "On the authority of the Registrar General".

Making of declaration under section 9 of the Act

24.—(1) The officer before whom a declaration for the purposes of section 9 of the Act (which relates to giving information to a person other than the registrar) may be made shall be—

(*a*) in a case where not more than 3 months have elapsed since the date of the birth of the child, any registrar of births and deaths, or

(*b*) in any other case, any superintendent registrar,

not being the superintendent registrar or the registrar of births and deaths for the district or sub-district in which the birth occurred.

(2) A registrar or a superintendent registrar before whom such a declaration is to be made shall ascertain from the informant the particulars to be registered concerning the birth, enter them in such declaration, using for the purpose a form provided by the Registrar General, read or show the form to the informant and, after correcting any error, require the informant to sign the declaration.

(3) Any such declaration shall be attested by the officer in whose presence it was signed.

(4) If it appears to the registrar of the sub-district in which the birth occurred that the particulars contained in any such declaration, as duly sent to him, are in any material respect not proper to be registered, he shall return the declaration to the officer before whom it was attested together with a note of the matters in which it appears to need amendment, and that officer shall in the presence of the declarant amend any error by striking out any incorrect particulars and inserting the correct particulars.

(5) Any amendment so made shall be initialled by the declarant, and the declaration shall be returned to the registrar of the sub-district in which the birth occurred.

(6) Subject to the provisions of paragraphs (7) and (8), when the said registrar receives a declaration which serves the purposes of section 9 of the Act (whether a declaration made solely for the purposes of that section or a declaration made in a case to which section 6 or 7 of the Act applies) he shall, if the birth has not to his knowledge already been registered, enter the particulars of the birth in his register in the following manner :—

(*a*) in spaces 1 to 13 of the entry, he shall enter the particulars as appearing in the corresponding spaces of the declaration, so, however, that where any particular has been corrected in pursuance of paragraph (4) he shall enter in the register only the particulars as corrected, omitting any incorrect particular which has been struck out and the initials of the declarant ;

(b) in space 14 (Signature of informant) he shall write the name of the declarant in the form in which it is signed in the declaration, and shall add the words "by declaration dated ....", inserting the date on which the declaration was made and signed.

(7) If more than 3 but less than 12 months have elapsed since the date of the birth of the child, the registrar shall make the entry in the presence of the superintendent registrar in whose district the birth occurred, and the superintendent registrar and registrar shall sign the entry, adding their official descriptions.

(8) If more than 12 months have elapsed since the date of the birth of the child, the registrar shall not make the entry until he has received the written authority of the Registrar General to register the birth; and below the date of registration in space 15 the registrar shall enter the words "On the authority of the Registrar General", and the superintendent registrar and registrar shall sign the entry, adding their official descriptions.

Alteration or giving of name after registration

25.—(1) An entry in pursuance of section 13 of the Act (which relates to registering or altering the name of a child) shall be made in space 17 of the entry of birth by the registrar or superintendent registrar having custody of the register in which the birth is registered.

(2) Where an entry is made in pursuance of the said section 13, the registrar or superintendent registrar, as the case may be, shall enter the name shown in the certificate given in pursuance of the said section followed by the surname recorded in space 2 of the entry and—

(a) if the entry is made on production of a certificate in form 2 that a name was given in baptism, add the words "by baptism on ....", inserting the date on which the child was baptised ;

(b) if the entry is made on production of a certificate in form 3 that a name was given otherwise than in baptism, add the words "on certificate of naming dated ....", inserting the date on which the certificate was signed.

PART V
RE-REGISTRATION OF BIRTHS OF LEGITIMATED PERSONS

Attendance of parent

26. Where under Section 14 of the Act the Registrar General authorises the re-registration of the birth of a legitimated person, a parent of the legitimated person shall, if required by the Registrar General, attend personally within such time as the Registrar General may specify at the office of the registrar of births and deaths for the sub-district in which the birth occurred.

Relevant date for particulars

27. The provisions of regulation 17 shall apply to this Part of these regulations except that the surname to be recorded in respect of the mother of a child shall be her surname immediately after her marriage to the father.

Making of entry where parent attends

28.—(1) The registrar of the sub-district in which such a birth occurred shall read or show to the parent the particulars entered in the Registrar General's authority, and if it appears that there is any error or omission therein shall correct it in such manner as the Registrar General may direct.

(2) The registrar shall in the presence of the parent copy the particulars recorded in the spaces of the authority into the corresponding spaces of the entry so, however, that where any particular has been corrected in pursuance of paragraph (1) he shall enter only the particular as corrected, omitting any incorrect particular which has been struck out.

(3) The registrar shall enter in the register the qualification of the informant as "father" or "mother", as the case may be, and call upon the parent to verify the particulars as entered and to sign the entry.

(4) The registrar shall enter the date on which the entry is made and add the words "On the authority of the Registrar General".

(5) When the registrar has signed the entry in space 16 he shall add his official description.

Making of declaration where parent does not attend

29.—(1) A parent who is in England or Wales may with the consent of the Registrar General verify the particulars required to be registered on the re-registration of the birth of a legitimated person by making and signing before a registrar other than the registrar for the sub-district in which the birth occurred a declaration of the particulars, on a form provided for the purpose by the Registrar General ; and any such declaration shall be attested by the registrar before whom it was made and sent by him to the registrar for the sub-district in which the birth occurred.

(2) A parent who is not in England or Wales may with the consent of the Registrar General verify the particulars required to be registered as aforesaid by making and signing before an authority specified in paragraph (3), (4) or (5), as the case may be, and sending to the Registrar General, a declaration of the particulars on a form provided for the purpose by the Registrar General.

(3) In the case of a parent who is in Scotland, Northern Ireland, the Isle of Man, the Channel Islands or any other country of the Commonwealth or in the Irish Republic, the authorities before whom a declaration may be made are a notary public and any other person lawfully authorised to administer oaths in that country or place.

(4) In the case of a parent who is not in England or Wales or in any country or place mentioned in paragraph (3), the authorities before whom a declaration may be made are one of Her Majesty's consular officers, a notary public and any other person lawfully authorised to administer oaths in that country or place ; but a declaration made before an authority other than one of Her Majesty's consular officers shall be authenticated by such an officer, if the Registrar General so requires.

(5) In the case of a parent who is a member of Her Majesty's Forces and who is not in the United Kingdom, the authorities before whom a declaration may be made shall include any officer who holds a rank not below that of Lieutenant-Commander, Major, or Squadron-Leader.

Making of entry in pursuance of declaration

30.—(1) On receiving the Registrar General's authority and consent to re-register a birth under regulation 29 and the declaration made for the purposes thereof, the registrar for the sub-district in which the birth occurred shall copy the particulars recorded in the spaces of the declaration into the corresponding spaces of the entry and shall enter the qualification of the informant as "father" or "mother", as the case may be ; and he shall enter in space 14 the words "by declaration dated ...." and the date on which the declaration was made and signed.

(2) After entering such particulars the registrar shall complete the entry in the manner provided in regulation 28(4) and (5).

Making of entry when particulars not verified by parent

31. Where so directed by the Registrar General the registrar for the sub-district in which the birth of a legitimated person occurred shall re-register the birth in such manner as the Registrar General in his authority may direct, although the particulars to be registered are not verified by a parent ; and in any such case the registrar shall enter in the space for the signature the words "On the authority of the Registrar General" without any further entry in that space.

Noting of previous entry

32. The superintendent registrar or the registrar having the custody of the register in which the birth was previously registered shall, when so directed by the Registrar General, note the previous entry of the birth with the words "Re-registered under section 14 of the Births and Deaths Registration Act 1953 on ....", inserting the date of re-registration, and shall make a certified copy of the previous entry, including a copy of the note, and send the copy to the Registrar General.

Certified copies of re-registered entries

33. Where application is made to a registrar or a superintendent registrar for a certified copy of the entry of the birth of a legitimated person whose birth has been re-registered in a register in his custody, he shall supply a certified copy of the entry of re-registration ; and no certified copy of the previous entry shall be given except under the direction of the Registrar General.

Declaration in respect of a person born at sea

34. Where information is furnished to the Registrar General for the re-registration of the birth of a legitimated person who was born at sea and whose birth was included in a return sent to the Registrar General, a parent of the legitimated person may verify the particulars required to be registered on the re-registration of the birth of that person by making and signing a declaration of such particulars, on a form provided by the Registrar General for the purpose, before any registrar in England and Wales or such authority specified in regulation 29(3), (4) or (5) as may be applicable, and sending that declaration to the Registrar General.

Entry in respect of a person born at sea

35. A person deputed for the purpose by the Registrar General, on receiving his authority to re-register the birth of a legitimated person who was born at sea and whose birth was included in a return sent to the Registrar General, shall make the entry in a register to be kept at the General Register Office in form 4, in such manner as the Registrar General may direct.

Noting of previous entry

36. Where an entry is made under regulation 35, a person deputed as afore-said shall note any previous record of the birth in the custody of the Registrar General with the words "Re-registered under section 14 of the Births and Deaths Registration Act 1953, on ....", inserting the date of re-registration, and shall send a copy of the previous record, including a copy of the note, certified under the seal of the General Register Office, to the authority from whom that record was received by the Registrar General.

PART VI

BIRTH ENTRIES OF ADOPTED CHILDREN

Marking of birth entry of adopted child

37.—(1) A superintendent registrar or a registrar shall, when so directed by the Registrar General acting pursuant to the Adoption Acts 1958 to 1968(a)—

(a) mark any entry specified in the direction with the word "Adopted" or, as the case may be, the words "Provisionally adopted", followed imme-diately, if the direction so specifies, by the name, in brackets, of the country in which the adoption order was made ;

(b) add his signature and official description ; and

(c) make and send to the Registrar General a certified copy of the entry showing the marking.

(2) A superintendent registrar or a registrar shall, when so directed by the Registrar General acting pursuant to the Adoption Acts 1958 to 1968—

(a) strike through any marking as to adoption in the margin of any entry specified in the direction and underneath write, as may be specified in the direction, the words "Adoption order quashed", "Adoption order revoked", "Appeal against adoption order allowed", or "Direction for the marking of this entry revoked" ;

(b) add his signature and official description ; and

(c) make and send to the Registrar General a certified copy of the entry showing the cancelled marking and the note with respect to its cancella-tion.

Reproduction of marking in certified copy

38. Where a certified copy of an entry of birth relating to an adopted person is given under the provisions of sections 30, 31, or 32 of the Act (which relate to searches of registers and indexes) the certified copy shall include a copy of the marking made in pursuance of regulation 37(1).

PART VII

REGISTRATION OF STILL-BIRTHS

Application to still-births of certain provisions relating to births

39. The proviso to section 1(1) of the Act (which requires a registrar to register the birth of a living new-born child found exposed in his sub-district) shall apply to a still-born child as it applies to a live-born child ; and section 3

(a) 7 & 8 Eliz. 2. c. 5; 1960 c. 59; 1964 c. 57; 1968 c. 53

of the Act (which requires information of birth particulars to be given when a living new-born child is found exposed) shall apply to a still-born child as it applies to a live-born child, subject to the modification that the words "and of any person in whose charge the child may be placed" shall be omitted.

Particulars to be registered

40. The particulars concerning a still-birth required to be registered pursuant to section 1 of the Act shall subject to the provisions of this Part of these regulations be the particulars required in spaces 1 to 13 in form 5 ; and form 5 shall be the prescribed form for still-birth registration for the purposes of section 5 of the Act.

Manner of registration

41.—(1) In the case of any still-birth with respect to which there has been delivered to the registrar :—

(*a*) a written certificate in form 6 of a medical practitioner or midwife as referred to in section 11(1)(*a*) of the Act (which section makes special provision as to registration of still-births) or

(*b*) a declaration as referred to in section 11(1)(*b*) thereof, in form 7,

the registrar, on receiving from an informant, at any time within 3 months after the date of the still-birth, information of the particulars required by regulation 40, shall (unless he takes action under regulation 43) register the still-birth in the presence of the informant by completing spaces 1 to 13 in form 5.

(2) Subject to the provisions of regulation 42, the provisions of regulations 17 to 21 shall, with any necessary modifications, apply to completing form 5 as they apply to completing form 1 ; but an informant shall not be required to verify space 2 on form 5.

Entry of nature of evidence of still-birth

42.—(1) Where the still-birth is registered on the production of a written certificate of a medical practitioner or a midwife, the registrar shall enter in space 2 the cause of death precisely as stated therein, followed by the words "Certified by ...." and the name and qualification of the medical practitioner or, as the case may be, the name of the midwife and the words "Certified Midwife".

(2) Where the still-birth is registered on the production of a declaration as referred to in section 11(1)(*b*) of the Act, the registrar shall enter in space 2 the words "Declaration by informant".

Reference to coroner

43. Where a registrar, on being given information as for a still-birth, has reason to believe that the child was born alive, he shall report the matter to the coroner on a form provided by the Registrar General.

Registration of still-birth where no inquest is held

44.—(1) Where, before the expiration of 3 months from the date of a still-birth which has not already been registered, a registrar receives from a coroner a notification that he does not intend to hold an inquest thereon, the registrar shall, subject to the provisions of paragraph (2), take such steps as may be required to register the still-birth in accordance with regulations 41 and 42.

(2) Where the coroner certifies in his notification that an examination made by his direction has disclosed that the child was still-born or that there was not sufficient evidence to show that the child was born alive, and delivers to the registrar a certificate showing the result of that examination, the registrar shall enter in space 2 the cause of death precisely as stated therein, followed by the words "Certified by ......" and the name and qualification of the medical practitioner who made the examination, and the words "after post-mortem held by direction of ......" and the name and description of the coroner.

Registration of still-birth after inquest

45. Where, before the expiration of 3 months from the date of a still-birth which he is required to register, a registrar receives a coroner's certificate upon an inquest from which it appears that the child was still-born or that there was not sufficient evidence to show that the child was born alive, the registrar shall register the still-birth as follows :—

(a) in spaces 1 and 3 to 10 he shall enter the particulars contained in the coroner's certificate, precisely as stated therein, as particulars to be entered in those spaces respectively ;

(b) in space 2 he shall enter the cause of death as stated in the coroner's certificate, precisely as stated therein, followed by the words "Certificate after inquest held on ....". and the date of the inquest as stated in the certificate ;

(c) in space 11 he shall enter the name and description of the coroner ;

(d) in space 15 he shall enter the date on which the entry is made, and in space 16 he shall sign the entry and add his official description.

Annotation of previous entry

46. If, in any case to which regulation 45 applies, the registrar ascertains that an entry in respect of the child has previously been made in any register of births, still-births or deaths he shall, after registering the still-birth in accordance with the said regulation—

(a) if the previous entry is in a still-birth register in his custody, write in the margin of the previous entry "Re-registered on coroner's certificate at entry No. ...." and the number of the new entry, and add his initials ;

(b) if the previous entry is in a birth or death register in his custody, write in the margin of the previous entry "This entry relates to a still-birth and is registered at entry No. .... in the still-birth register" and the number of the new entry, and add his initials.

PART VIII

DISPOSAL OF BODIES OF STILL-BORN CHILDREN

Certificate for disposal

47.—(1) The form of a certificate of a registrar under section 11(2) of the Act (which relates to preliminaries to disposal of bodies) that he has registered a still-birth shall be form 8.

(2) A certificate of a registrar under section 11(2) of the Act that he has received notice of a still-birth shall be given on a form provided by the Regis-

trar General but a registrar shall not give such a certificate except for the purpose of burial in a burial ground in England or Wales, and then only—

(a) where the case is one which is not required to be reported to the coroner, or

(b) where the case has been reported to the coroner and the registrar has been informed by the coroner that he has completed any investigations which he intends to make and has not issued any order or certificate for the purpose of the disposal of the body.

Part IX
Death Registration

Particulars to be registered and certificate of cause of death

48.—(1) The particulars concerning a death required to be registered pursuant to section 15 of the Act (which requires prescribed particulars of deaths to be registered) shall, subject to the provisions of this Part of these regulations, be the particulars required in spaces 1 to 8 in form 9 ; and form 9 shall be the prescribed form for the purposes of section 20 of the Act (which provides for registration of death free of charge).

(2) The form of a certificate of cause of death shall be form 10.

(3) The form of notice required by section 22(2) of the Act to be given by a medical practitioner to a qualified informant shall be form 11.

Registration without reference to coroner

49.—(1) In the case of any death which occurred in the registrar's sub-district with respect to which a certificate of cause of death has been delivered to the registrar and which has not been and is not required to be reported to the coroner the registrar shall, on receiving from an informant, at any time within 12 months of the date of the death, information of the particulars required by regulation 48(1), register the death in the presence of the informant by completing spaces 1 to 8 in form 9.

(2) Where a child lived for less than 24 hours, the registrar shall enter after the date of the child's death the word "Aged ......" and the age in completed hours or, if less than one hour, in minutes.

(3) Where the death relates to a dead body in relation to which the date and place of death are unknown, the registrar shall enter in space 1 the words "Dead body found on ...." and the date of finding the body, followed by "at ...." and the place of finding.

(4) Where the deceased was a child under the age of 15, the registrar shall enter in space 6 the words "son (or daughter) of ......" and the name and occupation of the father or, if the name and occupation of the father is not given, the words "son (or daughter) of ......" and the name and occupation of the mother.

(5) Where the deceased was a female aged 15 or over, the registrar shall enter—

(a) in the case of a married woman or widow, her own occupation and the words "wife (or widow) of ......" and the name and occupation of her husband or deceased husband ;

(b) in any other case, her own occupation.

(6) The registrar shall enter in space 8 the cause of death precisely as certified in the medical certificate, followed by the words 'Certified by ......" and the name and qualification of the medical practitioner who gave the medical certificate.

Verification of particulars

50.—(1) After completing spaces 1 to 8 in the entry, the registrar shall call upon the informant to verify the particulars entered in spaces 1 to 7 ; and if it appears that any error has been made in those particulars, the registrar shall thereupon in the presence of the informant make the necessary correction in the manner provided in regulation 72.

(2) The registrar shall then call upon the informant to sign the entry in space 9 ; and when the registrar has signed the entry in space 11 he shall add his official description.

Registration upon reference to coroner

51.—(1) Where a registrar is informed of the death of any person before the expiration of 12 months from the date of the death, he shall report the death to the coroner on a form provided by the Registrar General if the death is one—

(*a*) in respect of which the deceased was not attended during his last illness by a medical practitioner ; or

(*b*) in respect of which the registrar has been unable to obtain a duly completed certificate of cause of death ; or

(*c*) with respect to which it appears to the registrar, from the particulars contained in such a certificate or otherwise, that the deceased was seen by the certifying medical practitioner neither after death nor within 14 days before death ; or

(*d*) the cause of which appears to be unknown ; or

(*e*) which the registrar has reason to believe to have been unnatural or to have been caused by violence or neglect, or by abortion, or to have been attended by suspicious circumstances ; or

(*f*) which appears to the registrar to have occurred during an operation or before recovery from the effect of an anaesthetic ; or

(*g*) which appears to the registrar from the contents of any medical certificate to have been due to industrial disease or industrial poisoning.

(2) Where the registrar has reason to believe, with respect to any death of which he is informed or in respect of which a certificate of cause of death has been delivered to him, that the circumstances of the death were such that it is the duty of some person or authority other than himself to report the death to the coroner, he shall satisfy himself that it has been reported.

(3) The registrar shall not register any death which he has himself reported to the coroner, or which to his knowledge it is the duty of any other person or authority to report to the coroner, or which to his knowledge has been reported to the coroner, until he has received a coroner's certificate or a notification that the coroner does not intend to hold an inquest.

Registration where inquest is not held

52. Where, before the expiration of 12 months from the date of a death which it is his duty to register, the registrar is notified by the coroner that he does not intend to hold an inquest thereon, the registrar shall, unless the death has already been registered, register the death in accordance with regulations 49 and 50 :

Provided that—

(*a*) if the coroner in his notification certifies the cause of death disclosed by any report on a post-mortem examination of the body made by his direction under section 21 of the Coroners (Amendment) Act 1926(**a**), the entry in space 8 of the cause of death shall be of the cause of death as so certified, followed by the words "Certified by ......", the name and description of the coroner and the words "after post-mortem without inquest" ; and

(*b*) if it appears from the coroner's notification that no post-mortem examination was held by his direction, and the registrar is unable to obtain delivery of a certificate of cause of death, the entry in space 8 of the cause of death shall be of the cause of death as stated in the coroner's notification, or if none is stated therein as stated to the registrar by the informant, without any further or other entry in that space.

Procedure on coroner's notification of cause of death, when death already registered

53.—(1) Where a registrar receives a coroner's notification that he does not intend to hold an inquest in respect of a death which the registrar has already registered on the information of an informant, and the coroner certifies in that notification the cause of death as disclosed by any report on a post-mortem examination made by his direction, the registrar shall, without altering the entry of the death, enter in the margin of that entry the words "Post-mortem without inquest held by the direction of ......" and the name and description of the coroner and the words "and cause of death disclosed as ......" and the cause of death as certified by the coroner, and shall add his initials and the date.

(2) If the register containing the entry is in the custody of the superintendent registrar, the registrar shall deliver the notification to the superintendent registrar, who shall enter in the margin of the entry the particulars required by paragraph (1) and add his initials and the date.

Registration of death after inquest

54.—(1) Subject to the provisons of paragraph (2), where, before the expiration of 12 months from the date of a death which it is his duty to register, a registrar receives a coroner's certificate upon an inquest with reference to that death, the registrar shall register the death as follows :—

(*a*) in spaces 1 to 6 and 8 he shall enter the particulars contained in the certificate, precisely as stated therein. as particulars to be entered in those spaces respectively :

Provided that if any person is named in the certificate as having caused the death, the name of that person shall be omitted ;

(*b*) in space 7 he shall enter the words "Certificate received from ......" and the name and description of the coroner. and the words "Inquest held ......" and the date of the inquest as stated in the certificate ;

(*c*) in space 10 he shall enter the date on which the entry is made and in space 11 he shall sign the entry and add his official description.

(**a**) 1926 c. 59.

(2) Where the coroner's certificate relates to an inquest which has been adjourned and not resumed, the registrar shall register the death in accordance with the foregoing provisions of this regulation with the following modifications : —

(a) in space 8 he shall enter the cause of death as stated in the certificate, and where it appears that the inquest was adjourned under section 20 of the Coroners (Amendment) Act 1926 and a person has been charged with the murder, manslaughter or infanticide of the deceased person, the registrar shall enter after the entry of the cause of death the result of the criminal proceedings as stated in the certificate:

Provided that if any person is named in the certificate as having been so charged, the name of that person shall be omitted ; and

(b) in space 7, instead of the words "Certificate received from" the registrar shall enter—

(i) if the inquest was adjourned and not resumed, the words "Certificate on inquest adjourned and not resumed received from ..."; and

(ii) if the inquest was adjourned sine die, the words "Certificate on inquest adjourned sine die received from ..."

Registration on coroner's certificate of death already registered

55. Where a registrar has received a coroner's certificate upon an inquest relating to the death of any person in respect of whom an entry has previously been made in a register of still-births or deaths on the information of an informant, the registrar shall make a fresh entry in respect of the death in accordance with regulation 54, and the officer having custody of the register containing the previous entry shall write in the margin of that entry "Re-registered on coroner's certificate at entry No. ......", and the number of the new entry, particulars of the register in which it is contained and his initials.

Registration after 12 months

56.—(1) Where a registrar is informed that the death of a person who died more than 12 months previously has not been registered, the registrar shall make a report to the Registrar General stating to the best of his knowledge and belief the particulars required to be registered concerning the death, the source of his information and the name and address of any qualified informant available to give information for the registration, and shall send with the report any certificate of the cause of death and any coroner's notification that he does not intend to hold an inquest or coroner's certificate after an inquest held with reference to the death.

(2) On receiving the Registrar General's written authority to register the death on the information of an informant, the registrar shall arrange for the informant specified in the authority to attend at his office and shall register the death in the presence of the informant ; and the provisions of regulations 49 and 50 shall, subject to the modifications set out in paragraph (3), apply as they apply to the registration of a death within 12 months.

(3) On receiving the Registrar General's authority to register a death which occurred more than 12 months previously in respect of which the registrar has received a coroner's certificate after an inquest, the registrar shall register the death ; and the provisions of regulation 54 shall apply as they apply to the registration of a death within 12 months, subject to the modification that in space 10 the registrar shall, after entering the date on which the entry is made, enter the words "On the authority of the Registrar General".

Part X

Disposal of Bodies of Deceased Persons

Interpretation of Part X

57. In this Part of these regulations—

"certificate for disposal after registration" means a certificate of a registrar under section 24(1) of the Act that he has registered a death ;

"certificate for disposal before registration" means a certificate of a registrar under the said subsection that he has received notice of a death ;

"certificate for disposal" means either of the above-mentioned certificates ;

"notification of disposal" means a notification as to the date, place and means of disposal of the body of a deceased person which a person effecting the disposal is required by section 3 of the Births and Death Registration Act 1926 to deliver to the registrar ; and

"person effecting the disposal" has the same meaning as in section 12 of that Act.

Certificates for disposal

58.—(1) A registrar shall give a certificate for disposal on a form provided by the Registrar General, and such certificate shall embody a form of notification of disposal, for use of the person effecting the disposal, in form 12.

(2) A registrar shall not give a certificate for disposal before registration except for the purpose of burial in England or Wales, and then only—

(*a*) where the death is one which is not required to be reported to the coroner, or

(*b*) where the death has been reported to the coroner and the registrar has been informed by the coroner that he has completed any investigations which he intends to make and has not issued any order or certificate for the purpose of the disposal of the body.

Certificate that death is not required to be registered

59. The form of a certificate of a registrar in pursuance of section 24(2) of the Act that a death is not required to be registered in England and Wales shall be form 13.

Declaration that registrar's certificate or coroner's order for disposal has been issued

60. The form of a declaration for the purposes of the proviso to section 1(1) of the Births and Deaths Registration Act 1926 that a certificate of the registrar or order of the coroner has been issued in respect of a deceased person shall be form 14.

Notification of disposal

61. The person effecting the disposal of the body of a deceased person, or some responsible person deputed to act on his behalf, shall write, sign and date the notification of disposal embodied in the certificate for disposal or in the coroner's order with respect to the deceased person, and then detach the notification and deliver it to the registrar ; or, where a declaration has been made as referred to in regulation 60, the person effecting the disposal shall notify the registrar in writing in the terms used in form 12.

Enquiry in default of notification of disposal

62.—(1) The period after the issue of a registrar's certificate for disposal or a coroner's order authorising the disposal of the body on the expiration of which the registrar, if he has not previously received a notification of disposal, is required under section 24(5) of the Act to make such enquiry as is therein mentioned shall be a period of 14 days from the date of the issue of the certificate or order.

(2) Where in response to such an enquiry the registrar is informed that the body of the deceased person to whom the enquiry relates has not been disposed of, he shall, unless he is informed that the body is being held for the purposes of the Anatomy Acts 1832(a) and 1871(b), report the matter to the medical officer of health for the district in which the body is lying.

(3) Where after such an enquiry it appears to the registrar that the body has been disposed of and notification of disposal has not been made to him within the time required by law, he shall make immediate application for such notification to the person effecting the disposal of the body, and if the notification is not received within 3 days he shall report the matter to the Registrar General.

PART XI

REGISTRATION OF MARRIAGE

Form of notice of marriage

63.—(1) The form of notice of marriage to be given under section 27(1) of the Marriage Act 1949 where a marriage is intended to be solemnized on the authority of a certificate of a superintendent registrar without licence shall be form 15 or, where either party to the marriage is under the age of 21 years, and not a widower or widow, form 16.

(2) The form of notice of marriage to be given under section 27(2) of the Marriage Act 1949 where a marriage is intended to be solemnized on the authority of a certificate of a superintendent registrar by licence shall be form 17, or where either party of the marriage is under the age of 21 years, and not a widower or widow, form 18.

Endorsement on notice of marriage

64. The form of endorsement on the notice of marriage to be made under section 35(1) of the Marriage Act 1949 where a marriage is intended to be solemnized in a registered building which is not within a registration district in which either of the persons to be married resides shall be form 19.

Form of certificate and form of certificate and licence for marriage

65.—(1) The form of certificate for marriage to be issued by a superintendent registrar under section 31 of the Marriage Act 1949 shall be form 20.

(2) The form of certificate and licence for marriage to be issued by a superintendent registrar under section 32 of the Marriage Act 1949 shall be form 21.

(a) 1832 c. 75.   (b) 1871 c. 16.

*Form of instructions for solemnization of a marriage in a registered building
without the presence of a registrar*

66. The form of instructions to be given under sections 31 and 32 of the
Marriage Act 1949 to one of the persons whose marriage is to be solemnized
in a registered building for which an authorised person has been appointed,
where no notice has been given requiring a registrar to be present at the
marriage, shall be form 22.

Particulars to be registered

67.—(1) The particulars relating to a marriage required to be registered pursuant to section 55(1) of the Marriage Act 1949 shall, subject to the provisions
of regulations 68 to 70, be the particulars required in Part I of form 23 and the
particulars of attestation required by Part II of form 23 which are appropriate
to the place and manner of solemnization.

(2) Where a registrar is required to register a marriage pursuant to the said
section 55(1), he shall register it, in the manner prescribed by law, in some part
of the registered building or superintendent registrar's office where it was
solemnized and according to the provisions of this Part of these regulations.

Manner of registration

68.—(1) In column 3 in form 23 the registrar, if unable to ascertain the exact
age of either party, shall enter an age which accords with such information in
that respect as he is able to obtain, or, failing any such information, the words
"of full age" or the word "minor", as the case may be ;

(2) In column 4 in form 23 the registrar shall enter the condition of the
. parties to the marriage in the following manner—

    (*a*) if a party has not previously been married, he shall enter the word
    "Bachelor" or "Spinster", as the case may be, and if a party's previous
    marriage was terminated by the death of the previous wife or husband
    the word "Widower" or "Widow", as the case may be ;

    (*b*) if a party's previous marriage was terminated by divorce, he shall enter
    the words "Previous marriage dissolved";

    (*c*) if the marriage is between two parties who have previously been through
    a form of marriage with each other (not being a marriage which is known
    to have been null and void) and neither of whom has since married a
    third person, then—

        (i) if that marriage was terminated by divorce, he shall enter the words
        "Previously married at ...... on ...... Marriage dissolved on ......",
        inserting particulars of the place and date of marriage and the date
        of its dissolution ; or

        (ii) if the ceremony was performed for the avoidance of doubt as to the
        validity of a previous ceremony, he shall enter the words "Previously
        went through a form of marriage at ...... on ......", inserting par-
        ticulars of the place and the date of the previous ceremony ;

    and no further entry shall be made in column 4.

(3) In column 6 in form 23, if either of the parties has removed into another
district since the notice of marriage was given, the registrar shall enter the
words "Late of .... but now residing at ....", together with the full
address of both residences ;

(4) In column 7 in form 23, if either father is deceased, the registrar shall
enter the word "deceased" after the surname.

Entry of attestation

69. In the form of attestation set out in Part II of form 23 the registrar shall—

(*a*) if the marriage has been solemnized in a registered building according to the rites and ceremonies of any religious body or denomination, enter in the places respectively provided for the purpose the description of the registered building, the title of the body or denomination according to the rites and ceremonies of which the marriage has been solemnized, and the word "certificate" or "licence", as the case may be ;

(*b*) if the marriage has been solemnized in a superintendent registrar's office, enter in the places respectively provided for the purpose the words "register office" and the word "certificate" or "licence", as the case may be.

Signing the register

·**70.**—(1) After entering the required particulars the registrar shall call upon the parties to the marriage to verify those particulars ; and if it appears that any error has been made, the registrar shall thereupon in the presence of the parties make the necessary correction in the manner provided in regulation 72.

(2) When the required particulars have been verified in accordance with paragraph (1) the registrar shall call upon the parties to sign the register in the spaces provided ; and after the parties have signed the register the registrar shall call upon the witnesses to sign similarly.

(3) The registrar shall then call upon the minister or other person, if any, or the superintendent registrar by or before whom the marriage was solemnized to sign the register in the space provided and to add his official designation or description.

(4) The registrar shall then sign the register in the space provided and add his official description.

PART XII

CORRECTION OF ERRORS

Time when entry is complete

71. An entry of a birth, still-birth, death or marriage shall for the purposes of these regulations be deemed to have been completed when the registrar by whom it is made has signed the entry and added his official description.

Correction of entry before completion

72.—(1) Where under these regulations a registrar is required to correct an error in an entry of a birth, still-birth, death or marriage before the completion of the entry, he shall, subject to the provisions of paragraph (2), make the correction in the following manner—

(*a*) if a word is incorrect, he shall strike it out by a line drawn through it, so, however, that the word remains legible, and write the correct word above it ;

(*b*) if in any group of figures one or more figures is incorrect, he shall strike out all the figures in the group by a line drawn through them, so, however, that they remain legible, and write the correct figures above them ;

(c) if a word has been omitted, he shall place a caret where the omission occurs and above the caret he shall write the word omitted, or if there is space to write the word omitted in the place of the omission, he shall write the word therein and underline it ;

(d) all errors corrected as aforesaid shall be numbered consecutively by the registrar from the beginning of the register starting with "one", and on making any such correction the registrar shall write the number of the error in figures against the correction in the body of the entry and shall repeat the same number in words in the margin of the entry and add his initials ;

(e) if the particulars required to be entered in any two spaces or columns have been inadvertently transposed, the registrar shall, without any other correction, write in the margin of the entry a note of the error in the following form: "The particulars in .... and .... inadvertently transposed", and add his initials.

(f) if the particulars required to be entered in respect of the parties to a marriage, or the fathers of the parties, have been inadvertently transposed, the registrar shall, without any other correction, write in the margin of the entry a note to that effect, specifying the particulars to which the note relates, and add his initials.

(2) If it appears that an error has been made in the signature of the informant or of one of the parties or witnesses to a marriage, the signatory and not the registrar shall make the correction, and the registrar shall number the error and make an entry in the margin as provided in paragraph (1)(d).

Correction of minor clerical errors after completion

73.—(1) Where it appears to the superintendent registrar or the registrar, as the case may be, that there is in any completed entry in a register of births, still-births or deaths in his custody any error or omission to which this regulation applies (in this part of these regulations called a "Class I clerical error"), he shall correct the error in the manner prescribed in regulation 72(1), (a), (b), (c) or (e), whichever is appropriate.

(2) The clerical errors to which this regulation applies are—

(a) in a case where the particulars have been entered otherwise than by copying from a document specified in sub-paragraph (f) of this paragraph, any error in spelling any word which is not the name or surname of any person, or the misplacement or incorrect repetition of any such word ;

(b) the incorrect statement or omission of the year of the birth, still-birth or death to which an entry relates or of the year of registration (but not of both) ;

(c) the incorrect statement or omission of the month in the date of registration, where it is evident from the preceding and succeeding entries what month should have been inserted ;

(d) the omission of the words "by declaration dated .... " in space 14 of a birth entry made in pursuance of regulation 24 ;

(e) the omission of any of the words "by baptism on ...." or "on certificate of naming dated ....", as the case may be. following the entry of a name in space 17 of a birth entry made in pursuance of section 13 of the Act (which relates to registration or alteration of name after registration of birth) ;

(*f*) any error or omission in copying any particulars required to be copied from—

(i) a declaration made in pursuance of regulation 24 ;

(ii) a certificate of name given in baptism, or a certificate of name given otherwise than in baptism, delivered in pursuance of the said section 13 ;

(iii) a certificate of cause of death ;

(iv) a doctor's or midwife's certificate of still-birth ;

(v) a coroner's notification after post-mortem without inquest ;

(vi) a coroner's certificate after inquest.

(3) Where a registrar makes any correction under paragraph (1), he shall make the correction in the presence and with the concurrence of the superintendent registrar or Inspector of Registration, and shall write in the margin of the entry a note in the following form : —

"Clerical error (or omission) in ...... corrected on .... 19......
by me .... Registrar, in the presence of ....
Superintendent Registrar (or Inspector of Registration)" ;

and shall complete and sign the note in the places provided ; and the superintendent registrar or Inspector of Registration, as the case may be, shall thereupon sign the note in the place provided.

(4) Where a superintendent registrar makes a correction under paragraph (1), he shall write in the margin of the corrected entry a note in the following form—

"Clerical error (or omission) in ...... corrected on .... 19......
by me .... Superintendent Registrar" ;

and shall complete and sign the note in the places provided.

(5) Where a registrar or a superintendent registrar is authorised by the Registrar General to correct, as if it were a Class I clerical error, a clerical error or omission of a kind other than those specified in paragraph (2), he shall correct the error or omission in the manner provided in regulation 72(1), (*a*), (*b*), (*c*) or (*e*), whichever is appropriate, and shall write in the margin of the entry a note in the following form or in such other form as the Registrar General may in any particular case direct—

"Clerical error (or omission) in .... corrected on .... 19......
by me .... Registrar (or Superintendent Registrar) on the authority of the Registrar General" ;

and shall complete and sign the note in the places provided.

Correction of other clerical errors

74.—(1) Where it appears or is represented to a superintendent registrar or a registrar that there is in a completed entry made on the information of an informant in a register of births, still-births or deaths in his custody a clerical error other than a Class I clerical error, he shall send a report to the Registrar General about the alleged error, including in that report—

(*a*) such evidence as the Registrar General may require for the purpose of verifying the facts;

(*b*) the name of a qualified informant who will be available to witness a correction of the error; and

(*c*) a copy of the entry.

(2) On receiving the authority of the Registrar General to correct such an error, the superintendent registrar or the registrar, as the case may be, shall, in the presence of a qualified informant specified in the authority for the purpose, correct the error in the manner provided in regulation 72 (1), (*a*), (*b*), (*c*) or (*e*), whichever is appropriate.

(3) Where any correction is made under this regulation, the superintendent registrar or the registrar, as the case may be, shall write in the margin of the entry a note in the following form —

"Clerical error (or omission) in.........corrected on...............19......by me
............Superintendent Registrar (or Registrar), in the presence of............
..............................on the authority of the Registrar General";

and shall complete and sign the note in the places provided; and the informant shall sign the note in the place provided and the superintendent registrar or registrar shall add to the signature of the informant his qualification.

Errors of fact or substance

75.—(1) Where it appears or is represented to a superintendent registrar or a registrar that there is an error of fact or substance in a completed entry in a register of births, still-births or deaths in his custody, not being an entry made in pursuance of a coroner's certificate after inquest, he shall send a report to the Registrar General about the alleged error, giving such information as the Registrar General may require, together with a copy of the entry, and shall comply with any particular instruction which the Registrar General may give for the purpose of verifying the facts of the case and ascertaining whether there are available two persons qualified to make a statutory declaration required by section 29(3) of the Act (which relates to the correction of errors in registers).

(2) On being informed by the Registrar General that the alleged error may be corrected on production of a statutory declaration made by the two persons aforesaid in such terms as satisfy the requirements of the said section 29(3), the superintendent registrar or the registrar, as the case may be, shall on production to him of the statutory declaration correct the error in the following manner—

(*a*) he shall underline the erroneous matter in the entry; and

(*b*) he shall, unless otherwise directed by the Registrar General, write in the margin of the entry a note in the following form—

"In No..........in.........for...............read.....................................
Corrected on.....................19......by me..............Superintendent
Registrar (or Registrar) on production of a statutory declaration made
by ....and................................";

and he shall enter the particulars of the correction and of the declarants and complete and sign the note in the places provided.

Correction on coroner's certificate

76.—(1) Where the superintendent registrar or the registrar having the custody of a register containing an entry made in pursuance of a coroner's certificate after inquest receives a certificate relating to that entry given by the coroner authorising the correction of the entry, he shall send a report to the Registrar General about the error, together with a copy of the entry and any coroner's certificate relating to the entry.

(2) Where the error is a clerical error, the superintendent registrar or the registrar, as the case may be, shall correct the error in the manner provided in regulation 72 (1), (*a*), (*b*), (*c*), or (*e*), whichever is appropriate, and shall write in the margin of the said entry a note in the following form—

"Clerical error (or omission) in............corrected on....................19......
by me...............Superintendent Registrar (or Registrar) on the authority of a certificate from the Coroner";

and shall complete and sign the note in the places provided.

(3) Where the error is one of fact or substance, the superintendent registrar or the registrar, as the case may be, shall—

(*a*) underline the erroneous matter in the entry; and

(*b*) write in the margin of the entry a note in the following form—

"In No.............in............for............read................................
Corrected on...............19......by me....................Superintendent Registrar (or Registrar) on the authority of a certificate from the Coroner";

and shall complete and sign the note in the places provided.

Correction of marriage entry

77. Where it appears or is represented to the superintendent registrar or the registrar that there is in a completed entry in a register of marriages in his custody an error to which section 61 of the Marriage Act 1949 relates, he shall send a report to the Registrar General about the alleged error, giving such information as the Registrar General may require, together with a copy of the entry, and shall comply with any instruction which the Registrar General may give for the purpose of verifying the facts of the case and of ascertaining whether the parties or witnesses will be available to witness a correction of the entry.

Part XIII

Miscellaneous

Quarterly certified copies

78.—(1) For the purposes of section 26(1) of the Act (which requires registrars to make quarterly returns to superintendent registrars)—

(*a*) the forms of true copy of all the entries of births, still-births and deaths made in the registers during a period shall be forms 1, 5 and 9 respectively, and such a copy shall be certified in form 24; and

(*b*) the form of certificate that no birth, still-birth or death has been registered in a sub-district during that period shall be form 25.

(2) For the purposes of section 57(2) of the Marriage Act) (which requires registrars to make quarterly returns to superintendent registrars), the form of certification by a registrar—

(*a*) of a true copy of all entries of marriages made in the marriage register book during a period, shall be form 26, and

(*b*) that no marriage has been registered in that book during that period, shall be form 27.

Certificate of registration of birth or still-birth

79. For the purposes of section 12 of the Act (which relates to certificates of registration of birth) the form of certificate that a registrar has registered a birth or still-birth shall be form 28.

Section 33 of Act not to apply to still-births

80. Section 33 of the Act (which relates to short certificates of birth) shall not apply in relation to still-births.

Application for short certificate of birth

81. For the purposes of section 33(1) of the Act (which relates to short certificates of birth) the particulars to be furnished on an application for a short certificate of birth shall be the following particulars relating to the registered person:—

    (i) his name and surname;

    (ii) the date and place of his birth;

    (iii) the name and surname of his father; and

    (iv) the name, surname and maiden surname of his mother;

Provided that—

(*a*) no particulars shall be required if the application is made at the time of registering the birth;

(*b*) any of the said particulars may be omitted if in the opinion of a superintendent registrar or registrar to whom the application is made it is not reasonably practicable for the applicant to furnish such particular.

Compilation of short certificate of birth

82.—(1) For the purposes of section 33(2) of the Act—

(*a*) the form of a short certificate of birth shall be form 29;

(*b*) the manner of compilation of such a form from registers in the custody of the superintendent registrar or registrar shall be as described in paragraphs (2) to (4); and

(*c*) the particulars to be contained therein shall be the particulars shown in the said form 29:

Provided that where the place of birth is not recorded in the birth entry, the superintendent registrar or registrar shall remit the application to the Registrar General.

(2) Opposite the words "Name and Surname "there shall be entered the name and surname of the person as recorded in space 17 or, if there is no name and surname therein, in space 2; and if more than one surname is so recorded there shall be entered such one of those surnames as the applicant may request.

(3) Opposite the words "Sex" and "Date of birth" respectively there shall be inserted the particulars thereof in the entry.

(4) Opposite the words "Place of birth" there shall be inserted the name of the registration district and sub-district in which the birth was registered.

Certificates of death for purposes of Industrial Assurance and Friendly Societies Act 1948

83.—(1) Where a person wishes to make an application for the issue of a certificate of death for the purposes of Schedule 1 to the Industrial Assurance and Friendly Societies Act 1948 (in this regulation called "the Act of 1948") the registrar shall provide that person with a form of application supplied by the Registrar General.

(2) A superintendent registrar or a registrar shall not issue such a certificate to an applicant unless the applicant certifies in the application that he is the child, grandchild or stepchild, within the meaning of the Act of 1948, of the person to whose death the application relates and that he is entitled to claim under an insurance taken out by him on or after 1st January 1924 on the life of that person.

(3) Except as mentioned in paragraph (4), more than one certificate of death for the purposes of Schedule 1 to the Act of 1948 shall not be issued to the same person; and to ensure compliance with this provision every superintendent registrar and registrar shall keep a record in the form provided by the Registrar General of the number of the entry in the register in respect of which each such certificate is issued, the serial number of the certificate and the name and relationship to the deceased person of the person to whom that certificate is issued.

(4) If a person to whom a death certificate has been issued for the purposes of the Act of 1948 makes and delivers to the superintendent registrar or the registrar having custody of the register in which the death was registered a statutory declaration stating—

(*a*) that the certificate has been lost or destroyed; and

(*b*) whether any endorsement has been made on the certificate and, if so, by what society or company; and

(*c*) that if the original is recovered he will surrender it to the superintendent registrar or the registrar;

the superintendent registrar or the registrar shall issue to that person a duplicate of the certificate on a form provided for the purpose by the Registrar General.

(5) A superintendent registrar or a registrar who issues a duplicate certificate under this regulation in a case where it appears from the statutory declaration that an endorsement had been made on the lost or destroyed certificate by any society or company shall record on the duplicate certificate a requirement that it is to be produced to that society or company for the endorsement to be repeated on the duplicate.

Applications for certificates under various enactments

84.—(1) Where a person wishes to make an application or present a requisition to a registrar for a certificate of any birth, death or marriage for the purposes of any enactment referred to in paragraph (2), the registrar may on request provide that person with a form of application or requisition supplied by the Registrar General—

(2) The enactments referred to in paragraph (1) are—

(*a*) Savings Bank Act 1887**(a)**, section 10;

(*b*) Friendly Societies Act 1896**(b)**, section 98(5);

(*c*) Savings Certificate Regulations 1933**(c)**, regulation 30;

(d) Young Persons (Employment) Act 1938(a), section 5;

(e) Shops Act 1950(b), section 35;

(f) Premium Bonds Regulations 1956(c), regulation 21;

(g) National Insurance Act 1965(d), section 91(3) (including that sub-section as applied by—

(i) Family Allowances Act 1965(e), section 12; and

(ii) Industrial Injuries and Diseases (Old Cases) Act 1967(f), section 13).

PART XIV

ACCOUNTING

Duties which may be performed without pre-payment of fee

85.—(1) An officer, if authorised by the clerk in a particular case, may comply with an application made to him for any purpose for which a fee is payable under any enactment notwithstanding that the fee or, in the case of a non-salaried officer, so much of the fee as is payable by him to the council, has not been paid to him and, if so directed by the clerk in the particular case, he shall not refuse to comply with such an application on the ground that the fee or, in the case of a non-salaried officer, so much of the fee as is payable by him to the council has not been paid to him.

(2) The clerk may delegate his duties under this regulation, so far as they relate to applications made to a registrar, to the superintendent registrar within whose district that registrar has been appointed to act.

Recovery of fees, etc.

86.—(1) Save as provided in regulation 85, an officer shall refuse to comply with an application voluntarily made to him until there shall have been paid to him the fee chargeable or, if he is a non-salaried officer, so much of the fee as is payable by him to the council.

(2) In any case where, in pursuance of regulation 85 an officer complies with an application without prior payment of the fee or, as the case may be, so much of the fee as is payable by him to the council, he shall report the circumstances to the council within 7 days thereafter and shall, on receiving from the council an indemnity in respect of all costs and expenses which he may incur, take such steps as the council may require to recover the fee or, as the case may be, so much of the fee as is payable by him to them.

Rendering of accounts

87.—(1) A principal officer shall within 14 days after the expiration of each period of 3 months ending on the last day of March, June, September and December respectively render to the Registrar General on a form provided by him for the purpose an account of all fees or parts of fees for which the officer is required under any enactment to account to the Registrar General in respect of that period.

(2) A principal officer shall also submit any special account which the Registrar General may require with respect to the said fees.

(a) 1938 c. 69.   (b) 1950 c. 28.
(c) S.I. 1956/1657 (1956 I, p. 1489).   (d) 1965 c. 51
(e) 1965 c. 53.   (f) 1967 c. 34.

PART XV

OFFENCES

Offences and proceedings

88.—(1) If it appears to any officer that any offence under or breach of the Act, the Population (Statistics) Act 1938(a) or the Marriage Act 1949 or, so far as they relate to marriages or to the registration of births, still-births and deaths, the Perjury Act 1911(b) or the Forgery Act 1913(c) has been committed, he shall report the matter to the Registrar General.

(2) Save in accordance with any instructions given to him by the Registrar General, a superintendent registrar shall not commence any proceedings in respect of an offence under the Act or the Population (Statistics) Act 1938 or under section 76(1) or (2) of the Marriage Act 1949, (which relates to offences in the registration of marriage).

PART XVI

REVOCATIONS

Revocations and saving for existing forms

89. The regulations specified in schedule 2 are hereby revoked:

Provided that—

(*a*) such revocation shall not affect anything duly done or suffered or any right, privilege, obligation or liability acquired, accrued or incurred under any of those regulations;

(*b*) where any action is required to be taken in relation to any entry made before the commencement of these regulations, it shall be taken as if these regulations had not been made;

(*c*) notwithstanding anything in these regulations, any form lawfully used immediately before the commencement of these regulations for any of the purposes for which these regulations provide may be used for the like purpose until 1st April 1970.

(a) 1938 c. 12.   (b) 1911 c. 6.
(c) 3 & 4 Geo. 5 c. 27.

SCHEDULE 1

PRESCRIBED FORMS

CONTENTS

Form	Relevant Regulation	Description	Statutory purpose
1	16	Particulars of birth	Births and Deaths Registration Act 1953, Section 1(1)
2	25(2)	Certificate that name was given in baptism	,, Section 13(1)
3	25(2)	Certificate that name was given otherwise than in baptism	,, Section 13(1)
4	35	Particulars of birth at sea	,, Section 14(4)
5	40	Particulars of still-birth	,, Section 1(1)
6	41(1)(a)	Medical certificate of still-birth	,, Section 11(1)
7	41(1)(b)	Declaration as to still-birth	,, Section 11(1)(b)
8	47(1)	Certificate that registrar has registered still-birth	,, Section 11(2)
9	48(1)	Particulars of death	,, Section 15
10	48(2)	Certificate of cause of death	,, Section 22(1)
11	48(3)	Medical practitioner's notice to informant of death	,, Section 22(2)
12	58(1)	Notification of disposal	Births and Deaths Registration Act 1926, Section 3(1)
13	59	Certificate that death is not required to be registered	Births and Deaths Registration Act 1953, Section 24(2)
14	60	Declaration that certificate or order has been issued	Births and Deaths Registration Act 1926, Section 1(1)
15	63(1)	Notice of marriage without licence	Marriage Act 1949, Section 27(1)
16	63(1)	Notice of marriage without licence	,, Section 27(1)
17	63(2)	Notice of marriage with licence	,, Section 27(2)
18	63(2)	Notice of marriage with licence	,, Section 27(2)
19	64	Endorsement on notice of marriage	,, Section 35(1)
20	65(1)	Certificate for marriage	,, Section 31
21	65(2)	Certificate and licence for marriage	,, Section 32

Form	Relevant Regulation	Description	Statutory purpose
22	66	Form of instructions	Marriage Act 1949, Sections 31 & 32
23	67	Form of marriage entry	,, Section 55(1)
24	78(1)	Quarterly return of births, still-births and deaths	Births and Deaths Registration Act 1953, Section 26(1)(a)
25	78(1)	Certificate of no registration	,, Section 26(1)(b)
26	78(2)	Quarterly return of marriages	Marriage Act 1949, Section 57(2)
27	78(2)	Certificate of no registration	,, Section 57(2)
28	79	Certificate of registration of birth	Births and Deaths Registration Act 1953, Section 12
29	82(1)	Short certificate of birth	,, Section 33

FORM 1

Particulars of birth

Regulation 16   Births and Deaths Registration Act 1953, S.1(1)

NHS Number	BIRTH	Entry No.

Registration district   Administrative area

Sub-district

CHILD

1. Date and place of birth

---

2. Name and surname   3. Sex

FATHER

4. Name and surname

---

5. Place of birth

---

6. Occupation

MOTHER

7. Name and surname

---

8. Place of birth

---

9. (a) Maiden surname   (b) Surname at marriage
                                    if different from
                                    maiden surname

---

10. Usual address
    (if different from
    place of child's birth)

INFORMANT

11. Name and surname (if not the   12. Qualification
    mother or father)

---

13. Usual address (if different from that in 10 above)

---

14. I certify that the particulars entered above are true to the best of my knowledge
    and belief
                                                          Signature
    .... of informant

---

15. Date of registration   16. Signature of registrar

---

17. Name given
    after registration,
    and surname

FORM 2

Certificate that name was given in baptism

Regulation 25(2)   Births and Deaths Registration Act 1953, S.13(1)

I.. of ....

do hereby certify that [according to the register of Baptisms for.............................

............now in my custody]* the $\frac{male†}{female}$ child stated to have been born on the............

day of............................19......to ....

and...was on the............................

day of............................19......baptised by ....

in the name...

Witness my hand this...........................day of....................................19......

Signature...

†Officiating Minister/Person having custody of register.

* To be deleted where the certificate is given by the person who baptised the child.

† Strike out whichever does not apply.

FORM 3

Certificate that name was given otherwise than in baptism

Regulation 25(2)   Births and Deaths Registration Act 1953, S.13(1)

I.. of ....

being the....................of the $\frac{male*}{female}$ child born to...

and...on the...........................day of

............................19......whose birth was registered in the register of births for the

sub-district of...on the...........................

day of............................19......do hereby certify that the said child not having been

given a name in baptism was within twelve months after the registration of $\frac{his*}{her}$ birth

given the name..

Witness my hand this...........................day of....................................19......

*Strike out whichever does not apply.

FORM 4

Particulars of birth at sea

Births and Deaths Registration Act 1953, S.14(4)

Regulation 35

Columns: 1	2	3	4	5	6	7	8	9	10	11	12
No. Name of ship and Port of Registry	Official Number	Date of Birth	Name (if any) of child	Sex	Name and Surname of Father	Occupation of Father	Name, Surname and maiden surname of Mother	Name. Surname and description of informant	Date of registration	Signature of officer deputed by the Registrar General to make the entry	Name entered after registration

FORM 5

Particulars of still-birth

Regulation 40   Births and Deaths Registration Act 1953, S.1(1)

STILL-BIRTH	Entry No.
Registration district Administrative area Sub-district	

CHILD
1. Date and place of birth

2. Cause of death and nature of evidence that child was still-born	3. Sex

FATHER
4. Name and surname
5. Place of birth
6. Occupation

MOTHER
7. Name and surname
8. Place of birth

9. (a) Maiden surname	(b) Surname at marriage if different from maiden surname
10. Usual address (if different from place of child's birth)	

INFORMANT	
11. Name and surname (if not the mother or father)	12. Qualification
13. Usual address (if different from that in 10 above)	

14. I certify that the particulars entered above are true to the best of my knowledge and belief

                     Signature

....of informant

15. Date of registration	16. Signature of registrar

FORM 6

Medical certificate of still-birth

Regulation 41(1)(a)　　　　　Births and Deaths Registration Act 1953, S.11(1)
as amended by the Population (Statistics) Act 1960.

*I was present at the still-birth of a $\frac{\text{male*}}{\text{female}}$ child born

*I have examined the body of a $\frac{\text{male*}}{\text{female}}$ child which I am informed and believe was born

on the............day of.........................19...... to..
　　　　　　　　　　　　　　　　　　　　　　(NAME OF MOTHER)

at ....
　　　　(PLACE OF BIRTH)

I hereby certify that

　(i) the child was not born alive, and

　(ii) to the best of my knowledge and belief the cause of death and the estimated
　　　 duration of pregnancy of the mother were as stated below.

CAUSE OF DEATH

I	I	
DIRECT CAUSE State foetal or maternal condition directly $\}$ *(a)* .... causing death		Estimated duration of pregnancy
ANTECEDENT CAUSES State foetal and/or maternal conditions, $\rceil$ due to *(b)*............... if any, giving rise to the above cause *(a)* $\}$ stating the underlying cause last $\rfloor$ due to *(c)*...............		
II	II	.... Weeks
OTHER SIGNIFICANT CONDITIONS of foetus or mother which may have $\rceil$ contributed to but, in so far as is known, $\}$ .... were not related to direct cause of death $\rfloor$		

　　┌ 1. The certified cause of death has been confirmed by post-mortem.
†┤ 2. Post-mortem information may be available later.
　　└ 3. Post-mortem not being held.

Signature..　　Date..........................

Qualification as registered by General Medical Council, or $\}$ ....
Registered No. as Certified Midwife

Residence...

　　* Strike out the words which do not apply.
　　† Ring appropriate digit.

FORM 7

Declaration as to still-birth

Regulation 41(1)(b)   Births and Deaths Registration Act 1953, S.11(1)(b)

1. Date of still-birth..

2. Place of still-birth...

3. Name and surname of parents of]
    still-born child, or in case of } ....
    an illegitimate child, of the
    mother only   ] ....

4. Residence of mother of child...

5. Reason why a certificate that the child was not born alive cannot be obtained from a registered medical practitioner or certified midwife:

    ....

    ....

    ....

    I, the undersigned, declare that the particulars above stated are true to the best of my knowledge and belief, and that the child above mentioned was not born alive.

          Signature ....

          State whether "Mother" "Father", of the child or in what other capacity liable to give information concerning the still-birth.

          Date....................................

FORM 8

Certificate that registrar has registered still-birth

Regulation 47(1)   Births and Deaths Registration Act 1953, S.11(2)

To be delivered to the person effecting the disposal of the body

    I, the undersigned registrar, do hereby certify that I have this day registered the birth of the still-born child of..

....

which took place on...at..

Entry No..........Signature of registrar..

          Date...

Registration District........................... Sub-District...................................

FORM 9

Particulars of death

Regulation 48(1)   Births and Deaths Registration Act 1953, S. 15.

DEATH	Entry No.
Registration district Administrative area	
Sub-district	
1. Date and place of death	
2. Name and surname	3. Sex
	4. Maiden surname of woman who has married
5. Date and place of birth	
6. Occupation and usual address	
7. (a) Name and surname of informant	(b) Qualification
(c) Usual address	
8. Cause of death	
9. I certify that the particulars given by me above are true to the best of my knowledge and belief.......................................Signature of informant	
10. Date of registration	11. Signature of registrar

FORM 10

Certificate of cause of death

Regulation 48(2) Births and Deaths Registration Act 1953, S.22(1)

Name of deceased...

Date of death as stated to me...............day of...............19...Age as stated to me...

Place of Death...

Last seen alive by me...................................day of...................................19...

*⎰ 1 The certified cause of death takes ⎰ a Seen after death by me.
⎱   account of information obtained ⎱ b Seen after death by another medical
    from post-mortem.   practitioner but not by me.
* 2 Information from post-mortem * c Not seen after death by a medical
    may be available later.   practitioner.
  3 Post-mortem not being held.

	These particulars not to be entered in death register.
CAUSE OF DEATH	Approximate interval between onset and death.

I	I	
Disease or condition directly leading to death†	(a)	....
....	due to (or as a consequence of)	
Antecedent causes. Morbid conditions, if any, giving rise to the above cause stating the underlying condition last.	(b) .... due to (or as a consequence of)	....
	(c)	....
II	II	
Other significant conditions, contributing to the death, but not related to the disease or condition causing it.	....	....

I hereby certify that I was in medical attendance during the above-named deceased's last illness, and that the particulars and cause of death above written are true to the best of my knowledge and belief.

Signature .... Qualifications as ⎤
                        registered by ⎬.........................
                        Medical Council ⎦

Residence .... Date ....

*Please ring appropriate digit and letter.

†This does not mean the mode of dying, such as heart failure, asphyxia, asthenia, etc.; it means the disease, injury, or complication which caused death.

FORM 11

Medical practitioner's notice to informant of death

Regulation 48(3)   Births and Deaths Registration Act 1953, S.22(2)

I hereby give notice that I have this day signed a medical certificate of cause of death
of ....
Signature...   Date................................

This notice is to be delivered by the informant to the registrar of births and deaths for
the sub-district in which the death occurred.

FORM 12

Notification of disposal

Regulation 58(1)   Births and Deaths Registration Act 1926, S.3(1)

This is to notify that the body of...deceased,
who died on..at..
was buried/cremated* on...at...............................
Signature...
on behalf of...
Date...

*Strike out whichever does not apply

FORM 13

Certificate that death is not required to be registered

Regulation 59   Births and Deaths Registration Act 1953, S.24(2)

I, the undersigned registrar, hereby certify that, on the information declared before me,
it appears that the death of...
is not required by law to be registered in England or Wales.
Date...   Signature..
Registrar of Births and Deaths
Registration District................................   Sub-District...........................

FORM 14

Declaration that certificate or order has been issued

Regulation 60   Births and Deaths Registration Act 1926, S.1(1)

I .... of ....
in pursuance of the Births and Deaths Registration Act 1926, declare:—

(1) That I am the person procuring the burial of the body of...........................
who died at.................................on the.....................................

(2) that a $\frac{\text{registrar's certificate*}}{\text{coroner's order}}$ authorising burial was issued by the
$\frac{\text{registrar*}}{\text{coroner}}$ .... at................................
to..living at ....
on...; and,

(3) that the reason why the said document cannot be delivered before burial is that
....
....
....
....

I make this declaration believing the same to be true.
Signature of declarant.....................................
Date................................
*Strike out whichever does not apply.

FORM 15

Notice of marriage without licence

Regulation 63(1)　　　　　　　　　　　　　　　　　Marriage Act 1949, S.27(1)

PARTICULARS RELATING TO THE PERSONS TO BE MARRIED

Name and surname (1)	Age (2)	Marital status (3)	Occupation (4)	Place of residence (5)	Period of residence (6)	Church or other building in which the marriage is to be solemnized (7)	District and county of residence (8)

To the Superintendent Registrar of the district of ....in the county.......................

1. I, the above-named......................., give you notice that I and the other person above named intend to be married by certificate without licence within three months from the date of entry of this notice.

2. I solemnly declare that I believe there is no impediment of kindred or alliance or other lawful hindrance to the marriage, and that I and the other person named above have for the period of seven days immediately preceding the giving of this notice had our usual places of residence within the districts named in column 8 above.

3. And I further declare that I am not under the age of twenty-one years or, if under that age, am a widower or widow, and that the other person named above is not under the age of twenty-one years, or, if under that age, is a widower or widow.

4. I declare that to the best of my knowledge and belief the declarations which I have made above and the particulars relating to the persons to be married are true. I understand that if any of the declarations are false I MAY BE LIABLE TO PROSECUTION UNDER THE PERJURY ACT 1911.

5. I also understand that if, in fact, there is an impediment of kindred or alliance or other lawful hindrance to the intended marriage the marriage may be invalid or void and the contracting of the marriage may render one or both of the parties GUILTY OF A CRIME AND LIABLE TO THE PENALTIES OF BIGAMY OR SUCH OTHER CRIME AS MAY HAVE BEEN COMMITTED.

(Signed)...(Date)...............

In the presence of.....................................(Signature of registration officer)

Official designation ....

Registration district of...

Place of residence..

FORM 16

Notice of marriage without licence

Regulation 63(1)   Marriage Act 1949, S.27(1)

PARTICULARS RELATING TO THE PERSONS TO BE MARRIED

Name and surname (1)	Age (2)	Marital status (3)	Occupation (4)	Place of residence (5)	Period of residence (6)	Church or other building in which the marriage is to be solemnized (7)	District and county of residence (8)
	years						
	years						

To the Superintendent Registrar of the district of.. in the county...............

1. I, the above-named..give you notice that I and the other person named above intend to be married by certificate without licence within three months from the date of entry of this notice.

2. I solemnly declare that I believe there is no impediment of kindred or alliance or other lawful hindrance to the said marriage, and that I and the other person named above have for the period of seven days immediately preceding the giving of this notice had our usual places of residence within the districts named in column 8 above.

3. And I further declare that in respect of myself—   and in respect of the said‡....................

*(i) the consent of†...whose consent only is required by law has been obtained;

(ii) the necessity of obtaining the consent of†...has been dispensed with as provided by law;

(iii) there is no person whose consent to my marriage is required by law;

(iv) I am over the age of twenty-one years or if under that age am a widow/widower;

*(i) the consent of†....................................whose consent only is required by law has been obtained;

(ii) the necessity of obtaining the consent of†...............................has been dispensed with as provided by law;

(iii) there is no person whose consent to his/her marriage is required by law;

(iv) he/she is over the age of twenty-one years or if under that age is a widow/widower;

FORM 16—continued

Notice of marriage without licence

Regulation 63(1)　　　　　　　　　　　　　　　　Marriage Act 1949, S.27(1)

4. I declare that to the best of my knowledge and belief the declarations which I have made above and the particulars relating to the persons to be married are true. I understand that if any of the declarations are false I MAY BE LIABLE TO PROSECUTION UNDER THE PERJURY ACT 1911.

5. I also understand that if, in fact, there is an impediment of kindred or alliance or other lawful hindrance to the intended marriage the marriage may be invalid or void and the contracting of the marriage may render one or both of the parties GUILTY OF A CRIME AND LIABLE TO THE PENALTIES OF BIGAMY OR SUCH OTHER CRIME AS MAY HAVE BEEN COMMITTED.

(Signed) ....(Date) ....

In the presence of...(Signature of registration officer)

Official designation ....

Registration district of..

Place of residence..

*Delete the alternatives which do not apply; if none applies (e.g. the............Court has consented to the marriage) insert the appropriate declaration as to consent in the space provided.

†Insert the name(s) of the person(s) whose consent is/are required.

‡Insert the name of the other party.

FORM 17

Notice of marriage with licence

Regulation 63(2)　　　　　　　　　　　　　　　　　Marriage Act 1949, S.27(2)

PARTICULARS RELATING TO THE PERSONS TO BE MARRIED

Name and surname (1)	Age (2)	Marital status (3)	Occupation (4)	Place of residence (5)	Period of residence (6)	Church or other building in which the marriage is to be solemnized (7)	District and county of residence (8)

To the Superintendent Registrar of the district of..in the county.................

1. I, the above-named.........................., give you notice that I and the other person named above intend to be married by certificate and licence within three months from the date of entry of this notice.

2. I solemnly declare that I believe there is no impediment of kindred or alliance or other lawful hindrance to the said marriage, and that *I have/the other person named above has for the period of fifteen days immediately preceding the giving of this notice had *my/his/her usual place of residence within the above-mentioned district of...............................

3. And I further declare that I am not under the age of twenty-one years or, if under that age, am a widower or widow, and that the other person named above is not under the age of twenty-one years, or, if under that age, is a widower or widow.

4. I declare that to the best of my knowledge and belief the declarations which I have made above and the particulars relating to the persons to be married are true. I understand that if any of the declarations are false I MAY BE LIABLE TO PROSECUTION UNDER THE PERJURY ACT 1911.

FORM 17—continued

Notice of marriage with licence

Regulation 63(2)   Marriage Act 1949, S.27(2)

5. I also understand that if, in fact, there is an impediment of kindred or alliance or other lawful hindrance to the intended marriage the marriage may be invalid or void and the contracting of the marriage may render one or both of the parties, GUILTY OF A CRIME AND LIABLE TO THE PENALTIES OF BIGAMY OR SUCH OTHER CRIME AS MAY HAVE BEEN COMMITTED.

(Signed) ....(Date)

In the presence of.......................(Signature of registration officer)

Official designation........................

Registration district of........................

Place of residence........................

*Delete the alternatives which do not apply.

FORM 18

Notice of marriage with licence

Regulation 63(2) Marriage Act 1949, S.27(2)

PARTICULARS RELATING TO THE PERSONS TO BE MARRIED

Name and surname (1)	Age (2)	Marital status (3)	Occupation (4)	Place of residence (5)	Period of residence (6)	Church or other building in which the marriage is to be solemnized (7)	District and county of residence (8)
	years						
	years						

To the Superintendent Registrar of the district of..in the county................................

1. I, the above-named..., give you notice that I and the other person named above intend to be married by certificate and licence within three months from the date of entry of this notice.

2. I solemnly declare that I believe there is no impediment of kindred or alliance or other lawful hindrance to the said marriage, and that *I have/the other person named above has for the period of fifteen days immediately preceding the giving of this notice had* my/his/her usual place of residence within the above-mentioned district of... and in respect of the said‡.......................................

3. And I further declare that in respect of myself—

*(i) the consent of†.....................whose consent only ....whose consent only is required by law has been obtained; is required by law has been obtained;

(ii) the necessity of obtaining the consent of† (ii) the necessity of obtaining the consent of†...... ....has been dispensed with as provided by law; ....has been dispensed with as provided by law;

(iii) there is no person whose consent to my marriage is required by law; (iii) there is no person whose consent to his/her marriage is required by law;

(iv) I am over the age of twenty-one years or if under that age am a widow/widower; (iv) he/she is over the age of twenty-one years or if under that age is a widow/widower;

FORM 18—continued

Notice of marriage with licence

Regulation 63(2)   Marriage Act 1949, S.27(2)

4. I declare that to the best of my knowledge and belief the declarations which I have made above and the particulars relating to the persons to be married are true. I understand that if any of the declarations are false I MAY BE LIABLE TO PROSECUTION UNDER THE PERJURY ACT 1911.

5. I also understand that if, in fact, there is an impediment of kindred or alliance or other lawful hindrance to the intended marriage the marriage may be invalid or void and the contracting of the marriage may render one or both of the parties GUILTY OF A CRIME AND LIABLE TO THE PENALTIES OF BIGAMY OR SUCH OTHER CRIME AS MAY HAVE BEEN COMMITTED.

(Signed) ....(Date) ....
In the presence of............................(Signature of registration officer)
Official designation...
Registration district of..
Place of residence...

*Delete the alternatives which do not apply; if none applies (e.g. the ....Court has consented to the marriage), insert the appropriate declaration as to consent in the space provided.
†Insert the name(s) of the person(s) whose consent is/are required.
‡Insert the name of the other party.

FORM 19

Endorsement on notice of marriage

Regulation 64   Marriage Act 1949, S.35(1)

I declare that I and the other person named in this notice desire our intended marriage to be solemnized according to the form, rite or ceremony of the (i)................................to which (ii)................................belong(s); and that to the best of my belief there is not within the superintendent registrar's district in which (iii)................................reside(s) any registered building in which marriage is solemnized according to that form, rite or ceremony; and that the nearest district to (iv)................................place of residence in which there is a registered building in which marriage may be so solemnized is the superintendent registrar's district of (v)................................and that we intend to solemnize our marriage in the registered building described in this notice and which is situated within that district.

Signed................................

Date................................

  (i) Insert here the name of the body or denomination of Christians or other persons meeting for religious worship according to the form, rite or ceremony of which the parties desire the marriage to be solemnized.

 (ii) Insert here "I" or "the said ...." (followed by the name of the other party) as the case may be.

(iii) Insert here "I" or "the other person named in this notice", as the case may be.

(iv) Insert here "my", "his" or "her" according to the insertion in (iii).

 (v) Insert here the name of the district in which is situated the registered building in which the intended marriage is to take place.

FORM 20

Certificate for marriage

Regulation 65(1)   **Marriage Act 1949, S.31**

I,.., Superintendent Registrar of the district of..........................
in the county...............................of...............................hereby certify that on the...................................
day of...............................19......notice was duly entered in the Marriage Notice Book of the said district of the
marriage intended to be solemnized between the parties hereinafter named and described.

Name (1)	Age (2)	Marital status (3)	Occupation (4)	Place of residence (5)	Period of residence (6)	Church or other building in which the marriage is to be solemnized (7)	District and county of residence (8)
	years						
	years						

I further certify that the issue of this certificate has not been forbidden by any person authorised to forbid the issue thereof.

Date..   Signature...
                                                                        Superintendent Registrar

NOTE:
This certificate will be void if the marriage is not solemnized within three months from the date of entry of notice given above.

FORM 21

Certificate and licence for marriage

Regulation 65(2)   **Marriage Act 1949, S.32**

I,.., Superintendent Registrar of the district of..........................
in the county...............................of...............................hereby certify that on the...................................
day of...............................19......notice was duly entered in the Marriage Notice Book of the said district of the
marriage intended to be solemnized between the parties hereinafter named and described.

Name (1)	Age (2)	Marital status (3)	Occupation (4)	Place of residence (5)	Period of residence (6)	Church or other building in which the marriage is to be solemnized (7)	District and county of residence (8)
	years						
	years						

I further certify that the issue of this certificate has not been forbidden by any person authorised to forbid the issue thereof.
Now therefore I, the said Superintendent Registrar, grant to the above-named parties licence to contract and solemnize their intended marriage.

Date..   Signature...
                                                                        Superintendent Registrar

NOTE:
This certificate and licence will be void if the marriage is not solemnized within three months from the date of entry of notice given above.

FORM 22

Form of instructions

Regulation 66   Marriage Act 1949, Ss.31 & 32

Instructions for the solemnization of a marriage in a registered building without the presence of a registrar

1. This marriage must take place in the registered building named in the superintendent registrar's certificate or superintendent registrar's certificates for marriage, *and nowhere else.*

2. The authorised person duly appointed for the registered building named in the certificate or certificates, or an authorised person for some other registered building in the same registration district, must be present at the marriage.

3. At least two witnesses must also be present, and the doors of the registered building must be open. (The doors need not be actually open provided they are not so closed as to prevent persons from entering that part of the building in which the marriage is solemnized.)

4. Any certificate or certificates issued by a superintendent registrar as the legal authority for the marriage must be delivered to the authorised person in whose presence the marriage is to be solemnized. Unless this document (or these documents) are in his possession the authorised person must on no account allow the marriage to take place.

5. It is absolutely essential to the validity of the marriage that in some part of the ceremony each of the parties shall make the following declaration:—

> "I do solemnly declare that I know not of any lawful impediment why I, A.B., may not be joined in matrimony to C.D."

and that each of them shall say to the other either—

> "I call upon these persons here present to witness that I, A.B., do take thee, C.D., to be my lawful wedded wife [*or* husband]"; or

> "I A.B., do take thee, C.D., to be my wedded wife [*or* husband]".

6. These declaratory and contracting words must be said in the presence of the authorised person acting on the occasion and of the witnesses to the marriage.

7. Immediately after the marriage is solemnized the authorised person must register all the particulars prescribed by law in the duplicate marriage register books of the registered building in which the marriage has taken place; the entry in both books must be signed by the parties married, by at least two witnesses and by the authorised person.

8. After the registration of the marriage a certified copy of the entry thereof may be obtained from the authorised person on payment of the prescribed fee.

FORM 23

Form of marriage entry

Regulation 67   Marriage Act 1949, S.55(1)

PART I

Particulars of marriage

19........ Marriage solemnized at..in the...................................

of...in the ....

No.	1 When married	2 Name and surname	3 Age	4 Condition	5 Rank or profession	6 Residence at the time of marriage	7 Father's name and surname	8 Rank or profession of father

PART II

Particulars of Attestation

(i) For marriage according to the rites and ceremonies of the Church of England or of the Church in Wales.

Married in the...............................according to the rites and ceremonies of the.....................by............
or after...by me,

This marriage was solemnized between us, { .... } in the presence of us, { .... } ....
{ .... } { .... } ....

(ii) For marriage in a superintendent registrar's office.

Married in the...............................by..before me,

This marriage was solemnized between us, { .... } in the presence of us, { .... } ....
{ .... } { .... } ....

(iii) For marriage in a registered building in the presence of a registrar.

Married in the...according to the rites and ceremonies of the
....by..by me,

This marriage was solemnized between us, { .... } in the presence of us, { .... } ....
{ .... } { .... } ....

(iv) For marriage in a registered building in the presence of an authorised person.

Married in the...............................according to the rites and ceremonies of the ....by..........

This marriage was solemnized between us, { .... } in the presence of us, { .... } and in the.................
{ .... } { .... } presence of Authorised Person for
....

(v) For marriage according to the usages of the Society of Friends.

Married in the...............................according to the usages of the.....................by..........

This marriage was solemnized between us, { .... } in the presence of us, { .... } ....
{ .... } { .... }

(vi) For marriage according to the usages of the Jews.

Married in the ....according to the usages of the.....................by..........

This marriage was solemnized between us, { .... } in the presence of us, { .... } ....
{ .... } { .... }

FORM 24

Quarterly return of births, still-births and deaths

Regulation 78(1)   Births and Deaths Registration Act 1953, S.26(1)(a)

I,...registrar of
births and deaths in the sub-district of..,
in the *..., do hereby certify
that this is a true copy of the register book(s) of births/still-births/deaths† within the
said sub-district from entry no.............., book no..
to entry no...........................book no......................................

Signature of registrar.................................

Date...............................

I have examined the copies of the above entries, have compared them with the said
register book(s) and hereby certify them to be true copies.

Signature of superintendent registrar.............................

Date.............................

*Insert particulars as in headings in register book.
†Strike out whichever does not apply.

FORM 25

Certificate of no registration

Regulation 78(1)   Births and Deaths Registration Act 1953, S.26(1)(b)

Registration District............................. Sub-District.....................................
I hereby certify that no birth [still-birth, death] has been registered in the birth [still-birth, death] register now kept by me in the above-named sub-district during the quarter
ended....................................19......

The number of the last entry recorded in the register before that date is...............

Date............................. Signature of registrar.......................................

FORM 26

Quarterly return of marriages

Regulation 78(2)   Marriage Act 1949, S.57(2)

I,..., Registrar of the district of
.... in the ....
do hereby certify that this is a true copy of the entry (entries) of marriage registered in the
said district from the entry of the marriage of...
and..number ....to the entry of
the marriage of...and..
number......................

Date............................. Signature of registrar..

FORM 27

Certificate of no registration

Regulation 78(2)   Marriage Act 1949, S.57(2)

Registration District......................................

I hereby certify that no marriage has been registered in the marriage register book now kept by me in the above-named district during the quarter ended....................
19............

The number of the last entry recorded in the register book prior to that date is......

Date.............................. Signature of registrar...

(Countersigned)..
Superintendent Registrar

FORM 28

Certificate of registration of birth

Regulation 79   Births and Deaths Registration Act 1953, S.12

I, the undersigned, do hereby certify that the birth of a $\frac{male*}{female}$ child (still-) born on the....................................19......has been duly registered by me at Entry No.......
in my Register No..........
Name of informant...
Qualification of informant...

Date.............................. Signature of registrar...

District....................................... Sub-District...
*Strike out whichever does not apply.

FORM 29

Short certificate of birth

Regulation 82(1)   Births and Deaths Registration Act 1953, S.33

Name and Surname...
Sex..
Date of Birth..
Place of Birth..
I, ...
Superintendent Registrar for
————————————————————————————————— the
Registrar of Births and Deaths for the sub-district of.....................................in
Registration District of ....do hereby certify that the above particulars have been compiled from an entry in a register in my custody.

Date..............................   ....
                                    Superintendent Registrar
                                    Registrar of Births and Deaths

SCHEDULE 2

Regulations 89

REVOCATIONS

Column 1	Column 2	Column 3
Regulations revoked	References	Extent of revocation
The Marriage (Prescription of Forms) Regulations 1949	S.I. 1949/2414 (1949 I, p.3586).	The whole regulations
The Registration (Births, Stillbirths and Deaths) Prescription of Forms Regulations 1953	S.I. 1953/1347 (1953 II, p.1739).	,,
The Registration (Births, Stillbirths, Deaths and Marriages) Consolidated Regulations 1954	S.I. 1954/1596 (1954 II, p.1871).	,,
The Marriage (Prescription of Forms) (Amendment) Regulations 1954	S.I. 1954/1644 (1954 I, p.1189).	,,
The Registration (Births, Stillbirths Deaths and Marriages) Amendment Regulations 1959	S.I. 1959/528 (1959 II, p.2300).	,,
The Registration (Births, Stillbirths and Deaths) (Prescription of Forms) Regulations 1960	S.I. 1960/1603 (1960 III, p.2837).	,,
The Registration (Births, Stillbirths, Deaths and Marriages) Amendment Regulations 1960	S.I. 1960/1604 (1960 III, p.2841).	,,
The Registration of Deaths (Prescription of Forms) Regulations 1962	S.I. 1962/2582 (1962 III, p.3467).	,,
The Registration (Births, Stillbirths, Deaths and Marriages) Amendment Regulations 1964	S.I. 1964/2065 (1964 III, p.5175).	,,
The Registration of Births (Amendment) Regulations 1967	S.I. 1967/1819 (1967 III, p.4844).	Regulation 9

Given under my hand on 17th December 1968.

Michael Reed,
Registrar General.

I approve

R. H. S. Crossman,
Secretary of State for Social Services.

18th December 1968.

EXPLANATORY NOTE

(This Note is not part of the Regulations.)

The Acts relating to registration of births, deaths and marriages (The Births and Deaths Registration Act 1953, the Marriage Act 1949 and the Registration Service Act 1953) empower the Registrar General to prescribe various forms and procedures necessary for the operation of those Acts. Also, the last mentioned Act empowers the Registrar General to prescribe the duties of registration officers in the execution of any enactment, their qualifications for appointment and other matters affecting these officers. These Regulations consolidate with amendments the earlier regulations which prescribed these forms, procedures and duties, etc. They do not, therefore, themselves contain a complete code of registration, but are supplementary to the Acts referred to.

The regulations deal with the following main matters:—

1. Qualifications for office as registration officer, and other general matters affecting such officers (Regulations 4 to 12)

2. Registration of birth (more detailed procedure being involved if the interval between birth and registration exceeds 3 months) and re-registration after legitimation (Regulations 16 to 36)

3. Birth entries of adopted children (Regulations 37 and 38)

4. Registration of still-births (Regulations 39 to 47)

5. Registration of death (including prescription of the notices, etc., required to be issued by general practitioners) (Regulations 48 to 56)

6. Disposal of bodies of deceased persons (including prescription of the necessary certificates) (Regulations 57 to 62)

7. Registration of marriage (including the preliminary notices etc., and the manner of registration) (Regulations 63 to 70)

8. Correction of errors in any entry in a register (Regulations 71 to 77)

9. Short certificates of birth (Regulations 81 and 82)

10. Applications for birth or death certificates for purposes of certain other Acts (Regulations 84 and 85)

The principal changes from the earlier regulations are that numerous points of detail affecting only registration officers have been omitted and that new forms of entry are introduced for births, still-births and deaths (forms 1, 5 and 9 in schedule 1).

These are divided into spaces instead of columns as before, and now require particulars about the place of birth of parents and of a deceased person.

STATUTORY INSTRUMENTS

1968 No. 2050

REGISTRATION OF BIRTHS, DEATHS, MARRIAGES, ETC.

ENGLAND AND WALES

The Birth Certificate (Shortened Form) Regulations 1968

Made - - -	*18th December* 1968
Coming into Operation	*1st April* 1969

ARRANGEMENT OF REGULATIONS

1. Title and commencement.
2. Interpretation.
3. Application for short certificate of birth.
4. Form of short certificate of birth.
5. Compilation of short certificate of birth.
6. Entry of name and surname.
7. Entry of sex.
8. Entry of date of birth.
9. Entry of place of birth.
10. Revocations.

The Registrar General, in exercise of the powers conferred on him by section 33 of the Births and Deaths Registration Act 1953(a), and section 39 of that Act as extended by section 5(2) of the Foundling Hospital Act 1953(b), and of all other powers enabling him in that behalf, with the approval of the Secretary of State for Social Services, hereby makes the following regulations :—

Title and commencement

1. These regulations may be cited as the Birth Certificate (Shortened Form) Regulations 1968 and shall come into operation on 1st April 1969.

Interpretation

2.—(1) In these regulations, unless the context otherwise requires—

"short certificate of birth" means a certificate of birth the form of which is prescribed by regulation 4 ;

"registered person" means a person in respect of whose birth an application for a short certificate of birth is made and whose birth is registered or recorded in any register or record in the custody of the Registrar General ;

"the entry" in relation to a registered person means the entry relating to him in any such register or record as aforesaid ;

"adopted" means adopted under the Adoption Act 1968(c), the Adoption Act 1958(d), or any enactment repealed by the latter Act.

(a) 1953 c. 20.	(b) 1953 c. xxxvi.
(c) 1968 c. 53.	(d) 7 & 8 Eliz. 2. c. 5.

(2) The Interpretation Act 1889(**a**), shall apply to the interpretation of these regulations as it applies to the interpretation of an Act of Parliament and as if these regulations and the regulations hereby revoked were Acts of Parliament.

Application for short certificate of birth

3. For the purposes of section 33 of the Births and Deaths Registration Act 1953 (which relates to short certificates of birth), the particulars to be furnished to the Registrar General on an application for a short certificate of birth (other than a certificate issued under section 5 of the Foundling Hospital Act 1953), shall be the following particulars relating to the registered person—

(*a*) where the registered person has been adopted and the certificate is to be in respect of him as an adopted person—

(i) his name and surname ;

(ii) the date of his birth ;

(iii) the name and surname of his adopter or, as the case may be, his adopters ; and

(iv) the date upon which, and the name of the court by which, the adoption order was made ;

(*b*) in any other case—

(i) the name and surname of the registered person ;

(ii) the date of his birth ;

(iii) the name and surname of his father ;

(iv) the name, surname and maiden surname of his mother ; and

(v) the place of his birth or the place at which his birth was registered :

Provided that the Registrar General may dispense with the furnishing of any of the said particulars which in his opinion it is not reasonably practicable for the applicant to furnish.

Form of short certificate of birth

4. The form of short certificate of birth to be issued by the Registrar General under section 33 of the Births and Deaths Registration Act 1953, or under section 5 of the Foundling Hospital Act 1953, shall be the form set out in the Schedule to these regulations.

Compilation of short certificate of birth

5. A short certificate of birth issued by the Registrar General under the enactments mentioned in the last preceding regulation shall be compiled in accordance with, and shall contain the particulars required by, regulations 6 to 9.

Entry of name and surname

6.—(1) In a short certificate of birth issued under section 5 of the Foundling Hospital Act 1953, opposite the words "Name and Surname" there shall be entered the name and surname given to the registered person on his admission to the Foundling Hospital.

(**a**) 1889 c. 63.

(2) In a short certificate of birth issued under section 33 of the Births and Deaths Registration Act 1953, opposite the words "Name and Surname" there shall be entered—

(a) where the name and surname of the registered person are recorded as such in the entry, that name and surname (or, if there is more than one such surname, such one as the applicant may request);

(b) where the name but not the surname of the registered person is recorded as such in the entry, that name and immediately thereafter—

(i) if the entry contains a surname which appears from the entry to have been used by his father or mother at or after the date of birth, that surname (or, if there is more than one such surname, such one as the applicant may request);

(ii) if the entry contains a surname of his adopter or adopters, and the applicant so requests, that surname (or, if there is more than one such surname, such one as the applicant may request).

Entry of sex

7. Opposite the word "Sex" there shall be entered such particulars thereof as are contained in the entry.

Entry of date of birth

8. Opposite the words "Date of Birth" there shall be entered the date of birth recorded in the entry:

Provided that, if no date of birth is recorded in the entry, there shall be entered such date, (if any), as may appear to the Registrar General from the information recorded in the entry to be the probable date of birth.

Entry of place of birth

9.—(1) In a short certificate of birth issued under section 5 of the Foundling Hospital Act 1953, opposite the words "Place of Birth" there shall be entered particulars of the country of birth of the registered person.

(2) In a short certificate of birth issued under section 33 of the Births and Deaths Registration Act 1953, opposite the words "Place of Birth" there shall be entered such, (if any), of the following particulars as may be appropriate—

(a) where the register or other record containing the entry includes particulars of the registration district and sub-district in which the registered person's birth occurred or in which the birth is treated under any enactment as having occurred, the name of that registration district and sub-district;

(b) where the registered person's birth is recorded as having occurred on a British ship, the words "At Sea" followed by the name of the ship on which the birth occurred;

(c) where the registered person's birth is recorded as having occurred in an aircraft, the words "In an aircraft" followed by the particulars as to place of birth in the entry;

(d) in any other case where the entry contains particulars as to the place of the registered person's birth, those particulars;

(e) where the entry contains no particulars as to the place of the registered person's birth, such particulars, (if any), as to the country of birth of the registered person as the Registrar General is satisfied can be obtained from any register or record in his custody.

Revocation of existing regulations

10. The Birth Certificate (Shortened Form) Regulations 1959(a), are hereby revoked, but without prejudice to anything duly done or suffered or to any right, privilege, obligation or liability acquired, accrued or incurred under any of those regulations.

SCHEDULE

FORM OF SHORT CERTIFICATE OF BIRTH FOR ISSUE BY THE REGISTRAR GENERAL

Name and Surname	
Sex	
Date of Birth	
Place of Birth	

Certified to have been compiled from records in the custody of the Registrar General. Given at the General Register Office, Somerset House, London, under the Seal of the said Office, the   day of   19   .

Given under my hand on 17th December 1968.

Michael Reed,
Registrar General.

I approve.

R. H. S. Crossman,
Secretary of State for Social Services.

18th December 1968.

EXPLANATORY NOTE

(This Note is not part of the Regulations.)

These Regulations prescribe the form of short certificates of birth to be issued by the Registrar General (regulation 4 and Schedule); the particulars to be furnished by applicants for such certificates (regulation 3); and the manner in which the certificates are to be compiled (regulations 5 to 9).

The form of certificate and the particulars to be furnished remain as prescribed in the Birth Certificate (Shortened Form) Regulations 1959 (which are revoked by regulation 10); but a number of minor variations are made in the prescribed manner of compilation, largely because of changes to be made in the content and format of birth registers.

The new form of birth register will come into use on 1st April 1969 and these regulations accordingly take effect from that date (regulation 1).

(a) S.I. 1959/529 (1959 II, p. 2296).

STATUTORY INSTRUMENTS

1968 No. 2052

JUSTICES OF THE PEACE

The Justices (Supplemental List) Rules 1968

Made - - -		*20th December* 1968
Coming into Operation		*1st January* 1969

The Lord Chancellor, in exercise of the powers conferred on him by section 4 of the Justices of the Peace Act 1949(**a**) and by virtue of section 2 of the Justices of the Peace Act 1968(**b**), hereby makes the following Rules :—

1.—(1) These Rules may be cited as the Justices (Supplemental List) Rules 1968 and shall come into operation on 1st January 1969 :

Provided that, as regards the year 1969 and the three following years, the references in paragraphs (*a*) and (*b*) in Rule 3 to the age of 70 years shall be deemed to be references for 1969 to an age of 74 years, for 1970 to an age of 73 years, for 1971 to an age of 72 years and for 1972 to an age of 71 years ; and if, at the beginning of any of these years or of the year 1973, a person is of or over the age relevant for that year to those paragraphs, he shall be treated for the purposes of those paragraphs as having held since attaining that age any office mentioned in the said paragraph (*a*)(i) which he holds at the beginning of that year.

(2) The Interpretation Act 1889(**c**) applies to the interpretation of these Rules as it applies to the interpretation of an Act of Parliament.

2. Subject to the provisions of these Rules, there shall be kept in connection with every Commission of the Peace issued by Her Majesty a list to be called the "Supplemental List".

3. Subject to the provisions of these Rules, the Clerk of the Peace for every county and in the City of London and, in every borough having a separate Commission of the Peace, the Town Clerk, or, as the case may be, the Clerk of the Peace or other officer having the custody of the Commission, shall enter in the Supplemental List kept for that county or borough the name of any person appointed a Justice by the Commission or being an Alderman of the City of London—

(*a*) who is of the age of 75 years or over and neither—

  (i) on attaining the age of 70 years holds or has held office as chairman or deputy chairman of a court of quarter sessions or as a recorder of a borough (including Recorder of Liverpool or Manchester) ; nor

  (ii) holds or has held high judicial office within the meaning of the Appellate Jurisdiction Act 1876(**d**) ; or

---

(**a**) 1949 c. 101.   (**b**) 1968 c. 69.
(**c**) 1889 c. 63.   (**d**) 1876 c. 59.

(b) who, after attaining the age of 70 years while holding an office mentioned in paragraph (a)(i) above, no longer holds any such office and who neither holds nor has held high judicial office ; or

(c) who is of the age of 75 years or over ; or

(d) who applies to have his name entered therein and obtains the approval of the Lord Chancellor for such entry to be made ; or

(e) whose name is directed by the Lord Chancellor to be so entered in pursuance of section 4(4) of the Justices of the Peace Act 1949.

4. The Clerk of the Peace, Town Clerk or other officer shall remove from the Supplemental List—

(a) any name which the Lord Chancellor may direct him to remove from that list ; or

(b) the name of any person who has ceased to be a Justice.

5. These Rules shall apply to a Justice of the Peace whether appointed before or after the coming into operation of the Rules.

6. These Rules shall not extend to Scotland nor apply to the County Palatine of Lancaster or to any Commission of the Peace issued in connection with the County of Lancaster or any borough within that county having a separate Commission of the Peace.

7.—(1) The Justices (Supplemental List) Rules 1950(a) are hereby revoked.

Dated 20th December 1968.

Gardiner, C.

EXPLANATORY NOTE

(*This Note is not part of the Rules.*)

These Rules replace the Justices (Supplemental List) Rules 1950 so as to give effect to section 2 of the Justices of the Peace Act 1968, which lowers the retiring age of Justices from 75 to 70 years.

(a) S.I. 1950/594 (1950 I, p.1149).

STATUTORY INSTRUMENTS

1968 No. 2053

TRANSPORT

The National Freight Corporation (Transfer of Additional Securities) Order 1968

Made - - - -	*19th December* 1968
Coming into Operation	*20th December* 1968

The Minister of Transport makes this Order in exercise of his powers under section 4(2) of the Transport Act 1968(a) and of all other enabling powers :—

1. This Order may be cited as the National Freight Corporation (Transfer of Additional Securities) Order 1968, and shall come into operation on the 20th December 1968.

2. There shall be added to Part I of Schedule 3 to the Transport Act 1968 the following bodies, namely—

British Express Carriers Limited,

Road-Air Freight Express Limited,

Containerbase Federation Limited,

Containerbase (Leeds) Limited,

Containerbase (Scotland) Limited,

Containerbase (London East) Limited,

Containerbase (Liverpool) Limited,

Containerbase (Manchester) Limited,

West of England Freight Terminal Limited,

(being bodies whose activities are similar to those of the bodies already listed in the said Schedule and whose securities are beneficially owned by the Transport Holding Company).

Sealed with the Official Seal of the Minister of Transport the 19th December 1968.

(L.S.)

G. R. W. Brigstocke,
An Under Secretary of the
Ministry of Transport.

(a) 1968 c. 73.

EXPLANATORY NOTE

(This Note is not part of the Order.)

This Order adds nine companies to the list of bodies in Part I of Schedule 3 to the Transport Act 1968 whose securities are to be transferred to the National Freight Corporation by virtue of section 4(1) of the Transport Act 1968 and of the Transport Act 1968 (Commencement No. 1) Order 1968 (S.I. 1968/1822).

STATUTORY   INSTRUMENTS

1968 No. 2060

PRICES AND INCOMES

The Awards and Settlements (Temporary Continuation of Standstill) (No. 3) Order 1968

Made - - - -	30th December 1968
Laid before Parliament	3rd January 1969
Coming into Operation	4th January 1969

Whereas by virtue of a reference to the National Board for Prices and Incomes under section 2(1) of the Prices and Incomes Act 1966(a) (the text whereof was published on 10th September 1968 in the London Gazette) the implementation of the award described in Article 2 hereof relating to terms and conditions of employment in the road passenger transport undertaking of the Great Yarmouth County Borough Council was forbidden by section 15(2) of that Act ;

And whereas before the said implementation ceased to be so forbidden a Report of the Board on the said reference was published(b) with a recommendation adverse to the implementation of the said award ;

And whereas by virtue of the said recommendation and subsections (1) and (2)(a) of section 1 of the Prices and Incomes Act 1967(c) the said section 15(2) continued to apply to the implementation of the said award as it applied up to the date of publication of the said Report :

Now, therefore, the Secretary of State having given notice under section 1(2)(a) of the said Act of 1967 within a period of ten days after the date of the said publication of a proposal to make this Order, and having taken into consideration representations duly made in pursuance of the said notice, in exercise of the powers conferred on her by section 1(2)(b) of the said Act of 1967, as amended by section 3(2) of the Prices and Incomes Act 1968(d), and of all other powers enabling her in that behalf, hereby makes the following Order :—

1.—(1) This Order, which may be cited as the Awards and Settlements (Temporary Continuation of Standstill) (No. 3) Order 1968, shall come into operation on 4th January 1969.

(2) The Interpretation Act 1889(e) shall apply for the interpretation of this Order as it applies for the interpretation of an Act of Parliament.

2. The Secretary of State hereby directs that section 15(2) of the Prices and Incomes Act 1966 shall continue to apply to forbid the implementation up to and including 9th August 1969 of the award made on 4th September 1968 of a bonus payment of 10s. per week to employees in the transport undertaking of the Great Yarmouth County Borough Council in connection with the extension of one-man operation during the 1968 summer season.

Signed by order of the Secretary of State.
30th December 1968.

Harold Walker,

Joint Parliamentary Under Secretary of State,
Department of Employment and Productivity.

(a) 1966 c. 33.   (b) Report No. 96 entitled "Pay of Busmen employed by the Corporation of Great Yarmouth" (Cmnd. 3844) published 6th December 1968.   (c) 1967 c. 53.   (d) 1968 c. 42.   (e) 1889 c. 63.

EXPLANATORY NOTE

(This Note is not part of the Order.)

This Order, which has effect from 4th January 1969, provides for the further continuation until 9th August 1969 of the standstill on the implementation of an award relating to terms and conditions of employment in the road passenger transport undertaking of the Great Yarmouth County Borough Council.

STATUTORY INSTRUMENTS

1968 No. 2061 (S.187)

REGISTERS AND RECORDS, SCOTLAND
Act of Sederunt (Amendment of Fees in the Department of the Registers of Scotland) 1968

Made - - - - 20th December 1968
Coming into Operation 1st February 1969

The Lords of Council and Session, in respect that amended tables of fees to be charged in the Department of the Registers of Scotland have been prepared and approved in terms of section 25 of the Land Registers (Scotland) Act 1868(a) as amended by section 6 of the Lord Clerk Register (Scotland) Act 1879(b), section 5 of the Reorganisation of Offices (Scotland) Act 1928(c), and section 1 of the Public Registers and Records (Scotland) Act 1948(d), by virtue of the powers vested in them do hereby enact and declare as follows:—

1. The fees to be charged in the Department of the Registers of Scotland shall be those specified in the Schedule hereto.

2. The Act of Sederunt (Amendment of Fees in the Department of the Registers of Scotland) 1966(e) is hereby repealed.

3. This Act of Sederunt may be cited as the Act of Sederunt (Amendment of Fees in the Department of the Registers of Scotland) 1968, and shall come into operation on 1st February 1969.

And the Lords appoint this Act of Sederunt to be inserted in the Books of Sederunt.

J. L. Clyde,
I. P. D.

Edinburgh,
20th December 1968.

(a) 1868 c. 64. (b) 1879 c. 44. (c) 1928 c. 34. (d) 1948 c. 57.
(e) S.I. 1966/1304 (1966 III, p. 3620).

SCHEDULE

TABLES OF FEES IN THE DEPARTMENT OF THE REGISTERS OF SCOTLAND

A. GENERAL REGISTER OF SASINES

REGISTRATION FEES

Conveyance including *absolute* conveyance, voluntary or judicial, either for a price or as a gift or in implement of trust or other purpose, completion of title by decree or by Notice of Title, feu-right, lease, deed creating a ground annual or other yearly or periodical payment where there is a transfer of heritable property not in security, and generally all deeds transferring an absolute right to heritable subjects.

Where (*a*) the consideration, (*b*) the value of the heritable subjects transferred or passing, (*c*) the capitalised amount* of (i) feu duty, (ii) rent, or (iii) ground annual or other yearly or periodical sum, *plus* the consideration (if any),

			£								£	s.	d.
does not exceed			500	...	...	...	...	...	...	...	1	0	0
,,	,,	,,	1,000	...	...	...	...	...	...	...	1	10	0
,,	,,	,,	2,000	...	...	...	...	...	...	...	2	10	0
,,	,,	,,	3,000	...	...	...	...	...	...	...	3	15	0
,,	,,	,,	4,000	...	...	...	...	...	...	...	5	0	0
,,	,,	,,	5,000	...	...	...	...	...	...	...	6	10	0
,,	,,	,,	7,000	...	...	...	...	...	...	...	10	0	0
,,	,,	,,	10,000	...	...	...	...	...	...	...	14	0	0
,,	,,	,,	20,000	...	...	...	...	...	...	...	20	0	0
,,	,,	,,	50,000	...	...	...	...	...	...	...	25	0	0
,,	,,	,,	100,000	...	...	...	...	...	...	...	30	0	0
exceeds			100,000	...	...	...	...	...	...	...	60	0	0

NOTE.—Reconveyances *other than* to the original borrower (or his or her Trustees or Executors) are included under the heading "Conveyance", and the fee will be charged on the value of the subjects.

Securities including their constitution, transfer, postponement, corroboration and extinction and advances secured by *ex facie* absolute conveyances (but excluding ground annuals created by bilateral deed).

Where the amount of the security or securities created, transferred, postponed, corroborated or discharged or the amount of the securities affected by any combination of transfer, postponement, corroboration and discharge, or, in the case of a sum payable annually, the capitalised value† of such security or securities created, transferred, postponed, corroborated or discharged at the time (excluding ground annuals created by bilateral deed),

			£								£	s.	d.
does not exceed			500	...	...	...	...	...	...	...		15	0
,,	,,	,,	1,000	...	...	...	...	...	...	...	1	0	0
,,	,,	,,	2,000	...	...	...	...	...	...	...	1	10	0
,,	,,	,,	3,000	...	...	...	...	...	...	...	2	5	0
,,	,,	,,	4,000	...	...	...	...	...	...	...	3	0	0
,,	,,	,,	5,000	...	...	...	...	...	...	...	3	10	0
,,	,,	,,	7,000	...	...	...	...	...	...	...	5	0	0
,,	,,	,,	10,000	...	...	...	...	...	...	...	7	0	0
,,	,,	,,	20,000	...	...	...	...	...	...	...	14	0	0
,,	,,	,,	50,000	...	...	...	...	...	...	...	20	0	0
,,	,,	,,	100,000	...	...	...	...	...	...	...	25	0	0
exceeds			100,000	...	...	...	...	...	...	...	30	0	0

NOTES

1. Where two or more *ex facie* absolute conveyances or reconveyances are recorded in respect of one loan, a fee for the full amount of the loan will be charged on one writ

---

*Calculated at 20 years' purchase.

†Calculated (a) for perpetual annuities at 20 years' purchase and (b) for liferent annuities according to value of expectancy.

and a fee of 15s. will be charged on each of the others. This arrangement *only* applies to security conveyances or reconveyances.

2. In the case of a Discharge and Deed of Restriction, the fee will be charged upon the amount of the Discharge.

3. In the case of a Deed of Restriction there will be a fixed fee of 15s.

	£	s.	d.
Miscellaneous Writs not coming under "Conveyance" or "Securities"			
Where the writ affects an absolute right in any heritable subjects	1	0	0
Where the writ affects a security right in any heritable subjects		15	0

Writs Recorded by Memorandum

	£	s.	d.
Fee for each Memorandum		10	0

Receipts registered in terms of section 34 of the Industrial and Provident Societies Act, 1965 c. 12

	£	s.	d.
For each Receipt (inclusive fee)		5	0

SEARCHING FEES

Searches

For every search for Incumbrances over subjects in one County, included in one Search:—

For any period	Value of subjects not exceeding £500	Value of subjects exceeding £500
	£ s. d.	£ s. d.
Not exceeding 5 years	10 0	18 0
From 6 to 10 years	16 0	1 4 0
„ 11 „ 15 „	1 6 0	1 19 0
„ 16 „ 20 „	1 16 0	2 14 0
„ 21 „ 25 „	2 6 0	3 9 0
„ 26 „ 30 „	2 16 0	4 4 0
„ 31 „ 35 „	3 6 0	4 19 0
„ 36 „ 40 „	3 16 0	5 14 0

In any Search for a period exceeding 40 years a fee of 2s. or 3s. respectively according to value shall be charged for each year or part of a year beyond 40 years.

When a Search shall be required in respect of subjects situated in more than one County, the fees above specified shall be charged for one County calculated on the *cumulo* value of the subjects in the Search, and half fees at the same rate shall be charged for each additional County to which the Search shall apply.

When fees for a Search in the Register of Sasines have been paid in the Record Office no fee will be charged in the Sasine Office in respect of a continuation of such Search by the current Indexes of Persons and/or Places.

Interim Reports

	£	s.	d.
Interim Reports prior to completion of Search		15	0

Reports from Search Sheets

	£	s.	d.
For searching of any Search Sheet affecting one property:—			
Not exceeding 5 years		5	0

1s. additional for each year or part of a year beyond 5 years.
Half fees for each County after the first.
There is no charge for notes made by the party searching the Search Sheet.

B. GENERAL REGISTER OF HORNINGS
REGISTRATION FEES

	£	s.	d.
For each page or part thereof		10	0

C. REGISTER OF INHIBITIONS AND ADJUDICATIONS
REGISTRATION FEES

	£	s.	d.
(a) Registration fee		10	0
(b) For each page of Record		3	0

When fees for a Search in the Register of Inhibitions and Adjudications have been paid in the Record Office no fee will be charged in the Sasine Office in respect of a continuation of such Search in the current year's Index.

SEARCHING FEES

	£	s.	d.
For any period not exceeding 5 years		5	0
For each additional year or part of a year beyond 5 years		1	0

Where the number of names searched against exceeds 6, a further charge of 5s. for each period of 5 years or part thereof shall be made for every 6 additional or fewer names.

D. REGISTER OF ENTAILS
REGISTRATION FEES

	£	s.	d.
For each page or part thereof		10	0
For Certificate of Registration	2	2	0

E. REGISTER OF DEEDS, &c., REGISTER OF PROTESTS, AND REGISTER FOR ENGLISH AND IRISH JUDGMENTS
REGISTRATION FEES

	£	s.	d.
1. Registration of Deeds and Certificates of English and Irish Judgments:—			
(a) Registration or Preservation Fee, each deed or certificate		10	0
(b) For each page of Record		3	0
2. Recording Protest of a Bill or Promissory Note		5	0

F. H.M. CHANCERY

	£	s.	d.
For extracting Decrees of Service (including recording) each page of Extract or part thereof		10	0

NOTE: "Page" in Chancery Registers means a page of Record Volume.

G. REGISTER OF THE GREAT SEAL

	£	s.	d.
For a Charter of Incorporation	25	0	0
For a Charter of Novodamus or other Crown Grant of land...	5	0	0
For a Commission	55	10	0
For each page or part thereof		10	0
For each page of recording or part thereof		5	0

CACHET SEAL

	£	s.	d.
For each impression		5	0

H. REGISTER OF THE PRINCE'S SEAL

	£	s.	d.
For a Charter of Novodamus or other grant of land by the Prince and Steward of Scotland	5	0	0
For each page or part thereof		10	0
For each page of recording or part thereof		5	0

I. REGISTER OF THE QUARTER SEAL

	£	s.	d.
For each Gift of *Ultimus Haeres*	2	0	0
For each page or part thereof		10	0
For each page of recording or part thereof		5	0

J. PRECEPT RECORD (CROWN) AND PRECEPT RECORD (PRINCE AND STEWARD OF SCOTLAND)

	£	s.	d.
For each Writ of Clare Constat or other Grant	5	0	0
For each page or part thereof		10	0
For each page of recording or part thereof		5	0

K. RECORD OF CROWN GRANTS

	£	s.	d.
For each Minute		10	0
For each copy certified in addition to the principal		5	0

FEES APPLICABLE TO ALL REGISTERS
I. INSPECTION FEES

	£	s.	d.
For the inspection of each index, volume (except the Search Sheet), document or process		3	0

II. COPYING FEES

The following fees are in addition, where appropriate, to the fees for registration or preservation, recording in the Record Volume, searching and authentication.

1. For official extracts (except first Extracts of Decrees of Service) certified copies, plain copies, duplicates and excerpts:—

	£	s.	d.
(a) by Xerography, or similar method per sheet		1	0
(b) by Photostat per sheet		3	0
(c) by Typing per sheet		3	0
(d) by Writing per sheet		3	0

2. Authentication:—

	£	s.	d.
For each official extract or certified copy		5	0

III. OTHER SERVICES

	£	s.	d.
1. For a record retransmitted or transmitted to any court, or exhibited therein, at the instance of a party, in accordance with the Rules of Court governing such transmissions or exhibitions	1	5	0
2. For attendance by an officer of the Department at any court to produce a record in evidence, for each day or part of a day, in addition to travelling expenses	10	0	0
3. For each Certificate issued under the Judgments Extension Act 1863 (31 & 32 Vict. c. 54)	1	0	0
4. For each Certificate of Custody that a deed is retained for permanent preservation		10	0

EXPLANATORY NOTE

(This Note is not part of the Act of Sederunt.)

This Act of Sederunt prescribes new fees in the Department of the Registers of Scotland for registration of deeds, searches and other services.

STATUTORY INSTRUMENTS

1968 No. 2062 (S.188)

REGISTERS AND RECORDS, SCOTLAND

Act of Sederunt (Amendment of Fees in the Scottish Record Office) 1968

Made -   -   -   -   *20th December* 1968

Coming into Operation   *1st February* 1969

The Lords of Council and Session, under and by virtue of the powers conferred upon them by section 10 of the Public Records (Scotland) Act 1937(a), as amended by section 1(7) of the Public Registers and Records Act (Scotland) 1948(b), and of all other powers competent to them in that behalf, and with the approval of the Treasury, do hereby enact as follows:—

1. The fees to be charged in the Scottish Record Office for inspection of records, for copies thereof, and for other services relating thereto shall be those set out in the Schedule to this Act of Sederunt.

2. Section 2 of the Act of Sederunt (Amendment of Fees in the Departments of the Registers of Scotland and of the Records of Scotland) 1956(c) and sections 2 and 3 of the Act of Sederunt (Amendment of Fees in the Departments of the Registers of Scotland and of the Records of Scotland) 1962(d) are hereby repealed.

3. This Act of Sederunt may be cited as the Act of Sederunt (Amendment of Fees in the Scottish Record Office) 1968 and shall come into operation on the 1st day of February 1969.

And the Lords appoint this Act of Sederunt to be inserted in the Books of Sederunt.

J. L. Clyde,
I. P. D.

Edinburgh,
20th December 1968.

(a) 1937 c. 43.   (b) 1948 c. 57.
(c) S.I. 1956/530 (1956 II, p.1961).   (d) S.I. 1962/2842 (1962 III, p.4065).

SCHEDULE

I. INSPECTION FEES

		£	s.	d.

1. For the inspection of each volume, document or process 0 3 0

2. For the inspection of minute books and indexes of the Registers of Sasines, Registers of Inhibitions and Adjudications and other public records, and for the inspection of Valuation Rolls, for the following periods:

    not exceeding 1 year 0 5 0

    1—10 years 0 10 0

    11—20 years 0 15 0

    21—40 years 1 0 0

    exceeding 40 years, a further fee at the same rates as above.

Note: Fees are remitted for the inspection of records for historical or literary purposes in terms of section 10 of the Public Records (Scotland) Act 1937.

II. COPYING FEES

1. Reprographic Charges (to which will be added, as appropriate, handling, authentication, and postage and packing charges as below):

    (1) *Copies by Xerography, or similar method:*

    Per sheet 0 1 0

    (2) *Photostat Copies:*

    Negative, per sheet 0 5 0

    Positive, per sheet 0 8 0

    Positive, from exixsting negative, per sheet 0 3 0

    (3) *Microfilms:*

    Standard charge, per exposure 0 0 6

    minimum charge 1 0 0

    Duplicate copies of existing film, per reel of 100 feet 5 0 0

    per foot 0 2 0

    minimum charge 1 0 0

2. Handling Charge:

    Per volume or document, in addition to reprographic charge ... 0 7 0

Note: The handling charge is remitted for 'quick copy' orders, by Xerography or similar method, placed personally in the Search Rooms with documents clearly identified, and where an inspection fee has already been incurred or remitted. The handling charge may also be remitted at the discretion of the Keeper of the Records of Scotland for approved educational or historical purposes.

£ s. d.

3. *Authentication:*

For each Extract or Certified Copy, in addition to reprographic
charge and handling charge 0 5 0

Note: No authentication is given for microfilms or for 'quick copy' orders.

4. Postage and Packing:
Per order 0 1 0

Note: Air-mail postage is charged additionally.

III. OTHER SERVICES

1. For a record retransmitted or transmitted to any court, or exhibited
therein, at the instance of a party, in accordance with the Rules of
Court governing such transmissions or exhibitions 1 5 0

2. For attendance by an officer of the Scottish Record Office at any court
to produce a record in evidence, for each day or part of a day, in
addition to travelling expenses 10 0 0

3. For each Certificate issued under the Judgments Extension Act 1868
(31 & 32 Vict. c.54) 1 0 0

4. For each Certificate of Custody that a deed is retained for permanent
preservation 0 10 0

EXPLANATORY NOTE

(*This note is not part of the Act of Sederunt*)

This Act of Sederunt prescribes new fees in the Scottish Record Office for
inspection of records, for copies thereof, and for other services relating thereto.

STATUTORY INSTRUMENTS

1968 No. 2063

CUSTOMS AND EXCISE

The Anti-Dumping Duty (No. 2) Order 1968

Made - - - -	*30th December* 1968
Laid before the House of Commons - -	*2nd January* 1969
Coming into Operation	*3rd January* 1969

The Board of Trade, in pursuance of the powers conferred upon them by sections 1, 2 and 3 of the Customs Duties (Dumping and Subsidies) Act 1957(**a**), as amended by the Customs Duties (Dumping and Subsidies) Amendment Act 1968(**b**), hereby make the following Order:—

1. This Order may be cited as the Anti-Dumping Duty (No. 2) Order 1968 and shall come into operation on 3rd January 1969.

2.—(1) In this Order—

" flat file " means a file of rectangular cross-section but tapering in width and thickness for approximately that third of its length furthest from the tang, double cut on its two wider sides and single cut on its two narrower sides ;

" hand file " means a file of rectangular cross-section and a uniform width but tapering in thickness for approximately that third of its length furthest from the tang, double cut on its two wider sides, single cut on one of its narrower sides and uncut on the other ; and

references to the length of a file are references to its length along its centre line excluding the tang and any other part above the shoulder.

(2) The provisions of Schedule 3 to this Order shall have effect for the purpose of defining certain cuts of files mentioned in Schedule 1 to this Order.

(3) The Interpretation Act 1889(**c**) shall apply to the interpretation of this Order as it applies to the interpretation of an Act of Parliament.

3. There shall be charged upon the import into the United Kingdom of any goods of a description specified in the second column of Schedule 1 or Schedule 2 hereto (being goods classified in accordance with the Customs Tariff 1959(**d**) under the heading mentioned in the first column in those Schedules) a duty of customs at the relevant rate specified in the third column.

(**a**) 1957 c. 18.   (**b**) 1968 c. 33.   (**c**) 1889 c. 63.   (**d**) See S.I. 1968/679 (1968 I, p. 1519).

4. Section 3 of the Customs Duties (Dumping and Subsidies) Act 1957 (which provides for the giving of relief from duty where goods are shown not to be dumped or where the margin of dumping is shown to be less than the amount of duty payable on them) shall apply in relation to the duty imposed by this Order.

Edmund Dell,
Minister of State,
Board of Trade.

30th December 1968.

SCHEDULE 1

Goods originating in Portugal

Relevant tariff heading	Description of goods	Rate of duty
82.03 (B)	Files and rasps, with or without handles, originating in Portugal:	
	(1) Of a length of 4 inches or less	
	(a) Hand files and flat files	
	(i) Bastard cut or coarser	1s. 6d. per dozen
	(ii) Of a cut finer than bastard ...	4s. 0d. per dozen
	(b) Other	5d. per dozen
	(2) Of a length exceeding 4 inches but not exceeding 6 inches	
	(a) Hand files and flat files	
	(i) Bastard cut or coarser	5s. 6d. per dozen
	(ii) Of a cut finer than bastard ...	9s. 0d. per dozen
	(b) Other	3s. 0d. per dozen
	(3) Of a length exceeding 6 inches but not exceeding 8 inches	
	(a) Hand files and flat files	
	(i) Bastard cut or coarser	11s. 0d. per dozen
	(ii) Of a cut finer than bastard ...	14s. 6d. per dozen
	(b) Other	7s. 0d. per dozen
	(4) Of a length exceeding 8 inches but not exceeding 10 inches	
	(a) Hand files and flat files	
	(i) Bastard cut or coarser	15s. 0d. per dozen
	(ii) Of a cut finer than bastard ...	23s. 0d. per dozen
	(b) Other	13s. 6d. per dozen
	(5) Of a length exceeding 10 inches but not exceeding 12 inches	
	(a) Hand files and flat files	
	(i) Bastard cut or coarser	20s. 6d. per dozen
	(ii) Of a cut finer than bastard ...	30s. 6d. per dozen
	(b) Other	23s. 0d. per dozen
	(6) Exceeding 12 inches in length	
	(a) Hand files and flat files	
	(i) Bastard cut or coarser	25s. 0d. per dozen
	(ii) Of a cut finer than bastard ...	35s. 0d. per dozen
	(b) Other	23s. 6d. per dozen

SCHEDULE 2

Goods originating in Australia

Relevant tariff heading	Description of goods	Rate of duty
82.03 (B)	Files and rasps, with or without handles, originating in Australia:	
	(1) Of a length not exceeding 4 inches ...	4s. 0d. per dozen
	(2) Of a length exceeding 4 inches but not exceeding 6 inches	7s. 6d. per dozen
	(3) Of a length exceeding 6 inches but not exceeding 8 inches	10s. 0d. per dozen
	(4) Of a length exceeding 8 inches but not exceeding 10 inches...	12s. 6d. per dozen
	(5) Of a length exceeding 10 inches but not exceeding 12 inches...	15s. 0d. per dozen
	(6) Of a length exceeding 12 inches	20s. 0d. per dozen

SCHEDULE 3

1. In Schedule 1 to this Order, " bastard cut or coarser " means having not more than the relevant number of up-cuts mentioned in the table set out in this Schedule and " of a cut finer than bastard " means having more than the said relevant number of up-cuts.

Length of file	Number of up-cuts per inch of the centre line of the double cut sides
4 inches or less	40
over 4 inches but not exceeding 6 inches	32
over 6 inches but not exceeding 8 inches	26
over 8 inches but not exceeding 10 inches	24
over 10 inches but not exceeding 12 inches	21
over 12 inches but not exceeding 14 inches	19
over 14 inches but not exceeding 16 inches	18
over 16 inches	17

EXPLANATORY NOTE

(This Note is not part of the Order.)

This Order imposes anti-dumping duties on certain files and rasps of Portuguese or Australian origin.

The rate of the duties varies in the case of different descriptions of files and rasps and the rates in relation to files and rasps originating in Portugal (set out in Schedule 1) are different from those in relation to files and rasps originating in Australia (which are set out in Schedule 2).

The Order applies section 3 of the Customs Duties (Dumping and Subsidies) Act 1957 in relation to the duties. The application of this section allows the Board of Trade to grant relief from duty where they are satisfied that goods on which duty is payable have not been dumped or that the margin of dumping is less than the duty.

STATUTORY INSTRUMENTS

1968 No. 2070

CIVIL AVIATION

The Rules of the Air and Air Traffic Control (Seventh Amendment) Regulations 1968

Made - - - *30th December* 1968

Coming into Operation *9th January* 1969

The Board of Trade, in exercise of their powers under Article 59(1) of the Air Navigation Order 1966(a), as amended (b), and of all other powers enabling them in that behalf, hereby make the following Regulations.

1. These Regulations may be cited as the Rules of the Air and Air Traffic Control (Seventh Amendment) Regulations 1968, and shall come into operation on 9th January 1969.

2. The Interpretation Act 1889(c) applies for the purpose of the interpretation of these Regulations as it applies for the purpose of the interpretation of an Act of Parliament.

3. The Schedule to the Rules of the Air and Air Traffic Control Regulations(d), as amended (e), shall be further amended as follows :

(1) At the end of Rule 20 there shall be added the following proviso :
"Provided that this Rule shall not apply to a helicopter following the Motorway M4 on a route from West Drayton to Osterley Lock." ;

(2) In Rule 28 the following paragraphs shall be substituted for paragraph (3) :

"(3) The commander of the aircraft shall fly in conformity with

(*a*) the air traffic control clearance issued for the flight, as amended by any further instructions given by an air traffic control unit ; and

(*b*) the holding and instrument approach procedures notified in relation to the aerodrome of destination, unless he is otherwise authorised by the air traffic control unit there :

Provided that he shall not be required to comply with the foregoing provisions of this paragraph if:

(i) he is able to fly in uninterrupted Visual Meteorological Conditions for so long as he remains in controlled airspace, and

(ii) he has informed the appropriate air traffic control unit of his intention to continue the flight in compliance with Visual Flight Rules and has requested that unit to cancel his flight plan.

(3A) If for the purpose of avoiding immediate danger any departure is made from the provisions of paragraph (3) of this Rule (as is permitted by Article 59(3) of the Order) the commander of the aircraft shall, in

---

(a) S.I. 1966/1184 (1966 III, p. 3073).
(b) There is no relevant amending instrument.
(c) 1889 c. 63.   (d) S.I. 1966/1257 (1966 III, p. 3431).
(e) The relevant amending instrument is S.I. 1968/1837 (1968 III, p. 4846).

addition to causing particulars to be given in accordance with Article 59(4) of the Order, as soon as possible inform the appropriate air traffic control unit of the deviation.";

(3) In Rule 38 the following paragraph shall be substituted for paragraph (5):

"(5) In relation to Liverpool Airport the following special rules shall apply:

Except as it may otherwise be authorised by the air traffic control unit at the aerodrome:

(a) an aircraft shall not fly within the relevant airspace during the notified hours of watch of the air traffic control unit at the aerodrome unless the commander of the aircraft before so flying obtains the permission of the air traffic control unit at the aerodrome and informs the air traffic control unit, on the notified radio frequency appropriate to the circumstances, of the aircraft's position, level and track ; and

(b) while the aircraft is within the relevant airspace at any time during the said hours of watch the commander of the aircraft shall cause a continuous watch to be maintained on that frequency and comply with any instructions which the air traffic control unit at the aerodrome may give in the particular case.

For the purposes of this paragraph the "relevant airspace" means the airspace from the surface to 1,250 feet above mean sea level within the area defined by a straight line joining the points 53°19'00"N, 02°37'00"W and 53°22'00"N, 02°39'00"W and thence by tangents from those points to the circle with radius of six nautical miles centred on 53°20'20"N, 02°53'00"W." ;

(4) In Rule 60(1)(b) for "becomes pregnant" there shall be substituted "in the case of a woman, has reason to believe that she is pregnant,".

J. H. Riddoch,
An Under Secretary
of the Board of Trade.

30th December 1968.

EXPLANATORY NOTE

(This Note is not part of the Regulations.)

These Regulations further amend the Schedule to the Rules of the Air and Air Traffic Control Regulations 1966. In addition to some minor and drafting amendments the following changes are made:

(1) The right-hand traffic rule is amended so as not to apply to helicopters flying on a route following the Motorway M4 (Rule 20).

(2) The Instrument Flight Rules are amended so as to provide that the commander of an aircraft need not comply with the notified holding and instrument approach procedures at the destination aerodrome if he is otherwise authorised by the air traffic control unit there. (Rule 28(3)).

(3) The Zone centred on Liverpool Airport in which Special Rules apply, is extended. (Rule 38(5)).

(4) A drafting amendment is made in the requirement that a female air traffic controller must inform the Board of her pregnancy. (Rule 60(1)).

STATUTORY INSTRUMENTS

1968 No. 2071

PENSIONS

The Superannuation (Public and Judicial Offices) (Amendment) Rules 1968

Made - - -		*24th December* 1968
Laid before Parliament		*7th January* 1969
Coming into Operation		*8th January* 1969

The Minister for the Civil Service, in exercise of the powers conferred on him by section 38 of the Superannuation Act 1965(**a**) and article 2(1)(*c*) of the Minister for the Civil Service Order 1968(**b**), and of all other powers enabling him in that behalf, hereby makes the following Rules :—

1. The Superannuation (Public Offices) Rules 1967(**c**) shall be amended by substituting, in Rule 1(3)(*a*) thereof (which provides that a person shall be deemed to have been continuously employed in two public offices if he was employed in the first public office in a pensionable capacity and he became employed in the second public office within 31 days of ceasing to be employed in the first), for the figures "31" the figures "32".

2. The Superannuation (Judicial Offices) Rules 1968(**d**) shall be amended—

(*a*) by substituting, in Rule 1(3) thereof (which provides that a person shall be deemed to have been continuously employed in two judicial offices if he became employed in the second office within 31 days of ceasing to be employed in the first), for the figures "31" the figures "32"; and

(*b*) by substituting for paragraph (1) of Rule 4 thereof (which defines the expression "judicial office") the following paragraph : —

"(1) In these Rules, unless the context otherwise requires, the expression "judicial office" means any office which—

(*a*) is a public office within the meaning of section 39 of the Superannuation Act 1965, and

(*b*) is listed, or treated by virtue of any enactment as listed, in Schedule 1 to the Administration of Justice (Pensions) Act 1950(**e**),

but does not, in relation to any person, include any such office if the Superannuation Act 1965 applies to him in respect of his service in that office."

3. The Interpretation Act 1889(**f**) shall apply for the interpretation of these Rules as it applies for the interpretation of an Act of Parliament.

4. These Rules may be cited as the Superannuation (Public and Judicial Offices) (Amendment) Rules 1968, and shall come into operation on 8th January 1969.

(a) 1965 c.74.
(b) S.I. 1968/1656 (1968 III, p. 4485).
(c) S.I. 1967/364 (1967 I, p.1243).
(d) S.I. 1968/1363 (1968 II, p. 3792).
(e) 1950 c.11 (14 & 15 Geo. 6).
(f) 1889 c.63.

Given under the official seal cf the Minister for Civil Service on 24th December 1968.

(L.S.)

J. E. Herbecq,
Authorised by the Minister
for the Civil Service.

EXPLANATORY NOTE

(This Note is not part of the Rules.)

These Rules amend the Superannuation (Public Offices) Rules 1967 and the Superannuation (Judicial Offices) Rules 1968, which make provision for pensions payable to persons who have served in two or more public offices and two or more judicial offices respectively.

For the removal of doubt, both sets of Rules, by increasing from 31 days to 32 days the period within which persons to whom the Rules apply must, after ceasing to be employed in one office, become employed in another office, ensure that an interval of up to a full calendar month may be ignored.

In the 1968 Rules the definition of "judicial office" is amended so as to make it clear that the definition covers only judicial offices which are public offices within the meaning of s.39 of the Superannuation Act 1965.

STATUTORY INSTRUMENTS

1968 No. 2075

SEA FISHERIES

BOATS AND METHODS OF FISHING

The Fishing Nets (North-East Atlantic) Order 1968

Made - -	*30th December* 1968
Laid before Parliament	*7th January* 1969
Coming into Operation	*8th January* 1969

The Minister of Agriculture, Fisheries and Food and the Secretaries of State for Scotland and the Home Department (being the Secretaries of State respectively concerned with the sea-fishing industry in Scotland and Northern Ireland) in exercise of the powers conferred upon them by sections 3 and 15 of the Sea Fish (Conservation) Act 1967(a) and of all other powers enabling them in that behalf hereby make the following Order :—

Citation and Commencement

1. This Order may be cited as the Fishing Nets (North-East Atlantic) Order 1968 and shall come into operation on 8th January 1969.

Interpretation

2.—(1) In this Order—

"the area dividing line" means a line drawn east from the meridian of 44° west longitude along the parallel of 59° north latitude to the meridian of 42° west longitude, thence south to the parallel of 48° north latitude, thence east to the meridian of 18° west longitude, thence north to the parallel of 60° north latitude, thence east to the meridian of 15° west longitude, thence north to the parallel of 62° north latitude, thence east to the meridian of 10° west longitude, thence north to the parallel of 63° north latitude, thence east to the meridian of 4° west longitude, thence south to the parallel of 62° north latitude, thence east to the meridian of 51° east longitude ;

"British Sea-Fishery Officer" means any person who is for the time being a British Sea-Fishery Officer by virtue of section 11(2) of the Sea Fisheries Act 1883(b) as amended or extended by or under any subsequent enactment ;

"the Faroes area" means the area bounded by a line drawn east from the meridian of 15° west longitude along the parallel of 60° north latitude to the meridian of 5° west longitude, thence north to the parallel of 60° 30′ north latitude, thence east to the meridian of 4° west longitude, thence north to the parallel of 63° north latitude, thence west to the meridian of 10° west longitude, thence south to the parallel of 62° north latitude, thence west to the meridian of 15° west longitude, thence south to the parallel of 60° north latitude ;

(a) 1967 c. 84.   (b) 1883 c. 22.

"foreign fishing boat" has the meaning assigned to it by the Fishery Limits Act 1964(a) ;

"fishing boat" means a vessel of whatever size and in whatever way propelled which is for the time being employed in sea-fishing or in the sea-fishing service ;

"the Irish Sea" means the area bounded on the north by the parallel of 54° 38′ north latitude, on the east by the western coasts of England and Wales, on the south by the parallel of 51° north latitude and on the west by the meridian of 7° west longitude and the eastern coasts of the Republic of Ireland and Northern Ireland ;

"net" means any net constructed to take fish whilst being towed or hauled at or near the bottom of the sea by or from a fishing boat ;

"topside chafer" means a piece of netting attached to the upperside of the cod-end of a net for the purpose of preventing or reducing wear and tear.

(2) The Interpretation Act 1889(b) shall apply to the interpretation of this Order as it applies to the interpretation of an Act of Parliament, and as if this Order and the Order hereby revoked were Acts of Parliament.

Revocation of Previous Orders

3. The Sea-Fishing Industry (Nets on British and Foreign Fishing Boats) Order 1967(c) is hereby revoked.

Areas in relation to which this Order has application

4. This Order has application in relation to those areas of the Atlantic and Arctic Oceans and seas adjacent to those oceans which lie north of the parallel of 36° north latitude, between the meridians of 42° west longitude and 51° east longitude and north of 59° north latitude between 44° west longitude and 42° west longitude (but excluding the Mediterranean and Baltic Seas and Belts lying to the south and east of lines drawn from Hasenore Head, Denmark, to Gniben Point, Denmark, from Korshage, Denmark, to Spodsbierg, Denmark and from Gilbierg Head, Denmark, to Kullen, Sweden).

Sizes of Mesh of Nets

5.—(1) Except as hereinafter provided, there shall not be carried, in any British fishing boat registered in the United Kingdom for the purpose of fishing for sea-fish in any of the waters referred to in the first column of Schedule 1 to this Order any net or part of a net of a type specified in the second column of Schedule 1 opposite the reference to the said waters unless it has in all its parts meshes of such dimensions that when any mesh is stretched diagonally lengthwise of the net a flat gauge 2 millimetres thick, and of a width specified in the third column of Schedule 1 opposite the reference to that type of net, will pass easily through the mesh whether the net is wet or dry.

(2) Except as hereinafter provided, there shall not be carried, by any foreign fishing boat within the fishery limits of the British Islands adjacent to the United Kingdom for the purpose of fishing for sea-fish in any of the waters in relation to which this Order has application, any net or part of a net of a type specified in the first column of Schedule 2

(a) 1964 c. 72. (b) 1889 c. 63.
(c) 1967/1859 (1967 III, p. 4991).

to this Order unless it has in all its parts meshes of such dimensions that when any mesh is stretched diagonally lengthwise of the net a flat gauge 2 millimetres thick, and of a width specified in the second column of Schedule 2 opposite the reference to that type of net, will pass easily through the mesh whether the net is wet or dry.

Obstruction of mesh

6.—(1) Except as hereinafter provided, there shall not be carried in—

(a) any British fishing boat registered in the United Kingdom, or

(b) any foreign fishing boat within the fishery limits of the British Islands adjacent to the United Kingdom,

for the purpose of fishing for sea-fish in any waters to which this Order has application, any net having a covering of canvas or other material attached to it, or in respect of which any artifice may have been employed in such a manner that the mesh in any part of the net is obstructed or otherwise diminished in effect.

(2) Nothing in this Order shall be deemed to prohibit the attachment to the underside of the cod-end of a net of any canvas, netting or other material for the purpose of preventing or reducing wear and tear.

Topside Chafers

7. There shall not be carried in any British fishing boat registered in the United Kingdom any net to which a topside chafer is attached unless the net in question is a trawl net, the attachment is made for the purpose of fishing in waters north of the area dividing line, and the chafer complies with one of the following specifications :—

(1) a piece of netting rectangular in shape having in all its parts meshes the dimensions of which are not less that those of the meshes of the cod-end whether the netting and the cod-end respectively be wet or dry :

provided that :—

(a) the piece of netting shall in width be at least one and a half times the width of the part of the cod-end which is covered by it, such widths being measured at right angles to the long axis of the cod-end, and

(b) the piece of netting shall not be fastened to the cod-end except along the forward and lateral edges of the piece of netting and shall be so fastened that

(i) if there is a splitting strop, the piece of netting begins at a distance of not more than four of the meshes to which it is attached forward of the splitting strop and ends at a distance of not less than four of such meshes forward of the cod-line mesh, or

(ii) if there is no splitting strop, the piece of netting extends for not more than one-third of the length of the cod-end and ends at a distance of not less than four of the meshes of the net to which it is attached forward of the cod-line mesh ; or

(2) pieces of netting having in all their parts meshes the dimensions of which are not less than those of the meshes of the cod-end whether the netting and the cod-end respectively be wet or dry :
provided that :—

(*a*) each piece of netting

(i) is fastened by its forward edge only across the cod-end at right angles to the long axis of the cod-end ;

(ii) is of a width of at least the width of the cod-end (such width being measured at right angles to the long axis of the cod-end at the point of attachment), and

(iii) is not more than ten meshes long ; and

(*b*) the aggregate length of all the pieces of netting so attached does not exceed two-thirds of the length of the cod-end ; or

(3) a piece of netting made of the same material as the cod-end, having in all its parts meshes whereof the dimensions are twice the dimensions of the meshes of the cod-end, whether the netting and the cod-end respectively be wet or dry, and fastened to the cod-end along the forward, lateral and rear edges only of the netting, in such a way that each mesh of the piece of netting coincides with four meshes of the cod-end.

Defences—British Fishing Boats

8. In any proceedings in respect of a contravention of Article 5(1) of this Order it shall be a sufficient defence to prove that the net to which the proceedings relate :—

(1) was being carried solely for the purpose of fishing in waters situated north of the area dividing line for mackerel, clupeoid fish, sand-eels (Ammodytes), Norway pout (Gadus esmarkii), smelts, eels, great weevers (Trachinus draco), capelin (Mallotus villosus), blue whiting (Gadus poutassou), horse mackerel (Trachurus trachurus), Polar Cod, (Boreogadus saida), shrimps, prawns, nephrops or molluscs other than squids ; or

(2) had in no part of its cod-end meshes of such dimensions that when any mesh was stretched diagonally lengthwise of the net a flat gauge of 50 mm. broad and 2 mm. thick would pass easily through it whether the net was wet or dry and was being carried solely for the purpose of fishing :—

(*a*) for mackerel, clupeoid fish, sand-eels (Ammodytes), Norway pout (Gadus esmarkii), smelts, eels, great weevers (Trachinus draco), capelin (Mallotus villosus), Polar Cod (Boreogadus saida), shrimps, prawns or molluscs other than squids in waters south of the area dividing line, or

(*b*) for horse mackerel (Trachurus trachurus) in waters south of the area dividing line and north of the parallel of 48° north latitude, or

(*c*) for blue whiting (Gadus poutassou) in waters south of the area dividing line and north of the parallel of 48° north latitude other than such part of those waters as lies between the parallels of 52° 30′ north latitude and 48° north latitude and between the meridians of 7° west longitude and 18° west longitude, or

(*d*) for Nephrops norvegicus (commonly known as Norway lobster or Dublin Bay prawn) in the Irish Sea, and that none of the sea-fish taken in the course of the voyage on which the net to which the proceedings relate was carried, was landed, or was to be landed, at a place other than one bordering upon the Irish Sea ; or

(3) (*a*) had in all its parts meshes of such dimensions that when any mesh was stretched diagonally lengthwise of the net a flat gauge 60 mm. broad and 2 mm. thick would pass easily through it whether the net was wet or dry, and

(*b*) was carried solely in that part of the Irish Sea which lies between the parallels of 53° and 54° 30′ north latitude and west of the meridian of 5° 15′ west longitude for the purpose of fishing for whiting, and

(*c*) was carried in a fishing boat operating from and landing its catch at a port or place bordering upon the said part of the Irish Sea.

Defences—Foreign Fishing Boats

9. In any proceedings in respect of a contravention of Article 5(2) of this Order it shall be a sufficient defence to prove that the net to which the proceedings relate :—

(*a*) had in no part of its cod-end meshes of such dimensions that when any mesh was stretched diagonally lengthwise of the net a flat gauge 50 mm. broad and 2 mm. thick would pass easily through it whether the net was wet or dry, and that it was being carried solely for the purpose of fishing for mackerel, clupeoid fish, sand-eels (Ammodytes), Norway pout (Gadus esmarkii), smelts, eels, great weevers (Trachinus draco), capelin (Mallotus villosus), horse mackerel (Trachurus trachurus), blue whiting (Gadus poutassou), Polar Cod (Boreogadus saida), shrimps, prawns, nephrops or molluscs, or

(*b*) being a net of a type specified in the first column of Schedule 3, had in all its parts meshes of such dimensions that when any mesh was stretched diagonally lengthwise of the net a flat gauge 2 mm. thick and of a width specified in the second column of Schedule 3 opposite the reference to that type of net would pass easily through the mesh whether the net was wet or dry, and that it was being carried solely for the purpose of fishing south of the parallel of 48° north latitude.

Powers of British Sea-Fishery Officers

10. For the purpose of enforcing the provisions of this Order a British Sea-Fishery Officer may :—

(1) with respect to any British fishing boat registered in the United Kingdom wherever it may be and with respect to any foreign fishing boat within the fishery limits of the British Islands adjacent to the United Kingdom

(*a*) go on board the boat ;

(*b*) examine all fishing implements belonging to the boat ;

(*c*) make any examination or inquiry which he deems necessary to ascertain whether any contravention of the provisions of this Order has been committed ;

(2) with respect only to a foreign fishing boat within the fishery limits of the British Islands adjacent to the United Kingdom when it appears to him that a contravention of the provisions of this Order has been committed, without summons, warrant or other process take the offender and the boat to which he belongs to the nearest or most convenient port and bring him before a competent court and detain him and the boat in the port until the alleged contravention has been adjudicated upon.

In witness whereof the Official Seal of the Minister of Agriculture, Fisheries and Food is hereunto affixed on 17th December 1968.

(L.S.)

Cledwyn Hughes,
Minister of Agriculture,
Fisheries and Food.

Given under the seal of the Secretary of State for Scotland on 19th December 1968.

(L.S.)

William Ross,
Secretary of State for Scotland.

Given under the Hand of the Secretary of State for the Home Department on 30th December 1968.

James Callaghan,
Secretary of State for the
Home Department.

SCHEDULE 1

Article 5(1)

Column 1	Column 2	Column 3
Waters	Net	Appropriate width of gauge
(a) Waters of the areas north of the area dividing line	(1) Seine net	110 millimetres
	(2) Such part of any trawl net as is made of cotton, hemp, polyamide fibres or polyester fibres	120 millimetres
	(3) Such part of any trawl net as is made of any other material	130 millimetres
(b) Waters of the Faroes area	(1) Seine net	95 millimetres
	(2) Such part of any trawl net as is made of manila or sisal	100 millimetres
	(3) Such part of any trawl net as is made of any other material	95 millimetres
(c) All other waters of the areas in relation to which this Order has effect	(1) Seine net, or such part of any trawl net as is made of single twine and contains no manila or sisal	70 millimetres
	(2) Such part of any trawl net as is made of double twine and contains no manila or sisal	75 millimetres
	(3) Such part of any trawl net as made of manila or sisal	80 millimetres

SCHEDULE 2

Article 5(2)

Column 1	Column 2
Net	Appropriate width of gauge
(1) Seine net, or such part of any trawl net as is made of single twine and contains no manila or sisal	70 millimetres
(2) Such part of any trawl net as is made of double twine and contains no manila or sisal	75 millimetres
(3) Such part of any trawl net as is made of manila or sisal	80 millimetres

SCHEDULE 3

Article 9

Column 1	Column 2
Net	Appropriate width of gauge
(1) Such part of any net as is made of single twine synthetic fibre	60 millimetres
(2) Such part of any net as is made of double twine synthetic fibre	65 millimetres
(3) Such part of any net as is made of manila or sisal	70 millimetres

EXPLANATORY NOTE

(This Note is not part of the Order.)

This Order supersedes the Sea-Fishing Industry (Nets on British and Foreign Fishing Boats) Order 1967. It prescribes minimum sizes of mesh for the fishing nets carried by registered British fishing boats for fishing in areas specified in the Order and by foreign fishing boats within the fishery limits of the British Islands adjacent to the United Kingdom.

The principal changes are:—

1. Polar cod is added to the category of fish for the catching of which the use of a small mesh net is permitted.

2. The minimum permissible sizes of mesh in nets carried by foreign vessels within United Kingdom limits for use in fishing in certain southern waters are varied according to the materials used in the construction of the nets.

3. The Order modifies the requirements in relation to attachments to nets.

STATUTORY INSTRUMENTS

1968 No. 2076

SEA FISHERIES

LANDING AND SALE OF SEA FISH

The Immature Cod and Haddock (Distant Waters) Order 1968

Made -	-	-	-	*30th December* 1968
Laid before Parliament				*7th January* 1969
Coming into Operation				*8th January* 1969

The Minister of Agriculture, Fisheries and Food and the Secretaries of State for Scotland and the Home Department (being the Secretaries of State respectively concerned with the sea fishing industry in Scotland and Northern Ireland) in exercise of the powers conferred upon them by section 6 of the Sea Fish (Conservation) Act 1967(**a**) and of all other powers enabling them in that behalf, and after consultation with the Board of Trade, hereby make the following Order:—

1. This Order may be cited as the Immature Cod and Haddock (Distant Waters) Order 1968 and shall come in operation on 8th January 1969.

2.—(1) In this Order—

"length" means the length of the whole fish measured from tip of snout to extreme end of tail fin;

"the specified waters" means the waters of the Atlantic and Arctic Oceans which lie to the north of a line drawn east from the meridian of 44° west longitude along the parallel of 59° north latitude to the meridian of 42° west longitude, thence south to the parallel of 48° north latitude, thence east to the meridian of 18° west longitude, thence north to the parallel of 60° north latitude, thence east to the meridian of 5° west longitude, thence north to the parallel of 60° 30′ north latitude, thence east to the meridian of 4° west longitude, thence north to the parallel of 62° north latitude, thence east to the meridian of 51° east longitude;

(2) The Interpretation Act 1889(**b**) shall apply for the interpretation of this Order as it applies for the interpretation of an Act of Parliament, and as if this Order and the Orders hereby revoked were Acts of Parliament.

3. The Sea-Fishing Industry (Landing of Immature Cod and Haddock) Order 1964(**c**) and the Sea-Fishing Industry (Landing of Immature Cod and Haddock) (Variation) Order 1964(**d**) are hereby revoked.

4. The landing in the United Kingdom of sea fish of the following descriptions, being fish caught in the specified waters, is hereby prohibited:—

Cod (Gadus morhua) of a length of 30 centimetres and over but less than 34 centimetres; and

Haddock (Melanogrammus aeglefinus) of a length of 27 centimetres and over but less than 31 centimetres.

(a) 1967 c. 84.
(c) S.I. 1964/422 (1964 I, p. 706).
(b) 1889 c. 63.
(d) S.I. 1964/1808 (1964 III, p. 3940).

In witness whereof the Official Seal of the Minister of Agriculture, Fisheries and Food is hereunto affixed on 18th December 1968.

(L.S.)   *Cledwyn Hughes,*

Minister of Agriculture, Fisheries and Food.

Given under the Seal of the Secretary of State for Scotland on 19th December 1968.

(L.S.)   *William Ross,*

Secretary of State for Scotland.

Given under the Hand of the Secretary of State for the Home Department on 30th December 1968.

James Callaghan,

Secretary of State for the Home Department.

EXPLANATORY NOTE

(This Note is not part of the Order.)

This Order supersedes the Sea-Fishing Industry (Landing of Immature Cod and Haddock) Order 1964 as varied by the Sea-Fishing Industry (Landing of Immature Cod and Haddock) (Variation) Order 1964. It prohibits the landing in the United Kingdom of cod and haddock between specified lengths caught in defined waters. (The landing of cod and haddock below the lower specified lengths is prohibited by the Immature Sea-Fish Order 1968 (1968, No. 1618).)

The lengths specified in this Order are the same as those prescribed in the 1964 Orders but the defined waters cover a larger area of the North Atlantic, including the Faroes area.

STATUTORY INSTRUMENTS

1968 No. 2077

PLANT BREEDERS' RIGHTS

The Plant Breeders' Rights (Applications in Designated Countries) Order 1968

Made - - - -	*30th December* 1968
Coming into Operation	*9th January* 1969

The Minister of Agriculture, Fisheries and Food, the Secretary of State for Scotland and the Secretary of State for the Home Department (being the Secretary of State concerned with agriculture in Northern Ireland), acting jointly, in exercise of the powers conferred on them by paragraph 2(7) of Part I of Schedule 2 to the Plant Varieties and Seeds Act 1964(a), as extended to Northern Ireland by the Plant Varieties and Seeds (Northern Ireland) Order 1964(b), and of all other powers enabling them in that behalf, hereby make the following Order:—

Citation, commencement and interpretation

1.—(1) This Order may be cited as the Plant Breeders' Rights (Applications in Designated Countries) Order 1968 and shall come into operation on 9th January 1969.

(2) The Interpretation Act 1889(c) shall apply to the interpretation of this Order as it applies to the interpretation of an Act of Parliament.

Designated countries in respect of applications for plant breeders' rights

2. The Netherlands, the Federal Republic of Germany and Denmark are hereby designated as countries to which paragraph 2 of Part I of Schedule 2 to the Plant Varieties and Seeds Act 1964 (which paragraph provides that an application for a grant of plant breeders' rights which is made in a country to which the paragraph applies shall, if the conditions of the paragraph are satisfied, be treated as if made under the Plant Varieties and Seeds Act 1964) applies.

In Witness whereof the official seal of the Minister of Agriculture, Fisheries and Food is hereunto affixed on 17th December 1968.

(L.S) *Cledwyn Hughes,*
Minister of Agriculture, Fisheries and Food.

Given under the seal of the Secretary of State for Scotland on 19th December 1968.

(L.S) *William Ross,*
Secretary of State for Scotland.

Given under the hand of the Secretary of State for the Home Department on 30th December 1968.

James Callaghan,
Secretary of State for the Home Department.

(a) 1964 c. 14.
(b) S.I. 1964/1574 (1964 III, p. 3543).
(c) 1889 c. 63.

EXPLANATORY NOTE
(This Note is not part of the Order.)

Paragraph 2 of Part I of Schedule 2 to the Plant Varieties and Seeds Act 1964 enables an application for a grant of plant breeders' rights, made in a country to which that paragraph applies, to be treated as if made in the United Kingdom. This Order designates, as countries to which the paragraph applies, the Netherlands, the Federal Republic of Germany and Denmark.

APPENDIX
OF CERTAIN INSTRUMENTS
NOT REGISTERED AS S.I.

Orders in Council,
Letters Patent
and Royal Instructions

relating to the Constitutions etc. of
Overseas Territories or to appeals to the Judicial
Committee,

Royal Proclamations, etc.

CARIBBEAN AND NORTH ATLANTIC TERRITORIES

The British Honduras Letters Patent (No. 2) 1968

LETTERS PATENT passed under the Great Seal of the Realm amending the British Honduras Letters Patent 1964.

Dated: 26th September, 1968.

ELIZABETH THE SECOND, by the Grace of God of the United Kingdom of Great Britain and Northern Ireland and of Our other Realms and Territories Queen, Head of the Commonwealth, Defender of the Faith.

TO ALL TO WHOM THESE PRESENTS SHALL COME, GREETING!

Know Ye that We have declared and do hereby declare Our will and pleasure as follows:—

Citation, construction and commencement. 1.—(1) These Our Letters may be cited as the British Honduras Letters Patent (No. 2) 1968 and shall be included among the Letters Patent that may be cited together as the British Honduras Letters Patent 1964 and 1968.

(2) These Our Letters shall be construed as one with the British Honduras Letters Patent 1964(a) (hereinafter called " the principal Letters Patent "), as amended by the British Honduras Letters Patent 1968(b).

(3) These Our Letters shall be published in the Gazette and shall come into operation upon the date of such publication(c).

Amendment of Article 11 of principal Letters Patent. 2. Paragraph (5)(b) of Article 11 of the principal Letters Patent is revoked and the following substituted :—

"(b) if, at the first sitting of the House of Representatives after a general election, the holder of the office is not a member of either House of the National Assembly."

Insertion of new Article 17A in principal Letters Patent. 3.—(1) The principal Letters Patent are amended by the insertion therein immediately after Article 17 of the following Article :—

"Parliamentary Secretaries. 17A.—(1) The Governor, acting in accordance with the advice of the Premier, may appoint Parliamentary Secretaries from among the members of the two Houses of the National Assembly to assist Ministers in the performance of their duties :

Provided that if occasion arises for making an appointment while the Legislature is dissolved, a person who was a member of either House of the National Assembly immediately before the dissolution may be appointed as a Parliamentary Secretary.

(2) The provisions of paragraphs (5) and (6) of Article 11 of these Our Letters shall apply to the office of a Parliamentary Secretary as they apply to the office of a Minister."

(a) S.I. 1964 I, p. 1136.   (b) S.I. 1968 II, p. 4104.   (c) Day published 3.1.69.

4. Article 18 of the principal Letters Patent is amended by the deletion of the word " Minister " and the substitution therefor of the words " Minister or Parliamentary Secretary ".

Amendment of Article 18 of principal Letters Patent.

5. We do hereby reserve to Ourself full power and authority to amend or revoke these Presents.

Power reserved to Her Majesty.

In Witness whereof We have caused these Our Letters to be made Patent.

Witness Ourself at Westminster the twenty-sixth day of September in the seventeenth year of Our Reign.

By Warrant under The Queen's Sign Manual.

Dobson.

BY THE QUEEN

A PROCLAMATION

ALTERING CERTAIN DAYS APPOINTED FOR BANK HOLIDAYS
IN THE YEAR 1969

ELIZABETH R.

Whereas We consider it inexpedient that in Scotland the first Monday in May, or in England and Wales the first Monday in August, should be Bank Holidays in the year 1969:

Now, therefore, We, in exercise of the powers conferred on Us by section 5 of the Bank Holidays Act 1871(**a**), section 3 of the Holidays Extension Act 1875(**b**), section 1 of the Revenue Offices (Scotland) Holidays Act 1880(**c**), and section 3(3) of the Customs and Excise Act 1952(**d**), do hereby, by and with the advice of Our Privy Council, declare and appoint as follows:—

1. In Scotland in the year 1969 the first Monday in May shall not be a Bank Holiday, and instead the last Monday in May shall be a Bank Holiday.

2. In England and Wales in the year 1969 the first Monday in August shall not be a Bank Holiday, and instead the first Monday in September shall be a Bank Holiday.

3. In this Proclamation the expression " Bank Holiday " shall include a public holiday in the Inland Revenue Offices and a holiday in the Customs and Excise.

Given at Our Court at Buckingham Palace, this twenty-second day of November in the year of our Lord one thousand nine hundred and sixty-eight, and in the seventeenth year of Our Reign.

GOD SAVE THE QUEEN

(**a**) 34 & 35 Vict. c. 17.   (**b**) 38 & 39 Vict. c. 13.
(**c**) 43 & 44 Vict. c. 17.   (**d**) 15 & 16 Geo. 6 & 1 Eliz. 2. c. 44.

ROAD TRAFFIC

The Breath Test Device (Approval) (Scotland) Order 1968

In terms of section 7(1) of the Road Safety Act 1967(a) I, the Right Honourable William Ross, one of Her Majesty's Principal Secretaries of State, do by this order approve, for the purpose of breath tests as defined in the said section 7(1), the type of device described in the Schedule hereto.

William Ross,
One of Her Majesty's Principal
Secretaries of State.

St. Andrew's House,
  Edinburgh.

16th December, 1968.

SCHEDULE

The device known as the Alcotest, comprising an indicator tube (marked with the name " Alcotest "), mouth piece and measuring bag, and supplied to police forces in Scotland in a container marked with the name "ALCOTEST®80".

(a) 1967 c. 30.

BY THE QUEEN

A PROCLAMATION

CALLING IN ALL HALF-CROWNS

ELIZABETH R.

Whereas under section eleven of the Coinage Act 1870(a) We have power, with the advice of Our Privy Council, by Proclamation to call in coins of any date or denomination :

And Whereas it now appears to Us desirable to call in all half-crowns :

We, therefore, with the advice of Our Privy Council and in pursuance of section eleven of the Coinage Act 1870, do hereby call in by the thirty-first day of December One thousand nine hundred and sixty-nine all half-crowns and direct that after such thirty-first day of December One thousand nine hundred and sixty-nine such coins shall not be current or legal tender within Our United Kingdom of Great Britain and Northern Ireland.

Given at Our Court at Buckingham Palace, this twentieth day of December, in the year of our Lord One thousand nine hundred and sixty-eight, and in the seventeenth year of Our Reign.

GOD SAVE THE QUEEN

(a) 1870 c. 10.

BY THE QUEEN

A PROCLAMATION

DETERMINING THE SPECIFICATIONS AND DESIGN FOR, AND GIVING CURRENCY TO, A FIFTY NEW PENCE COIN

ELIZABETH R.

Whereas by virtue of section 2 (3) of the Decimal Currency Act 1967(a) We have power, with the advice of Our Privy Council, by Proclamation under section 11 of the Coinage Act 1870(b), to determine the weight and composition of coins of the new decimal currency to be made at Our Mint and to determine the remedy to be allowed in the making of such coins:

And Whereas under section 11 of the said Act of 1870 We have power by Proclamation to determine the dimension of and design for any coin:

And Whereas by virtue of section 2 (4) of the said Act of 1967 We have power, by Proclamation under section 11 of the said Act of 1870, to direct that coins made in accordance with section 2 of the said Act of 1967 may be issued for use before the fifteenth day of February One thousand nine hundred and seventy-one (being the day appointed under section 1 of that Act) as current coins of such denominations as may be specified :

And Whereas it appears to Us desirable to order that a new coin of cupro-nickel of the denomination of fifty new pence should be made at Our Mint and should be issued for use before the fifteenth day of February One thousand nine hundred and seventy-one as a current coin of the denomination of ten shillings :

We, therefore, in pursuance of section 11 of the Coinage Act 1870, as extended by section 2 (3) and (4) of the Decimal Currency Act 1967, and of all other powers enabling Us in that behalf, do hereby, by and with the advice of Our Privy Council, proclaim, direct and ordain as follows :—

1.—(1) A new coin of cupro-nickel of the denomination of fifty new pence shall be made, being a coin of a standard weight of 13·5 grammes, a standard diameter of 30 millimetres and a standard composition of seventy-five per cent copper and twenty-five per cent nickel, and being in the shape of an equilateral curve heptagon.

(2) In the making of the said coin a remedy (that is, a variation from the standard weight, diameter or composition specified above) shall be allowed of an amount not exceeding the following, that is to say :—

(*a*) a variation from the said standard weight of an amount per coin (measured as the average of a sample of not more than one kilogramme of the coin) of 0·08 grammes ; and

(*b*) a variation from the said standard diameter of 0·1 millimetres per coin ; and

(*c*) a variation from the said standard composition of one per cent.

2. The design for the said coin shall be as follows :—

Every fifty new pence shall have for the obverse impression Our effigy with the inscription " D·G·REG·F·D·ELIZABETH II " and the date of the year, and for the reverse a figure of Britannia, seated beside a lion, with a

---

(**a**) 1967 c. 47.   (**b**) 1870 c. 10.

shield resting against her right side, holding a trident in her right hand and an olive branch in her left hand ; and the inscription " 50 NEW PENCE ". The coin shall have a plain edge.

3. The said coin may be issued for use before the fifteenth day of February One thousand nine hundred and seventy-one as a current cupro-nickel coin of the denomination of ten shillings issued by Our Mint in accordance with the provisions of the Coinage Act 1946(a).

4. This Proclamation shall come into force on the twenty-seventh day of December One thousand nine hundred and sixty-eight.

Given at Our Court at Buckingham Palace, this twentieth day of December, in the year of our Lord One thousand nine hundred and sixty-eight, and in the seventeenth year of Our Reign.

GOD SAVE THE QUEEN

(a) 1946 c. 74.

CLASSIFIED LIST

OF THE

LOCAL

STATUTORY INSTRUMENTS

REGISTERED DURING

1968

TABLE OF CONTENTS

NOTES

1. In the following list the number in brackets after the date of each instrument is the S.I. number of that instrument in the 1968 series.

2. Instruments indicated with an asterisk were not printed and sold by H.M.S.O. Copies will usually be obtainable from the local authority or Government Department concerned.

3. The list does not show ministerial orders (including special procedure orders) which are not statutory instruments. Information as to any such orders may be obtained from the local authority or Government Department concerned.

CLASS 1.—ROADS, BRIDGES, ROAD TRAFFIC AND RIGHTS OF WAY

(1) *Bridges and tunnels.*
(2) *Establishment as highways.*
(3) *Parking places.*

(4) *Rights of way (extinguishment, stopping up, etc.).*
(5) *Traffic regulation.*

(1) Bridges and tunnels

Minister of Transport—Confirmation Instruments under Highways (Miscellaneous Provisions) Act 1961 (c. 63), s. 3†.

City of Chester (Shropshire Union Canal Bridge) Scheme 1968; 11 Nov. (1811).
County of Cambridgeshire and Isle of Ely (River Nene Bridge, Wisbech) Scheme 1967; 13 Mar. (452).
*Reading (River Kennet Bridge) Scheme 1968; 25 June (1019).

(2) Establishment as highways

(a) TRUNK ROADS

Restriction of traffic on trunk roads—*see* (5) below.

Trunk roads in built-up areas—*see* (5) below.

(i) England and Wales

Minister of Transport—Orders under Highways Act 1959 (c. 25), s. 7†.

Bootle–South of Preston Trunk Road (Greaves Hall Diversion); 5 Apr. (632).
Doncaster–Kendal Trunk Road (Ardsley Junction); 4 Dec. (1942).
King's Lynn–Newark Trunk Road (Swineshead Bridge); 29 Nov. (1923).
London–Bristol Trunk Road (Ivy Lane and Other Roads, Chippenham); 6 June (904).
London–Fishguard Trunk Road—
(Roundabout at Beaconsfield); 29 Jan. (130).
(Sherborne Park Lodges Diversion); 19 July (1161).
London–Great Yarmouth Trunk Road—
(Kelvedon By-Pass Slip Roads); 26 Apr. (697).
(Stratford St. Mary By-Pass Slip Roads); 29 Feb. (336).
(Witham By-Pass Slip Roads); 18 Mar. (451).
London–Penzance Trunk Road (Cricketers Bridge, Bagshot, Slip Roads); 20 Mar. (460).
London–Southend Trunk Road (Hall Lane Flyover, Upminster, Slip Road); 11 June (924).
London–Thurso Trunk Road (Link Roads); 18 Nov. (1876).
Newport–Shrewsbury Trunk Road (Queeny Bridge Diversion); 26 July (1229).
Newport–Worcester Trunk Road (Whitchurch and other Diversions) (De-Trunking); 27 Aug. (1437).
Norman Cross–Grimsby Trunk Road (City of Peterborough New Trunk Road (No. 2) De-trunking); 26 Apr. (692).
North of Newcastle-under-Lyme–Tarvin Trunk Road (Diversion near Dean's Lane); 21 Nov. (1877).
Warwick Road–Bridgefoot Link Road, Stratford-upon-Avon, Trunk Road; 30 Oct. (1765).
West of Maidenhead–Oxford Trunk Road (Sandford Link Slip Roads, Trunking); 24 Apr. (670).
Widmerpool–Howden Trunk Road (Whitewater Lane, Ollerton Diversion); 18 July (1162).
Workington–Barons Cross Road (Trunking); 5 Mar. (346).

---

*Not printed for sale in the S.I. series.
†Orders made under this section are liable to special parliamentary procedure.

Class 1.—Roads, Bridges, Road Traffic and Rights of Way—*cont.*

(2) Establishment as highways—*cont.*

(*a*) TRUNK ROADS—*cont.*

(*i*) *England and Wales—cont.*

Secretary of State—Orders under Highways Act 1959 (c. 25), s. 7†.

London–Holyhead Trunk Road—
(Bron Ryffydd, Betws-y-Coed Diversion); 21 Mar. (499).
(Golf Club Bends, Llangollen); 10 Oct. (1658).
St. Clears–Nash (South Pembrokeshire) Trunk Road; 10 Jan. (34).

Minister of Transport—Orders under Highways Act 1959 (c. 25), ss. 7†, 20†.

London–Great Yarmouth Trunk Road (Lowestoft Inner Harbour Bridge Diversion);
17 July (1137).
Widmerpool–Howden Trunk Road (Thorne Bridge); 21 Oct. ¶1703).

Minister of Transport—Orders under Highways Act 1959 (c. 25), ss. 7†, 44.

Carlisle–Sunderland Trunk Road (Lowmoor-Edmond Castle); 2 July (1070).
Exeter–Leeds and Nottingham–Stoke-on-Trent Trunk Roads (Mickleover By-
Pass and Link Road); 22 Aug. (1369).
Ipswich–Weedon Trunk Road (Eltisley By-Pass); 11 July (1134).
London–Inverness Trunk Road—
(Kendal Link); 29 Oct. (1766).
(Manchester Road, Westhoughton); 3 May (731).
London North Circular Trunk Road (Neasden Lane Underpass) (Slip Roads);
12 Nov. (1823).
London–Penzance Trunk Road and the South-West of Basingstoke–Southampton
Trunk Road (Popham–Dummer); 25 Mar. (503).
London–Thurso Trunk Road (Tickencote to South Witham Slip Roads); 15 Aug.
(1329).
London–Tilbury Trunk Road (Tilbury Docks Approach Road) (Slip Roads);
19 July (1172).
Penrith–Middlesbrough Trunk Road (Green Brough Diversion); 4 Sept. (1436).

PENRITH–MIDDLESBROUGH TRUNK ROAD (STOCKTON AND THORNABY SOUTHERN
BY-PASS) (REVN.) O., made by Minister of Transport under Highways Act 1959
(c. 25), ss. 7†, 20†, 286(2); 23 Sept. (1525).

CARDIFF–LLANGURIG TRUNK ROAD (NANTGARW TO GLYNTAF, PONTYPRIDD SLIP
ROADS) O., made by Secretary of State under Highways Act 1959 (c. 25), ss. 7†, 44;
20 May (866).

LONDON–GREAT YARMOUTH TRUNK ROAD (STANWAY BY-PASS) (SLIP ROADS)
(VARIATION) O., made by Minister of Transport under Highways Act 1959 (c. 25),
ss. 7†, 44, 286; 21 Aug. (1367).

LONDON–FISHGUARD TRUNK ROAD (CARMARTHEN DIVERSION) (VARIATION NO. 2)
O., made by Secretary of State under Highways Act 1959 (c. 25), ss. 7†, 44, 286;
1 Feb. (148).

LONDON–GREAT YARMOUTH TRUNK ROAD (STANWAY BY-PASS) (VARIATION) O.,
made by Minister of Transport under Highways Act 1959 (c. 25), ss. 7†, 44, 286, sch.
24 para. 29; 21 Aug. (1368).

DOLGELLAU–SOUTH OF BIRKENHEAD TRUNK ROAD (PONT-Y-LAFAR, NEAR BALA,
DIVERSION) O., made by Secretary of State under Highways Act 1959 (c. 25), ss. 7†,
286; 1 Oct. (1595).

---

†Orders made under this section are liable to special parliamentary procedure.

Class 1.—Roads, Bridges, Road Traffic and Rights of Way—*cont.*

(2) Establishment as highways—*cont.*

(*a*) TRUNK ROADS—*cont.*

(*i*) *England and Wales—cont.*

LIVERPOOL–HULL TRUNK ROAD (WEST GARFORTH DIVERSION AND WEST GARFORTH TO PECKFIELD BAR SIDE ROADS) (REVN.) O., made by Minister of Transport under Highways Act 1959 (c. 25), s. 286, sch. 24, para. 29; 19 Apr. (664).

LONDON–BRIGHTON TRUNK ROAD (MERSTHAM, REDHILL AND HORLEY BY-PASS) (REVN.) O., made by Minister of Transport under Highways Act 1959 (c. 25), sch. 24 para. 29; 24 Oct. (1715).

Minister of Transport—Orders under Highways Act 1959 (c. 25), s. 7† and Local Government Act 1966 (c. 42), s. 27.

Basingstoke–Newbury Trunk Road (Cheap Street, Market Place and Mansion House Street, Newbury, De-trunking); 26 Apr. (702).

Birmingham–Great Yarmouth Trunk Road (Crown Road and Neatherd Road, East Dereham); 29 Feb. (337).

East of Snaith–Sunderland Trunk Road (Ryhope Grange–Ryhope Dene); 28 May (878).

London–Bristol and Bath–Lincoln Trunk Roads (London Road and Gloucester Road, Bath) (Detrunking); 19 Mar. (437).

London–Inverness Trunk Road (Buckwell Street Diversion, Desborough); 8 Feb. (158).

Penrith–Middlesbrough Trunk Road (Blackwell Bridge–Blands Corner); 17 July (1171).

Secretary of State—Orders under Highways Act 1959 (c. 25), s. 7† and Local Government Act 1966 (c. 42), s. 27.

Dolgellau–South of Birkenhead Trunk Road (Llanfor Diversion); 31 Oct. (1769).

Swansea–Manchester Trunk Road (Arddleen By-Pass); 10 Dec. (1981).

Minister of Transport—Orders under Highways Act 1959 (c. 25), ss. 7†, 44 and Local Government Act 1966 (c. 42), s. 27.

East of Snaith–Sunderland Trunk Road and the West of Dishforth–Thirsk Trunk Road (Thirsk By-Pass); 10 Apr. (651).

King's Lynn–Newark Trunk Road (Beckingham By-Pass); 4 June (896).

Liverpool–Leeds Trunk Road (Whalley and Clitheroe By-Pass); 15 May (811).

London–Inverness Trunk Road (Gretna Diversion); 21 Mar. (506).

London–Penzance Trunk Road (Plympton By-Pass); 18 Apr. (633).

London–Thurso Trunk Road (Balderton Diversion); 11 Nov. (1812).

Secretary of State—Orders under Highways Act 1959 (c. 25), ss. 7†, 44 and Local Government Act 1966 (c. 42), s. 27.

Fishguard–Bangor (Menai Suspension Bridge) Trunk Road (Caernarvon Inner Relief Road); 6 Nov. (1800).

Neath–Abergavenny Trunk Road (Glyn–Neath By-Pass); 7 Nov. (1816).

Newport–Worcester Trunk Road—
  (Raglan–Usk Diversion); 26 Jan. (138).
  (Usk– Coldra Diversion); 12 Dec. (1991).

Shrewsbury–Dolgellau Trunk Road (Pont Minllyn, Dinas Mawddwy); 30 Sept. (1594).

HUNGERFORD–HEREFORD TRUNK ROAD (COVINGHAM FARM AND COMMON HEAD DIVERSIONS) O., made by Minister of Transport under Highways Act 1959 (c. 25), ss. 7†, 44, 286 and Local Government Act 1966 (c. 42), s. 27; 5 Mar. (356).

---

†Orders made under this section are liable to special parliamentary procedure.

Class 1.—Roads, Bridges, Road Traffic and Rights of Way—*cont.*

(2) Establishment as highways—*cont.*

(a) TRUNK ROADS—*cont.*

(ii) Scotland

Secretary of State—Orders under Trunk Roads Act 1946 (c. 30), s. 1(2)†.

Dennyloanhead–St. Andrews Trunk Road (Check Bar Slip Roads) (Trunking);
24 June (1009).

Edinburgh–Glasgow Trunk Road (Baillieston Diversion); 25 Sept. (1548).

Fort William–Mallaig Trunk Road (Sgeir nan Ron and Other Diversions); 28 Feb.
(319).

Gretna–Stirling Trunk Road—
(Castlecary Slip Roads) (Trunking); 24 June (1008).
(Revenshall and Kirkdale Diversions); 18 June (964).

Invergarry–Kyle of Lochalsh Trunk Road (Inverinate Village Diversions); 19 June
(980).

Kincardine–St. Andrews Trunk Road (Rossie Diversion); 13 June (952).

London–Inverness Trunk Road (Alexandria Bypass Stage II Slip Roads); 27 June
(1025).

Tyndrum–Oban Trunk Road (Alexandra Road–Corran Parks) (Trunking); 19 June
(979).

FORT WILLIAM–MALLAIG TRUNK ROAD (BANAVIE BRIDGE) TRUNKING O., made by
Secretary of State under Trunk Roads Act 1946 (c. 30), ss. 1(2)†, 6(1)†; 19 Dec. (2054).

*Secretary of State—Orders under Trunk Roads Act 1946 (c. 30), s. 1(2)† and Local
Government (S.) Act 1966 (c. 51), s. 28(2).*

Dennyloanhead–St. Andrews Trunk Road (Sheriff's Toll to Kirkcaldy Burgh
Boundary Trunking and Detrunking); 16 Apr. (638).

Glasgow–Monkton Trunk Road (Greenock Burgh Boundary to Inverkip Trunking
and Detrunking); 13 May (768).

Gretna–Stirling Trunk Road (Gretna Diversion); 25 Mar. (495).

London–Inverness Trunk Road (Gretna Diversion); 25 Mar. (494).

GRETNA–STIRLING TRUNK ROAD (OLD INN JUNCTION DIVERSION, SLIP ROADS AND
DE-TRUNKING) (AMDT.) O., made by Secretary of State under Trunk Roads Act 1946
(c. 30), ss. 1(2)†, 11(4) and Trunk Roads Act 1936 (c. 5), s. 13(2); 9 May (753).

INVERGARRY–KYLE OF LOCHALSH TRUNK ROAD (ARDELVE AND AUCHTERTYRE
DIVERSIONS) O., made by Secretary of State under Trunk Roads Act 1946 (c. 30),
s. 1(2)† and Special Roads Act 1949 (c. 32), s. 14(5); 22 July (1182).

LONDON–THURSO TRUNK ROAD (HELMSDALE DIVERSION) O., made by Secretary of
State under Trunk Roads Act 1946 (c. 30), ss. 1(2)†, 6(1)†, Special Roads Act 1949
(c. 32), s 14(5) and Local Government (S.) Act 1966 (c. 51), s. 28(2); 11 Nov. (1818).

(b) SPECIAL ROADS

(i) England and Wales

*Minister of Transport—Special Roads Schemes under Highways Act 1959 (c. 25),
ss. 11†, 12, 14, 20†, 286.*

Beaconsfield and Gerrards Cross By-Pass Connecting Roads; 29 Jan. (129).

Birtley By-Pass; 13 Feb. (192).

Catthorpe–Castle Bromwich Motorway Connecting Roads (Castle Bromwich);
1 Nov. (1754).

---

†Orders made under this section are liable to special parliamentary procedure.

Class 1.—Roads, Bridges, Road Traffic and Rights of Way—*cont.*

(2) Establishment as highways—*cont.*

(*b*) SPECIAL ROADS—*cont.*

(*i*) *England and Wales*—*cont.*

Cheshire County Council (Ringway Airport Link) Motorway Confirmation; 25 Apr. (693).

City of Birmingham Aston Expressway Special Road Confirmation; 16 May (817).

Lancashire County Council and Rochdale Borough Council (Rochdale–Lancashire Yorkshire Motorway–Oldham) Confirmation; 21 Nov. (1893).

London–King's Lynn Trunk Road (Little Thetford Diversion) (Revn.); 13 Mar. (408).

M.3 Motorway—
(Basingstoke to Hawley Section) Connecting Roads; 15 Mar. (409).
(Chertsey and Sunbury) (Variation); 7 Oct. (1592).
(Hawley to Lightwater Section) Connecting Roads; 5 June (879).
(Popham to Basingstoke Section) Connecting Roads, 25 Mar. (504).
(Thames Bridge); 2 Feb. (147).
(Virginia Water to Sunbury Cross Section) Connecting Roads; 25 Oct. (1716).

M.4 Motorway—
(Poughley to Wickham Section) Connecting Roads; 1 Oct. (1572).
(Theale to Winnersh Section) Connecting Roads; 18 Sept. (1486).
(Winnersh to Holyport Section); 6 Aug. (1274).

M.5 Motorway (Easton-in-Gordano–Edithmead Section) Connecting Roads; 25 Sept. (1584).

M.18 Motorway (Thorne Section); 17 Sept. (1487).

M.23 London–Crawley Motorway; 13 May (763).

M.25 South Orbital Motorway (Leatherhead–Godstone Section); 13 May (764).

M.53 Motorway—
(Bidston Moss Section); 23 Dec. (2064).
(Wallasey/Birkenhead Boundary to Woodchurch Section)—
23 Dec. (2068).
Connecting Roads; 23 Dec. (2069).
(West Kirby/Seacombe Railway to Wallasey/Birkenhead Boundary Section); 23 Dec. (2065).
(Woodchurch to Hooton Section)—
23 Dec. (2066).
Connecting Roads; 23 Dec. (2067).

M.56 North Cheshire Motorway (Wythenshawe–Bowdon Section); 14 Mar. (410).

M.62 Lancashire–Yorkshire Motorway—
(Croft to Worsley Section); 19 Sept. (1518).
(Eccles Interchange); 28 Nov. (1901).
(Outlane and Ainley Top) Connecting Roads; 8 Nov. (1791).
(Tarbock to Croft Section); 13 June (948).

M.62 North of Worsley–West of Moss Moor Motorway Connecting—
Roads (Castleton); 2 May (708).
Road (Simister); 18 Sept. (1517).

Outlane–Lofthouse Special Roads (Variation); 2 Dec. (1931).

South of Aylesford–East of Wrotham Special Road Connecting Roads; 29 Apr. (683).

(*ii*) *Scotland*

Secretary of State—Special Roads Schemes under Special Roads Act 1949 (c. 32), ss. 1†, 2, 9, 17.

Glasgow Inner Ring Road (West and North Flanks)—
Confirmation; 21 Feb. (240).
(Connecting Roads) Confirmation; 21 Feb. (241).

---

†Orders made under this section are liable to special parliamentary procedure.

Class 1.—Roads, Bridges, Road Traffic and Rights of Way—*cont.*

(2) Establishment as highways—*cont.*

(b) SPECIAL ROADS—*cont.*

(ii) Scotland —*cont.*

Kinross and Milnathort Bypass; 21 Mar. (477).
Maryville to West of Mollinsburn—
15 Feb. (201).
(Connecting Roads)—
25 Sept. (1546).
(No. 2); 25 Sept. (1547).
Newbridge to Dechmont—
(Connecting Roads) (Variation); 13 May (770).
(Variation); 6 May (769).
Newbridge to Lathallan (Connecting Roads)—
4 Apr. (560).
(Variation); 12 Sept. (1462).
Stirling Bypass—
26 Feb. (277).
(Connecting Roads); 6 May (760).

(c) METROPOLITAN ROADS*

London Government (Metropolitan Roads) Orders made by Minister of Transport under London Government Act 1963 (c. 33), s. 17.
22 Apr. (669).
(No. 2); 6 Dec. (1955).

(d) COUNTY ROADS*

County Roads Cesser Orders made by Minister of Transport under Highways Act 1959 (c. 25), s. 22.
Hertford—
(No. 2); 5 Aug. (1277).
(No. 3); 8 Oct. (1635).
(No. 4); 10 Dec. (2043).
Leicester (No. 1); 23 May (915).

(3) Parking places

PARKING PLACES AND CONTROLLED PARKING ZONE (MANCHESTER) (1966) (VARIATION) O., made by Minister of Transport under Road Traffic Regulation Act 1967 (c. 76), ss. 35, 36, 37, 39; 11 Nov. (1813).

(4) Rights of way (extinguishment, stopping up, etc.)*

Stopping up of Highways Orders made by Secretary of State under Town and Country Planning (S.) Act 1947 (c. 53), s. 46†.

Coatbridge: 3 July (1133).
Dalkeith; 30 May (873).
East Kilbride; 20 Sept. (1519).
Edinburgh; 4 June (893).
Glasgow—
(Brace Street); 28 Oct. (1744).
(Earlston Avenue); 1 Oct. (1600).
(Laurieston/Gorbals No. 3); 1 Oct. (1590).
(Millburn Street); 1 Oct. (1589).
(Townhead and Cowcaddens No. 1); 16 July (1136).

Grangemouth; 31 July (1259).
Greenock; 15 Nov. (1850).
Kincardine; 27 June (1054).
Rutherglen; 24 Oct. (1707).

---

*Not printed for sale in the S.I. series.
†Orders made under this section are liable to special parliamentary procedure.

Class 1.—Roads, Bridges, Road Traffic and Rights of Way—*cont.*

(5) Traffic regulation

(*a*) *England and Wales*   (*b*) *Scotland*

(*a*) ENGLAND AND WALES*

(*i*) General regulation

Minister of Transport—Orders under Road Traffic Regulation Act 1967 (c. 76), ss. 1, 2, 3, 6, 9, 10.

BOX JUNCTIONS—
Beddingham Level Crossing; 4 June (877).
Bedford, High Street; 8 Nov. (1788).
Camberley, London Road; 6 Dec. (1951).
Cambridge, Trumpington Street and Trumpington Road; 29 Mar. (566).
Lancaster, Various Roads; 29 Nov. (1924).
Lowestoft, Pier Terrace and London Road North; 29 Oct. (1726).
Maidenhead, Bath Road; 5 Nov. (1777).
Nantwich, London Road; 6 May (744).
Peterborough, Various Roads; 12 Nov. (1809).
Redhill, High Street; 20 Sept. (1516).
Sale, Cross Street and Washway Road; 18 July (1190).
Strood, London Road, and Rochester, High Street; 24 Oct. (1704).

COMPULSORY RIGHT TURNS—
Coventry—
Dunchurch and Fletchamstead Highways; 16 May (793).
Kenpas and Fletchamstead Highways; 21 May (823).
Dartford, Princes Road; 23 May (842).

NO RIGHT TURN—
Bedford, Various Roads; 24 Sept. (1531).
Crosby, Crosby Road South; 22 Mar. (502).
Haydock Interchange; 14 Aug. (1323).
Tyldesley, East Lancashire Road; 18 Jan. (87).

NO U TURNS—
Haydock Interchange; 14 Aug. (1323).

ONE-WAY—
Abingdon, Various Roads; 5 July (1083).
Bedford, Various Roads; 24 Sept. (1531).
Beverley, Various Streets; 14 June (932).
Boston, Various Streets (Amdt.); 23 Jan. (109).
Bury St. Edmunds, Westgate Street; 25 Mar. (522).
Coventry By-Pass; 24 May (853).
Dover, Various Roads; 31 Oct. (1747).
Earley, Berks, London Road and Shepherds Hill; 22 Nov. (1878).
Little Thetford Corner, Cambridgeshire; 19 June (970).
Lowestoft, Various Streets; 30 Sept. (1574).
Mitcham's Corner, Cambridge; 27 Nov. (1895).
Norwich, Carrow Road; 19 Jan. (90).
Royston, Various Roads; 4 Sept. (1445).
Sawtry, Huntingdonshire (Revn.); 12 Aug. (1308).
South Molton, Devon, Various Streets; 18 Nov. (1873).
Southfleet, Kent, Park Corner; 10 Oct. (1628).
Stafford, Foregate Street; 29 Aug. (1416).
Stratford-upon-Avon, Various Roads; 27 Mar. (518).

PRESCRIBED ROUTES—
Bagshot, Surrey; 16 Apr. (635).
Barham, Kent; 4 Sept. (1446).
Coventry, Dunchurch Highway, Junction with Brookside Avenue; 21 May (837).
Havering, Southend Arterial Road—
18 Oct. (1667).
(No. 2); 5 Nov. (1775).
Wincanton, Market Place; 5 Nov. (1774).

PROHIBITION OF CYCLING—
Chelmsford, Princes Road, Pedestrian Subway; 22 Nov. (487).
Dartford, Princes Road, Footbridges; 17 June (946).
Gloucester, Estcourt Road; 30 Sept. (1573).
Maghull, Northway, Subway; 2 Feb. (149).

PROHIBITION OF DRIVING—
Bootle, Dunnings Bridge Road—
22 Apr. (663).
(No. 2); 20 Nov. (1872).
Chester-le-Street, Plawsworth Road; 10 May (777).
Chester Moor, Front Street; 29 Aug. (1411).
Colney Heath, North Orbital Road; 4 July (1078).
Coventry—
Fletchamstead Highway, Junctions with—
Cannon Close and Cannon Park Road; 17 May (822).
Cannon Hill Road, Charter Avenue and Canley Road; 21 May (820).
Prior Derem Walk and Burnsall Road; 16 May (794).
Standard Avenue and Torrington Avenue; 16 May (792).
Kenpas Highway, Junctions with—
Beanfield Avenue; 17 May (807).
Grasmere Avenue and Woodside Avenue; 16 May (804).
Green Lane; 17 May (808).
Stonebridge Highway, Junctions with—
Baginton Road; 16 May (805).
Howes Lane and Leaf Lane; 22 May (832).
Dockacres, Carnforth to Milnthorpe Road; 3 May (719).
Felling, Felling By-Pass; 6 May (743).
Filton, Cycle Tracks; 5 June (895).
Lancing, Old Shoreham Road; 30 Sept. (1568).
Meriden—
Birmingham Road, Junctions with Pickford Green Lane and Brickhill Lane; 12 Aug. (1302).
Coventry Road, Junction with—
Church Lane; 12 Aug. (1303).
Goodway Road; 9 Aug. (1304).
Middle Bickenhill Lane—
12 Aug. (1305).
(Amdt.); 27 Sept. (1550).
Meriden By-Pass, Junction with Maxstoke Lane; 9 Aug. (1307).
Middle Aston, Oxfordshire; 16 Apr. (629).
Patchway, Gloucestershire, Gloucester Road; 30 Sept. (1579).
Royston, Various Roads; 4 Sept. (1445).
St. Helens, East Lancashire Road; 18 Sept. (1500).
Stretford, Chester Road, Junction of Longford Road; 15 Feb. (215).
Strood, London Road; 12 Jan. (63).
Thrussington, Leicestershire; 5 Jan. (28).
Winwick, Winwick Road; 21 May (843).

PROHIBITION OF ENTRY—
Chesterfield, Holywell Street, Junction with Devonshire Street; 7 June (902).
Folkestone, Sandgate Road; 27 Nov. (1907).
Froxfield, Wiltshire; 12 Feb. (181).
High Wycombe, Oxford Street; 12 July (1129).
Kilverstone, London–Norwich; 26 Apr. (690).
Wardley, Chorley Road, Swinton and Manchester Road; 3 Sept. (1424).

PROHIBITION OF ENTRY AND EXIT—
Aldingbourne, Chichester; 19 Sept. (1499).
Dartford, Princes Road; 23 May (842).

PROHIBITION OF LOADING AND UNLOADING—
Andover, Bridge Street and London Street; 11 Nov. (1806).
Dover—
1 Mar. (321).
(Amdt.); 25 Mar. (486).

*Not printed for sale in the S.I. series.

Class 1.—Roads, Bridges, Road Traffic and Rights of Way—*cont.*

(5) Traffic regulation—*cont.*

(a) ENGLAND AND WALES*—*cont.*

(i) General regulation—*cont.*

PROHIBITION OF LOADING AND UNLOADING—*cont.*
Market Harborough; 10 Apr. (608).
Norwich, Eaton Street; 22 Jan. (89).
Salisbury, Various Roads; 5 June (894).
Stony Stratford, High Street and London Road; 4
July (1069).
Stratford-on-Avon, Various Roads; 25 July (1215).
Tamworth, Various Roads; 4 Dec. (1940).

PROHIBITION OF RIGHT TURNS—
Bagshot, Surrey; 16 Apr. (635).
Chelmsford, London Road; 17 Dec. (2026).
Coventry—
   Dunchurch and Fletchamstead Highways; 16
   May (793).
   Kenpas and Fletchamstead Highways; 21 May
   (823).
High Wycombe—
   High Street; 12 Mar. (381).
   Oxford Road; 4 July (1059).
Plymouth, Plymouth Road; 30 May (869).
Rayleigh, Southend Arterial Road; 6 Sept. (1447).
Ringwood; 27 Sept. (1552).
Stratford-upon-Avon, Various Roads; 27 Mar.
(518).
Stretford, Chester Road; 29 Feb. (329).
Thruxton; 7 June (916).
Thurrock, Lodge Lane; 18 Dec. (2039).
Tilbury, Various Roads; 5 Nov. (1776).
Ware, Bridge Foot; 7 Aug. (1279).
Watford, North Western Avenue; 14 May (821).

PROHIBITION OF U TURNS—
Bickenhill, Coventry Road; 14 Nov. (1830).
Coventry—
   Dunchurch and Fletchamstead Highways; 16
   May (793).
   Fletchamstead Highway, Junction with Tile Hill
   Lane; 22 May (833).
   Kenpas and Fletchamstead Highways; 21 May
   (823).
Felling, Felling By-Pass; 6 May (743).
Hatfield Peverel By-Pass; 5 Aug. (1269).
Salisbury, Rampart Road; 12 Jan. (59).

PROHIBITION OF VEHICLES—
Aycliffe, High Street; 26 July (1216).
Chilton, Durham Road/Hunter Terrace; 12 July
(1135).

PROHIBITION OF WAITING—
Abingdon, Various Roads; 5 July (1083).
Alfreton, Chesterfield Road, King Street and Derby
Road; 11 Jan. (42).
Andover, Bridge Street and London Street; 11
Nov. (1806).
Ashton-in-Makerfield, Various Roads; 26 Sept.
(1567).
Bakewell, Derbyshire, Various Roads; 6 Aug.
(1278).
Beckhampton to West Kennett, Wiltshire; 5 Apr.
(582).
Bexhill, Little Common Roundabout; 2 Oct. (1580).
Bexhill-on-Sea, Belle Hill and Little Common
Road; 11 Nov. (1805).
Bingley, Main Street and Keighley Road; 14 June
(934).
Blackburn, Accrington Road and Whitebirk Road;
18 Apr. (649).
Blackwater, Hampshire (Amdt.); 6 Mar. (351).
Boston, Market Place, South Street and South
Square; 12 Aug. (1306).
Brackley, High Street; 9 Apr. (606).
Bradford, Whitehall Road; 19 Aug. (1341).
Broughton, High Street; 8 Mar. (359).
Broxbourne, High Road—
   19 Jan. (88).
   (No. 2); 22 Feb. (262).
Buxton, Fairfield Road; 16 Sept. (1472).

PROHIBITION OF WAITING—*cont.*
Camberley, London Road—
   13 Mar. (376).
   (Amdt.); 19 Apr. (640).
Camborne–Redruth; 8 Mar. (360).
Cheltenham—
   Bath Road; 22 Oct. (1705).
   Lansdown Road and Montpelier Walk; 5 Jan.
   (14).
   Various Roads (Amdt.); 15 Aug. (1330).
Chesterfield, Various Roads; 17 Dec. (2027).
Chilton, Durham Road; 26 Sept. (1566).
Clayton-le-Woods, Preston Road; 29 Oct. (1732).
Clow Bridge, Burnley Road; 9 Apr. (631).
Denbigh Corner–Lichfield Road, Warwickshire
   (Revn.); 8 Mar. (401).
Denton, Hyde Road (Amdt.); 20 Aug. (1345).
Dilton, Kent, London Road; 10 July (1113).
Dover—
   1 Mar. (321).
   (Amdt.); 25 Mar. (486).
   Douro Place and Marine Parade; 5 Apr. (583).
   Various Roads; 30 Apr. (696).
Downham Market, Church Road—
   29 Nov. (1905).
   (No. 2); 13 Dec. (1983).
Esher; 10 Jan. (31).
Folkestone—
   (Amdt.); 16 Feb. (214).
   Honiton, Clearways; 19 Sept. (1514).
   Pavilion Road; 5 Apr. (581).
Gillingham and Chatham; 16 Apr. (634).
Hartley Wintney; 21 Aug. (1346).
Hazel Grove, Macclesfield Road; 22 Oct. (1693).
Heckington, High Street and Boston Road; 28
May (856).
Henley-in-Arden, High Street; 19 Apr. (650).
Henley-on-Thames, Various Roads; 4 July (1068).
High Wycombe, Various Roads; 17 Jan. (67).
Hindhead, London Road; 25 Sept. (1532).
Huntingdon and Godmanchester, Various Streets;
29 Feb. (311).
Hyde, Market Street; 16 Feb. (211).
Hythe, High Street; 1 Jan. (9)
Ipswich – Newmarket – Cambridge – St. Neots –
   Bedford – Northampton – Weedon, Clearways
   (Amdt.); 21 Mar. (476).
Kegworth, Derby Road; 27 Feb. (274).
Keighley, Bradford Road; 23 May (847).
Kenilworth, Warwick Road and Waverley Road;
6 May (722).
Leek, Various Roads; 19 Dec. (2056).
Leominster, Bridge Street (Revn.); 10 Apr. (607).
Liverpool – Warrington – Stockport – Sheffield –
   Lincoln–Skegness, Clearways; 6 Feb. (154).
London–Birmingham, Clearways; 18 Sept. (1501).
London–Bristol, Clearways; 16 July (1174).
London–Edinburgh–Thurso, Clearways; 18 Nov.
(1833).
London–Great Yarmouth, Clearways; 22 Nov.
(1904).
London–Norwich, Clearways; 12 Nov. (1824).
London–Portsmouth, Clearways; 5 Dec. (1949).
Longtown, Bridge Street, Hight Street and English
Street; 29 Apr. (695).
Ludlow, Bull Ring, Corve Street and Coronation
Avenue; 22 May (835).
Lydney; 25 Jan. (122).
Maidenhead, Bridge Road; 8 Mar. (382).
Market Harborough; 10 Apr. (608).
Market Weighton, Market Place and High Street;
19 Aug. (1339).
Minster Lovell, Oxfordshire; 29 Apr. (689).
Morley, Various Roads; 19 June (971).
Nailsworth, Gloucestershire, Various Roads;
13 Aug. (1311).
Newbury, Berkshire, Oxford Road; 17 Dec. (2024).
Newport, Salop, Various Streets; 15 Feb. (212).

*Not printed for sale in the S.I. series.

Class 1.—Roads, Bridges, Road Traffic and Rights of Way—*cont.*

(5) Traffic regulation—*cont.*

(a) ENGLAND AND WALES*—*cont.*

(i) General regulation—*cont.*

PROHIBITION OF WAITING—*cont.*
Newton-le-Willows, Ashton Road, High Street and Church Street; 28 May (857).
North-East of Birmingham–Nottingham, Clearways; 23 Aug. (1396).
North Hykeham, Newark Road; 7 Feb. (156)
Norwich—
Carrow Road; 19 Jan. (90).
Eaton Street; 22 Jan. (89).
Oadby, Harborough Road; 11 Nov. (1808).
Oxford–Northampton–Stamford–Market Deeping, Clearways; 24 Oct. (1709).
Petersfield, Dragon Street; 31 Oct. (1748).
Rainham, High Street; 2 Aug. (1276).
Rainhill, Warrington Road; 28 May (858).
Ripley, Various Roads; 27 Mar. (519).
Royston, Various Roads; 4 Sept. (1445).
St. Albans, Park Street; 10 Jan. (41).
Sale and Stretford (Amdt.); 17 May (836).
Salisbury, Various Roads; 5 June (894).
Saxmundham, North Entrance, High Street and South Entrance 28 Nov. (1906).
Skipton, Various Roads; 5 Dec. (1943).
Slough, Bath Road Service Road; 4 July (1058).
South Molton, Devon, Various Streets; 18 Nov. (1873).
South-West of Basingstoke–Southampton, Clearways; 1 Aug. (1267).
Southam, Two Gates–Banbury Road (Revn.); 16 Jan. (85).
Southwick, Old Shoreham Road; 26 Apr. (682).
Stony Stratford, High Street and London Road; 4 July (1069).
Stratford-on-Avon—
Bardon Hill (Revn.); 19 Feb. (236).
Various Roads; 25 July (1215).
Tamworth, Various Roads; 4 Dec. (1940).
Thornaby-on-Tees, Mandale Road and Middlesbrough Road; 24 June (996).
Thorne, Various Roads; 1 Mar. (322).
Tollerton, Melton Road; 20 Mar. (459).
Towcester, Watling Street—
28 Mar. (540).
(Amdt.); 29 Apr. (688)
Ulverston, Various Streets; 2 Aug. (1268).
Wadebridge, Molesworth Street (Amdt.); 9 Apr. (604).
Warwick By-Pass, Clearways; 17 Dec. (2057).
West Bridgford, Melton Road; 10 May (762).
West of Southampton–Salisbury–Bath, Clearways; 22 Aug. (1372).
Wincanton—
High Street, Market Place and Church Street; 20 Sept. (1515).
South Street and Tout Hill; 18 Dec. (2040).
Winchester–Preston, Clearways; 5 Apr. (603).

RESTRICTION OF DRIVING—
Coventry, Kenpas Highway, Junction with Bathway Road; 17 May (834).
Derby, Osmaston Park Road; 27 Mar. (520).
Market Harborough, High Street; 19 Aug. (1340).

RESTRICTION OF LOADING AND UNLOADING—
Derby, Osmaston Park Road; 15 Feb. (213).
Dover—
1 Mar. (321).
(Amdt.); 25 Mar. (486).
Fareham, Hampshire; 6 Mar. (341).
Lewes—
High Street; 8 Apr. (605).
South Street and Cliffe High Street; 7 Feb. (168).
Market Harborough; 10 Apr. (608).
Rainham, High Street; 2 Aug. (1276).
Redhill, High Street; 12 Jan. (45).
Salisbury, Various Roads; 5 June (894).
Stony Stratford, High Street and London Road; 4 July (1069).
Stratford-on-Avon, Various Roads; 25 July (1215).
Sutton Coldfield, Various Roads; 16 July (1156).

RESTRICTION OF WAITING—
Abingdon, Various Roads; 5 July (1083).
Alfreton, Chesterfield Road, King Street and Derby Road; 11 Jan. (42).
Ashbourne, Station Street and Derby Road; 22 Mar. (485).
Axminster; 23 Aug. (1395).
Bakewell, Derbyshire, Various Roads; 6 Aug. (1278).
Bexhill, Little Common Roundabout; 2 Oct. (1580).
Brackley, High Street; 9 Apr. (606).
Bridgwater—
18 Mar. (432).
(Amdt.); 11 July (1112).
Bury St. Edmunds, Various Roads; 14 June (933).
Camborne and Redruth, Illogan Highway; 30 Apr. (691).
Chesterfield, Various Roads; 17 Dec. (2027).
Derby, Osmaston Park Road; 15 Feb. (213).
Dover—
1 Mar. (321).
(Amdt.); 25 Mar. (486).
Various Roads; 30 Apr. (696).
Downham Market, Church Road—
29 Nov. (1905).
(No. 2); 13 Dec. (1983).
Dymchurch; 18 Jan. (81).
Fareham, Hampshire; 6 Mar. (341)
Hartley Wintney; 21 Aug. (1346).
Hayle, Fore Street; 5 Jan. (12).
Henley-on-Thames; 4 July (1068).
Huntingdon and Godmanchester, Various Streets; 29 Feb. (311).
Leek, Various Roads; 19 Dec. (2056).
Lewes—
High Street; 8 Apr. (605).
South Street and Cliffe High Street; 7 Feb. (168).
Lowestoft, Various Roads (Consolidation); 20 Feb. (235).
Ludlow—
Bull Ring, Corve Street and Coronation Avenue; 22 May (835).
Old Street (Amdt.); 16 May (809).
Lydney; 25 Jan. (122).
Market Deeping, High Street and Deeping St. James, Bridge Street; 11 Dec. (1984).
Market Harborough; 10 Apr. (608).
Market Weighton, Market Place and High Street; 19 Aug. (1339).
Needham Market, High Street; 22 Mar. (528).
New Romney; 8 Jan. (20).
Newport, Salop, Various Streets; 15 Feb. (212).
Norwich, Carrow Road; 19 Jan. (90).
Okehampton; 6 June (903).
Petersfield, Dragon Street, 31 Oct. (1748).
Radlett, Watling Street; 25 Oct. (1712).
Rainham, High Street; 2 Aug. (1276).
Redhill, High Street; 12 Jan. (45).
Ripley, Various Roads; 27 Mar. (519).
Rushden, High Street and Church Parade; 27 June (1031).
Salisbury, Various Roads; 5 June (894).
Saxmundham, North Entrance, High Street and South Entrance; 28 Nov. (1906).
Skipton, Various Roads; 5 Dec. (1943).
South Molton, Devon, Various Streets; 18 Nov. (1873).
Stony Stratford, High Street and London Road; 4 July (1069).
Stratford-on-Avon, Various Roads; 25 July (1215).
Sutton Coldfield, Various Roads; 16 July (1156).
Swaffham, Lynn Road and Market Place; 26 June (1018).
Tilbury, Various Roads; 5 Nov. (1776).
Towcester, Watling Street—
28 Mar. (540).
(Amdt.); 29 Apr. (688).
West Bridgford, Melton Road; 10 May (762).
Wickham Market, Various Roads; 11 July (1119).

*Not printed for sale in the S.I. series.

Class 1.—Roads, Bridges, Road Traffic and Rights of Way—*cont.*

(5) Traffic regulation—*cont.*

(a) ENGLAND AND WALES*—*cont.*

(i) General regulation—*cont.*

RESTRICTION OF WAITING—*cont.*
Wigton, West Street, Market Place and King Street;
29 Mar. (556).
Wincanton, South Street and Tout Hill; 18 Dec.
(2040).

ROADS RESTRICTION—
Billingham, Durham, Various Roads (Revn.);
22 Mar. (484).
Kent (Amdt.); 29 Feb. (291).
Tothill Bridge, Hampshire (Revn.); 15 Mar. (403).
West Sussex (Amdt.); 7 June (917).

TRAFFIC REGULATION—
Durham (Revn.); 30 Aug. (1423).
Lincoln, Parts of Kesteven (Amdt.); 16 Jan. (65).
Nuneaton, Various Roads; 9 Aug. (1312).
Sutton Coldfield and Aldridge (Revn.); 25 Mar.
(521).
Wansford By-Pass (Revn.); 20 Sept. (1507).
Warwick (Revn.); 27 Mar. (529).
Willoughby, Warwick (Revn.); 16 Jan. (66).

WEIGHT RESTRICTION—
Chesterfield, Sheffield Road Bridge; 29 May (870).

Secretary of State—Orders under Road Traffic Regulation Act 1967 (c. 76), ss. 1, 3, 108.

NO RIGHT TURN—
Galon Uchaf; 19 Feb. (243).
Laleston, Well Road; 2 Dec. (1938).
Raglan, Usk Road; 11 Apr. (627).

ONE-WAY—
Galon Uchaf; 19 Feb. (243).

PROHIBITION OF CYCLING—
Wye Bridge Pedestrian Underpass; 6 May (737).

PROHIBITION OF LOADING AND UNLOADING—
Cardiff, Cowbridge Road West; 24 Oct. (1719).
Wrexham, Various Roads; 22 Mar. (500).

PROHIBITION OF WAITING—
Ammanford, Tycroes Square; 2 Dec. (1937).
Bangor, Various Roads; 13 June (944).
Brecon, High Street and Bulwark; 9 Oct. (1627).
Caernarvon, Bangor Street and North Road; 19
Feb. (221).
Cardiff, Cowbridge Road West; 24 Oct. (1719).
Conway, Castle Street; 17 Apr. (647).
Dolgellau, Various Roads; 15 May (814).
Glyn–Neath—
High Street; 9 Oct. (1626).
Various Roads; 14 June (943).
Haverfordwest (Amdt.); 1 Nov. (1768).
Letterston; 10 Dec. (1993).
Llanfairfechan, Aber Road and Penmaenmawr
Road, 13 Dec. (1992).

PROHIBITION OF WAITING—*cont.*
Llanidloes, Various Roads; 28 Aug. (1413).
Newport–Monmouth–Ross-on-Wye–Worcester,
Clearways (No. 1); 18 Mar. (429).
Newport–Shrewsbury, Clearways—
(No. 1); 30 May (881).
(No. 2); 31 Dec. (2079).
Pyle; 19 Sept. (1494).
Wrexham, Various Roads; 22 Mar. (500).

RESTRICTION OF LOADING AND UNLOADING—
Cardiff, Cowbridge Road West; 24 Oct. (1719).
Wrexham, Various Roads; 22 Mar. (500).

RESTRICTION OF WAITING—
Bangor, Various Roads; 13 June (944).
Blaenau Ffestiniog, Church Street and High Street;
27 May (867).
Cardiff, Cowbridge Road West; 24 Oct. (1718).
Conway, Castle Street; 17 Apr. (647).
Dolgellau, Various Roads; 15 May (814).
Fishguard, High Street; 23 Feb. (253).
Holyhead, Various Roads; 19 Feb. (222).
Llandeilo; 24 Jan. (108).
Loggerheads; 19 Feb, (223).
Old Colwyn, Colwyn Bay, Abergele Road; 4
July (1086).
Rhayader, Various Roads; 30 Apr. (705).
Wrexham, Various Roads; 22 Mar. (500).

Miscellaneous restrictions

Trunk Roads (Restricted Roads) Orders made by Minister of Transport under Road Traffic Regulation Act 1967 (c. 76), ss. 72(3), 73(1)(4)(5), 74(1)(6).

No. 1.   A.4.   Thatcham; 1 Jan. (2).
No. 2.   A.23.   Merstham; 4 Jan. (13).
No. 3.   A.27.   Emsworth; 16 Jan. (86).
No. 4.   A.3.   Kingston-upon-Thames; 21 Feb.
                  (273).
No. 5.   A.3.   Liphook; 4 Mar. (352).
No. 6.   A.49.   Hereford; 8 Mar. (358).
No. 7.   A.46.   Braunstone; 27 Mar. (535).
No. 8.   A.49.   Bromfield; 19 Apr. (648).
No. 9.   A.18.   Edenthorpe; 9 May (773).
No. 10. A.5, 47. Hinkley; 9 May (774).
No. 11. A.49.   Leominster; 9 May (775).
No. 12. A.6.   Bakewell, Darley Dale and Mat-
                  lock Bath; 9 July (1115).
No. 13. A.419.   Aldbourne; 9 July (1085).
No. 14. A.47.   Honingham; 23 July (1192).
No. 15. A.567.   Litherland; 6 Aug. (1290).
No. 16. A.567.   Bootle; 6 Aug. (1291).
No. 17. A.1.   Belford; 6 Aug. (1292).

No. 18. A.516.   Hilton; 21 Aug. (1370).
No. 19. A.6.   Bamber Bridge and Walton-le-
                  Dale; 22 Aug. (1403).
No. 20. A.3.   Ripley; 29 Aug. (1432).
No. 21. A.45.   Flore; 5 Sept. (1449).
No. 22. A.12.   Wickham Market; 9 Sept. (1471).
No. 23. A.41.   Boxmoor; 23 Sept. (1524).
No. 24. A.49.   Ashton-in-Makerfield; 23 Sept.
                  (1523).
No. 25. A.4.   Slough; 27 Sept. (1553).
No. 26. A.465.   Pontrilas; 7 Oct. (1629).
No. 27. A.34.   Shipston-on-Stour; 7 Oct. (1630).
No. 28. A.259.   Westham; 10 Oct. (1638).
No. 29. A.12.   Yoxford; 21 Oct. (1691).
No. 30. A.5.   Dunstable; 21 Oct. (1708).
No. 31. A.3.   Kingston-upon-Thames; 6 Nov.
                  (1793).
No. 32. A.20.   Dover; 12 Nov. (1825).
No. 33. A.10.   Enfield; 30 Dec. (2078).

Trunk Roads (Restricted Roads) Orders made by Secretary of State under Road Traffic Regulation Act 1967 (c. 76), ss. 72(3), 73(1), 108.

No. 1.   A.487.   Llanrhystyd; 8 Jan. (22).

No. 2.   A.40.   Whitemill; 30 July (1245).

*Not printed for sale in the S.I. series.

Class 1.—Roads, Bridges, Road Traffic and Rights of Way—*cont.*

(5) Traffic regulation—*cont.*

(a) ENGLAND AND WALES*—*cont.*

(i) General regulation—cont.

Miscellaneous restrictions—cont.

URBAN DISTRICT OF SUTTON-IN-ASHFIELD (RESTRICTED ROADS) O., made by Minister of Transport under Road Traffic Act 1967 (c. 76), ss. 72(3), 73(1)(4); 22 Feb. (290).

Trunk Roads (40 m.p.h. Speed Limit) Orders made by Minister of Transport under Road Traffic Regulation Act 1967 (c. 76), s. 74.

No.			No.		
No. 1.	A.30.	Zelah; 30 Jan. (146).	No. 31.	A.27.	West End; 28 Aug. (1433).
No. 2.	A.3.	Kingston-upon-Thames and Merton; 22 Feb. (272).	No. 32.	A.57.	Hyde; 26 Sept. (1564).
No. 3.	A.4.	Speen; 28 Feb. (289).	No. 33.	A.12.	Hooton; 26 Sept. (1565).
No. 4.	A.6.	Oadby; 28 Feb. (288).	No. 34.	A.38.	Tideford; 30 Sept. (1581).
No. 5.	A.38.	Sutton Coldfield; 4 Mar. (349).	No. 35.	A.12.	Havering; 30 Sept. (1582).
No. 6.	A.452.	Aldridge and Sutton Coldfield; 4 Mar. (350).	No. 36.	A.47.	Thorpe; 30 Sept. (1583).
			No. 37.	A.5.	Shrewsbury; 3 Oct. (1619).
No. 7.	A.20.	Larkfield, Dilton and Aylesford; 7 Mar. (377).	No. 38.	A.38.	Droitwich; 4 Oct. (1620).
			No. 39.	A.63.	Newport; 7 Oct. (1621).
No. 8.	A.46.	Thurmaston; 12 Mar. (411).	No. 40.	A.6.	Whaley Bridge and New Mills; 14 Oct. (1639).
No. 9.	A.158.	Horncastle; 12 Mar. (412).			
No. 10.	A.1079.	Bishop Burton; 13 Mar. (413).	No. 41.	A.4.	Newbury and Thatcham; 14 Oct. (1640).
No. 11.	A.46.	Braunstone; 27 Mar. (536).			
No. 12.	A.38.	South Brent; 29 Mar. (537).	No. 42.	A.6120.	Leeds; 14 Oct. (1641).
No. 13.	A.49.	Ludlow; 29 Mar. (538).	No. 43.	A.30.	Connor Downs; 14 Oct. (1642).
No. 14.	A.35.	Tolpuddle; 24 Apr. (675).	No. 44.	A.66.	Cockermouth; 14 Oct. (1643).
No. 15.	A.35.	Honiton; 6 May (723).	No. 45.	A.30.	Long Rock; 14 Oct. (1644).
No. 16.	A.1.	Alnwick; 6 May (757).	No. 46.	A.630.	Thrybergh; 17 Oct. (1687).
No. 17.	A.6.	Oadby; 6 May (758).	No. 47.	A.34.	Tittensor; 21 Oct. (1688).
No. 18.	A.47.	Hinckley; 9 May (776).	No. 48.	A.12.	Yoxford; 21 Oct. (1689).
No. 19.	A.56.	Thelwall and Grappenhall; 15 May (802).	No. 49.	A.5.	Dunstable; 21 Oct. (1690).
			No. 50.	A.41.	Brent Cross Flyover; 30 Oct. (1772).
No. 20.	A.5111.	Derby; 15 May (803).	No. 51.	A.4.	Newbury and Speen; 1 Nov. (1773).
No. 21.	A.39.	Horns Cross; 13 June (956).	No. 52.	A.50.	Church Lawton; 6 Nov. (1782).
No. 22.	A.40.	Charlton Kings; 14 June (957).	No. 53.	A.2.	Boughton; 6 Nov. (1783).
No. 23.	A.6.	Ambergate, Cromford, Matlock Bath, Darley Dale and Bakewell; 9 July (1114).	No. 54.	A.16.	Spilsby; 14 Nov. (1829).
			No. 55.	A.49.	Holmer; 18 Nov. (1838).
No. 24.	A.47.	Narborough; 6 Aug. (1286).	No. 56.	A.14.	Great Stukeley and Little Stukeley; 22 Nov. (1902).
No. 25.	A.567.	Litherland; 6 Aug. (1287).	No. 57.	A.58.	Spenborough; 22 Nov. (1903).
No. 26.	A.567.	Bootle; 6 Aug. (1288).	No. 58.	A.34.	Shipston-on-Stour; 5 Dec. (1950).
No. 27.	A.47.	Weet Walton; 6 Aug. (1289).	(Amdt.) Kingston-upon-Thames and Merton; 6 Nov. (1792).		
No. 28.	A.59.	Clitheroe; 22 Aug. (1392).			
No. 29.	A.6.	Chorley; 22 Aug. (1393).			
No. 30.	A.6.	Clayton Green and Whittle-le-Woods; 22 Aug. (1394).			

Trunk Roads (40 m.p.h. Speed Limit) Orders made by Secretary of State under Road Traffic Regulation Act 1967 (c. 76), ss. 74, 108.

No.			No.		
No. 1.	A.487.	Furnace and Eglwysfach; 6 Aug. (1294).	No. 4.	A.487.	Llannon; 2 Aug. (1272).
No. 2.	A.48.	Pwllmeyric; 9 Sept. (1456).	No. 5.	A.48.	Llanddarog; 4 Oct. (1625).
No. 3.	A.487.	Penparc; 2 Aug. (1273).	No. 6.	A.40.	Goodwick; 1 Aug. (1246).

BOROUGH OF STALYBRIDGE (40 M.P.H. SPEED LIMIT) O., made by Minister of Transport under Road Traffic Regulation Act 1967 (c. 76), ss. 72, 73, 74; 11 Dec. (1977).

LONDON (TRUNK ROADS) (40 M.P.H. SPEED LIMIT) (NO. 1) O., made by Minister of Transport under Road Traffic Regulation Act 1967 (c. 76), s. 74; 17 Jan. (82).

Trunk Roads (50 m.p.h. Speed Limit) Orders made by Minister of Transport under Road Traffic Regulation Act 1967 (c. 76), s. 74.

No.			No.		
No. 1.	A.45.	Thurlaston and Dunchurch; 25 June (1004).	No. 2.	A.38.	Willand; 25 June (1006).

TRUNK ROADS (50 M.P.H. SPEED LIMIT) (WALES) O., made by Secretary of State under Road Traffic Regulation Act 1967 (c. 76), ss. 74, 108; 28 Mar. (543).

---

*Not printed for sale in the S.I. series.

Class 1.—Roads, Bridges, Road Traffic and Rights of Way—*cont.*

(5) Traffic regulation—*cont.*

(a) ENGLAND AND WALES*—*cont.*

(ii) Temporary restrictions

Minister of Transport—Orders under Road Traffic Regulation Act 1967 (c. 76), s. 12.

ONE-WAY—
Measham, Ashby Road; 11 Sept. (1457).
Whitfield, Gloucestershire—
18 Apr. (661).
20 Sept. (1506).

PRESCRIBED ROUTES—
Barnet, North Circular Road; 22 Nov. (1879).
Edmonton, Silver Street and Bull Lane; 7 Oct. (1611).

PROHIBITION OF DRIVING—
Southend Arterial Road; 9 Apr. (636).

PROHIBITION OF RIGHT TURNS—
Edgware Road, Edgware Brook Bridge; 16 Oct. (1668).

PROHIBITION OF TRAFFIC—
Arundel, Tarrant Street and High Street; 5 Jan. (16).
Bacons End, Warwickshire; 19 Jan. (93).
Bamber Bridge Level Crossing—
2 Feb. (151).
(No. 2); 18 Mar. (433).
Barnet, Watford Way; 11 Oct. (1631).
Bicester Level Crossing; 2 Aug. (1243).
Birmingham–Preston Motorway; 23 Aug. (1371).
Black Dog Railway Bridge; 17 Apr. (654).
Blythe Bridge Level Crossing; 9 Sept. (1450).
Bootle, Dunnings Bridge Road; 23 Feb. (275).
Countess Wear, Exeter, Bridge Road; 27 May (854).
Curdworth River Bridge; 30 Aug. (1412).
Ealing, Western Avenue—
27 Sept. (1537).
(No. 2); 25 Oct. (1706).
East Ilsley By-Pass to Beedon Hill—
26 June (1005).
(No. 2); 15 Aug. (1322).
Flemingate Level Crossing; 29 Mar. (539).
Gittisham, Iron Bridge; 8 Mar. (353).
Gobowen Level Crossing; 26 Nov. (1894).
Hambrook Spur Motorway; 13 Sept. (1469).
Kenton Bankfoot; 27 Sept. (1549).
Lancaster By-Pass; 13 Sept. (1468).
Ludlow, Ludford Bridge; 5 Apr. (806).
Malton Level Crossing; 4 Jan. (15).
Meriden, Chester Road; 14 Oct. (1636).
Morley, Tingley Common; 2 Jan. (3).
M.5 Motorway near Droitwich; 2 Aug. (1250).
Newark—
and Tuxford By-Passes; 17 Sept. (1482).
Cromwell and Tuxford By-Passes; 19 Aug. (1332).

PROHIBITION OF TRAFFIC—*cont.*
North of Chepstow Bridge; 4 Mar. (317).
Northampton Road; 3 May (721).
Onibury Level Crossing; 27 Sept. (1551).
Painswick, Gloucestershire, New Street; 18 Nov. (1834).
Pewsham to Beckhampton, Wiltshire; 21 Oct. (1692).
Rawtenstall, Bank Street—
18 June (958).
(No. 2); 9 Aug. (1297).
Ross Spur Motorway; 28 June (1028).
Standish, High Street; 2 Feb. (150).
Tilbury Docks Approach Road; 10 Sept. (1458).
Tring, High Street; 25 Oct. (1711).
Winthorpe, Lincoln Road—
15 July (1128).
(No. 2); 14 Oct. (1637).
Worsbrough Bridge, Level Crossing; 22 Feb. (278).

RESTRICTION OF DRIVING—
Ashley, Hampshire; 25 Oct. (1710).

RESTRICTION OF TRAFFIC—
Bexley, Rochester Way; 9 Aug. (1324).
Bideford Long Bridge; 22 Mar. (483).
Fenny Bridges; 30 July (1227).
Hereford, Edgar Street; 17 May (810).
Kingston-upon-Thames, Malden Way; 23 Sept. (1505).
Marsh, Newhaven Bridge; 30 July (1228).
Preston By-Pass Motorway; 21 June (993).
St. Albans By-Pass; 27 May (855).
Sawtry, Great North Road; 11 Apr. (628).
Shrewsbury, Whitchurch Road; 23 Feb. (250).
Tamworth, Silver Street and Aldergate—
29 Aug. (1417).
(No. 2); 19 Dec. (2045).
Washbrook By-Pass; 17 Sept. (1488).
Wellington, Watling Street—
18 July (1155).
(No. 2); 9 Aug. (1313).
Wibtoft, Watling Street; 29 Apr. (720).
Wiveliscombe, West Street; 19 Apr. (662).

SPEED LIMIT—
Carlisle-Sunderland; 19 Nov. (1839).

WEIGHT RESTRICTION—
Beverley, North Bar; 16 Sept. (1483).
Edgware Road, Edgware Brook Bridge; 16 Oct. (1668).

Secretary of State—Orders under Road Traffic Regulation Act 1967 (c. 76), ss. 12, 108.

PROHIBITION OF OVERTAKING—
Penrhos, Holyhead; 27 Nov. (1900).

PROHIBITION OF TRAFFIC—
Llanfarian Railway Bridge; 21 Mar. (478).

WEIGHT RESTRICTION—
Ruthin Railway Bridge; 18 Jan. (76).

TRUNK ROAD (CHEPSTOW BRIDGE, CHEPSTOW AND GLOUCESTER) (TEMPORARY PROHIBITION OF TRAFFIC) O., made by Secretary of State under Road Traffic Regulation Act 1967 (c. 76), ss. 12, 108 and Minister of Transport under Road Traffic Regulation Act 1967 (c. 76), s. 12; 4 Mar. (316).

---

*Not printed for sale in the S.I. series.

Class 1.—Roads, Bridges, Road Traffic and Rights of Way—*cont.*

(5) Traffic regulation—*cont.*

(a) ENGLAND AND WALES*—*cont.*

(iii) *Experimental traffic schemes*

Minister of Transport—Orders under Road Traffic Regulation Act 1967 (c. 76), ss. 3, 9, 10.

NO RIGHT TURN—
  Stretford, Chester Road; 3 Oct. (1593).

ONE-WAY—
  Attleborough, High Street, Exchange Street and Church Street; 7 June (918).
  Bedford, St. John's Street; 17 Dec. (2025).
  Kendal, Various Roads—
    28 Mar. (517).
    Variation; 19 July (1191).

PRESCRIBED ROUTES—
  Enfield, Bowes Road; 2 Dec. (1918).

PROHIBITION OF LOADING AND UNLOADING—
  Maidenhead, High Street and Bridge Road; 13 May (761).

PROHIBITION OF RIGHT TURNS—
  Bletchley, Bucks; 11 Sept. (1465).
  Burpham; 9 Sept. (1459).

PROHIBITION OF WAITING—
  Maidenhead, High Street and Bridge Road; 13 May (761).

RESTRICTION OF LOADING AND UNLOADING—
  Highbridge, Church Street; 2 Aug. (1293).
  Maidenhead, High Street and Bridge Road; 13 May (761).

RESTRICTION OF WAITING—
  Kendal, Various Roads—
    28 Mar. (517).
    Variation; 19 July (1191).
  Maidenhead, High Street and Bridge Road; 13 May (761).

TRAFFIC REGULATION—
  Bude, Cornwall (Amdt.); 30 Jan. (126).

VARIATION—
  Bournemouth, Christchurch Road; 15 Mar. (402).

Secretary of State—Orders under Road Traffic Regulation Act 1967 (c. 76), ss. 9, 10, 108.

PROHIBITION OF WAITING—
  Brecon, Builth Wells; 1 July (1049).
  Carmarthen, Various Roads—
    10 May (788).
    Variation; 10 Sept. (1461).

RESTRICTION OF WAITING—
  Brecon, Builth Wells; 1 July (1049).
  Carmarthen, Various Roads—
    10 May (788).
    Variation; 10 Sept. (1461).

(b) SCOTLAND*

(i) *General regulation*

Secretary of State—Orders under Road Traffic Regulation Act 1967 (c. 76), ss. 1, 3, 12.

BOX JUNCTIONS—
  Irvine. Fullarton Place and Fullarton Street; 16 Feb. (209).

CLEARWAYS—
  Glasgow–Stirling and Dennyloanhead–Kincardine; 12 June (926).

NO LEFT TURN—
  Creetown; 4 Nov. (1770).
  Glasgow–Stirling; 12 Sept. (1475).

PROHIBITION OF TRAFFIC—
  Blackford; 4 Oct. (1599).
  Linlithgow; 7 May (801).

PROHIBITION OF WAITING—
  Arrochar; 1 May (700).
  Ayton Village; 14 Nov. (1832).
  Hawick, Various Streets; 10 Jan. (37).

PROHIBITION OF WAITING—*cont.*
  Kinross. High Street; 23 May (859).
  Oban. Various Streets; 29 Aug. (1414).
  Pitlochry, Atholl Road; 6 Feb. (162).
  Vale of Leven; 26 Aug. (1398).

PROHIBITION OF WAITING AND LOADING—
  Auchterarder, High Street; 27 Dec. (2059).
  Largs; 8 July (1088).

RESTRICTION OF WAITING—
  Banff; 18 July (1176).
  Montrose, Northesk Road, Murray Street and High Street; 6 Nov. (1804).

RESTRICTION OF WAITING AND LOADING—
  Glasgow–Inverness (Fort William); 16 Feb. (217).
  Langholm, High Street and Market Place; 23 May (846).

Miscellaneous restrictions

Trunk Roads (Restricted Roads) Orders made by Secretary of State under Road Traffic Regulation Act 1967 (c. 76), ss. 72, 73.

No. 1.	A.7.	Canonbie; 7 Feb. (153).	No. 4.	A.82.	Dunbarton, County of; 27 Aug. (1401).
No. 2.	A.9.	Helmsdale; 19 Feb. (224).			
No. 3.	A.78.	Wemyss Bay; 18 July (1165).			

Trunk Roads (40 m.p.h. Speed Limit) Orders made by Secretary of State under Road Traffic Regulation Act 1967 (c. 76), s. 74.

No. 1.	A.73.	Lanark, County of; 16 Feb. (216).	No. 4.	A.82,	Glasgow–Fort William–Inverness
No. 2.	A.830.	Corpach; 21 May (840).		A.830.	and Fort William–Mallaig; 21
No. 3.	A.78.	Wemyss Bay; 18 July (1167).			Oct. (1680).

*Not printed for sale in the S.I. series.

Class 1.—Roads, Bridges, Road Traffic and Rights of Way—*cont.*

(5) Traffic regulation—*cont.*

(*b*) SCOTLAND*—*cont.*

(*i*) *General regulation*—*cont.*

Miscellaneous restrictions—*cont.*

TRUNK ROADS (50 M.P.H. SPEED LIMIT) (S.) O., made by Secretary of State under Road Traffic Regulation Act 1967 (c. 76), s. 74; 10 Dec. (1967).

GLASGOW INNER RING ROAD (WEST AND NORTH FLANKS) (SPEED LIMIT) REGS., made by Secretary of State under Road Traffic Regulation Act 1967 (c. 76), s. 13; 14 Mar. (419)†.

(*ii*) *Temporary restrictions*

Secretary of State—Orders under Road Traffic Regulation Act 1967 (*c. 76*), *ss. 12, 77.*

ONE-WAY—
Glasgow–Inverness; 16 Dec. (1999).

SPEED LIMIT—
Glasgow–Inverness (30 m.p.h.); 21 June (992).
Stirling, Inner Relief Road, Phase I (40 m.p.h.); 17 Dec. (2041).

WEIGHT RESTRICTION—
Connel–Glencoe (Ferlochan Burn Culvert); 17 Oct. (1666).

(*iii*) *Experimental traffic schemes*

Secretary of State—Orders under Road Traffic Regulation Act 1967 (*c. 76*), *s. 9.*

PROHIBITION OF DRIVING—
Nairn, King Street and St. Ninian Road; 12 Sept. (1476).

PROHIBITION OF WAITING—
Maybole; 20 Mar. (450).

CLASS 2.—RAILWAYS, TRAMWAYS AND TROLLEY VEHICLES

Light Railway Orders made by Minister of Transport under Light Railways Act 1896 (*c. 48*), *ss. 7, 9, 10, 24 as amended by Light Railways Act 1912* (*c. 19*) *and Railways Act 1921* (*c. 55*), *Pt. V.*

British Railways Bd. (Keighley and Worth Valley) (Transfer); 17 May (819).

Festiniog Railway (Amdt.); 9 Feb. (178).

Jarrow East End (Leasing); 22 Feb. (242).

---

*Not printed for sale in the S.I. series.
†This instrument (419) was printed and put on sale.

CLASS 3.—RIVERS AND INLAND WATERWAYS

(1) *Land drainage schemes and orders.*　　(3) *Rivers (prevention of pollution).*
(2) *River authorities.*　　　　　　　　　　(4) *Salmon and freshwater fisheries.*

(1) Land drainage schemes and orders

Minister of Agriculture, Fisheries and Food—Orders under Land Drainage Act 1930 (c. 44), ss. 4†, 14 as applied by Water Resources Act 1963 (c. 38).

Essex River Authority (Alteration of Boundaries of the—
　Chelmer and Blackwater Internal Drainage District); 25 July (1520).
　Maldon, Wivenhoe and Clacton Internal Drainage District); 11 Mar. (637).
　North Fambridge Internal Drainage District); 1 Feb. (380).
Great Ouse River Authority—
　(Alteration of Boundaries of the Lakenheath Internal Drainage District); 29 Nov. 1967 (254).
　(Feltwell Fen Second District Internal Drainage District); 15 Mar. (741).
　(Middle Fen and Mere Internal Drainage District); 1 Oct. (2073).
　(Mildenhall Internal Drainage District); 21 Nov. (249).
　(Snettisham Internal Drainage District); 27 Feb. (553).
Gwynedd River Authority Transfer; 16 Dec. (2074).
Lincolnshire River Authority—
　(Alteration of Boundaries of the—
　　Ancholme Internal Drainage District); 27 Aug. (1671).
　　Black Sluice Internal Drainage District); 19 Oct. 1967 (57).
　　Skegness District Internal Drainage District); 19 Oct. 1967 (62).
　　Upper Witham Internal Drainage District); 13 Oct. 1967 (56).
　　Witham First District Internal Drainage District); 4 Jan. (646).
　(Tetford Internal Drainage District); 13 Oct. 1967 (58).
Trent River Authority (Crowle Area Internal Drainage District); 25 Aug. 1967 (550).
Yorkshire Ouse and Hull River Authority (Goole and Airmyn Internal Drainage District); 25 Jan. (513).

GENERAL DRAINAGE CHARGE (ASCERTAINMENT) REGS., made by Minister of Agriculture, Fisheries and Food under Land Drainage Act 1961 (c. 48), s. 2† as adapted by Water Resources Act 1963 (c. 38), s. 5, sch. 3 para. 4; 26 Feb. (283).

(2) River authorities

WELLAND AND NENE AND THE LINCOLNSHIRE RIVER AUTHORITIES (ALTERATION OF AREAS) O., made by Minister of Housing and Local Government and Minister of Agriculture, Fisheries and Food acting jointly under Water Resources Act 1963 (c. 38), s. 10; 18 Nov. (1836).

MERSEY AND WEAVER RIVER AUTHORITY (EXCEPTIONS FROM CONTROL) O., made by Minister of Housing and Local Government under Water Resources Act 1963 (c. 38), s. 25; 10 June (910).

River Authority Constitution Orders made by Minister of Housing and Local Government and Minister of Agriculture, Fisheries and Food acting jointly under Water Resources Act 1963 (c. 38), ss. 3, 7, 8, 134.

Devon (Amdt.); 24 June (985).
Northumbrian (Amdt.); 31 Oct. (1742).

Water Board Orders made by Minister of Housing and Local Government under Water Resources Act 1963 (c. 38), s. 133.

Croydon; 21 Oct. (1669).
Rombalds; 8 May (735).

LLANELLI AND DISTRICT WATER BOARD O., made by Secretary of State under Water Resources Act 1963 (c. 38), s. 133; 20 June (998).

†Orders made under this section are liable to special parliamentary procedure.

Class 3.—Rivers and Inland Waterways—*cont.*

(3) Rivers (prevention of pollution)

River Purification Board (Prevention of Pollution) (Tidal Waters) Orders made by Secretary of State under Rivers (Prevention of Pollution) (S.) Act 1951 (c. 66), s. 29 and Rivers (Prevention of Pollution) (S.) Act 1965 (c. 13), s. 8.

Ayrshire; 22 Nov. (1892).
Clyde; 22 Nov. (1891).

(4) Salmon and freshwater fisheries

(*a*) ENGLAND AND WALES

NORTHUMBRIAN RIVER AUTHORITY AREA (FISHERIES) O., made by Minister of Agriculture, Fisheries and Food under Salmon and Freshwater Fisheries Act 1923 (c. 16), ss. 37†, 38†; 19 Jan. (326).

GREAT OUSE RIVER AUTHORITY (FISHERIES) O., made by Minister of Agriculture, Fisheries and Food under Salmon and Freshwater Fisheries Act 1923 (c. 16), ss. 37†, 38† as applied by Water Resources Act 1963 (c. 38), s. 5; 17 Oct. (2008).

Diseases of Fish (Injected Area) Orders made by Minister of Agriculture, Fisheries and Food under Diseases of Fish Act 1937 (c. 33), s. 2.

No. 1; 24 Jan. (141).
No. 2; 26 Jan. (161).
No. 3; 8 May (784).
No. 4; 8 May (785).

No. 5; 4 June (940).
No. 6; 3 Oct. (1606).
No. 7; 28 Nov. (1928).

(*b*) SCOTLAND

Annual Close Time Orders made by Secretary of State under Salmon Fisheries (S.) Act 1868 (c. 123), s. 9.

District of—
Loch Roag; 2 Dec. (1960).
the River Creed or Stornoway and Laxay; 29 Nov. (1959).
the River Stinchar; 21 Oct. (1679).

CLASS 4.—SHIPPING, HARBOURS, DOCKS, PORTS, &c.

(1) *Harbour development and improvement.*
(2) *Marine works.*
(3) *Port health authorities.*
(4) *Port of London.*
(5) *Revision of charges.*

(1) Harbour development and improvement

Harbour Revision Orders made by Minister of Transport under Harbours Act 1964 (c. 40), s. 14†.

Clyde Port Authority; 2 Jan. (778).
Grangemouth Docks; 26 Feb. (974).
King's Lynn Conservancy Bd; 28 Aug. (1976).
Lancaster Port Commission; 21 Nov. 1967 (532).
Mallaig; 16 May (1202).
Newport (Isle of Wight); 18 Apr. (1084).
Shoreham Port Authority; 10 Oct. (2042).

Harbour Reorganisation Scheme Confirmation Orders made by Minister of Transport under Harbours Act 1964 (c. 40), s. 18†, sch 4.

Humber; 24 Nov. 1967 (237).
Port of Tyne; 2 Apr. (942).
Southampton; 2 Apr. (941).

†Orders made under this section are liable to special parliamentary procedure.

Class 4.—Shipping, Harbours, Docks, &c.—*cont.*

(1) Harbour development and improvement—*cont.*

NEWLYN PIER AND HARBOUR REVISION O., made by Minister of Agriculture, Fisheries and Food under Sea Fish Industry Act 1951 (c. 30), s. 21 and Harbours Act 1964 (c. 40), s. 14†; 5 July (1886).

(2) Marine works

Secretary of State—Orders made under General Pier and Harbour Act 1861 (c. 45), s. 15† as applied by Harbours, Piers and Ferries (S.) Act 1937 (c. 28), ss. 4, 5.

Gourdon Harbour; 1 Nov. (2017).
Zetland County Council (Symbister Harbour); 18 Nov. (2058).

SOUTH KILLINGHOLME JETTY EMPOWERMENT O., made by Minister of Transport under Harbours Act 1964 (c. 40), s. 16†; 29 Mar. (986).

(3) Port health authorities

BRIDGWATER PORT O., made by Minister of Health under Public Health Act 1936 (c. 49), s. 9†; 19 Mar. (445).

(4) Port of London

PORT OF LONDON ACT 1964 (SECOND APPOINTED DATE) O., made by Minister of Housing and Local Government under Rivers (Prevention of Pollution) Act 1961 (c. 50), s. 1 as applied by Port of London Act 1964 (c. xxxvi), s. 6; 9 May (738).

*PORT OF LONDON AUTHORITY (MANNER OF BORROWING) O., made by Minister of Transport under Port of London (Consolidation) Act 1920 (c. clxxiii), s. 95 as amended by Port of London Act 1964 (c. xxxvi), s. 24; 7 June (901).

(5) Revision of charges*

Minister of Transport—Orders under Transport Charges &c. (Miscellaneous Provisions) Act 1954 (c. 64), s. 6.

Great Yarmouth Port and Haven; 22 Mar. (474).
Renfrew Ferry; 27 Feb. (312).

CLASS 5.—LOCAL GOVERNMENT

(1) *Accounts and audit.*
(2) *Adaptation of enactments.*
(3) *Clean air.*
(4) *Fire services.*
(5) *Local government areas.*

(6) *Police.*
(7) *Powers and duties of local authorities.*
(8) *Sunday cinematograph entertainments.*
(9) *Miscellaneous.*

(1) Accounts and audit*

Amalgamation of Funds Orders made by Minister of Housing and Local Government under Local Government (Miscellaneous Provisions) Act 1953(c. 26), s. 1.

Blackpool; 16 July (1131).
Bolton; 29 Oct. (1733).
Fylde; 11 Mar. (369).
Gloucester; 27 Sept. (1544).

---

*Not printed for sale in the S.I. series.
†Orders made under this section are liable to special parliamentary procedure.

Class 5.—Local Government—*cont.*

(2) Adaptation of enactments*

GREENOCK CORPORATION ACTS 1909 TO 1927 ETC. (AMDT.) O., made by Secretary of State under Local Government (S.) Act 1947 (c. 43), ss. 368, 381; 8 May (756).

(3) Clean air*

Suspension of Smoke Control—Orders made by Minister of Housing and Local Government under Clean Air Act 1956 (c. 52), s. 11.

Hammersmith; 24 Jan. (96).
Sutton-in-Ashfield; 8 Feb. (160).

(4) Fire services

LANARKSHIRE FIRE AREA ADMINISTRATION AMDT. SCHEME O., made by Secretary of State under Fire Services Act 1947 (c. 41), s. 36; 12 June (951).

SUFFOLK AND IPSWICH FIRE SERVICES (COMBINATION) (AMDT.) O., made by Secretary of State under Fire Services Act 1947 (c. 41), ss. 5, 9; 28 Nov. (1915).

(5) Local government areas

(a) ENGLAND AND WALES

(i) County electoral divisions

County (Electoral Divisions)—Orders made by Secretary of State under Local Government Act 1933 (c. 51), s. 11 as amended by Local Government Act 1958 (c. 55), sch. 8 para. 3.

Berkshire; 23 Sept. (1522).
Dorset; 21 Mar. (461).
Hertfordshire; 20 Nov. (1855).
Kent; 19 Mar. (442).

Lancaster—
  19 Mar. (453).
  (No. 2); 11 Nov. (1797).
Somerset; 9 Feb. (169).
West Sussex; 16 Dec. (2004).

(ii) City, Borough and Metropolitan borough wards

*Orders in Council made under Local Government Act 1933 (c. 51), s. 25.

Bedford; 4 Mar. (297).
Carlisle; 14 Feb. (186).
Ellesmere Port; 26 Jan. (115).
Leeds; 22 Mar. (466).
Macclesfield; 22 Nov. (1865).
Maidenhead; 26 Jan. (116).

New Windsor; 16 Oct. (1653).
Oxford; 12 July (1095).
Swinton and Pendlebury; 4 Mar. (298).
Widnes; 4 Mar. (299).
Wigan; 22 Nov. (1866).

GREATER LONDON, KENT AND SURREY O., made by Minister of Housing and Local Government under London Government Act 1963 (c. 33), ss. 6, 85; 19 Dec. (2020).

Secretary of State—Orders under London Government Act 1963 (c. 33), sch. 1 Pt. III paras. 2, 6.

Barking; 9 Apr. (591).

Southwark; 5 Mar. (324).

(iii) Alteration of areas

Minister of Housing and Local Government—Orders under Local Government Act 1958 (c. 55), ss. 23, 29, 38, 41, 60.

Cornwall—
  (Lostwithiel); 3 Jan. (5).
  (Padstow); 3 Jan. (6).
Derby; 12 Jan. (44).

Kingston upon Hull; 31 Jan. (128).
Norwich; 19 Jan. (68).
Teesside (Amdt.); 1 Mar. (526).

*Not printed for sale in the S.I. series.

Class 5.—Local Government—*cont.*

(5) Local government areas—*cont.*

(*a*) ENGLAND AND WALES—*cont.*

(*iii*) *Alteration of areas*—*cont.*

BOOTLE (EXTENSION) O., made by Minister of Housing and Local Government under Local Government Act 1933 (c. 51), s. 140† as amended by Local Government Act 1958 (c.55), sch. 8 para. 7; 27 Feb. (527).

ISLE OF WIGHT REVIEW (AMDT.) O., made by Minister of Housing and Local Government under Local Government Act 1929 (c. 17), ss. 46, 131; 12 Jan. (33).

(*b*) SCOTLAND*

Local Government (S.) Orders made by Secretary of State under Local Government (S.) Act 1947 (c. 43).

(*i*) *County councils and electoral divisions* (*ss. 4, 13, 361, 372*)
County of Inverness Electoral Divisions; 9 July (1127).
Dunbarton Electoral Divisions and Representation of the Burgh of Cumbernauld; 2 May (732).
Zetland County Council (Representation of the Burgh of Lerwick); 10 Apr. (609).

(*ii*) *Burgh councils and wards* (*ss. 21, 361*)
Burgh of Barrhead Wards; 13 Dec. (2018).

(*iii*) *District councils scheme* (*s. 38*)
County of Dunbarton District Council; 16 May (789).
County of Stirling District Council; 10 Apr. (610).

(6) Police

Police (Amalgamation)—Orders made by Secretary of State under Police Act 1964 (c. 48), ss. 21, 22, 23.

Devon and Cornwall (Amdt.); 14 Mar. (387).
Durham; 20 Aug. (1337).
Dyfed-Powys; 21 Mar. (475).
Essex and Southend-on-Sea; 8 Nov. (1786).
Lancashire; 27 Nov. (1899).
Liverpool and Bootle (Amdt.); 27 June (1026).

Manchester and Salford; 13 Feb. (190).
Sussex (Amdt.); 25 Jan. (121).
Thames Valley; 25 Mar. (496).
West Yorkshire; 4 July (1065).
York and North-East Yorkshire; 2 Apr. (555).

Police (Amalgamation)—Orders made by Secretary of State under Police (S.) Act 1967 (c. 77), s. 20.

Ayrshire; 22 Feb. (264).

Inverness; 5 Aug. (1282).

(7) Powers and duties of local authorities

(*a*) GENERAL POWERS

(*i*) *Borough and district councils*

Minister of Housing and Local Government—Orders under Public Health Act 1875 (c. 55), s. 276.

Bingham; 25 Mar. (511).
Hemsworth; 11 June (922).

Louth; 18 Mar. (446).
Worksop; 27 Mar. (498).

*SPILSBY RURAL DISTRICT (URBAN POWERS) O., made by Secretary of State under Public Health Act 1875 (c. 55), s. 276; 20 Aug. (1350).

---

*Not printed for sale in the S.I. series.
†Orders made under this section are liable to special parliamentary procedure.

Class 5.—Local Government—*cont.*

(7) Powers and duties of local authorities—*cont.*

(*a*) GENERAL POWERS—*cont.*

(*i*) *Borough and district councils—cont.*

* Minister of Housing and Local Government—Orders under Public Health Act 1875 (c. 55), s. 276 and Public Health Act 1925 (c. 71), s. 4.

Bedford; 12 Sept. (1466).   Thorney; 17 June (949).
Richmond; 10 Jan. (27).

*WAYLAND RURAL DISTRICT (URBAN POWERS) O., made by Minister of Housing and Local Government under Public Health Act 1875 (c. 55), s. 276, Public Health Act 1925 (c. 71), s. 4 and Local Government Act 1933 (c. 51), s. 190; 1 Mar. (310).

* Minister of Housing and Local Government—Orders under Public Health Act 1875 (c. 55), s. 276 and Local Government Act 1933 (c. 51), s. 148 as applied by Parish Councils Act 1957 (c. 42), s. 3.

Newark; 6 Mar. (330).   Newent; 19 Feb. (202).

* Minister of Housing and Local Government—Orders under Public Health Act 1875 (c. 55), s. 276, Local Government Act 1933 (c. 51), s. 148 as applied by Parish Councils Act 1957 (c. 42), s. 3 and Local Government Act 1933 (c. 51), s. 190.

Chelmsford; 24 June (984).   Preston—
                                                          22 Feb. (229).
                                                          26 Nov. (1887).

* Minister of Housing and Local Government—Orders under Public Health Act 1875 (c. 55), s. 276 and Local Government Act 1933 (c. 51), s. 190.

Eton; 10 Apr. (589).   Malmesbury—
Loddon; 13 Dec. (1985).   23 Oct. (1685).
                                                          (No. 2); 28 Nov. (1897).

* Secretary of State—Declarations under Public Health Acts Amdt. Act 1890 (c. 59), s. 5.

Ampthill; 8 Oct. (1613).   Luton; 30 Aug. (1418).
Aylesbury; 25 July (1203).   Melton and Belvoir; 1 Nov. (1767).
Banbury; 14 Mar. (406).   New Forest; 16 Oct. (1661).
Bedford; 20 Aug. (1347).   Newton Abbot; 19 June (963).
Biggleswade; 20 Aug. (1348).   Ploughley; 8 Oct. (1612).
Deben; 17 Sept. (1491).   Richmond; 4 Apr. (561).
Devizes; 19 Sept. (1497).   Stokesley; 21 Mar. (472).
Droitwich; 30 Apr. (685).   Tenterden; 20 Aug. (1349).
Gainsborough; 10 Jan. (29).   Weobley; 12 Jan. (49).

* Pleasure Boats Orders made by Secretary of State under Public Health Acts Amdt. Act 1907 (c.53), s.3.

No. 1; 6 Feb. (152).   No. 5; 17 June (945).
No. 2; 9 Feb. (167).   No. 6; 31 July (1238).
No. 3; 9 Apr. (595).   No. 7; 16 Sept. (1473).
No. 4; 10 June (920).

* Minister of Housing and Local Government—Orders under Public Health Act 1936 (c. 49), s. 13.

Bullingdon; 26 Apr. (672).   Spilsby; 12 Nov. (1819).

* Secretary of State—Orders under Highways Act 1959 (c. 25), s. 290.

Llandrindod Wells; 12 June (925).   Rhondda; 28 June (1042).

(*Advance Payments for Street Works*) *Orders made by Minister of Housing and Local Government under Highways Act 1959 (c. 25), sch. 14 para. 6.*

Devon; 9 Feb. (194).   Nottinghamshire; 8 Feb. (193).
Lincoln, Parts of Lindsey; 17 Oct. (1665).

GLAMORGAN (ADVANCE PAYMENTS FOR STREET WORKS) O., made by Secretary of State under Highways Act 1959 (c. 25), sch. 14 para. 6; 20 Feb. (269).

---

*Not printed for sale in the S.I. series.

Class 5.—Local Government—*cont.*

(7) Powers and duties of local authorities—*cont.*

(*a*) GENERAL POWERS—*cont.*

(*i*) *Borough and district councils—cont.*

*Refuse Dumps (Postponement) Orders made by Minister of Housing and Local Government under Civic Amenities Act 1967 (c. 69), s. 18.

Axminster; 18 July (1142).
Dudley; 22 July (1151).
Dulverton; 24 July (1178).
Mansfield; 18 July (1141).

Trowbridge; 18 July (1143).
Wing; 22 July (1152).
Winslow; 18 July (1144).

*Civic Amenities Act 1967 (Section 20) (Extension of Period) Orders made by Minister of Transport under Civic Amenities Act 1967 (c. 69), s. 20.

No. 1; 23 July (1193).
No. 2; 23 July (1194).
No. 3; 23 July (1195).

No. 4; 23 July (1186).
No. 5; 23 July (1187).
No. 6; 23 July (1189).

CIVIC AMENITIES ACT 1967 (SECTION 20) (EXTENSION OF PERIOD) (VALLEY RURAL DISTRICT) O., made by Secretary of State under Civic Amenities Act 1967 (c. 69), ss. 20, 30; 16 July (1140).

(*ii*) *Special expenses*

*Minister of Housing and Local Government—Orders under Local Government Act 1933 (c. 51), s. 190.

Barnstaple—
  23 Jan. (95).
  26 Apr. (671).
Basford; 16 Jan. (60).

Brixworth; 9 Jan. (23).
Droxford; 12 Nov. (1815).
Eton; 27 Mar. (510).
Watford; 6 June (897).

See also 4 orders listed under *Borough and district councils* above under Public Health Act 1875 (c. 55), s. 276 and Local Government Act 1933 (c. 51), s. 190.

(*b*) EXTENSION OF POWERS

*Minister of Housing and Local Government—Orders under Local Government Act 1933 (c. 51), s. 271.

Bideford; 19 Feb. (210).
Burnham-on-Sea; 5 June (882).

Hinckley; 18 Mar. (421).
York; 28 June (1022).

(8) Sunday cinematograph entertainments*

Secretary of State—Orders under Sunday Entertainments Act 1932 (c. 51), s. 1.

Middleton; 17 May (959).
Pickering; 21 Mar. (684).

Pocklington; 16 July (1204).
Skipton; 6 Feb. (335).

(9) Miscellaneous

Water Undertaking (Valuation) Orders made by Minister of Housing and Local Government under General Rate Act 1967 (c. 9), sch. 4 para. 10.

Barnsley; 3 Sept. (1427).
Southampton; 3 Sept. (1426).

West Somerset; 27 Mar. (501).

GREATER LONDON COUNCIL (ALLOWANCES TO MEMBERS) REGS., made by Minister of Housing and Local Government under Local Government Act 1948 (c. 26), s. 117 as extended by Greater London Council (General Powers) Act 1966 (c. xxviii), s. 23; 2 July (1043).

ISLES OF SCILLY (PREVENTION OF DAMAGE BY PESTS) O., made by Minister of Housing and Local Government under Local Government Act 1933 (c. 51), s. 292; 8 May (736).

TAF FECHAN WATER UNDERTAKING (VALUATION) O., made by Secretary of State under General Rate Act 1967 (c. 9), sch. 4 para. 10; 25 Apr. (699).

---

*Not printed for sale in the S.I. series.

CLASS 6.—PUBLIC HEALTH

(1) *Authorities.*
(2) *Food and drugs.*

(3) *National Health Service.*

(1) Authorities

*CAMBRIDGESHIRE UNITED DISTRICTS (MEDICAL OFFICER OF HEALTH) REVN. O., made by Minister of Health under Local Government Act 1933 (c. 51), s. 112†; 18 July (1145).

STEVENAGE NEW TOWN SEWERAGE (AMDT.) O., made by Minister of Housing and Local Government under New Towns Act 1965 (c. 59), s. 34; 5 Jan. (18).

(2) Food and drugs

Milk (Special Designations) (Specified Areas) (S.)—Orders made by Secretary of State under Milk (Special Designations) Act 1949 (c. 34), s. 5.
29 Feb. (374).   (No. 2); 5 Dec. (1957).

Slaughterhouses (Hygiene) Regs. (Appointed Day)—Orders made by Minister of Agriculture, Fisheries and Food under Slaughterhouses (Hygiene) Regs. 1958 **(a)**, *reg. 1 as amended* **(b)**.
2 Feb. (142).   (No. 2); 30 Sept. (1557).

(3) National Health Service

(a) ENGLAND AND WALES

National Health Service—Orders made by Minister of Health under National Health Service Act 1946 (c. 81), s. 11.

Betley Court Rehabilitation Centre; 19 Jan. (73).
Colinswood Maternity Home; 26 Apr. (673).
Deanhouse Hospital; 17 May (791).
Freeland Hospital; 20 June (972).
George Street Maternity Home; 25 July (1197).
Heath Lane Hospital; 14 Feb. (191).
Heathfield Road Maternity Hospital; 6 May (712).
Holloway Sanatorium; 15 July (1123).
Homewood Convalescent Home; 20 June (973).
Littlemore and Warneford and Park Hospitals;
  26 Mar. (489).

Moorview Hospital; 28 Oct. (1720).
Manchester and Cheshire Hospitals; 23 Sept. (1512).
North Devon Hospitals; 19 Aug. (1331).
North Tees-side Maternity Hospitals; 28 Mar. (546).
South Shields District Clinics; 27 Sept. (1540)
Spittlesea Isolation Hospital; 28 June (1027).
Taunton Maternity Home; 16 Aug. (1325).
Victoria Maternity Hospital; 6 Sept. (1435).
West Somerset Hospitals; 12 Sept. (1460).

NATIONAL HEALTH SERVICE (GLENTHORNE ANNEXE) O., made by Secretary of State under National Health Service Act 1946 (c. 81), s. 11; 17 Dec. (2000).

(b) SCOTLAND

Secretary of State—Orders under National Health Service (S.) Act 1947 (c. 27), s. 8.
Glasgow Victoria and Leverndale Hospitals; 17 Sept. (1503).
Glasgow Western and Gartnavel Hospitals; 11 Apr. (630).

**National Health Service* (Appointment of Boards of Management—Consequential Provisions) (S.)—Orders made by Secretary of State under National Health Service (S.) Act 1947 (c. 27), s. 11.*
29 Feb. (462).
(No. 2); 22 July (1175).

(No. 3); 18 Dec. (2055).

---

*Not printed for sale in the S.I. series.
†Orders made under this section are liable to special parliamentary procedure.
  (a) S.I. 1958/2168 (1958 I, p. 1182).   (b) S.I. 1966/1318 (1966 III, p. 3649).

CLASS 7.—TOWN AND COUNTRY PLANNING, OPEN SPACES, ACCESS TO THE COUNTRYSIDE

(1) *Designation of New Town Sites.*   (2) *Planning permission.*

(1) Designation of New Town Sites*

Minister of Housing and Local Government—Orders under New Towns Act 1965 (c. 59), ss. 1, 53.

Corby Amdt.; 21 Aug. (1343).
Dawley Amdt. (Telford); 29 Nov. (1912)†.
Northampton; 14 Feb. (179).
Warrington; 24 Apr. (665).

(2) Planning permission

Town and Country Planning (S.) (New Town of Irvine) (Special Development) O., made by Secretary of State under Town and Country Planning (S.) Act 1947 (c. 53), s. 11 and New Towns Act 1946 (c. 68), s. 3; 18 Mar. (482).

CLASS 8.—WATER SUPPLY

Minister of Housing and Local Government—Orders made under one or more of the following sections of Water Act 1945 (c. 42), Water Act 1948 (c. 22) and Compulsory Purchase Act 1965 (c. 56).

1945: *ss. 9‡, 10‡, 19, 23‡, 26‡, 32‡, 33‡, 40, 50.*
1948: *ss. 2‡, 3, 14.*
1965: *s. 33.*

Barnsley—
  17 Oct (1660).
  (Wharncliffe Estate); 17 May (790).
Bath Corporation (Water Charges); 6 Aug. (1270).
Birmingham and Coventry (Variation of Limits); 1 Jan. (1).
Bournemouth and District—
  7 Mar. (334).
  (No. 2); 20 Sept. (1504).
Bradford—
  20 Dec. (2051).
  (Brown Bank, Holden Beck and Aire Syphons); 25 Oct. (1814).
Brighton (Extension of Operation of Byelaws)— 23 Feb. (245).
  (No. 2); 29 Sept. (1569).
Chester (Borrowing Powers); 27 Mar. (507).
Colchester and District Water Bd. (Water Charges); 12 Jan. (32).
Colne Valley (Extension of Operation of Byelaws)– 4 Apr. (559).
  (No. 2); 1 Nov. (1750).
Cotswold Water Bd. (Charges); 30 Sept. (1570).
Craven and Fylde (Horton and Martons); 10 June (909).
Craven Water Bd. (Hawkswick Waterworks); 2 July (1038).
Cromer Urban District; 4 Apr. (558).
Dorset ; 11 Jan. (1154).
Durham County (Water Charges); 27 Mar. (508).
East Anglian—
  (Broome Common); 15 Mar. (393).
  (Financial Provisions); 4 Nov. (1752).
East Devon—
  27 Sept. (1543).
  (No. 2); 18 Oct (1664).
East Worcestershire—
  (Capital Powers); 6 Sept. (1438).
  (Evesham Sources); 2 July (1044).

East Worcestershire and—
  Cotswold (Variation of Limits); 22 Aug. (1359).
  North West Gloucestershire (Variation of Limits); 6 Sept. (1439).
Eastbourne—
  (Capital Powers); 4 Sept. (1431).
  (River Cuckmere); 16 Jan. (55).
Fylde Water Bd.; 15 Mar. (394).
Hanningfield; 15 Oct. (1735).
Hartlepools; 2 July (1039).
Lee Valley—
  17 Apr. (625).
  (No. 2) 6 Sept. (1440).
Leicester (Extension of Operation of Byelaws); 5 July (1067).
Lincoln and District Water Bd. (General Powers); 8 Oct. (1616).
Liverpool (Water Charges); 25 Sept. (1529).
Macclesfield District; 21 Feb. (220).
Malvern (Water Charges); 27 Mar. (509).
Manchester; 12 Feb. (175).
Mid Cheshire Water Bd. (Extension of Operation of Byelaws); 19 Jan. (91).
Mid Kent—
  (Canterbury); 17 July (1969).
  (New Sources); 15 Nov. (1828).
  (Rolvenden); 31 Oct. (1743).
Mid-Wessex; 8 Nov. (1785).
Middle Thames Water Bd. (Charges); 29 Feb. (287).
Nene and Ouse Water Bd.; 21 Oct. (1670).
Newcastle and Gateshead (Team Valley Industrial Estate); 29 Apr. (674).
North Devon—
  (Meldon Reservoir); 15 Nov. (1840).
  (Newhaven Pumping Station); 5 Feb. (144).
  (River Exe); 7 Nov. (1936).
North Lindsey (Barrow Haven); 30 Sept. (1554).

---

*Not printed for sale in the S.I. series.
†This instrument (1912) was printed and put on sale.
‡Orders made under this section are liable to special parliamentary procedure.

Class 8.—Water Supply—*cont.*

North West Gloucestershire and—
Herefordshire Water Bds. (Alteration of Limits of
Supply); 14 Aug. (1317).
Newport and South Monmouthshire (Variation of
Limits); 17 Oct. (1659).
North West Worcestershire Water Bd.—
(Chaddesley Corbett); 14 Mar. (395).
(Waresley Boreholes); 30 Oct. (1790).
North Wilts Water Bd. (Holt Borehole); 13 Nov.
(1817).
Northallerton and the Dales (Byelaws); 25 Sept.
(1528).
Norwich (Aylsham Pumping Station); 5 Apr. (569).
Portsmouth (Water Charges); 19 Feb. (204).
Rickmansworth and Uxbridge Valley (Extension of
Operation of Byelaws); 26 Mar. (492).
Rochdale (Extension of Operation of Byelaws); 26
Mar. (493).
Royal Tunbridge Wells (Extension of Operation of
Byelaws); 18 July (1139).
Rugby Joint Water Bd. (Charges); 12 Feb. (166).
Scarborough (Charges); 30 Sept. (1555).
Sheffield (Extension of Operation of Byelaws)—
23 Feb. (246).
(No. 2); 22 Aug. (1360).
South Essex—
(Extension of Operation of Byelaws)—
8 Mar. (347).
(No. 2); 17 Sept. (1478).
Waterworks (Roman River); 18 Jan. (64).
South Lincolnshire Water Bd.; 17 Apr. (813).
South Staffordshire (Seisdon and Uttoxeter); 20 Mar.
(447).
South West Worcestershire Water Bd.; 28 Apr. (1405).
Southampton Corporation—
(Andover Boreholes); 8 May (734).
(Kingsclere Borehole); 22 Aug. (1361).
(West Tytherley Waterworks); 20 May (812).
Spenborough (Extension of Operation of Byelaws);
14 June (929).

Sunderland and South Shields—
(Financial Provisions); 23 Apr. (655).
(Mill Hill Pumping Station); 1 Nov. (1751).
Swindon; 15 Aug. (1318).
Tees Valley and Cleveland—
31 Jan. (125).
(Water Charges); 27 June (1015).
Tendring Hundred—
10 Dec. (1962).
(Extension of Operation of Byelaws)—
10 June (919).
(No. 2); 16 Dec. (1990).
Thanet; 18 Oct. (1663).
Thorney (Extension of Operation of Byelaws); 8 May
(733).
Wakefield and District Water Bd.—
14 Nov. (1820).
(Charges); 19 Feb. (205).
(Victoria Reservoir); 11 Nov. (1789).
Warrington—
8 Apr. (584).
(No. 2); 18 July (1138).
(No. 3); 6 Sept. (1441).
(No. 4); 22 Nov. (1853).
West Pennine; 23 Feb. (512).
West Shropshire Water Bd.—
28 Mar. (515).
(Oakley Farm Borehole); 19 Dec. (2023).
West Suffolk Water Bd.—
18 Mar. (417).
(Shepherds Grove Airfield); 19 Sept. (1489).
West Wilts Water Bd.; 21 Nov. (1844).
Weymouth Waterworks (Extension of Operation of
Byelaws); 24 Oct. (1686).
Woking (Extension of Operation of Byelaws); 29 Jan.
(124).
Worthing; 14 Nov. (1821).
York—
12 June (923).
(Water Charges); 7 Mar. (331).

Bucks Water O., made by Minister of Housing and Local Government under Water Act 1945 (c. 42), s. 33† and Bucks Water Act 1937 (c. xcv), s. 93; 16 Dec. (1998).

Secretary of State—Orders made under one or more of the following sections of the Water Act 1945 (c. 42) and Water Act 1948 (c. 22).

1945: ss. 9†, 23†, 32†, 40, 50.
1948: s. 3.

Cardiganshire Water Bd.; 20 Mar. (441).
Eryi Water Bd. (Bwrdd Dwr Eryri) (Marchlyn Mawr);
21 Feb. (244).
Pontypool and District; 7 Mar. (340).
West Denbighshire and West Flintshire Water Bd.—
12 Mar. (372).
(No. 2); 11 Nov. (1810).

West Glamorgan Water Bd. (Llyn Brianne); 26 June
(1017).
Wrexham and East Denbighshire; 6 Dec. (1946).

*North Devon Water Bd. (Drought) O., made by Minister of Housing and Local Government under Water Act 1958 (c. 67), s. 1; 17 Sept. (1479).

Secretary of State—Orders made under one or more of the following sections of the Water (S.) Act 1946 (c. 42) as amended by Water (S.) Act 1949 (c. 31) and Water (S.) Act 1967 (c. 78).

1946: ss. 21†, 42†, 44†, 88†.
1949: s. 23.

Argyll County Council—
(Abhuinn Cheannain, Lochdonhead); 10 May (772).
(Allt Mor, Trislaig); 23 Apr. (667).
(Loch Fada, Ardfern); 23 Apr. (666).
Argyll Water Bd. (Allt Blaich Mhoir); 10 July (1121).
Ayr County Council—
(Loch Bradan); 14 May (798).
(Water of Girvan); 15 May (796).

Banff County Council (Tomintoul); 15 May (797).
County of Inverness (Loch a'Mhuilinn); 14 May (800).
Glasgow Corporation; 10 May (771).
Mid-Scotland Water Bd. (Longhill Weir); 1 Oct.
(1586).
Peterhead Town Council (Ugie); 15 May (799).
Zetland County Council (Sand Water, Mossbank);
8 Mar. (368).

---

*Not printed for sale in the S.I. series.
†Orders made under this section are liable to special parliamentary procedure.

Class 8.—Water Supply—*cont.*

Water Board (Financial Provisions)—Orders made by Secretary of State under Water (S.) Act 1967 (c. 78), s. 12.

Argyll; 6 May (739).
Ayrshire and Bute; 11 Mar. (367).
East of Scotland; 13 Mar. (383).
Fife and Kinross; 9 Apr. (612).
Inverness-shire; 9 May (749).
Lanarkshire; 27 Feb. (276).

Lower Clyde; 26 Feb. (268).
Mid-Scotland; 7 May (715).
North-East of Scotland; 14 May (782).
North of Scotland; 8 May (750).
Ross and Cromarty; 6 May (740).
South-East of Scotland; 29 Apr. (681).

CENTRAL SCOTLAND WATER DEVELOPMENT BD. (APPOINTED DAYS) O., made by Secretary of State under Water (S.) Act 1967 (c. 78), s. 3; 1 Mar. (313).

CENTRAL SCOTLAND WATER DEVELOPMENT BD. (SUPERANNUATION) O., made by Secretary of State under Water (S.) Act 1967 (c. 78), s. 23; 10 May (783).

MID-SCOTLAND WATER BD. (CONSTITUTION ETC.) AMDT. O., made by Secretary of State under Water (S.) Act 1967 (c. 78) ss. 8, 33; 29 Nov. (1932).

CLASS 9.—EDUCATION

Endowment Scheme Orders in Council under Education (S.) Act 1962 (c. 47), s. 127(1).

Catherine McCaig's Trust (Amdt.); 20 Dec. (2036).
George Heriot's Trust (Amdt.); 20 Dec. (2937).
Madras College (St. Andrews) Trust; 16 Oct. (1654).
Royal College of Science and Technology, Glasgow;
   12 July (1107).

University of St. Andrews (Scholarships and Bursaries) (Amdt.); 22 Nov. (1856).

CLASS 10.—LIGHTING, POWER AND HEATING

(1) *Gas.*   (2) *Mines and quarries.*

(1) Gas

GAS (SUPERANNUATION SCHEME) (WINDING UP) REGS., made by Minister of Power under Gas Act 1948 (c. 67), s. 58; 18 Mar. (415).

(2) Mines and quarries*

Minister of Power—regulations under Mines and Quarries Act 1954 (c. 70), ss. 141, 143 revoking special mines regs.

Bold; 12 Jan. (52).
Firbeck; 30 Jan. (127).
Hilton; 19 July (1160).

Lynemouth; 6 June (900).
New Stubbin; 5 Jan. (19).
Welbeck; 4 Apr. (567).

Mines—Special Regulations made by Minister of Power under Mines and Quarries Act 1954 (c. 70).

regs. relating to automatic shaft signalling (made under s. 141):

Brookhouse; 3 May (713).   Orgreave; 2 May (707).

regs. relating to cinematograph lighting (made under ss. 68, 141, 143):

Calverton; 30 Apr. (698).
Gedling; 29 Mar. (554).
Golborne; 1 May (701).
Kellingley; 30 Aug. (1410).

Lynemouth; 14 Aug. (1326).
Newstead; 17 Dec. (2013).
Westoe; 5 Apr. (568).

regs. relating to electric lighting (made under ss. 68, 141, 143):

Baddesley; 18 Oct. (1674).
Barrow; 19 July (1159).
Boldon; 14 Mar. (396).
Daw Mill; 20 June (975).
Havannah; 20 June (976).
Linby; 2 Aug. (1260);
Ollerton; 24 Oct. (1725).

Rawdon; 10 Dec. (1971).
Seafield; 22 Nov. (1888).
Sherwood; 17 Dec. (2014).
Silverwood; 31 Oct. (1756).
South Kirby; 21 Feb. (227).
Wearmouth; 11 Nov. (1796).
Westoe; 31 Oct. (1749).

*Not printed for sale in the S.I. series.

Class 10.—Lighting, Power and Heating—*cont.*

(2) Mines and quarries*—*cont.*

regs. relating to diesel or electric trolley locomotives (made under ss. 68, 83, 141):

Nangiles and the Janes; 30 May (868).   West Golds; 26 June (1024).

regs. relating to friction winding (made under ss. 141, 143):

Grimethorpe (Amdt.); 1 Nov. (1757).

regs. relating to lighting (made under ss. 68, 141):

Broadway New Pit Tunnel; 22 Jan. (103).   Preston Manor; 10 Jan. (38).
Chudleigh Knighton Tunnel; 10 Jan. (39).   West Golds; 10 Jan. (40).
Mainbow; 22 Jan. (104).

regs. relating to locomotives and diesel vehicles (made under ss. 39, 83, 141, 143):

Fauld; 8 Aug. (1295).   Sherburn; 21 Aug. (1351).
Oakley; 24 Oct. (1724).

regs. relating to precautions against inrushes (made under ss. 141, 143):

Gartenkeir; 20 June (977).   Ridge Heath; 26 July (1209).
Gartmorn; 24 July (1185).   Wearmouth; 23 Sept. (1527).

regs. relating to rope haulage (made under ss. 47, 141, 143):

Maltby; 15 Jan. (53).

regs. relating to winding and haulage appratus (made under ss. 141, 143):

Hawthorn; 18 Oct.'(1673).   Michael; 29 Oct. (1738).
Houghton; 2 Aug. (1261).   Sherwood; 3 May (714).
Lochhead; 13 Nov. (1831).   Silksworth; 26 June (1023).

CLASS 11.—ADMINISTRATION OF JUSTICE

(1) *Coroners' districts.*   (4) *Probation areas.*
(2) *Fixed penalty areas.*   (5) *Quarter Sessions.*
(3) *Petty sessional divisions.*

(1) Coroners' districts*

*Coroners' Districts—Orders made by Secretary of State under Coroners (Amdt.)
Act 1926 (c. 59), s. 12.*

Montgomeryshire (Amdt.); 11 Apr. (613).   York, East Riding (Amdt.); 21 May (829).

(2) Fixed penalty areas

*Fixed Penalty (Areas)—Orders made by Secretary of State under Road Traffic
Regulation Act 1967 (c. 76), s. 80.*

3 Jan. (10).   (No. 8); 9 Sept. (1455).
(No. 2); 6 Feb. (155).   (No. 9); 23 Oct. (1695).
(No. 3); 14 Mar. (385).   (No. 10); 20 Nov. (1843).
(No. 4); 9 Apr. (596).   (S.)—
(No. 5); 7 May (747).   23 Jan. (110).
(No. 6); 19 June (962).   (No. 2); 8 Feb. (174).
(No. 7); 20 Aug. (1338).

(3) Petty sessional divisions

(a) PETTY SESSIONS GENERALLY

*Petty Sessional Divisions—Orders made by Secretary of State under Justices of the
Peace Act 1949 (c. 101), s. 18.*

Bedfordshire; 31 July (1236).   Outer London—
Devon; 14 Feb. (199).   7 May (746).
Hertfordshire—   (No. 2); 31 July (1237).
  28 Nov. (1917).   Shropshire; 18 Sept. (1490).
  (No. 2); 30 Dec. (2072).   Somerset; 2 July (1057).

*Not printed for sale in the S.I. series.

Class 11.—Administration of Justice—*cont.*

(3) Petty sessional divisions—*cont.*

(*b*) JUVENILE COURT PANELS*

Juvenile Court Panel—Orders made by Secretary of State under Children and Young Persons Act 1933 (c. 12), sch. 2 paras. 6, 21.

Banbury Borough, Banbury and Bloxham and Chipping Norton; 30 May (871).
Birdforth, Bulmer West and Hallikeld; 30 May (872).
Dewsland, Haverfordwest and Milford Haven; 28 Nov. (1916).

Raglan and Trelech; 6 Nov. (1787).
Sheffield and Hallamshire; 1 July (1050).
West Riding of Yorkshire; 18 July (1153).
Worcestershire; 22 July (1208).

DEVON JUVENILE COURT PANELS (REVN.) O., made by Secretary of State under Children and Young Persons Act 1933 (c. 12), sch. 2 paras. 6, 20, 21 as amended by Children and Young Persons Act 1963 (c. 37), s. 17; 21 Mar. (479).

(4) Probation areas*

Probation and After-Care Area—Orders made by Secretary of State under Criminal Justice Act 1948 (c. 58), s. 76, sch. 5 paras. 1, 2.

East Sussex (Amdt.); 10 Apr. (611).

Hampshire; 12 Mar. (371).

(5) Quarter Sessions

ORDER IN COUNCIL made under Municipal Corporations Act 1882 (c. 50), granting a separate Court of Quarter Sessions in the County Borough of Teesside; 26 Jan. (119).

CLASS 12.—AGRICULTURE, FISHERIES AND FORESTRY

(1) *Diseases of trees and plants.*
(2) *Markets and fairs.*

(3) *Prevention of cruelty.*
(4) *Protection of birds.*

(1) Diseases of trees and plants

PROTECTION OF SEED CROPS (NORTH ESSEX) O., made by Minister of Agriculture, Fisheries and Food under Plant Varieties and Seeds Act 1964 (c. 14), s. 33; 19 Feb. (207).

(2) Markets and fairs*

Market (Exemption)—Orders made by Minister of Agriculture, Fisheries and Food under Food and Drugs Act 1955 (c. 16), s. 56.

Buxton; 3 July (1056).

Holmfirth; 13 Aug. (1301).

(3) Prevention of cruelty

Slaughter of Animals (Prevention of Cruelty) Regs. (Appointed Day)—Orders made by Minister of Agriculture, Fisheries and Food under Slaughter of Animals (Prevention of Cruelty) Regs. 1958 (a), regs. 2, 5, 15, 28.

2 Feb. (143).

(No. 2); 30 Sept. (1556).

(4) Protection of birds

Wild Birds (Sanctuary)—Orders made by Secretary of State under Protection of Birds Act 1954 (c. 30), ss. 3, 13.

Brean Down; 3 Apr. (562).
Charlton's Pond; 3 Apr. (564).
Fairburn Ings; 10 Dec. (1964).

Gibraltar Point; 3 Apr. (563).
Island of Fetlar; 8 May (755).

---

*Not printed for sale in the S.I. series.
(a) S.I. 1958/2166 (1958 I, p. 147).

CLASS 13.—MISCELLANEOUS

(1) Aerodrome Roads

Minister of Transport—Orders under Airports Authority Act 1965 (c. 16), s. 12.

Gatwick (Amdt.)—
12 Jan. (46).
(No. 2); 11 Mar. (363).
Heathrow (Amdt.)—
12 Jan. (47).
(No. 2); 11 Mar. (364).

Stansted (Amdt.)—
12 Jan. (48).
(No. 2); 11 Mar. (365).

AERODROME ROADS (PRESTWICK) (AMDT.) O., made by Secretary of State under Airports Authority Act 1965 (c. 16), s. 12; 19 Jan. (84).

(2) Charities

CHARITIES (WOBURN ALMSHOUSE CHARITY) O., made by Secretary of State under Charities Act 1960 (c. 58), s. 19; 23 Oct. (1694).

(3) Civil Aviation

Air Navigation (Restriction of Flying)—Regulations made by the Board of Trade under Air Navigation O. 1966 (a), art. 60.

Farnborough; 28 Aug. (1400).
R.A.F. Station at Abingdon; 6 June (880).

LONDON (HEATHROW) AIRPORT NOISE INSULATION GRANTS (AMDT.) SCHEME, made by the Board of Trade under Airports Authority Act 1965 (c. 16), s. 15; 21 Nov. (1842).

(4) Continental Shelf

CONTINENTAL SHELF (PROTECTION OF INSTALLATIONS) (No. 2) O., made by Minister of Power under Continental Shelf Act 1964 (c. 29), s. 2; 5 Mar. (323).

(5) Landlord and Tenant

LEASEHOLD REFORM ACT 1967 (APPLICATION OF SECTION 28 TO THE ROYAL COLLEGE OF ART) O., made by Minister of Housing and Local Government under Leasehold Reform Act 1967 (c. 88), s. 28; 18 Dec. (2022).

(6) National Gallery and Tate Gallery

National Gallery (Lending Outside the United Kingdom)—Orders made by Secretary of State for Education and Science under National Gallery and Tate Gallery Act 1954 (c. 65), s. 4.

(No. 1); 21 May (828).

(No. 2); 23 July (1179).

(7) Savings Banks

BIRMINGHAM MUNICIPAL BANK (AMDT.) O., made by the Treasury under Finance Act 1956 (c. 54), s. 9 as amended by Trustee Savings Banks Act 1958 (c. 8), s. 3; 30 July (1221).

(a) S.I. 1966/1184 (1966 III, p. 3073).

TABLES OF EFFECT

of the Statutory Instruments of 1968

(With certain additional information)

Table A

A CHRONOLOGICAL TABLE OF ACTS OF PARLIAMENT
WHOSE OPERATION WAS AFFECTED BY
STATUTORY INSTRUMENTS OF 1968

Public General Acts

Table B

A CHRONOLOGICAL TABLE OF SUBORDINATE LEGISLATION
(S.R. & O. AND S.I) AND CERTAIN PREROGATIVE INSTRUMENTS
WHOSE OPERATION WAS AFFECTED BY
LEGISLATION OF 1968 (ACTS AND INSTRUMENTS)

TABLE A

NOTES

1. For List of Abbreviations used in this Table, see p. ix.

2. A comprehensive table showing the effect of Acts, Measures and S.I. of 1968 on Acts and Measures is printed in the *Annual Volume of Public General Acts.*

EFFECT ON PUBLIC GENERAL ACTS

Short Title	How affected and Instrument by which affected
1847 Town Police Clauses Act 1847 (c. 89) ...	s. 46 **am.,** 1968/170.
1855 Places of Worship Registration Act 1855 (c. 81)	ss. 5, 7 **am.,** 1968/1242.
1856 Marriage and Registration Act 1856 (c. 119)	s. 24 **am.,** 1968/1242.
1860 Game Licences Act 1860 (c. 90)	ss. 2, 7, 13 **am.,** 1968/120.
1862 Juries Act 1862 (c. 107)	s. 11 **am.,** 1968/1253.
1871 Pedlars Act 1871 (c. 96)	s. 5 **am.(E.)** 1968/1970.
1872 Pawnbrokers Act 1872 (c. 93)	s. 37 **am.,** 1968/120.
1874 Births and Deaths Registration Act 1874 (c. 88)	s. 28 **am.,** 1968/1242.
1875 Explosives Act 1875 (c. 17)...	ss. 15, 18, 21 **am.** (E. and W.) 1968/170, (S.) 1968/248.
1876 Sheriff Cts. (S.) Act 1876 (c. 70)	s. 45 **am.,** 1968/140.
1881 Fugitive Offenders Act 1881 (c. 69) ...	**r.** (exc. s. 25) s. 25 **am.,** (Cayman Islands) 1968/112, (Falkland Islands and Dependencies) 1968/113, (British Indian Ocean Territory) 1968/183, (St. Helena) 1968/184, Turks and Caicos Islands 1968/185, (Pitcairn, Henderson, Ducie and Oeno Islands) 1968/884, (New Hebrides) 1968/1091.
1882 Settled Land Act 1882 (c. 38)	s. 25 **am.** (N.I.), 1968/703.
1883 Customs and Inland Revenue Act 1883 (c. 10)	s. 5 **am.,** 1967/120.
1887 Savings Bank Act 1887 (c. 40)	s. 10 **am.** (S.) 1968/1177, (E. and W.) 1968/1242.

Short Title	How affected and Instrument by which affected
1890 Foreign Jurisdiction Act 1890 (c. 37) ...	sch. 1 **am.** (Cayman Islands) 1968/112, (Falkland Islands and Dependencies) 1968/113, (British Indian Ocean Territory) 1968/183, (St. Helena) 1968/184, (Turks and Caicos Islands) 1968/185, (Pitcairn, Henderson, Ducie and Oeno Islands) 1968/884, (New Hebrides) 1968/1091.
Public Health Acts Amdt. Act 1890 (c. 59)	s. 51 para. 1 **am.**, 1968/170.
1892 Burgh Police (S.) Act 1892 (c. 55)	ss. 275, 396, sch. 5 para. 2 **am.**, 1968/248.
1896 Friendly Societies Act 1896 (c. 25) ...	s. 97 **am.** (S.) 1968/1177, (E. and W.) 1968 /1242.
1898 Merchant Shipping (Mercantile Marine Fund) Act 1898 (c. 44)	sch. 2 **am.**, 1968/580.
1907 Sheriff Cts. (S.) Act 1907 (c. 51)	s. 45 **am.**, sch. 1 rule 15A **inserted,** 1968/1149.
Public Health Acts Amdt. Act 1907 (c. 53)	s. 94 **am.**, 1968/170.
1909 Cinematograph Act 1909 (c. 30)	s. 2 **am.** (E. and W.) 1968/170, (S.)1968/ 248.
1915 Fugitive Offenders (Protected States) Act 1915 (c. 39)	**rep.** (Cayman Islands) 1968/112, (Falkland Islands and Dependencies) 1968 /113, (British Indian Ocean Territory) 1968/183, (St. Helena) 1968/184, (Turks and Caicos Islands) 1968/185, (Pitcairn, Henderson, Ducie and Oeno Islands) 1968/884, (New Hebrides) 1968/1091.
1916 New Ministries and Secretaries Act 1916 (c. 68)	ss. 1, 2, 10 **rep.**, 11 **am.**, 12, 14 **rep.** sch. **rep.** 1968/729.
1919 Ministry of Health Act 1919 (9 & 10 Geo. 5) (c. 21)	s. 1 **rep.**, 2 **am.**, 3 **rep.**, 6 **am.**, 7 **rep.**, 8, 11 **am.**, sch. 1 **rep.**, 1968/1699.
1920 Firearms Act 1920 (c. 43)	s. 6 (N.I.), functions transfd. to Secy. of State 1968/1200.
Official Secrets Act 1920 (c. 75)	s. 5 **am.** (E. and W.) 1968/170, (S.) 1968/248.
1923 Fees (Increase) Act 1923 (c. 4)	s. 9 **am.**, 1968/656.
1925 Settled Land Act 1925 (c. 18)	sch. 3 **am.**, 1968/704.
Performing Animals (Regulation) Act 1925 (c. 38)	s. 5 **am.** (E. and W.) 1968/170, (S.) 1968/248.
Supreme Ct. of Judicature (Consolidation) Act 1925 (c. 49)	sch. 2 **replaced,** 1968/1676.
Theatrical Employers Registration Act 1925 (c. 50)	s. 3 **am.** (E. and W.) 1968/170, (S.) 1968/248.
1926 Home Counties (Music and Dancing) Licensing Act 1926 (c. 31)	s. 3 **am.**, 1968/170.

Short Title	How affected and Instrument by which affected
1926 Fertilisers and Feeding Stuffs Act 1926 (c. 45)	sch. 1–5 **replaced,** 1968/218. sch. 1, 2, 4 **am.,** 1968/883.
Births and Deaths Registration Act 1926 (c. 48)	s. 9 **am.,** 1968/1699.
1927 Moneylenders Act 1927 (c. 21)	s. 1 **am.,** 1968/120.
1928 Petroleum (Consolidation) Act 1928 (c. 32)	sch. 1 **am.** (E. and W.) 1968/170, (S.) 1968/248.
1933 Pharmacy and Poisons Act 1933 (c. 25) ...	Pt. II **am.,** 1968/75. sch. 2 **am.,** 1968/1699.
Local Govt. Act 1933 (c. 51)	s. 290 **am.,** 1968/656.
Road and Rail Traffic Act 1933 (c. 53) ...	s. 47 **am.,** 1968/656.
1936 Petroleum (Transfer of Licences) Act 1936 (c. 27)	s. 1 **am.** (E. and W.) 1968/170, (S.) 1968/248.
Firearms (Amdt.) Act 1936 (c. 39) ...	s. 7 (N.I.), functions transfd. to Secy. of State, 1968/1200.
Public Health Act 1936 (c. 49)	s. 187 **am.,** 1968/102. s. 143 functions transfd. to the Bd. of Trade, 1968/2038.
1938 Young Persons (Employment) Act 1938 (c. 69)	s. 5 **am.** (S.) 1968/1177, (E. and W.) 1242.
Nursing Homes Registration (S.) Act 1938 (c. 73)	s. 1 **am.,** 1968/248.
1939 War Risks Insurance Act 1939 (c. 57) ...	Pt. I functions transfd. to the Bd. of Trade, 1968/2038.
Restriction of Advertisement (War Risks Insurance) Act 1939 (c. 120)	s. 1(2) **am.,** 1968/2038.
1940 Finance Act 1940 (c. 29)	s. 64(1) functions transfd. to the Bd. of Trade, 1968/2038.
1944 Education Act 1944 (c. 31)	s. 94 **am.,** 1968/1242.
1946 Statutory Instruments Act 1946 (c. 36) ...	ss. 8, 11 functions transfd. to Min. for the Civil Service, 1968/1656.
National Health Service Act 1946 (c. 81) ...	s. 67 **am.,** 1968/1699.
1947 Exchange Control Act 1947 (c. 14) ...	sch. 1 **am.,** 1968/333, 1399.
National Health Service (S.) Act 1947 (c. 27)	s. 66 **am.,** 1968/1699.
Local Govt. (S.) Act 1947 (c. 43)	s. 355 **am.,** 1968/656.
Crown Proceedings Act 1947 (c. 44) ...	s. 17 functions transfd. to Min. for the Civil Service, 1968/1656.

Short Title	How affected and Instrument by which affected
1948 National Assistance Act 1948 (c. 29) ...	s. 37 **am.** (E. and W.) 1968/102, (S.) 1968/248.
Radioactive Substances Act 1948 (c. 37) ...	ss. 3, 4 **am.**, 1968/1699.
Industrial Assurance and Friendly Societies Act 1948 (c. 39)	sch. 1 para. 7 **am.** (S.) 1968/1177, (E. and W.) 1968/1242.
1949 Special Roads Act 1949 (c. 32)	sch. 2 **am.**, 1968/1982.
Marriage Act 1949 (c. 76)	ss. 27, 29, 31, 32, 41, 51, 57, 63–65 **am.**, 1968/1242.
1950 Shops Act 1950 (c. 28)	s. 35 **am.** (S.) 1968/1177, (E. and W.) 1968/1242.
1951 Pet Animals Act 1951 (c. 35)	s. 1 **am.** (E. and W.) 1968/170, (S.) 1968/248.
Rag Flock and Other Filling Materials Act 1951 (c. 63)	ss. 2, 6, 7 **am.** (E. and W.) 1968/99, (S.) 1968/248.
1952 National Health Service Act 1952 (c. 25) ...	s. 2 **am.** (E. and W.) 1968/544, (S.) 1968/557.
Marine and Aviation Insurance (War Risks) Act 1952 (c. 57)	Functions transfd. to the Bd. of Trade, 1968/2038. s. 8 **am.**, 1968/2038.
1953 Births and Deaths Registration Act 1953 (c. 20)	ss. 5–7, 9, 11–14, 20, 21, 24, 29–33 **am.**, 1968/1242.
1955 Food and Drugs Act 1955 (4 & 5 Eliz. 2. c. 16)	sch. 10 **am.**, 1968/1699.
Aliens' Employment Act 1955 (4 & 5 Eliz. 2 c. 18)	s. 1 functions transfd. to Min. for the Civil Service, 1968/1656.
1956 Therapeutic Substances Act 1956 (c. 25) ...	ss. 4, 8, 9 **am.**, 1968/1699. sch. 1 **am.**, 1968/906, 907.
Restrictive Trade Practices Act 1956 (c. 68)	s. 7 **am.**, 1968/1036.
1957 House of Commons Disqualification Act 1957 (c. 20)	sch. 1 Pts. I, II, III **am.** 1968/187. sch. 2 **am.**, 1968/729, 1699. sch. 3 **am.**, 1968/187.
Dentists Act 1957 (c. 28)	sch. 1 **am.**, 1968/1699.
1958 Local Govt. Act 1958 (c. 55)	s. 60 functions transfd. to Min. for the Civil Service, 1968/1656.
Adoption Act 1958 (7 & 8 Eliz. 2. c. 5) ...	s. 30 **am.** (E. and W.) 1968/170, (S.) 1968/248.
1959 Highways Act 1959 (c. 25)	sch. 4 **am.**, 1968/1966.
1960 Road Traffic Act 1960 (c. 16)	s. 249 **am.**, 1968/656. s. 164 **mod.**, 1968/1168. ss. 212, 213 **am.** (E.) 1968/1970, (S.) 1968/1994.
Mental Health (S.) Act 1960 (c. 61) ...	s. 15 **am.**, 1968/248.
Professions Supplementary to Medicine Act 1960 (c. 66).	sch. 1 **am.**, 1968/1699.

Short Title	How affected and Instrument by which affected
1960 Ministers of the Crown (Parliamentary Secretaries) Act 1960 (9 & 10 Eliz. 2 c. 6)	sch. 1 **am.**, 1968/729, 1699.
1961 Factories Act 1961 (c. 34)	s. 176 **am.**, 1968/1530. s. 178 **am.** (S.) 1968/1177, (E. and W.) 1968/1242.
Trustee Investments Act 1961 (c. 62) ...	sch. Pt. I **am.**, 1968/470.
1962 Local Govt. (Financial Provns. etc.) (S.) Act 1962 (c. 9)	sch. 1 **am.**, 1968/198.
Vehicles (Excise) Act 1962 (c. 13)	s. 2 **am.**, 1968/439.
Commonwealth Immigrants Act 1962 (c. 21)	s. 4A **mod.**, 1968/284. s. 4A **mod.** (Jersey), 1968/315. s. 16 **am.**, 1968/1699.
Health Visiting and Social Work (Training) Act 1962 (c. 33)	s. 7 **am.**, 1968/1699.
Transport Act 1962 (c. 46)	s. 90 **am.**, 1968/656.
Education (S.) Act 1962 (c. 47)	s. 99 **am.**, 1968/1177.
1963 Betting, Gaming and Lotteries Act 1963 (c. 2)	sch. 2 para. 11, sch. 3 para. 12, sch. 6 para. 4, sch. 7 paras. 3, 9 **am.** (E. and W.) 1968/170, (S.) 1968/248.
Purchase Tax Act 1963 (c. 9)	sch. 1 Pt. I **am.**, 1968/709, 1511.
British Museum Act 1963 (c. 24)	sch. 3 Pt. I **am.**, 1968/1604.
Weights and Measures Act 1963 (c. 31) ...	s. 10 **am.**, 1968/1699. sch. 3 Pt. V **am.**, 1968/320.
London Government Act 1963 (c. 33) ...	sch. 12 paras. 3, 6 **am.**, 1968/170.
Animal Boarding Establishments Act 1963 (c. 43)	s. 1 **am.** (E. and W.) 1968/170, (S.) 1968/248.
Local Govt. (Financial Provns.) Act 1963 (c. 46)	s. 6 **am.**, 1968/491.
1964 Licensing Act 1964 (c. 26)	sch. 8 **am.** (W.), 1968/1542.
Emergency Laws (Re-enactments and Repeals) Act 1964 (c. 60)	ss. 4, 5 **am.**, 1968/1699.
Riding Establishments Act 1964 (c. 70) ...	s. 1 **am.** (E. and W.) 1968/170, (S.) 1968/248.
Ministers of the Crown Act 1964 (c. 98) ...	sch. 2 Pt. II **am.**, 1968/729, 1699.
1965 Dangerous Drugs Act 1965 (c. 15) ...	sch. Pt. I **am.**, 1968/1650.
Overseas Development and Service Act 1965 (c. 38)	s. 2 functions transfd. to Min. for the Civil Service, 1968/1656.

Short Title	How affected and Instrument by which affected
1965 National Insurance Act 1965 (c. 51) ...	s. **4 am.**, 1968/827. s. **91 am.** (S.) 1968/1177, (E. and W.) 1968/1242. ss. 79, 110 functions transfd. to Min. for the Civil Service, 1968/1656.
National Health Service Contributions Act 1965 (c. 54)	ss. 1, 3, **4 am.**, 1968/1699.
Ministerial Salaries Consolidation Act 1965 (c. 58)	s. **2 am.**, 1968/1699. sch. 1 **am.**, 1968/729, 1699.
Redundancy Payments Act 1965 (c. 62) ...	s. **27 am.**, 1968/1264, 1699 s. 41 functions transfd. to Min. for the Civil Service, 1968/1656. s. **29 am.**, 1968/1699.
1966 National Health Service Act 1966 (c. 8) ...	s. **11 am.**, 1968/1699.
Rating Act 1966 (c. 9)	s. **10 am.**, 1968/491. s. **7 am.** (S.), 1968/1079.
Ministry of Social Security Act 1966 (c. 20)	s. 1 **rep.**, 1968/1699. ss. 31, **32 am.**, 1968/1699. sch. 2 para. 23 **am.**, 1968/759, 818. sch. 2 paras. 9, 10 **replaced**, paras. 11—13 **am.**, 1968/1118.
Docks and Harbours Act 1966 (c. 28) ...	sch. 1 **am.**, 1968/1075.
Selective Employment Payments Act 1966 (c. 32)	s. 1 **am.**, 1968/1147. sch. 1 Pts. I—III **am.**, 1968/1388. sch. 1 Pt. II **am.**, 1968/1622.
Prices and Incomes Act 1966 (c. 33) ...	sch. 2 **replaced**, 1968/616.
1967 General Rate Act 1967 (c. 9)	s. **49 am.**, 1968/491. sch. 9 Pt. II **am.**, 1968/1066.
Parliamentary Commissioner Act 1967 (c. 13)	sch. 2 **am.**, 1968/1656, 1657, 1699, 1859.
National Insurance Act 1967 (c. 73) ...	s. **5 am.**, 1968/17.
1968 Commonwealth Immigrants Act 1968 (c. 9)	s. 5 **mod.** (Jersey) 1968/300, (Guernsey) 1968/301, (Is. of Man) 1968/302.
Public Expenditure and Receipts Act 1968 (c. 14)	s. 5, functions transfd. to Min. for the Civil Service, 1968/1656.
Firearms Act 1968 (c. 27)	ss. 32, 35 **am.**, (E. and W.) 1968/1753, (S.) 1968/1961.
Health Services and Public Health Act 1968 (c. 46)	ss. 59, 61 **am.**, 1968/1699.
Medicines Act 1968 (c. 67)	ss. 1, 5, 120 **am.**, 1968/1699.
Race Relations Act 1968 (c. 71)	s. 27, functions transfd. to Min. for the Civil Service, 1968/1656.
Transport Act 1968 (c. 73)	sch. 7 **am.**, 1968/1980. sch. 3 Pt. I **am.**, 1968/2053.

TABLE B

A CHRONOLOGICAL TABLE OF SUBORDINATE LEGISLATION

(S.R. & O. AND S.I. AND CERTAIN PREROGATIVE INSTRUMENTS)

WHOSE OPERATION WAS AFFECTED BY

LEGISLATION OF 1968 (ACTS AND INSTRUMENTS)

NOTES

1. For List of Abbreviations used in this Table, see p. IX.

2. In Col. 2, Volume references given in brackets after the titles of instruments have the following significance:—

" Rev., 1903 " indicates *Statutory Rules and Orders Revised* (2nd Edition, to 31 Dec. 1903).

" Rev." indicates *Statutory Rules and Orders and Statutory Instruments Revised* (3rd Edition, to 31 Dec. 1948).

Where neither of these appears, the reference is to the Annual Volume of S.R. & O. (1890 to 1947) or S.I. (1948 onwards) for the year shown (in heavy type) in col. 1.

The Roman numeral indicates the Volume or Part number of the Edition or year concerned.

Year and Number (or date)	Title or Description	How affected and Act or Instrument by which affected
1876 1 Apr.	Public Works Loans Act 1875—Regs. (Rev. XVIII, p. 899)	r., 1968/458.
1879 18 Dec.	Public Works Loans Act 1875—further Regs. (Rev. XVIII, p. 901)	r., 1968/458.
1888 *Instrt. not S.I.* 19 Jan.	Bermuda L. P. 1888 (Rev. III, p. 119)	r., 1968/182.
1889 31 May	Preparation, issue and cancellation of Treas. Bills—Minute (Rev. XXIII, p. 289)	r., 1968/414.
1897 884	Merchant Shipping Act 1894, exercise of powers of British Consular Officer in Gilbert and Ellice Is. and Solomon Is. O. in C. (Rev. XIV, p. 687)	r., 1968/293.
1900 695	Infectious Diseases, notification of Plague—O. 1900 (Rev. XVIII, p. 761)	r., 1968/1366.
1904 *Instrt. not S.I.* 24 Jan.	Tenders for Treas. Bills—Amdg. Minute (H. of C. Paper 1 (2 Feb. 1904))	r., 1968/414.

Year and Number (or date)	Title or Description	How affected and Act or Instrument by which affected
1908 227	Criminal Appeal Rules 1908 (Rev. V, p. 352)	**r.,** 1968/1262.
277	Criminal Appeal Rules 1908—Addnl. Rule (Rev. V, p. 400)	**r.,** 1968/1262.
1318	Merchant Shipping Act 1894, exercise of powers of British Consular Officer in Gilbert and Ellice Is. and Solomon Is. O. in C. 1908 (Rev. XIV, p. 688)	**r.,** 1968/293.
1910 1165	Prevention of plague—O. 1910 (Rev. XVIII, p. 800)	**r.,** 1968/1366.
1912 69	Irish Land (Finance) Rules, 1912 (1912, p. 405)	rule 16 **am.,** 1968/991.
1915 *Instrt. not S.I.* 13 Apr.	Preparation, issue and cancellation of Treasury Bills—Treas. Minute (H. of C. Paper 199 (15 Apr. 1915))	**r.,** 1968/414.
25 Nov.	Bermuda R. Instructions 1915	**r.,** 1968/182.
1917 146	Public Health (Small-pox Prevention) Regs. 1917 (Rev. XVIII, p. 804)	**r.,** 1968/1366.
1918 67	Public Health (Notification of Infectious Disease) Regs. 1918 (Rev. XVIII, p. 763)	**r.,** 1968/1366.
1919 767	Public Health (Cerebro-Spinal Fever) Regs. 1919 (Rev. XVIII, p. 795)	**r.,** 1968/1366.
1925 788	Post Office Register Regs. 1925 (Rev. XV, p. 448)	reg. 26 **am.,** 1968/1001.
1146	Theatrical Employers Registration Rules 1925 (Rev. XXII, p. 525)	rule 12 **replaced,** 1968/1342.
1219	Performing Animals Rules 1925 (Rev. II, p. 254)	rule 9 **replaced,** 1968/1464.
1926 971	Public Health (Ophthalmia Neonatorum) Regs. 1926 (Rev. XVIII, p. 767)	**r.,** 1968/1366.
1927 1184	Supreme Ct. Funds Rules 1927 (1927, p. 1638)	rule 78 **am.,** 1968/106.
1185	Land Charges Fees O. 1927 (Rev. XI, p. 814)	**r.,** 1968/677.

Year and Number (or date)	Title or Description	How affected and Act or Instrument by which affected
1928		
175	Superannuation and other Trust Funds (Interpretation) Regs. 1928 (Rev. XXI, p. 700)	r., 1968/1480.
668	Agricultural Credits Fees O. 1928 (Rev. I, p. 94)	r., 1968/678.
1094	Post Office Annuity Regs. 1928 (Rev. IX, p. 763)	reg. 6 am., 1968/1003.
1930 *Instrt. not S.I.* 9 June	Bermuda Addnl. Instructions 1930	r., 1968/182.
1931		
1097	Treasury Solicitor (Crown's Nominee) Rules 1931 (Rev. XXIII, p. 295)	rules 2, 3 am., 1968/1521.
1932		
1047	Public Health (Infectious Diseases) Regs. (S.) 1932 (Rev. XVIII, p. 837)	regs. 2, 5, 10 am., 1968/1493.
1933		
479	Scottish Milk Marketing Scheme (Approval) O. 1933 (Rev. I, p. 263)	sch. s. 16 am., 1968/391.
1149	Savings Certificates Regs. 1933 (Rev. XV, p. 309)	reg. 4 am., 1968/425. regs. 6, 27 am., 1968/995. regs. 30 am., 1968/1444.
1934		
674	Public Health (Treatment of Infectious Disease) Regs. 1934 (Rev. XVIII, p. 796)	r., 1968/1366.
1346	London Cab. O. 1934 (Rev. XIV, p. 795)	paras. 40 **replaced,** 41 **am.,** sch. E **replaced,** 1968/1929.
1936		
626	County Ct. Rules 1936 (1936 I, p. 282)	O. 2, 31 am., 1968/2010.
1937		
35	Public Health (Ophthalmia Neonatorum) Amdt. Regs. 1937 (Rev. XVIII, p. 767)	r., 1968/1366.
329	Public Health (Imported Food) Regs. 1937 (Rev. VIII, p. 118)	r., 1968/97.
509	Public Health (Imported Food) Regs. (S.) 1937 (Rev. VIII, p. 127)	r., 1968/1181.
993	Methylated Spirits (Sale by Retail) (S,) O. 1937 (Rev. XXI, p. 474)	art. 2 am., 1968/1126.
1937		
1227	Indian Military Widows' and Orphans' Fund Rules 1937 (Rev. X, p. 662)	rules 2, 8, 13, 13A, 19, 34, sch. 5 am., sch. 9 **replaced,** 1968/1492.
1938		
757	District Probate Registries O. 1938 (Rev. XXII, p. 241)	r., 1968/1676.

Year and Number (or date)	Title or Description	How affected and Act or Instrument by which affected
1938 1435	Foot and Mouth Disease (Controlled Areas Restrictions) General O. 1938 (Rev. II, p. 520)	art. 5 **am.**, 1968/51.
1939 877	Ministry of Supply (Transfer of Powers) (No. 1) O. 1939 (Rev. XV, p. 192)	art. 1–4 **r.**, Industrial Expansion Act 1968 (c. 32).
1298	Ministry of Supply (Transfer of Powers) (No. 2) O. 1939 (Noted Rev. XV, p. 192)	**r.**, Industrial Expansion Act 1968 (c. 32).
Instrt. not S.I. 9 Mar.	Emergency Powers O. in C. 1939 (see 1952 I, p. 621)	s. 2, sch. 1 **am.**, 1968/724. **r.** (Swaziland), 1968/1377. **r.** (Mauritius), O. 4.3.68.
1940 204	Measles and Whooping Cough Regs. 1940 (Rev. XVIII, p. 790)	**r.**, 1968/1366.
762	Minister of Aircraft Production (Transfer of Functions) O. 1940	**r.**, Industrial Expansion Act 1968 (c. 32).
1943 *Instrt. not S.I.* 30 Aug.	Bermuda Addnl. Instructions 1943	**r.**, 1968/182.
1945 248	County and Voluntary Schools (Notices) Regs. 1945 (Rev. VI, p. 375)	**r.**, 1968/615.
698	Provision of Milk and Meals Regs. 1945 (Rev. VI, p. 380)	reg. 8 **am.**, 1968/534. regs. 13, 14 **am.**, 1968/1251.
722	Public Works Loan Act 1875 s. 41— Regs. 1945 (Rev. XVIII, p. 903)	**r.**, 1968/458.
1946 374	Ministry of Aircraft Production (Dissolution) O. 1946 (Rev. XV, p. 189)	**r.**, Industrial Expansion Act 1968 (c. 32).
378	Transfer of Functions (Various Commodities O. 1946 (Rev. XV, p. 201)	art. 5 **am.**, Industrial Expansion Act 1968 (c. 32).
1094	Coal Industry Nationalisation (National Coal Bd.) Regs. 1946 (Rev. IV, p. 2)	reg. 9 **replaced,** 1968/1781.
1947 806	Double Taxation Relief (Taxes on Income) (Australia) O. 1947 (Rev. X, p. 347)	**superseded,** 1968/305.
865	Factories (Luminising) Special Regs, 1947 (Rev. VII, p. 384)	**r.**, 1968/780.
1443	Petroleum (Inflammable Liquids and Other Dangerous Substances) O. 1947 (Rev. XVIII. p. 5)	art. 1 **am.**, sch. Pt. 1 **r.**, 1968/570.
1750	Electricity (Central Authy. and Area Bds.) Regs. 1947 (Rev. VI, p. 833)	reg. 10 **replaced,** 1968/1780.

Year and Number (or date)	Title or Description	How affected and Act or Instrument by which affected
1947		
1774	Double Taxation Relief (Taxes on Income) (Cyprus) O. 1947 (Rev. X, p. 377)	sch. paras. 2, 6, 13 **am.**, 1968/1097.
2043	Exchange Control (Deposit of Securities) (Exemption) O. 1947 (Rev. VI, p. 1041)	**r.**, 1968/79.
2865	Double Taxation Relief (Taxes on Income) (Antigua) O. 1947 (Rev. X, p. 341)	sch. paras. 2, 6, 13 **am.**, 13A **inserted,** 1968/1096.
2866	Double Taxation Relief (Taxes on Income) (British Honduras) O. 1947 (Rev. X, p. 363)	sch. paras. 6, 13 **am.**, 1968/573.
2867	Double Taxation Relief (Taxes on Income) (Gambia) O. 1947 (Rev. X, p. 399)	sch. paras, 2, 6, 13 **am.**, 1968/1099.
2869	Double Taxation Relief (Taxes on Income) (Montserrat) O. 1947 (Rev. X, p. 433)	sch. paras. 1, 2, 6, 13 **am.**, 1968/576.
2873	Double Taxation Relief (Taxes on Income) (Sierra Leone) O. 1947 (Rev. X, p. 492)	sch. paras. 2, 6, 13 **am.**, 1968/1104.
2874	Double Taxation Relief (Taxes on Income) (Virgin Is.) O. 1947 (Rev. X, p. 537)	sch. paras. 1, 2, 6, 13 **am.**, 1968/578.
1948		
421	Measles and Whooping Cough (Amdt.) Regs. 1948 (Rev. XVIII, p. 790)	**r.**, 1968/1366.
886	Public Health (Imported Food) Amdt Regs. 1948 (Rev. VIII, p. 118)	**r.**, 1968/97
1121	Public Health (Imported Food) (Amdt. No. 2) Regs. 1948 (Rev, VIII, p. 118)	**r.**, 1968/97.
1261	National Insurance (Widows Benefit and Retirement Pensions) Regs. 1948 (Rev. XVI, p. 207)	reg, 6 **am.**, 1968/524.
1278	National Insurance (General Benefit) Regs, 1948 (Rev. XVI, p. 179)	regs. 5B **inserted,** 5C **am.**, 1968/524.
1390	National Health Service (Appointment of Medical and Dental Officers) (S.) Regs. 1948 (Rev. XV, p. 854)	reg. 7 **am.**, 1968/225.
1425	National Insurance (Classification) Regs. 1948 (Rev. XVI, p. 95)	reg. 1 **am.**, sch. 1 paras. 5B **inserted,** 10 **replaced,** sch. 3 **am.**, 1968/1684.
1434	Public Health (Imported Food) (Amdt.) (S.) Regs. 1948 (Rev. VIII, p. 127)	**r.**, 1968/1181.
1456	National Insurance (Industrial Injuries) (Insurable and Excepted Employments) Regs. 1948 (Rev. XVI, p. 423)	schs. 2 Pt. I, 3 **am.**, 1968/1723.

Year and Number (or date)	Title or Description	How affected and Act or Instrument by which affected
1948		
1781	Town and Country Planning (Tree Preservation O.) (S.) Regs. 1948 (Rev. XXII, p. 895)	regs. 2, 5, 8 **am.**, 1968/435.
2096	Town and Country Planning (Building Preservation O.) (S.) Regs. 1948 (Rev. XXII, p. 897)	regs. 2, 5, 8 **am.**, 1968/434.
2233	Gas (Area Bds. and Gas Council) Regs. 1948 (Rev. IX, p. 575)	reg. 10 **replaced**, 1968/1779.
2324	Superannuation and other Trust Funds (Amdt. of Interpretation) Reg. 1948 (Rev. XXI, p. 700)	**r.**, 1968/1480.
2361	Airways Corporations (General Staff Pensions) Regs. 1948 (Rev. I, p. 1275)	sch. **am.**, 1968/1577.
2517	National Health Service (Venereal Diseases) Regs. 1948 (Rev. XV, p. 574)	**r.**, 1968/1624.
2771	Industrial Assurance (Returns) Regs. 1948 (Rev. VIII, p. 916)	**r.** (saving), 1968/1585.
1949		
352	National Insurance (New Entrants Transitional) Regs. 1949 (1949 I, p. 2737)	sch. 2 **am.**, 1968/680.
359	Double Taxation Relief (Taxes on Income) (Dominica) O. 1949 (1949 I, p. 2256)	sch. paras. 2, 6, 13 **am.**, 1968/1098.
360	Double Taxation Relief (Taxes on Income) (Falkland Is.) O. 1949 (1949 I, p. 2262)	sch. paras. 6, 13 **am.**, 1968/575.
361	Double Taxation Relief (Taxes on Income) (Grenada) O. 1949 (1949 I, p. 2276)	sch. paras. 2, 6, 13 **am.**, 1968/1867.
366	Double Taxation Relief (Taxes on Income) (Saint Lucia) O. 1949 (1949 I, p. 2289)	sch. paras. 2, 6, 13 **am.**, 1968/1102.
367	Double Taxation Relief (Taxes on Income) (Saint Vincent) O. 1949 (1949 I, p. 2296)	sch. paras. 2, 6, 13 **am.**, 13A **inserted**, 1968/1103.
404	Food and Drugs (Whalemeat) Regs. 1949 (1949 I, p. 1754)	**r.**, 1968/97.
870	Food and Drugs (Whalemeat) (S.) Regs. 1949 (1949 I, p. 1760)	**r.**, 1968/1181.
875	National Insurance (Members of the Forces) Regs. 1949 (1949 I, p. 2731)	**r.**, 1968/827.
1205	Water (Adaptation and Mod. of the Local Govt. (S.) Act, 1947) (S.) Regs. 1949 (1949 I, p. 4724)	**r.**, 1968/711.

Year and Number (or date)	Title or Description	How affected and Act or Instrument by which affected
1949		
1417	Civil Defence Corps (S.) Regs. 1949 (1949 I, p. 645)	r., 1968/547.
1433	Civil Defence Corps Regs. 1949 (1949 I, p. 639)	r., 1968/541.
2058	County Ct. Districts O. 1949 (1949 I, p. 955)	sch. 1 am., 1968/404, 938, 1442.
2120	Civil Defence (Fire Services) Regs. 1949 (1949 I, p. 658)	reg. 2 am., 1968/542.
2167	Civil Defence (Fire Services) (S.) Regs. 1949 (1949 I, p. 659)	reg. 4 am., 1968/548.
2197	Double Taxation Relief (Taxes on Income) (Basutoland) O. 1949 (1949 I, p. 2242)	sch. gen. am., paras. 6, 14 am., 1968/1868.
2259	Public Health (Acute Poliomyelitis, Acute Encephalitis, and Meningococcal Infection) Regs. 1949 (1949 I, p. 3543)	r., 1968/1366.
2414	Marriage (Prescription of Forms) Regs. 1949 (1949 I, p. 3586)	r. (1.4.70), 1968/2049.
1950		
145	Superannuation (Transfers between the Civil Service and Local Govt.) Rules 1950 (1950 II, p. 277)	r., 1968/72.
189	Food and Drugs (Whalemeat) (Amdt.) Regs. 1950 (1950 I, p. 757)	r., 1968/97.
198	Food and Drugs (Whalemeat) (Admt.) (S.) Regs. 1950 (1950 I, p. 758)	r., 1968/1181.
376	Coal Industry Nationalisation (Superannuation) Regs. 1950 (1950 I, p. 356)	reg. 1 am., 1968/748.
533	Assurance Companies Rules 1950 (1950 I, p. 1121)	rules 2–11, 13–15 r., 1968/1408.
567	Justices (Lancashire Retired List) Rules 1950 (1950 I, p. 1148)	r., 1968/2021.
594	Justices (Supplemental List) Rules, 1950 (1950 I, p. 1149)	r. (S.) 1968/1997, (E.) 1968/2052.
643	Assurance Companies (Amdt.) Rules 1950 (1950 I, p. 1139)	r., 1968/1408.
748	Double Taxation Relief (Taxes on Income) (British Solomon Is. Protectorate) O. 1950 (1950 I, p. 997)	sch. paras. 6, 13 am., 1968/574.
749	Double Taxation Relief (Taxes on Income) (Fiji) O. 1950 (1950 I, p. 1029)	sch. paras. 6, 13 am., 1968/308.
750	Double Taxation Relief (Taxes on Income) (Gilbert and Ellice Is. Colony) O. 1950 (1950 I, p. 1036)	sch. paras. 6, 13 am., 1968/309.

Year and Number (or date)	Title or Description	How affected and Act or Instrument by which affected
1950 804	Register of Patent Agents Rules 1950 (1950 II, p. 209)	sch. 3 **replaced,** 1968/1741.
947	Water (Adaptation and Mod. of the Local Govt. (S.) Act, 1947). Amdt. (S.), Regs. 1950 (1950 II, p. 1509)	**r.,** 1968/711.
1195	Double Taxation Relief (Taxes on Income) (Denmark) O. 1950 (1950 I, p. 1019)	art. XVII, **mod.** (Faroe Is.), 1968/307.
1196	Double Taxation Relief (Taxes on Income) (Netherlands) O. 1950 (1950 I, p. 1044)	**superseded,** 1968/577.
1539	Superannuation (Transfers between the Civil Service and Public Bds.) Rules 1950 (1950 II, p. 291)	rules 7 **am.,** 8A, **inserted,** sch. **am.,** 1968/471.
1544	Industrial Assurance (Deposits, etc.) Rules 1950 (1950 I, p. 1102)	rules 11–13 **r.,** 1968/1571.
1596	Aerated Waters Wages Council (S.) Wages Regulation (No. 2) O. 1950 (1950 II, p. 1228)	**r.,** 1968/752.
1977	Double Taxation Relief (Taxes on Income) (Brunei) O. 1950 (1950 I, p. 1004)	sch. paras. 6, 12, **am.,** 1968/306.
1951 1081	Puerperal Pyrexia Regs. 1951 (1951 II, p. 315)	**r.,** 1968/1366.
1259	Civil Defence Corps (Scunthorpe) Regs. 1951 (1951 I, p. 256)	**r.,** 1968/541.
1309	District Probate Registries O. 1951 (Rev. XXII, p. 241)	**r.,** 1968/1676.
1388	Double Taxation Relief (Taxes on Income) (France) O. 1951 (1951 I, p. 1100)	**superseded,** 1968/1869.
1456	Food Standards (Fish Paste) O. 1951 (1951 III, p. 16)	**r.** (15.3.71), 1968/430.
1457	Food Standards (Meat Paste) O. 1951 (1951 III, p. 20)	**r.** (15.3.71), 1968/430.
1720	National Insurance (Members of the Forces) Amdt. Regs. 1951 (1951 I, p. 1491)	**r.,** 1968/827.
2241	Food Standards (Fish Paste) (Amdt.) O. 1951 (1951 III, p. 18)	**r.** (15.3.71), 1968/430.
2242	Food Standards (Meat Paste) (Amdt.) O. 1951 (1951 III, p. 22)	**r.** (15.3.71), 1968/430.
1952 194	Cts.—Martial (Appeals) Rules 1952 (1952 I, p. 648)	**r.,** 1968/1071.

Year and Number (or date)	Title or Description	How affected and Act or Instrument by which affected
1952		
649	National Insurance (Members of the Forces) Amdt. Regs. 1952 (1952 II, p. 2188)	r., 1968/827.
704	Public Health (Tuberculosis) Regs. 1952 (1952 III, p. 2736)	r., 1968/1366.
862	Japanese Treaty of Peace O. 1952 (1952 II, p. 2322)	art. 25 r., Industrial Expansion Act 1968 (c. 32).
1432	Detention Centre Rules 1952 (1952 I, p. 787)	rule 26 **replaced**, 1968/1014.
2113	Bankruptcy Rules 1952 (1952 I, p. 213)	Appx. 1 form 175 **replaced**, 1968/1935
2115	Industrial Assurance (Amdt. of Fees) Regs. 1952 (1952 I, p. 1231)	reg. 3 r., 1968/1571.
2184	National Insurance (Members of the Forces) Amdt. (No. 2) Regs. 1952 (1952 II, p. 2190)	r., 1968/827.
2190	Magistrates' Cts. Rules 1952 (1952 II, p. 1593.)	r. (1.3.69), 1968/1920.
2191	Magistrates' Cts. (Forms) Rules 1952 (1952 II, p. 1619)	r. (1.3.69), 1968/1920.
2209	Matrimonial Causes (Judgment Summons) Rules 1952 (1952 III, p. 3359)	r., 1968/219.
1953		
299	Public Health (Infectious Diseases) Regs. 1953 (1953 II, p. 1691)	r., 1968/1366.
392	Merchant Shipping (Light Dues) O. 1953 (1953 I, p. 1065)	art. 2 r., 1968/580.
493	Justices' Clerks (Accounts) Regs. 1953 (1953 I, p. 1006)	regs. 1, 3, 5, 6 **am.**, sch. **replaced**, 1968/1266.
1230	County and Voluntary Schools (Notices) Amdg. Regs. 1953 (1953 I, p. 604)	r., 1968/615.
1347	Registration (Births, Still-births and Deaths) Prescription of Forms Regs. 1953 (1953 II, p. 1739)	r. (1.4.70), 1968/2049.
1671	Aliens O. 1953 (1953 I, p. 94)	arts. 4, 20, 31, 33, sch. 1 **am.**, 1968/1649. arts. 30, 32, 33 **am.**, 1968/1699.
1928	Acute Rheumatism Regs. 1953 (1953 II, p. 1688)	r., 1968/1366.
Instrts. not S.I.		
16 May	Bermuda Addnl. Instructions 1953	r., 1968/182.
9 Nov.	Bermuda (Amdt.) L.P. 1953 (1953 II, p. 2777)	r., 1968/182.

Year and Number (or date)	Title or Description	How affected and Act or Instrument by which affected
1954 189	National Insurance (Maternity Benefit and Miscellaneous Provns.) Regs. 1954 (1954 I, p. 1387)	sch. 2 **am.**, 1968/827.
370	Pedestrian Crossings Regs. 1954 (1954 II, p. 1948)	sch. 1 **am.**, 1968/1196.
439	Wireless Telegraphy (General Licence Charges) Regs. 1954 (1954 II, p. 2376)	**r.**, 1968/1314.
609	Aerated Waters Wages Council (E. and W.) Wages Regulation (Holidays) O. 1954 (1954 II, p. 2491)	sch. para. 2 **am.**, 1968/422.
796	Non-Contentious Probate Rules 1954 (1954 II, p. 2202)	rules 2A **inserted,** 3, 4 **am.**, 1968/1675.
898	British Transport Commn. (Male Wages Grades Pensions) Regs. 1954 (1954 I, p. 175)	sch. rule 17A **inserted,** 1968/1249.
1028	Transfer of Functions (Ministry of Materials) O. 1954 (1954 I, p. 1242)	art. 4 **r.**, Industrial Expansion Act 1968 (c. 32).
1401	Welfare Foods (G.B.) O. 1954 (1954 II, p. 2119)	**r.**, 1968/389.
1402	Welfare Foods (N.I.) O. 1954 (1954 II, p. 2131)	**r.**, 1968/427.
1578	Savings Bank Annuities (Tables) O. 1954 (1954 I, p. 935)	sch. 2 **am.**, 1968/1731
1596	Registration (Births, Still-births, Deaths and Marriages) Consolidated Regs. 1954 (1954 II, p. 1871)	regs. 49 **r.**, 67 **am.**, 89, 93 **r.**, 1968/1241. **r.** (1.4.70), 1968/2049.
1635	Exchange Control (Declarations and Evidence) O. 1954 (1954 I, p. 818)	**r.**, 1968/1232.
1644	Marriage (Prescription of Forms) (Amdt.) Regs. 1954 (1954 I, p. 1189)	**r.** (1.4.70), 1968/2049.
1691	Puerperal Pyrenia (Amdt.) Regs. 1954 (1954 II, p. 1846)	**r.**, 1968/1366.
1955 127	Superannuation (Transfers between the Civil Service and Public Bds.) (Amdt.) Rules 1955 (1955 II, p. 1822)	rule 5 **r.**, 1968/471.
419	Savings Bank Annuities (Tables) O. 1955 (1955 I, p. 938)	sch. 2 **am.**, 1968/1731.
876	Transfer of Functions (Iron and Steel) O. 1955 (1955 I, p. 1196)	art. 6 **r.**, Industrial Expansion Act 1968 (c. 32).
1047	Pensions Commutation Regs. 1955 (1955 II, p. 1755)	**r.**, 1968/1163.
1369	Welfare Foods (G.B.) (Amdt.) O. 1955 (1955 II, p. 2511)	**r.**, 1968/389.

Year and Number (or date)	Title or Description	How affected and Act or Instrument by which affected
1955 1370	Welfare Foods (N.I.) (Amdt.) O. 1955 (1955 II, p. 2514)	r., 1968/427.
1542	Superannuation (Transfers between the Civil Service and Local Govt.) Amdt. Rules 1955 (1955 II, p. 1812)	r., 1968/72.
1796	Welfare Foods (G.B.) Amdt. (No. 2) O. 1955 (1955 II, p. 2512)	r., 1968/389.
Instrt. not S.I. 25 Aug.	Bermuda (Amdt.) L.P. 1955 (1955 II, p. 3179)	r., 1968/182.
1956 131	Laundry Wages Council (G.B.) Wages Regulation (Holidays) O. 1956 (1956 II, p. 2663)	r., 1968/1535.
162	Rules of Procedure (Army) 1956 (1956 I, p. 213)	rules 22, 93, 101, sch. 4 **am.**, 1968/1180. sch. 2 **am.**, 1968/1898.
163	Rules of Procedure (Air Force) 1956 (1956 II, p. 2020)	rules 22, 93, 101, sch. 4 **am.**, 1968/1173. sch. 2 **am.**, 1968/1921.
530	Act of Sederunt (Amdt. of Fees in the Departments of the Registers of Scotland and of the Records of Scotland) 1956 (1956 II, p. 1961)	s. 2 **r.**, 1968/2062.
619	Double Taxation Relief (Taxes on Income) (Federation of Rhodesia and Nyasaland) O. 1956 (1956, I, p. 1072)	sch. arts. VI, XIII, **am.** (Malawi), 1968/1101, (Zambia), 1968/1106.
715	Ulster and Colonial Savings Certificates (Income Tax Exemption) Regs. 1956 (1956 I, p. 1086)	reg. 3 **am.**, 1968/428.
894	Schools (S.) Code 1956 (1956 I, p. 735)	reg. 1, 4 **am.**, 1968/1055.
962	Foreign Compensation Commn. Rules 1956 (1956 I, p. 1021)	sch. rules 20A **inserted,** 38 am., 1968/164.
1130	Welfare Foods (G.B.) Amdt. O. 1956 (1956 II, p. 2266)	r., 1968/389.
1466	Housing (Improvement Grants) (Rate of Interest) Regs. 1956 (1956 I, p. 1064)	r., 1968/234.
1467	Housing (Rate of Interest) O. 1956 (1956 I, p. 1065)	**superseded,** 1968/233.
1468	Private Improvement Expenses (Rate of Interest) O. 1956 (1956 II, p. 1916)	**superseded,** 1968/232.
1469	Public Health (Rate of Interest) O. 1956 (1956 II, p. 1917)	**superseded,** 1968/231.
1471	Water (Rate of Interest on Deposits) Regs. 1956 (1956 II, p. 2951)	r., 1968/230.

Year and Number (or date)	Title or Description	How affected and Act or Instrument by which affected
1956		
1654	Registration of Restrictive Trading Agreements Regs. 1956 (1956 II, p. 1984)	r., 1968/1755.
1657	Premium Savings Bonds Regs. 1956 (1956 I, p. 1489)	reg. 4 **am.**, 1968/994. reg. 21 **am.**, 1968/1443.
1981	Imprisonment and Detention (Air Force) Rules 1956 (1956 II, p. 2118)	rule 14 **replaced**, 70, 96 **am.**, 97–99 **replaced**, 99A **inserted**, 100, 102–104, sch. 2 **am.**, 1968/874.
1999	Police (S.) Regs. 1956 (1956 II, p. 1766)	r., 1968/716.
1957		
8	Acute Rheumatism (Amdt.) Regs. 1957 (1957 II, p. 1932)	r., 1968/1366.
336	Police (S.) Amdt. Regs. 1957 (1957 II, p. 1879)	r., 1968/716.
393	Sheriff Cts. (Ross and Cromarty) O. 1957 (1957 II, p. 2277)	r., 1968/1601.
411	Welfare Foods (G.B.) Amdt. O. 1957 (1957 II, p. 2343)	r., 1968/389.
415	Welfare Foods (N.I.) (Amdt.) O. 1957 (1957 II, p. 2346)	r., 1968/427.
488	National Health Service (Designation of London Teaching Hospitals) O. 1957 (1957 I, p. 1452)	sch. 1 **am.**, 1968/490, 545, 1334, 1945.
603	Restrictive Practices Ct. Rules 1957 (1957 II, p. 1955)	rules 3, 4, 9 **am.**, 11–13, 16 **replaced**, 64A, 64B, 65 **am.**, 75A, 75B, 75C, 75D **inserted**, 76, 77 **am.**, 1968/1802.
619	Matrimonial Causes Rules 1957 (1957 II, p. 2406)	r. (exc. rules 73–77), 1968/219. rules 73–77 **r.**, 1968/1244.
742	Police (S.) Amdt. (No. 2) Regs. 1957 (1957 II, p. 1880)	r., 1968/716.
978	Wireless Telegraphy (General Licence Charges) Amdt. (No. 1) Regs. 1957 (1957 II, p. 2544)	r., 1968/1314.
1074	Motor Vehicles (International Circulation) O. 1957 (1957 II, p. 2154)	art. 5 **am.**, 1968/1111.
1077	Transfer of Functions (Misdescription of Fabrics) O. 1957 (1957 I, p. 1438)	art. 3 am., Industrial Expansion Act 1968 (c. 32).
1177	Matrimonial Causes (Amdt.) (No. 2) Rules 1957 (1957 II, p. 2461)	r. 1968/219.
1423	Ancillary Dental Workers Regs. 1957 (1957 I, p. 639)	r., 1968/357.
1429	Magistrates' Cts. Rules 1957 (1957 I, p. 1349)	r. (1.3.69). 1968/1920.

Year and Number (or date)	Title or Description	How affected and Act or Instrument by which affected
1957		
1759	Welfare Foods (G.B.) Amdt. (No. 2) O. 1957 (1957 II, p. 2344)	r., 1968/389.
1760	Welfare Foods (N.I.) (Amdt. No. 2) O. 1957 (1957 II, p. 2348)	r., 1968/427.
1781	Police (S.) Amdt. (No. 3) Regs. 1957 (1957 II, p. 1882)	r., 1968/716.
2011	Central Midwives Bd. for Scotland Rules 1957, Approval Instrument, 1957 (1957 I, p. 1381)	r., 1968/694.
2039	Police (S.) Amdt. (No. 4) Regs. 1957 (1957 II, p. 1883)	r., 1968/716.
2202	Matrimonial Causes (Maintenance Agreements) Rules 1957 (1957 II, p. 2462)	r., 1968/219.
2216	Spring Traps Approval O. 1957 (1957 I, p. 146)	sch. **am.**, 1968/645.
1958		
17	Acute Rheumatism (Amdt.) Regs. 1958 (1958 II, p. 2012)	r., 1968/1366.
73	Patents Rules 1958 (1958 II, p. 1713)	r., 1968/1389.
80	Housing (Register of Rents) (S.) Regs. 1958 (1958 I, p. 1255)	r. (saving), 1968/1463.
257	Petroleum (Carbon Disulphide) O. 1958 (1958 II, p. 1888)	art. 1 **am.**, 1968/571.
473	Public Service Vehicles (Conditions of Fitness) Regs. 1958 (1958 II, p. 2014)	regs. 3 **am.**, 8, 9 **r.**, 14, 21A, 26, 27, 29 **am.**, 29A **inserted**, 30, 32, 38, 43, 45, 50 **am.**, 1968/824. reg. 29A **am.**, 1968/1526.
519	Independent Schools Tribunal Rules 1958 (1958 I, p. 1006)	sch. 2 **am.**, 1968/588.
652	Criminal Appeal Rules 1958 (1958 I, p. 396)	r., 1968/1262.
926	Public Service Vehicles (Equipment and Use) Regs. 1958 (1958 II, p. 2036)	reg. 7 **replaced**, 1968/826.
957	Eggs (Protection of Guarantees) O. 1958 (1958 I, p. 80)	r., 1968/1986.
958	Fatstock (Protection of Guarantees) O. 1958 (1958 I, p. 84)	arts. 3, 6 **am.**, 10A **inserted**, sch. **am.**, 1968/399.
1192	Central Midwives Bd. for Scotland (Amdt.) Rules 1958 Approval Instrt. 1958 (1958 II, p. 1701)	r., 1968/694.
1780	Spring Traps Approval (S.) O. 1958 (1958 I, p. 160)	sch. **am.**, 1968/676.

Year and Number (or date)	Title or Description	How affected and Act or Instrument by which affected
1958 2009	Police (S.) Amdt. Regs. 1958 (1958 II, p. 1917)	r., 1968/716.
2082	Matrimonial Causes (Amdt.) Rules 1958 (1958 II, p. 2294)	r., 1968/219.
1959 60	Industrial Assurance Companies (Forms) Regs. 1959 (1959 I, p. 1472)	r. (saving), 1968/1571.
258	Rate-product Rules 1959 (1959 II, p. 2288)	r., 1968/491.
363	School Health Service Regs. 1959 (1959 I, p. 1582)	reg. 5A am., 1968/1252.
364	Schools Regs. 1959 (1959 I, p. 1584)	regs. 17 **am.**, 18 **replaced**, sch. II **am.**, 1968/1281.
477	Further Education (S.) Regs. 1959 (1959 I, p. 1068)	regs. 2 **am.**, 3 **r.**, 16 **am.**, 1968/1849.
496	Agriculture (Calculation of Value for Compensation) Regs. 1959 (1959 I, p. 1528)	sch. Pt. I **am.**, 1968/378.
528	Registration (Births, Still-births Deaths and Marriages) Amdt. Regs. 1959 (1959 II, p. 2300)	r. (1.4.70), 1968/2049.
529	Birth Certificate (Shortened Form) Regs. 1959 (1959 II, p. 2296)	r. (1.4.69), 1968/2050.
537	Foreign Service Fees O. 1959 (1959 I, p. 1411)	r., 1968/114.
622	Foreign Service Fees Regs. 1959 (1959 I, p. 1420)	r., 1968/137.
640	Foreign Compensation Commn. (Egyptian Claims) Rules 1959 (1959 I, p. 1368)	rules 21A **inserted**, 38 **am.** 1968/163.
747	Police (S.) Amdt. Regs. 1959 (1959 II, p. 2096)	r., 1968/716.
833	Grant Aided Secondary Schools (S.) Grant Regs. 1959 (1959 I, p. 1104)	regs. 3, 4 **am.**, 6 **r.**, sch. **inserted**, 1968/449.
962	Public Health Officers Regs. 1959 (1959 I, p. 1605)	reg. 15 **am.**, 1968/1366.
963	Public Health Officers (Port Health Districts) Regs. 1959 (1959 II, p. 2125)	reg. 12 **am.**, 1968/1366.
1253	Public Works Loan Commnrs. (Officers' Powers) Regs. 1959 (1959 I, p. 306)	r., 1968/458.
1296	Inter-governmental Maritime Consultative Organisation (Immunities and Privileges) O. 1959 (1959 I, p. 972)	r., 1968/1862.
1349	Housing (Register of Rents) (S.) Amdt. Regs. 1959 (1959 I, p. 1451)	r. (saving), 1968/1463.

Year and Number (or date)	Title or Description	How affected and Act or Instrument by which affected
1959		
1432	General Optical Council (Registration and Enrolment Rules) O. of C. 1959 (1959 II, p. 1984)	r., 1968/1965.
1768	Minister of Aviation O. 1959 (1959 I, p. 1793)	art. 3 **am.**, Industrial Expansion Act 1968 (c. 32).
1827	Service Departments Supply (No. 1) O. 1959 (1959 I, p. 1798)	r., Industrial Expansion Act 1968 (c. 32).
1832	Direct Grant Schools Regs. 1959 (1959 I, p. 1034)	regs. 4, 13 **am.**, 23, 24 **replaced**, 1968/1148.
1917	Police (S.) Amdt. (No. 2) Regs. 1959 (1959 II, p. 2098)	r., 1968/716.
1975	Service Departments Supply (No. 2) O. 1959 (1959 I, 1799)	r., Industrial Expansion Act 1968 (c. 32).
2201	Saint Vincent (Constitution) O. in C. 1959 (1959 I, p. 479)	ss. 12–14, 16 **am.**, 1968/1093.
2257	Police (S.) Amdt. (No. 3) Regs. 1959 . (1959 II, p. 2100)	r., 1968/716.
1960		
69	Coal and Other Mines (Shafts, Outlets and Roads) Regs. 1960 (1960 II, p. 2028)	regs. 18 **replaced**, 19 am. 1968/1037.
119	Nurses (Area Nurse—Training Ctees.) O. 1960 (1960 II, p. 2618)	sch. 2 **am.**, 1968/1430.
369	Police (S.) Amdt. Regs. 1960 (1960 II, p. 2750)	r., 1968/716.
477	Matrimonial Causes (District Registries) O. 1960 (1960 III, p. 3168)	r., 1968/219.
544	Matrimonial Causes (Amdt.) Rules 1960 (1960 III, p. 3163)	r., 1968/219.
726	Cinematograph Films (Collection of Levy) Regs. 1960 (1960 I, p. 555)	r., 1968/1077.
819	Superannuation (Civil Service and N.I. Local Govt.) Transfer Rules 1960 (1960 II, p. 2676)	rule 1 **am.**, 1968/779.
910	Housing (Declaration of Unfitness) (S.) Regs. 1960 (1960 II, p. 1613)	r., 1968/955.
1071	Trustee Savings Banks (Special Investments) Regs. 1960 (1960 III, p. 3069)	r., 1968/1029.
1083	Motor Vehicles (Tests) Regs. 1960 (1960 III, p. 2965)	r., 1968/1714.
1143	Housing (Forms) (S.) Regs. 1960 (1960 II, p. 1617)	reg. 3, sch. forms 1–46, 53–62 **r.**, 1968/955. regs. 1, 2, sch. forms 47–52 **r.**, 1968/1502.
1165	Fertilisers and Feeding Stuffs Regs. 1960 (1960 I, p. 185)	**r.** (1.10.70), 1968/218.

Year and Number (or date)	Title or Description	How affected and Act or Instrument by which affected
1960 1185	Cinematograph Films (Collection of Levy) (Amdt.) Regs. 1960 (1960 I, p. 558)	r., 1968/1077.
1213	Matrimonial Causes (District Registries) (No. 2) O. 1960 (1960 III, p. 3169)	r., 1968/219.
1260	Criminal Appeal Rules 1960 (1960 I, p. 862)	r., 1968/1262.
1261	Matrimonial Causes (Amdt.) (No. 2) Rules 1960 (1960 III, p. 3164)	r., 1968/219.
1431	Magistrates' Cts. Rules 1960 (1960 II, p. 1867)	r. (1.3.69), 1968/1920.
1530	Rate-product Rules 1960 (1960 III, p. 2831)	r., 1968/491.
1603	Registration (Births, Still-births and Deaths) (Prescription of Forms) Regs 1960 (1960 III, p. 2837)	r. (1.4.70), 1968/2049.
1604	Registration (Births, Still-births, Deaths and Marriages) Amdt. Regs. 1960 (1960 III, p. 2841)	r. (1.4.70), 1968/2049.
1622	Police (S.) Amdt. (No. 2) Regs. 1960 (1960 II, p. 2751)	r., 1968/716.
1989	Public Health (Infectious Diseases) Amdt. Regs. 1960 (1960 II, p. 2802)	r., 1968/1366.
2140	Removal of Vehicles (Charges) (E. and W.) O. 1960 (1960 III, p. 2925)	spent on commencement of 1968/43.
2220	Removal of Vehicles (Charges) (S.) O. 1960 (1960 III, p. 2927)	spent on commencement of 1968/43.
2325	Criminal Appeal (No. 2) Rules 1960 (1960 I, p. 879)	r., 1968/1262.
2331	Skimmed Milk with Non-Milk Fat Regs. 1960 (1960 II, p. 1483)	sch. 2 replaced, 1968/1474.
2404	Police (S.) Amdt. (No. 3) Regs. 1960 (1960 II, p. 2753)	r., 1968/716.
2433	Town and Country Planning (Grants) (S.) Regs. 1960 (1960 III, p. 3300)	r., 1968/392.
2437	Skimmed Milk with Non-Milk Fat (S.) Regs. 1960 (1960 II, p. 1491)	sch. 2 replaced, 1968/1495.
1961 64	Foreign Service Fees (Amdt.) O. 1961	r., 1968/114.
90	Eggs (Protection of Guarantees) (Amdt.) O. 1961	r., 1968/1986.
169	Magistrates' Cts. Rules 1961	r. (1.3.69), 1968/1920.

Year and Number (or date)	Title or Description	How affected and Act or Instrument by which affected
1961		
275	Police (S.) Amdt. Regs. 1961	**r.**, 1968/716.
352	Welfare Foods (G.B.) Amdt. O. 1961	**r.**, 1968/389.
367	Welfare Foods (N.I.) (Amdt.) O. 1961	**r.**, 1968/427.
485	Traffic Regulation Orders (Procedure) (E. & W.) Regs. 1961	**r.**, 1968/172.
543	Sea-Fishing Industry (Immature Sea-Fish) O. 1961	**r.**, 1968/1618.
577	Double Taxation Relief (Taxes on Income) (Sweden) O. 1961	arts. I, II **am.**, VII—IX **replaced**, X **am.**, XII, XXII, XXIII, XXV, **replaced**, XXVI **am.**, XXX **replaced**, 1968/2034.
1015	Cts.-Martial Appeal (Amdt.) Rules 1961	**r.**, 1968/1071.
1082	Matrimonial Causes (Amdt.) Rules 1961	**r.**, 1968/219.
1197	Foreign Service Fees (Amdt.) (No. 2) O. 1961	**r.**, 1968/114.
1214	Nurses Agencies Regs. 1961	reg. 4 **am.**, 1968/101.
1219	Nurses Agencies (S.) Regs. 1961	reg. 3 **am.**, 1968/247.
1249	Indian Military Widows' and Orphans' Fund (Amdt.) Rules 1961	**superseded**, 1968/1492.
1311	Police (S.) Amdt. (No. 2) Regs. 1961	**r.**, 1968/716.
1365	Dental Auxiliaries Regs. 1961	**r.**, 1968/357.
1462	Removal of Vehicles (E. and W.) Regs. 1961	**spent on commencement** of 1968/43.
1473	Removal of Vehicles (S.) Regs. 1961	**spent on commencement** of 1968/43.
1510	Foreign Service Fees (Amdt.) (No. 3) O. 1961	**r.**, 1968/114.
1524	Temporary Importation (Hired Vehicles) Regs. 1961	**r.**, 1968/1852.
1525	Temporary Importation (Private Vehicles Vessels and Aircraft) Regs. 1961	**r.**, 1968/1852.
1902	Police (S.) Amdt. (No. 3) Regs. 1961	**r.**, 1968/716.
2074	Welfare Foods (N. I.) (Amdt. No. 2) O. 1961	**r.**, 1968/427.
2307	Supreme Ct. Fees O. 1961	sch. 1 ss. I, IV, VI **am.**, 1968/388.
2316	Colonial Air Navigation O. 1961	arts. 2, 10, 14–16, 21, 22, 29A, 35, Pt. V heading, **am.**, arts. 43–45, 47–49, 55 **am.**, 61A **inserted**, 73, 78, 80, 81 **am.**, 82 **r.**, schs. 1, 2, 5, 6, 9–12 **am.**, 13, 15 **replaced**, 1968/1090. sch. 5 **am.** (1.6.69), 1968/1090.

Year and Number (or date)	Title or Description	How affected and Act or Instrument by which affected
1961		
2352	National Insurance (Members of the Forces) Amdt. Regs. 1961	r., 1968/827.
2364	Matrimonial Causes (Amdt. No. 2) Rules 1961	r., 1968/219.
1962		
146	Central Midwives Bd. for Scotland (Amdt.) Rules 1961, Approval Instrt. 1962	r., 1968/694.
196	Commonwealth Telegraphs (Cable and Wireless Ltd. Pension) Regs. 1962	reg. 2 am., 1968/1979.
623	Approved Schools (Contributions by Local Authies.) Regs. 1962	reg. 1 am., 1968/407.
667	Pensions Commutation (Amdt.) Regs. 1962	r., 1968/1163.
800	Mental Health (Constitution of State Hospital Management Ctee.) (S.) O. 1962	art. 4 am., 1968/1010.
824	Matrimonial Causes (Judgment Summons) (Amdt.) Rules 1962	r., 1968/219.
839	Matrimonial Causes (Amdt.) Rules 1962	r., 1968/219.
874	Police (S.) Amdt. Regs. 1962	r., 1968/716.
1338	International Wheat Council (Immunities and Privileges) O. 1962	r., 1968/1863.
1340	Commonwealth Immigrants (Jersey) O. 1962	art. 1, sch. 1, Pts. I, II, am., 1968/300.
1341	Commonwealth Immigrants (Guernsey) O. 1962	art. 1, sch. 1 Pts. I, II, am., 1968/301.
1342	Commonwealth Immigrants (Is. of Man) O. 1962	art. 1, sch. 1, Pt. II, am., 1968/302.
1393	Salmon and Migratory Trout (Drift-net Fishing) Licensing O. 1962	art. 4 am. (15.2.69), 1968/1974.
1394	Salmon and Migratory Trout (Drift-net Fishing) Restrictions on landing O. 1962	art. 3 am., 1968/1975.
1402	Housing (Forms) (S.) Amdt. Regs. 1962	r., 1968/955.
1592	Magistrates' Cts. (Forms) Rules 1962	r. (1.3.69), 1968/1920.
1765	Professions Supplementary to Medicine (Registration Rules) O. of C. 1962	sch. rules 18 r., 19 replaced, 1968/1973.
2044	Building Societies (Authorised Investments) O. 1962	art. 2 am., 3A inserted, sch. am., 1968/657.
2544	Cinematograph Films (Collection of Levy) (Amdt. No. 2) Regs. 1962	r., 1968/1077.

Year and Number (or date)	Title or Description	How affected and Act or Instrument by which affected
1962 2582	Registration of Deaths (Prescription of Forms) Regs. 1962	r. (1.4.70), 1968/2049.
2615	Matrimonial Causes (District Registries) O. 1962	r., 1968/219.
2713	Fertilisers and Feeding Stuffs (Amdt.) Regs. 1962	r. (1.10.70), 1968/218.
2741	Police (S.), Amdt. (No. 2) Regs. 1962	r., 1968/716.
2842	Act of Sederunt (Amdt. of Fees in the Departments of the Registers of Scotland and of the Records of Scotland) 1962	ss. 2, 3 r., 1968/2062.
Instrt. not S.I. 10 Jan.	Bermuda L.P., 1962 (1962 I, p. 1025)	r., 1968/182.
1963 230	Telephone (Channel Is.) Regs. 1963	r., 1968/1257.
483	Lands Tribunal Rules 1963	rules 2, 15, 16, 35, 51, sch. 1 forms 6, **am.**, 6X **inserted**, sch. 2 **am.**, 1968/1700.
525	Abstract of Factories Act (Docks, etc.) O. 1963	r., 1968/354.
596	Companies Registration Office (Fees) (No. 2) O. 1963	art. 3 r., 1968/659.
607	Telephone (Channel Is.) Amdt. (No. 1) Regs. 1963	r., 1968/1257.
700	Motor Vehicles (Tests) (Amdt.) Regs. 1963	r., 1968/1714.
709	Town and Country Planning General Development O. 1963	art. 4, sch. 1 **am.**, 1968/1623.
792	Location of Offices Bureau O.	gen. **am.**, s. 3 **am.**, Town and Country Planning Act 1968 (c. 72).
934	National Insurance (Industrial Injuries) (Colliery Workers Supplementary Scheme) Amdt. and Consolidation O. 1963	sch. 1 art. 12 **am.**, 1968/83, 1896.
948	Local Govt. (Rate Product) (S.) Rules 1963	rules 2, 3 **am.**, 1968/754.
989	Matrimonial Causes (Amdt.) Rules 1963	r., 1968/219.
999	Local Govt. (Compensation) Regs. 1963	regs. 2, 8 **am.**, 33A **inserted**, 34, 35 **am.**, 1968/913.
1026	Motor Vehicles (Driving Licences) Regs. 1963	reg. 17 **am.**, 1968/947.
1165	General Grant (Relevant Expenditure) (S.) Regs. 1963	r., 1968/392.
1178	Govt. Annuity Table O. 1963	sch. 2 **am.**, 1968/1731.

Year and Number (or date)	Title or Description	How affected and Act or Instrument by which affected
1963		
1222	General Optical Council (Regulation and enrolment Rules) Amdt. O. of C.	r., 1968/1965.
1263	Magistrates' Cts. (Forms) Rules 1963	r. (1.3.69), 1968/1920.
1283	Exchange Control (Deposit of Securities) (Exemption) (Amdt.) O. 1963	r., 1968/79.
1291	Livestock Rearing Land Improvement Grants (Standard Costs) Regs. 1963	**superseded**, 1968/282.
1342	Nurses (Regional Nurse-Training Ctees.) (S.) O. 1963	sch. 2 Pts. II, III **am.**, 1968/1448.
1375	Cinematograph Films (Collection of Levy) (Amdt. No. 3), Regs. 1963	r., 1968/1077.
1376	Cinematograph Films (Distribution of Levy) Regs. 1963	regs. 6, 13 **am.**, 1968/1076.
1456	Therapeutic Substances (Manufacture of Preparations of Human Blood) Regs. 1963	regs. 6, 37, 40–44 **am.**, 48 **renumbered** 49, new 48 **inserted**, Pt. XII (regs. 49–53) **replaced**, by new Pt. XII (regs. 50–54), Pts. XIII (regs. 55-58), XIV (regs. 59-62) **inserted**, 1968/908.
1709	Measuring Instruments (Liquid Fuel and Lubricants) Regs. 1963	regs. 27 **replaced**, 31 **am.**, 1968/1541.
1710	Weights and Measures Regs. 1963	sch. I, Pt. III **am.**, 1968/338.
1711	Weights and Measures (Local Standards: Limits of Error) Regs. 1963	sch. Pt. III **am.**, 1968/339.
1781	Motor Cycles (Protective Helmets) Regs. 1963	r., 1968/844.
1864	London Borough Council and Greater London Council Elections Rules 1963	rule 1, sch. 1 **r.**, 1968/497.
1891	Weights and Measures (Prescribed Stamp) Regs. 1963	r., 1968/1615.
1990	Matrimonial Causes (Amdt. No. 2) Rules 1963	r., 1968/219.
2040	Wages Regulation (Sack and Bag) (Holidays) O. 1963	r., 1968/1358.
2077	Police (S.) Amdt. Regs. 1963	r., 1968/716.
2121	Magistrates' Cts. Rules 1963	r. (1.3.69), 1968/1920.
1964		
26	Water Officers (Compensation) Regs. 1964	regs. 2, 8 **am.**, 33A **inserted**, 34, 35 **am.**, 1968/912.
71	Indian Military Widows' and Orphans' Fund (Amdt.) Rules 1964	**superseded**, 1968/1492.
105	London Cab O. 1964	**superseded**, 1968/1929.

Year and Number (or date)	Title or Description	How affected and Act or Instrument by which affected
1964		
142	Fertilisers and Feeding Stuffs (Amdt.) Regs. 1964	**r.** (1.10.70), 1968/218.
149	Police (S.) Amdt. Regs. 1964	**r.**, 1968/716.
168	Magistrates' Cts. Rules 1964	**r.** (1.3.69), 1968/1920.
193	District Probate Registries O. 1964	**r.**, 1968/1676.
205	Road Vehicles Lighting Regs. 1964	regs. 3 **am.**, 20–22, **replaced,** 22A **inserted.** 23, 23A **replaced,** 1968/1247.
228	Patents (Amdt.) Rules 1964	**r.**, 1968/1389.
388	Prison Rules 1964	rules 5 **replaced,** 50–52 **am.,** 53 **r.,** 54 **am.,** 65–71 **r.,** 1968/440.
404	Road Vehicles (Index Marks) Regs. 1964	sch. 2 **am.,** 1968/355.
409	Importation of Potatoes (Health) (G.B.) O. 1964	sch. 3 **replaced,** 1968/165.
422	Sea-Fishing Industry (Landing of Immature Cod and Haddock) O. 1964	**r.**, 1968/2076.
454	London Borough Council and Greater London Council Election Rules 1964	rule 1 **r.**, 1968/497.
461	Police (S.) Amdt. (No. 2) Regs. 1964	**r.**, 1968/716.
463	Fatstock (Guarantee Payments) O. 1964	arts. 14 **r.,** 15 **am.,** 16A **inserted,** sch. Pt. IV **am.,** 1968/398.
504	National Insurance (Industrial Injuries) (Benefit) Regs. 1964	regs. 4 **am.,** 13 **inserted,** 14 **am.,** 25 **replaced,** 1968/524. reg. 2 **replaced,** 1968/1007.
561	British Sugar Corporation Limited (Incentive Agreement) (No. 2) O. 1964	annex— sch. para. 3 **am.,** 1968/1513.
687	Price Stability of Imported Products (Minimum Import Price Levels) O. 1964	**r.**, 1968/1132.
690	Copyright (International Conventions) O. 1964	schs. 1, 6 **am.,** 1968/1858.
810	Price Stability of Imported Products (Minimum Import Price Levels) (Operative Date) O. 1964	**r.**, 1968/1132.
840	Cereals (Guarantee Payments) O. 1964	arts. 3, 4 **replaced,** 1968/767.
849	Wages Regulation (Flax and Hemp) (Holidays) O. 1964	**r.**, 1968/1485.
875	Town and Country Planning (Grants) Regs. 1964	**r.**, 1968/189.
889	Magistrates' Cts. (No. 2) Rules 1964	**r.** (1.3.69), 1968/1920.

Year and Number (or date)	Title or Description	How affected and Act or Instrument by which affected
1964		
907	Industrial Training (Wool Industry Bd.) O. 1964	sch. 1 **replaced,** 1968/898.
939	National Assistance (Professions Supplementary to Medicine) Regs. 1964	reg. 3 **am.,** 1968/271.
940	National Health Service (Professions Supplementary to Medicine) Regs. 1964	reg. 3 **am.,** 1968/270.
942	Hire-Purchase and Credit Sale Agreements (Control) O. 1964	art. 8 **r.,** 196/81678. schs. 1 Pt. 1 **replaced,** 3 Pt. 1 **am.,** 1968/1737.
943	Control of Hiring O. 1964	art. 10 **r.,** 1968/1677. art. 8 **am.,** sch. 1 **replaced,** 1968/1736.
973	Police (S.) Amdt. (No. 3) Regs. 1964	**r.,** 1968/716.
990	Price Stability of Imported Products (Minimum Import Price Levels) (Amdt.) O. 1964	**r.,** 1968/1132.
995	National Health Service (Professions Supplementary to Medicine) (S.) Regs. 1964	reg. 3 **am.,** 1968/279.
996	National Assistance (Professions Supplementary to Medicine) (S.) Regs. 1964	reg. 3 **am.,** 1968/280.
1002	Motorways Traffic (S.) Regs. 1964	reg. 10 (A) **inserted,** 1968/960.
1071	Civil Aviation (Navigation Services Charges) Regs. 1964	reg. 4 **am.,** 1968/423.
1086	Industrial Training (Engineering Bd.) O. 1964	sch. 1 **replaced,** 1968/1333.
1125	Matrimonial Causes (District Registries) O. 1964	**r.,** 1968/219.
1177	Local Govt. (Executive Councils) (Compensation) Regs. 1964	reg. 7 **am.,** 1968/1945.
1178	Road Vehicles (Registration and Licensing) Regs. 1964	reg. 47A **inserted,** 1968/594.
1211	Criminal Appeal Rules 1964	**r.,** 1968/1262.
1212	Matrimonial Causes (Amdt.) Rules 1964	**r.,** 1968/219.
1222	Wages Regulation (Button Manufacturing) O. 1964	**r.,** 1968/742.
1230	Anthrax Disinfection Fee Rules 1964	**r.,** 1968/1434.
1337	Patents (Amdt. No. 2) Rules 1964	**r.,** 1968/1389.
1341	Composite Goods O. 1964	**r.,** 1968/1381.

Year and Number (or date)	Title or Description	How affected and Act or Instrument by which affected
1964		
1354	Building Societies (Designation for Trustee Investment) Regs. 1964	reg. 1, sch. **am.,** 1968/480.
1410	Act of Adjournal (Criminal Legal Aid Fees) 1964	paras. 3, 12 **am.,** 13, 15 **replaced,** 1968/1933.
1475	Building Societies (Accounts and Annual Return etc.) Regs. 1964	**r.,** 1968/1954.
1662	Admiralty Jurisdiction (Montserrat) O. 1964	**r.,** 1968/1647.
1729	Fees of Appointed Factory Doctors (No. 1) O. 1964	**r.,** 1968/937.
1782	Industrial Training (Shipbuilding Bd.) O. 1964	sch. I **replaced,** 1968/1614.
1808	Sea-Fishing Industry (Landing of Immature Cod and Haddock) (Variation) O. 1964	**r.,** 1968/2076.
1842	Magistrates' Cts. (No. 3) Rules 1964	**r.** (1.3.69), 1968/1920.
1859	Traffic Signs (School Crossing Patrols) (E. and W.) Regs. 1964	**r.,** 1968/1826.
1890	Fees of Appointed Factory Doctors (No. 2) O. 1964	**r.,** 1968/937.
1953	London Govt. (Compensation) Regs. 1964	regs. 2, 8 **am.,** 33A **inserted,** 34, 35 **am.,** 1968/911.
1966	European Free Trade Assocn. (Origin of Goods) Regs. 1964	sch. 1 **am.,** 1968/653.
1969	Police (S.) Amdt. (No. 4) Regs. 1964	**r.,** 1968/716.
1979	Importation of Potatoes (Health) (G.B.) (Amdt.) O. 1964	**r.,** 1968/165.
1990	Nurses (Regional Nurse-Training Ctees.) (S.) Amdt. O. 1964	**superseded,** 1968/1448.
2015	Traffic Signs (School Crossing Patrols) (S.) Regs. 1964	**r.,** 1968/1826.
2030	Police (Common Police Services) (S.) O. 1964	**r.,** 1968/373.
2065	Registration (Births, Still-births, Deaths and Marriages) Amdt. Regs. 1964	**r.** (1.4.70), 1968/2049.
2077	Personal Injuries (Civilians) Scheme 1964	arts. 19, 31 **am.,** 63A **inserted,** 64 **am.,** 1968/1206. schs.3, 4 **am.,** 1968/176, 1206.
Instrts. not S.I. 1 Jan.	British Honduras L.P. 1964 (1964 I, p. 1136)	arts. 5, 21, 36 **am.,** L.P. 11.6.68.

Year and Number (or date)	Title or Description	How affected and Act or Instrument by which affected
1964 19 Sept.	Disablement and Death Pensions etc. (Military) 1914 World War Service, and Service subsequent to 2 Sept. 1939, R. Warrant 1964. (1964 III, p. 5257)	arts. 19, 33, 55 **am.**, 59A **inserted** 60 **am.**, R. Warrant 24.7.1968. schs. 6, 7 **am.**, R. Warrant 12.2.1968, R. Warrant 24.7.1968.
24 Sept.	Disablement and Death Pensions etc. (Air Forces), 1914 World War Service, and Service subsequent to 2 Sept. 1939 O. 1964 (1964 III, p. 5361)	arts. 19, 33, 55 **am.**, 59A **inserted,** 60 **am.**, O. 26.7.1968. schs. 6, 7 **am.**, O. 13.2.68, O. 26.7.1968.
25 Sept.	Disablement and Death Pensions etc. (Naval Forces), 1914 World War Service, and Service subsequent to 2 Sept. 1939, O. in C. 1964 (1964 III, p. 5466)	arts. 19, 33, 55 **am.**, 59A **inserted,** 60 **am.**, O. in C. 26.7.1968. schs. 6, 7 **am.**, O. in C. 14.2.1968, O. in C. 26.7.1968.
1965 5	Price Stability of Imported Products (Minimum Import Price Levels) (Amdt.) O. 1965	**r.,** 1968/1132.
40	National Insurance (Increase of Benefit and Miscellaneous Provisions) Regs. 1965	sch. A **am.,** I **r.,** 1968/827.
65	Plant Breeders' Rights Regs. 1965	sch. 2 Pt. XIII, XIV **inserted,** 1968/255. reg. 12 **am.,** sch. 2 Pts. XV–XXII **inserted,** 1968/622.
66	Plant Breeders' Rights (Fees) Regs. 1965	**r.,** 1968/619.
145	Transfer of Functions (Shipping and Construction of Ships) O. 1965	art. 3 **am.,** sch. 2 **r.,** Industrial Expansion Act 1968 (c. 32).
225	Telephone Regs. 1965	**r.,** 1968/1256.
259	General Optical Council (Registration and Enrolment Rules) (Amdt.) O. in C.	**r.,** 1968/1965.
318	Merchant Shipping (Light Dues) O. 1965	**r.,** 1968/580.
321	A.S. (Rules of Ct., consolidation and amdt.) 1965	rule 351 **replaced,** 1968/1016. rule 68A **inserted,** 1968/1150. rule 3 **replaced,** 1968/1602. Appx. form 23 **replaced,** 1968/1759. rule 347 **am.,** 1968/1760.
473	Town and Country Planning (Inquiries Procedure) Rules 1965	rule 2 **am.,** 3 **replaced,** 16 **am.,** 1968/1953.
536	Special Constables Regs. 1965	reg. 5 **am.,** 1968/899.
538	Police Regs. 1965	**r.** (exc. reg. 3, 62), 1968/26.
577	Fire Services (Appointments and Promotion) Regs. 1965	regs. 4, 7, 8 **am.,** 1968/614.
584	Juvenile Cts. (London) O. 1965	sch. **am.,** 1968/592.

Year and Number (or date)	Title or Description	How affected and Act or Instrument by which affected
1965		
619	Police Federation Regs. 1965	reg. 11 **am.**, 1968/24. reg. 10, sch. 3 Pt. II **am.**, 1968/2044.
621	London Authies. (Superannuation) O. 1965	art. 3 **am.**, 1968/488.
641	Removal of Vehicles (E. and W.) (Amdt.) Regs. 1965	**spent on commencement** of 1968/43.
704	Wages Regulation (Toy Manufacturing) (Holidays) O. 1965	**r.**, 1968/1847.
722	Probation (Conditions of Service) Rules 1965	schs. 1, 2 **replaced**, 1968/386. rule 4 **am.**, 1968/2003.
826	Police (S.) Amdt. Regs. 1965	**r.**, 1968/716.
827	Matrimonial Causes (Amdt.) Rules 1965	**r.**, 1968/219.
836	River Authies. (Compensation) Regs. 1965	regs. 2, 8 **am.**, 33A **inserted**, 34, 35 **am.**, 1968/914.
1023	Superannuation (Teaching and Public Bds.) Interchange Rules 1965	**r. (saving)**, 1968/1120.
1067	Merchant Shipping (Dangerous Goods) Rules 1965	rules 1, 2, 10 **am.**, sch. 2 **replaced**, 1968/332.
1128	Repatriation Fee O. 1965	**r.**, 1968/114.
1191	Telephone Amdt. (No. 1) Regs. 1965	**r.**, 1968/1256.
1192	Telex Regs. 1965	regs. 1A **inserted**, 3 **am.**, schs. 1 **replaced**, 4 **inserted**, 1968/1258.
1203	U.K. Forces (Jurisdiction of Colonial Cts.) O. 1965	**r. (Swaziland)**, 1968/1377.
1216	Repatriation Fee Regs. 1965	**r.**, 1968/137.
1227	Police (S.) Amdt. (No. 2) Regs. 1965	**r.**, 1968/716.
1352	Central Midwives Bd. for Scotland (Amdt.) Rules 1965 Approval Instrument 1965	**r.**, 1968/694.
1392	Wages Regulation (Licensed Residential Establishment and Licensed Restaurant) O. 1965	**r.**, 1968/54.
1404	University and Other Awards Regs. 1965	regs. 4, 5, 7, 8, **am.**, 8A **inserted**, 10–12, 14, 15, **am.**, 15A **inserted**, 16 **am.**, 17 **r.**, 19, schs. 1, 2 **am.**, 1968/1296.
1412	Milk (N.I.) O. 1965	sch. **replaced**, 1968/850.
1417	Sea Fisheries (S.), Byelaw (No. 72) 1965	**r.**, 1968/600.
1418	Sea Fisheries (S.) Byelaw (No. 73) 1965	**r.**, 1968/238.
1419	Sea Fisheries (S.) Byelaw (No. 74) 1965	**r.**, 1968/239.

Year and Number (or date)	Title or Description	How affected and Act or Instrument by which affected
1965 1500	County Ct. Funds Rules 1965	rules 24, 38 **am.**, 1968/107.
1520	Probation (Conditions of Service) (No. 3) Rules 1965	**superseded,** 1968/2003.
1578	Price Stability of Imported Products (Minimum Import Price Levels) (Amdt. No. 2) O. 1965	**r.**, 1968/1132.
1601	Magistrates' Cts. (Forms) Rules 1965	**r.** (1.3.69), 1968/1920.
1602	Magistrates' Cts. Rules 1965	**r.** (1.3.69), 1968/1920.
1693	Wages Regulation (Laundry) O. 1965	**r.**, 1968/1534.
1707	Mayor's and City of London Ct. Funds Rules 1965	rule 21 **am.**, 1968/105.
1722	Police (Amdt.) (No. 2) Regs. 1965	**r.**, 1968/26.
1734	British Commonwealth and Foreign Parcel Post Regs. 1965	regs. 3, 7, 24 **am.**, sch. 2 **replaced,** 1968/1255.
1735	British Commonwealth and Foreign Post Regs. 1965	regs. 3, 10, 15 **am.**, 22 **replaced,** 34 **am.**, sch. 1 Pts. 1, 2 **replaced,** 2 Pt. 1 **am.**, Pt. 2 **r.**, Pt. 3 **renumbered** Pt. 2, sch. 3, Pt. 1 **replaced,** sch. 5 **replaced,** 1968/1254.
1742	Fire Services (Appointments and Promotion) (S.) Regs. 1965	**r.**, 1968/1745.
1753	British Nationality Regs. 1965	regs. 5 **r.**, 9 **am.**, 26A **inserted,** schs. 7 **r.**, 14 **replaced,** 1968/448.
1776	Rules of the Supreme Ct. (Revision) 1965	Arrangement of orders— O. 104 **am.**, 112 **inserted,** 1968/1244. O. 1, 11, 30, 32, 41, 55, 59, 62, 67, 73, 80, 89, 93, 94, 100, 104 **am.**, O. 112 **inserted,** Appx. A form 53 **am.**, 1968/1244.
1803	Trustee Savings Banks (Rate of Interest) O. 1965	**r.**, 1968/765.
1861	Turks and Caicos Is. (Constitution) O. 1965	Annex. s. 19, **am.**, 1968/728.
1881	Continental Shelf (Jurisdiction) O. 1965	**r.**, 1968/892.
1887	Water Officers (Compensation) (S.) Regs. 1965	regs. 2–5, 7, 8, 13, 14, 17, 23, 33 **am.**, 33A **inserted,** 34, 35, 37, 38, 41 **am.**, 44 **replaced,** 1968/848.
1895	Motor Cycles (Protective Helmets) (Amdt.) Regs. 1965	**r.**, 1968/844.
1899	Police (S.) Amdt. (No. 3) Regs. 1965	**r.**, 1968/716.
1901	Housing (Forms) (S.) Amdt. Regs. 1965	**r.**, 1968/1502.
1920	British Indian Ocean Territory O. 1965	s. 2, schs. 2, 3 **am.**, 1968/111.

Year and Number (or date)	Title or Description	How affected and Act or Instrument by which affected
1965		
1971	Molluscan Shellfish (Control of Deposit) O. 1965	art. 4 **am.**, 1968/1164.
1976	Rent Regulation (Forms etc.) (E. and W.) Regs. 1965	form 3A **inserted,** 1968/1080.
1979	London Transport Bd. (Borrowing Powers) O. 1965	**superseded,** 1968/565.
2029	Rumuneration of Teachers (Farm Institutes) O. 1965	**r.,** 1968/345.
2030	Rumuneration of Teachers (Further Education) O. 1965	r., 1968/197.
2042	Rent Regulation (Forms, etc.) (S.) Regs. 1965	form 3A **inserted,** 1968/1081.
2046	Offices, Shops and Railway Premises Act 1963 (Exemption No. 3) O. 1965	r., 1968/1947.
2073	Wages Regulation (General Waste Materials Reclamation) O. 1965	r., 1968/8.
2135	Wages Regulation (Cotton Waste Reclamation) O. 1965	r., 1968/1355.
2136	Wages Regulation (Cotton Waste Reclamation) (Holidays) O. 1965	r., 1968/1356.
2137	Matrimonial Causes (Amdt.) (No. 2) Rules 1965	r., 1968/219.
2140	Southern Rhodesia (Petroleum) O. 1965	r., 1968/885.
2169	Wages Regulation (Baking) (E. and W.) O. 1965	sch. para. 2 **replaced,** 1968/327.
1966		
12	Public Health (Leprosy) Regs. 1966	r., 1968/1366.
20	Wages Regulation (Rope, Twine and Net) (Holidays) O. 1966	r., 1968/1051.
41	Southern Rhodesia (Prohibited Exports and Imports) O. 1966	r., 1968/885.
42	Southern Rhodesia (Prohibited Exports) (Chrome) O. 1966	r., 1968/885.
43	Wages Regulation (Ostrich and Fancy Feather and Artificial Flower) O. 1966	r., 1968/1926.
44	Wages Regulation (Ostrich and Fancy Feather and Artificial Flower) (Holidays) O. 1966	r., 1968/1927.
48	Town and Country Planning (Development Plans for Greater London) Regs. 1966	reg. 11 **am.,** 1968/815.

Year and Number (or date)	Title or Description	How affected and Act or Instrument by which affected
1966		
66	Postal Packets (Customs and Excise) Regs. 1966	reg. 9 **am.**, 1968/931.
115	Southern Rhodesia (Prohibited Exports) (Tobacco) O. 1966	**r.**, 1968/885.
132	Police Federation (S.) Regs. 1966	reg. 11 **am.**, 1968/590.
146	Police (Amdt.) Regs. 1966	**r.**, 1968/26.
159	Overseas Service (Pensions Supplement) Regs. 1966	reg. 11A **inserted,** 1968/745.
193	Removal of Vehicles (E.) (Amdt.) Regs. 1966	**spent on commencement** of 1968/43.
207	Fiduciary Note Issue (Extension of Period) O. 1966	**r.**, 1968/259.
245	Industrial Training (Carpet Bd.) O. 1966	sch. 1 **replaced,** 1968/1882.
262	Public Health (Ships) Regs. 1966	reg. 2 **am.**, 1968/1576.
266	Wages Regulation (Keg and Drum) O. 1966	sch. 1 para. 3 **replaced** 1968/1429.
292	Southern Rhodesia (Prohibited Exports) (Sugar) O. 1966	**r.**, 1968/885.
357	Teachers' Superannuation (Family Benefits) Regs. 1966	regs. 11 **am.**, 13 **r.**, 17 **am.**, 18 **replaced,** 36 **r.**, 46 **am.**, 49 **replaced,** 52, 57 **am.**, 1968/1914.
407	Southern Rhodesia (Prohibited Exports) (Iron Ore) O. 1966	**r.**, 1968/885.
409	Motor Cycles (Protective Helmets) (Amdt.) Regs. 1966	**r.**, 1968/844.
428	Industrial Training (Wool, Jute and Flax Bd.) O. 1966	**r.**, 1968/898.
437	Telephone (Channel Is.) Amdt. (No. 2) Regs. 1966	**r.**, 1968/1257.
452	Superannuation (Civil Service and N.I. Local Govt.) Transfer (Amdt.) Rules 1966	rule 1 **am.**, 1968/779.
484	Cereals (Guarantee Payments) (Amdt.) O. 1966	art 2 **am.**, 1968/767.
502	Therapeutic Substances (Manufacture of Hormone Products) Regs. 1966	Pts. XXI (regs. 79–87), XXII (regs. 88–91) **inserted,** 1968/907.
505	Therapeutic Substances (Manufacture of Antibiotics) Regs. 1966	Pt. XVII (regs. 89–93) **inserted,** 1968/906.
510	Removal of Vehicles (W.) (Amdt.) Regs. 1966	**spent on commencement** of 1968/43.

Year and Number (or date)	Title or Description	How affected and Act or Instrument by which affected
1966		
518	Price Stability of Imported Products (Rates of Levy) O. 1966	r., 1968/551.
551	Wages Regulation (Aerated Waters) (E. and W.) O. 1966	r., 1968/422.
554	Wages Regulation (Road Haulage) O. 1966	r., 1968/1130.
560	Matrimonial Causes (Amdt.) Rules 1966	r., 1968/219.
579	Local Land Charges Rules 1966	sch. 4 **replaced,** 1968/1212.
635	Police (Amdt.) (No. 2) Regs. 1966	r., 1968/26.
641	Plant Breeders' Rights (Fees) (Amdt.) Regs. 1966	r., 1968/619.
660	Southern Rhodesia (Prohibited Exports) (Asbestos) O. 1966	r., 1968/885.
661	Southern Rhodesia (Prohibited Exports) (Pig Iron) O. 1966	r., 1968/885.
667	Origin of Goods (Republic of Ireland) Regs. 1966	sch. 1 Pt. I, **am.,** 1968/988, 1223. Pt. II, **am.,** 1968/988. sch. 2 **am.,** 1968/988, 1223. reg. 1 **am.,** 1968/1223.
669	Wages Regulation (Hollow-ware) (Holidays) O. 1966	sch. **am.,** 1968/626.
709	Poison Rules 1966	r., 1968/75.
727	Post Office Savings Bank Regs. 1966	regs. 20, 46, 59, 60 **am.,** 1968/1064.
741	Transfer of Functions (Civil Aviation) O. 1966	art. 3 **am.,** Industrial Expansion Act 1968 (c. 32).
759	Registration of Births, Deaths and Marriages (Local Registration Authies'. Officers) Compensation (S.) Regs. 1966	regs. 2, 8 **am.,** 34A **inserted,** 35, 36 **am.,** 1968/1087.
779	Wages Regulation (Ready-made and Wholesale Bespoke Tailoring) O. 1966	r., 1968/660.
786	Wages Regulation (Shirtmaking) O. 1966	sch. Pts. II, III **replaced,** 1968/1319.
803	Wages Regulation (Corset) O. 1966	r., 1968/1420.
820	Wages Regulation (Paper Box) O. 1966	r., 1968/260.
831	Teachers' Salaries (S.) Regs. 1966	r., 1968/420.
846	Removal of Vehicles (S.) (Amdt.) Regs. 1966	**spent on commencement** of 1968/43.
850	Skimmed Milk with Non-Milk Fat (Amdt.) Regs. 1966	r., 1968/1474.

Year and Number (or date)	Title or Description	How affected and Act or Instrument by which affected
1966		
854	Wages Regulation (Hair, Bass and Fibre) O. 1966	r., 1968/133.
855	Wages Regulation (Dressmaking and Women's Light Clothing) (E. and W.) O. 1966	r., 1968/1327.
856	Horticultural Improvements (Standard Costs) Regs. 1966	**superseded,** 1968/282.
857	Telephone Amdt. (No. 2) Regs. 1966	r., 1968/1256.
858	Telephone (Channel Is.) Amdt. (No. 3) Regs. 1966	r., 1968/1257.
874	Mayor's and City of London Ct. Funds (Amdt.) Rules 1966	**superseded,** 1968/105.
875	County Ct. Funds (Amdt.) Rules 1966	**superseded,** 1968/107.
876	Supreme Ct. Funds (Amdt.) Rules 1966	**superseded,** 1968/106.
893	Motor Vehicles (Tests) (Amdt.) Regs. 1966	r., 1968/1714.
921	Import Duty Drawbacks (No. 6) O. 1966	r., 1968/1881.
966	Police (S.) Amdt. Regs. 1966	r., 1968/716.
975	Offices, Shops and Railway Premises Act 1963 (Exemption No. 4) O. 1966	r., 1968/1183.
997	Building Control (Cost Limit Exemption) O. 1966	r., 1968/781.
1003	National Insurance (Members of the Forces) Amdt. Regs. 1966	r., 1968/827.
1023	Building Societies (Accounts and Annual Return etc.) (Amdt.) Regs. 1966	r., 1968/1954.
1045	Firemen's Pension Scheme O. 1966	appx. 2 arts. 11 **replaced** by 11 and 11A, 13 **am.,** 17A **inserted,** 20, 63–65 **am.,** sch. 2 Pt. VI, **inserted,** 1968/157. appx. 2 art. 66 **am.,** 1968/397.
1081	Import Duty Drawbacks (No. 7) O. 1966	r., 1968/1881.
1083	Police (S.) Amdt. (No. 2) Regs. 1966	r., 1968/716.
1132	Rate-product (Amdt.) Rules 1966	r., 1968/491.
1156	Police (Amdt.) (No. 3) Regs. 1966	r., 1968/26.
1184	Air Navigation O. 1966	arts. 10, 17, 77, 83, sch. 9 Pts. A, B **am.,** 1968/1857.
1189	District Registries O. in C. 1966	sch. **am.,** 1968/579.
1206	Salad Cream (S.) Regs. 1966	reg. 2, sch. **am.,** 1968/263.

Year and Number (or date)	Title or Description	How affected and Act or Instrument by which affected
1966		
1210	National Health Service (General Medical and Pharmaceutical Services) Regs. 1966	sch. 4 Pt. I am., 1968/759.
1220	Import Duty Drawbacks (No. 8) O. 1966	r., 1968/1881.
1224	Plant Breeder's Rights (Fees) (Amdt. No. 2) Regs. 1966	r., 1968/619.
1233	National Health Service (General Medical and Pharmaceutical Services) (S.) Regs. 1966	sch. 4 Pt. I am., 1968/818.
1244	Police (S.) Amdt. (No. 3) Regs. 1966	r., 1968/716.
1254	Air Navigation (Restriction of Flying) Regs. 1966	reg. 4 am., 1968/1045, 1848. reg. 5 r., 1968/1045.
1255	Air Navigation (Fees) Regs. 1966	sch. paras. 2, 3, 5 am., 1968/424. para. 8 am., 1968/1871.
1257	Rules of the Air and Air Traffic Control Regs. 1966	sch. rules 59 am., 60 inserted, 1968/1837. rules 20, 28, 38, 50 am., 1968/2070.
1288	Motor Vehicles (Construction and Use) Regs. 1966	regs. 3 am., 21A inserted, 86 am., 87A inserted, schs. 9, 10 inserted, 1968/362. regs. 7 am., 19 replaced by 19, 19A, 58 replaced, 106, 109 am., sch. 8 Pt. I am., 1968/426. regs. 51 replaced, 95 am., 1968/523. regs. 3, 4 am., Pt. V (regs. 116–123) inserted, sch. 11 inserted, 1968/602. reg. 66 am., 1968/1248. reg. 21A, sch. 9 am., 1968/1632.
1289	Motor Vehicles (Authorisation of Special Types) General O. 1966	arts.11 r., 20 am., 1968/438. art. 22 am., 1968/839.
1302	Matrimonial Causes (District Registries) O. 1966	r., 1968/219.
1304	Act of Sederunt (Amdt. of Fees in the Department of the Registers of Scotland) 1966	r., 1968/2061.
1335	Import Duty Drawbacks (No. 9) O. 1966	r., 1968/1881.
1461	Redundancy Fund Contributions O. 1966	r., 1968/1264.
1462	Import Duty Drawbacks (No. 10) O. 1966	r., 1968/1881.
1471	Commons Registration (General) Regs. 1966	regs. 7 replaced, 8, 27, 29 am., 31A inserted, sch. 1 forms 7–10, 16, 17, 19 am., 1968/658. regs. 13 r., 14 am., sch. 1 forms 22–28 inserted, sch. 2 Pts. 1, 2 am., 1968/989.
1475	Motor Vehicles (Tests) (Amdt.) (No. 2) Regs. 1966	r., 1968/1714.

Year and Number (or date)	Title or Description	How affected and Act or Instrument by which affected
1966		
1481	European Free Trade Assocn. (Drawback) Regs. 1966	reg. 3 **am.,** 1968/100, 2001.
1482	Patents (Amdt.) Rules 1966	**r.,** 1968/1389.
1491	Wages Regulation (Aerated Waters) (E. and W.) Amdt. O. 1966	**r.,** 1968/422.
1493	Wages Regulation (Ready-made and Wholesale Bespoke Tailoring) (Holidays) O. 1966	sch. para. 2 **am.,** 1968/660.
1494	Wages Regulation (Wholesale Mantle and Costume) O. 1966	**r.,** 1968/1320.
1503	Wages Regulation (Dressmaking and Women's Light Clothing) (S.) O. 1966	**r.,** 1968/1609.
1504	Wages Regulation (Dressmaking and Women's Light Clothing) (S.) (Holidays) O. 1966	**r.,** 1968/173.
1505	Wages Regulation (Retail Bespoke Tailoring) (E. and W.) O. 1966	sch. paras. 3–7 **replaced,** 12 **am.,** 1968/1795.
1516	Wages Regulation (Milk Distributive) (E. and W.) O. 1966	**r.,** 1968/525.
1517	Wages Regulation (Paper Bag) O. 1966	**r.,** 1968/328.
1520	Wages Regulation (Hat, Cap and Millinery) O. 1966	**r.,** 1968/1562.
1521	Wages Regulation (Hat, Cap and Millinery) (Holidays) O. 1966	**r.,** 1968/1563.
1548	County Cts. (Bankruptcy and Companies Winding-up-Jurisdiction) O. 1966	sch. 1, 2 **am.,** 1968/939.
1555	Import Duties (General) (No. 11) O. 1966	**r.,** 1968/679.
1563	Import Duty Drawbacks (No. 11) O. 1966	**r.,** 1968/1881.
1570	Public Health (Ships) (S.) Regs. 1966	reg. 2 **am.,** 1968/1913.
1572	Police (Amdt.) (No. 4) Regs. 1966	**r.,** 1968/26.
1582	Police Pensions Regs. 1966	regs. 3, 14 **am.,** 27 **r.,** 54, 57, 59, 63, 86 **am.,** 96A **inserted,** 97, 100, sch. 3 Pts. III **am.,** V, VI **r.,** 1968/530.
1590	Special Constables (Pensions) Regs. 1966	reg. 15, sch. 1 **am.,** 1968/1989.
1595	Southern Rhodesia (Prohibited Trade and Dealings) O. 1966	**r.,** 1968/885.
1612	Rate Support Grant O. 1966	**superseded,** 1968/1956.

Year and Number (or date)	Title or Description	How affected and Act or Instrument by which affected
1966		
1619	Police (S.) Amdt. (No. 4) Regs. 1966	r., 1968/716.
1625	Special Constables (Pensions) (S.) Regs. 1966	reg. 2, sch. 1 **am.**, 1968/1995.
Instrt. not S.I. 21 Dec.	Mauritius Constitution O. 1966 (1966 III, p. 5190)	r., O. 4.3.68 (I, p. 1871).
1967		
18	Southern Rhodesia (Prohibited Trade and Dealings) (Overseas Territories) O. 1967	r. (certain territories), 1968/1094.
65	Probation (S.) Rules 1967	schs. 2, 3 **replaced,** 1968/418.
78	Import Duty Drawbacks (No. 1) O. 1967	r., 1968/1881.
79	Import Duties (General) (No. 1) O. 1967	r., 1968/679.
80	Redundant Assocn. Officers Compensation Regs. 1967	regs. 2, 3 **am.**, 1968/1701.
99	Southern Rhodesia (Prohibited Trade and Dealings) (Amdt.) O. 1967	r., 1968/885.
115	Royal Navy and Royal Marines Discharge by Purchase Regs. 1967	r., 1968/1801.
203	Import Duties (General) (No. 2) O. 1967	r., 1968/679.
204	Import Duty Drawbacks (No. 2) O. 1967	r., 1968/1881.
207	Approved Schools (Contributions by Education Authies.) (S.) Regs. 1967	r., 1968/196.
241	Swaziland Constitution O. 1967	r., 1968/1377.
246	Swaziland (Appeals to Privy Council) O. 1967	r., 1968/1377.
248	Southern Rhodesia (Prohibited Trade and Dealings) (Overseas Territories) (Amdt.) O. 1967	r. (certain territories), 1968/1094.
270	Rate Support Grant (S.) O. 1967	art. 3 **am.**, 1968/516.
279	Industrial Training (Engineering Bd.) O. 1967	r., 1968/1333.
334	Approved Schools (Contributions by Local Authies.) Regs. 1967	r., 1968/407.
364	Superannuation (Public Offices) Rules 1967	rule 1 **am.**, 1968/2071.
392	Patents (Amdt.) Rules 1967	r., 1968/1389.

Year and Number (or date)	Title or Description	How affected and Act or Instrument by which affected
1967		
394	Southern Rhodesia (Prohibited Trade and Dealings) (Amdt.) O. 1967	**r.,** 1968/885.
433	Telephone Amdt. (No. 3) Regs. 1967	**r.,** 1968/1256.
446	Inner London (Needs Element) Regs. 1967	**r.,** 1968/348.
454	Milk (N.I.) (Amdt.) O. 1967	**r.,** 1968/850.
455	Milk (G.B.) O. 1967	sch. 1, 2 **replaced,** 1968/457.
468	Import Duties (General) (No. 3) O. 1967	**r.,** 1968/679.
469	Import Duties (General) (No. 4) O. 1967	**r.,** 1968/679.
470	Import Duty Drawbacks (No. 3) O. 1967	**r.,** 1968/1881.
489	Teachers' Superannuation Regs. 1967	regs. 7, 16, 24, 43, 52, 70, 74 **am.,** 86 **replaced,** schs. 2 Pts. I, III **am.,** 3 **am.,** 1968/1353.
490	Police (Amdt.) Regs. 1967	**r.,** 1968/26.
525	Poisons List O. 1967	**superseded,** 1968/74.
526	Poison (Amdt.) Rules 1967	**r.,** 1968/75.
556	Exchange Control (Specified Currency and Prescribed Securities) O. 1967	art. 3A **inserted,** 1968/1233.
574	Composite Goods (Amdt.) O. 1967	**r.,** 1968/405.
578	Savings Certificates (Amdt.) Regs. 1967	**r.,** 1968/425.
618	Wages Regulation (Retail Drapery, Outfitting and Footwear) O. 1967	sch. paras. 2, 4 **replaced,** 1968/1428.
634	Wages Regulation (Made-up Textiles) O. 1967	**r.,** 1968/1421.
635	Wages Regulation (Made-up Textiles) (Holidays) O. 1967	**r.,** 1968/1422.
639	Wages Regulation (Sack and Bag) O. 1967	**r.,** 1968/1357.
642	Prices and Incomes (General Considerations) O. 1967	**r.,** 1968/616.
644	Wages Regulation (Licensed Non-residential Establishment) O. 1967	sch. Pts. I, III **am.,** 1968/1597.
645	Wages Regulation (Licensed Non-residential Establishment) (Managers and Club Stewards) O. 1967	sch. Pt. I **am.,** 1968/1598.
651	Import Duty Drawbacks (No. 4) O. 1967	**r.,** 1968/1881.

Year and Number (or date)	Title or Description	How affected and Act or Instrument by which affected
1967		
663	Wages Regulation (Aerated Waters) (S.) O. 1967	**r.,** 1968/751.
664	Wages Regulation (Flax and Hemp) O. 1967	**r.,** 1968/1484.
675	Export of Goods (Control) O. 1967	sch. 1 Pt. I **am.,** 1968/132, 370, 845, 1073. sch. 1 Pt. II **inserted,** 1968/132. art. 2 **am.,** 1968/1073.
715	Rate Support Grant (S.) Regs. 1967	reg. 2, 4 **am.,** 1968/1889.
744	Wages Regulation (Toy Manufacturing) O. 1967	**r.,** 1968/1846.
745	Wages Regulation (Retail Food) (E. and W.) O. 1967	sch. paras. 2 —5 **replaced,** 1968/1536.
757	Wages Regulation (Rope, Twine and Net) O. 1967	sch. 2 **r.,** 1968/1051.
758	Wages Regulation (Retail Bookselling and Stationery) O. 1967	sch. paras. 2, 3 **replaced,** 9 **am.,** 1968/1633.
765	Police (Promotion) Regs. 1967	**r.,** 1968/1074.
766	Police (Amdt.) (No. 2) Regs. 1967	**r.,** 1968/26.
772	Wages Regulation (Milk Distributive) (S.), O. 1967	paras. 2 **replaced,** 17 **am.,** 1968/1968.
774	Wages Regulation (Laundry) (Amdt.) O. 1967	**r.,** 1968/1534.
780	Import Duty Drawbacks (No. 5) O. 1967	**r.,** 1968/1881.
794	Farm Improvements (Standard Costs) Regs. 1967	**superseded,** 1968/282.
815	Commonwealth Countries and Republic of Ireland (Immunities) (No. 2) O. 1967	sch. 1 Pt. I **am.,** 1968/464, 1374.
816	Mauritius (Appeals to Privy Council) O. 1967	**r.,** 1968/294.
837	Matrimonial Causes (Amdt.) Rules 1967	**r.,** 1968/219.
838	Wages Regulation (Hairdressing) O. 1967	**r.,** 1968/1740.
844	National Insurance (Assessment of Graduated Contributions) Regs. 1967	regs. 2, 3, **mod.,** 1968/827.
859	Wages Regulation (Retail Food) (S.) O. 1967	sch. paras. 2–5 **replaced,** 1968/1851.
861	Canned Meat Product Regs. 1967	regs. 5, 6, 8 **am.,** 1968/2046.
862	Sausage and Other Meat Product Regs. 1967	regs. 3, 5 **am.,** 1968/2047.

Year and Number (or date)	Title or Description	How affected and Act or Instrument by which affected
1967		
869	Probation (Conditions of Service) (Amdt.) Rules 1967	**spent on commencement** of 1968/386.
886	Purchase Tax (No. 1) O. 1967	**r.**, 1968/1511.
889	Cinematograph Films (Collection of Levy) (Amdt. No. 5) Regs. 1967	**r.**, 1968/1077.
907	Wages Regulation (Retail Furnishing and Allied Trades) O. 1967	sch. paras. 2, 4, 5 **replaced,** 20 **am.,** 1968/1890.
908	Probation (S.) Amdt. Rules 1967	**spent on commencement** of 1968/418.
923	Police (Amdt.) (No. 3) Regs. 1967	**r.**, 1968/26.
926	Wages Regulation (Retail Bread and Flour Confectionery) O. 1967	sch. paras. 2, 4–7 **replaced,** 1968/1729.
928	Wages Regulation (Retail Bread and Flour Confectionery) (S.) O. 1967	sch. paras. 2, 4, 5 **replaced,** 1968/1730.
937	National Health Service (General Dental Services) Regs. 1967	sch. 6 paras. 1, 3 **replaced,** 1968/443.
944	Police (S.) Amdt. Regs. 1967	**r.**, 1968/716.
952	Import Duty Drawbacks (No. 6) O. 1967	**r.**, 1968/1881.
953	Import Duties (General) (No. 5) O. 1967	**r.**, 1968/679.
975	Swaziland Constitution (Amdt.) O. 1967	**r.**, 1968/1377.
980	Irish Land (Finance) (Amdt.) Rules 1967	**r.**, 1968/991.
1019	Grading of Produce (Pears) Regs. 1967	schs. 1–5 **am.,** 1968/1041.
1020	Grading of Produce (Apples) Regs. 1967	schs. 4, 5 **am.,** 1968/1040.
1021	Police (Discipline) (S.) Regs. 1967	reg. 14, sch. 1 **am.,** 1968/716.
1078	Sausage and Other Meat Product (S.) Regs. 1967	reg. 2 **am.,** 1968/139.
1112	Import Duties (General) (No. 6) O. 1967	**r.**, 1968/679.
1113	Import Duty Drawbacks (No. 7) O. 1967	**r.**, 1968/1881.
1127	Supplementary Benefit (Determination of Requirements) Regs. 1967	**superseded,** 1968/1118.
1132	White Fish and Herring Subsidies (U.K.) Scheme 1967	para. 10 **am.,** sch. 1, Pt. IIIA **inserted,** 1968/200.
1133	White Fish and Herring Subsidies (Aggregate Amount of Grants) O. 1967	**superseded,** 1968/1234.

Year and Number (or date)	Title or Description	How affected and Act or Instrument by which affected
1967		
1148	Summer Time O. 1967	art. 2 **am.**, 1968/117.
1165	Redundancy Fund (Advances out of the Consolidated Fund) O. 1967	**r.**, 1968/599.
1171	Patents (Amdt. No. 2) Rules 1967	**r.**, 1968/1389.
1192	Police (Amdt.) (No. 4) Regs. 1967	**r.**, 1968/26.
1198	Wages Regulation (Hollow-ware) O. 1967	**r.**, 1968/626.
1215	Wages Regulation (Cutlery) O. 1967	**r.**, 1968/1987.
1228	Family Allowances (Temporary Increase and Consequential Provns.) O. 1967	art. 3 **am.**, 1968/17.
1234	Criminal Justic Act 1967 (Commencement No. 1) O. 1967	sch. 3 **am.**, 1968/325.
1255	Import Duty Drawbacks (No. 8) O. 1967	**r.**, 1968/1881.
1265	National Insurance (Increase of Benefit and Miscellaneous Provns.) Regs. 1967	reg. 5 **am.**, 1968/524. schs. A **am.**, K **r.**, 1968/827.
1280	Wireless Telegraphy (Isle of Man) O. 1967	art. 1 sch. **am.**, 1968/118.
1289	Criminal Justice Act 1967 (Commencement) (S.) O. 1967	schs. 1, 4 **am.**, 1968/325.
1293	Hire-Purchase and Credit Sale Agreements (Control) (Amdt. No. 8) O. 1967	**superseded,** 1968/1737.
1294	Act of Sederunt (Alteration of Sheriff Ct. Fees) 1967	para. 12 **am.**, 1968/1166.
1303	Fugitive Offenders (Extension) O. 1967	**r.** (Cayman Islands), 1968/112, (Falkland Islands and Dependencies), 1968/113, (Pitcairn, Henderson, Ducie and Oeno Islands), 1968/884, (New Hebrides), 1968/1091.
1308	Wages Regulation (Fur) O. 1967	sch. paras. 1, 3, 5, 8, 11, 12, 15 **am.**, 1968/1578.
1315	Police (Promotion) (Amdt.) Regs. 1967	**r.**, 1968/1074.
1342	Police (S.) Amdt. (No. 2) Regs. 1967	**r.**, 1968/716.
1360	Wages Regulation (Cutlery) (Holidays) O. 1967	sch. paras. 7, 9 **am.**, 1968/1987.
1362	Wages Regulation (Corset) (Holidays) O. 1967	sch. 2 **r.**, 1968/1420.
1363	Wages Regulation (Wholesale Mantle and Costume) (Holidays) O. 1967	**r.**, 1968/1321.

Year and Number (or date)	Title or Description	How affected and Act or Instrument by which affected
1967 1385	Land Registration (District Registries) (No. 2) O. 1967	**r.**, 1968/344.
1405	British Sugar Corporation Limited (Incentive Agreement) (Variation) O. 1967	**superseded**, 1968/1513.
1416	Inland Post Regs. 1967	**r.**, 1968/1253.
1427	Industrial Training Levy (Engineering) (No. 2) O. 1967	arts. 2 **am.**, 3, 4 **replaced** by new 3, 5 **am.** and **renumbered** 4, 6 **replaced** by new 5, 7 **replaced** by new 6, 8 **am.** and **renumbered** 7, 9 **am.** and **renumbered** 8, 1968/1477.
1435	Import Duty Drawbacks (No. 9) O. 1967	**r.**, 1968/1881.
1455	Plant Breeders' Rights (Fees) (Amdt.) Regs. 1967	**r.**, 1968/619.
1480	Seychelles (Appeals to Privy Council) O. 1967	s. 2 **am.**, 1968/295. **r.** (Mauritius), O. 4.3.68 (I, p. 1871).
1515	Fire Services (Appointments and Promotion) (S.) Regs. 1967	**r.** 1968/1745.
1546	Special Constables (Pensions) (Amdt.) Regs. 1967	**superseded**, 1968/1989.
1553	Special Constables (Pensions) (S.) Amdt. Regs. 1967	**superseded**, 1968/1995.
1559	Beef Cow Subsidy Payment (E. and W.) O. 1967	art. 3 **am.**, 1968/967.
1561	Beef Cow Subsidy Payment (S.) O. 1967	art. 3 **am.**, 1968/983.
1562	Import Duties (General) (No. 7) O. 1967	**r.**, 1968/679.
1564	Import Duty Drawbacks (No. 10) O. 1967	**r.**, 1968/1881.
1566	Wireless Telegraphy (Broadcast Licence Charges) Regs. 1967	sch. 1 **am.**, 1968/1807.
1583	Exchange Control (Authorised Dealers and Depositaries) O. 1967	**r.**, 1968/1634.
1601	Wages Regulation (Dressmaking and Women's Light Clothing) (E. and W.) (Holidays) O. 1967	**r.**, 1968/1328.
1661	Magistrates' Cts. Rules 1967	**r.** (1.3.69), 1968/1920.
1702	Control of Hiring (Amdt. No. 7) O. 1967	**superseded**, 1968/1677.
1703	Hire-purchase and Credit Sale Agreements (Control) (Amdt. No. 9) O. 1967	**superseded**, 1968/1678.
1715	Betterment Levy (Waiver of Interest) (No. 2) Regs. 1967	reg. 3 **am.**, 1968/131.

Year and Number (or date)	Title or Description	How affected and Act or Instrument by which affected
1967		
1716	Sugar (Rates of Surcharge and Surcharge Repayments) (No. 11) O. 1967	**superseded,** 1968/285.
1717	Composite Sugar Products (Surcharge and Surcharge Repayments—Average Rates) (No. 11) O. 1967	**superseded,** 1968/286.
1718	Import Duties (General) (No. 8) O. 1967	**r.,** 1968/679.
1719	Import Duty Drawbacks (No. 11) O. 1967	**r.,** 1968/1881.
1729	Reports of Appointed Factory Doctors O. 1967	**r.,** 1968/2002.
1730	Fees of Appointed Factory Doctors (Amdt.) O. 1967	**r.,** 1968/937.
1747	Industrial Training Levy (Agricultural, Horticultural and Forestry) O. 1967	art. 3 **am.,** (temp.), 1968/343.
1765	Betterment Levy (Rate of Interest) (No. 5) O. 1967	**r.,** 1968/549.
1810	Matrimonial Causes (Amdt. No. 2) Rules 1967	**r.,** 1968/219.
1811	Criminal Appeal Rules 1967	**r.,** 1968/1262.
1819	Registration of Births (Amdt.) Regs. 1967	regs. 9 **r.** (1.4.70), 1968/2049.
1835	Import Duty Drawbacks (No. 12) O. 1967	**r.,** 1968/1881.
1847	Import Duties (Temporary Exemptions) (No. 9) O. 1967	**r.,** 1968/1948.
1859	Sea-Fishing Industry (Nets on British and Foreign Fishing Boats) O. 1967	**r.,** 1968/2075.
1872	Mink (Keeping) Regs. 1967	reg. 3, 4 **am.,** 1968/2007.
1873	Coypus (Keeping) Regs. 1967	reg. 4 **am.,** 1968/2006.
1904	Fugitive Offenders (Bahamas Is.) O. 1967	s. 3 **am.,** annex—s. 20 **inserted,** 1968/292. ss. 5, 19 **am.,** 1968/1375.
1905	Fugitive Offenders (Bermuda) O. 1967	s. 3 **am.,** annex–s. 20 **inserted,** 1968/292. ss. 5, 19 **am.,** 1968/1375. s. 13 **am.,** 1698/1696.
1906	Fugitive Offenders (British Honduras) O. 1967	s. 3 **am.,** annex—s. 20 **inserted,** 1968/292. ss. 5, 19 **am.,** 1968/1375.
1907	Fugitive Offenders (British Solomon Is. Protectorate) O. 1967	s. 3 **am.,** annex—s. 20 **inserted,** 1968/292. ss. 5, 19 **am.,** 1968/1375.
1908	Fugitive Offenders (Fiji) O. 1967	s. 3 **am.,** annex—s. 20 **inserted,** 1968/292. ss. 6, 19 **am.,** 1968/1375.
1909	Fugitive Offenders (Gibraltar) O. 1967	s. 3 **am.,** annex—s. 20 **inserted,** 1968/292. ss. 5, 19 **am.,** 1968/1375.

Year and Number (or date)	Title or Description	How affected and Act or Instrument by which affected
1967		
1910	Fugitive Offenders (Gilbert and Ellice Is.) O. 1967	s. 3 **am.**, annex—s. 20 **inserted,** 1968/292. ss. 5, 19 **am.,** 1968/1375.
1911	Fugitive Offenders (Hong Kong) O. 1967	s. 3 **am.,** annex—s. 20 **inserted,** 1968/292. ss. 5, 19 **am.,** 1968/1375.
1912	Fugitive Offenders (Mauritius) O. 1967	s. 3 **am.,** annex—s. 20 **inserted,** 1968/292.
1913	Fugitive Offenders (Montserrat) O. 1967	s. 3 **am.,** annex—s. 20 **inserted,** 1967/292. ss. 5, 19 **am.,** 1968/1375.
1914	Fugitive Offenders (Seychelles) O. 1967	s. 3 **am.,** annex—s. 20 **inserted,** 1968/292. ss. 5, 19 **am.,** 1968/375.
1915	Fugitive Offenders (Virgin Is.) O. 1967	s. 3 **am.,** annex—s. 20 **inserted,** 1968/292. ss. 5, 19 **am.,** 1968/1375.
1916	Fugitive Offenders (Sovereign Base Areas of Akrotiri and Dhekelia) O. 1967	s. 3 **am.,** annex—s. 20 **inserted,** 1968/292. ss. 5, 19 **am.,** 1968/1375.
1917	Air Force Act 1955 (Continuation) O. 1967	**expired,** 31.12.68.
1918	Army Act 1955 (Continuation) O. 1957	**expired,** 31.12.68.
1929	Land Registration (District Registeries) (No. 3) O. 1967	**r.,** 1968/344.
1946	Exchange Control (Authorised Dealers and Depositaries) (Amdt.) (No. 3) O. 1967	**r.,** 1968/1634.
1977 ·	Beef Cow Subsidy Payment (N.I.) O. O. 1967	art. 3 **am.,** 1968/968.
Instrts. not S.I. 12 Apr.	Mauritius Constitution (Amdt.) O. 1967 1967 (1967 I, p. 2132)	**r.,** O. 4.3.68 (I, p. 1871).
28 July	Mauritius Constitution (Amdt. No. 2) O. 1967 (1967 II, p. 3807)	**r.,** O. 4.3.68 (I, p. 1871).
10 Oct.	Seychelles Civil Appeals O. 1967 (1967 III, p. 5414)	s. 3 **am.,** O. 4.3.68 (I, p. 1949). **r.** (Mauritius), O. 4.3.68 (I, p. 1871).
28 Nov.	Mauritius Constitution (Amdt. No. 3) O. 1967 (1967 III, p. 5455)	**r.,** O. 4.3.68 (I, p. 1871).
1968 4	Wages Regulation (Ostrich and Fancy Feather and Artificial Flower) (Amdt.) O. 1968	**r.,** 1968/1926.
26	Police Regs. 1968	sch. 3 Pts. I, II **am.,** 1968/552, 1207. regs. 25 **am.,** 48 **replaced,** 54 **am.,** sch. 6 **replaced,** 1968/766. reg. 55, sch. 6 **am.,** 1968/1761.

Year and Number (or date)	Title or Description	How affected and Act or Instrument by which affected
1968		
50	Police (S.) Amdt. Regs. 1968	**r.,** 1968/716.
74	Poisons List O. 1968	**superseded,** 1968/1682.
75	Poisons Rules 1968	**r.,** 1968/1683.
77	Import Duties (General) (No. 1) O. 1968	**r.,** 1968/679.
78	Import Duty Drawbacks (No. 1) O. 1968	**r.,** 1968/1881.
80	Exchange Control (Declarations and Evidence) (Amdt.) O. 1968	**r.,** 1968/1232.
83	National Insurance (Industrial Injuries) (Colliery Workers Supplementary Scheme) Amdt. O. 1968	**superseded,** 1968/1896.
92	National Insurance (Industrial Injuries) (Benefit) Amdt. Regs. 1968	**r.,** 1968/1007.
94	Foot-and-Mouth Disease (Imported Meat) O. 1968.	**r.,** 1968/585.
112	Fugitive Offenders (Cayman Is.) O. 1968	s. 3 **am.,** annex—s. 20 **inserted,** 1968/292. ss. 5, 19 **am.,** 1968/1375.
113	Fugitive Offenders (Falkland Is. and Dependencies) O. 1968	s. 3 **am.,** annex—s. 20 **inserted,** 1968/292. ss. 5, 19 **am.,** 1968/1375.
123	Wages Regulation (Road Haulage) (Amdt.) O. 1968	**r.,** 1968/1130.
137	Consular Fees Regs. 1968	**r.,** 1968/456.
159	Exchange Control (Authorised Dealers and Depositaries) (Amdt.) O. 1968	**r.,** 1968/1634.
173	Wages Regulation (Dressmaking and Women's Light Clothing) (S.) (Holidays) O. 1968	**r.,** 1968/1610.
182	Bermuda Constitution O. 1968	Annex— s. 43 **am.,** 1968/463. s. 7A **inserted,** 1968/726.
183	Fugitive Offenders (British Indian Ocean Territory) O. 1968	s. 3 **am.,** annex—s. 20 **inserted,** 1968/292. ss. 5, 19 **am.,** 1968/1375.
184	Fugitive Offenders (St. Helena) O. 1968	s. 3 **am.,** annex—s. 20 **inserted,** 1968/292. ss. 5, 19 **am.,** 1968/1375.
185	Fugitive Offenders (Turks and Caicos Is.) O. 1968	s. 3 **am.,** annex—s. 20 **inserted,** 1968/292. ss. 5, 19 **am.,** 1968/1375.
218	Fertilisers and Feeding Stuffs Regs. 1968	schs. 1 Pt. II, 2 Pt. II, 4 Pt. II, 7 paras. 1, 5, 13, sch. 8 paras. 1, 5, 14, sch. 11 Pt. II **am.** 1968/883.
238	Sea Fisheries (S.) Byelaw (No. 77) 1967	**r.,** 1968/1011.
239	Sea Fisheries (S.) Byelaw (No. 78) 1967	**r.,** 1968/1012.

Year and Number (or date)	Title or Description	How affected and Act or Instrument by which affected
1968		
251	Import Duty Drawbacks (No. 2) O. 1968	r., 1968/1881.
252	Import Duties (Temporary Exemptions) (No. 1) O. 1968	r., 1968/1948.
256	Plant Breeders' Rights (Fees) (Amdt.) Regs. 1968	r., 1968/619.
267	Measuring Instruments (Liquid Fuel and Lubricants) (Amdt.) Regs. 1968	r., 1968/1541.
285	Sugar (Rates of Surcharge and Surcharge Repayments) O. 1968	**superseded,** 1968/586.
286	Composite Sugar Products (Surcharge and Surcharge Repayments—Average Rates) O. 1968	**superseded,** 1968/587.
314	Divorce County Cts. O. 1968	schs. 1, 2 **am.,** 1968/1934.
379	General Optical Council (Registration and Enrolment Rules) (Amdt.) O. of C. 1968	r., 1968/1965.
389	Welfare Foods O. 1968	art. 3 **am.,** 1968/1605.
405	Composite Goods (Amdt.) O. 1968	r., 1968/1381.
481	Import Duty Drawbacks (No. 3) O. 1968	r., 1968/1881.
533	Inland Post Amdt. (No. 1) Regs. 1968	r., 1968/1253.
549 ·	Betterment Levy (Rate of Interest) O. 1968	r., 1968/1591.
586	Sugar (Rates of Surcharge and Surcharge Repayments) (No. 2) O. 1968	**superseded,** 1968/999.
587	Composite Sugar Products (Surcharge and Surcharge Repayments-Average Rates) (No. 2) O. 1968	**superseded,** 1968/1000.
593	Telephone Amdt. (No. 4) Regs. 1968	r., 1968/1256.
599	Redundancy Fund (Advances out of the National Loans Fund) O. 1968	r., 1968/1263.
600	Sea Fisheries (S.) Byelaw (No. 80) 1968	r., 1968/1013.
601	Goods Vehicles (Plating and Testing) Regs. 1968	reg. 2, sch. 2 **am.,** 1968/1169, 1854. reg. 57 **inserted,** 1968/1854. sch. 3 Pts.I, II **am.,** 1968/1169.
641	Import Duties (Temporary Exemptions) (No. 2) O. 1968	r., 1968/1948.
642	Import Duties (General) (No. 2) O. 1968	r., 1968/679.
643	Import Duties (General) (No. 3) O. 1968	r., 1968/679.

Year and Number (or date)	Title or Description	How affected and Act or Instrument by which affected
1968 644	Import Duty Drawbacks (No. 4) O. 1968	r., 1968/1881.
668	Exchange Control (Authorised Dealers and Depositaries) (Amdt.) (No. 2) O. 1968	r., 1968/1634.
679	Import Duties (General) (No. 4) O. 1968	sch. 1 c. 40, 58–62, 65, 94 **am.**, 1968/950. c. 2, 5, 7–9, 18–21, 25, 40, 41, 44, 71 **am.**, 1968/1030. c. 56 **am.**, 1968/1158. c. 36, 90 **am.**, 1968/1383. c. 15, 63 **am.**, 1968/1509. c. 28, 38 **am.**, 1968/1510. c. 3 **am.**, 1968/1778. c. 70 **am.**, 1968/1880.
716	Police (S.) Regs. 1968	sch. 6 **am.**, 1968/1963.
727	Swaziland Constitution (Amdt.) O. 1968	r., 1968/1377.
759	National Health Service (Charges for Drugs and Appliances) Regs. 1968	regs. 2A **inserted**, 4, 7, 8 **am.**, 1968/1588.
816	Awards and Settlements (Temporary Continuation of Standstill) (No. 1) O. 1968	art. 2 **am.**, 1968/1188.
818	National Health Service (Charges for Drugs and Appliances) (S.) Regs. 1968	regs. 2A **inserted**, 4, 7, 8 **am.**, 1968/1607.
861	Public Health (Infective Jaundice) Regs. 1968	r., 1968/1366.
865	Companies (Disclosure of Directors' Interests) (Exceptions) No. 2 Regs. 1968	reg. 1 **am.**, 1968/1533.
884	Fugitive Offenders (Pitcairn) O. 1968	Annex. ss. 5, 19 **am.**, 1968/1375.
885	Southern Rhodesia (United Nations Sanctions) O. 1968	r., 1968/1020.
930	Import Duty Drawbacks (No. 5) O. 1968	r., 1968/1881.
937	Fees of Appointed Factory Doctors O. 1968	arts. 4, 5 **am.**, 1968/1771.
978	Import Duties (Temporary Exemptions) (No. 3) O. 1968	r., 1968/1948.
999	Sugar (Rates of Surcharge and Surcharge Repayments) (No. 3) O. 1968	**superseded**, 1968/1124.
1000	Composite Sugar Products (Surcharge and Surcharge Repayments—Average Rates) (No. 3) O. 1968	**superseded**, 1968/1125.
1002	Exchange Control (Authorised Dealers and Depositaries) (Amdt.) (No. 3) O. 1968	r., 1968/1634.

Year and Number (or date)	Title or Description	How affected and Act or Instrument by which affected
1968 1105	Double Taxation Relief (Taxes on Income) (Sweden) O. 1968	**superseded,** 1968/2034.
1124	Sugar (Rates of Surcharge and Surcharge Repayments) (No. 4) O. 1968	**superseded,** 1968/1335.
1125	Composite Sugar Products (Surcharge and Surcharge Repayments—Average Rates) (No. 4) O. 1968	**superseded,** 1968/1336.
1157	Import Duty Drawbacks (No. 6) O. 1968	**r.,** 1968/1881.
1213	Price Stability of Imported Products (Rates of Levy) O. 1968	**r.,** 1968/1587.
1225	Price Stability of Imported Products (Rates of Levy No. 2) O. 1968	**r.,** 1968/1467.
1242	Registration of Births, Deaths and Marriages (Fees) O. 1968	art. 1 **am.,** 1968/1309.
1335	Sugar (Rates of Surcharge and Surcharge Repayments) (No. 5) O. 1968	**superseded,** 1968/1717.
1336	Composite Sugar Products (Surcharge and Surcharge Repayments—Average Rates) (No. 5) O. 1968	**superseded,** 1968/1718.
1354	Price Stability of Imported Products (Rates of Levy No. 3) O. 1968	**r.,** 1968/1467.
1363	Superannuation (Judicial Offices) Rules 1968	rules 1, 4 **am.,** 1968/2071.
1384	Import Duties (Temporary Exemptions) (No. 4) O. 1968	**r.,** 1968/1948.
1385	Import Duty Drawbacks (No. 7) O. 1968	**r.,** 1968/1881.
1389	Patents Rules 1968	rule 146 **am.,** 1968/1702.
1390	Price Stability of Imported Products (Rates of Levy No. 4) O. 1968	**r.,** 1968/1391.
1391	Price Stability of Imported Products (Rates of Levy No. 5) O. 1968	**r.,** 1968/1713.
1404	Price Stability of Imported Products (Rates of Levy) (Amdt.) O. 1968	**r.,** 1968/1467.
1425	Price Stability of Imported Products (Rates of Levy No. 6) O. 1968	**r.,** 1968/1545.
1442	County Ct. Districts (Miscellaneous) O. 1968	sch. 1 Pt. IV **am.,** 1968/1596.
1508	Import Duty Drawbacks (No. 8) O. 1968	**r.,** 1968/1881.
1545	Price Stability of Imported Products (Rates of Levy No. 7) O. 1968	**r.,** 1968/1587.

Year and Number (or date)	Title or Description	How affected and Act or Instrument by which affected
1968 1587	Price Stability of Imported Products (Rates of Levy No. 8) O. 1968	**r.**, 1968/1713.
1617	Price Stability of Imported Products (Rates of Levy No. 9) O. 1968	**r.**, 1968/1939.
1634	Exchange Control (Authorised Dealers and Depositories) O. 1968	sch. 2 **am.**, 1968/2019.
1713	Price Stability of Imported Products (Rates of Levy No. 10) O. 1968	**r.**, 1968/1746.
1717	Sugar (Rates of Surcharge and Surcharge Repayments) (No. 6) O. 1968	**superseded,** 1968/1883.
1718	Composite Sugar Products (Surcharge and Surcharge Repayments—Average Rates) (No. 6) O. 1968	**superseded,** 1968/1884.
1721	Import Duties (Temporary Exemptions) (No. 5) O. 1968	**r.**, 1968/1948.
1722	Import Duty Drawbacks (No. 9) O. 1968	**r.**, 1968/1881.
1746	Price Stability of Imported Products (Rates of Levy No. 11) O. 1968	**r.**, 1968/1803.
1803	Price Stability of Imported Products (Rates of Levy No. 12) O. 1968	**r.**, 1968/1939.
1883	Sugar (Rates of Surcharge and Surcharge Repayments) (No. 7) O. 1968	**superseded,** 1968/2015.
1884	Composite Sugar Products (Surcharge and Surcharge Repayments—Average Rates) (No. 7) O. 1968	**superseded,** 1968/2016.
Instrts. not S.I.		
12 Feb.	Disablement and Death Pensions etc. (Military) 1914 World War Service, and Service subsequent to 2 Sept. 1939, Amdt. R. Warrant 1968 (1968 I, p. 1857)	**superseded,** R. Warrant 24.7.1968.
13 Feb.	Disablement and Death Pensions etc. (Air Force), 1914 World War Service, and Service subsequent to 2 Sept. 1939, Amdt. O. 1968 (1968 I, p. 1861)	**superseded,** O. 26.7.1968.
14 Feb.	Disablement and Death Pensions etc. (Naval Forces), 1914 World War Service, and Service subsequent to 2 Sept. 1939, Amdt. O. 1968 (1968 I, p. 1865)	**superseded,** O. in C. 26.7.1968.

NUMERICAL LIST

of those Statutory Instruments of 1968 which were printed and sold under the Statutory Instruments Act 1946

[*Note.*—With respect to each instrument listed, two dates are shown; the first is the date on which it was made, and the second, which is in square brackets, is the date on which it was first issued by Her Majesty's Stationery Office.]

No.	SUBJECT	Part	Page
1	Birmingham and Coventry (Variation of Limits) Water, 1 Jan. [10 Jan.]	(n) III,	5655
4	Wages Regulation (Ostrich and Fancy Feather and Artificial Flower), 3 Jan. [12 Jan.]	I,	1
5	Cornwall (Lostwithiel), 3 Jan. [15 Jan.]	(n) III,	5650
6	Cornwall (Padstow), 3 Jan. [12 Jan.]	(n) III,	5650
7	Grading of Produce (Cucumbers), 3 Jan. [10 Jan.]...	I,	3
8	Wages Regulation (General Waste Materials Reclamation), 4 Jan. [16 Jan.]	I,	8
10	Fixed Penalty (Areas), 3 Jan. [11 Jan.]	(n) III,	5658
11	Import Duties (Process), 8 Jan. [12 Jan.]	I,	15
17	Family Allowances and National Insurance Act 1967 (Commencement) 5 Jan. [19 Jan.]	I,	17
18	Stevenage New Town Sewerage, 5 Jan. [16 Jan.] ...	(n) III,	5654
21	Shot Guns, 8 Jan. [15 Jan.]	I,	20
24	Police Federation, 10 Jan. [16 Jan.]	I,	29
25	Police Cadets, 10 Jan. [17 Jan.]	I,	31
26	Police, 10 Jan. [18 Jan.]	I,	38
30	Industrial Training Levy (Carpet), 11 Jan. [22 Jan.]	I,	88
32	Colchester and District Water Bd. (Water Charges), 12 Jan. [19 Jan.]	(n) III,	5655
33	Isle of Wight Review, 12 Jan. [18 Jan.]	(n) III,	5651
34	St. Clears-Nash (South Pembrokeshire) Trunk Road, 10 Jan. [23 Jan.]	(n) III,	5634
35	Assistance for House Purchase and Improvement (Housing Associations), 12 Jan. [18 Jan.] ...	I,	92
36	A.S. (Sessions of Ct.), 11 Jan. [29 Jan.]	I,	95
43	Removal and Disposal of Vehicles, 12 Jan. [23 Jan.]	I,	96
44	Derby, 12 Jan. [23 Jan.]	(n) III,	5650
46	Aerodrome Roads (Gatwick), 12 Jan. [23 Jan.] ...	(n) III,	5660
47	Aerodrome Roads (Heathrow), 12 Jan. [23 Jan.]...	(n) III,	5660
48	Aerodrome Roads (Stansted), 12 Jan. [23 Jan.] ...	(n) III,	5660
50	Police (S.), 11 Jan. [23 Jan.]...	I,	110
51	Foot-and-Mouth Disease (Controlled Areas Restrictions), 15 Jan. [18 Jan.]	I,	114

(n) Instrument classified as local, noted in the Classified List of Local S.I. at the page shown above, but not set out in full.

(n) Instrument classified as local, noted in the Classified List of Local S.I. at the page shown above, but not set out in full.

(n) Instrument classified as local, noted in the Classified List of Local S.I. at the page shown above, but not set out in full.

(n) Instrument classified as local, noted in the Classified List of Local S.I. at the page shown above, but not set out in full.

(n) Instrument classified as local, noted in the Classified List of Local S.I. at the page shown above, but not set out in full.

(n) Instrument classified as local, noted in the Classified List of Local S.I. at the page shown above, but not set out in full.

(n) Instrument classified as local, noted in the Classified List of Local S.I. at the page shown above, but not set out in full.

No.	Subject	Part	Page
309	Double Taxation Relief (Taxes on Income) (Gilbert and Ellice Islands Colony), 4 Mar. [11 Mar.] ...	I,	937
313	Central Scotland Water Development Bd. (Appointed Days), 1 Mar. [21 Mar.]	(n) III,	5657
314	Divorce County Cts., 4 Mar. [8 Mar.]	I,	940
315	Commonwealth Immigrants (Exemption from Restrictions on Landing) (Jersey), 5 Mar. [8 Mar.] ...	I,	943
318	Field Drainage (Ditching) (Standard Costs), 4 Mar. [13 Mar.]	I,	946
319	Fort William–Mallaig Trunk Road (Sgeir nan Ron and Other Diversions), 28 Feb. [18 Mar.] ...	(n) III,	5636
320	Weights and Measures (Additional Metric Weights), 6 Mar. [13 Mar.]	I,	952
323	Continental Shelf (Protection of Installations), 5 Mar. [13 Mar.]	(n) III,	5660
324	London Borough of Southwark (Wards), 5 Mar. [14 Mar.]	(n) III,	5650
325	Criminal Justice Act 1967 (Commencement), 5 Mar. [13 Mar.]	I,	952
326	Northumbrian River Authority Area (Fisheries), 19 Jan. [14 Mar.]	(n) III,	5648
327	Wages Regulation (Baking) (E. and W.), 6 Mar. [18 Mar.]	I,	957
328	Wages Regulation (Paper Bag), 6 Mar. [18 Mar.] ...	I,	961
331	York (Water Charges), 7 Mar. [15 Mar.] ...	(n) III,	5656
332	Merchant Shipping (Dangerous Goods), 6 Mar. [15 Mar.]	I,	969
333	Exchange Control (Scheduled Territories), 6 Mar. [11 Mar.]	I,	971
334	Bournemouth and District Water, 7 Mar. [15 Mar.]	(n) III,	5655
336	London–Great Yarmouth Trunk Road (Stratford St. Mary By-Pass Slip Roads), 29 Feb. [25 Mar.]	(n) III,	5633
337	Birmingham–Great Yarmouth Trunk Road (Crown Road and Neatherd Road, East Dereham), 29 Feb. [25 Mar.]	(n) III,	5635
338	Weights and Measures, 7 Mar. [14 Mar.]	I,	972
339	Weights and Measures (Local Standards: Limits of Error), 7 Mar. [14 Mar.]	I,	974
340	Pontypool and District Water, 7 Mar. [15 Mar.] ...	(n) III,	5656
342	Industrial Training Levy (Ceramics, Glass and Mineral Products), 7 Mar. [18 Mar.]	I,	976
343	Industrial Training Levy (Agricultural, Horticultural and Forestry), 7 Mar. [18 Mar.] ...	I,	982
344	Land Registration (District Registries), 5 Mar. [14 Mar.]	I,	984
345	Remuneration of Teachers (Farm Institutes), 8 Mar. [15 Mar.]	I,	990
346	Workington–Barons Cross Road (Trunking), 5 Mar. [25 Mar.]	(n) III,	5633
347	South Essex Water (Extension of Operation of Byelaws), 8 Mar. [18 Mar.]	(n) III,	5656
348	Inner London (Needs Element), 8 Mar. [21 Mar.] ...	I,	992

(n) Instrument classified as local, noted in the Classified List of Local S.I. at the page shown above, but not set out in full.

(n) Instrument classified as local, noted in the Classified List of Local S.I. at the page shown above, but not set out in full.

(n) Instrument classified as local, noted in the Classified List of Local S.I. at the page shown above, but not set out in full.

(n) Instrument classified as local, noted in the Classified List of Local S.I. at the page shown above, but not set out in full.

(n) Instrument classified as local, noted in the Classified List of Local S.I. at the page shown above, but not set out in full.

No.	Subject	Part	Page
514	Market Development (Extension of Period), 20 Feb. [4 Apr.]	I,	1238
515	West Shropshire Water Bd., 28 Mar. [5 Apr.] ...	(n) III,	5656
516	Rate Support Grant (Increase) (S.), 4 Mar. [8 Apr.]	I,	1240
523	Motor Vehicles (Construction and Use), 27 Mar. [9 Apr.]	I,	1242
524	Family Allowances, National Insurance and Industrial Injuries (Consequential), 29 Mar. [4 Apr.]	I,	1246
525	Wages Regulation (Milk Distributive) (E. and W.), 28 Mar. [10 Apr.]	I,	1255
526	Teesside, 1 Mar. [8 Apr.]	(n) III,	5650
527	Bootle (Extension), 27 Feb. [8 Apr.]	(n) III,	5651
530	Police Pensions, 29 Mar. [8 Apr.]	I,	1269
531	Calf Subsidies (U.K.), 28 Mar. [9 Apr.]	I,	1274
532	Lancaster Port Commission Revision, 21 Nov. 1967 [17 Apr.]	(n) III,	5648
533	Inland Post, 29 Mar. [8 Apr.]	I,	1278
534	Provision of Milk and Meals, 1 Apr. [9 Apr.] ...	I,	1280
541	Civil Defence Corps, 29 Mar. [5 Apr.]	I,	1282
542	Civil Defence (Fire Services), 29 Mar. [5 Apr.] ...	I,	1283
544	National Health Service (Charges for Dental Treatment), 29 Mar. [10 Apr.]	I,	1284
545	National Health Service (Hydestile Hospital), 29 Mar. [8 Apr.]	I,	1286
546	National Health Service (North Tees-side Maternity Hospitals), 28 Mar. [9 Apr.]	(n) III,	5654
547	Civil Defence Corps (S.), 29 Mar. [8 Apr.] ...	I,	1289
548	Civil Defence (Fire Services) (S.), 29 Mar. [8 Apr.]...	I,	1290
549	Betterment Levy (Rate of Interest), 2 Apr. [10 Apr.]	I,	1292
550	Trent River Authority (Crowle Area Internal Drainage District), 25 Aug. 1967 [9 Apr.] ...	(n) III,	5647
551	Price Stability of Imported Products (Levy Revn.), 2 Apr. [5 Apr.]	I,	1293
552	Police, 2 Apr. [9 Apr.]	I,	1294
553	Great Ouse River Authority (Snettisham Internal Drainage District), 27 Feb. [16 Apr.]	(n) III,	5647
555	York and North-East Yorkshire Police (Amalgamation), 2 Apr. [11 Apr.]	(n) III,	5651
557	National Health Service (Charges for Dental Treatment) (S.), 2 Apr. [10 Apr.]	I,	1296
558	Cromer Urban District Water, 4 Apr. [16 Apr.] ...	(n) III,	5655
559	Colne Valley Water (Extension of Operation of Byelaws), 4 Apr. [16 Apr.]	(n) III,	5655
560	Newbridge to Lathallan (Connecting Roads) Special Roads, 4 Apr. [17 Apr.]	(n) III,	5638
562	Wild Birds (Brean Down Sanctuary), 3 Apr. [11 Apr.]	(n) III,	5659
563	Wild Birds (Gibraltar Point Sanctuary), 3 Apr. [16 Apr.]	(n) III,	5659
564	Wild Birds (Charlton's Pond Sanctuary), 3 Apr. [16 Apr.]	(n) III,	5659

(n) Instrument classified as local, noted in the Classified List of Local S.I. at the page shown above, but not set out in full.

No.	Subject	Part	Page
565	London Transport Bd. (Borrowing Powers), 4 Apr. [16 Apr.]	I,	1298
569	Norwich (Aylsham Pumping Station) Water, 5 Apr. [17 Apr.]	(n) III,	5656
570	Petroleum (Inflammable Liquids), 8 Apr. [17 Apr.]	I,	1300
571	Petroleum (Carbon Disulphide), 8 Apr. [17 Apr.] ...	I,	1308
572	Double Taxation Relief (Shipping and Air Transport Profits) (Brazil), 8 Apr. [17 Apr.]	I,	1310
573	Double Taxation Relief (Taxes on Income) (British Honduras), 8 Apr. [17 Apr.]	I,	1312
574	Double Taxation Relief (Taxes on Income) (British Solomon Islands Protectorate), 8 Apr. [17 Apr.]	I,	1316
575	Double Taxation Relief (Taxes on Income) (Falkland Islands), 8 Apr. [17 Apr.]	I,	1319
576	Double Taxation Relief (Taxes on Income) (Montserrat), 8 Apr. [17 Apr.]	I,	1322
577	Double Taxation Relief (Taxes on Income) (Netherlands), 8 Apr. [18 Apr.]	I,	1326
578	Double Taxation Relief (Taxes on Income) (Virgin Islands), 8 Apr. [17 Apr.]	I,	1342
579	District Registries, 8 Apr. [17 Apr.]	I,	1345
580	Merchant Shipping (Light Dues), 8 Apr. [17 Apr.]	I,	1347
584	Warrington Water, 8 Apr. [17 Apr.]	(n) III,	5656
585	Foot-and-Mouth Disease (Imported Meat), 9 Apr. [11 Apr.]	I,	1349
586	Sugar (Rates of Surcharge and Surcharge Repayments), 9 Apr. [17 Apr.]	I,	1351
587	Composite Sugar Products (Surcharge and Surcharge Repayments—Average Rates), 9 Apr. [17 Apr.]	I,	1354
588	Independent Schools Tribunal, 9 Apr. [18 Apr.] ...	I,	1358
590	Police Federation (S.), 5 Apr. [19 Apr.]	I,	1360
591	London Borough of Barking (Wards), 9 Apr. [19 Apr.]	(n) III,	5650
592	Juvenile Cts. (London), 9 Apr. [19 Apr.]	I,	1361
593	Telephone, 10 Apr. [16 Apr.]	I,	1362
594	Road Vehicles (Registration and Licensing), 8 Apr. [22 Apr.]	I,	1364
596	Fixed Penalty (Areas), 9 Apr. [18 Apr.]	(n) III,	5658
597	London Cab Act 1968 (Commencement), 9 Apr. [18 Apr.]	I,	1366
598	Public Expenditure and Receipts Act 1968 (Commencement), 10 Apr. [16 Apr.]	I,	1367
599	Redundancy Fund (Advances out of the National Loans Fund), 9 Apr. [22 Apr.]	I,	1368
600	Sea Fisheries (S.), 22 Feb. [22 Apr.]	I,	1370
601	Goods Vehicles (Plating and Testing), 10 Apr. [25 Apr.]	I,	1372
602	Motor Vehicles (Construction and Use), 10 Apr. [25 Apr.]	I,	1415
612	Fife and Kinross Water Bd. (Financial Provisions), 9 Apr. [23 Apr.]	(n) III,	5657

(n) Instrument classified as local, noted in the Classified List of Local S.I. at the page shown above, but not set out in full.

(n) Instrument classified as local, noted in the Classified List of Local S.I. at the page shown above, but not set out in full.

No.	SUBJECT	Part	Page
655	Sunderland and South Shields Water (Financial Provisions), 23 Apr. [2 May]	(n) III,	5656
656	Fees for Inquiries, 23 Apr. [29 Apr.]	I,	1486
657	Building Societies (Authorised Investments), 24 Apr. [2 May]	I,	1488
658	Commons Registration (General), 24 Apr. [2 May]	I,	1490
659	Companies Registration Office (Business Names) (Fees), 24 Apr. [30 Apr.]	I,	1498
660	Wages Regulation (Ready-made and Wholesale Bespoke Tailoring), 24 Apr. [6 May]	I,	1500
664	Liverpool–Leeds–Hull Trunk Road (West Garforth Diversion and West Garforth to Peckfield Bar Side Roads), 19 Apr. [13 May]	(n) III,	5635
666	Argyll County Council (Loch Fada, Ardfern) Water, 23 Apr. [3 May]	(n) III,	5656
667	Argyll County Council (Allt Mor, Trislaig) Water, 23 Apr. [3 May]	(n) III,	5656
668	Exchange Control (Authorised Dealers and Depositaries), 25 Apr. [30 Apr.]	I,	1511
670	West of Maidenhead–Oxford Trunk Road (Sandford Link Slip Roads, Trunking), 24 Apr. [17 May]	(n) III,	5633
673	National Health Service (Colinswood Maternity Home), 26 Apr. [2 May]	(n) III,	5654
674	Newcastle and Gateshead Water (Team Valley Industrial Estate), 29 Apr. [8 May]	(n) III,	5655
676	Spring Traps Approval (S.), 29 Apr. [2 May] ...	I,	1513
677	Land Charges Fees, 26 Apr. [3 May]	I,	1515
678	Agricultural Credits Fees, 26 Apr. [3 May] ...	I,	1517
679	Import Duties (General), 30 Apr. [14 May] ...	I,	1519
680	National Insurance (New Entrants Transitional), 29 Apr. [2 May]	I,	1851
681	South-East of Scotland Water Bd. (Financial Provisions), 29 Apr. [9 May]	(n) III,	5657
683	South of Aylesford–East of Wrotham Special Road Connecting Roads, 29 Apr. [8 May]	(n) III,	5637
686	Grading of Produce (Tomatoes), 30 Apr. [8 May]...	II,	1953
687	Grading of Produce (Cauliflowers), 30 Apr. [8 May]	II,	1960
692	Norman Cross–Grimsby Trunk Road (City of Peterborough New Trunk Road De-trunking), 26 Apr. [9 May]	(n) III,	5633
693	Cheshire County Council (Ringway Airport Link) Motorway, 25 Apr. [14 May]	(n) III,	5637
694	Central Midwives Bd. for S., 29 Apr. [14 May]	II,	1967
697	London–Great Yarmouth Trunk Road (Kelvedon By-Pass Slip Roads), 26 Apr. [9 May]	(n) III,	5633
699	Taf Fechan Water Undertaking (Valuation), 25 Apr. [10 May]	(n) III,	5653
702	Basingstoke–Newbury Trunk Road (Cheap Street, Market Place and Mansion House Street, Newbury, De-trunking), 26 Apr. [20 May] ...	(n) III,	5635

(n) Instrument classified as local, noted in the Classified List of Local S.I. at the page shown above, but not set out in full.

(n) Instrument classified as local, noted in the Classified List of Local S.I. at the page shown above, but not set out in full.

(n) Instrument classified as local, noted in the Classified List of Local S.I. at the page shown above, but not set out in full.

(n) Instrument classified as local, noted in the Classified List of Local S.I. at the page shown above, but not set out in full.

(n) Instrument classified as local, noted in the Classified List of Local S.I. at the page shown above, but not set out in full.

(n) Instrument classified as local, noted in the Classified List of Local S.I. at the page shown above, but not set out in full.

(n) Instrument classified as local, noted in the Classified List of Local S.I. at the page shown above, but not set out in full.

No.	SUBJECT	Part	Page
1027	National Health Service (Spittlesea Isolation Hospital), 28 June [5 July]	(n) III,	5654
1029	Trustee Savings Banks (Special Investments), 1 July [5 July]	II,	2704
1030	Import Duties (General), 2 July [9 July]	II,	2706
1032	Industrial Training (Distributive Bd.), 1 July [12 July]	II,	2709
1033	Industrial Training (Food, Drink and Tobacco Bd.), 1 July [12 July]	II,	2721
1034	Industrial Training Levy (Furniture and Timber), 1 July [10 July]	II,	2732
1035	Industrial Training Levy (Water Supply), 1 July [12 July]	II,	2737
1036	Iron and Steel (Restrictive Trading Agreements), 1 July [4 July]	II,	2741
1037	Coal and Other Mines (Shafts, Outlets and Roads), 1 July [9 July]	II,	2743
1038	Craven Water Bd. (Hawkswick Waterworks), 2 July [11 July]	(n) III,	5655
1039	Hartlepools Water, 2 July [11 July]...	(n) III,	5655
1040	Grading of Produce (Apples), 2 July [9 July] ...	II,	2745
1041	Grading of Produce (Pears), 2 July [9 July] ...	II,	2748
1043	Greater London Council (Allowances to Members), 2 July [10 July]	(n) III,	5653
1044	East Worcestershire Water (Evesham Sources), 2 July [11 July]	(n) III,	5655
1045	Air Navigation (Restriction of Flying), 2 July [10 July]	II,	2751
1046	Docks and Harbours Act 1966 (Commencement), 1 July [10 July]	II,	2753
1047	Offices, Shops and Railway Premises Act 1963 (Exemption), 2 July [10 July]	II,	2754
1048	Agricultural Land Tribunals (Transitional Provisions), 3 July [10 July]	II,	2756
1051	Wages Regulation (Rope, Twine and Net) (Holidays), 3 July [15 July]	II,	2761
1052	Merchant Shipping (Load Lines) (Transitional Provisions), 4 July [12 July]	II,	2769
1053	Merchant Shipping (Load Line), 4 July [15 July]...	II,	2774
1055	Schools (S.) Code, 2 July [12 July]	II,	2849
1057	Petty Sessional Divisions (Somerset), 2 July [11 July]	(n) III,	5658
1060	Family Allowances and National Insurance Act 1968 (Commencement), 5 July [12 July] ...	II,	2851
1061	Industrial Training Levy (Construction Bd.), 4 July [15 July]	II,	2854
1062	Ports Welfare Amenities (Inquiries Procedure), 4 July [15 July]	II,	2859
1063	Ports Welfare Amenities (Objections and Appeals), 4 July [15 July]	II,	2866
1064	Post Office Savings Bank, 5 July [12 July]... ...	II,	2868
1065	West Yorkshire Police (Amalgamation), 4 July [15 July]	(n) III,	5651

(n) Instrument classified as local, noted in the Classified List of Local S.I. at the page shown above, but not set out in full.

(n) Instrument classified as local, noted in the Classified List of Local S.I. at the page shown above, but not set out in full.

(n) Instrument classified as local, noted in the Classified List of Local S.I. at the page shown above, but not set out in full.

(n) Instrument classified as local, noted in the Classified List of Local S.I. at the page shown above but not set out in full.

(n) Instrument classified as local, noted in the Classified List of Local S.I. at the page shown above, but not set out in full.

(n) Instrument classified as local, noted in the Classified List of Local S.I. at the page shown above, but not set out in full.

(n) Instrument classified as local, noted in the Classified List of Local S.I. at the page shown above, but not set out in full.

(n) Instrument classified as local, noted in the Classified List of Local S.I. at the page shown above, but not set out in full.

(n) Instrument classified as local, noted in the Classified List of Local S.I. at the page shown above, but not set out in full.

(n) Instrument classified as local, noted in the Classified List of Local S.I. at the page shown above, but not set out in full.

No.	SUBJECT	Part	Page
1493	Public Health (Infectious Diseases) (S.), 19 Sept. [25 Sept.]	III,	4247
1495	Skimmed Milk with Non-Milk Fat (S.), 12 Sept. [25 Sept.]	III,	4249
1496	Crofting Counties Agricultural Grants (S.), 16 Sept. [30 Sept.]	III,	4253
1498	British Transport Police (Transfers from Pension), 19 Sept. [27 Sept.]	III,	4256
1502	Housing (Forms) (S.), 5 Sept. [27 Sept.]	III,	4259
1503	Glasgow Victoria and Leverndale Hospitals Endowments, 17 Sept. [27 Sept.]	(n) III,	5654
1504	Bournemouth and District Water, 20 Sept. [2 Oct.]	(n) III,	5655
1508	Import Duty Drawbacks, 23 Sept. [27 Sept.] ...	III,	4268
1509	Import Duties (General), 23 Sept. [27 Sept.] ...	III,	4270
1510	Import Duties (General), 23 Sept. [30 Sept.] ...	III,	4272
1511	Purchase Tax, 23 Sept. [27 Sept.]	III,	4274
1512	National Health Service (Manchester and Cheshire Hospitals), 23 Sept. [30 Sept.]	(n) III,	5654
1513	British Sugar Corporation Limited (Incentive Agreement), 23 Sept. [30 Sept.]	III,	4290
1517	M.62 North of Worsley–West of Moss Moor Motorway Connecting Road (Simister), 18 Sept. [4 Oct.]	(n) III,	5637
1518	M.62 Lancashire–Yorkshire Motorway (Croft to Worsley Section), 19 Sept. [3 Oct.]	(n) III,	5637
1520	Essex River Authority (Alteration of Boundaries of the Chelmer and Blackwater Internal Drainage District), 25 July [2 Oct.]	(n) III,	5647
1521	Treasury Solicitor (Crown's Nominee), 25 Sept. [30 Sept.]	III,	4293
1522	County of Berkshire (Electoral Divisions), 23 Sept. [2 Oct.]	(n) III,	5650
1525	Penrith–Middlesbrough Trunk Road (Stockton and Thornaby Southern By-Pass), 23 Sept. [11 Oct.]...	(n) III,	5634
1526	Public Service Vehicles (Conditions of Fitness), 23 Sept. [2 Oct.]	III,	4295
1528	Northallerton and the Dales Water (Byelaws), 25 Sept. [7 Oct.]	(n) III,	5656
1529	Liverpool (Water Charges), 25 Sept. [7 Oct.] ...	(n) III,	5655
1530	Engineering Construction (Extension of Definition), 24 Sept. [3 Oct.]	III,	4297
1533	Companies (Disclosure of Depositors' Interests) (Exceptions) 26 Sept. [3 Oct.]	III,	4299
1534	Wages Regulation (Laundry), 26 Sept. [9 Oct.] ...	III,	4301
1535	Wages Regulation (Laundry) (Holidays), 26 Sept. [9 Oct.]	III,	4310
1536	Wages Regulation (Retail Food) (E. and W.), 26 Sept. [9 Oct.]	III,	4319
1538	Docks and Harbours Act 1966 (Commencement), 23 Sept. [4 Oct.]	III,	4324
1539	Agriculture Act 1967 (Commencement), 26 Sept. [1 Oct.]	III,	4325

(n) Instrument classified as local, noted in the Classified List of Local S.I. at the page shown above, but not set out in full.

(n) Instrument classified as local, noted in the Classified List of Local S.I. at the page shown above, but not set out in full.

(n) Instrument classified as local, noted in the Classified List of Local S.I. at the page shown above, but not set out in full.

(n) Instrument classified as local, noted in the Classified List of Local S.I. at the page shown above, but not set out in full.

(n) Instrument classified as local, noted in the Classified List of Local S.I. at the page shown above, but not set out in full.

(n) Instrument classified as local, noted in the Classified List of Local S.I. at the page shown above, but not set out in full.

No.	SUBJECT	Part	Page
1790	North West Worcestershire Water Bd. (Waresley Boreholes), 11 Nov. [20 Nov.]	(n) III,	5656
1791	M.62 (Lancashire–Yorkshire) Motorway (Outlane and Ainley Top) Connecting Roads, 8 Nov. [18 Nov.]	(n) III,	5637
1794	Teaching Council (S.) Act 1965 (Commencement), 8 Nov. [15 Nov.]	III,	4806
1795	Wages Regulation (Retail Bespoke Tailoring) (E. and W.), 11 Nov. [21 Nov.]	III,	4807
1797	County of Lancaster (Electoral Divisions), 11 Nov. [18 Nov.]	(n) III,	5650
1798	Remuneration of Teachers (Further Education), 11 Nov. [19 Nov.]	III,	4811
1799	Remuneration of Teachers (Primary and Secondary Schools), 11 Nov. [19 Nov.]	III,	4813
1800	Fishguard–Bangor (Menai Suspension Bridge) Trunk Road (Caernarvon Inner Relief Road), 6 Nov. [21 Nov.]	(n) III,	5635
1801	Armed Forces (Discharge by Purchase), 12 Nov. [18 Nov.]	III,	4816
1802	Restrictive Practices Ct., 12 Nov. [18 Nov.] ...	III,	4819
1803	Price Stability of Imported Products (Rates of Levy), 12 Nov. [14 Nov.]	III,	4824
1807	Wireless Telegraphy (Broadcast Licence Charges), 11 Nov. [19 Nov.]	III,	4827
1810	West Denbighshire and West Flintshire Water Bd., 11 Nov. [22 Nov.]	(n) III,	5656
1811	City of Chester (Shropshire Union Canal Bridge), 11 Nov. [25 Nov.]	(n) III,	5633
1812	London–Edinburgh–Thurso Trunk Road (Balderton Diversion), 11 Nov. [22 Nov.]	(n) III,	5635
1813	Parking Places and Controlled Parking Zone (Manchester), 11 Nov. [21 Nov.]	(n) III,	5638
1814	Bradford Water (Brown Bank, Holden Beck and Aire Syphons), 25 Oct. [20 Nov.]	(n) III,	5655
1816	Neath–Abergavenny Trunk Road (Glyn–Neath By-Pass) 7 Nov. [22 Nov.]	(n) III,	5635
1817	North Wilts Water Bd. (Holt Borehole), 13 Nov. [22 Nov.]	(n) III,	5656
1818	London–Edinburgh–Thurso Trunk Road (Helmsdale Diversion), 11 Nov. [27 Nov.]	(n) III,	5636
1820	Wakefield and District Water Bd., 14 Nov. [22 Nov.]	(n) III,	5656
1821	Worthing Water, 14 Nov. [22 Nov.]	(n) III,	5656
1822	Transport Act 1968 (Commencement), 14 Nov. [21 Nov.]	III,	4830
1823	London North Circular Trunk Road (Neasden Lane Underpass) (Slip Roads), 12 Nov. [22 Nov.]	(n) III,	5634
1826	Traffic Signs (School Crossing Patrols), 13 Nov. [21 Nov.]	III,	4837
1827	Building Control (Suspension of Control), 18 Nov. [19 Nov.]	III,	4840
1828	Mid Kent Water (New Sources), 15 Nov. [25 Nov.]	(n) III,	5655

(n) Instrument classified as local, noted in the Classified List of Local S.I. at the page shown above, but not set out in full.

No.	Subject	Part	Page
1835	Industrial Training Levy (Road Transport), 19 Nov. [29 Nov.]	III,	4841
1836	Wellard and Nene and the Lincolnshire River Authorities (Alteration of Areas), 18 Nov. [27 Nov.]	(n) III,	5647
1837	Rules of the Air and Air Traffic Control, 20 Nov. [27 Nov.]	III,	4846
1840	North Devon (Meldon Reservoir) Water, 15 Nov. [4 Dec.]	(n) III,	5655
1841	Race Relations (Prescribed Public Bodies), 21 Nov. [25 Nov.]	III,	4848
1842	London (Heathrow) Airport Noise Insulation Grants, 21 Nov. [28 Nov.]	(n) III,	5660
1843	Fixed Penalty (Areas), 20 Nov. [28 Nov.]	(n) III,	5658
1844	West Wilts Water Bd., 21 Nov. [2 Dec.]	(n) III,	5656
1845	Surcharge on Revenue Duties, 22 Nov. [22 Nov.] ...	III,	4850
1846	Wages Regulation (Toy Manufacturing), 20 Nov. [2 Dec.]	III,	4852
1847	Wages Regulation (Toy Manufacturing) (Holidays), 20 Nov. [2 Dec.]	III,	4859
1848	Air Navigation (Restriction of Flying), 20 Nov. [29 Nov.]	III,	4869
1849	Further Education (S.), 19 Nov. [2 Dec.]	III,	4870
1851	Wages Regulation (Retail Food) (S.), 21 Nov. [2 Dec.]	III,	4873
1852	Temporary Importation (Hired Vehicles and Private Vehicles, Vessels and Aircraft), 20 Nov. [2 Dec.]	III,	4879
1853	Warrington Water, 22 Nov. [2 Dec.]	(n) III,	5656
1854	Goods Vehicles (Plating and Testing), 22 Nov. [29 Nov.]	III,	4880
1855	County of Hertfordshire (Electoral Divisions), 20 Nov. [29 Nov.]	(n) III,	5650
1856	University of St. Andrews (Scholarships and Bursaries), 22 Nov. [2 Dec.]	(n) III,	5657
1857	Air Navigation, 22 Nov. [28 Nov.]	III,	4883
1858	Copyright (International Conventions), 22 Nov. [28 Nov.]	III,	4887
1859	Parliamentary Commissioner (Departments and Authorities), 22 Nov. [28 Nov.]	III,	4889
1860	Commission of the European Communities (Immunities and Privileges), 22 Nov. [29 Nov.] ...	III,	4890
1861	Consular Conventions (People's Republic of Bulgaria), 22 Nov. [28 Nov.]	III,	4895
1862	Inter-Governmental Maritime Consultative Organisation (Immunities and Privileges), 22 Nov. [29 Nov.]	III,	4897
1863	International Wheat Council (Immunities and Privileges), 22 Nov. [29 Nov.]	III,	4903
1864	Tokyo Convention Act 1967 (Overseas Territories), 22 Nov. [28 Nov.]	III,	4909
1867	Double Taxation Relief (Taxes on Income) (Grenada), 22 Nov. [29 Nov.]	III,	4917

(n) Instrument classified as local, noted in the Classified List of Local S.I. at the page shown above, but not set out in full.

(n) Instrument classified as local, noted in the Classified List of Local S.I. at the page shown above, but not set out in full.

(n) Instrument classified as local, noted in the Classified List of Local S.I. at the page shown above, but not set out in full.

(n) Instrument classified as local, noted in the Classified List of Local S.I. at the page shown above, but not set out in full.

(n) Instrument classified as local, noted in the Classified List of Local S.I. at the page shown above, but not set out in full.

(n) Instrument classified as local, noted in the Classified List of Local S.I. at the page shown above, but not set out in full.

(n) Instrument classified as local, noted in the Classified List of Local S.I. at the page shown above, but not set out in full.

Index to Parts I, II and III

The date shown against each title is the date of making.

SBN 11 840020 7